D1238277

The Medical Implications of
NUCLEAR WAR

INSTITUTE OF MEDICINE

NATIONAL ACADEMY OF SCIENCES

Fredric Solomon, M.D., and Robert Q. Marston, M.D.
Editors

With a Foreword by Lewis Thomas, M.D.

NATIONAL ACADEMY PRESS
Washington, D.C. 1986

NATIONAL ACADEMY PRESS   2101 CONSTITUTION AVENUE, NW   WASHINGTON, DC 20418

Library of Congress Cataloging-in-Publication Data

The medical implications of nuclear war.

Based on papers presented at a symposium held at the National Academy of Sciences, Washington, D.C., Sept. 20–22, 1985 and organized under the auspices of the Institute of Medicine.

Includes index.

1. Nuclear warfare—Hygienic aspects—Congresses.   2. Emergency medical services—Congresses.   3. Nuclear warfare—Environmental aspects—Congresses. 4. Nuclear warfare—Psychological aspects—Congresses.   5. Nuclear warfare— Social aspects—Congresses.   I. Solomon, Fredric.   II. Marston, Robert Q., 1923–   .   III. Institute of Medicine (U.S.)

[DNLM: 1. Nuclear Warfare—congresses.   2. Radiation Injuries—congresses. 3. Radioactive Fallout—adverse effects—congresses.   WN 610 M4865 1985]

RA648.3.M445 1986   363.3'498   86-18134

ISBN 0-309-03692-5

ISBN 0-309-03636-4 (pbk.)

Cover photo: Nagasaki, 10 August 1945, 11 A.M. The heavy overcast of smoke from fires cut off the sunlight. The narrow path, along which the wounded are being carried on stretchers, leads to Nagasaki Railway Station. (Photograph by Yōsuke Yamahata.) Copyright © 1981 by Hiroshima City and Nagasaki City. Reprinted by permission of Basic Books, Inc., Publishers.

A videotape digest of symposium highlights is available. For information, write the Institute of Medicine, Office of Information, at 2101 Constitution Avenue, NW, Washington, DC 20418.

Printed in the United States of America

INSTITUTE OF MEDICINE

Steering Committee for the Symposium on the Medical Implications of Nuclear War

ROBERT Q. MARSTON, M.D. (IOM), *Chairman,* President Emeritus, University of Florida, Gainesville

HERBERT L. ABRAMS, M.D. (IOM), Visiting Professor, Department of Diagnostic Radiology, Stanford University School of Medicine, and Stanford Center for International Security and Arms Control

WILLIAM R. BEARDSLEE, M.D., Clinical Director, Department of Psychiatry, Children's Hospital Medical Center, and Assistant Professor, Harvard Medical School

K. SUNE D. BERGSTROM, M.D., Ph.D. (IOM, NAS), Professor of Chemistry, Karolinska Institute

THOMAS C. CHALMERS, M.D. (IOM), Distinguished Service Professor of Medicine, President and Dean Emeritus, The Mount Sinai Medical Center, New York City

DAVID S. GREER, M.D. (IOM), Dean of Medicine and Professor of Community Health, Brown University

ALEXANDER LEAF, M.D. (IOM, NAS), Ridley Watts Professor of Preventive Medicine, Harvard Medical School, and Chairman, Department of Preventive Medicine and Epidemiology, Massachusetts General Hospital

JENNIFER LEANING, M.D., Chief of Emergency Services, Harvard Community Health Plan

GILBERT S. OMENN, M.D., Ph.D. (IOM), Dean, School of Public Health and Community Health, and Professor of Medicine and Environmental Health, University of Washington

JEANNE PETERSON, United Nations Office of Population

CHESTER M. PIERCE, M.D. (IOM), Professor of Education and Psychiatry in the Faculty of Medicine, the Graduate School of Education, and the Faculty of Public Health, Harvard University

THEODORE A. POSTOL, Ph.D., Science Fellow, Stanford Center for International Security and Arms Control

---

IOM, Member of the Institute of Medicine
NAS, Member of the National Academy of Sciences

Contents

Part I
Nuclear War with Modern Weapons:
Physical Effects and Environmental Consequences

Part II
Health Consequences of Nuclear War

**Part III
Medical Resource Needs and Availability
Following Nuclear War**

**Part IV
Images and Risks of Nuclear War:
Psychosocial Perspectives**

Part V
**Long-Term Consequences of and Prospects for
Recovery from Nuclear War: Two Views**

Concluding Remarks

Foreword

I was in Europe at the time of the Institute of Medicine's symposium, and I read the accounts of the meeting in the headlines of the French, German, and British newspapers. Banner headlines, lead stories, front pages everywhere. The announcement was that a nuclear war would cause AIDS.

No matter that the real AIDS is caused by a virus. The concept of immune deficiency as a consequence for the survivors of radiation, malnutrition, burns, grief, and other assaults of nuclear bombardment was compelling.

It was as though the problem of hydrogen bombs had suddenly turned into something the writers could lay hands on. Something to sit down and think about, and compose a front page story about; something different from all those unthinkable matters. To be sure, there were some lines at the bottom of the stories, continued on inside pages, giving some new estimates of the numbers of people to be killed outright by blast and burns, the utter impossibility of any health care system doing anything even marginally useful, and some mention of the "nuclear winter" scenario. But it was AIDS that caught the attention of the press, AIDS that *made* the story.

When I got back to New York a few days later, the whole story had vanished from the papers, but I found clippings from most of the earlier reports that had appeared in the national papers and news magazines. Same story: AIDS.

And then that was the end of the matter. No more stories in the days and weeks that followed, not about the medical consequences of nuclear war. Back to normal: the stuck inconclusive Geneva talks, the harangues by statesmen hungry for television, the talk of new talks, arms control talks, treaty violation talks, editorials saying that neither side can trust the other or ever will, endless bewildering columns on the SDI and the talk about SDI. Wretched, dishonest, evasive talk, political talk, with no mention anywhere of burnt blasted vaporized human beings in the billions and half the planet frozen and irradiated. The same turning away from real life and real death danger that we have all been tolerating, some of us even encouraging, since we and the Russians began building our "arsenals," as we like to call the things to make it seem like old times, same old clash of arms, same excitements. The British and the French with theirs, and the Chinese and Indians and God only knows who else with theirs, all of humanity caught up in the craziness like lemmings running headlong toward the cliff, everyone muttering *unthinkable*.

We behave as if we really believe these are weapons—even, burn our tongues, weapons of "defense." We brandish them, display them like the spears and banners of primitive tribes shouting insults across a river boundary, getting ready to fight, to defend, to burn up the earth for the honor. Maybe holding back, but only for the moment, at the thought of catching AIDS. And then, next day, that thought gone.

When I complain, as I bitterly do, to my journalist friends about all this, they say what on earth do you expect us to do? We can't run front page stories every day about the world coming to an end, they say. People won't read things like this, they say.

I raise my voice, yell sometimes, what the hell are newspapers for? You're supposed to provide information, real news, and this is the news of the world, the news of the end of the world, print more of it for God's sake before it's too late, I say. Put the nuclear winter up there on the front page every day, give it the biggest blackest headlines you've got, make it the main story, run it and run it. I say all that, and things like that, and they look at me with embarrassment.

But AIDS! And then nothing. And in that one day of stories, down at the bottom, winding things up, a short paragraph saying 56 million Americans would be killed outright in a 100-megaton attack on cities; not much better in an attack on military targets (our "assets," we call them), 38 million if they do that. That's from 100 megatons, the equivalent of a warning shot over the heads of a crowd considering that we and the Soviets have between us 20,000 megatons or whatever the number now is.

I complain to my journalist friends in a voice as reasonable as I can make it, even good-natured, can't you at least do more to get the public thinking hard about nuclear winter? Too much uncertainty, they say, you can't be sure about the weather, can't predict it until it really happens. Anyway, people don't want to read about it, be told about it. Not a good thing to think about. And anyway, what can be worse than 2.2 billion sudden human deaths? They ask me that, then say, that's the closest estimate available for the deaths in a really full-scale nuclear war, when everything is let fly. How can you get people (the "reading public," they say) to think about a lot of clouds, even the extinction of some other kinds of life on the planet, when you've got a number that is at least half the human species? Then they use the word that has become the cliche of late twentieth century statecraft: *unthinkable*.

That is the center of the trouble, I see that. Nuclear war is for sure, beyond question, dead certainly, literally, figuratively, any way you don't want to think about it: *unthinkable*.

If we go on this way, unthinking, putting it out of our minds, leaving it to statecraft of the kind we've got all over the world, or leaving it to the editorial writers, the columnists, the TV newsmen, or the military people, first thing you know some crafty statesman or some other crafty unbalanced military personage, one side or the other, is going to do something wrong, say something wrong, drop something, misread some printout, and there will go 30,000 years of trying ever since Lascaux right up to Bach and beyond into this benighted century—all civilization, gone without a trace. Not even a thin layer of fossils left of us, no trace, no memory.

Pay attention to George Kennan and Solly Zuckerman and their books along with this one. They have thought longer and more clearly than most people close to the complexities. Solly Zuckerman, with years of experience as science adviser to the British cabinet, says we're in trouble because of the weapons-scientists ("technicians," he calls them, with austere and adult contempt), and the lack of anyone with the authority and power and real brains (brains, not easy cleverness or clever craziness) to tell them what to do, or more importantly what not to do. Tell them: that's enough now, don't improve the technology, don't make anything technically sweeter or smarter, go home and we'll pay you to stay there.

Unthinkable is the word for whatever is in front of our eyes but too big to figure out, too frightening. Pay attention, in this book, to the doctors and the scientists here assembled.

Everything needed for thinking clearly, wincing all the way but thinking anyway, is written down in these chapters. Anyone, any age, can read what's here and understand what we could be in for if we stay on this road. What to do is another matter, but at least the facts of the matter are laid out here. You'd better bet your life it's thinkable.

Lewis Thomas, M.D.
President Emeritus
Memorial Sloan-Kettering
Cancer Center

Preface

On August 6, 1945, a 15-kiloton atomic bomb ignited the center of the Japanese city of Hiroshima, flattening it and killing more than 100,000 people. Just three days later, a second bomb was exploded over the city of Nagasaki, resulting in the deaths of another 70,000. For months after the attack, many survivors developed symptoms that puzzled doctors: blood cell abnormalities, high fevers, chronic fatigue, diarrhea, vomiting, and depression. Physicians began to term these symptoms "radiation sickness." It would eventually be revealed that survivors were experiencing an increased incidence of certain forms of cancer.

Now, forty-one years later, the destructive power of a 15-kiloton bomb (equivalent to 15,000 tons of TNT) is dwarfed by weapons of megaton force (1 million tons of TNT). Although development of ever more destructive weapons continues, scientific examination of the effects of nuclear weapons upon the short- and long-term health of survivors, as well as upon the environment, has lagged until very recently.

In 1981, Paul Crutzen and John Birks calculated the effects on the Earth's atmosphere of large-scale fires that would result from a major nuclear exchange. A subsequent series of analyses expanded on the concept of a mid-day twilight or "nuclear winter" that might follow in the weeks and months after a nuclear war. This led to a fundamental reassessment of postwar environmental conditions, especially those affecting food production. The early 1980s also saw the beginning of new efforts by physicians and by scientists from many disciplines and many nations to examine the indirect health-related effects of nuclear war, including intermediate-term consequences for survivors and effects on persons living far away from anticipated war zones. More comprehensive appraisals were produced of the catastrophic social, economic, and psychological sequelae of nuclear war. Scholars began anew to examine the psychosocial dimensions of nuclear arms competition, international conflict, and the threat of nuclear war.

The time seemed propitious, therefore, to convene an international group of scholars in the autumn of 1985 to review the medical implications of these and other new studies. In addition to considering the direct and indirect health effects of nuclear attack, these physicians and scientists were asked to examine the availability of medical resources and the psychological issues surrounding nuclear weapons and war. It was fitting that this conference was organized under the auspices of the Institute of Medicine in Washington, D.C. Since being chartered by the National Academy of Sciences in 1970, the Institute has devoted itself to examining developments in science, health care, and public policy that affect the health of the public. Indeed, it has asserted that nothing can have greater potential impact on health than a nuclear war. A statement adopted by the IOM membership in 1982 reflects that concern: "Nuclear war is the single event that could terminate all our efforts to improve the human condition. That possibility seems particularly ironic at a time when great strides are being made in alleviating human ills, and even greater advances are in prospect. . . . The only preventive medicine we know that can avoid the medical consequences of nuclear war is to prevent nuclear war itself."

It is also fitting that this symposium occurred during Frederick Robbins's tenure as president of the Institute of Medicine. Dr. Robbins has long been concerned with the threat of nuclear war, and this symposium last fall was an appropriate tribute to his five years of leadership. In fact, the symposium has had the support and guidance of three Institute presidents. David Hamburg, who was Fred Robbins's predecessor, contributed in several ways to the success of the symposium—through the support of the Carnegie Corporation of New York, which he now heads, through his advice on the program as it was being developed, and through the extraordinary chapter that opens this book. Finally, Samuel Thier, the current president of the Institute, has directed the review and dissemination of the results of the symposium, including this volume.

In his opening remarks to the conferees, Frank Press, president of the National Academy of Sciences and chairman of the National Research Council, emphasized the value of vigorous scientific debate on this topic: "The profundity of the consequences of nuclear war are such that symposia of this type—building up momentum for these issues and for public concern and disseminating the kind of information and knowledge that is generated at a conference like this—are a most valuable public service."

Moreover, Dr. Press reminded the audience that, despite the level of internal government activities, many of the best ideas for the control of nuclear weapons and the best estimates of the consequences of nuclear war have come from scientists and scholars working outside official circles. Indeed, during that September weekend, more than 80 scientists from nine countries were joined by concerned members of the general public. Thirty papers were presented which, after subsequent refinement, have become the contents of this volume. The authors come not only from government laboratories but also from private consulting firms, hospitals, and academia.

In the months that have passed since the symposium, the failures of U.S. and European space launch vehicles and the accident at the Soviet nuclear power plant have dramatized an important point: there are difficulties inherent in the design, maintenance, and operation of complex fail-safe systems. The tragedies at Cape Canaveral and Chernobyl seem to underscore certain conclusions in David Hamburg's opening chapter and in Part IV of this volume: namely, we cannot depend indefinitely upon technology, prudence, or good luck to safeguard mankind from the risk of nuclear war. In fact, it is argued, the hazards of nuclear weapons and modern strategic systems are so complex and permit so little margin for human error or misunderstanding in a time of crisis, that even the most sophisticated efforts of crisis management might fail us in a nuclear confrontation. In the long run, strategic military crises must be prevented from developing among the nuclear powers of the world, because neither human judgment nor technology can be relied upon to avoid nuclear war in the event of a prolonged and complex confrontation.

This volume is divided into five parts. The first provides an overview of the physical and environmental effects of nuclear war, setting the stage for later sections that address the medical impact of various types of nuclear attack. Among the papers in Part I is a disturbing report by Theodore Postol from the Stanford Center for International Security and Arms Control. Based on the properties of modern nuclear weapons, he estimates that firestorms triggered by nuclear explosions would kill two to four times as many people in or near cities than have been predicted by standard government studies. Unlike Hiroshima and Nagasaki, where many of the survivors were able to walk out of the blast zones and seek help, contemporary weapons would produce vast "hurricanes of fire," making escape impossible over wide areas.

Other contributors to Part I review the physics of large urban fires and update projections of nuclear winter. "Nuclear famine" is also described, drawing on the very recent work of SCOPE (The Scientific Committee on Problems of the Environment of the International Council of Scientific Unions). Because of the dependence of third-world countries on rice, wheat, and corn harvests, as well as on agricultural support from the world's superpowers, a nuclear attack that destroyed crop harvests and stockpiles and interrupted distribution systems might kill more people in noncombatant nations than in combatant ones. And new ecological concerns are raised—for example, the toxicity of an environment laden with the by-products of burning plastics and other man-made materials.

In Part II, the consequences of nuclear war are considered from a standpoint of deaths, injuries, and, especially, the health of survivors. In preparation for this symposium, a Princeton University research team developed the first detailed computer model outside the classified literature for calculating U.S. casualties from a nuclear war. This model was then used to examine the sensitivity of casualty estimates to various assumptions about nuclear weapons effects. The work indicates that if some heretofore standard assumptions are revised—as proposed in several of the other papers in this volume (e.g., greater lethality of firestorms or of radiation exposure)—a "limited" attack solely on strategic nuclear targets would kill tens of millions, a figure much greater than earlier government estimates. The Princeton group also demonstrates that it is virtually meaningless for military analysts to distinguish between attacks in which nuclear weapons are used on military-related industries but not on civilian targets and attacks in which cities are targeted per se: the toll is nearly as great in either case because such industries are so frequently located within or adjacent to major population centers.

Also in this section, physicians and scientists describe problems of triage and care of the injured survivors of nuclear war. They provide new estimates of the lethality of radiation exposure under wartime conditions, consider the effects of food shortages and malnutrition on the prospects for survival, and discuss the psychological consequences of surviving major disasters. Scientists from Norway and the Soviet Union offer estimates of the long-term genetic and carcinogenic effects of nuclear weapons use. In a provocative new synthesis, the combined effects of high levels of ionizing and ultraviolet radiation, burns and physical trauma, malnutrition, and psychological stress upon human immunology are examined; investigators from Brown University argue that these multiple insults would impair the cell-mediated immune capability of a great many survivors, making them likely to succumb to diseases such as pneumonia, tuberculosis, and cancer—diseases that are prevalent among today's victims of the virus-caused immune deficiency known as AIDS.

Part III reviews the demand for medical resources after a nuclear attack and estimates the actual supply likely to be available. If a single one-megaton bomb were exploded over the city of Detroit, for example, it is calculated that survivors would need about forty times the number of burn beds currently available throughout the entire United States. They would also need twice the number of intensive care beds currently available, and the need for blood transfusions would exceed the existing supply many times over. A more extensive nuclear exchange involving the United States, Europe, and the Soviet Union and its allies would wipe out most of the world's supply of pharmaceuticals, medical equipment, and food. Also in Part III, two social scientists offer an economic and social perspective on the consequences of nuclear war.

Contributors to Part IV address the nuclear arms race from a psychosocial point of view: How does the threat of nuclear war affect the attitudes and behavior of adults and children? Studies provide evidence that many young children are worried about the possibility of nuclear war; most learn about nuclear war from television or the media and rarely discuss it with their parents. One study indicates that people in their late teens are somewhat less concerned than younger children; and surveys of adult attitudes consistently indicate that although most people believe a nuclear war has a moderate chance of occurring within their lifetime (and also believe they will not survive it), they take no action toward preventing it.

The maintenance of hope and the denial of responsibility in the nuclear age are also discussed in Part IV. Furthermore, a review of the demands on managers of nuclear weapons systems leads to serious concern that there might be a breakdown of leadership in the case of a nuclear attack. The attitudes of world leaders toward war and power are examined, as is the history of decision-makers' behavior under the stress of international crises.

Finally in this section is a call for improving the screening system used to select nuclear weapons handlers. Although psychological problems are supposedly discerned before candidates are chosen, a psychiatric interview for weapons handlers is not required, and more than 3,000 previously screened armed forces personnel are removed each year from weapons handling because of alcohol or drug abuse, mental disorders, and other psychosocial problems.

Rounding out the book are remarks by Carl Sagan and Lynn Anspaugh, who offer contrasting viewpoints on the prospects for recovery from nuclear war and on the use of scientific information in policy-oriented discussions in this area. Many scientists, like Sagan, emphasize the importance of assuming "worst-case" analyses as the basis for policy discussions—much as military planners assume worst-case scenarios in projecting defense needs—while others agree with Anspaugh that the uncertainties in any discussions of the consequences of nuclear war are so numerous, and so fundamental, that they preclude the application of these studies to policy debates. There seems to be wide agreement that the biological and environmental effects of nuclear war are not fully understood and that our knowledge of these issues will continue to grow as research continues; however, compared with research expenditures on the physical aspects of nuclear weapons effects, biological, psychosocial, and ecological studies appear to be underfunded and late in starting.

Herbert Abrams, a member of the symposium's steering committee, closes the volume with a powerful, personal summary of lessons to be learned from the Institute of Medicine's conference.

The value of this symposium is, in large part, a credit to the steering committee, which worked many long, hard hours despite ongoing responsibilities at universities, hospitals, and research facilities. All the members of the committee, along with the authors of these chapters, share a deep commitment to the importance of this work and made many extraordinary efforts to make the symposium successful. Special recognition is due Marc Messing, who served as symposium coordinator, and the staff of the National Academy Press, which transformed the symposium papers into this attractive volume. It was our pleasure to work with them.

The symposium could not have taken place nor could this volume have been published without the generous support of the Carnegie Corporation of New York. We also want to thank the National Research Council for its financial assistance.

We believe that the papers presented here constitute the most comprehensive and authoritative review to date of health-related issues associated with modern nuclear weapons and the threat of nuclear war. Moreover, as a result of preparation for the symposium and interaction at the conference itself, new calculations and hypotheses emerged that are potentially of far-reaching importance. It is our hope that this volume will increase public understanding of the risks and consequences of nuclear war and will inspire scientific efforts and government actions designed to avoid such a catastrophe.

Robert Q. Marston, M.D.
Chairman
Fredric Solomon, M.D.
Project Director

The Medical Implications of
NUCLEAR WAR

The Medical Implications of Nuclear War, Institute of
Medicine. © 1986 by the National Academy of Sciences.
National Academy Press, Washington, D.C.

Understanding and Preventing Nuclear War: The Expanding Role of the Scientific Community

DAVID A. HAMBURG, M.D.
Carnegie Corporation, New York, New York

The consequences of nuclear war constitute the central facts of our age. Everything else in contemporary experience hinges on them, depends on them, follows from them. Therefore, it is exceedingly important to get the facts straight. We deal with a metric that our species has never had to deal with in the millions of years of its history—a metric involving the sudden elimination of tens or hundreds of millions of people and perhaps the deaths of billions in a matter of months. That is something we have never had to accommodate, and I am not sure we can. Grasping the meaning of these numbers is a very difficult thing to do, for it constitutes a qualitative break with the experience of the species. It is not just World War II written large. It is a fundamentally and profoundly different experience. So I believe that the facts that scientists are clarifying here represent the most important facts our species has ever had to deal with.

We all like to see the caring, loving, creating side of human experience. We want to believe that this side will dominate in world affairs, and perhaps it will. Indeed, an occasion like this gives some hope that it will, but let us recall George Bernard Shaw's incisive remark: "We cannot help it because we are so constituted that we always believe finally what we wish to believe. The moment we want to believe something, we suddenly see all the arguments for it and become blind to the arguments against it. The moment we want to disbelieve anything we have previously believed, we suddenly discover not only that there is a mass of evidence against, but that this evidence was staring us in the face all the time."

The tendencies to wishful thinking, to complacency in the face of hard

1

reality, to avoidance of facts, to denial of the significance of facts—these are perhaps our worst enemies in the nuclear arena. There are people who believe that we can manage any kind of crisis, take any kind of risk, treat nuclear weapons like any other weapons, and still come away from every brink in good shape.

Beyond the fact of the large scale of killing throughout human history, and the unprecedented scale of killing that now lies before us, is an underlying fact that deserves our serious attention. Human societies have a pervasive tendency to distinguish between apparently good and bad people, heroes and villains, or, more generally, between in-groups and out-groups. Historically, it has been easy for us to put ourselves at the center of the universe, attaching a strong positive value to ourselves and our group, while attaching a negative value to certain other people and their groups. It is prudent to assume that we are all, to some extent, susceptible to egocentric and ethnocentric tendencies. The human species is one in which individuals and groups easily learn to blame others for whatever difficulties exist, but in terms of the nuclear predicament, blaming is at best useless and most likely counterproductive. We have seen all too much finger-pointing between the superpowers, and for that matter, among nations throughout the world.

The crux of my presentation is that the circumstances surrounding nuclear war call for a new level of commitment by the scientific community to reduce the risk of nuclear war. What the world requires is really a mobilization—something akin to a wartime mobilization of the best possible intellectual, technical, and moral resources over a wide range of knowledge and perspectives. We need a science-based effort to maximize the analytical capability, the objectivity, the respect for evidence that is characteristic of the scientific community worldwide, and indeed the worldwide perspective that is itself an integral part of the scientific community.

These efforts should bring together scientists, scholars, and practitioners to clarify the many facets of avoiding nuclear war. To generate new options for decreasing the risk, we need analytical work by people who know the weaponry and its military uses. But that is far from enough to do the job. We also need scholars who know the superpowers in depth; people who know other nuclear powers; people who know third-world flash points; people who know international relations very broadly; people who know a lot about policy formation and implementation, especially in the superpowers; people who understand human behavior under stress, especially leadership under stress; people who understand negotiation and conflict resolution—and much more. In other words, the relevant knowledge and skills cut right across all the sciences—physical, biological, behavioral, social.

Analytical studies of this kind are likely to be much more useful if they are informed by the perspective of policymakers, and policymakers can benefit greatly from having such studies—new ideas, a wider range of options, and deeper insights—in other words, a continuing dynamic interplay between the scientific community and the world of policy.

I want to refer to a few examples of the emerging generation of rather complex, serious, analytical efforts in the scientific and scholarly communities on the issue of avoiding nuclear war, bringing in heavy intellectual and technical firepower for peace, not for war. I cite examples that are primarily taking place in the United States because I am more familiar with them and have actually been involved in some. U.S. activity has been rapidly increasing in recent years, and I hope there will be similar upsurges in many countries. Now let us consider some examples of international scientific cooperation for avoiding nuclear war.

Since this conference is a medical one, it is appropriate to point out the recent activity of medical organizations in this field. A serious, worldwide effort has been made to stimulate public awareness of the harsh facts of nuclear war. Many different facets of the problem have been illuminated by analytic work and education of the public on the basis of best available information. Prominent in this effort have been the Physicians for Social Responsibility, International Physicians for the Prevention of Nuclear War, World Health Organization, British Medical Association, and the American Medical Association; others have contributed as well. The central point is that a kind of awakening has occurred in the medical community to the responsibility of addressing the immense nature of the threat to public health.

The present meeting is an activity of the National Academy of Sciences, which in 1980 established the Committee on International Security and Arms Control (CISAC), chaired for several years by Marvin Goldberger and now headed by Wolfgang Panofsky, both distinguished physicists. There is a counterpart "CISAC" in the Soviet Academy of Sciences, chaired by academician E. P. Velikhov, also a physicist of note. Both committees are staffed by people with rich backgrounds in arms control and international security. CISAC's main function is to meet with its Soviet counterpart twice a year, once here and once in the Soviet Union, with a good deal of preparation between meetings. The discussions have dealt with almost all the major topics of the arms control field; in fact, CISAC has primarily been an arms control committee. These meetings have made it possible to consider in an open-minded, exploratory way a variety of major issues between our two countries. There has been a minimum of boilerplate; a minimum of hostile rhetoric; and a good deal of serious, thoughtful discussion based on the facts of the awesome nuclear stockpiles: ways to reduce those stockpiles, ways to balance them, ways to increase their stability, and ways to enhance safety in their maintenance.

CISAC has also had the useful function of educating the members of the National Academy of Sciences. For the past 3 years, it has conducted in-depth seminars immediately preceding the annual meeting of the Academy, and hundreds of Academy members have participated in both occasions. The first was a broad coverage of the arms control field and the second a specific focus on strategic defense. CISAC also put together a volume called *Nuclear Arms Control: Background and Issues,* published by the National Academy Press in 1984. Indeed, it has been altogether a constructive and stimulating body both in its activities in this country and in its interchange with Soviet counterparts over its history. And 1986 should see further extension in the range of its activities.

In 1985, there was a new initiative in the National Academy of Sciences—the creation of a Committee on the Contributions of the Behavioral and Social Sciences to Avoiding Nuclear War. This group explores in depth some of the topics that are represented in this meeting as well as others. It is an enterprise of great potential importance and we may well find it useful to approach the Soviet Academy in due course about some counterpart group.

Now let us move to another important organization in this country, the American Association for the Advancement of Science (AAAS). This is a very interesting organization because it is a kind of broad umbrella group covering all the sciences. It is deeply engaged in national science policy and is an important articulator of relationships between the scientific community and the government, a useful link between that community and the society at large, and in recent years a very active participant in the arms control and national security fields.

In 1981, AAAS established the Committee on Science, Arms Control and National Security to encourage its own members to become more informed on these matters and more deeply involved in them and, also, to provide links between the scientific community and the policy community. It has been very effective, in my judgment, in fostering a lively interplay between scientists and policymakers on arms control and international security issues.

The AAAS annual meeting is a very large gathering that evokes a great deal of public interest and media coverage. AAAS also holds about 10 major symposia each year on reducing the risk of nuclear war. They cover arms control, of course, but also approaches beyond arms control, such as *crisis prevention,* about which I will say more later.

The official journal of the AAAS, *Science,* has increasingly given extended coverage to the issues under discussion at this meeting and related ones. Under its new editor, Daniel Koshland, there is a commitment to increase even further the coverage of subjects pertinent to the avoidance of nuclear war. In November 1985, AAAS's magazine for the lay reader, *Science 85,* had a special issue on science, technology, and peace. Coinciding with its publication was a symposium for journalists based on this issue.

AAAS also sponsors seminars for members of Congress and their staffs. The most recent one centered on crisis prevention and nuclear risk reduction. This year, for the first time, AAAS will have a highly visible and very-high-quality meeting that will be the first of an annual series of national colloquia on avoiding nuclear war, bringing together the scientific and scholarly communities with a wide cross-section of national leaders and the public at large.

Now I turn to another organization, the American Academy of Arts and Sciences, based in Cambridge, Massachusetts. Its Committee on International Security Studies (CISS) has just completed a major study of weapons in space, reported in the most recent issue of *Daedalus.* A book based on this project is forthcoming. CISS is also completing a project on Crisis, Stability and Nuclear War, conducted jointly with Cornell University, that looks particularly at crisis management issues, command and control communication questions for both U.S. and Soviet nuclear forces, delegation of authority in time of crisis, and the very dangerous interplay of military alerts between the superpowers.

The American Academy will soon be publishing a volume that analyzes whether the superpowers place too much emphasis on the technical aspects of weaponry and not enough on underlying political and psychological factors that exacerbate conflict. It aims to illuminate underlying factors in the U.S.-Soviet relationship that make the weapons so dangerous.

The American Academy is actively supporting Pugwash. Pugwash, of course, was the pioneering international forum in this field. Active interest continues, and one phenomenon of the American participation is a growing involvement of young scholars. Pugwash is dealing with critical issues: conventional deterrence in Europe, regional conflicts that can lead to nuclear war, and the ramifications for Europe of strategic defense.

The American Academy is also trying to enlarge the role of U.S. universities and colleges in addressing nuclear issues. It has started a Kistiakowsky visiting scholar program honoring the late scientist who was the President's Science Adviser in the Eisenhower administration. In this program, distinguished scholars visit smaller colleges and universities that are starting courses and other activities in this field. Perhaps the most striking of the American Academy's outreach efforts occurred some months ago in a meeting held jointly with the Planetary Society and with the cooperation of the National Academy of Sciences. The meeting was devoted to ballistic missile defense (BMD) and antisatellite (ASAT) matters, including effects of the BMD and ASAT programs on U.S.-Soviet political relations, on the superpowers' strategic stability, and on civilian uses of space. This meeting was covered extensively by the national news media in this country. Finally, in connection with the American Academy's Weapons in Space Project, there is a U.S.-Soviet activity led on the Soviet side by academicians Velikhov and Segdaev, together with Professor Frank Long of Cornell University.

Let me now mention a set of studies being supported by the Carnegie Corporation of New York on different facets of strategic defense and to some extent dealing also with the way the Strategic Defense Initiative (SDI) impinges on other security uses of space and on civilian uses of space. This is, after all, an exceedingly complex area: technical feasibility, economic considerations, strategic considerations, international relations; there are so many facets affected by SDI that it is important to have a set of objective, analytical, science-based, independent studies. These studies are open to full critique, will be published, and should be useful to governments and the public. I have already sketched the American Academy of Arts and Sciences study. There is another being done in the University of California system headed by Professor Herbert York and involving various campuses of the university, as well as the special laboratories associated with the University of California. The American Physical Society is also conducting a study with the cooperation of the U.S. Department of Defense. And the Johns Hopkins School of Advanced International Studies, headed by the former Secretary of Defense, Dr. Harold Brown, and the United Nations Association of the United States are each conducting their own studies. The earliest such study came from Stanford University, with Drell and Farley as the principal authors. More recently, the Stanford group completed a report on a specific space defense research program that would be consistent with the Anti-Ballistic Missile (ABM) Treaty and with improved U.S.-Soviet relations.

The crisis prevention approach deserves mention here. In essence, it is an antidote to complacency in the spirit of science: raising questions, challenging assumptions in seeking ways to reduce the risk of the use of nuclear weapons, looking at factors that influence the use of these weapons. Basically it is preoccupied with the prevalence of error and misjudgment in human affairs.

Crisis prevention simply says that it is too dangerous to think that we can manage nuclear confrontations like the Cuban Missile Crisis time after time and get away with it. There are too many sources of both human and mechanical error and, above all, the interaction between human and mechanical error that is enormously exacerbated in time of crisis.

It is appropriate in this medical meeting to reflect on the wider significance of the growing research literature on iatrogenic illness. For those of you not close to medicine, the term refers to medically induced illness. Most of the studies indicating the serious nature of this problem are coming out of our very finest hospitals. Even with splendid institutions, a science-based profession, and highly disciplined teams of workers, tragic mistakes are made. Our power is greater than ever before, both for better and for worse, and not just in medicine. It has been my personal good fortune to relate to leaders in government, science, technology, medicine, and business. They have earned my respect. Yet I have witnessed serious mistakes in each of these spheres.

In the nuclear war arena, we have only one mistake to make. This is the first time in history that we really cannot afford one serious mistake. Over the long term it is vanishingly improbable that, in this field where the stakes are much higher than any other, we could operate indefinitely in an error-free environment. That is what the crisis prevention approach addresses. It involves a variety of strategies and techniques.

One fundamental point of crisis prevention is to avoid subjecting either superpower to any threatening surprises. The upgrading of the Hotline is a useful step in that direction. Another idea of crisis prevention is to reach agreements that deal effectively with situations that are predictably sensitive and potentially explosive; perhaps the best case in point involves the rules of sea agreement between the U.S. and Soviet navies. It is highly probable that, during the course of this meeting, somewhere on the high seas U.S. and Soviet naval vessels or naval aircraft have encountered each other. They might have had a very nasty, unpleasant, dangerous exchange if not for the fact that the rules for such encounters are well established, codified in books on the ships at sea, and updated and clarified every year at a high-level conference between the two navies. All this is done in a professional, low-key manner that has survived political vicissitudes between the two nations.

Similarly we had a recent agreement on nuclear terrorism, a very appropriate subject to worry about between the U.S. and Soviet governments. It is only a start, but a step in the right direction. This year, too, we have had systematic regional consultations where we tried to clarify vital interests in touchy situations. It may not mean anything more than informal understandings about what are crucial interests, but it too is a step in the right direction. Finally, in this crisis prevention approach, one needs institutional mechanisms that provide a professional exchange of information and ideas on a regular basis about matters that could become highly dangerous. In this domain, the best example is the Standing Consultative Commission (SCC). The SCC has worked well for more than a decade. Various suggestions about risk reduction centers in Washington and Moscow are now under active consideration; they build on the SCC experience and could provide a useful long-term mechanism for crisis prevention.

Crisis prevention endeavors go beyond arms control. They do not make assumptions about the levels of stockpiles or the hostility between the two nations, only hope that both will change for the better. That would be a highly desirable therapeutic outcome, but the question is, what do we do until the doctor comes? Until that fundamental change in the relationship occurs, can we alter the circumstances surrounding the likelihood of use of nuclear weapons?

We in the scientific community are beginning to give the problem the attention it deserves. There is so much more to be done. When we leave this meeting, I fervently hope that each of us will ask, What more can I do? Who can I enlist in the effort? How can I widen that network? What tasks are being neglected? What organizations and institutions am I familiar with that could do more useful work in this field?

One more point and a vital one: the scientific community must address the sources of conflict; it must go beyond the manifestations of conflict or the weapons that make so much damage possible. What is there in human nature and human interaction that increases the risk of hatred and destruction, and what can be done to resolve conflicts?

Scientific study of human conflict is only beginning to expand. It is being stimulated now by the deep concerns that we all share at this meeting, and yet the status accorded this field of inquiry has been low, the support has been minimal, and the institutional arrangements have often been inadequate. I regard it as one of the greatest challenges of science policy in the remainder of this century to find ways to understand the nature and sources of human conflict and, above all, to develop effective ways of resolving it short of disaster.

The world is now, as it has been for a long time, awash in a sea of ethnocentrism, prejudice, and violent conflict. The historical record is full of every sort of slaughter based on invidious distinctions pertaining to religion, race, nationality, and so on. The human species seems to have a virtuoso capacity for making invidious distinctions and for justifying violence on whatever scale the current technology permits.

That is old; but what is new—indeed, very new and very threatening—is the destructive power of our weaponry; not only nuclear but enhanced conventional, chemical, and biological. What else is new is the worldwide spread of technical capability. Thus, it is possible almost everywhere to make or at least to use effectively the weapons of high technology. What is also new is the miniaturization of weapons, which opens up all kinds of dangerous possibilities for terrorism. And the technology that permits the widely broadcast justifications for violence is new, too. Moreover, there is an upsurge of fanatical behavior. Taken together, these developments provide a set of conditions that give us a growing capacity to make life everywhere absolutely miserable and disastrous, even aside from the fact that two nations probably have the capacity to render human life extinct.

In this kind of world, the scientific community must pull together in a reasonably unified way so that the physical, biological, behavioral, and social sciences can address these profound and pervasive problems. This will require cooperative engagement over a wide range of scientific activity and will necessitate overcoming some of our own internal barriers within the scientific community.

There is one final feature about the scientific community that is worth bearing in mind. I think it is fair to say that the scientific community is the closest approximation we now have to a truly international community, sharing certain fundamental interests, values, and standards, as well as certain fundamental curiosities about the nature of matter, life, behavior, and the universe. The shared quest for understanding is one that knows no national boundaries, has no inherent prejudices, no necessary ethnocentrism, and no barriers to the free play of information and ideas. So, to some extent the scientific community can provide a model for human relations that might transcend some of the biases and dogmatisms that have torn us apart throughout our history and have recently become so much more dangerous than ever before. Science can contribute greatly to a better future through its ideals and its processes—as well as through the specific content of its research—and all these need to be brought to bear now on the problem of human conflict. As I see it, the essential scientific outlook flows from some very old and cardinal features of human adaptation through our long history as a species. The evolution that is distinctively human centers around our increasing capacity for learning, for communication chiefly by language, for cooperative problem solving, for complex social organization, and for advanced toolmaking and tool using. These attributes have gotten us here by enormously enhancing our capabilities, not only to adapt to the widest variety of habitats, but also to modify our habitats profoundly in ways that suit our purposes. Now we are challenged as never before to find ways in which these unique capacities can be used to prevent us from destroying ourselves and especially to prevent the final epidemic; to prevent that will make possible the search for a decent quality of life for everyone on the planet. If we have lost our sense of purpose in the modern world, perhaps this perspective can help us regain it.

BIBLIOGRAPHY

Some Recent Books Published by Scientific Organizations Concerned with Nuclear War

Adams, R., and S. Cullen, eds. 1981. The Final Epidemic: Physicians and Scientists on Nuclear War (Physicians for Social Responsibility). Chicago, Ill.: University of Chicago Press.

American Psychiatric Association. 1982. Psychosocial Aspects of Nuclear Developments (APA Task Force Report No. 20). Washington, D.C.: American Psychiatric Association.

British Medical Association. 1983. The Medical Effects of Nuclear War. New York and Chichester: John Wiley & Sons.

Cassel, C., M. McCally, H. Abraham. 1984. Nuclear Weapons and Nuclear War: A Source Book for Health Professionals (Physicians for Social Responsibility). New York: Praeger.

Chivian, E., S. Chivian, R. J. Lifton, and J. E. Mack, eds. 1982. Last Aid: The Medical Dimensions of Nuclear War (International Physicians for the Prevention of Nuclear War). San Francisco, Calif.: W. H. Freeman and Company.

The Committee for the Compilation of Materials on Damage Caused by the Atomic Bombs in Hiroshima and Nagasaki. 1981. Hiroshima and Nagasaki: The Physical, Medical, and Social Effects of the Atomic Bombings. New York: Basic Books. (Translated by Eisei Ishikawa and David L. Swain.)

Ehrlich, P., C. Sagan, D. Kennedy, W. O. Roberts. 1984. The Cold and the Dark: The World After Nuclear War (Center on the Consequences of Nuclear War). New York: W. W. Norton.

Griffiths, F., and J. Polanyi, eds. 1979. The Dangers of Nuclear War (A Pugwash Symposium). Toronto: University of Toronto Press.

Harwell, M. A., and T. C. Hutchinson, with W. P. Cropper, Jr., C. C. Harwell, and H. D. Grover, eds. 1986. Environmental Consequences of Nuclear War. Volume II: Ecological and Agricultural Effects. SCOPE 28 (Scientific Committee on Problems of the Environment, International Council of Scientific Unions). New York and Chichester: John Wiley & Sons.

Leaning, J., and L. Keyes, eds. 1984. The Counterfeit Ark: Crisis Relocation for Nuclear War (Physicians for Social Responsibility). Cambridge: Ballinger.

London, J., and G. F. White, eds. 1984. The Environmental Effects of Nuclear War (American Association for the Advancement of Science Selected Symposium No. 98). Boulder, Colo.: Westview Press.

Long, F. A., D. Hafner, and J. J. Boutwell, eds. 1986. Weapons in Space (American Academy of Arts and Sciences). New York: W. W. Norton.

National Academy of Sciences, Committee on International Security and Arms Control. 1985. Nuclear Arms Control: Background and Issues. Washington, D.C.: National Academy Press.

National Research Council. 1985. The Effects on the Atmosphere of a Major Nuclear Exchange. Washington, D.C.: National Academy Press.

Peterson, Jeanne, ed. 1983. The Aftermath: The Human and Ecological Consequences of Nuclear War (Royal Swedish Academy of Sciences). New York: Pantheon Books.

Pittock, A. B., T. P. Ackerman, P. J. Crutzen, M. C. MacCracken, C. S. Shapiro, and R. P. Turco, eds. 1986. Environmental Consequences of Nuclear War. Volume I: Physical Atmospheric Effects. SCOPE 28 (Scientific Committee On Problems of the Environment, International Council of Scientific Unions). New York and Chichester: John Wiley & Sons.

Thompson, James. 1985. Psychological Aspects of Nuclear War (The British Psychological Society). New York and Chichester: John Wiley & Sons.

World Health Organization. 1984. Effects of Nuclear War on Health and Health Services: Report of the International Committee of Experts in Medical Services and Public Health. WHO Pub. A36.12. Geneva: World Health Organization.

PART I

Nuclear War with Modern Weapons: Physical Effects and Environmental Consequences

The Medical Implications of Nuclear War, Institute of
Medicine. © 1986 by the National Academy of Sciences.
National Academy Press, Washington, D.C.

Possible Fatalities from Superfires Following Nuclear Attacks in or near Urban Areas

THEODORE A. POSTOL, PH.D.
Stanford University, Stanford, California

INTRODUCTION

During the period of peak energy output, a 1-megaton (Mt) nuclear weapon can produce temperatures of about 100 million degrees Celsius at its center, about four to five times that which occurs at the center of the Sun.

Because the Sun's surface is only about 6,000°C and it heats the Earth's surface from a range of more than 90 million miles (about 145 million km), it should be clear that such a nuclear detonation would be accompanied by enormous emanations of light and heat.

So great is the amount of light and heat generated by a 1-Mt airburst, that if one were to occur at a high enough altitude over Baltimore, observers in Washington, D.C., might see it as a ball of fire many times brighter than the noonday Sun. Even if such a detonation were to occur near dawn over Detroit, out of line of sight because of the Earth's curvature, enough light could well be scattered and refracted by atmospheric effects for it to be observed as a glare in the sky from Washington, D.C.

This intense light and heat from nuclear detonations is capable of setting many simultaneous fires over vast areas of surrounding terrain. These fires, once initiated, could efficiently heat large volumes of air near the Earth's surface. As this heated air buoyantly rises, cool air from regions beyond the vast burning area would rush in to replace it. Winds at the ground could reach hurricane force, and air temperatures within the zone of fire could exceed that of boiling water.

15

The ferocious hurricane of fire would also be accompanied by the release of large amounts of potentially lethal toxic smoke and combustion gases, creating an environment of extreme heat, high winds, and toxic agents in target areas.

Although the smoke from these fires has been the subject of considerable attention, as it is possible that significant climate effects could result from its sudden injection into the upper atmosphere, there has been no comprehensive evaluation of the implications of these fires for those in target areas.

In this paper, the potential implications of these fire environments on casualty estimates is assessed.

The standard model for calculating deaths and nonfatal injuries from hypothetical nuclear attacks assumes that the same casualty rates will occur at each level of blast overpressure as that which occurred at Hiroshima. This methodology, which will henceforth be referred to as *blast effect,* or simply *blast scaling,* is the standard methodology used by government agencies to estimate casualties in nuclear war.

The preliminary analysis presented in this paper indicates that if fire effects are included in assessments of possible fatalities from nuclear attacks using megaton or near megaton airbursts in or near urban areas, about two to four times more fatalities might be expected relative to those which might be expected from blast scaling calculations.

This enormous increase in projected fatalities is partly a result of the very large expected range of superfires, which would extend well beyond that in which large numbers of blast fatalities would be expected, and partly because of the high lethality in the blast-disrupted and fire-swept environments within the burning region.

The very great uncertainties in the speculated differences between blast and fire scaling are due to the great uncertainties in the radius of the potential fire zone, as well as to uncertainties in the exact nature of the environments within these zones.

Another feature that emerges from the analysis is that the projected number of injured requiring medical treatment would be drastically reduced relative to that projected by blast scaling, as many injured that would otherwise require treatment would be consumed in the fires. This is consistent with the findings of German review commissions[1] which were set up during World War II to evaluate the effects of large-scale incendiary raids against their cities and with the findings of the U.S. Strategic Bombing Survey after World War II.[2] Both reviews found that the ratio of fatalities to injuries was much higher when the effects of incendiaries, rather than high explosives, was the major source of damage from air raids.

In this paper, the following will be discussed. First, the blast and incendiary effects that would accompany the detonation of a 1-Mt airburst will be described. A baseline estimate of the radius of potential incendiary effects from the airburst will then be established; and the distinctive characteristics of the resulting giant area fires, high winds, and unusually high average air temperatures will be described. Evidence is presented to show that contrary to what has been previously believed,[3-5] attacks on lightly built-up, sprawling American cities, where the amount of combustible material per unit area is relatively low, could well result in extreme conditions somewhat comparable to those of the firestorms experienced in Japan and Germany during World War II. Estimates of noxious gas concentrations then will be made using data presented in the previous section, and it will be shown that the combination of these toxic agents within the fire zone are likely to be lethal to all unprotected individuals. Anecdotal and medical observations from World War II firestorm experiences will be reviewed, and a very crude cookie cutter model will be discussed. It is argued that more sophisticated models are unjustified in view of the large uncertainties in possible fire radius but that the simplicity of this model still allows a preliminary assessment of the importance of fire effects. The currently standard blast effect scaling method will be reviewed and compared and contrasted with the fire effect scaling method. Projections of casualties using both blast and fire scaling will then be presented for airburst antipopulation attacks. This establishes a reference case for the comparison of casualty projections by both methods and for different target sets. It will be shown that blast scaling may underestimate fatalities from airburst attacks in or near urban areas by factors of about two to four. Casualty projections are then compared for the antipopulation reference attack and a very limited anti-industrial attack, which is not designed to kill large numbers of people. However, the inclusion of superfires in casualty predictions indicates that this more limited attack might actually result in about two to three times more fatalities than that predicted by the government for the antipopulation attack. This serves to underscore the need for a better understanding of these weapons effects.

INCENDIARY EFFECTS OF NUCLEAR WEAPONS

In this section, the events associated with the detonation of a 1-Mt airburst are described. Because the weapons' effects of interest here, blast and thermal radiation (heat emanating from the fireball), do not change drastically with yield and because many of the weapons in today's arsenals are of comparable yield, this discussion will provide background information that will allow the reader to construct a picture of an urban target area following a nuclear attack.

When a nuclear weapon is detonated, an enormous amount of energy is released in an extraordinarily short interval of time. Nearly all of this energy is initially released in the form of fast-recoiling nuclear matter which is then deposited into the surrounding environment within hundredths of millionths of a second.

Unlike a comparable chemical explosion, in which almost all the explosive power is in expanding gaseous bomb debris, more than 95 percent of the explosive power is at first in the form of intense light. Since this intense light is of very short wavelength (it is soft x-rays), it is efficiently absorbed by the air immediately surrounding the weapon, heating it to very high temperatures creating a "ball" of fire.

Because the early fireball is so hot, it quickly begins to violently expand, initially moving outward at several millions of miles per hour while it also radiates tremendous amounts of light and heat. This rate of expansion slows rapidly, and by the time the fireball begins to approach its maximum size, its average speed of expansion is no more than 5,000 to 10,000 miles/h (about 8,000 to 16,000 km/h).

During the course of its expansion, almost all of the air that originally occupies the volume within and around it is compressed into a thin shell of superheated, glowing, high-pressure gas. This shell of gas, which continues to be driven outward by hot expanding gases in the fireball interior, itself compresses the surrounding air, forming a steeply fronted luminous shock wave of enormous extent and power (see Figure 1A).

By the time a 1-Mt fireball is near its maximum size, it is a highly luminous ball of more than 1 mile (1.6 km) in diameter. At 0.9 second after detonation begins, it is at its brightest. Its surface, which masks the much hotter interior of the fireball from the surroundings, still radiates two and a half to three times more light and heat than that of a comparable area of the Sun's surface.

By taking into account atmospheric attenuation (12-mile [about 19.3-km] visibility), at a distance of 6 miles (about 9.7 km), it would be 300 times brighter than a desert Sun at noon; and at 9 miles (about 14.5 km), it would still be 100 times brighter. Thus, extensive fire ignitions would accompany such an airburst over an urban/industrial area.

Figure 1 shows the development of a 1-Mt airburst detonated at an altitude of 6,500 feet (about 2 km) at five distinct points of time during the process.[6]

At 1.8 seconds (Figure 1A), the fireball is no longer expanding very rapidly, although it is still like a giant luminous and buoyant bubble in the Earth's atmosphere. It has already passed the time of maximum brightness, and the shock wave has broken away from it, already reaching a range of more than 0.5 mile (about 0.8 km) from its point of origin. When the primary shock wave from the explosion reaches the ground (see Figure 1B), a secondary shock wave is generated by reflection. The primary and secondary shock waves then propagate outward along the ground, forming a single vertical shock wave called the reinforced Mach front (see Figure 1C). The overpressure in this shock is roughly twice that of either the primary or the secondary shock.

By judicious choice of height of burst, it is possible to maximize the area over which this Mach front delivers a predetermined level of destructive overpressure. For the choice of burst height in this example, the area over which 15 pounds per square inch (psi) or more occurs has been maximized.

Figure 1C shows the situation at roughly 11 seconds after detonation. The shock wave would be about 3 miles (about 4.8 km) from the point on the Earth's surface over which the detonation occurred (this point is called ground zero), and the peak shock overpressure would be 6 psi. In the next 5 seconds, the shock would reach a range of 4 miles (about 6.4 km) and decay to a peak overpressure of 5 psi.

Figure 2 shows the sequence of events as they might occur at a wood frame house at a distance of 4 miles. Since the shock wave would take 16 seconds to arrive at the 4-mile range, when the detonation begins, a bright flash of growing intensity would be observed at the house within tenths of seconds. Because the shock wave would take a long time to arrive, this is the only initial indication of a detonation (see Figure 2A). Hence, sounds and noise levels around the house, at least at this moment, would be relatively unaltered.

The fireball, of course, continues to grow in brightness. Within 1 second, it is at its maximum brightness, appearing 800 to 900 times brighter than a desert Sun at noon. The tremendous rate of arrival of radiant power would result in the effusion of black smoke from the front of the house, as paint would be burned off the wood surfaces (see Figure 2B). If the building has interior household materials in it, and they are in the line of sight of the fireball, they would explode into violently burning fires almost instantly.

Fifteen seconds after the peak in the thermal pulse, the shock wave arrives (see Figures 2D, 2E, and 2F). Unlike a shock wave of comparable peak overpressure from a high explosive bomb, which persists for about 0.1 second as it passes, this shock wave persists for nearly 3 seconds. As a result, it is accompanied by winds of more than 150 miles/h (about 241 km/h). The shock wave therefore would first strike the building and then envelope it in a region of high-pressure air and high winds. The building

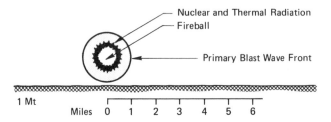

A　　1 MEGATON AIR BURST—1.8 SECONDS

Nuclear and Thermal Radiation
Fireball

Primary Blast Wave Front

1 Mt
Miles　0　1　2　3　4　5　6

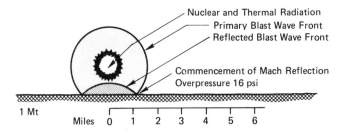

B　　1 MEGATON AIR BURST—4.6 SECONDS

Nuclear and Thermal Radiation
Primary Blast Wave Front
Reflected Blast Wave Front

Commencement of Mach Reflection
Overpressure 16 psi

1 Mt
Miles　0　1　2　3　4　5　6

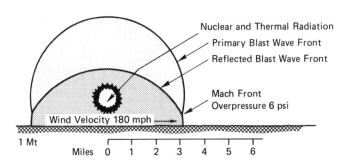

C　　1 MEGATON AIR BURST—11 SECONDS

Nuclear and Thermal Radiation
Primary Blast Wave Front
Reflected Blast Wave Front

Mach Front
Overpressure 6 psi

Wind Velocity 180 mph

1 Mt
Miles　0　1　2　3　4　5　6

FIGURE 1　The sequence of events for a 1-Mt airburst detonated at 6,500 feet (about 2 km) altitude are shown in A through E. This altitude maximizes the range from ground zero at which the primary and secondary shock waves coalesce

D

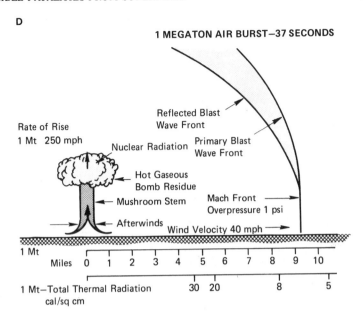

1 MEGATON AIR BURST–37 SECONDS

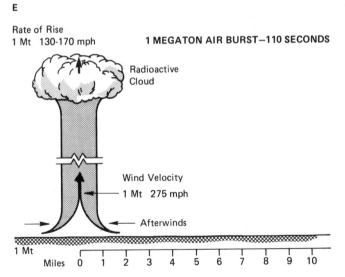

1 MEGATON AIR BURST–110 SECONDS

to give a 15-psi peak overpressure on the ground (see text). By adjusting the detonation altitude to 11,000 feet (about 3,353 m), the 5-psi distance could be increased from 3.8 to 4.3 miles (about 6 to 7 km), but the 15-psi range would shrink to near zero. Source: Glasstone (1962).[6]

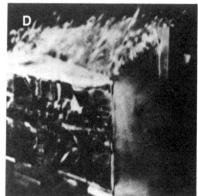

FIGURE 2   The sequence of prompt nuclear effects as observed at a range of about 4 miles (about 6.5 km). Light from the fireball begins to illuminate the structure a few tenths of seconds after the detonation (A). As the brightness of the fireball increases (B), the front of the house gives off a thick black smoke as paint is burned off by the heating action of the very intense light. After the paint is burned off, the house is bathed in light of decreasing intensity as the fireball rises and cools (C). About 16 seconds after the detonation, the shock wave arrives (D). As it propagates across the building, the front wall begins to cave in, and tiles are stripped from the roof. When the building is completely engulfed by the passing shock wave (E and F), the high pressure that now surrounds the building crushes the structure, and the high winds cause further damage to the building as it collapses. Source: Glasstone and Dolan (1977)[3] and Glasstone (1962).[6]

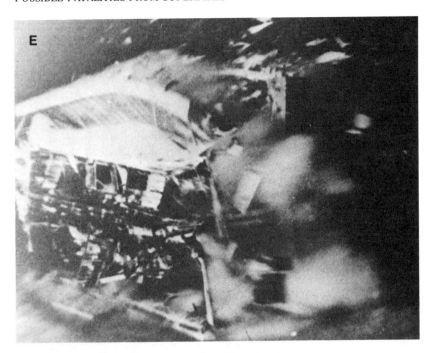

thus would be simultaneously knocked down and crushed as the shock wave propagates past.

Figures 3A and 3B show typical urban residential structures that have been subjected to overpressures of about 5 psi from nuclear bursts at the Nevada Test Site. Because these structures were constructed to study the effects of blast, precautions were taken to prevent them from burning. The exteriors were painted white to reflect rather than to absorb light from the fireball, windows facing the explosion were equipped with light-reflecting aluminum finish, metal venetian blinds, and roofs were made of light gray asbestos cement shingles. Also, there were no utilities (gas lines, electric lines, stoves, etc.) that could be sources of secondary fires from blast effects.

Of course, if fires from thermal and secondary blast effects had been allowed to initiate in these structures, they would clearly burn with great efficiency.

It would take 37 seconds from the time of detonation for the shock wave to reach a distance of about 9.5 miles (about 15.3 km). At this distance, 35 to 36 seconds before its arrival, the fireball would be about 100 times brighter than the Sun at noon. This is bright enough to cause first- or second-degree skin burns on those in line of sight. It is also possible, but much less certain, that some scattered fires could be set in very highly combustible items (possibly some dry grass, leaves, or newspapers, and also interior curtains and other lightweight materials).

When the shock wave finally arrives, it will have a peak overpressure between 1 and 1.5 psi, which would knock windows (possibly with their frames) out, along with many interior building walls and some doors (see Figures 4 through 7 and their figure captions).

By 110 seconds, the characteristic mushroom cloud will have reached about 7 miles (about 11.3 km) altitude (see Figure 1E). However, from the ground within the target area, it might be difficult to observe, as great amounts of dust kicked up by the blast wave and the accompanying high winds, as well as smoke from the fires initiated by the bright thermal flash of the fireball, could obscure the vision of those inclined to look. For those in the target area who are uninjured or still alert enough to be aware of their surroundings, the drama would not yet be over, as fires would begin to simultaneously develop and intensify over a vast area.

The situation in the target area therefore would be one of extremely severe blast damage to a range of 3 to 4 miles (about 4.8 to 6.4 km) from ground zero and very slowly diminishing levels of serious damage out to ranges well beyond 10 miles (about 16 km). Streets would be blocked with debris, water pressure would drop to zero, gas lines would be opened in places, and power would be off. Essentially all windows would have been broken, buildings that were not knocked down would have suffered

FIGURE 3   The effects of 5 psi of overpressure from a nuclear detonation are shown for two structures (A and B) that are typical of those in the United States. Since the structures were built to study the effects of blast, precautions were taken to minimize the possibility that fires would be initiated by light from the fireball or blast disruption effects. For this reason, neither of the buildings contained utilities of any kind. In addition, the roofs were made of light gray asbestos shingles, and windows facing the blast were equipped with metal venetian blinds with an aluminum finish. Source: Glasstone (1962).[6]

FIGURE 4   The effects of a nuclear detonation-generated blast of 1.7 psi on a wood-frame building. Figure 2A shows a similar structure before the blast and Figure 3B shows that structure after a blast of 5 psi. Although the building shown in this figure was not knocked down, the front door was broken into pieces and the kitchen and basement doors were torn off their hinges. In addition, many of the windows, including their frames, were blown into the building interior. Such a building, if ignited by blast or thermal effects associated with a detonation, might burn with great efficiency. Source: Glasstone (1962).[6]

extensive interior and wall damage (see Figures 4 through 7), and fires of varying intensity would have been initiated at many points within the target area.

Figures 8 through 10 show plots of the overpressure and thermal fluence as a function of range for airbursts of 1-, 0.5-, and 0.1-Mt yields. Each graph assumes a visibility of 12 miles (about 19.3 km), and for purposes of comparison, each graph is also accompanied by a plot of the over-pressure and thermal energy that occurred at Hiroshima.

It should be noted that the ratio of thermal to blast effects change drastically in Figures 8 through 10, as the scales of each of these two quantities are different with changes in weapon yield. The reasons for this are as follows.

Blast energy from a detonation fills the volume surrounding it. A det-onation would therefore fill a volume with blast energy in direct proportion to its yield. Since the size of the sphere's radius varies as the cube root of its volume, so does the range at which a given peak overpressure occurs. Hence, the range at which a given peak overpressure occurs scales as the cube root of the yield.

Thermal energy, unlike blast energy, instead radiates out into the surroundings. Thermal energy from a detonation will therefore be distributed over a hypothetical sphere that surrounds the detonation point. If the sphere's area is larger in direct proportion to the yield of a detonation, then the amount of energy per unit area passing through its surface would be unchanged. The radius of this hypothetical sphere varies as the square root of its area. Hence, the range at which a given amount of thermal energy per unit area is deposited varies as the square root of the yield.

FIGURE 5   The first floor joists of a strengthened wood-frame building that has been subjected to a 4-psi blast from a nuclear detonation. If the building structure had not been strengthened, the blast would likely have caused it to collapse. At the 4-psi range, the light from the fireball of a 1-Mt detonation could be 500 to 700 times brighter than a desert sun at noon. Such intense light would ignite furnishings and curtains in the building, which could then ignite the rest of the damaged structure. Source: Glasstone (1962).[6]

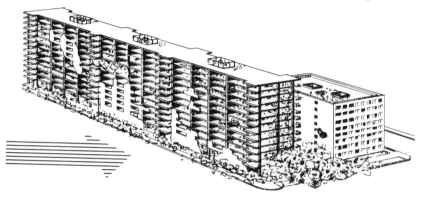

FIGURE 6   Illustration of the possible appearance of a building whose exterior walls are predicted to collapse when loaded at normal incidence with a 1.5-psi blast from a nuclear detonation. Ignitions caused by the light of the fireball or blast disruption could potentially result in the rapid development of well-aerated and extremely intense fires in such structures. Adapted from J. Wiersma and S. B. Martin, 1973. An Evaluation of the Nuclear Fire Threat to Urban Areas, Contract DAHC20-70-C-0219, Menlo Park, Calif.: Stanford Research Institute.

This square root scaling is further modified by absorption and scattering of light in the air, and so it would vary with weather and visibility.

As a result of these different scaling rules, at any range at which a given overpressure were to occur, the ratio of thermal to blast energy would vary with weapon yield. For almost all ranges of interest here, in which fires can be set by light from the fireball, unless visibility is significantly less than 12 miles (about 19.3 km), the ratio of thermal to blast effects would increase with an increase in weapon yield. Hence, weapons of higher yield are yet better incendiaries than those of lower yield.

SUPERFIRES AND THEIR ENVIRONMENTS

Figure 11 shows the area over which simultaneous fires could be initiated by the light from a 1-Mt airburst if visibility is good (10 to 12 miles [about 16 to 19.3 km]). The radius of the circle is 12 km.

At this range the 2 psi of peak overpressure from the blast wave would be sufficient to knock nonsupporting interior walls out of most buildings (see Figure 7). It may shatter or badly damage exterior nonsupporting walls on many buildings as well. Secondary fires from overturned stoves, broken gas lines, and electrical shorts could then be expected with low but significant frequency. In addition, the 10 calories per square centimeter (cal/cm^2) deposited by the fireball would ignite some light fabrics, curtains, and perhaps other easily combustible items.

At the center of Figure 11 is a silhouette of the area that burned in the firestorm following the atomic attack of August 6, 1945, on Hiroshima. A box with sides of 1 mile (about 1.6 km) length puts the scale of the possible fire region in perspective.

Under the assumptions used in the construction of Figure 11, an area of about 175 mile^2 (about 450 km^2), about 40 times larger than that at Hiroshima, would simultaneously contain fires. It is emphasized, however, that the area over which ignitions could play an important role in the development of a mass fire is highly uncertain.

If clouds or heavy fog were in the path of radiant energy from the

FIGURE 7 The interior of the Hiroshima District Monopoly Bureau building, about 2.3 km from the hypocenter. The building was probably subjected to a blast of about 3 psi, which did not knock it down but caused heavy interior damage. Because of the different way blast and thermal effects scale with weapon yield, the amount of thermal energy from the fireball of a 1-Mt detonation would be greater than that which occurred at the 3-psi range at Hiroshima. At the 3-psi range from a 1-Mt detonation, the amount of thermal energy delivered by the fireball would be about 3 times greater than that which occurred at Hiroshima. This would greatly increase the likelihood of fire ignitions in the building interior. Adapted from The United States Strategic Bombing Survey, Physical Damage Division, 1947.

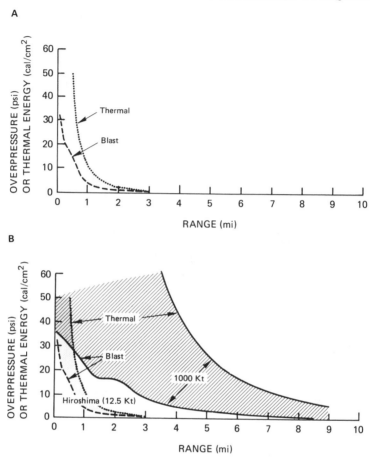

FIGURE 8   The peak blast overpressure and the total amount of thermal energy per square centimeter are plotted as a function of range from detonation. (A) Range dependence of peak overpressure and thermal energy from a 12.5-kt detonation at a height of burst of about 1,800 to 2,000 feet (about 550 to 610 m). (B) Similar curves for a 1,000-kt detonation at a height of burst of about 8,000 feet (about 2,440 m). Because the two heights of burst are chosen so that they are related by the ⅓ power of the ratio of the two yields [1,000 kt/12.5 kt$^{1/3}$ = 4.3], the range at which a given overpressure in B occurs is simply 4.3 times that in A. However, as can be seen from a comparison of these graphs, the thermal energy per square centimeter does not scale in the same way as the peak overpressure. For the 1,000-kt weapon (and assuming 12 miles [about 19 km] visibility), the thermal energy at a range which results in a given overpressure is much higher than that which occurs at the same peak overpressure for the smaller detonation. Thus, the use of blast scaling alone as a method of defining the environments in which casualties may occur could potentially lead to predictions that could seriously be in error.

fireball, the range of thermal ignitions shown in Figure 11 would likely be reduced (however, secondary ignitions from blast effect would likely be affected little). If the target area were instead experiencing dry summer weather, many fires could be set in grass and leaves at a greater range. In winter, if there were snow cover, this could not occur. But the snow would reflect additional fireball light into the low-relative-humidity interiors of houses, where fires would then be more likely.

Also influencing the nature and scale of mass fire dynamics is blast damage from the shock wave. The blast from the detonation would knock down some buildings and leave others standing. In standing buildings, windows would be shattered and many interior walls and doors would be

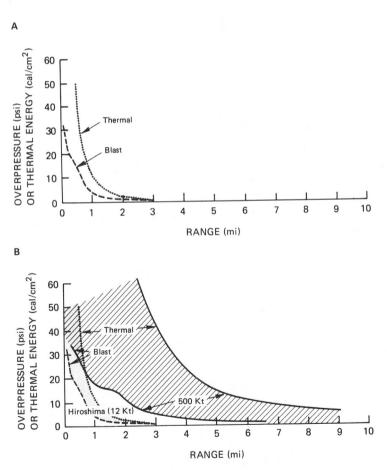

FIGURE 9 The two graphs are similar to those shown in Figure 8, except the choice of yields is 12.5 (A) and 500 (B) kt.

blown out or badly damaged, making the buildings and their interiors more combustible (see Figures 4, 5, and 7). In other standing buildings, exterior walls could also be knocked down or badly damaged (see Figure 6). These buildings could provide a well-aerated structure for fire development.

In addition, the blast wave could also initiate secondary fires, as gas mains would be broken, electrical shorts would be created, stoves would be knocked over, and the like.

Thus, highly uncertain sources of ignition and conditions of fire spread could influence the extent of a mass fire region, its development over time, and its intensity following an airburst over or near an urban/industrial

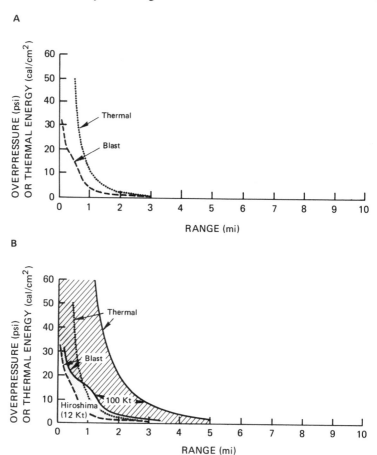

FIGURE 10   The two graphs are similar to those shown in Figures 8 and 9, except the choice of yields is 12.5 (A) and 100 (B) kt.

FIGURE 11   The area over which a mass fire could be initiated from the combined blast and thermal effects of a 1,000-kt detonation at a height of burst of 8,000 feet (about 2,440 m). The outer circle is highly speculative, as 10 calories/cm^2 from the fireball might only initiate scattered and isolated fires in highly combustible exposed materials. However, the 2-psi blast would result in considerable interior and exterior damage to structures of the type shown in Figures 4 through 7. The disruption from blast effects could then initiate many secondary fires that could also contribute to the growth of a mass fire of unprecedented scale. By comparison, the silhouette shown in the center of the diagram is the area that burned following the atomic bombing of Hiroshima.

area.[7] Nevertheless, as individual fires burn and intensify over a vast region, the volume of heated and buoyantly rising air from the fire zone could increase to significant levels. If a sufficiently intense source of air heating were created within the fire zone, the expanding hot air from that region could begin to lift the vertical column of cooler air above it (see Figure 12A). If the rate of air heating were very high, this pumping action could be very great. Conversely, if it were very low, the pumping action could be insignificant relative to that of other forces influencing the motion of the air above.

Conceptually, as such a fire develops and as each layer of air in the column is pushed upward to a slightly higher altitude, that layer would bear a greater weight of air above it than that of the outside air at the same altitude (Figure 12A). Because air pressure at each altitude would be a result of this weight, the pressure within the air column would be initially greater than that of the surroundings, resulting in an outward horizontal expansion of the air in the column (see Figure 12B).

As this occurs, the weight of air above the ground within the column would decrease, while it would increase above the ground outside the column. In response, the air pressure at ground level within the column would also decrease, and the air pressure external to the column would increase. Air would then begin to flow into the fire zone from the surrounding regions at ground level.

At upper altitudes, the buoyantly rising heated air from the fire zone would still create outward driving pressure differentials, and a gigantic circulating air flow would develop with winds moving outward at high altitudes and inward at low altitudes.

On the ground, the resulting fire winds would begin to fan the individual fires, causing them to burn more intensely, radiating greater heat, and generating firebrands. This action then would cause the fires to spread and intensify yet more rapidly, increasing the rate of air heating within the fire zone and generating still more intense fire winds, further fanning fires of still greater intensity. Thus, a fire of gigantic scale and ferocity could develop, resulting in very high average air temperatures and winds near the ground.

Figure 13 shows the circulating air motion predicted by two exploratory numerical simulations of extremely intense firestorms.[8] Such numerical simulations contain many assumptions that can result in artifacts; and hence, their predictions should be taken as illustrative, and detailed results should be viewed with appropriate caution.

The calculations assume heat inputs per unit area comparable to those of the Dresden firestorm (about 250 kilowatts per meter squared), but over a circle of much larger radius (10 km). Of interest is the circulating vortices which occur at about a 10-km altitude in Figure 13A and at a 5-km altitude in Figure 13B.

In Figure 14 the two different assumptions about the rate of change of temperature with altitude used in these calculations are shown. The simulated result in Figure 13A assumed a dry adiabatic lapse rate* of -9.8 °K/km, while the simulated result shown in Figure 13B assumes a standard U.S. atmosphere, with a tropospheric lapse of -6.5 °K/km (see Figure 14).

The additional buoyancy generated by the colder atmosphere simulation in Figure 13A relative to that in 13B is likely the cause in the upward

---

*The lapse rate is the rate at which the atmospheric temperature changes with altitude.

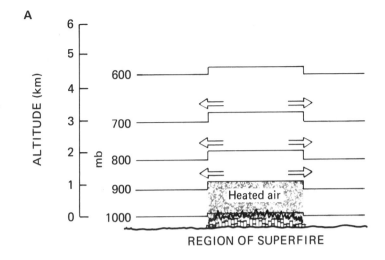

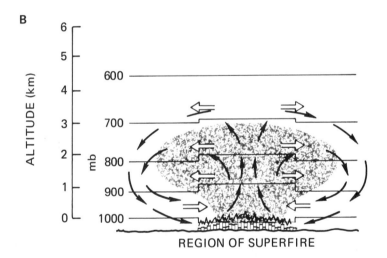

FIGURE 12   The drawings show how a mass fire that burns simultaneously over
a large area can generate high ground winds. In A, buoyantly rising air from a
fire zone pushes air at higher altitudes upward and outward. Eventually this action
can result in the establishment of a macroscopic flow field of enormous power
and extent (B). If the heat output per unit area from combustion is reduced, but
the area over which the heat output is produced is increased, such a large circulating
pattern might still occur. Thus, predictions of ground winds and air temperatures
from mass fires must consider both the scale of the fire and the heat input per
unit area in the region where such fires burn.

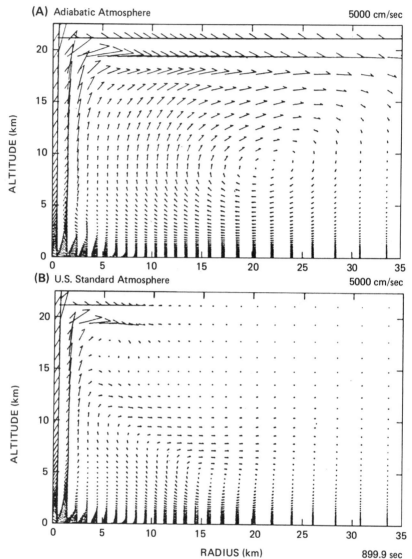

FIGURE 13 Two numerical simulations reported in note 8 of flow patterns from a very intense mass fire that results in 250 kw/m^2 of heat input over a circle of radius 10 km are shown. The two simulations assume different vertical temperature profiles (shown in Figure 14). Although the large-scale atmospheric motions for the two different vertical temperature profiles differ, the predicted ground winds near and within the fire region are almost identical. It is therefore possible that subtle details of weather may not be an important factor in the creation of severe ground conditions in and around a sufficiently intense mass fire. Source: Hassig and Rosenblatt (1983).[8]

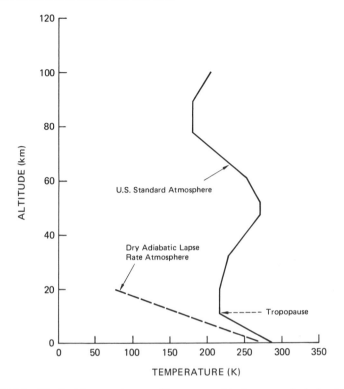

FIGURE 14 Vertical temperature profiles assumed in the numerical simulations shown in Figure 13. Source: Hassig and Rosenblatt (1983).[8]

shift of the circulating vortices. However, in spite of the very different physical assumptions about conditions in the upper atmosphere, the winds at lower altitudes are essentially unchanged, indicating that the postulated energy input at ground level dominates the dynamics in both circumstances.

Also noteworthy is that the average winds predicted near ground level would be over 100 miles per hour (about 161 km per hour) at many ranges, and the circulating vortices in both calculations would be of the order of 15 km from the center of the fire region. This suggests that fires separated by 20 to 30 km could distort each other's flow field, resulting in pressure differentials that could cause these fires to merge.

However, as noted above, these calculations are numerical simulations, and of necessity they require the application of boundary conditions as well as numerical simplifications of very complex hydrodynamic processes. The above observations must therefore be viewed as being only of the most qualitative nature.

A conceptual demonstration of fire interactions on a much smaller scale is shown in photographs of a fire experiment with candles (see Figure 15). The flow fields from the separate fires clearly interact, as the fires and their plumes begin to merge, resulting in a mass fire of enormously greater scale.

It is therefore possible, at least conceptually, that intense regions of fire initiated from multiple attacks with low-yield nuclear weapons could also generate mass fires of enormous scale and intensity, possibly indistinguishable from those initiated by larger-yield weapons.

Small, Larson, and Brode have constructed a hydrothermodynamic theory that permits exploratory scaling studies of possible near surface environments in regions of mass fire.[9-17] The average ground temperatures predicted in some of their calculations are shown in Figure 16.

In these calculations, it is assumed that a mass fire would burn out to a range of 12 km. Heating rates that are appropriate for fuel loadings found in lightly built-up cities of the type found in the western United States are assumed as input for the results presented in Figure 16A (average heat input rates of about 25 to 30 kw/m^2), and rates more appropriate to heavily built-up eastern industrial cities are used as input in Figure 16B (average heat input rates of about 75 to 80 kw/m^2). Other assumptions of a blast-modified versus unmodified city assume that centers of the fire regions would be so heavily damaged by blast that much of the combustible material would be buried in rubble and, hence, would not be sufficiently exposed to burn.

A most striking prediction of these calculations is that the average ground level air temperatures would be above the boiling point of water throughout the fire zones, even if the city were lightly built-up. The calculation for the lightly built-up city also predicts average winds of 35 to 40 miles/h (about 56.3 to 64.4 km/h), which is comparable to those that are known to have occurred at Hamburg. Predictions for a heavily built-up city estimate that there would be average wind speeds near 60 miles/h (about 96.5 km/h). Channeling of such average winds down streets or over terrain features for either case could well result in hurricane-force winds at the street level.

ESTIMATES OF NOXIOUS GAS CONCENTRATIONS WITHIN THE MASS FIRE REGION

The physical environments discussed in the previous sections are average environments. Actual physical conditions could differ substantially from location to location within a fire zone. However, areas that experience winds less than the average may experience temperatures higher than the

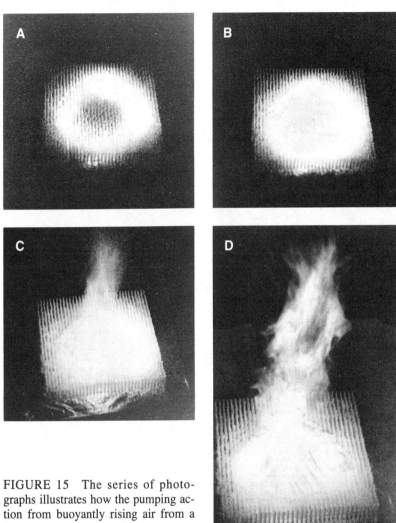

FIGURE 15 The series of photographs illustrates how the pumping action from buoyantly rising air from a collection of individual fires can create large-scale air currents that would not result if each fire were to burn in isolation. In A, a circle of candles that are part of a matrix of candles separated by 0.5 inch (1.27 cm) are lit. Buoyantly rising air from individual fires immediately results in large-scale air currents that bend the flames toward the center of the burning circle. In B through D, the inward air motion becomes increasingly well established, resulting in fire spread to the entire area surrounded by the original circle of flames. Reprinted from A "Fire Book" on Fire Safety in the Atomic Age. © 1952 National Fire Protection Association, Quincy, Mass. Reprinted with permission.

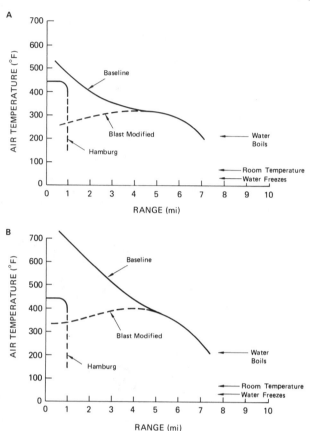

FIGURE 16   Calculations of average air temperatures for modeled mass fires in lightly (A) and heavily (B) built-up cities. The lightly built-up city is assumed to consist of a 3- to 12-km outer belt where 15 percent of the area is covered by buildings of 1.5 stories average height. The average fuel loading per story is assumed to be 16 lbs/ft^2. It is further assumed that 90 percent of the fuel is consumed within 3 hours and each pound of fuel consumed releases 8,000 BTUs of energy. In the central region of radius 3 km, the average fuel loadings are higher. The heavily built-up city shows similar results for a city that consists of a 6- to 12-km outer belt with 25 percent of the area covered by buildings of 2.5 stories average height. The fuel loading per story is also 16 lbs/ft^2, and the region within 6 km of the city center is still more built up. The solid curve shows average air temperatures (in degrees Fahrenheit) for the cities if all materials are assumed to burn according to these rules. The dashed curves are predictions of the model if it is assumed that the centers of the cities mostly do not burn, due to rubble from blast burying most that is combustible. Adapted from Larson and Small (1982).[16]

average, as heat generated by local fires might not be carried off as efficiently. In addition, other toxic effects of a mass fire may play an important role in determining whether or not those within the fire zone could survive. It is therefore of interest to examine and identify some of the other possible threats to those in a fire zone.

Because heating rates from combustion in the fire zone would result in high ground winds, there would be considerable mixing of large volumes of air with combustion products. A detailed calculation of combustion gas concentrations therefore requires a computationally powerful simulation or hydrothermodynamic modeling techniques of the kind discussed in the previous section.

However, because these techniques already provide estimates of the average air temperature and heating rates within the fire zone, they can be used to derive a very crude estimate of average gas concentrations as well.

In addition to estimates of the average air temperature and heat input for both the lightly and heavily built-up cities, estimates of the average output of energy and noxious gases per unit weight of burned material are also required. With these inputs, a very rough estimate of gas concentrations can be made for the postulated regions of mass fire.

The procedure for doing this is as follows. First, the average air temperature and heat input data from the hydrothermodynamic calculations are used to estimate the mass of air that would be heated per unit weight of material burned. The mass of material that must be burned to produce this energy and the amount of gas that would be given off in the process of combustion are then calculated. The ratio of the mass of combustion products to that of the heated air then gives a rough measure of the gas concentration.

Quantitative estimates of carbon monoxide and carbon dioxide generation in open fires vary by about an order of magnitude, ranging from about 600 pounds of carbon monoxide per ton (about 273 kg per metric ton) to about 50 pounds per ton (about 23 kg per metric ton).[18,19] Values for the ratio of carbon dioxide to carbon monoxide produced in different combustion experiments also vary considerably (from 10 to 50).[20-22] Using these extremely varied data on combustion product outputs and the heating rate/average air temperature relationships calculated by Small, Brode, and Larson,[9-17] the range of average carbon monoxide and carbon dioxide concentrations can be estimated for the area within the region of combustion.

Neglecting radiative losses, the amount of energy required to raise the temperature of a mass of air in the combustion zone by T degrees is governed by the heat capacity of air:

$$
\begin{array}{c}
\text{Energy} \\
\text{required to} \\
\text{raise a} \\
\text{mass of} \\
\text{air by} \\
T^\circ \text{ F}
\end{array}
=
\begin{array}{c}
\text{Mass} \\
\text{of air}
\end{array}
\times
\begin{array}{c}
\text{Heat capacity} \\
\text{per unit mass}
\end{array}
\times
\begin{array}{c}
\text{Change in} \\
\text{air} \\
\text{temperature}
\end{array}
\qquad (1)
$$

or $E = M \times C_M \times T$, where E is the amount of energy in British thermal units (BTUs) required to raise a mass of M pounds of air by T° F; M is the mass of air to be heated in pounds; C_M is the heat capacity of air, which is equal to 0.24 BTU/pound/°F; and T is the change in air temperature from its ambient value.

This energy equation (equation 1) can, of course, also be used to estimate the mass of air (per unit time) that is heated within the combustion region of the superfire:

$$
M = \frac{E}{C_M T} \qquad (2)
$$

For the lightly built-up city environment, the average temperature would be raised from around room temperature to slightly more than 200°F (about 93°C) (hence, $T = 130 - 150°F$) by a postulated heating rate of 6.55 kcal/m^2/s = 26 BTU/m^2/s. This results in the heating of a mass of air per unit time of about $M = 26$ BTU/s/m^2/[(0.24 BTU/lb/°F)(150°F)] = 0.72 lbs/s/m^2.

Because about 8,000 BTU of energy is released per pound of burning material, and between 50 and 1,000 pounds of carbon monoxide is released per ton of material burned (about 23 and 455 kg per metric ton), the rate at which carbon monoxide (CO) might be produced is between

$$
\text{Mass of CO produced/m}^2\text{/s} = \frac{(26 \text{ BTU/m}^2\text{/s})(50 \text{ lb CO/ton})}{(8,000 \text{ BTU/lb})(2,000 \text{ lbs/ton})}
$$
$$
= 8.1 \times 10^{-5} \text{ lb/m}^2\text{/s}
$$

and

$$
\text{Mass of CO produced/m}^2\text{/s} = \frac{(26 \text{ BTU/m}^2\text{/s})(1,000 \text{ lb CO/ton})}{(8,000 \text{ BTU/lb})(2,000 \text{ lbs/ton})}
$$
$$
= 1.6 \times 10^{-3} \text{ lb/m}^2\text{/s}
$$

The fraction of carbon monoxide that could be present may therefore be between $8.1 \times 10^{-5}/0.72 = 0.0001$, or 0.01 percent, and $1.6 \times 10^{-3}/0.72 = 0.0022$, or 0.22 percent.

Because the estimates given here are so rough, the range of carbon dioxide to carbon monoxide ratios quoted earlier is applied to estimate the carbon dioxide concentrations. This suggests that at the lower end of the carbon monoxide production, the amount of carbon dioxide in the air could be of order 0.1 to 0.5 percent. At the higher end the average concentration could be as high as several percent.

The reader may wish to note, when reviewing the contents of the next section on combined toxic effects of fire gases, that a carbon dioxide to carbon monoxide ratio of about 30 results in both thresholds for human collapse being reached simultaneously.

In addition, it is known that a variety of relatively typical building materials (Douglas fir and red oak woods) can produce hydrogen cyanide and sulfur dioxide when they burn. Ratios of hydrogen cyanide to carbon monoxide production of about 0.0025 to 0.005 have been observed experimentally.[23] Similar ratios have also been observed for sulfur dioxide. These ratios suggest that if these materials are common, average hydrogen cyanide and sulfur dioxide levels could be in concentrations of parts per million to tens of parts per million.

The estimates given above are very crude, and they therefore should be considered with appropriate caution.

The efficiency of combustion, for example, would vary strongly with circumstances at each location within the fire zone. When materials are exposed to high air temperatures and winds, they burn differently than when they are confined to closed spaces or under rubble.

On the other hand, the calculations given above underestimate the mass of material that is burned per mass of heated air, as the radiative energy is not included in the energy balance equation (equation 1).

COMBINED TOXIC EFFECTS OF FIRE GASES AND ELEVATED TEMPERATURES

The combined toxic effects of heat, combustion gases, aerosols (smoke from fires and dust heated and carried by hot winds), and physiological stresses created by fear, hysteria, and strenuous attempts to escape can result in a serious threat to the lives of unsheltered individuals within a region of mass fires. Even sheltered individuals may be threatened by a similar array of toxic effects, as shelters must be carefully designed to protect occupants from the effects of infiltration of poisonous gases and from heating by fire and hot rubble.[24-26]

During World War II in Germany, for example, the infiltration of carbon monoxide into shelters was the apparent immediate cause of death of many in the shelters. It was further judged to be the cause of death in 70 to 80 percent of reported fatalities from large-scale incendiary raids. However, such statistics have great potential to be misleading.[1,2]

TABLE 1   Physiological Effects from Exposure to Elevated
Temperatures (Hyperthermia)

Exposure Level	Physiological Effects
100°F (38°C)	Danger of heat prostration and heat stroke.
110°F (43°C)	Body heat balance cannot be long maintained.
120°F (49°C)	Three to five hours tolerance time.
130°F (54°C)	Danger of heat prostration and stroke within tens of minutes.

For instance, after the extremely successful allied incendiary air attack of July 26 and 27, 1943, on Hamburg, the heating of rubble from the fire made it impossible to enter the main area of the firestorm for 2 days following the raid. In fact, the heat content of the debris was so great that nearly a month after the raids (up to August 25), hosing of hot rubble and smoldering fires had to be carried out at different locations every day.[27] Thus, even if sheltered individuals had escaped death from the carbon monoxide that infiltrated the shelters, they may have instead met death in the extreme temperatures of shelters buried under fire-heated smoldering debris.

Some of the physiological effects of exposure to various levels of excessive heat, oxygen starvation, carbon monoxide, and carbon dioxide are summarized in Tables 1 through 5 and Figures 17 through 20. The Figures are derived from those published previously,[22,24,28] and Tables are derived from data published previously.[22,28–34] It is unlikely that these toxic agents would be encountered singly in the environment of a mass fire.

TABLE 2   Physiological Effects from Exposure to Carbon Dioxide

Exposure Level	Physiological Effects
2% CO_2	Breathing becomes deeper.
4% CO_2	Considerable discomfort with quickened and deeper breathing.
7% CO_2	Extremely labored breathing, accompanied by headache, dizziness, and sweating; may also be accompanied by nausea.
8% CO_2	Dizziness, stupor, and unconsciousness within about 4 hours.
9% CO_2	Labored respiration and extreme shortness of breath accompanied by congestion; loss of blood pressure and death within about 4 hours.
10% CO_2	Unconsciousness occurs within about 10 minutes.

TABLE 3   Physiological Effects from Exposure to Carbon Monoxide

Exposure Level	Physiological Effects
0.01% CO	No appreciable effects if exposure limited to several hours.
0.02% CO	Headache after 2 to 3 hours, followed by collapse within 4 to 5 hours.
0.03% CO	Headache within about 1.5 hours, followed by collapse within about 3 hours.
0.04% CO	Headache within 1 hour, followed by collapse within 2 hours and death within about 3 to 4 hours.

TABLE 4   Physiological Effects from Exposure to Oxygen Starvation (Anoxia)

Exposure Level	Physiological Effects
17% O_2	Respiration volume increases, muscular coordination diminishes, attention and clear thinking require greater discipline.
14% O_2	Dizziness, shortness of breath, headache, numbness, quickened pulse, efforts fatigue quickly
11% O_2	Nausea and vomiting, exertion impossible, paralysis of motion
8% O_2	Symptoms become serious and stupor sets in, unconsciousness occurs

The most immediate threat to individuals caught within a zone of mass fire is excessive heating of the body (hyperthermia) due to extended exposure to high-temperature air and to radiant energy from combusting materials (Tables 1 and 5 and Figure 20).

When the body carries a burden of excess heat and the air temperature is elevated, it is difficult for the body to radiate, convect, or evaporate away this excess energy to the environment. The body reacts to this circumstance by increasing its respiration and heart rate, which then results

TABLE 5   Estimated Levels of Toxic Agents Causing Death in 4 Hours

Variable	Estimated Lethal Levels
Temperature	130°F (54°C; hyperthermia)
Oxygen	8.00% (anoxia)
Carbon monoxide	0.04%
Carbon dioxide	20.00%

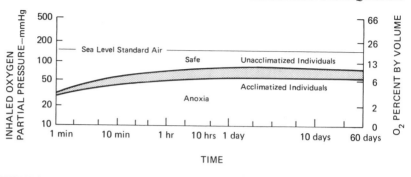

FIGURE 17   Human tolerance to variations in oxygen levels as a function of time. The lower band represents the minimum oxygen partial pressure that can be tolerated in the air entering the lungs. The reaction to changes in oxygen levels depends both on the magnitude of the change and the time over which the change occurs. When oxygen levels drop gradually from the normal sea level value, the usual symptoms are sleepiness, headache, fatigue, altered respiration, psychologic impairment, inability to perform even simple tasks, and eventual loss of consciousness. When oxygen levels instead drop suddenly, the intermediate symptoms are bypassed, and humans rapidly lose consciousness and go into spasms or convulsions. Adapted from Wilton et al. (1976)[22] and Bucheim (1958).[45]

in increased sweat production followed by the transport of excess body heat to the environment by evaporation. If the metabolic rate is increased from strenuous activity or excitement, a significant additional burden of body heat is added to that which already must be conducted to the environment. In addition, evaporative cooling in humid air is much less efficient than that in dry air, and there is a constant biological need for the replacement of essential body water throughout this process.

Thus, even if only the effects of elevated air temperature are considered, a combination of apparently nonthreatening contingencies can still result in a serious, near certain threat to life from heat prostration or stroke.

Keeping this in mind, note that exposure to air temperatures much above 130 to 140°F (54.4 to 60°C) for several hours will result in death from excessive body heating, even if the individual were calmly resting.

If, as expected, the regulator of the breathing function, carbon dioxide, is also present in the fire, it will cause the body to react by further increasing the respiration rate (Tables 2 and 5 and Figure 18).

In isolated circumstances, when carbon dioxide concentrations rise above about 2 percent, breathing becomes deeper. At a 5 percent carbon dioxide concentration, extremely labored breathing is induced, and this is possibly also accompanied by nausea. The human carbon dioxide tolerance level is usually considered to be between 7 and 9 percent, with unconsciousness generally occurring within 10 minutes when the concentration level is about 10 percent.

Carbon dioxide is found in fire environments because it is formed in the process of combustion. It may also be accompanied by small but biologically significant concentrations of carbon monoxide, which is also formed in the process of combustion.

Carbon monoxide, which is a chemical asphyxiant, is an extremely dangerous combustion product of fires (Tables 3 and 5 and Figure 19), and it bonds to the hemoglobin in red blood cells with an affinity of between 200 and 300 times that of oxygen. Because of this high affinity, very small concentrations of this material can cause a considerable decrease in the oxygen-carrying capability of the blood, as well as in the blood's ability to eliminate its presence by subsequent exposure to oxygen.

When the body respiration rate is increased by exposure to both carbon

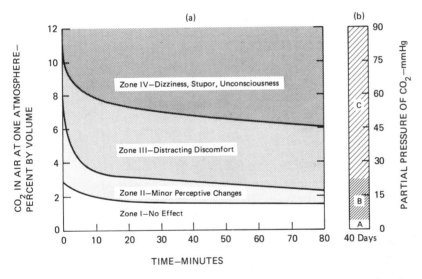

FIGURE 18   Human tolerance to variations in carbon dioxide levels as a function of time. As with exposure to changes in the level of oxygen, if changes are gradual, tolerances and symptoms are different than when changes are sudden. In Zone I, no psychophysiological effects occur in most subjects. In Zone II, a perceptible doubling in the depth of breathing will occur and small threshold hearing losses occur. In Zone III, mental depression, headache, dizziness, nausea, air hunger, and decreases in visual discrimination occur. In Zone IV, deterioration results in inability to take steps for self-preservation. Dizziness and stupor is then followed by unconsciousness. Adapted from Wilton et al. (1976)[22] and Bucheim (1958).[45]

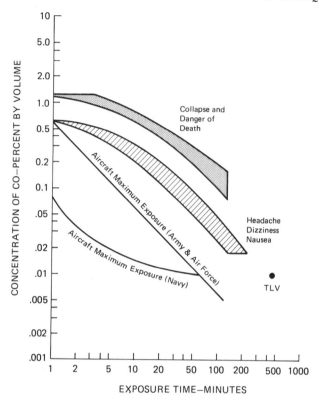

FIGURE 19   The effects of carbon monoxide as a function of concentration and exposure time. Milder effects are shown in the lower band of concentrations and exposure times, while dangerous or lethal times and concentrations are delineated by the upper band. The solid lines are exposure limits set by the military services. The point marked TLV at 0.01 percent (100 ppm) and 480 minutes is the Threshold Level Value, which is the allowed 8-hours-a-day exposure in industry. Adapted from Wilton et al. (1976).[22]

dioxide and elevated temperatures and its excess heat burden is further stressed by an elevated metabolic state from excitement or strenuous activity, enhanced take up of carbon monoxide by the body occurs.

Furthermore, if there is carbon dioxide and other gases in the air, these gases will displace oxygen, adding still another insult of oxygen starvation to the body burden (Tables 4 and 5 and Figure 17).

Other less well understood noxious threats include soot and smoke, which can cause inflammation and blockage within the respiratory system and which can transport poisonous materials into the respiratory tracts; sulfur dioxide and nitrogen dioxide, each of which can induce physiolog-

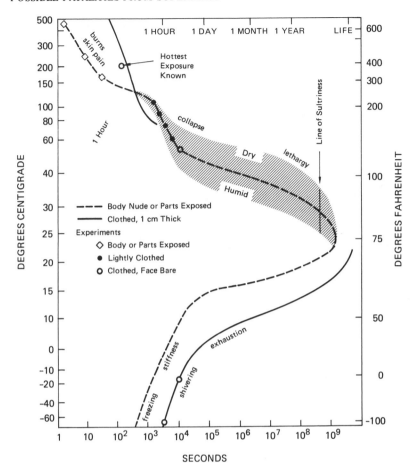

FIGURE 20 The safe exposure time for humans in high-temperature environments is highly dependent on relative humidity and water consumption. It is also dependent on the level of activity, acclimatization, and body weight. For example, at 100°F (38°C) and low humidity, lethargy may not occur. In high humidity it might instead occur within an hour of exposure. However, for a human to function in the 100°F temperatures for an extended period, required water consumption would roughly increase by about a factor of 4 over that which would be required at an air temperature of about 70°F. At 120°F (49°C) a 6 to 8 times higher water consumption might be needed to sustain an individual. Adapted from Wilton et al. (1976)[22] and Bucheim (1958).[45]

ical effects in humans at concentrations as low as 1 to 5 parts per million; hydrogen cyanide, which is also a threat at trace concentrations; and many other materials that can be generated by the combustion of both synthetic and natural materials found in urban and commercial areas.

The combined effects of exposure to elevated temperatures and different concentrations of carbon monoxide, carbon dioxide, and oxygen are shown in Table 6. These data were derived from those published previously[34] by extrapolation from experiments performed on adult albino Swiss mice, and therefore, they should only be regarded as indicative of trends.

The experimental studies reported previously[34] indicate the possibility of strong synergisms among the identified toxic agents produced in fires. In particular, some combustion products of synthetic materials like polyvinyl chloride (PVC) plastic pipe could be 50 times more toxic when exposures occur in combination with other combustion agents. However, at this time much additional work is required before useful insights along these lines will be available.

TABLE 6   Estimated Combined Levels of Toxic Agents
Causing Death in 4 Hours

Toxic Agents	Estimated Lethal Levels
Combination of Two	
Carbon monoxide + temperature	0.02% CO + 120°F (49°C)
Carbon dioxide + temperature	14% CO_2 + 120°F (49°C)
Oxygen + carbon monoxide	17% O_2 + 0.02% CO
	14% O_2 + 0.01% CO
Oxygen + carbon dioxide	14% O_2 + 14% CO_2
Carbon monoxide + carbon dioxide	0.02% CO + 14% CO_2
Combination of Three	
Oxygen + carbon monoxide + carbon dioxide	14% O_2 + 0.01% CO + 5% CO_2
	17% O_2 + 0.01% CO + 14% CO_2
Oxygen + carbon dioxide + temperature	11% O_2 + 5% CO_2 + 120°F (49°C)
	14% O_2 + 7% CO_2 + 120°F (49°C)
	17% O_2 + 10% CO_2 + 120°F (49°C)
Carbon monoxide + carbon dioxide + temperature	0.01% CO + 5% CO_2 + 120°F (49°C)
	0.01% CO + 10% CO_2 + 110°F (43°C)
	0.02% CO + 7% CO_2 + 110°F (43°C)
Oxygen + carbon monoxide + temperature	17% O_2 + 0.01% CO + 110°F (43°C)

MASS FIRE EXPERIENCES OF WORLD WAR II*

Although it is known that firestorms occurred at Hamburg, Kassel, Darmstadt, and Dresden in Germany and at Hiroshima and other cities in Japan, there are little quantitative data from these experiences, and much information is in fact contradictory.

The firestorm resulting from the second of three highly successful saturation incendiary raids at Hamburg is the most well documented to date.[1,35-37] The German Fire Protection Police reports indicate that between 50,000 and 60,000 people in the fire zone were killed. At the peak of the fire's intensity, 5 to 6 mile^2 (about 12.9 to 15.4 km^2) were simultaneously in flames, and estimates suggest that its power output reached 1 million or 2 million megawatts (MW).

By comparison, a mass fire initiated by a 1-Mt airburst over a typical urban area in the United States could involve areas considerably larger than 100 mile^2 (about 259 km^2) and have peak intensities of perhaps 15 to 50 million MW. Because of this considerable difference in scale and the instantaneous way fire and high levels of blast damage would be delivered by airbursts with weapons of megaton or fractional megaton yield, comparisons with these much smaller fire experiences of World War II could be misleading. This possibility is at least suggested by the casualty data obtained from studies of the atomic attack on Hiroshima. In that attack, the report of the U.S. Strategic Bombing survey noted that the near simultaneous initiation of fires, collapse of buildings, blockage of streets, and loss of water and power over an area of about 4.4 mile^2 (about 11.3 km^2) made escape from the aftermath of the attack considerably less likely, resulting in the very high casualty rates.

In support of this view, about the same number of people were killed in the incendiary saturation raid of March 9 and 10, 1945, against Tokyo (84,000 people were killed in the Tokyo raid, and between 70,000 and 80,000 are believed to have been killed at Hiroshima).

Although a much larger, more heavily populated area of nearly 16 mile^2 (about 41 km^2) of Tokyo was subject to an intense fire, which was sometimes accompanied by winds that were described as hurricane force, many were able to escape, presumably because street access was relatively

---

*This section draws heavily on the extraordinary accounts of allied fire protection engineers in World War II, who not only felt a duty to plan the incendiary attacks against Germany and Japan in war but also felt a duty to report their consequences in peace. I have also benefited greatly from numerous conversations with Horatio Bond, who has shared much of his knowledge and time with grace and generosity.

unimpaired and the fire developed and propagated over a much longer time period.

It should also be noted that more recent analyses of the most successful incendiary attacks of World War II indicate a high correlation of success with raid intensity.[38] When raids delivered large amounts of ordnance in short intervals of time, casualties were extremely high, as was the total damage. In this sense, a nuclear weapon could be considered the nearly ideal example of an incendiary weapon.

In the period between July 24 and July 30, 1943, there were three large raids against Hamburg.[39] The first of these raids occurred on July 24 and 25 and destroyed about 1.5 mile^2 (about 4 km^2) of the west section of the city; the next raid occurred on July 27 and 28 and resulted in the famous firestorm that destroyed 5 to 6 mile^2 (about 13 to 15.4 km^2) of the city's southeast section; and the last raid occurred on July 29 and 30, involving about 2 mile^2 (about 5 km^2) of the city's south section, while many units were still involved in fighting the great firestorm started 2 days earlier.

Each of these great raids involved about 700 planes, delivering about 1,300 tons (about 1,181 metric tons) of high-explosive bombs, 500 tons (about 455 metric tons) of oil incendiaries, and 600 tons (about 545 metric tons) of 4-pound (about 1.8-kg) magnesium incendiaries.

The incendiaries were designed to penetrate roof and floors into the interior of buildings, where tests had shown that fires were most efficiently set. High explosives were used to block access roads with rubble and craters and to break waterlines that might be utilized by firefighters. In addition, contrary to the advice of experts, military analysts believed that high explosives would also open buildings so they would burn more rapidly and with greater efficiency.[40]

Delivery of high-explosive bomb loads was spaced out over the entire period of the raid, so that firefighters would be kept in shelters, creating time for fires set by incendiaries to intensify. In addition, small high-explosive air mines with delayed fusing were dropped along with incendiaries to deter attempts to put out newly initiated fires.

In the second and most successful of the great raids at Hamburg, the raid of July 27 and 28, 1943, within about 20 minutes, two of three buildings within a 4.5-mile^2 (11.6-km^2) area were on fire, and a major fire was in progress.[35] As the individual fires grew and increased in intensity, sparks and radiated heat reached combustible interiors of nearby uninvolved buildings through shattered and undamaged windows. The fires thereby increased in volume and intensified for a period of about 3 hours and then raged at full force for another 3 hours.

During the period of intensification, a tremendous hurricane of fire developed; this was accompanied by irregular intervals of squall. As air was drawn toward the fire from all directions, the pumping action from different sections of the fire may have resulted in the unusual shifts of winds noted by firefighters in their reports. The rapidly shifting winds and fire spread foiled attempts to establish firebreaks. At the edge of the fire, the winds were sufficiently intense to uproot trees 3 feet (about 1 m) in diameter and to prevent firemen from coming within hose range.

In the air above the intensifying storm of fire, pilots encountered turbulent flying conditions, presumably due to the buoyantly rising heated air that was causing the intense ground winds below.[1,2] The intensity of these turbulent updrafts from fires could even have posed a threat to those in the bombers above.

In incendiary raids over Japan, for example, B-29 pilots reported that rising columns of hot air from mass fires below could bounce the planes from 15,000 to 17,000 feet (about 4,572 to 5,182 m) in a matter of seconds. Such violent air disturbances were sometimes encountered 3 or 4 miles (about 4.8 or 6.4 km) laterally from the center of a mass fire. Because these air disturbances were quite violent and it was believed that several B-29s had been lost due to encounters with them, missions were planned so that planes could drop their bombs and turn away before reaching areas of danger downwind.

The extremely intense ground winds at Hamburg, in combination with the fire, soon caused buildings to collapse into streets, further preventing the movement of firefighting units and the escape of people (Figure 21B shows a fire truck buried in the debris of a Hamburg street, and Figure 21C shows debris piled at the edges of formerly blocked streets). In some cases, units were trapped by debris and could not withdraw, resulting in the loss of both equipment and the lives of firemen. With many simultaneous large fires burning unchecked and with winds tending to go toward the center of the firestorm region, many streets became filled with flames, acting as gigantic channels for the high-velocity fire winds. Because of the terrific heat and showers of embers, existing open spaces, even parks, could not be used as sanctuaries by firefighters. In some cases, even strong men had to crawl on their hands and knees, hugging street curbs, to move against the wind.

Even though warning had been adequate and people had entered shelters by the time the raid began, thousands still died in the streets.

As the raid and fires intensified, heat and smoke became intense within shelters, and panic broke out in many places. Those who remained calm still had to choose between the increasingly unviable circumstance of the shelter and the intensifying hurricane of fire in the streets.

For most people there was no question of getting away. The areas hit were so great that once the fire intensified, the long travel time to the perimeter made it physically impossible for them to escape.

From areas where fire-filled regions could be observed, hundreds of

FIGURE 21   A, B, and C show various street scenes after the great incendiary
raids at Hamburg in late July of 1943. A shows a district near the city center
after streets have been partially cleared of debris. This section was not in the
firestorm. B shows the condition of streets in a firestorm area after the attack.
This street acted like a channel, creating very high winds which carried flames,
firebrands, and debris. The buried vehicles in the middle of the picture are fire-
trucks that were trapped by falling debris. Since the lives of their crews were
threatened by the heat and high winds, the vehicles had to be abandoned. C shows
a street level view of the firestorm-devastated area after debris was cleared from

the streets. During the firestorm, and for 2 days afterward, such streets were impassable even with tracked vehicles, as they were covered with high-temperature rubble from collapsed buildings. D is a picture of a burning section of London taken from the dome of St. Paul's on 29 December 1940. The relatively ineffective German incendiary raids early in World War II alerted allied military decision makers to the potential effectiveness of incendiaries for destruction. Reprinted from Fire and the Air War.© 1946 National Fire Protection Association, Quincy, Mass. Reprinted with permission.

FIGURE 22   A through E show some of the ways hundreds of thousands died in mass fires resulting from large-scale incendiary raids during World War II. A through C are photos of the dead found in shelters. The sequence of events varied, but it appears that those in shelters most often succumbed to carbon monoxide that filtered into shelters from partially combusting debris around shelters. A and C show corpses that were desiccated from the effects of extreme heating of shelters from surrounding rubble of collapsed buildings. In some cases shelter heating may have been the cause of death, but it is believed most victims in shelters were killed by carbon monoxide poisoning. However, even if carbon monoxide poisoning could have been avoided, the heating of many shelters from overburdens of fire-heated rubble would have almost certainly killed the occupants at a later time. D shows a victim who attempted to flee the fire zone rather than stay in a

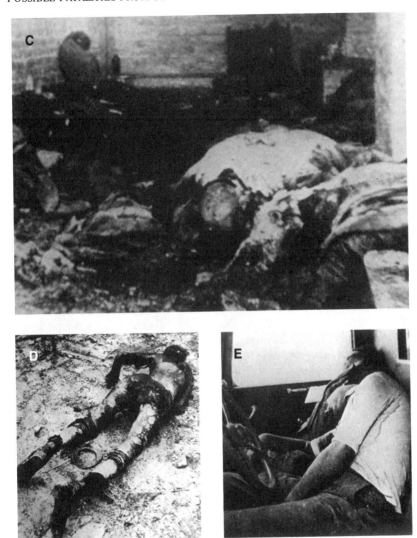

shelter. Since the street winds and temperatures were so high, hyperthermia, possibly in combination with combustion product poisoning, killed many thousands in the streets of Hamburg. E shows corpses in a truck. These victims were probably overcome by heat and carbon monoxide as they attempted to escape a fire zone. Reprinted from Fire and the Air War.© 1946 National Fire Protection Association, Quincy, Mass. Reprinted with permission.

people were seen leaving shelters. After traveling short distances in the open, they would slowly collapse, as if exhausted. In some cases they did not immediately become motionless, but they tried to get up. In other cases their clothes burst into flames as they were engulfed in tornado-like fire whirls that propagated unpredictably down streets. Many killed in this manner were found to be naked (see Figure 22D).

Those who stayed in their shelters faced a different fate. As buildings collapsed under the heat of fire and the force of winds, many shelters became overburdened with debris (Figures 22A, B, and C). In many cases, death came easily (Figure 22A), as people slipped calmly into unconsciousness in carbon monoxide-infiltrated shelters. In other cases, there were signs of panic and attempts to escape.

Many shelters that had been closed off by rubble also suffered very high heating rates from an overburden of hot rubble and burning debris (Figure 22B). In these shelters, shrunken bodies were often found lying in a thick greasy black mass, which appeared to be melted body fat. In many shelters in which shrunken bodies were found, there were also bodies that had been reduced to bits of ashes.

Since many of the shrunken bodies burned to ash within a few weeks of exposure to air, it may be that oxidation exposure or temperatures differed markedly even within the same shelter.

In all cities that were subjected to successful Allied incendiary attacks and surveyed by German medical teams, carbon monoxide poisoning was regarded as the primary cause of death or injury, sometimes reaching to as much as 80 percent of all incendiary raid casualties. Air blast was found to be a relatively infrequent cause of death, generally affecting only those within a radius of about 30 meters of the explosions.

I was unable to find any unambiguous data on survival rates within the region of mass fire at Hamburg. It is interesting to note that a figure of 15,000 to 18,000 lives is often quoted as the number of people saved from the Hamburg fire storm. However, a review of Hamburg Fire Department records[37] reveals no data regarding survival in the fire zone, although documents do indicate that 18,000 people were rescued during the period from July 25 to August 4.

There is a reference to the fact that hundreds of thousands of people possibly escaped the fire, presumably in its early phases, and there are additional personal reports[35] of people who survived in bomb craters, in which the water table was sufficiently high that body parts could be covered with water-soaked clothing, and in public bunkers, which apparently were thick-walled, freestanding structures that were removed from the areas covered with the debris of collapsed buildings. However, the location of these bunkers in the fire zone and the numbers of people saved by them were not reported.

At this time, the complete absence of any tabulated data for a circumstance that is relatively well documented remains conspicuous.

MODEL FOR ESTIMATING FATALITIES FROM SUPERFIRES

As should be evident from the three previous sections, the environment resulting from a mass fire over vast blast-disrupted regions of a nuclear target area could plausibly kill all or most people who could not escape the region of fire.

Even in the case of lightly built-up cities, average air temperatures could be well over 200°F (93°C) over nearly all of an involved region. At these temperatures, even resting individuals would be subject to serious threat of death from excess body heating within tens of minutes. Those with elevated metabolic rates due to hysteria, stress, panic, or strenuous activity would be threatened in still shorter times. The heated environment, elevated metabolic states, and the presence of carbon dioxide would induce increased respiration activity which would, in turn, increase body uptake of carbon monoxide, sulfur dioxide, nitrogen dioxide, toxic smoke, and other materials. Superheated, hurricane-force winds would do further damage to uncollapsed structures. Firebreaks of many hundreds of feet would have no inhibiting effect on the spread of mass fire.

In outlying concrete-reinforced structures that may be seriously damaged but not initially knocked down by the blast, basements would offer apparent refuge. However, winds generated by the pumping action of rising heated air over large areas would be most severe in these outlying regions near the edge of the superfire.

Burning debris and overburdens of rubble could trap sheltered individuals. Carbon monoxide and other toxic gases could, with very high probability, infiltrate such shelters, and serious delayed thermal heating could occur either from burning overburden or hot rubble from collapsed sections of buildings. In addition, high-temperature winds in combination with fire could bring down sections of many structures and spread hot and burning debris around shelter entrances and ventilation accesses.

Given this situation and the enormous range of uncertainties associated with the possible scale of such fires, even a qualitative estimate of the potential consequences of superfires on fatality and casualty estimates is necessarily uncertain. Nevertheless, as will be evident from the discussion in the two sections that follow, even qualitative, speculative estimates strongly indicate that superfires would be a threat of major importance.

Consider the baseline fire radius hypothesized at the beginning of the section Superfires and Their Environments and consider the possibility that within the baseline fire radius of 7.455 miles (12 km) the superfire calculations performed by Small, Brode, and Larson would apply.[7,15] Then, speculate further that all individuals are killed.

Both the assumed fraction of those killed and the radius within which superfires might rage are, of course, highly uncertain numbers.

As noted many times above, the fraction of those killed within the superfire depends on numerous as yet unresolved physical uncertainties and scenario-dependent details. The radius within which a superfire might occur would depend on the type of combustible material at different ranges, its distribution, atmospheric visibility at the time of attack, whether the ground is desert or covered with dry combustible vegetation or noncombustible but highly reflecting snow, whether or not cloud heights are such that fireball light is reflected back toward the Earth or away from it, and a host of other uncertain contingencies.

For example, if there is either snow cover on the ground or clouds at heights that reflect thermal radiation back to the Earth, the range at which a major mass fire might occur (assuming that all other assumptions remain unchanged) might instead be 9 to 10.5 miles (15 to 17 km). This would increase (or decrease in the opposite circumstance) the area of superfire by 1½ to 2 times.

Thus, if a population were uniformly distributed over the target area, the number of predicted fatalities, assuming a 12-km lethal radius in which all would die and a 17-km radius in which only half would die, results in the same prediction of fatalities. In light of the very great range of uncertainties and the severe environmental conditions within the region of fire, it is therefore reasonable to scope out the possibilities by assuming a cookie cutter* fatality condition.

FATALITY POTENTIAL OF SUPERFIRES
The Influence of Casualty Rules on Predictions of Deaths and Injuries from Nuclear Attacks

In order to estimate the number of fatalities and injuries resulting from a nuclear attack, it is necessary to know where weapons would fall in relationship to population, as well as the probability that individuals would suffer death or injury from each of many possible weapons effects. For a presumed set of detonations, such calculations therefore require both population distribution data and rules for estimating the probabilities of death or injury from each attack.

---

*By cookie cutter it is meant that all individuals caught within the fire zone are assumed to be killed by fire effects, while all individuals outside the fire zone are assumed to survive fire effects.

Figures 23A, 23B, and 23C show such a set of rules for an assumed 1-Mt airburst detonated at about a 2.2-km altitude (this is the same scaled height of burst used at Hiroshima). Because the height of burst is such that the likelihood of fallout in the target area would be relatively low, the weapons effects that pose major threats of death or injury would be blast, heat from the fireball, and fires that follow in the aftermath of the detonation.

Each of the three graphs in Figure 23 shows several curves for the probability of fatality, casualty (fatality plus nonfatal injury), or nonfatal injury as a function of range from the detonation. The solid curves are those used by the U.S. Congress Office of Technology Assessment (OTA) in its 1979 study *The Effects of Nuclear War*[41] to estimate deaths and injuries from airbursts on urban and other targets. Since OTA's assumptions about casualties and injuries are similar to those used by the Department of Defense (DOD),[42,43] they also give results similar to those of the standard DOD methodology.

The broken curves plotted in Figures 23A and 23B are derived from fatality and casualty data from Hiroshima (as noted above, casualties are the sum of fatalities and nonfatal injuries). The Hiroshima data are scaled by assuming that the probability of injury or death at each range from the 1-Mt detonation is only a function of the peak blast wave overpressure.

For example, the peak overpressure at 0.95 miles (1.5 km) from ground zero at Hiroshima was about 5 psi, and the probability of being killed was about 0.3. For the 1-Mt airburst, this same overpressure would occur at about 4 miles (6.5 km). Therefore, it is assumed that the probability of being killed would also be about 0.3.

In order to understand the potential implications of these rules for death and injury estimates, it is necessary to choose a set of targets. Obviously, if the targets are chosen in sparsely populated areas, casualties will be lower than for a choice of targets in heavily populated areas.

For purposes of analysis, a reference case of 100 1-Mt warheads on the 100 largest city centers in the United States is of interest.

This reference case results in no overlap of areas that are subject to the effects of multiple weapons, as could be the case in many imaginable nuclear attacks; and it applies the casualty rules to circumstances similar to those from which the data were derived. It is therefore a baseline measure of the potential influence of casualty rules on predictions of deaths and injuries from nuclear attacks, which can then be used as a reference against alternative possibilities of interest to analysts.

Thus, it is emphasized that the above choice of targets is chosen for its analytic interest; it is not a scenario, and I attach no significance to this target set beyond that of a baseline reference.

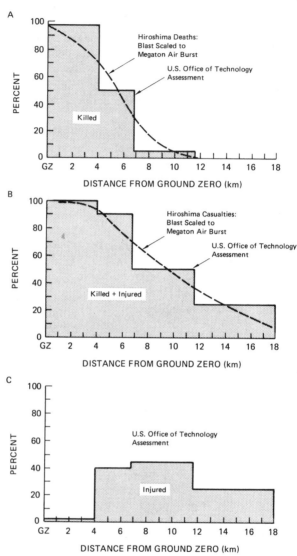

FIGURE 23   The three graphs show an application of rules used by the OTA to estimate fatalities and injuries from a 1-Mt airburst over an urban area. The solid curve in A shows the assumed probability of death as a function of range from ground zero. The broken curve shows fatality data from Hiroshima scaled by assuming that the probability of death is purely a function of the peak overpressure at each range from the detonation. In B similar curves are shown for total casualties, which is defined to be the sum of those killed and those injured. In C the OTA rules for those injured (but not killed) are shown as a function of range from ground zero.

The calculations that I performed for the presumed 100-city attack, using first the OTA/DOD rules and then a blast scaling of Hiroshima data, gave identical predictions within a few percent. It is therefore clear that the government rules for estimating fatalities and injuries are virtually indistinguishable from blast scaling of data from Hiroshima.

Figure 24 shows the range dependence of the government's probability of injury assumptions for a 1-Mt airburst. At selected ranges below the horizontal axis, the overpressure and thermal energy deposited from the fireball of a 1-Mt airburst is shown (12-mile [19.3-km] visibility). Above the axis is the thermal fluence which occurred at a similar overpressure

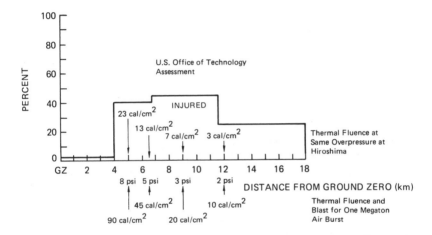

FIGURE 24 Some aspects of the physical environment that could influence the probability of death at different ranges from a ground zero are compared for 1-Mt and 12.5-kt detonations. The solid curve shows the probability of blast injury as a function of range from ground zero derived by applying the OTA rules to the case of a 1-Mt airburst. (These rules are also discussed in the legend to Figure 23 and the text.) The 3-psi range at Hiroshima occurred at about 1.5 miles (about 2.3 to 2.4 km) from ground zero. As indicated on the upper side of the range axis, the amount of thermal radiation delivered along with the blast was about 7 cal/cm². Individuals subjected to these effects at Hiroshima would not have been in the region of mass fire that occurred after the attack. At the 3-psi range for a 1-Mt airburst, about 20 cal/cm² could be delivered along with the blast. Many fires would be set at this range, and many additional fires might even be set at much greater range (perhaps at the 12-km range or greater). Individuals injured by the 3-psi blast at the 9-km range might therefore have to walk 3 or more km through a zone heavily damaged by blast and with fires of increasing intensity. By comparison, an injured individual who survived blast and radiation effects at ground zero in Hiroshima would have had to walk less than 2 km to escape the fire zone. It is therefore clear that using blast alone as the criterion for estimating fatalities could well result in a serious underestimate of the probability of death.

at Hiroshima. Thus, at Hiroshima, about 12 to 13 calories per square centimeter was deposited at the range at which 5 psi occurred. In contrast, at the 5-psi range for the 1-Mt airburst, about 45 cal/cm^2 occurs.

Because this environment is created at about 6.5 km from the detonation point and, as shown earlier, it is plausible that a mass fire could rage to a range of 12 km, it appears unlikely that a simple scaling rule of the kind used in the OTA/DOD methodology adequately accounts for the circumstance of those at the 6.5-km range.

Figure 25 shows estimates of fatalities and casualties for the 100-city reference case. Blast scaling predicts that there would be 14 million to 15 million fatalities and 22 million to 23 million injured.

An alternative postulate, discussed in the previous section, is that superfires of uncertain scale would occur, killing all within a range of 6 to 8 miles (9.5 to 13 km) from each ground zero. For the area outside the range of the superfire, then, it can be postulated that the blast injury rules derived from Hiroshima data apply.

Under these assumptions, the number of outright fatalities increases by a factor of between 2.5 and 4, resulting in a prediction of from 36 million to 56 million fatalities, while the number of injured decreases dramatically to between 3 million and 11 million. This is in accord with German experiences during World War II, in which medical surveys determined that incendiary raids always resulted in a much higher ratio of killed to injured.

The reason for this dramatic change in distribution of fatalities and injuries can be quickly grasped from Figure 23C. The result of the new assumption is that many who would be counted as injured in the blast methodology instead are counted as dead; it also counts uninjured individuals within the fire zone among the dead as well. The only nonfatal injured are therefore those who are injured by the effects of the blast but are outside the perimeter of the superfire.

Even though the scale, ferocity, and effects of these superfires are as yet highly uncertain, it is not difficult to test the sensibility of this hypothetical casualty estimate.

Because the area covered by such fires is proportional to the square of the fire radius, if the average fire radius were to increase or decrease by 10 to 15 percent, the result would be an increase or decrease in the affected area of about 20 to 30 percent. The population density is, to a first approximation, relatively constant for such small changes in fire radius.[44] This means that a 10 or 15 percent increase or decrease in fire radius results in about a 20 to 30 percent increase or decrease in predicted fatalities.

Thus, the minimum postulated superfire radius used in the calculations

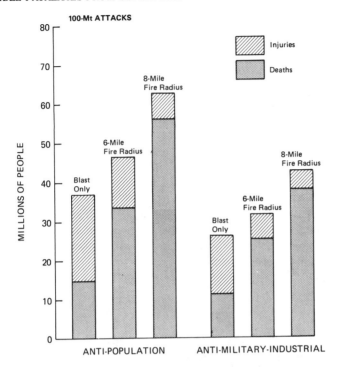

FIGURE 25   The potential effects of differing assumptions about the causes of fatalities and injuries. A reference attack that assumes that a single 1-Mt detonation occurs over the population center of each of the 100 largest metropolitan areas is used to determine the potential significance of differing fatality and injury rules. When only blast scaling from Hiroshima is used to estimate fatalities and injuries, about 14 million fatalities and 23 million injured are projected. If it is assumed that mass fires kill everyone within 6 miles (about 9.7 km) of the ground zeros and injuries beyond that range occur because of blast at the same rate as that which occurred at Hiroshima, 33 million would be killed and 12 to 13 million would be injured. If the fire zone extends to 8 miles (about 12.9 km) instead, 56 million would be killed and 6 to 7 million would be injured. Similar results are also shown for a reference attack that does not seek to kill population but only attempts to destroy 100 of the most important industrial facilities that would provide military products that could directly support a war effort.

summarized in Figures 25 and 26 (6 miles or 9.5 km) would have to be reduced by a factor of somewhat less than the square root of two before predictions of fatalities could be similar to those of blast scaling methodologies.

High survival rates at a range of about 4 miles (6.5 km) would therefore be required. At this range, however, the thermal fluence from the fireball would be about 45 cal/cm², which is enough to set almost any interior household material in line of sight of the fireball on fire immediately (Figure 2B shows the emission of smoke from the front of a wood frame house from 25 cal/cm²).

If, instead, it is assumed that all those who are not injured by blast could miraculously escape the hostile effects of near-hurricane-force winds and air temperatures above that at which water boils, and only those who are injured according to the blast scaling rules shown in Figure 23C die in superfires of radius 6 to 8 miles (9.5 to 13 km), then the number of deaths would increase by a factor of around two, to 27 million to 33 million.

It is therefore difficult to see how casualty rules that do not include the hostile effects of mass fires over such vast areas can result in projections more plausible than even those that follow from the preliminary speculations contained in this study.

COMPARISON OF OTHER TARGET SETS WITH THE REFERENCE CASE

Daugherty, Levi, and von Hippel[44] have made a very complete and uniquely systematic study of possible fatalities and injuries from nuclear attacks against the United States. They have not only systematically examined a wide range of possibilities by varying the assumptions about the biological consequences of given nuclear environments (for example, variations in the 50 percent lethal dose [LD_{50}] for radiation exposure) and the behavior of individuals within these environments (how fallout protection factors, and hence casualties, differ if sheltered people make short excursions from their shelters), but they have also examined the potential consequences of plausible variations in the nuclear environment itself (how injury and fatality estimates vary if populations are subject to fires as well as to blast).

Furthermore, they have systematically examined the implications of their assumptions for different potential target classes on both an individual and multiply aggregated basis. By doing this, they have created a menu of possibilities from which analysts or decision makers may choose to contemplate, or to reject as implausible, any of a wide range of potential nuclear attacks.

This kind of analysis is, so far, absent from studies and results of studies published by government agencies.

Two interesting reference cases studied by Daugherty et al.[44] are noteworthy:

1. An attack of 100 single 1-Mt airbursts on 100 U.S. urban centers.
2. An attack of 101 nuclear airbursts on 101 key military-industrial targets.

As noted by Daugherty et al., because the first reference case has no areas of overlap from the effects of multiple weapons detonations, the 100-city reference case provides a baseline of analytic interest for comparison with other cases in their menu of possibilities.

In addition, if the reference case is calculated using blast scaling casualty rules derived from data following an attack on a city center (Hiroshima), an unambiguous estimate of the potential significance of fire effects is established.

The second reference case is of interest relative to the first since it provides just such a comparative case from their menu.

This attack is of interest not only because of its central role in many policy statements and deliberations but also because it does not target population per se. Instead it uses essentially the same number of warheads (101 versus 100) to attack a small number of very-high-value military-industrial end product facilities, and therefore represents what some might argue is a minimal attack that could quickly interrupt U.S. conventional war production capabilities.

As shown in Figure 26, if I assume that the 100 detonations are airbursts of 1-Mt yield and that the hypothesized superfire casualty rules of the previous section apply, 25 million to 37 million deaths and 2 million to 7 million injured would result. Thus, if fires kill substantial numbers of people in target areas, the attack that does not target population per se might result in the death of between 1.5 and 2.5 times more people than the blast scaling would predict for the antipopulation attack of a similar size.

It is also of interest to examine the potential effects of choice of weapon yield. If the rules for guessing the radius of superfire are scaled by assuming that the fire radius occurs at the 10-cal/cm^2 range (12-mile [19.3-km] visibility), then Figure 27 shows the predicted results for the anti-industrial attack, assuming that the attack is instead executed with 101 weapons of either 500- or 100-kiloton (kt) yield.

In this case, the 500-kt attack would kill 23 million people, 1.5 times that predicted by blast scaling for the antipopulation reference attack, and the 100-kt attack would kill about 8 million people, about two-thirds that predicted by the application of blast scaling to the antipopulation reference attack.

However, it is noteworthy that the fire radius derived for the 100-kt weapon is about 4.5 km, and the already speculative cookie cutter fire

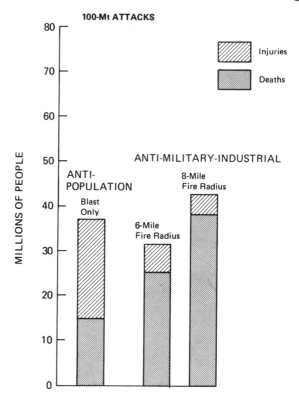

FIGURE 26   Some of the results shown in Figure 25 are rearranged to illustrate that when the proposed alternative method of assessing casualties is applied to attacks aimed at industrial facilities rather than population centers, the result could be greater casualties than in the antipopulation attack. Since such attacks have sometimes been proposed as relatively limited, and hence more sensible and more plausible than antipopulation attacks, this comparison serves to underscore the potentially misleading character of such arguments.

model is still more speculative, as it is more likely that many of those who would not have been severely injured would have some chance to attempt to escape the fire region.

CONCLUSION

During World War II the extraordinary power of science was turned to building a weapon that could create energy densities and temperatures comparable to those that normally exist in the interiors of stars. Today,

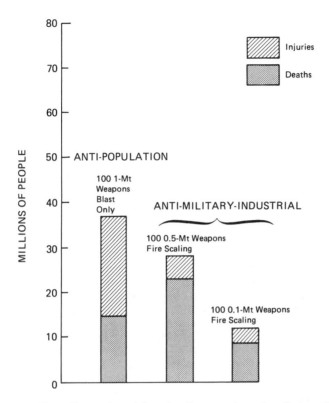

FIGURE 27 The effects of applying the fire casualty rules discussed in the legend to Figure 25 and the text to attacks that utilize weapons of lower yield. The predicted casualties when 100 0.5-Mt weapons are substituted for 1-Mt weapons are only slightly diminished. When 0.1-Mt weapons (100 kt) are substituted, casualties drop significantly. It should be noted, however, that for these much lower yield detonations, blast scaling from Hiroshima data may be no less uncertain than alternative rules discussed in this paper.

the results of those and subsequent efforts have given us weapons with effects that are of vast and nonintuitive scales.

One of these effects is superfires; they would accompany nuclear detonations in or near urban areas and might result in two to four times as many fatalities as that predicted by standard government blast scaling rules.

The effects of such fires, while recognized by many during and at the end of World War II, has remained an issue of discussion and research only among a small group of dedicated researchers. As such, an understanding of their effects and the possible scale of unpredictable consequences that could accompany the use of nuclear weapons in many applications remains poorly understood, or absent, from the cognition of planners and decision makers. Without this understanding, the probability of misjudgment and miscalculation could be considerable.

NOTES

[1]Bond, H., ed. 1946. Fire and the Air War. National Fire Protection Association.

[2]The U.S. Strategic Bombing Survey. 1946. Washington, D.C.: U.S. Government Printing Office.

[3]Glasstone, S., and P. J. Dolan, eds. 1977. The Effects of Nuclear Weapons. Report no. O-213-794. Washington, D.C.: U.S. Government Printing Office.

[4]Federal Emergency Management Agency. 1982. Attack Environment Manual. CPG-2-1A2. Washington, D.C.: Federal Emergency Management Agency.

[5]Defense Civil Preparedness Agency. 1973. DCPA Attack Manual. CPG-2-1A1. Washington, D.C.: Department of Defense.

[6]Glasstone, S., ed. 1962. The Effects of Nuclear Weapons. Washington, D.C.: U.S. Government Printing Office.

[7]Brode, H. L., and R. D. Small. 1983. Fire Damage and Strategic Targeting. PSR Note 567. Los Angeles, Calif.: Pacific-Sierra Research Corp.

[8]Hassig, P. J., and M. Rosenblatt. 1983. Firestorm Formation and Environment Characteristics After a Large-Yield Nuclear Burst. Proceedings of the 17th Asilomar Conference on Fire and Blast Effects of Nuclear Weapons. CONF-8305107, May 30-June 3.

[9]Brode, H. L., D. A. Larson, and R. D. Small. 1983. Hydrocode Studies of Flows Generated by Large Area Fires. Proceedings of the 17th Asilomar Conference on Fire and Blast Effects of Nuclear Weapons. CONF-8305107. May 30-June 3.

[10]Larson, D. A., and R. D. Small. 1983. The Large Urban Fire Environment: Trends and Model City Predictions. Proceedings of the 17th Asilomar Conference on Fire and Blast Effects of Nuclear Weapons. CONF-8305107. May 30-June 3.

[11]Small, R. D., and D. A. Larson. 1983. Analysis of the Large Urban Fire Environment. Proceedings of the 17th Asilomar Conference on Fire and Blast Effects of Nuclear Weapons. CONF-8305107. May 30-June 3.

[12]Small, R. D., D. A. Larson, and H. L. Brode. 1983. Fluid dynamics of large area fires. In Fire Dynamics and Heat Transfer. J. G. Quintiere, R. L. Alpert, and R. A. Altenkirch, eds. New York: The American Society of Mechanical Engineers.

[13]Brode, H. L., and R. D. Small. 1983. Fire Damage and Strategic Targeting. PSR Note 567. Los Angeles, Calif.: Pacific-Sierra Research Corp.

[14]Small R. D., and H. L. Brode. 1980. Physics of Large Urban Fires. PSR Report 1010. Los Angeles, Calif.: Pacific-Sierra Research Corp.

[15]Larson, D. A., and R. D. Small. 1982. Analysis of the Large Urban Fire Environment: Part I. Theory. PSR Report 1210. Los Angeles, Calif.: Pacific-Sierra Research Corp.

[16]Larson, D. A., and R. D. Small. 1982. Analysis of the Large Urban Fire Environment: Part II. Parametric Analysis and Model City Simulations. PSR Report 1210. Los Angeles, Calif.: Pacific-Sierra Research Corp.

[17]Brode, H. L. 1980. Large-Scale Urban Fires. PSR Note 348. Los Angeles, Calif.: Pacific-Sierra Research Corp.

[18]Feldstein, M., S. Duckworth, H. C. Wohlers, and B. Linsky. 1963. The contribution of the open burning of land clearing debris to air pollution. J. Air Pollut. Control Assoc. 13:(11).

[19]Darley, E. F., F. R. Burleson, E. H. Mateer, J. T. Middleton, and V. P. Osterli. 1966. Contribution of burning of agricultural wastes to photochemical air pollution. J. Air Pollut. Control Assoc. 11:(12).

[20]Gerstle, R. W., and D. A. Kemnitz. 1967. Atmospheric emissions from open burning. J. Air Pollut. Control Assoc.

[21]Wiersma, S. J. 1975. Characteristics of fires in structural debris. Silver Spring, Md.: Naval Surface Weapons Center.

[22]Wilton, C., K. Kaplan, B. Gabrielsen, and J. Zaccor. 1976. Blast/Fire Interaction, Blast Translation, and Toxic Agents. Final Report, URS 7030-6. Redwood City, Calif.: URS Research Co. See also note 45.

[23]Pryor, A. J., D. E. Johnson, and N. N. Jackson. 1969. Hazards of Smoke and Toxic Gases Produced in Urban Fires. San Antonio, Tex.: Southwest Research Institute.

[24]Takata, A. N., and T. E. Waterman. 1972. Fire Laboratory Tests—Phase II, Interaction of Fire and Simulated Blast Debris, IITRI-J6217(2). Chicago, Ill.: IIT Research Institute.

[25]Longinow, A., T. E. Waterman, and A. N. Takata. 1982. Assessment of Combined Effects of Blast and Fire on Personnel Survivability. Chicago, Ill.: IIT Research Institute.

[26]Lee, W., H. C. Leong, C. Jee, and M. Gayle Hershberger. 1966. Design of Tests for the Effects of Mass Fires on Shelter Occupants. Final Report. Palo Alto, Calif.: Isotopes, Inc.

[27]Police President of Hamburg. 1971. Short Version of Report on Experiences of the Hamburg Fire Department During the Air Attacks from July 24 to August 3, 1943. Reprinted as Appendix 1 in Fire Fighting Operations in Hamburg, Germany During World War II, by C. F. Miller, Final Report, URS 7030-6. Redwood City, Calif.: URS Research Company.

[28]Christian, W. J., and R. C. Wands, eds. 1972. An Appraisal of Fire Extinguishing Agents. Proceedings of a Symposium at the National Academy of Sciences, April 11–12. Washington, D.C.: National Academy of Sciences.

[29]Goodale, T. 1971. An Attempt to Explore the Effect of High Blast Overpressures on the Persistence of Smouldering Combustion in Debris. Summary Report, URS 7030-6. Redwood City, Calif.: URS Research Company.

[30]Braker, W., and A. L. Mossman. 1971. Matheson Gas Data Book, 5th ed. East Rutherford, N.J.

[31]Jacobs, M. B. 1949. The Analytic Chemistry of Industrial Poisons, Hazards, and Solvents, 2nd ed. New York: Interscience Publishers, Inc.

[32]Jacobs, M. B. 1967. Chemical Analysis XXII, The Analytic Toxicology of Industrial Inorganic Poisons. New York: Interscience Publishers, Inc.

[33]Henderson and Haggard. 1943. Noxious Gases and the Principles of Respiration Influencing Their Action, 2nd ed. Oxford, England: Clarendon Press.

[34]Pryor, A. J., D. E. Johnson, and N. N. Jackson. 1969. Hazards of Smoke and Toxic Gases Produced in Urban Fires. San Antonio, Tex.: Southwest Research Institute.

[35]Kehrl, Police President of Hamburg. 1946. Secret Report by the Police President of Hamburg on the Heavy Raids on Hamburg in July/August 1943, I.O.(t)45 (translated and published by the United Kingdom Home Office, Civil Defense Department, Intelligence Branch, Document Number 43097, January 1946).

[36]Report of the Technical Services Division of the Hamburg Fire Protection Police During the Major Catastrophe and Summary of Reports on Actions During the Air Attacks on Hamburg from July 24 to August 3, 1943. 1971. Reprinted as Appendix 2 in Fire Fighting Operations in Hamburg, Germany During World War II, by C. F. Miller, Final Report, URS 7030-6. Redwood City, Calif.: URS Research Company.

[37]Miller, C. F. 1971. Fire Fighting Operations in Hamburg, Germany During World War II. Final Report, URS 7030-6. Redwood City, Calif.: URS Research Co.

[38]Taylor, D. H. 1978. Methodology for Estimating High Intensity Attacks. SAI-77-803-LJ. La Jolla, Calif.: Science Applications Inc.

[39]In fact, a fourth raid occurred on August 3, 1943; however, it took place during a severe thunderstorm. Police reports indicate that the substantial numbers of available fire fighting forces were not overwhelmed, as was the case in the three previous raids.

It should be kept in mind, however, that the most successful attacks are known to have been those of highest intensity, since they started so many potentially controllable fires so quickly, that by the time some fires were put out, others had grown beyond control. The weather's major contribution could well have been interference with the placement of bombs, rather than expungement of fires.

In Japan, reports indicate that successful incendiary attacks were made even during periods of light rain and often within hours of heavier rain. For example, 37 percent of the Nishinomiya-Mikage area was destroyed in a single raid despite the fact that heavy rain had fallen for the previous 48 hours.

On the other hand, German cities were much more fire resistant than Japanese (and incidentally American) cities, as building construction was cellular, relying on internal and external masonry walls to protect against fire propagation. Hence, in the absence of more complete data on these events, the effects of weather must be considered to be quite ambiguous.

[40]Horatio Bond, private communication. National Fire Protection Association.

[41]U.S. Congress, Office of Technology Assessment. 1979. The Effects of Nuclear War. Washington, D.C.: U.S. Government Printing Office.

[42]Peter Sharfman, private communication, project director of The Effects of Nuclear War, U.S. Congress Office of Technology Assessment.

[43]British Medical Association. 1983. The Medical Effects of Nuclear War. The Report of the British Medical Association's Board of Science Education. London: John Wiley and Sons.

[44]Daugherty, W., B. Levi, and F. von Hippel. Casualties Due to the Blast, Heat and Radioactive Fallout from Various Hypothetical Nuclear Attacks on the United States. This volume.

[45]Bucheim, R. W., and the staff of the Rand Corporation. 1958. Space Handbook: Astronautics and Its Applications. New York: Random House.

The Medical Implications of Nuclear War, Institute of
Medicine. © 1986 by the National Academy of Sciences.
National Academy Press, Washington, D.C.

A Review of the Physics of Large Urban Fires

H. L. BRODE, PH.D., and R. D. SMALL, PH.D.
Pacific-Sierra Research Corporation, Los Angeles, California

INTRODUCTION

A review of historical urban fires can help to illustrate the nature of
large fires and the devastation that they can cause. The observations and
descriptions of those fires provide the basis for understanding the much
larger fires that would result from a nuclear explosion. The focus of this
paper is on the major physical factors that are relevant to the characterization of such fires. Atmospheric responses in the vicinity of a large smoke
column are addressed, and the hazards expected to accompany nuclear
fires are briefly discussed.

HISTORY OF URBAN FIRES

Disastrous urban fires have occurred throughout history. In wartime,
cities have been bombarded, sacked, and burned. Fires have also resulted
from earthquake damage, hurricane winds, accidents, explosions, and
arson. Firebombing in World War II was aimed at the destruction of cities
and industries in both Europe and Japan. Despite the large number of city
fires, the available data are mostly anecdotal. Most of the empirical knowledge of nuclear explosion fires has been obtained from the nuclear bursts
at Hiroshima and Nagasaki.

Table 1 lists several major urban fires, beginning with the London fire
of 1666. Although it destroyed an area of nearly 2 km², only eight people
were killed because the fire moved slowly. The Chicago fire of 1871 killed

TABLE 1   Some Past Large-Scale Urban Fires

City	Year	Deaths	Area Burned (km²)	Comments
London	1666	8	1.8	Burned 4 days; 32,000 homes lost
New York City	1835			
Charleston, S.C.	1838			
Pittsburgh	1845			
Philadelphia	1865			
Portland, Maine	1866			
Chicago	1871	50	8.6	Burned 1 day; 98,500 homeless; 17,500 homes lost
Boston	1872			
San Francisco	1906	452	12.0	Earthquake-generated explosions and fires; 30 ignitions; burned 3 days; 100,000 homeless
Halifax, Nova Scotia	1917	2,000		
Tokyo	1923			
	1925			
	1932			
Niigata, Japan	1925			
Yamanaka, Japan	1931			
Hakodate, Japan	1934	2,000		Generated fire storm
Takaoka, Japan	1938			
Boston	1942	1,000		Explosion and fire; burned 3 days; 3,000 injured; 300 missing
Muramatsu, Japan	1946[a]			
Texas City	1947	510		Fertilizer ship explosion
Chungking, China	1949	1,000		
Brussels	1967	250		Burned 6 hours
Chelsea (London, England)	1973			400 homes lost
Anaheim, California	1982			500 apartments and 1 firehouse destroyed
Philadelphia	1985			2 blocks of row houses gutted

[a]Approximate date.

more people and burned a larger area in less time. The San Francisco fire, following the 1906 earthquake, resulted in greater casualties and left 100,000 homeless. The Halifax, Nova Scotia, explosion started many fires; the casualty figures include those from the explosion and the fires. Many people died in the intense Hakodate, Japan, fire storm in 1934. The explosion of a fertilizer ship in Galveston Bay caused many fires in the adjoining Texas City, Tex.

Even modern cities are vulnerable to urban fires. In April 1982, some 500 apartments were destroyed in a few hours as a wind-whipped fire swept through Anaheim, Calif. A flash bomb on a row house in Philadelphia in early 1985 led to the burnout of two city blocks. In September 1985, an arson fire virtually destroyed an industrial section of Passaic, N.J.

These few examples illustrate that major urban fires can be started in many different ways. In most of these fires, there were few casualties, although property damage was extensive. When the fires spread from one or a few ignition points, evacuation and movement from the threat was possible.

In World War II, European cities suffered extensive fire damage. In several of the German cities attacked with incendiary weapons, fire storms developed (Bond, 1946). In particular, Dresden, Hamburg, Kassel, Heilbronn, Darmstadt, and Brunswick suffered intense area fires (see Table 2). When intense area fires occurred, damage and casualties were significantly higher.

In the more than 70 firebombed German cities, it is estimated that 500,000 to 800,000 people were killed. In intensity and magnitude, the worst fire occurred in Dresden (February 1945) with 135,000 to 250,000 deaths. Hamburg experienced 34,000 to 100,000 deaths in the raids of July 1943. Fire storms frequently killed more than 5 percent of the population at risk; less intense or isolated fires seldom killed as many as 1 percent of those at risk. Berlin was repeatedly bombed, but its defenses prevented concentrated attacks, and the resulting fires never coalesced into the inferno of a fire storm.

In the raids on Hamburg, the explosive and incendiary bombing was concentrated in an old part of the city, comprised of a high density of four- and five-story buildings. Almost all buildings in the area burned simultaneously; the destruction was nearly complete, and for many escape was impossible. Virtually all combustibles were burned out; only crumbled ruins or empty masonry shells of multistory buildings remained. Figure 1 is an overhead photograph of a gutted section of Hamburg.

A similar, old section was burned in Dresden. Buildings were an average of three to five stories high, were closely spaced, and were heavily loaded with combustibles. The lack of an organized air defense allowed the Royal Air Force (RAF) to concentrate its bombing, which led to many simultaneous fire starts. The intense fire completely and nearly simultaneously burned out all the buildings in a broad area.

The concentrated B-29 firebombing of Japanese cities lasted about six months—from February to August of 1945. Firebombing raids were made on 65 cities. Tokyo was the first city attacked, and that fire was perhaps the most disastrous of all, burning nearly two-thirds of that city plus Yokahama with great loss of life (perhaps 200,000 dead). Major fires

TABLE 2   German Cities Burned in World War II

City	Population (in thousands)	Deaths (in thousands)	Percentage of Population Killed	Remarks
Dresden	600–2,000	135–250	20	Fire storm
Hamburg	1,760	34–100	5	Fire storm
Berlin	4,420	52	1	Many small fires, many raids, no fire storm
Darmstadt	109	8–15	10	Fire storm, 90 percent asphyxiation deaths
Kassel	228	6–9	4	Fire storm
Heilbronn	78	6–8	10	Fire storm
Cologne	757	5.6	<1	
Wuppertal	395	2.6–5.2	1	65 percent fire deaths
Duisburg	410	1.5–2.6	<1	
Bremen	434	1.2	0.3	
Pirmasens	50	0.6	1	
Brunswick	216	0.56	0.3	Fire storm; 23,000 rescued
59 others				49 cities lost 39 percent residential units

FIGURE 1   Photo of gutted Hamburg buildings on July 24, 1943, after a raid
by the Royal Air Force. Reprinted from Fire and the Air War. © 1946 National
Fire Protection Association, Quincy, Mass. Reprinted with permission.

occurred at Osaka, Kobe, Kyoto, Nagoya, Nishinomiya, Kawasaki, Shi-
zuoka, and Kumagaya (the last city attacked).

The atomic bomb dropped on Hiroshima instantaneously lit many fires
throughout the city. Three to five minutes after the burst, dust and smoke
from the already burning city could be seen following the rising nuclear
fireball cloud.

Figures 2 and 3 are previously unpublished views of Hiroshima taken
in September 1945. Despite some reconstruction, an enormous amount of
rubble and devastation is evident. Only the skeletons of reinforced concrete
buildings and massive masonry structures or chimneys remained standing.
In the center of the city, fire damage was nearly complete.

The sketch of the damage areas at Hiroshima (Figure 4) shows that for
more than 1 mile in radius (about 1.6 km) around ground zero, the destruction was heavy; nearly all buildings were burned out. An appreciable
number of additional buildings were burned out to 2 miles (about 3 km);
even as much as 3 miles (about 5 km) away, some damage was experienced
and a few fires occurred. The yield of the Hiroshima bomb is now estimated
at about 15 kilotons (kt). The height of the burst was at an altitude of
1,860 feet (about 567 m). Modern strategic weapons have yields in the
hundreds and thousands of kilotons. Today, an attack on a city like Hi-

FIGURE 2   View of central Hiroshima in September 1945 showing rubble and reconstruction. (From the private collection of W. Shephard.)

FIGURE 3   View of Hiroshima, September 1945. (From the private collection of W. Shephard.)

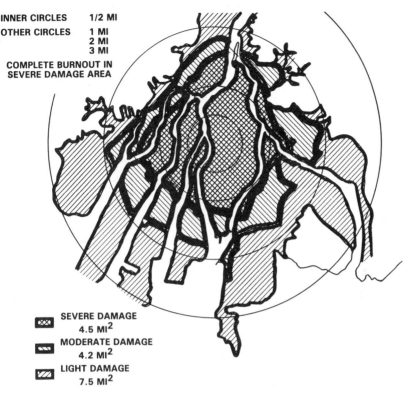

INNER CIRCLES 1/2 MI
OTHER CIRCLES 1 MI
2 MI
3 MI

**COMPLETE BURNOUT IN
SEVERE DAMAGE AREA**

SEVERE DAMAGE
4.5 MI^2

MODERATE DAMAGE
4.2 MI^2

LIGHT DAMAGE
7.5 MI^2

FIGURE 4   Map of damaged areas in Hiroshima.

roshima would probably employ one or more weapons with much larger yields, in keeping with either U.S. or Soviet targeting philosophy and weapon availability.

Figure 5 illustrates the percentage of buildings that were burned as a function of distance from ground zero at Hiroshima. At a range of more than 1 nautical mile,* more than half the buildings were gutted by fire. At that point, the peak overpressure of the nuclear blast wave was about 3 psi, and the fireball heat or thermal fluence was about 8 or 9 cal/cm^2. The surveyed area was composed mainly of industrial or commercial buildings, with some residential structures intermingled among them.

The bomb that was dropped on Nagasaki also caused intense fires, though not as widespread as those at Hiroshima because the bomb was exploded over an industrial area, much of which was not highly built up.

---

*One nautical mile is about 6,076 feet, 1,851 meters, or 1.15 miles.

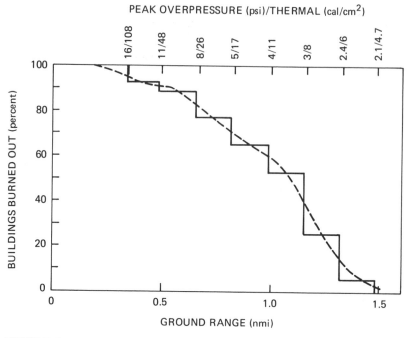

FIGURE 5   Hiroshima fire destruction (nmi = nautical miles).

A number of enclaves of residential and commercial development, however, were scenes of intense fires.

From the limited past experience, it is clear that nuclear-caused urban fires can do extensive damage over very wide areas. Although such fires would be influenced by many factors, intense and widespread fires appear inevitable in the event of a nuclear attack on urban areas. Our understanding, based on historical evidence and a study of nuclear explosions, is summarized in Table 3.

CHARACTERISTICS OF LARGE-SCALE URBAN FIRES

Several obvious facets of large-scale urban fires are unusual and deserve characterization. Some of these unusual features are attributable to the uncommonly large size of such fires. An intense large-area fire could exhaust most of the urban-area fuel in a matter of a few hours; some stores of flammables such as underground oil storage tanks or large stocks of rubber goods could, however, continue to smolder and burn for days. And fire in the rubble of collapsed buildings may burn more slowly.

TABLE 3　Summary of Large-Scale Urban Fire Experience

Nonnuclear
> Most urban war damage is due to fire.
> Much fire damage occurs due to accidents and natural disasters.

Hiroshima
> The central area was nearly completely burned out.
> Firebreaks were not effective.
> Some fires spread beyond the initial ignition area.
> Possibly, many blast-induced ignitions took place (overturned hibachis or charcoal braziers).

Nagasaki
> Target layout led to smaller, separate fires.
> Some areas developed small fire storms.
> Weather and topography influenced damage.

Nuclear tests
> No large-area fire experiments were conducted.
> Numerous ignition thresholds were measured.
> Thermal phenomena were studied extensively.

Intense large-area fires have been known to create unusual drafts, with winds approaching hurricane velocities. Air temperatures in and near these huge fires may exceed the temperature of spontaneous ignition for most burnables. The rising column of hot air, smoke, ash, and combustion gases from a large urban fire can be expected to rise more rapidly, cool more slowly, and otherwise behave differently from that of a single house fire.

Table 4 lists some of the parameters and factors needed to characterize large-scale fires. The burning area may be described in terms of the height of the flames, the rate of burning or rate of heat released, the nature of combustion gases, average temperatures, and the amount of buoyancy created by the fires. Those factors, interactively combined with the city layout, can yield a large-scale urban fire model.

The column above the burning region can be described in terms of its rate of rise, the altitude that it achieves, the periodic or transient toroidal motions, the radiation and chemistry of the gases and particulates that are carried aloft, and their interaction with winds and temperature changes in the atmosphere.

City fires after a nuclear burst are different from fires that spread from a point or along a front: large areas would burn simultaneously. The diameter of such fires can be comparable in scale to the height of the atmosphere. Area fires that are many kilometers in diameter can generate high winds and raise a column of smoke and water vapor that can reach

TABLE 4   Large-Scale Fire Features for Which Models Are Needed

Fire size (area)	Gas/smoke/ash
Duration	Plume heights
Surface winds	Plume dynamics
Air temperatures	Vorticities
Flame heights	Atmospheric/meteorologic influences
Fuel densities	Blast damage influences on fire propagation
Combustion rates	Multiple burst effects
Heat release	

the tropopause.* This fire-generated plume can pump smoke and ash into upper levels of the atmosphere, forming large, spreading clouds. Conceivably, firebrands could be dropped at great distances from the fire itself, leading to additional fires.

Many parameters should be considered in predicting fire damage from such large-scale urban fires. Table 5 lists some of these factors. Fires can result from either blast disruption or thermal (fireball radiation) ignitions. For the latter, the atmospheric transmission of visible and infrared light is important, as are the reflection and scattering of light from snow cover or cloud decks. For blast-induced ignitions, the frequency of open flames, electrical discharges, or sparks from electrostatic discharge or metal friction from motions induced by the blast wave can be correlated with the density, type, usage, and content of buildings and their surroundings and fire suppression measures.

In some cases, the blast can blow out an incipient thermal ignition, but it can also fan and spread an established fire. The blast can expose fuels by breaking up structures, thus leading to the possibility of additional ignitions by subsequent nuclear bursts.

Multiple bursts on or near the same urban area can exacerbate the fire damage. A second burst can more readily light fires in the debris of a preceding burst. It can also scatter burning debris from the first burst and thus contribute to the spread.

High-altitude bursts could burn cities yet cause relatively little direct blast damage. A city protected by a low-altitude antiballistic missile defense system could thus be damaged even though no missiles or bombs actually reach it.

A surface burst radiates about half as effectively as an air burst. In addition, its fireball lies lower on the horizon, and at large ranges, burnable

---

*The tropopause is the altitude at which the air ambient temperature begins increasing with altitude; it is viewed as the dividing line between the lower atmosphere and the stratosphere.

material is more likely to be shielded from it. Yet even surface bursts are capable of causing large fires by thermal and blast-disruption ignitions. A surface burst also leaves a crater, throws ejecta, and causes intense local radiation fallout.

Rain and snow have helped suppress natural fires, but intense urban-area fires may not be subject to weather effects—most of the combustibles in a city are inside the buildings and thus are dry. The disastrous Dresden fire occurred in February with snow on the ground and clouds overhead.

Civil defense preparations could make considerable difference at fire peripheries, but most passive measures are of limited value. Window coverings will be blown away. Firebreaks are otherwise of little value if fires start on both sides of them or large numbers of wind-borne burning firebrands are carried across them. Even with electrical and gas utilities turned off, spark ignition from static electricity discharges or metal scraping on stone or other metal during blast disruption can light leaking volatile fuels or other flammable materials. The removal of all gasoline or diesel vehicles could help, but short of tearing down a city, it is hard to greatly reduce a city's propensity for burning. Active firefighting during or after a nuclear attack seems quite impractical due to the overwhelming number of ignitions, blast-caused debris, and the continued hazards to firefighters.

The bulk of the heat that emanates from a nuclear fireball comes out mostly in a major pulse whose power is illustrated in Figure 6 (left-hand scale). The integral of that pulse, or the total accumulated amount of radiated heat, is indicated by the upper curve with the right-hand scale. For a 1-megaton (Mt) explosion, the peak occurs at about 1 second, and the pulse lasts some 7 or 8 seconds. It is a brief, but intense, release of heat. Roughly one-third of the total weapon yield shines away in this thermal pulse.

TABLE 5   Variables in Fire Damage Prediction

Weapon yield	Blast-induced fires
Burst height	Building construction
Thermally induced fires	Building contents/usage
Visibility/transmittance	Building density
Ignition thresholds	Firespread
Fire propagation probabilities	Firebreaks
Clouds/snow cover reflectance	Topography
Multiple bursts	Weather
Blast-fire interactions	Countermeasures/civil defense
	Preparation/evacuation
	Fire fighting
	Repair/recovery

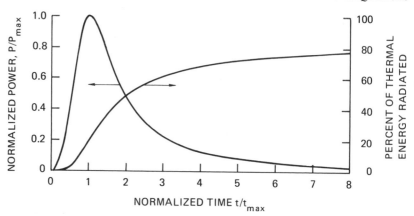

FIGURE 6   Thermal radiation. Source: Glasstone and Dolan (1977).

The normalized power curve of Figure 6 can be approximated by the analytic formula

$$P \simeq P_{max} \left(\frac{2\tau^2}{1 + \tau^4} \right),$$

(1)

in kilotons per second, in which $\tau = t/t_{max}$, and t is the time (in seconds). The time to peak power and the maximum power are approximated by

$$t_{max} \simeq 0.0417 W^{0.44}_{kt},$$

(2)

$$P_{max} \simeq 3.18 W^{0.56}_{kt}.$$

(3)

In equations 2 and 3, W_{kt} is the weapon yield (in kilotons).

The total heat (E, in kilotons) released by the fireball up to time t after burst is the integral of this power:

$$E \simeq \int_0^t P dt,$$

(4)

in which P is the thermal power and dt the time increment.

The ignition of combustibles can be related to this total energy. The ignition threshold energy level for a particular material depends on the weapon yield. The time of the pulse increases with yield, and for longer pulses more energy is needed to ignite materials. Threshold ignition levels Q_T for common susceptible materials in an urban environment increase with yield roughly as

$$Q_T \sim 3.5 W_{kt}^{0.113}. \quad (cal/cm^2)$$

(5)

Relatively simple formulas can be used to estimate the amount of heat per unit area, or the number of calories per square centimeter, that will be felt at various distances. This in turn can be used to predict where fires will develop. Equation 6 indicates that the fluence decreases as the inverse square of the distance from the burst.

$$Q \simeq 1.07 W_{kt} T/R^2, \qquad (\text{cal/cm}^2) \qquad (6)$$

where R is the slant range from the burst (in miles), and T is the transmissivity or attenuation due to passage through the intervening air.

The transmissivity, and thus fluence, decreases exponentially because of absorption by moisture or pollutants in the air (equation 7). Some increases can occur, however, by forward scattering of light. A linear term corrects for this scattering enhancement. The transmissivity can be approximated by

$$T \simeq (1 + 1.9R/V) \exp(-2.9R/V), \qquad (7)$$

where V is the visibility in miles (12-mile [about 19 km] visibility is considered a clear day).

As indicated by equation 5, the levels of thermal fluence, or the amount of heat that it takes to light various susceptible fuels, is a matter of a few calories per square centimeter. Table 6 lists thresholds for a few materials. From 3 to 10 cal/cm^2 should prove sufficient to light likely fuels at yields from 20 to 100 kt. At the larger yields, it takes somewhat more total energy in calories per square centimeter to ignite susceptible materials.

Factors that can influence the development and spread of fires in urban areas are listed in Table 7. Although they represent a number of complex factors, recent studies (Brode and Small, 1984) have attempted to model

TABLE 6   Approximate Threshold Radiant Exposure Needed for Ignition

Fuel	Threshold Radiant Exposure (cal/cm^2)	
	35-kt Yield	1,400-kt Yield
Dry leaves	4	6
Dry grass	5	8
Newspaper (text)	6	8
Cardboard carton	16	20
Rayon (black)	9	14
Canvas	12	18
Cotton shirt	14	21
Heavy cotton drapes	15	18
Black rubber	10	20

SOURCE: Glasstone and Dolan (1977).

TABLE 7   Factors in Target Susceptibility to Fire

Construction (related fire susceptibilities)
Contents (fuel load and ignition sources)
Adjacent structure susceptibility, proximity
Proximity of vehicles
Window area
Weather conditions (cloud cover, snow cover)
Terrain (uphill spread/shadowing)
Disruption sources (open fires, electrical transformers, etc.)
Fuel volatility and dispersion
Multiple burst/exposure factors
   Exposing susceptible fuel to second burst
   Blowing firebrands
Fire suppression

their influences. These studies reveal that, in general, fires tend to burn out the entire center of the area around ground zero and create at least some probability of damage out to many miles.

A number of these variables (see also Table 5) were assigned ranges or uncertainties and were combined statistically. The probabilities for fire damage as a function of distance from ground zero for a generic city are plotted in Figure 7 for 50-kt and 1-Mt explosions. For a 1-Mt explosion, the mean distance to the point at which 50 percent probability of damage would occur is about 7 miles (about 11 km), but the range could be greater or, under certain circumstances, much smaller. The two-sigma values bound 95 percent of the expected variations, i.e., the damage would be expected to fall outside of these extreme curves only 5 percent of the time. Only 1 time in 40 might one expect an urban area to be 50 percent burned out at less than 2 miles (about 3 km) or to be 50 percent destroyed beyond 6 miles (about 10 km) from a 50-kt airburst.

The results shown in Figures 6 and 7 are for generic cities. The range of possible fire sizes could be narrowed by choosing specific cities and weather conditions. Nevertheless, there are many variables that influence the prediction of fire size, and thus there may remain considerable uncertainty in damage or casualty prediction. While it may be prudent to assume and plan for the worst case, it should be noted that smaller values may be equally probable.

MODELING LARGE-FIRE ENVIRONMENTS

Despite the rather large number of disastrous area fires, there exist little technical data. Observations by survivors are, in most cases, sketchy and seldom provide sufficient information to construct and verify theoretical

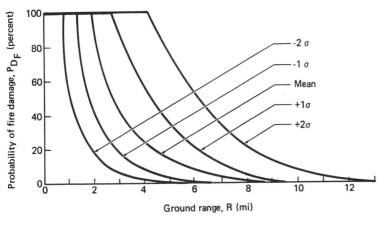

Fire damage range summation curves: all parameters, W = 50 KT.

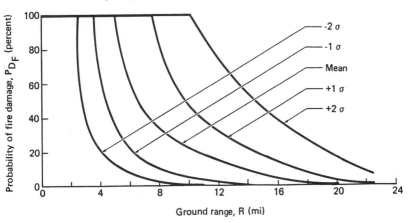

Fire damage range summation curves: all parameters, W = 1 MT

FIGURE 7   Fire damage range summation curves.

models. Nevertheless, when whole areas have burned simultaneously, unusual and extreme conditions have resulted. Survivors of the fire storms at Hamburg, Dresden, Hiroshima, and other cities recall similar experiences. Extreme temperatures and high-velocity fire winds were reported in each of these fires.

We have developed analytical models that explain many of the phenomena observed in the World War II city fires and predict what might occur for a large-yield nuclear attack on an urban area. Basically, the models consider the simultaneous ignition of fires over a large area and the resulting distribution of buoyancy (Small et al., 1984, 1985). The buoyancy initiates a chain of interrelated effects. Pressure forces are created, and as a consequence, a broad upward motion supported by a high-velocity inward flow (the fire winds) is produced (Smith et al., 1975; Cox and Chitty, 1980; Zukoski et al., 1981). This simple view neglects many important transient features of large fires. Nevertheless, analysis of such flows explains many of the observed phenomena. Higher velocities could occur, however, if a swirling column develops (Carrier et al., 1982) from, for example, topography, ambient wind shears, or fire-generated entropy gradients (Weihs and Small, in preparation). Such flows rarely seem to occur. In general, motions resulting from the fire-generated strong buoyancy account for the high-velocity fire winds.

From our analyses, it appears that large-area city fires in World War II, as well as those that might result from nuclear weapon explosions over urban areas, are different from small laboratory-scale fires or isolated building fires. In many of the large World War II fires, all combustibles were consumed. This is not always the case for an ordinary building fire, a fire involving several buildings, or spreading fires that burn along a front. Furthermore, fires with radii approaching 5 to 10 km will have convection columns or plumes that are almost as wide as they are high. In fact, for low inversion heights in the atmosphere or strong ambient winds, the plume may have greater width than vertical dimension.

An analysis of large-area fires should include at least three special features. First, plume motions stem directly from fire dynamics, and therefore, the fire source must be modeled in some detail. Second, since the plume is likely to be fairly broad relative to its height, edge entrainment of ambient air is not likely to be a major factor influencing the plume equilibrium in the atmosphere. Third, the plumes above large-area fires are more seriously influenced by atmospheric gradients, inversion heights, and upper atmosphere crosswinds.

Our approach has been to develop a detailed analytical model of the fire region and to calculate (in numerical experiments) the atmospheric responses to widespread fires or, in modeling terms, large heat additions in a finite surface volume.

The fire or source-region analysis (Larson and Small, 1982a,b; Small et al., 1984, 1985) relates the heat addition to the production of buoyancy and to the induction (and turning upward) of the fire winds. The analysis is valid only in the vicinity of a large fire. Even though transient features are neglected, this analytical view provides some insight into the principal persistent features of large fires. In addition, the steady-state analysis provides some insight and guides the formulation of time-dependent calculations. Some sample results are shown in Figures 8 through 10. Tem-

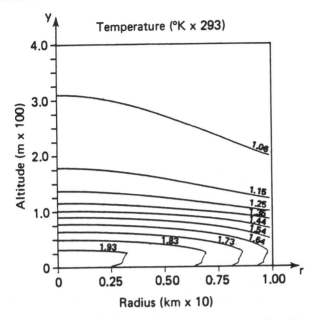

FIGURE 8   Source-region temperature contours: 10-km radius fire.

perature ratios for the fire region are given in Figure 10. Those ratios
represent the average of both the burning structure and street air temperatures. The street air temperatures are, of course, lower than the fire
temperatures; nevertheless, the predicted mean values indicate an extremely hostile thermal environment for survivors of the blast. Figures 11
and 12 show that large fires can indeed generate hurricane-force winds.
Velocities on the ground approach 90 miles per hour (40 m/s) for the
largest fires. These derived velocities are averaged over space and time.
Actual velocities in streets or channels may be larger. In general, the fire
wind velocities are greater at the fire edge than in the center of the burning
area. Survivors attempting to escape the burning zone would meet progressively higher wind speeds.

We have also simulated the time-dependent dynamics of such large-
scale fires and the resulting atmospheric responses. A two-dimensional
implicit hydrodynamics program was used for numerical calculations that
modeled the dynamics of very large fires (Small et al., 1984, 1985). Such
calculations employ finite difference methods to approximate the differential equations of motion. The model accounted for radiation, the buoyancy generated by the heating by the fire, and the subsequent rising of
the plume in the atmosphere. The results show high velocities near the

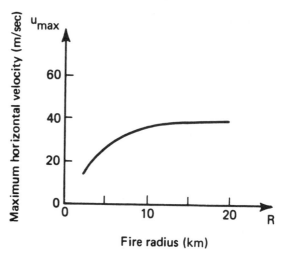

FIGURE 9   Fire wind dependence on radius.

ground surface, a rapid decay of buoyancy above the flames, significant periodic vortex motions around the rising column, and occasional penetrations of the tropopause by the plume. Significantly, the bulk of the column and cloud (containing the smoke and ash) remains below the tropopause, i.e., it does not penetrate into the stratosphere where it might remain for long periods. Clearly, the structure of the atmosphere plays a major role in limiting the plume rise.

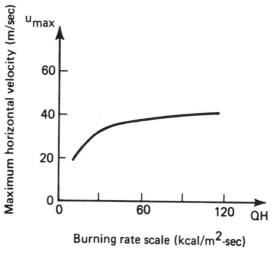

FIGURE 10   Fire wind dependence on burning rate: 10-km radius fire.

An example calculation shown in Figures 11 through 15 models a fire with a 10-km radius. Such a fire would be representative of a 1-Mt yield explosion over a very large urban area. In the first 15 minutes, the intensity of the burning is linearly increased and then held constant at 100 kW/m². This simulates the development of a superfire of many thousands of ignitions. Initially (Figure 11), there is evidence of a very turbulent motion with several distinct rotating cells. The motions extend several kilometers above the fire.

At 25 minutes, the fire winds are well established and extend beyond the fire region (Figure 12). Notable in the solutions are complex transient motions. Some local vortex motions account for periodically high centerline velocities that may loft combustion products through the tropopause; other vortices influence the ambient air induction (fire winds) and the plume rise. These vortex motions vary somewhat periodically with time. There is, however, a uniformity and an overall persistence to the flow.

The calculated plume motions show that the atmosphere plays a major role in the equilibrium height attained by the fire products. The lofting of fire products is limited; the tropopause effectively caps the flow (see Figures 13 and 14).

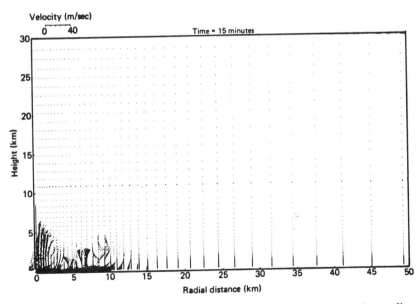

FIGURE 11   Velocity vectors at 15 minutes after the start of a 10-km radius fire.

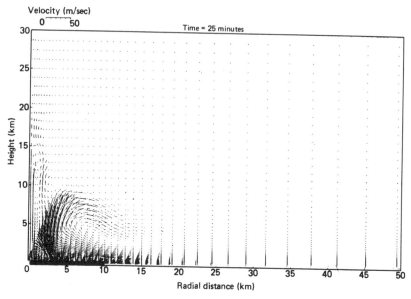

FIGURE 12   Velocity vectors at 25 minutes after the start of a 10-km radius fire.

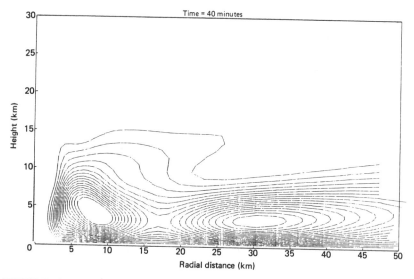

FIGURE 13   Stream lines in atmospheric circulation generated by a 10-km radius fire 40 minutes after ignition.

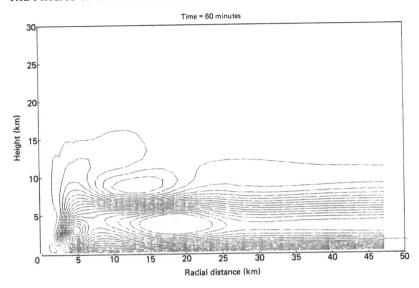

FIGURE 14   Stream lines in atmospheric circulation created by a 10-km radius fire 1 hour after ignition.

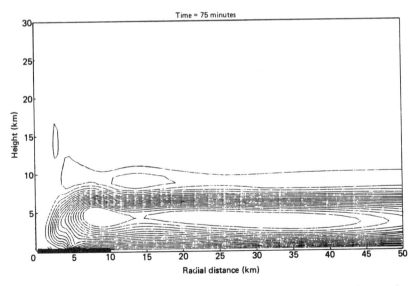

FIGURE 15   Stream lines above a 10-km radius fire at 1 hour 15 minutes after ignition.

At 75 minutes (Figure 15), the bulk of the circulation is well below the tropopause but it extends many kilometers beyond the 10-km fire radius. Evident above the main flow is another layer containing combustion products that originally penetrated to higher altitudes and then fell back. Both layers are contained in the lower atmosphere.

Both the steady-state source-region analysis and the time-dependent numerical simulations portray physically consistent flow fields. There are, however, a number of simplifications and assumptions contained in both models. That there is reasonable agreement between theory and experiment lends confidence to these models. Nevertheless, it is important to recognize deficiencies: processes such as turbulence, radiation, and heat release require improved modeling. The development of these models is continuing.

SUMMARY

The concentrated attacks on urban centers during World War II resulted in several city fires in which large areas burned simultaneously. Extreme temperatures and wind fields were created by those fires. Despite a well-organized German civil defense, firefighting, rescue operations, and emergency medical aid were severely limited in many of the fires and totally ineffective in the intense fire storms.

Even larger area fires are likely to result from nuclear weapon bursts. A 1-Mt yield weapon can start fires over several hundred square kilometers—a fire area many times larger than those in Hiroshima, Hamburg, or Dresden. In fact, a greater area may be damaged by fire than by blast.

High mean temperatures, hurricane-force winds, and toxic gases would characterize the street-level environment. Analysis shows that the fire wind velocities increase with the size and intensity of the burning city and peak at approximately 90 miles per hour (40 m/s). Local wind values in natural channels, between buildings, or in streets may be somewhat higher; and gusts to even higher speeds can be expected. Intense fires, and thus a more severe fire environment, are likely in the more densely built cities.

Our calculations show that large-area fires will produce high mean air temperatures. Flame convection and radiative heating would produce a hostile temperature environment throughout an intensely burning city, even in the streets. Extreme thermal conditions and noxious gas accumulations would also be likely in shelters not properly designed to diffuse or dissipate the heat load and filter the smoky and poisonous air.

The induced fire winds would be drawn into the burning city from surrounding areas. Measurable velocities may be felt as far as 40 km from the fire, and significant wind speeds may be felt as far as 10 km from the fire edge. This inflow would feed and fan the fires and replace the gases of the rising plume or smoke column. The smoke would mostly be contained in the lower atmosphere, although some may be injected to higher altitudes. The possible long-term or climatic effects of these fires are currently being investigated by a number of agencies and laboratories. The smoke load injected into the atmosphere by a nuclear war is the subject of a continuing study by us. A previously published study provided detailed estimates of smoke from attacks on nonurban targets (military strategic forces) (Small and Bush, 1985).

REFERENCES

Bond, Horatio, ed. 1946. Fire and the Air War. Boston: National Fire Protection Association.

Brode, H. L., and R. D. Small. 1984. Fire Damage and Strategic Targeting. PSR Note 567 (DNA-TR-84-272). Santa Monica, Calif.: Pacific-Sierra Research Corp.

Carrier, G. F., F. E. Fendell, and P. S. Feldman. 1982. Firestorms. TRW Report 38163-6001-UT-00. Redondo Beach, Calif.: TRW Systems.

Cox, G., and R. Chitty. 1980. A study of the deterministic properties of unbounded fire plumes. Combust. Flame 39:191–209.

Glasstone, S., and P. J. Dolan. 1977. The Effects of Nuclear Weapons. Washington, D.C.: U.S. Department of Defense and U.S. Department of Energy.

Larson, D. A., and R. D. Small. 1982a. Analysis of the Large Urban Fire Environment. II. Parametric Analysis and Model City Simulations. PSR Report 1210. Santa Monica, Calif.: Pacific-Sierra Research Corp.

Larson, D. A., and R. D. Small. 1982b. Analysis of the Large Urban Fire Environment. I. Theory. PSR Report 1210. Santa Monica, Calif.: Pacific-Sierra Research Corp.

Nielsen, H. J. 1970. Mass Fire Data Analysis. DASA Report No. 2018. Chicago, Ill.: IIT Research Institute.

Small, R. D., and H. L. Brode. 1983. Thermal radiation from a nuclear weapon burst. LLNL-CONF-8305107. Pp. 211–216 in Proceedings of the 17th Asilomar Conference on Fire and Blast Effects of Nuclear Weapons. Monterey, Calif.: Lawrence Livermore National Laboratory.

Small, R. D., and B. W. Bush. 1985. Smoke production from multiple nuclear explosions in nonurban areas. Science 229:465–469.

Small, R. D., D. A. Larson, and H. L. Brode. 1984. Asymptotically large area fires. J. Heat Trans. 106:318–324.

Small, R. D., D. Remetch, and H. L. Brode. 1985. Atmospheric motions from large fires. American Institute of Aeronautics and Astronautics Paper 85-0458. Paper presented at the 23rd Aerospace Sciences Meeting, Reno, Nev., January 14–17.

Smith, R. K., R. B. Morton, and L. M. Leslie. 1975. The role of dynamic pressure in generating fire wind. J. Fluid Mech. 68:1–19.

Weihs, D., and R. D. Small. In preparation. On the possibility of large area fires swirling. Los Angeles, Calif.: Pacific-Sierra Research Corp.

Zukoski, E. E., T. Kubota, and B. Cetegen. 1981. Entrainment in the Near Field of a Fire Plume. Report NBS-GCR-81-346. Washington, D.C.: National Bureau of Standards.

The Medical Implications of Nuclear War, Institute of
Medicine. © 1986 by the National Academy of Sciences.
National Academy Press, Washington, D.C.

Recent Assessments of the Environmental Consequences of Nuclear War

RICHARD P. TURCO, PH.D.
R&D Associates, Marina del Rey, California

NEW FINDINGS

Since late 1984 a number of important scientific studies have considered
the global-scale consequences of a major nuclear war. These studies look
beyond the immediate and direct effects of nuclear explosions (blast,
thermal radiation, and local radioactive fallout) to investigate the more
widespread effects of dispersed radioactivity and severe climatic disturbances—the nuclear winter (Crutzen and Birks, 1982; Turco et al., 1983).
Assessments of the relevant phenomena have been carried out by the U.S.
National Research Council (NRC, 1985), the Royal Society of Canada
(1985), and the Scientific Committee on Problems of the Environment
(SCOPE) of the International Council of Scientific Unions (Pittock et al.,
1986; Harwell and Hutchinson, 1985). Numerous physicists, atmospheric
scientists, biologists, and physicians from around the world have contributed to these projects. In each case the findings are similar. While cau-
tioning that significant uncertainties remain to be resolved, each report
concludes that a nuclear winter is a clear possibility following a nuclear
exchange. The SCOPE report goes even further, describing the biological,
ecological, and human implications of a nuclear war and its aftermath.
This unique treatise is summarized in the paper by M. Harwell in this
volume (also see Harwell and Hutchinson, 1985).

The SCOPE executive summary of findings on the physical and atmospheric effects of nuclear war is reproduced in the appendix to this
paper. The report confirms that the coexistence of immense nuclear ar-

senals (about 24,000 warheads carrying some 12,000 megatons of explosives) and abundant combustible fuels concentrated in industrial and urban areas (up to several thousand million tons of petroleum and petroleum products and more than ten thousand million tons of wood and wood products) could bring about a global nuclear winter in the event of nuclear exchange. The physical mechanism would involve the ignition of large fires by nuclear bursts, followed by the insertion of unprecedented quantities of smoke into the atmosphere, where it could divert sunlight and trigger climatic perturbations.

In addition to the major national and international studies mentioned above, a number of important individual scientific contributions to the nuclear winter problem have been made recently. Small and Bush (1985) reassessed the potential quantity of fuel that might burn in nuclear detonations over rural (nonurban) targets. They found quantities 10 to 100 times smaller than previous estimates (Crutzen and Birks, 1982; Turco et al., 1983; NRC, 1985). Although the methodology of the study by Small and Bush is more thorough than earlier approaches, some of the key assumptions have been questioned; a subsequent analysis increases the fuel estimates of Small and Bush by a factor of about 10 (Pittock et al., 1986). Regardless of the resolution to this problem, wildland fire smoke remains a secondary contributor to a nuclear winter, with industrial and urban smoke being the primary contributor.

The heights of deposition of smoke in large fire plumes have been studied by Cotton (1985) and Manins (1985). It now seems clear that smoke from large nuclear-initiated fires would be injected into the upper troposphere, with some directly reaching the stratosphere. Most of the smoke injection would be above the low-altitude zone of normally rapid washout. However, the fraction of the smoke that might be removed immediately in the induced "black rain" is currently unknown; fractions of 30 to 50 percent assumed in recent assessments seem reasonable (NRC, 1985; Pittock et al., 1986).

Even if the smoke is not initially injected into the stratosphere, several new studies show that heating produced by the absorption of sunlight will cause the smoke to rise into this region (Haberle et al., 1985). Such studies also indicate that solar heating could lead to the stabilization of elevated smoke layers and accelerate their spread into the Southern Hemisphere. The result would be more widespread and prolonged climatic disturbances.

The expected climatic impacts of dense smoke layers include land surface temperature decreases of up to 35°C within one week during the summer half of the year, major shifts in global wind patterns, and substantial decreases in precipitation in many continental regions (Thompson, 1985; Cess et al., 1985; Malone et al., 1986). When proper comparisons are made between these new results and the original nuclear winter calculations of Turco et al. (1983), the predicted temperature declines are found to be very similar.* The latest physical modeling of the radiative and climatic effects of dense clouds of smoke (Cess et al., 1985; Covey et al., 1985; Ramaswamy and Kiehl, 1985) reinforce the cooling mechanisms postulated for a nuclear winter.

In summary, a growing body of detailed technical analyses supports the general principles of the nuclear winter theory. Thus, although substantial work remains to be done, the theory now stands on a much firmer scientific basis than ever before. In light of these newest confirmations of the possible physical aftermath of a major nuclear war, greater emphasis should be placed on understanding the biological and ecological consequences, particularly the agricultural and human impacts. These are, after all, of the most urgent concern to the global community (Harwell and Hutchinson, 1985).

POTENTIAL CONTRIBUTION OF PLASTICS TO NUCLEAR WINTER

Modern civilization is finding more uses for plastics in construction, durable goods, and packaging. When burned, plastics typically generate a sooty toxic smoke (and could therefore contribute to a nuclear winter). The industrialized world is producing plastics and noncellulosic synthetic fibers at the rate of about 60 million metric tons, or teragrams (1 teragram [Tg] $= 10^{12}$ g), per year (U.N. Statistical Yearbook, 1981; Handbook of Economic Statistics, 1984). In the United States, plastics output is projected to increase by up to 5 to 6 percent per year through this decade (U.S. Industrial Outlook, 1985). Worldwide output has grown roughly 10-fold over the last two decades, and at current rates of growth output could redouble by the turn of the century. In 1983, production in the North Atlantic Treaty Organization (NATO) and Warsaw Pact alliances and Japan amounted to about 46 Tg of plastics and 8 Tg of noncellulosic fibers. Plastics are derived primarily from petroleum and account for about 2 percent of total petroleum consumption.

The breakdown of production and usage for various plastics in the United States is given in Table 1. Considering the 70 percent of all plastics represented by the data in Table 1, about one-third goes into each of the packaging and construction industries, about one-quarter into consumer durables, and the rest into the transportation industry. These statistics are

---

*That is, by taking into account the moderating effect of oceans on land temperatures and the normal seasonal differences in initial land temperatures.

TABLE 1   Plastics Production, Use, and Properties

Plastics	Production/Use[a] (Tg/yr) Packaging	Construction	Consumer Durables	Transportation	Fraction of Total Production[b] Represented	Specific Extinction Coefficient of Smoke[c] (m^2/g-plastic)
Polyethylene	2.87	0.77	0.70	0.12	0.70	0.5
Polyvinylchloride	0.30	1.89	0.49	0.10	0.81	1.0
Polystyrene	0.74	0.15	0.48	0	0.63	1.5
Polypropylene	0.42	0.04	0.87	0.16	0.68	0.5
Polyurethane	0	0.18	0.39	0.19	0.86	0.5
Polyester	0.40	0.15	0.33	0.09	0.95	1.0
Phenolic	0	0.99	0.08	0	0.91	0.5
Acrylonitrile-butadiene-styrene	0	0.09	0.16	0.11	0.69	1.2
Epoxy/Melamine	0	0.49	0.25	0	0.90	0.3
Total	4.73	4.75	3.75	0.77	0.70[d]	
Weighted-average[e] specific extinction coefficient of smoke (m^2/g-plastic)	0.73	0.78	0.75	0.73		

NOTE: Data on production and consumption apply to the United States in 1984 and are taken from Modern Plastics (1985). Only the predominant families of plastics are considered.

[a]Packaging includes containers, wrappers, fillers, bottles, caps, cups, and so on. Construction materials include pipes, panels, insulation, wiring, tiles, moldings, fixtures, and so forth. Consumer durables include appliances, electronic gear, housewares, toys, records, tapes, and the like. Transportation refers to plastics used in cars, trucks, buses, aircraft, and so on.

[b]The fraction of production of each type of plastic that is included in the four use categories (i.e., excluding miscellaneous uses—for which statistics are unavailable—and exports).

[c]The specific extinction (scattering plus absorption) coefficients apply at visible wavelengths. The values are based on laboratory data obtained from the references cited in the text, but have a substantial uncertainty. (The coefficient for phenolics is only estimated.) The extinction coefficient, when multiplied by the quantity of a particular type of plastic that may be burned, and divided by the area over which the smoke may be dispersed, provides an estimate of the extinction optical depth of the resulting smoke layer.

[d]This is the fraction of the *total* production of plastics (all types and all uses) represented by the data in the table. According to Modern Plastics (1985), total U.S. plastics consumption in 1984 was nearly 20 Tg.

[e]The average extinction coefficient corresponding to the specific mix of plastics in each use category.

consistent with other surveys of plastics consumption (U.S. Statistical Abstracts, 1985).

There are two lifetimes of plastics that are of interest: their functional lifetime from manufacture to disposal as trash and their lifetime in the environment after disposal. It is assumed that plastics used in packaging (about 33 percent of the total produced, or 16 Tg/year at present) have an average functional lifetime of 3 months. Thus, relatively little packaging material is stockpiled at any time. Of the remaining plastics, it is assumed that equal thirds have functional lifetimes of 10, 20, and 40 years (i.e., about 22 percent of total production, or 10 Tg/year of each type at present). The longer-lived materials would be used mainly in construction as well as in certain items of furniture and appliances. In addition, polymeric fibers, used principally in carpeting, are assigned a lifetime of 10 years (8 Tg/year is produced at present). While the useful lifetimes of plastics in society are difficult to determine accurately, our estimates based on broad use categories should be adequate.

In disposal, plastics may be burned, buried, or simply discarded as loose rubbish. Only about 10 percent of all collected municipal waste is burned, and thus incineration represents a minor sink for plastics (Guillet, 1973). No meaningful recycling of plastics occurs. Most polymers are also immune to decomposition in soils. However, solar ultraviolet radiation causes bond incisions in many polymers, leading to chemical activity and degradation, although continuous direct exposure to sunlight is required for effective decomposition (Guillet, 1973). Today, discarded plastics continue to accumulate in dumps, salvage yards, and landfills. Some of this material would be accessible to burning in a nuclear war.

Production records indicate that about 750 Tg of plastics and noncellulosic fibers were manufactured from 1963 to 1983 in the United States, Europe, the USSR, and Japan. With the assumed lifetimes discussed above, it is estimated that about 400 Tg of polymers are in use today.

Given the production rates and lifetimes of various plastics products and the amounts available in 1983, estimates of future accumulations can be made (Figure 1). If production were to remain constant at the 1983 level, the quantity of plastics in use would continue to grow, approaching 700 Tg in several decades. If production were to increase by 5 percent per year until the turn of the century (as might be anticipated based on past performance; U.S. Industrial Outlook, 1985), about 800 Tg could be in use in the NATO and Warsaw Pact alliances by the turn of the century, with the quantities in use in these countries continuing to grow well into the century. Greater amounts would have been produced and discarded, and much of this would be accessible at trash disposal sites. More than 1,600 Tg of plastics and fibers will have been manufactured in the countries of interest by the turn of the century.

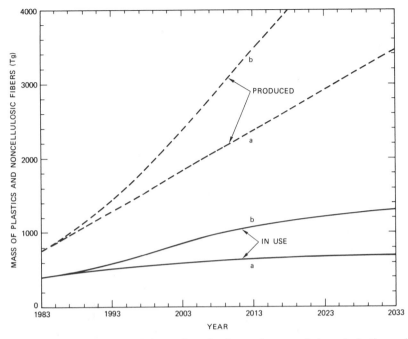

FIGURE 1   Projections of the total production and accumulation of plastics and noncellulosic fibers in the United States, Europe, the U.S.S.R., and Japan. The calculations correspond to the following assumptions about future plastics production: (a) production is constant at the 1983 rate for an indefinite period, and (b) production grows annually by 5 percent of the 1983 rate from 1983 to 2003 and is constant thereafter. The assumed plastics lifetimes are discussed in the text.

The smoke produced by burning polymers has been studied in the laboratory (Tewarson, 1982; Seader and Einhorn, 1976; Morikawa, 1978; Hilado and Machado, 1978; Quintiere, 1982; Bankston et al., 1981). For the materials in Table 1, measured smoke emission factors (grams of smoke per gram of material burned) range from several percent to 20 percent or more. Under smoldering conditions, as much as 50 percent of some plastics may be converted into smoke particles. Under flaming conditions, the smoke is typically black and sooty, with a large optical absorption coefficient.

Table 1 summarizes data on the specific extinction coefficient of the smoke generated by a variety of plastics during flaming combustion (the specific extinction coefficient is expressed in terms of the square meters of cross section produced by each gram of material burned). The values for individual plastics differ by a factor of 5 or more. However, the average weighted coefficients corresponding to the four principal use categories in Table 1 are very similar. On this basis, a specific extinction coefficient of 0.75 m^2/g-plastics burned may be employed to make estimates of optical effects.

Plastics can be treated with flame retardants and smoke retardants. In the United States in 1984, 200,000 tons of flame retardants were used (about 1 percent of the weight of the plastics produced) (Modern Plastics, 1984). Flame retardants do not generally reduce the smoke emissions of plastics and can increase emissions dramatically in some cases (Bankston et al., 1981). Practical and economical smoke retardants for plastics have not yet been developed. Such retardants may eventually reduce the smoke emissions of certain plastics by up to 50 percent (Modern Plastics, 1984) but will never eliminate the smoke altogether.

Accumulated plastics are concentrated in urban zones where, because of their variety, utility, and durability, they find countless practical uses. In the United States, the top 277 metropolitan areas hold about 75 percent of the population (U.S. Statistical Abstracts, 1985) and, presumably, at least this fraction of all plastics. The burning of hundreds of teragrams of plastics would produce enough sooty smoke to contribute to a nuclear winter, perhaps even leading to one in the absence of other sources of smoke and dust. Of course, a substantial portion of the urban areas of the warring nations would have to be ignited in fires, as has been postulated in a number of recent studies (Crutzen and Birks, 1982; Turco et al., 1983; NRC, 1985; Pittock et al., 1986).

Table 2 defines a plausible range of optical perturbations that might result from plastics combustion in a future nuclear war. The range of potential global-average absorption optical depths resulting from plastics smoke—accounting for a plausible range of parameter variations—is about 0.1 to 1.2. It has been shown that smoke injections leading to equivalent global absorption optical depths of ~0.2 could greatly perturb the climate (Thompson, 1985; Cess et al., 1985; Malone et al., 1986). The baseline scenario of Turco et al. (1983) projected an equivalent global absorption

TABLE 2   Projected Smoke Potential of Plastics in 2000 A.D.

Mass of Plastics (Tg)	1,000–2,000
Total Extinction Cross-section (10^{12} m^2)	750–1,500
Fraction Activated by Fires[a]	1/8–1/2
Equivalent Global Extinction Optical Depth[b]	0.2–1.5
Global Absorption Optical Depth[c]	0.1–1.2
TTAPS Baseline Urban Smoke Absorption Optical Depth (global)	~0.5

[a]This factor assumes that one-fourth to two-thirds of all plastics in the warring nations could be burned in a major nuclear war and that one-fourth to one-half of the smoke would be removed immediately by precipitation (Pittock et al., 1986).

[b]This assumes that the smoke is uniformly distributed around the entire planet.

[c]This corresponds to a range of 0.2 to 0.5 for the single-scatter albedo of the smoke.

optical depth of about 0.5, which produced a nuclear winter. Accordingly, smoke and toxic gases from plastics alone would seem to guarantee some nuclear winter-like environmental effects in the event of a future nuclear conflict. Additional sources of climate-altering aerosols would be soot from oil and structure fires, smoke from wildfires, and dust from surface detonations.

The estimates presented here are uncertain because, among other things, extrapolations of trends in plastics consumption have been extended several decades into the future. However, the drift toward greater worldwide dependence on plastics and synthetic fibers is very clear. Nuclear arsenals may be reduced substantially in the coming decades, but there is currently little reason for optimism. Thus, in a politically divided world, we must seriously consider how advanced technologies may someday interact to threaten the future of mankind.

REFERENCES

Bankston, C. P., B. T. Zinn, R. F. Browner, and E. A. Powell. 1981. Aspects of the mechanisms of smoke generation by burning materials. Comb. Flame 41:273–292.

Cess, R. D., G. L. Potter, S. J. Ghan, and W. L. Gates. 1985. The climatic effects of large injections of atmospheric smoke and dust. J. Geophys. Res. 90:12937–12950.

Cotton, W. R. 1985. Atmospheric convection and nuclear winter. Am. Sci. 73:275–280.

Covey, C., S. L. Thompson, and S. H. Schneider. 1985. "Nuclear winter": A diagnosis of atmospheric general circulation model simulations. J. Geophys. Res. 90:5615–5628.

Crutzen, P. J., and J. W. Birks. 1982. Twilight at noon: The atmosphere after a nuclear war. Ambio 11:114–125.

Guillet, J. (ed.). 1973. Polymers and ecological problems. Polymer Science and Technology, Volume 3. New York: Plenum.

Haberle, R. M., T. P. Ackerman, O. B. Toon, and J. L. Hollingsworth. 1985. Global transport of atmospheric smoke following a major nuclear exchange. Geophys. Res. Lett. 12:405–408.

Handbook of Economic Statistics, 1984. 1984. Washington, D.C.: U.S. Government Printing Office.

Harwell, M. A., and T. C. Hutchinson. 1985. Environmental Consequences of Nuclear War, Volume II: Ecological and Agricultural Effects. SCOPE 28. Chichester, U.K.: John Wiley & Sons.

Hilado, C. J., and A. M. Machado. 1978. Smoke studies with the Arapahoe chamber. J. Fire Flammability 9:240–244.

Malone, R. C., L. H. Auer, G. A. Glatzmaier, M. C. Wood, and O. B. Toon. 1986. Nuclear winter: Three-dimensional simulations including interactive transport, scavenging and solar heating of smoke. J. Geophys. Res. 91:1039–1053.

Manins, P. C. 1985. Cloud heights and stratospheric injections resulting from a thermonuclear war. Atmos. Environ. 19:1245–1255.

Modern Plastics. 1984. 61:62–64.

Modern Plastics. 1985. Materials '85. 62:61–71.

Morikawa, T. 1978. Evolution of soot and polycyclic aromatic hydrocarbons in combustion. J. Comb. Toxicol. 5:349–360.

National Research Council (NRC). 1985. The effects on the atmosphere of a major nuclear exchange. Washington, D.C.: National Academy Press.

Pittock, A. B., T. P. Ackerman, P. J. Crutzen, M. C. MacCracken, C. S. Shapiro, and R. P. Turco. 1986. Environmental Consequences of Nuclear War, Volume I: Physical and Atmospheric Effects. SCOPE 28. Chichester, U.K.: John Wiley & Sons.

Quintiere, J. G. 1982. An assessment of correlations between laboratory and full-scale experiments for the FAA aircraft fire safety program. Part 1: Smoke. National Bureau of Standards Report NBSIR 82-2508. Washington, D.C.: National Bureau of Standards.

Ramaswamy, V., and J. Kiehl. 1985. Sensitivities of the radiative forcing due to large loadings of smoke and dust. J. Geophys. Res. 90:5597–5613.

Royal Society of Canada. 1985. Nuclear winter and associated effects: A Canadian appraisal of the environmental impact of nuclear war. Ottawa, Canada: Royal Society of Canada.

Seader, J. D., and I. N. Einhorn. 1976. Some physical, chemical, toxicological and physiological aspects of fire smokes. Pp. 1423–1445 in Proceedings of the 16th International Symposium of the Combustion Institute, Pittsburgh, Pa.

Small, R. D., and B. W. Bush. 1985. Smoke production from multiple nuclear explosions in nonurban areas. Science 229:465–469.

Tewarson, A. 1982. Experimental evaluation of flammability parameters of polymeric materials. Pp. 97–153 in Flame Retardant Polymeric Materials, Vol. 3., M. Lewin, S. M. Atlas, and E. M. Pierce, eds. New York: Plenum.

Thompson, S. L. 1985. Global interactive transport simulations of nuclear war smoke. Nature 317:35–39.

Turco, R. P., O. B. Toon, T. P. Ackerman, J. B. Pollack, and C. Sagan. 1983. Nuclear winter: Global consequences of multiple nuclear explosions. Science 222:1283–1292.

U.N. Statistical Yearbook, 1979/1980. 1981. New York: United Nations.

U.S. Industrial Outlook, 1985. 1985. Washington, D.C.: Department of Commerce.

U.S. Statistical Abstracts 1984. 1985. Washington, D.C.: Department of Commerce.

APPENDIX
SCOPE/ENUWAR Executive Summary

The executive summary of the SCOPE (Scientific Committee on Problems of the Environment) ENUWAR (Environmental Effects of Nuclear War) Report, Volume I: Physical and Atmospheric Effects (Pittock et al., 1986), reviews the most important findings of recent detailed scientific studies of the nuclear winter phenomenon (SCOPE 28, Volumes I and II, John Wiley & Sons, Ltd., Chichester—available also from Wiley, Inc. for North America). The summary is reproduced here in its entirety by permission of SCOPE.

Executive Summary

This volume presents the results of an assessment of the climatic and atmospheric effects of a large nuclear war. The chapters in the volume follow a logical sequence of development, starting with discussions of nuclear weapons effects and possible characteristics of a nuclear war. The report continues with a treatment of the consequent fires, smoke emissions, and dust injections and their effects on the physical and chemical processes of the atmosphere. This is followed by a chapter dealing with long-term radiological doses. The concluding chapter contains recommendations for future research and study.

In assessments of this type, a variety of procedural options are available, including, for example, "worst case" analyses, risk analyses, and "most probable" analyses. All of these approaches have relevance for the subject addressed here due to the large uncertainties which surround many aspects of the problem. Some of these uncertainties are inherent in studies of nuclear war and some are simply the result of limited information about natural physical processes. In general, in making assumptions about scenarios, models, and magnitudes of injections, and in estimating their atmospheric effects, an attempt has been made to avoid "minimum" and "worst case" analyses in favor of a "middle ground" that encompasses, with reasonable probability, the atmospheric and climatic consequences of a major nuclear exchange.

The principal results of this assessment, arranged roughly in the same order as the more detailed discussions contained in the body of this volume, are summarized below. The Executive Summary of Volume II (Harwell and Hutchinson, 1985), which describes the ecological and agricultural consequences of a nuclear war, is included as Appendix 1 at the end of this volume. A Glossary is included as Appendix 2 and a list of participants in the study is included as Appendix 3.

1. DIRECT EFFECTS OF NUCLEAR EXPLOSIONS

The two comparatively small detonations of nuclear weapons in Japan in 1945 and the subsequent higher yield atmospheric nuclear tests preceding the atmospheric test ban treaty of 1963 have provided some information on the direct effects of nuclear explosions. Typical modern weapons carried by today's missiles and aircraft have yields of hundreds of kilotons or more. If detonated, such explosions would have the following effects:

• In each explosion, thermal (heat) radiation and blast waves would result in death and devastation over an area of up to 500 km^2 per megaton of yield, an area typical of a major city. The extent of these direct effects depends on the yield of the explosion, height of burst, and state of the local environment. The destruction of Hiroshima and Nagasaki by atomic bombs near the end of World War II provides examples of the effects of relatively *small* nuclear explosions.

• Nuclear weapons are extremely efficient incendiary devices. The thermal radiation emitted by the nuclear fireball, in combination with the accidental ignitions caused by the blast, would ignite fires in urban/industrial areas and wildlands of a size unprecedented in history. These fires would generate massive plumes of smoke and toxic chemicals. The newly recognized atmospheric effects of the smoke from a large number of such fires are the major focus of this report.

• For nuclear explosions that contact land surfaces (surface bursts), large amounts (of the order of 100,000 tonne per megaton of yield) of dust, soil, and debris are drawn up with the fireball. The larger dust particles, carrying about half of the bomb's radioactivity, fall back to the surface mostly within the first day, thereby contaminating hundreds of square kilometers near and downwind of the explosion site. This local fallout can exceed the lethal dose level.

• All of the radioactivity from nuclear explosions well above the surface (airbursts) and about half of the radioactivity from surface bursts would be lofted on particles into the upper troposphere or stratosphere by the rising fireballs and contribute to longer term radioactive fallout on a global scale.

• Nuclear explosions high in the atmosphere, or in space, would generate an intense electromagnetic pulse capable of inducing strong electric currents that could damage electronic equipment and communications networks over continent-size regions.

2. STRATEGIES AND SCENARIOS FOR A NUCLEAR WAR

In the forty years since the first nuclear explosion, the five nuclear powers, but primarily the U.S. and the U.S.S.R., have accumulated very large arsenals of nuclear weapons. It is impossible to forecast in detail the evolution of potential military conflicts. Nevertheless, enough of the general principles of strategic planning have been discussed that plausible scenarios for the development and immediate consequences of a large-scale nuclear war can be derived for analysis.

• NATO and Warsaw Pact nuclear arsenals include about 24,000 strategic and theatre nuclear warheads totaling about 12,000 megatons. The arsenals now contain the equivalent explosive power of about one million "Hiroshima-size" bombs.

• A plausible scenario for a global nuclear war could involve on the order of 6000 Mt divided between more than 12,000 warheads. Because of its obvious importance, the potential environmental consequences of an exchange of roughly this size are examined. The smoke-induced atmospheric consequences discussed in this volume are, however, more dependent on the number of nuclear explosions occurring over cities and industrial centers than on any of the other assumptions of the particular exchange.

- Many targets of nuclear warheads, such as missile silos and some military bases, are isolated geographically from population centers. Nevertheless, enough important military and strategic targets are located near or within cities so that collateral damage in urban and industrial centers from a counterforce nuclear strike could be extensive. As a result, even relatively limited nuclear attacks directed at military-related targets could cause large fires and smoke production.

- Current strategic deterrence policies imply that, in an escalating nuclear conflict, many warheads might be used directly against urban and industrial centers. Such targeting would have far-reaching implications because of the potential for fires, smoke production, and climatic change.

3. THE EXTENT OF FIRES AND GENERATION OF SMOKE

During World War II, intense city fires covering areas as large as 10 to 30 square kilometers were ignited by massive incendiary bombing raids, as well as by the relatively small nuclear explosions over Hiroshima and Nagasaki. Because these fires were distributed over many months, the total atmospheric accumulation of smoke generated by these fires was small. Today, in a major nuclear conflict, thousands of very intense fires, each covering up to a few hundred kilometers, could be ignited simultaneously in urban areas, fossil fuel processing plants and storage depots, wildlands, and other locations. Because there have never been fires as large and as intense as may be expected, no appropriate smoke emission measurements have been made. Estimates of emissions from such fires rely upon extrapolation from data on much smaller fires. This procedure may introduce considerable error in quantifying smoke emissions, especially in making estimates for intense fire situations.

- About 70% of the populations of Europe, North America and the Soviet Union live in urban and suburban areas covering a few hundred thousand square kilometers and containing more than ten thousand million tonne of combustible wood and paper. If about 25–30% of this were to be ignited, in just a few hours or days, tens of millions to more than a hundred million tonne of smoke could be generated. About a quarter to a third of the emitted smoke from the flaming combustion of this material would be amorphous elemental carbon, which is black and efficiently absorbs sunlight.

- Fossil fuels (e.g., oil, gasoline, and kerosene) and fossil fuel-derived products (including plastics, rubber, asphalt, roofing materials, and organochemicals) are heavily concentrated in cities and industrial areas; flaming combustion of a small fraction (~25–30%) of the few thousand million tonne of such materials currently available could generate 50–150 million tonne of very sooty smoke containing a large fraction (50% or greater) of amorphous elemental carbon. The burning of 25–30% of the combustible materials of the developed world could occur with near total burnout of less than one hundred of the largest industrialized urban areas.

• Fires ignited in forests and other wildlands could consume tens to hundreds of thousands of square kilometers of vegetation over days to weeks, depending on the state of the vegetation, and the extent of fire-spread. These fires could produce tens of millions of tonne of smoke in the summer half of the year, but considerably less in the winter half of the year. Because wildland fire smoke contains only about 10% amorphous elemental carbon, it would be of secondary importance compared to the smoke created by urban and industrial fires, although its effects would not be negligible.

• The several tens of millions of tonne of sub-micron dust particles that could be lofted to stratospheric altitudes by surface bursts could reside in the atmosphere for a year or more. The potential climatic effects of the dust emissions, although substantially less than those of the smoke, also must be considered.

4. THE EVOLUTION AND RADIATIVE EFFECTS OF THE SMOKE

The sooty smoke particles rising in the hot plumes of large fires would consist of a mixture of amorphous elemental carbon, condensed hydro-carbons, debris particles, and other substances. The amount of elemental carbon in particles with effective spherical diameters on the order of 0.1 μm to perhaps 1.0 μm would be of most importance in calculating the potential effect on solar radiation. Such particles can be spread globally by the winds and remain suspended for days to months.

• Large hot fires create converging surface winds and rapidly rising fire plumes which, within minutes, can carry smoke particles, ash and other fire products, windblown debris, and water from combustion and the surrounding air to as high as 10–15 kilometers. The mass of particles deposited aloft would depend on the rate of smoke generation, the intensity of the fire, local weather conditions, and the effectiveness of scavenging processes in the convective column.

• As smoke-laden, heated air from over the fire rises, adiabatic expansion and entrainment would cause cooling and condensation of water vapor that could lead, in some cases, to the formation of a cumulonimbus cloud system. Condensation-induced latent heating of the rising air parcels would help to loft the smoke particles to higher altitudes than expected from the heat of combustion alone.

• Although much of the water vapor drawn up from the boundary layer would condense, precipitation might form for only a fraction of the fire plumes. In the rising fire columns of such fires, soot particles would tend to be collected inefficiently by the water in the cloud. Smoke particles however, are generally composed of a mixture of substances and might, at least partially, be incorporated in water droplets or ice particles by processes not now well understood. Smoke particles that are captured could again be released to the atmosphere as the ice or water particles evaporate in the cloud anvils or in the environment surrounding the convective clouds. Altogether, an unknown fraction of the smoke entering the cloud would be captured in droplets and promptly removed from the atmosphere by precipitation.

• Not all fires would, however, induce strong convective activity. This depends on fuel loading characteristics and meteorological conditions. It is assumed in current studies that 30–50% of the smoke injected into the atmosphere from all fires would be removed by precipitation within the first day, and not be available to affect longer-term large-scale, meteorological processes. This assumption is a major uncertainty in all current assessments. For the fire and smoke assumptions made in this study, the net input of smoke to the atmosphere after early scavenging is estimated to range from 50 to 150 million tonne, containing about 30 million tonne of amorphous elemental carbon.

• Smoke particles generated by urban and fossil fuel fires would be strong absorbers of solar radiation, but would be likely to have comparatively limited effects on terrestrial longwave radiation, except perhaps under some special circumstances. If 30 million tonne of amorphous elemental carbon were produced by urban/industrial fires and spread over Northern Hemisphere mid-latitudes, the insolation at the ground would be reduced by at least 90%. The larger quantities of smoke that are possible in a major nuclear exchange could reduce light levels under dense patches to less than 1% of normal, and, on a daily average, to just several percent of normal, even after the smoke has spread widely.

• Because of the large numbers of particles in the rising smoke plumes and the very dense patches of smoke lasting several days thereafter, coagulation (adhering collisions) would lead to formation of fewer, but somewhat larger, particles. Coagulation of the particles could also occur as a result of coalescence and subsequent evaporation of rain droplets or ice particles. Because optical properties of aerosols are dependent on particle size and morphology, the aggregated aerosols may have different optical properties than the initial smoke particles, but the details, and even the sign, of such changes are poorly understood. The optical properties of fluffy soot aggregates that may be formed in dense oil plumes, however, seem to be relatively insensitive to their size. This is not the case for more consolidated particle agglomerates.

• Little consideration has yet been given to the possible role of meteorological processes on domains between fire plume and continental scales. Mesoscale and synoptic-scale motions might significantly alter, mix, or remove the smoke particles during the first several days. Studies to examine quantitatively the microphysical evolution of smoke particles during this period are needed. While changes in detailed understanding are expected, a significant fraction of the injected smoke particles is likely to remain in the atmosphere and affect the large-scale weather and climate.

5. SMOKE-INDUCED ATMOSPHERIC PERTURBATIONS

In a major nuclear war, continental scale smoke clouds could be generated within a few days over North America, Europe, and much of Asia. Careful analysis and a hierarchy of numerical models (ranging from one-dimensional global-average to three-dimensional global-scale models) have been used to estimate the transport, transformation, and removal of the smoke particles and the effects of the smoke on temperature, precipitation, winds, and other important atmospheric properties. All of the simulations indicate a strong potential for large-scale weather disruptions as a result of the smoke injected by extensive post-nuclear fires. These models, however, still have important simplifications and uncertainties that may affect the fidelity and the details of their predictions. Nonetheless, these uncertainties probably do not affect the general character of the calculated atmospheric response.

• For large smoke injections reaching altitudes of several kilometers or more and occurring from spring through early fall in the Northern Hemisphere, average land surface temperatures beneath dense smoke patches could decrease by 20–40°C below normal in continental areas within a few days, depending on the duration of the dense smoke pall and the particular meteorological state of the atmosphere. Some of these patches could be carried long distances and create episodic cooling. During this initial period of smoke dispersion, anomalies could be spatially and temporally quite variable while patchy smoke clouds strongly modulate the insolation reaching the surface.

• Smoke particles would be spread throughout much of the Northern Hemisphere within a few weeks, although the smoke layer would still be far from homogeneous. For spring to early fall injections, solar heating of the particles could rapidly warm the smoke layer and lead to a net upward motion of a substantial fraction of the smoke into the upper troposphere and stratosphere. The warming of these elevated layers could stabilize the atmosphere and suppress vertical movement of the air below these layers, thereby extending the lifetime of the particles from days to perhaps several months or more.

• Average summertime land surface temperatures in the Northern Hemisphere mid-latitudes could drop to levels typical of fall or early winter for periods of weeks or more with convective precipitation being essentially eliminated, except possibly at the southern edge of the smoke pall. Cold, near-surface air layers might lead initially to fog and drizzle, especially in coastal regions, lowland areas, and river valleys. In continental interiors, periods of very cold, mid-winter-like temperatures are possible. In winter, light levels would be strongly reduced, but the initial temperature and precipitation perturbations would be much less pronounced and might be essentially indistinguishable in many areas from severe winters currently experienced from time to time. However, such conditions would occur simultaneously over a large fraction of the mid-latitude region of the Northern Hemisphere and freezing cold air outbreaks could penetrate southward into regions that rarely or never experience frost conditions.

• In Northern Hemisphere subtropical latitudes, temperatures in any season could drop well below typical cool season conditions for large smoke injections. Temperatures could be near or below freezing in regions where temperatures are not typically strongly moderated by warming influence from the oceans. The convectively driven monsoon circulation, which is of critical importance to subtropical ecosystems, agriculture, and is the main source of water in these regions, could be essentially eliminated. Smaller scale, coastal precipitation might, however, be initiated.

• Strong solar heating of smoke injected into the Northern Hemisphere between April and September would carry the smoke upwards and equatorward, strongly augmenting the normal high altitude flow to the Southern Hemisphere (where induced downward motions might tend to slightly suppress precipitation). Within one or two weeks, thin, extended smoke layers could appear in the low to mid-latitude regions of the Southern Hemisphere as a precursor to the development of a more uniform veil of smoke with a significant optical depth (although substantially smaller than in the Northern Hemisphere). The smoke could induce modest cooling of land areas not well buffered by air masses warmed over nearby ocean areas. Since mid-latitudes in the Southern Hemisphere would already be experiencing their cool season, temperature reductions would not likely be more than several degrees. In more severe, but less probable, smoke injection scenarios, climatic effects in the Southern Hemisphere could be enhanced significantly, particularly during the following austral spring and summer.

• Much less analysis has been made of the atmospheric perturbations following the several week, acute climatic phase subsequent to a nuclear war involving large smoke injections. Significant uncertainties remain concerning processes governing the longer-term removal of smoke particles by precipitation scavenging, chemical oxidation, and other physical and chemical factors. The ultimate fate of smoke particles in the perturbed atmospheric circulation is also uncertain, both for particles in the sunlit and stabilized upper troposphere and stratosphere and in the winter polar regions, where cooling could result in subsidence that could move particles downward from the stratosphere to altitudes where they could later be scavenged by precipitation.

• Present estimates suggest that smoke lofted to levels (either directly by fire plumes or under the influence of solar heating) which are, or become, stabilized, could remain in the atmosphere for a year or more and induce long-term (months to years) global-scale cooling of several degrees, especially after the oceans have cooled significantly. For such conditions, precipitation could also be reduced significantly. Reduction of the intensity of the summer monsoon over Asia and Africa could be a particular concern. Decreased ocean temperatures, climatic feedback mechanisms (e.g., ice-albedo feedback), and concurrent ecological changes could also prolong the period of meteorological disturbances.

6. ATMOSPHERIC CHEMISTRY IN A POST-NUCLEAR-WAR ENVIRONMENT

Nuclear explosions and the resultant fires could generate large quantities of chemical compounds that might themselves be toxic. In addition, the chemicals could alter the atmospheric composition and radiative fluxes in ways that could affect human health, the biosphere, and the climate.

• Nitrogen oxides (NO_x) created by nuclear explosions of greater than several hundred kilotons would be lofted into the stratosphere. Depending on the total number of high yield weapons exploded, the NO_x would catalyze chemical reactions that, within a few months time, could reduce Northern Hemisphere stratospheric ozone concentrations by 10 to 30% in an atmosphere free of aerosols. Recovery would take several years. However, if the atmosphere were highly perturbed due to smoke heating and by injection of gaseous products from fires, the long-term ozone changes could be enhanced substantially in ways that cannot yet be predicted.

• Ozone reductions of tens of percent could increase surface intensities of biologically-active ultraviolet (UV) radiation by percentages of up to a few times as much. The presence of smoke would initially prevent UV-radiation from reaching the surface by absorbing it. The smoke, however, might also prolong and further augment the long-term ozone reduction as a result of smoke-induced lofting of soot and reactive chemicals, consequent heating of the stratosphere, and the occurrence of additional chemical reactions.

• Large amounts of carbon monoxide, hydrocarbons, nitrogen and sulfur oxides, hydrochloric acid, pyrotoxins, heavy metals, asbestos, and other materials would be injected into the lower atmosphere near the surface by flaming and smoldering combustion of several thousand million tonne of cellulosic and fossil fuel products and wind-blown debris. Before deposition or removal, these substances, some of which are toxic, could be directly and/or indirectly harmful to many forms of life. In addition, numerous toxic chemical compounds could be released directly into the environment by blast and spillage, contaminating both soil and water. This complex and potentially very serious subject has so far received only cursory consideration.

• If the hydrocarbons and nitrogen oxides were injected into an otherwise unperturbed troposphere, they could enhance average background ozone concentrations several-fold. Such ozone increases would not significantly offset the stratospheric ozone decrease, which also would be longer lasting. It is highly questionable, however, whether such large ozone increases could indeed occur in the presence of smoke because ozone generation in the troposphere requires sunlight as well as oxides of nitrogen. It is possible that, in the smoke perturbed atmosphere, the fire-generated oxides of nitrogen could be removed before photochemical ozone production could take place.

• Precipitation scavenging of nitrogen, sulfur, and chlorine compounds dispersed by the fire plumes throughout the troposphere could increase rainfall acidity by about an order of magnitude over large regions for up to several months. This increased acidity could be neutralized to some degree by alkaline dust or other basic (as opposed to acidic) compounds.

• Rapid smoke-induced cooling of the surface under dense smoke clouds could induce the formation of shallow, stable cold layers that might trap chemical emissions from prolonged smoldering fires near the ground. In such layers, concentrations of CO, HCl, pyrotoxins, and acid fogs could reach dangerous levels. The potential for local and regional effects in areas such as populated lowland areas and river valleys merits close attention.

7. RADIOLOGICAL DOSE

Near the site of an explosion, the health effects of prompt ionizing radiation from strategic nuclear warheads would be overshadowed by the effects of the blast and thermal radiation. However, because nuclear explosions create highly radioactive fission products and the emitted neutrons may also induce radioactivity in initially inert material near the detonation, radiological doses would be delivered to survivors both just downwind (local fallout) and out to hemispheric and global scales (global fallout).

• Local fallout of relatively large radioactive particles lofted by the number of surface explosions in the scenario postulated in this study could lead to lethal external gamma-ray doses (assuming no protective action is taken) during the first few days over about 7 percent of the land areas of the NATO and Warsaw Pact countries. Areas downwind of missile silos and other hardened targets would suffer especially high exposures. Survivors outside of lethal fallout zones could still receive debilitating radiation doses (exposure at half the lethal level can induce severe radiation sickness). In combination with other injuries or stresses, such doses could increase mortality. If large populations could be mobilized to move from highly radioactive zones or take substantial protective measures, the human impact of fallout could be greatly reduced.

• The uncertainty in these calculations of local fallout is large. Doses and areas for single nuclear explosions could vary by factors of 2–4 depending on meteorological conditions and assumptions in the models. A detailed treatment of overlapping fallout plumes from multiple explosions could increase the areas considerably (by a factor of 3 in one sample case). Results are also sensitive to variations in the detonation scenario.

• Global fallout following the gradual deposition of the relatively small radioactive particles created by strategic air and surface bursts could lead to average Northern Hemisphere lifetime external gamma ray doses on the order of 10 to 20 rads. The peak values would lie in the northern midlatitudes where the average doses for the scenarios considered would be about 20 to 60 rads. Such doses, in the absence of other stresses, would be expected to have relatively minor carcinogenic and mutagenic effects (i.e., increase incidence at most a few percent above current levels). Smoke-induced perturbations that tend to stabilize the atmosphere and slow deposition of radioactive particles might reduce these estimated average doses by perhaps 15%.

• Intermediate time scale and long term global fallout would be deposited unevenly, largely because of meteorological effects, leading to "hotspots" of several hundred thousand square kilometers in which average doses could be as high as 100 rads, and, consequently, large areas where doses would be lower than the average value.

• In the Southern Hemisphere and tropical latitudes, global fallout would produce much smaller, relatively insignificant, radiological doses about one-twentieth those in the Northern Hemisphere, even if cross-equatorial transport were accelerated by the smoke clouds. Additional local fallout would be important only within a few hundred kilometers downwind of any surface burst in the Southern Hemisphere.

• Additional considerations not factored into the above estimates are possible from several sources. Doses from ingestion or inhalation of radioactive particles could be important, especially over the longer term. Beta radiation could have a significant effect on the biota coming into contact with the local fallout. Fission fractions of smaller modern weapons could be twice the assumed value of 0.5; adding these to the scenario mix could cause a 20% increase in areas of lethal fallout. General tactical and theater nuclear weapons, ignored in these calculations, could also cause a 20% increase in lethal local fallout areas in certain geographical regions, particularly in Europe. The injection into the atmosphere of radionuclides created and stored by the civilian nuclear power industry and military reactors, a possibility considered remote by some, could increase estimates of long-term local and global radiological doses to several times those estimated for weapons alone.

8. TASKS FOR THE FUTURE

Extensive research and careful assessment over the past few years have indicated that nuclear war has the potential to modify the physical environment in ways that would dramatically impair biological processes. The perturbations could impact agriculture, the proper functioning of natural ecosystems, the purity of essential air and water resources, and other important elements of the global biosphere. Because current scientific conclusions concerning the response of the atmosphere to the effects of nuclear war include uncertainties, research can and should be undertaken to reduce those uncertainties that are accessible to investigation.

• Laboratory and field experiments are needed to improve estimates of the amount and physical characteristics of the smoke particles that would be produced by large fires, particularly by the combustion of fossil fuels and fossil fuel-derived products present in urban and industrial regions.

Experimental conditions should be designed to emulate as much as possible the effects of large-scale fires.

• Laboratory, field, and theoretical studies are needed to determine the potential scavenging rates of smoke particles in the convective plumes of large fires and the scavenging processes that operate on intermediate and global scales as the particles disperse.

• Further theoretical calculations of the seasonal response of the atmosphere to smoke emissions from large fires are needed, particularly of the extent of the perturbation to be expected at early times, when the smoke is freshly injected and patchy. Simulations must be made for later times from months to a year or more, when the atmosphere has been highly perturbed and a substantial fraction of the smoke may have been lofted to high altitudes. Closer attention should be paid to the possible effects in low latitudes and in the Southern Hemisphere, where the climatic effects are likely to be much more important than the direct effects of the nuclear detonations, which are expected to be confined largely to the Northern Hemisphere.

• Laboratory and theoretical studies are needed of the potential chemical alterations of the atmosphere on global and local scales, and of the extent that smoke particles could affect and might be removed by chemical reactions high in the atmosphere.

• Radiological calculations should be undertaken using models that more realistically treat the overlap of fallout plumes, complex meteorological conditions, and that consider both external and internal doses. Patterns of land use and likely targeting strategy should be used in estimating the potential significance of various scenarios. The question of the possible release of radioactivity from nuclear fuel cycle facilities in a nuclear war should be explored more thoroughly.

Nuclear Famine: The Indirect
Effects of Nuclear War

MARK A. HARWELL, PH.D., and
CHRISTINE C. HARWELL, J.D.
Cornell University, Ithaca, New York

INTRODUCTION

Over a 2-year period, the Scientific Committee on Problems of the
Environment (SCOPE)–Environmental Effects of Nuclear War (ENU-
WAR) project involved the participation of about 100 physical and atmospheric scientists and an additional 200 agricultural and ecological
scientists from more than 30 countries around the world in a unique
undertaking to assess the global consequences of nuclear war. The atmospheric scientists convened in a series of workshops, taking stock of
their ongoing research and identifying the next issues to be examined with
their computer models. From this emerged the characterization of the
projected nuclear war-induced disturbances in the global atmosphere, with
specified uncertainties and research needs (Pittock et al., 1985). We on
the biological side did not have the luxury of existing funded laboratory
and modeling research projects on the consequences of nuclear war; instead, our mission was to inspect the current information, models, and
understanding of how biological systems respond to stress. From these
data and models, developed for reasons far removed from considerations
of nuclear war, we synthesized a portrait of the global world after nuclear
war (Harwell and Hutchinson, 1985). The focus was on human population
impacts mediated by disruptions in ecological, agricultural, and other life-
support systems.

The consensus that developed was stark: the *indirect* effects of a large-
scale nuclear war would probably be far more consequential than the *direct*

117

effects; and the primary mechanism for human fatalities would likely not be from blast effects, not from thermal radiation burns, and not from ionizing radiation, but, rather, from mass starvation. Whereas the direct effects of such a nuclear war could result in several hundred million human fatalities, according to several studies (e.g., Bergstrom et al., 1983; Ambio, 1982), the indirect effects could lead to the loss of one to four billion lives.

This conclusion is derived from considerations of the vulnerabilities of ecological and agricultural systems to the types of disturbances potentially associated with the occurrence of a large-scale nuclear war. Thus, the biological analyses were not linked to any specific nuclear war scenario or to any single specific projection of alterations in the physical environment. This disassociation with particular scenarios was sought to avoid being limited by the current uncertainties of the physical estimates. Many of these uncertainties are irreducible, such as the specific details of an actual nuclear war, details that would only become certain as the war itself developed. Other uncertainties can be reduced by further investigations, such as the processes controlling smoke emissions and scavenging in the atmosphere. However, we cannot delay making biological and, especially, human impact assessments until such issues become fully resolved. By examining the vulnerabilities of biological systems to classes of perturbations, our results can be applied to a full range of possible physical outcomes of nuclear war. Moreover, since the biological systems were found to be so sensitive to nuclear war-induced stresses, consensus was reached on biological responses and human impacts with perhaps less uncertainty than remains for the physical estimates.

The categories of potential physical nuclear war-induced stresses that were examined are listed in Table 1. There was an emphasis on the effects from climatic disturbances, discussed in detail below, but other mechanisms for indirect effects were examined, including, in particular, effects from ionizing radiation and from increased levels of ultraviolet light. The climatic stresses were categorized with respect to the types of biological issues of importance. Specifically, an acute phase of climatic disturbance characterized by an abrupt onset of lowered temperatures and associated reductions in sunlight was identified as representing the potential environment in the first few days to weeks after a nuclear war. No single temperature or light decline was assumed; rather, the vulnerability of biological systems to brief episodes of chilling or freezing temperatures was examined. Similarly, for chronic-phase climatic disturbances, the vulnerability of biological systems to a few degrees' (Celsius) reduction in average temperatures persisting over the growing season, accompanied by 5–20 percent reductions in sunlight and possible decreases in precipitation, was evaluated.

TABLE 1   Nuclear War-Induced Stresses Examined

Climatic
  Acute
    Temperature—episodes of chilling or freezing
    Light—episodes of 1-10 percent normal insolation
  Chronic
    Temperature—average decreases of 1°C, 3°C, 5°C, 7°C, 10°C
      below normal over growing season
    Light—associated reductions in insolation by 5–20 percent
    Precipitation—reductions by 25–50 percent

Radiation
  Local fallout
  Global fallout
  Focus on external gamma doses

Other stresses
  Fire
  Ultraviolet-B radiation
  Atmospheric pollutants

In order to make these evaluations, no single set of experimental data was available; instead, a number of lines of reasoning were drawn on to exploit the full range of relevant information, including historical analogs, statistical analyses, laboratory physiological studies, simulation models, and expert judgment. The historical approach involved examination of specific episodes of environmental stresses and responses which have actually been experienced. For instance, incidents of freezing events in subtropical regions (e.g., Florida and southern Texas) were examined for their effects on fish populations, fruit trees, and other biological systems. Statistical analyses were done on data representing multiple years and multiple locations to determine the relationships among the physical environment and biological systems. For instance, the relationship between the average air temperature experienced over growing seasons and the length of the frost-free period (a measure of growing season duration) was characterized statistically. Laboratory data were evaluated for physiological-level information, such as the growth rates of crop plants under laboratory conditions of different levels of temperature, light, moisture availability, and air pollutant exposures. Computer simulation models of ecological and agricultural systems were used for assessing the effects of chronic alterations in climate on crop yields and ecosystem productivity. And the judgment of scientists with expertise in specific agricultural and ecological systems was relied on to identify and evaluate available data and models and to extrapolate beyond the current experimental and historical records to obtain the best estimates of biological system responses to nuclear war. For the most part, the physiological-level data and expert judgment were used to evaluate acute vulnerabilities, and the less extreme perturbations associated with chronic-phase conditions were more suited to historical, statistical, and computer simulation analyses.

These approaches were applied to each major biome type (Table 2 and Figure 1), covering freshwater, marine, and terrestrial ecosystems from the Arctic to the Southern Ocean and including the main grain crops in the northern temperate, tropical, and southern temperate regions of Earth. A number of international conferences were convened, each of which specifically addressed particular system types: northern temperate ecosystems were addressed at Toronto, Canada; northern temperate agriculture at Essex, United Kingdom; tropical ecological and agricultural systems at Caracas, Venezuela; Southern Hemisphere extratropical ecological and agricultural systems at Melbourne, Australia; and general biological responses to radiation at Paris, France. Other conferences dealing with more generic biological issues were held in Stockholm, Sweden; New Delhi, India; Leningrad, USSR; and Essex, United Kingdom. A special conference on the experiences and extrapolations from the Japanese nuclear bombings was convened in Hiroshima and Tokyo, Japan. At each conference, as broad a consensus as possible was sought among the experts,

TABLE 2   Biome Approach to the Ecological Evaluations

Northern Hemisphere terrestrial ecosystems
   Arctic and boreal
   Deciduous forests
   Coniferous forests
   Grasslands
   Arid and semiarid

Northern Hemisphere aquatic ecosystems
   Freshwater
   Marine
   Estuarine

Tropical ecosystems
   Evergreen rainforests
   Deciduous forests
   Montane-cloud forests
   Alpine
   Grasslands and savannahs
   Mangroves

Southern Hemisphere extratropical ecosystems
   Australian ecosystems
   New Zealand ecosystems
   Southern Ocean and Antarctica

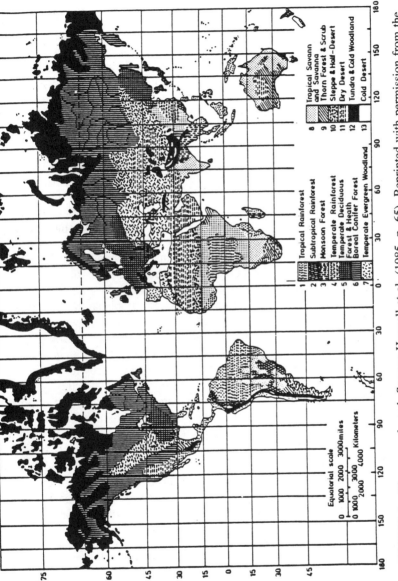

FIGURE 1   Biomes evaluated. Source: Harwell et al. (1985, p. 65). Reprinted with permission from the Scientific Committee on Problems of the Environment (SCOPE).

with identification of unresolved issues and research needs. Many of the latter were addressed within the ENUWAR project itself, with specific statistical and computer simulation analyses being initiated. We used the reports of the various conferences, the results of the commissioned analyses, and additional studies conducted by the ENUWAR teams at Cornell University and the University of Toronto as the bases for writing Volume II of the ENUWAR report. This was subjected to an extensive review process, during which we ensured faithful representation of the consensus of the participants of the conferences; the completed book (Harwell and Hutchinson, 1985) provides the technical basis for the conclusions presented here.

ECOSYSTEM VULNERABILITIES

The vulnerabilities of ecological systems were found to differ among ecosystems, types of disturbances, and time of year. For example, temperate forests were found to be most sensitive to acute, extreme temperature changes that occur during the spring or summer, whereas marine ecosystems were quite tolerant to changes in air temperatures. However, marine ecosystems were found to be very vulnerable to disruptions in the levels of incident sunlight, with acute reductions in insolation resulting in the collapse of phytoplankton and, perhaps, zooplankton populations on a large scale. Grassland ecosystems and the wheat-growing areas of Australia were assessed to be most vulnerable to chronic disturbances in precipitation, which is during the summer in the case of African grasslands and during the winter in the case of Australian wheat-growing areas.

These conclusions were based primarily on the understanding of plant responses to light, temperature, and moisture levels; by contrast, animal responses, especially with respect to propagation of effects from one species to another through species-species interactions, were considered to be more speculative and probably never fully predictable. It is clear that inadequate data bases and simulation model resources exist for precise characterization of ecosystem responses, particularly to the less extreme range of physical disturbances. Nevertheless, the various approaches outlined above suggest the cross-system vulnerability estimates provided in Table 3.

Other analyses addressed the prospects for recovery for various ecosystems and the processes by which recovery could be affected. The consensus was that nuclear war-induced disturbances to the environment would include virtually every environmental problem of concern today— habitat destruction, species extinction, air pollutants, toxic chemicals, acid precipitation, ozone depletion—only on a scale of totally unprecedented extent and intensity. Precisely what the full ecological ramifications of such stresses would be and the specific pathways that subsequent recovery would follow are urgently in need of a concerted research effort in the general field of stress ecology. Other considerations, however, show clearly that even without any disturbance to ecosystems, these natural systems could support only a very small fraction, on the order of 1 percent or less, of the current human population on Earth. The reason for this is that there would simply not be the base of utilizable energy sufficient to maintain 5 billion people if we did not have agricultural and other human-controlled systems to rely on. Thus, the carrying capacity of natural ecosystems is greatly exceeded by the current human population, and disruptions in human support systems that would force humans to rely substantially on natural systems for sustenance would necessarily lead to reductions in the human population. This fact provides the overriding incentive to examine the vulnerability of agricultural and food distribution systems to disruptions following a nuclear war.

AGRICULTURAL VULNERABILITIES

An examination of the vulnerabilities of agricultural systems showed that these systems are the most sensitive of any biological systems to changes in climatic conditions. There are several mechanisms by which climatic alterations translate into reductions or loss of crop yields. For most agricultural crops, temperature is the critical variable, although many crops are also sensitive to changes in precipitation and others can be limited by insufficient sunlight. Our studies focused on grain crops because these contribute the majority of the caloric inputs into the human diet on the global scale and because these crops are more effectively stored than most other food crops (e.g., fruits), a factor that could be critical in the aftermath of a nuclear war. Considering first the effects of temperature on grain yields, a number of factors are important:

1. Brief episodes of chilling or freezing temperatures—The occurrence of even short-duration events of freezing temperatures during the growing season leads to loss of grain yields, as demonstrated in laboratory experiments and in the historical record; for example, in 1816 (the year without a summer) a series of frosts occurred during June through September, resulting in the loss of grain crops in the northeastern United States, eastern Canada, and western Europe. The occurrence of such episodes following a nuclear war could be expected to happen during the acute period, when average temperatures might be reduced by tens of degrees Celsius for days to weeks. Because of cloud patchiness during the period of early smoke cloud development, it could be expected that even greater tem-

TABLE 3 Summary of Consequences for Ecological Systems

System Type	Stress and Responses[a]						
	Temperature	Light	Precipitation	Radiation	UV-B	Air pollutants	Fire
Agriculture	●●●	●	●●●	●●	●	●●	● ● ○
Tundra/alpine	◆ ◇	● ◇	● ○	● ○	● ○	● ○	● ○
Boreal forests	●● ○	● ○	● ○	●● ○	● ○	● ○	● ○
Temperate forests							
Deciduous	●● ○	● ○	●● ○	●● ○	● ○	●● ○	●● ○
Coniferous	●● ○	● ○	●● ○	●●● ○	● ○	● ○	●● ○
Tropical forests	●●● ○○○	● ○	●● ○○	● ○	●● ○○	● ○	●● ○○

Grasslands

Lakes and streams

Estuaries

Marine

aHighly generalized representation of consequences of various physical stresses on biological systems resulting from nuclear war. Includes both acute and chronic stresses and reflects large-scale effects rather than localized situations. Stresses are temperature, air temperature reductions; light, incident sunlight reductions; precipitation, precipitation reductions; radiation, fallout radiation; UV-B, increased ultraviolet-B from ozone depletion; air pollutants, toxic gases (e.g., O_3, SO_2, NO_x); fire, initiated by nuclear detonations or from increased frequency later. Symbols in the chart reflect both the extent of the stress on the specified system and the vulnerability of that system to the specified stress. Open symbols represent consequences if stresses occurred in winter, closed symbols are those for stresses in summer. Symbols indicate essentially no effect ($\blacklozenge$,$\lozenge$); low effect ($\bullet$,$\circ$); medium effect ($\bullet\bullet$,$\circ\circ$); large effect ($\bullet\bullet\bullet$,$\circ\circ\circ$); extremely large effect ($\bullet\bullet\bullet\bullet$,$\circ\circ\circ\circ$).

SOURCE: Harwell et al. (1985, p. 251). Reprinted with permission from the Scientific Committee on Problems of the Environment (SCOPE).

perature reductions could occur for brief periods of time. Furthermore, during the chronic period that would extend into growing seasons one or more years after a nuclear war, average temperature reductions of relatively small amounts (in the range of 1°C–5°C) would be associated with episodes of chilling or freezing events. The historical record indicates that years with extreme low temperatures during the growing season (e.g., 1816) had average temperature reductions of less than 1°C, which nonetheless caused large crop losses.

2. Insufficient growing season length—Associated with the average reduction in temperatures over the spring-summer months, which is expected during a chronic post-nuclear-war period, would be a shortening of the length of the growing season, with delay in the occurrence of the last day of freezing temperatures in the spring and an early onset of freezing temperatures in the fall. Several lines of evidence indicate that in the Northern Hemisphere continental regions of the mid-latitudes (i.e., the main grain-producing areas), on average, a 1°C reduction in average temperature correlates to a 10-day reduction in the growing season length. For example, Figure 2 shows the average temperatures and growing season lengths for several locations in the United States over a several-year period. The importance of this phenomenon can be seen when a growing season is shorter than the growing season length requirements of the crop in order for it to reach maturity and produce a yield. Exacerbating this problem is the fact that reduced growing season temperatures result in the slower development of crop plants, thereby increasing the growing season length requirements for the crop to reach maturity. More on the growing season limitation aspects will be discussed below.

3. Insufficient growing degree-days—The term *thermal time* is used as a measure of the number of hours during the growing season that air temperatures exceed a specified base level by various amounts and is calculated by multiplying the amount of time that the air temperature exceeds the base level times the increment of temperature above that level. For example, for a base level of 10°C, 2 days with a temperature of 20°C would have the same thermal time as 1 day with a temperature of 30°C (i.e., 20 degree-days). As with growing season requirements, each variety of crop plant has a particular requirement for a total amount of thermal time, measured as growing degree-days, that is needed in order for the crop to mature. Below the threshold for thermal time, maturity does not occur and grain yields are lost. Again, during the chronic period after a nuclear war, the thermal times may be too low for grain production.

4. Insufficient integrated sunlight time—A similar situation exists for the numbers of hours during the growing season during which sunlight levels exceed a certain amount. Simulations of Canadian wheat production showed that reductions in insolation by about 20 percent over the growing

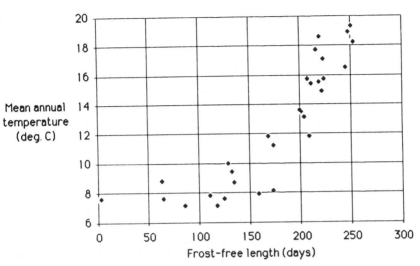

FIGURE 2   Relationship between mean annual temperature and duration of frost-free period. Source: Harwell et al. (1985, p. 279). Reprinted with permission from the Scientific Committee on Problems of the Environment (SCOPE).

season led to a total loss of yield because the required threshold level was not exceeded.

Thus far we have looked at mechanisms by which temperature and light reductions would lead to a total loss of crops for the growing season. In addition, the altered climate could be sufficiently benign so that some productivity remained possible, but the yields could be substantially reduced from current levels. The mechanisms are as follows:

5. Reduced productivity in response to the physical environment—Laboratory data show those circumstances under which the thresholds of stress that would eliminate production are not exceeded, but less than optimal conditions reduce yields. These can result from reduced temperatures, reduced light levels, and reduced precipitation levels. As an example of the latter, the historical record and computer simulations indicated that wheat yields in Australia are essentially linearly reduced with reductions in rainfall; i.e., a 25 percent reduction in precipitation could be expected to result in at least a 25 percent reduction in yields.

6. Disruptions in energy inputs to agriculture—The considerations to this point have focused on the yields that would be possible assuming continued high levels of energy inputs to agriculture, e.g., inputs of fer-

tilizers, pesticides, herbicides, fuel for tilling and harvesting, machinery, etc. However, in the aftermath of a large-scale nuclear war, the availability of these subsidies to agriculture, in combatant countries and in noncombatant countries that rely on other countries for energy and commodity imports, would be severely disrupted or eliminated. Current yields of grains are heavily dependent on such energy subsidies, as demonstrated in Figure 3, which shows the tremendous increase in yields over the last four decades. This is largely in response to increases in energy subsidies. Assessments indicate that even in the absence of any climatic disturbances, disruptions in agricultural subsidies could lead to reductions in crop production by up to 50 percent.

The Agriculture Canada model of spring wheat production illustrates the potential effects of chronic climatic alterations on crop production following a nuclear war (Figure 4). A map of the wheat-producing provinces of western Canada shows the current boundaries for wheat production and the boundaries associated with a reduction in temperatures over the growing season on average by 1°C, 2°C, 3°C, and 5°C. The 1°C reduction in average temperature results in a decrease in the potential growing area by a relatively small amount, but a 2°C reduction in average temperature

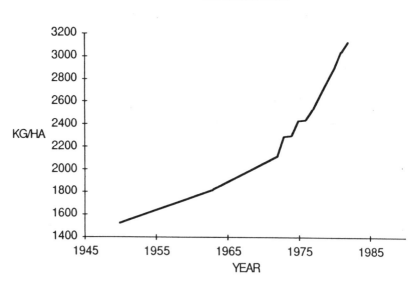

FIGURE 3   Mean rice yield. Source: Harwell et al. (1985, p. 343). Reprinted with permission from the Scientific Committee on Problems of the Environment (SCOPE).

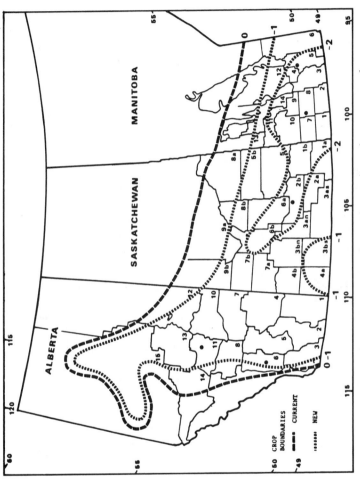

FIGURE 4 Reduction in area capable of maturing spring wheat as annual temperature decreases from the 1951–1980 period of normal values in western Canada. Source: Harwell et al. (1985, p. 305). Reprinted with permission from the Scientific Committee on Problems of the Environment (SCOPE).

eliminates the majority of the growing areas; a 3°C reduction would result in the complete elimination of any wheat production in Canada. This effect follows both from the reduction in the growing season length and in the insufficient levels of thermal time. Similar results were found for all other crops simulated, including crops that grow in much warmer climates such as soybeans (for which only a 4°C–6°C reduction in average temperature would eliminate yields in the southern United States).

Rice was evaluated in particular because of its large share of the human diet on a worldwide basis and because a disproportionate number of immediate post-nuclear-war survivors would live in tropical and subtropical regions. We found that rice is the most sensitive of the grains to temperature reductions and that rice yields can be eliminated even in the absence of frost. In fact, at certain times during the growing season, temperatures below 15°C lasting for only one or two nights would be adequate not to kill the rice plants but to preclude the formation and maturation of the rice grains. The historical evidence of rice production in Japan adds considerable support to the conclusion that rice is extremely sensitive to temperature; for example, when average summer temperatures are reduced in Japan by 1°C–2°C, crop failure occurs.

From these and many other analyses and considerations, the strong consensus that emerged among the agricultural scientists associated with ENUWAR is that the acute phase of climatic disturbances could eliminate grain production in the Northern Hemisphere following a large-scale nuclear war that occurred in the spring or summer and perhaps at other times of the year. Furthermore, the chronic-phase climatic conditions could also be expected to result in severe reductions or total elimination of yields of Northern Hemisphere grain crops, and Southern Hemisphere crops could also be adversely affected. Superimposed on these responses would be severe reductions in yields in response to the loss of energy subsidies, reductions in precipitation, and loss of arable land in combatant countries because of radioactive fallout. Additional yield reductions could follow enhanced levels of ultraviolet light and air pollutants. Clearly, there are multiple mechanisms by which food production could be disrupted on at least a hemispheric scale. A critical point in this is that these disruptions would occur at climatic disturbances at the very low end of the range of climatic changes projected to be likely to occur; thus, many of the uncertainties associated with climatic projections are irrelevant to the impacts on food production, since the levels of temperature changes under discussion (e.g., tens of degrees Celsius average decreases in air temperatures in the grain-producing areas of the Northern Hemisphere for a spring-summer nuclear war) well exceed the thresholds necessary for elimination of grain yields.

VULNERABILITY TO DISRUPTIONS IN FOOD AVAILABILITY

These conclusions of the potential for massive disruptions in food production must be examined to assess the potential impact on humans. Since we cannot predict precisely by how much food production would be affected, because of the climatic and nuclear war scenario uncertainties discussed above, we again focused on the vulnerability of the human population to disruption in food production for 1 or more years. The key issue here is the amount and duration of food stores distributed around the world.

In order to make this assessment, we examined data from the U.N. Food and Agriculture Organization and other sources for 15 countries on the quantities of grains stored, the current and estimated immediate post-nuclear-war population levels, the age structure of the population, and the minimal caloric consumption rates that humans require for subsistence. These 15 countries include about 65 percent of the human population and were selected to represent the range of situations in the world, including highly industrialized nations, likely combatants, underdeveloped countries, Northern and Southern Hemisphere locations, tropics and temperate regions, and various population densities. Included in the analyses are the United States, the USSR, China, India, Australia, Japan, Costa Rica, Nigeria, and others. In addition, we acquired less extensive data to analyze the situation in 120 other countries, representing almost the entire world's population. Some simplifying assumptions were required: (1) grains were assumed to be fed only to humans, diverting the large quantities that currently are designated for animal feed; (2) the diet was assumed to change to primary reliance on grains as opposed to current patterns of consumption; (3) no imports or exports of grains or energy supplies were assumed to occur in the aftermath of a large-scale nuclear war; (4) grain stores in combatant countries were assumed to be destroyed approximately in proportion to the loss of human life from direct effects of nuclear detonations; and (5) within each country, food distribution was assumed to work perfectly, such that each person would receive exactly the minimal amount needed for survival; furthermore, if it was found that there would be insufficient food to keep the full population in the country alive for 1 year, then the maximum numbers of people that could be maintained were assumed to consume all the food stores, and no food was assumed to be eaten at all by those eventually doomed to starvation. Clearly this last set of assumptions provides a very considerable overestimate of the number of people that the food stores would actually keep alive and provides the physically limited upper value for population maintenance. The issues of societal disruption and other factors that could lead to a less-than-perfect distribution of food in the aftermath of a nuclear war were not analyzed but require a concerted scientific study.

The picture that emerged from the calculations of the food supply is as follows:

1. For a very few countries, specifically those that are the major grain exporters, such as the United States, Canada, and Australia, the grain stores are, in principle, sufficient to keep the surviving population alive for a few years. Again, other factors might change this conclusion if food were not appropriately distributed, and long-term sole reliance on such grains could lead to nutrient deficiencies that were not calculated in our analyses. Also, these would likely be combatant countries, so the direct effects of nuclear detonations would be extensive.

2. For the rest of the world, including the vast majority of countries and of the human population, there is less than 1 year's food supply typically available during the year; for most countries the food duration is on the order of half a year or less. Furthermore, if the war were to occur prior to harvest (i.e., when food supplies were at their minimum levels), most of the stores would last only a matter of weeks to a few months.

3. Consequently, if food production were disrupted for one or more growing seasons, there simply would be not enough food to keep most of the survivors alive. Starvation, and the diseases and societal disruptions associated with starvation, would account for global declines in the human population.

An indication of the extreme vulnerability of the Earth's human population to sole reliance on food stores is seen in Figures 5a-c. Figure 5a shows the current population, as distributed within latitude bands, and the population distribution expected after a large-scale nuclear war (based on other analyses involving a severe-case impact on cities). Figure 5b compares the current population with the number of people who could be kept alive for one year under the assumptions discussed above if food stores were at their median level at the time of the nuclear war; Figure 5c shows the same, but for food stores at their minimum levels. These benchmark calculations make clear the extent of human vulnerabilities on a global scale.

One other analysis is also noteworthy. Even if there were no impacts on food production at all, but only direct food and energy imports were disrupted, many countries would still be severely affected. Japan is the most striking case (Figure 6), where cessation in food imports would result in the loss of half the total population in Japan, even if 100 percent of current agricultural productivity could be maintained and if no nuclear detonations occurred in the country. In the much more likely situation of

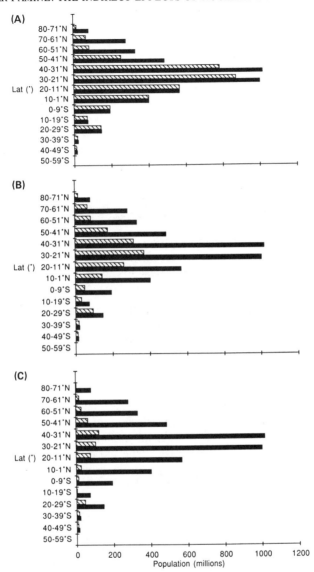

FIGURE 5   1982 population (solid bars) versus survivors of a nuclear war (hatched bars). A: Current population, as distributed within latitude bands, and population distribution expected after a large-scale nuclear war. B: Current population in comparison with how many people could be kept alive for one year if food stores were at their median level at the time of nuclear war. C: Same as in B, except for food stores at their minimum level. Source: Harwell et al. (1985, pp. 472 and 480). Reprinted with permission from the Scientific Committee on Problems of the Environment (SCOPE).

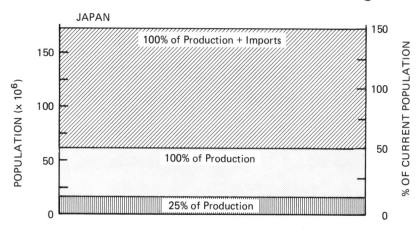

FIGURE 6   Post-nuclear-war chronic phase agricultural effects in Japan. Source: Harwell et al. (1985, p. 475). Reprinted with permission from the Scientific Committee on Problems of the Environment (SCOPE).

food production impacts, such as from energy input disruptions or from mild climatic alterations, then 25 percent of current grain production could keep only about 15 percent of the population alive in Japan.

CONCLUSION

The indirect effects of a nuclear war, especially as mediated by disruption in food availability, could be much more extensive than the direct effects. Furthermore, this risk is especially severe for noncombatant countries—for the 4 billion or so humans expected to survive the immediate period after a nuclear war relatively physically unharmed. Thus, a fundamentally different picture of the post-nuclear-war world results, where a large-scale nuclear war between the United States and the Soviet Union would probably result in more eventual fatalities in India than in the United States and the Soviet Union combined, and more people would die on the African continent than in all of Europe. Rather than reflecting images of Hiroshima and Nagasaki, a modern nuclear war would, for most of the people of the world, much more resemble current images of Ethiopia and the Sudan.

ACKNOWLEDGMENTS

This report represents the findings of the International Council of Scientific Unions' SCOPE-ENUWAR project, which involved the contributions of many scientists from all over the world (see Harwell and Hutchinson, 1985; Pittock et al., 1985). We especially recognize the contributions by Wendell P. Cropper, Jr., Cornell University, and Thomas C. Hutchinson, University of Toronto. We wish to acknowledge the financial support provided by the SCOPE-ENUWAR Unit, Essex University, United Kingdom, and by Cornell University, Ithaca, New York.

REFERENCES

Ambio. 1982. Nuclear War: The Aftermath. Special Issue of Ambio Vol. XI(2–3):75–176.

Bergstrom, S., D. Black, N. P. Bochkov, S. Eklund, R. J. H. Kruisinga, A. Leaf, O. Obasanjo, I. Shigematsu, M. Tubiana, and G. Whittembury. 1983. Effects of Nuclear War on Health and Health Services. Report of the International Committee of Experts in Medical Sciences and Public Health, World Health Organization. World Health Organization Pub. A36.12. Geneva: World Health Organization.

Harwell, M. A., and T. C. Hutchinson, with W. P. Cropper, Jr., C. C. Harwell, and H. D. Grover. 1985. Environmental Consequences of Nuclear War. Volume II. Ecological and Agricultural Effects. SCOPE 28. Chichester, U.K.: John Wiley & Sons.

Pittock, A. B., T. P. Ackerman, P. J. Crutzen, M. C. MacCracken, C. S. Shapiro, and R. P. Turco. 1985. Environmental Consequences of Nuclear War. Volume I. Physical and Atmospheric Effects. SCOPE 28. Chichester, U.K.: John Wiley & Sons.

The Medical Implications of Nuclear War, Institute of Medicine. © 1986 by the National Academy of Sciences. National Academy Press, Washington, D.C.

Nuclear Winter: The State of the Science

GEORGE F. CARRIER, PH.D.
Harvard University, Cambridge, Massachusetts

During the past year, it has become widely known that a major exchange of nuclear weapons could result in, among other consequences, a significant contamination of a large portion of the earth's atmosphere (NRC, 1985; Crutzen and Birks, 1982; Turco et al., 1983; and Sagan, 1983–1984). This contamination, preliminary calculations have suggested, could lead to cooling of significant portions of the earth's surface—a "nuclear winter." There is little doubt that atmospheric modifications of this character would occur. But their extent and duration—and hence their potential impact on people, food supplies, and other biological systems—are very difficult to determine, and they remain controversial. In the following, I describe the principal types of contamination and the uncertainties attendant upon calculations of the atmospheric effects, given our present, limited knowledge.

The fireballs caused by nuclear weapons directed against hardened military targets and therefore detonated at ground level would contain large numbers of dust particles in the submicron size—that is, with typical dimensions of less than one ten-thousandth of a centimeter—as well as large amounts of nitrogen oxides (NO_x). A major portion of both of these substances would be carried into the stratosphere where, in otherwise unmodified circumstances, most would remain for a considerable period (on the order of one year) while being gradually removed by natural processes. The nitrogen oxides would deplete stratospheric ozone and increase the flux of ultraviolet radiation reaching the lower atmosphere; the dust would reduce somewhat the total amount of sunlight reaching the lower atmosphere.

Of greater concern are potential modifications to the lower atmosphere. Weapons directed at targets in or close to cities and detonated in the air would ignite intense, extensive fires. The fires in turn would generate large numbers of smoke particles also of submicron size. The smoke would rise to moderately high altitudes (four to nine kilometers), where it could impede the passage of sunlight and alter many of the details of the heat balance and motions of the atmosphere. In particular, published reports say, temperatures near the ground could be significantly lowered. It is also possible that modifications of the winds at high altitudes could delay or speed the removal of NO_x and dust from the stratosphere.

Any assessment of this potential threat depends on quantitative estimates of the numbers of weapons that might be used against the various types of targets, the yields of those weapons, the amounts of contaminants (dust, NO_x, and smoke) that would be produced, and their lateral and vertical distribution in the atmosphere. The assessment also depends on calculations of the atmosphere's response to the presence of those contaminants— that is, the evolving temperature distributions and motions. However, any attempt to make such calculations with today's knowledge and today's understanding of many of the pertinent phenomena is severely impeded by a large number of major uncertainties.

To understand the extent of those uncertainties and their role in attempts to estimate the degree of the atmospheric degradation that would follow a nuclear war, it may be useful to consider the ways in which uncertainties would be compounded in the events that accompany a major weapons exchange. There are three types of uncertainties. These concern the nuclear weapons scenario, the production of smoke and its injection into the atmosphere, and the atmospheric response to contaminants on the scale envisioned.

The first set of uncertainties cannot be removed. One cannot know in advance of the nuclear phase of the postulated hostilities, for example, the numbers of weapons that any combatant would actually use, the distributions of targets against which those weapons would be directed, or the number of those weapons that would reach their targets and detonate successfully. One can postulate, however, a plausible hypothetical exchange and the time of year at which it is to occur and then try to estimate the atmospheric degradation caused by that exchange.

In contrast, the second set of uncertainties can be estimated by a process illustrated in the following example. A moderate amount of observational data exists concerning large fires in irregularly littered solid fuel, such as would be found in a city in the aftermath of a nuclear explosion (McMahon, 1983). These data suggest that between 2 and 6 percent of the fuel actually burned would be converted to smoke. The data do not imply that the fraction converted to smoke cannot be larger; in fact, if the fuel largely consisted of synthetic organic materials, it is known that the smoke production could be much larger than 6 percent. Alternatively, distributions of fuel and air supply are possible for which smoke production can be much lower than 6 percent. Nevertheless, no competing arguments seem to refute the 2 to 6 percent range, which we will refer to as the uncertainty range. Furthermore, because the largest number in this range is three times the smallest, we will say that the uncertainty factor is three.

The size of the smoke particles and the height to which they rise in the atmosphere are important because a given mass of larger particles will impede the passage of solar radiation less effectively than will the same mass of smaller particles. Furthermore, larger particles and those injected at lower altitudes will be more rapidly removed. To estimate the amount of submicron smoke that would rise above this altitude requires quantitative estimates for the amount of fuel in the regions where burning would occur (the fuel supply), the fraction of the fuel supply that would burn, and the fraction of the fuel burned that would emerge as smoke. It also requires estimates of the fraction of smoke particles that would remain at submicron size during their ascent in the smoke plume, despite their coagulation and incorporation into moisture condensation droplets that would form at the higher altitudes. I would assert that the uncertainty factor for the fuel supply is not less than two, that the uncertainty factor in the fraction burned is not less than two, that the uncertainty factor in the fraction of fuel burned that becomes smoke is not less than three, and that the uncertainty factor in the nonagglomerated fraction of the total smoke is not less than three. Thus, the composite uncertainty factor associated with this second set of uncertainties is not less than 36. Still other uncertainties are not included in this estimate: the height of the smoke plume (and hence the height at which the smoke is injected); the optical properties of the smoke (the more opaque the smoke, the more it obscures sunlight); and changes in the smoke's optical properties over a period of time.

In the National Research Council's recent report, *The Effects on the Atmosphere of a Major Nuclear Exchange*, a particular scenario for a nuclear exchange in which somewhat less than half (6,500 megatons) of the world's arsenal is expended was adopted as a baseline case. In other words, this scenario was used to illustrate the process of estimating the atmospheric effects of a nuclear exchange. No pretense is made that this is a "most likely exchange." It is merely a plausible assumption whose estimated consequences can give some guidance regarding possible atmospheric degradation. For this assumed nuclear exchange, the amount of submicron smoke that would survive the ascent in the fire plume is between 20 million tons and 650 million tons. These numbers are generally consistent with the uncertainty factors given above. (Some small and unimportant discrepancies arise, however, because this discussion is a highly simplified recasting of the National Research Council's report.) In that report, for purposes of inquiry, the investigators chose to assume that 180 million tons of submicron smoke were injected at altitude (four to nine kilometers) in the atmosphere.

The third set of uncertainties—those dealing with the atmosphere's response—complicates the final stage of analysis. Atmospheric scientists have at their disposal a variety of computational procedures designed to reproduce some of the large-scale features of the atmosphere's response to various conditions. These mathematical models are designed to deal with relatively small variations in normal atmospheric behavior. The modeling of small-scale processes (such as precipitation, particle removal, the mixing effects of turbulence, to name a few) are chosen and refined so that they satisfactorily represent the large-scale consequences of those small-scale processes. They are satisfactory because they are designed, insofar as possible, to conform to the observed behavior of the normal atmosphere. In the phenomena of interest here, however, the conditions include strong and abnormal temperature gradients and millions of tons of smoke particles at an altitude of several kilometers, yet there are no observations of an atmosphere in such a severely modified state that could be used to validate the models. Accordingly, it is especially difficult to assess quantitatively the inaccuracies that may result when making calculations with existing mathematical models. Clearly, it is eminently sensible to use these models to estimate the order of magnitude of the temperature change caused by smoke, but the results can only be regarded as suggestive. They are definitely not predictions.

A variety of computational models have been applied to the baseline war scenario described above and to some variations on that case (NRC, 1985; Crutzen and Birks, 1982; Turco et al., 1983; McCracken, 1983; Thompson et al., 1984). The results must be interpreted with care, but they boil down to the suggestion that the atmospheric response to smoke injection on the order of 180 million tons, as estimated using currently available computational models, would include temperature changes that could be of serious concern. In particular, the results suggest that for an exchange occurring in the summer, with all of the foregoing quantitative uncertainty, intermittent temperature drops in the northern temperate zone could be on the order of 20 degrees centigrade and might continue for a few weeks. Although it is even more uncertain, smaller temperature drops might occur in the tropics of the northern hemisphere. It is even possible that areas in the southern hemisphere could experience longlasting temperature drops of several degrees.

From this discussion and the studies on which it is based, I find unavoidable the following three-part conclusion:

1. The uncertainties that pervade the quantitative assessment of the atmospheric effects of a major nuclear exchange are so numerous and so large that no definitive description of those effects is possible at this time. Nevertheless:

2. The model calculations that can be made suggest temperature changes of a size that could have very severe consequences. This possibility cannot and must not be ignored. Therefore:

3. It is incumbent on agencies having resources that can be allocated to such matters and on appropriate members of the scientific and technological community to support and conduct investigations that can narrow many of the uncertainties. Only in this way can we approach a posture from which a more definitive assessment can be made.

Subsequent to the appearance of the foregoing article, in Issues in Science and Technology (Winter 1985:114–117), the response of the atmosphere has been recalculated several times using models which should replicate some features of the real phenomena in a more realistic way. The results of these calculations do differ in some of their details from the earlier results but those differences and the uncertainties that remain are such that no changes in the conclusions cited above are justified.

REFERENCES

Crutzen, P. J., and J. W. Birks. 1982. The atmosphere after a nuclear war: Twilight at noon. Ambio 11:114–125.

McCracken, M. 1983. Nuclear War: Preliminary Estimates of the Climatic Effects of a Nuclear Exchange. Paper presented at the Third Conference on Nuclear War, Erice, Sicily, August 12–23.

McMahon, C. K. 1983. Characteristics of Forest Fuels, Fires, and Emissions. Paper presented at the 76th Annual Meeting of the Air Pollution Control Association, Atlanta, Georgia, June 19–24.

National Research Council. 1985. The Effects on the Atmosphere of a Major Nuclear Exchange. Washington, D.C.: National Academy Press.

Sagan, C. 1983–1984. Foreign Affairs (Winter):257–292.

Thompson, S. L., V. V. Aleksandrov, G. L. Gtenchikov, S. H. Schneider, C. Covey, and R. M. Chervin. 1984. Global consequences of nuclear war: Simulations with three dimensional models. Ambio 13(4):236–243.

Turco, R. P., O. B. Toon, T. P. Ackerman, J. B. Pollock, and C. Sagan. 1983. Nuclear winter: Global consequences of multiple nuclear explosions. Science December 23:1283–1292.

Atmospheric Perturbations of Large-Scale Nuclear War

ROBERT C. MALONE, PH.D.
Los Alamos National Laboratory, Los Alamos, New Mexico

Several of the papers in this volume have discussed nuclear winter, large fires, and the dynamics of smoke plumes from large fires. I would like to elaborate on this theme by describing new computer simulations of the atmospheric consequences of the injection of a large quantity of smoke. I will focus on what might happen to the smoke after it enters the atmosphere and what changes or perturbations could be induced in the atmospheric structure and circulation by the presence of a large quantity of smoke.

To help in understanding the significance of these atmospheric perturbations and the manner in which they arise, I will start by breaking the nuclear winter phenomenon into its component parts. A very simplified view of nuclear winter is represented in Figure 1A, in which is shown a vertical column of processes and a box to the side that represents smoke injected into the atmosphere. Ignoring the rest of Figure 1 for the moment, it can be seen that there are two basic ingredients to nuclear winter: sunlight coming into the earth's atmosphere and smoke that has been injected into the atmosphere by fires. The smoke absorbs some of the incoming sunlight, causing a reduction in sunlight reaching the earth's surface. A radiation

---

The material on which this presentation is based is drawn from two papers (Malone et al., 1985, 1986). Readers interested in a more comprehensive discussion that includes historical background, related research, technical details of the model, and more extensive references should consult these articles, particularly the latter.

All figures are reprinted from Malone, R. C., et al., 1986, Nuclear winter: three-dimensional simulations including interactive transport, scavenging, and solar heating of smoke, J. Geophys. Res. 91 (D1):1039–1053, © 1986 by the American Geophysical Union. Reprinted with permission.

deficit at the surface results because the surface continues to emit infrared radiation (heat). The smoke particles do not trap infrared radiation effectively, so the heat goes out into space (not indicated in Figure 1). This continuing heat loss to space combined with reduced incoming sunlight causes the surface to cool. This is the origin of the so-called nuclear winter effect.

It is apparent that the magnitude of the cooling would depend on the amount of smoke injected and that the duration of the cooling would depend on how long smoke remained in the atmosphere.

The latter point brings us to the next element of complication in this picture, which is the removal of smoke from the atmosphere by rainfall (Figure 1B). Precipitation scavenging of smoke, as this is also called, was considered in the TTAPS study of nuclear winter (Turco et al., 1983) and

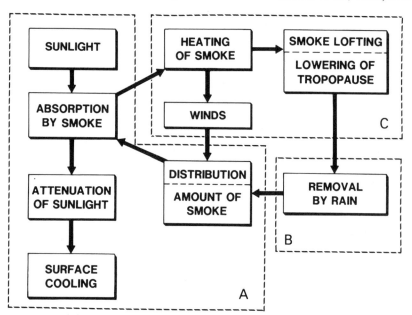

FIGURE 1   Interconnection of the processes which control the distribution and residence time of smoke in the atmosphere and the resulting surface climatic change. Some arrows indicate that one process *causes* another; other arrows indicate only that a process *influences* the operation of the process to which the arrow points. For example, the presence of smoke in the atmosphere results in the absorption of sunlight, which causes heating, which causes both lofting of the smoke and lowering of the tropopause. These two effects influence (decrease) the efficiency with which precipitation removes smoke by changing the vertical distribution of both smoke and precipitation. Removal by rain changes the amount of smoke. Heating also modifies the winds, which influence the distribution of smoke. Source: Malone et al. (1986, p. 1040).

also in the report on this subject by the National Academy of Sciences (1985). However, with the models that were available at the time, it was necessary to assume that the removal of smoke by rainfall occurred at a rate that was prescribed based on the observed lifetime of smoke particles in the unperturbed atmosphere. Although it was recognized that changes in the atmosphere would occur, it was not possible to take these changes into account in the models.

It has now become possible to investigate these atmospheric changes with more complicated models that have been developed in the last few years. These changes are quite important because they influence the ability of precipitation to remove smoke from the atmosphere and, therefore, the duration of the climatic effects of smoke. Now the last elements can be added to the diagram (Figure 1C). The principal ingredient in Figure 1C is heating of smoke-filled air due to absorption of sunlight by smoke particles. This heating causes changes in the atmospheric circulation and structure (also indicated in Figure 1C)—the atmospheric perturbations alluded to in the title of this paper.

The first of these perturbations is a major change in the atmospheric circulation patterns that causes the heated air and the entrained smoke particles to rise. This carries some smoke particles well above the altitudes to which they were injected initially by the fires. The second change is one that takes place in the vertical thermal structure of the atmosphere, which is also brought about by the heating of smoke-filled air. As I will show in this paper, both of these effects inhibit the ability of the atmosphere to purge itself of smoke. Specifically, they reduce the efficiency of smoke removal by precipitation.

In fact, there is a competition between rainfall, which removes smoke from the atmosphere, and these atmospheric perturbations, which act to isolate smoke from removal by rainfall. Precipitation scavenging begins to act as soon as smoke is injected into the atmosphere. In the model calculations, precipitation is able to remove a substantial amount of smoke during the first two weeks. During that time these perturbations develop and, at least for summertime conditions and large smoke injections, can become dominant.

These changes in the atmospheric structure and circulation are important in their own right, but it should be noted that they form a feedback loop in which elements of Figures 1A, 1B, and 1C are interconnected. In the full diagram, the amount (and spatial distribution) of smoke remaining in the atmosphere at any time is influenced by the changes caused by solar heating of the smoke itself. In a given season of the year, the intensity of heating depends on the amount (concentration) of smoke. Consequently, if larger injections of smoke are postulated, stronger heating results and causes larger atmospheric perturbations and greater inhibition of smoke removal by rain. Thus, the larger the amount of smoke injected, the greater is its ability to modify the atmosphere and, thereby, to inhibit its own removal. (For very large smoke injections, another effect, discussed by Malone et al. [1986], modifies this conclusion.) For a given amount of injected smoke, the intensity of heating depends on the amount of sunlight that is available. Assuming that smoke would be initially injected only in the Northern Hemisphere, the heating of smoke and the resultant atmospheric perturbations would be greater in July than in January, simply because there is more sunlight in the Northern Hemisphere in July than in January.

The computer model that we used for our studies is a general circulation model or global climate model, or simply a GCM. It is a three-dimensional model that solves on a computer the mathematical equations describing the evolution in time of the winds, temperature, moisture, and other quantities throughout the earth's global atmosphere.

To study the nuclear winter problem, the capability of transporting aerosols (very small particles) with the simulated winds of the model was added. The model's solar radiation scheme was modified to allow for the absorption by smoke particles of sunlight coming into the atmosphere. A very simplified treatment of the removal of smoke from the atmosphere by rainfall was also added. For this rainfall was used as predicted by the model itself, so that changes in rainfall caused by the heat-induced atmospheric perturbations could be taken into account.

In the computer simulation studies that I will describe, smoke was injected into the model atmosphere over the United States, Europe, and the western part of the Soviet Union. The injection rate decreased linearly to zero at day 7. Half of the smoke was injected during the first two days. The sensitivity of smoke transport and removal to the assumed initial vertical distribution of smoke was considered by using two profiles: a low injection with smoke distributed between 2- and 5-km altitude in the lower troposphere, and an NAS injection (so-called because of its use in the study done by the National Academy of Sciences) with constant smoke mass density between the surface and a 9-km altitude (NAS, 1985) but still within the unperturbed troposphere. Both January and July conditions were used to reveal seasonal differences. The behavior of aerosols in the normal atmosphere was studied with a passive tracer which, like smoke, is transported by the model's winds and removed by the predicted rainfall but, unlike smoke, does not absorb sunlight. This last characteristic permits the model atmosphere to evolve unperturbed by the presence of the passive tracer. The contrasting behaviors of interactive smoke and passive tracer illustrate clearly the importance of atmospheric heating due to sunlight absorbed by smoke particles.

The amount of smoke that is assumed to be injected into the atmosphere is an important parameter, but estimates of this quantity are quite uncertain. The study by the National Academy of Sciences (NAS, 1985) estimated a range from 20 teragrams (Tg; 1 Tg = 10^{12} grams = 1 million metric tons) up to as much as 640 Tg of smoke. I will present only results for 170 Tg, a value close to the NAS baseline value; results for other smoke amounts can be found in Malone et al. (1986).

Now I would like to explain more fully some of the elements of Figure 1. Using July conditions, because the atmospheric changes are larger and more easily seen, I will first describe smoke lofting and then show how the structure of the atmosphere is changed. Next I will describe how these effects influence the removal of smoke by rainfall and the lifetime of smoke in the atmosphere. Finally, I will describe briefly the findings about the climatic impact of smoke.

Figure 2 contains a comparison of two calculations that illustrate nicely the influence of solar heating on the dynamics of smoke. One calculation was done with interactive smoke; the results from it are shown with solid contours. The second calculation was done with a passive tracer; its results

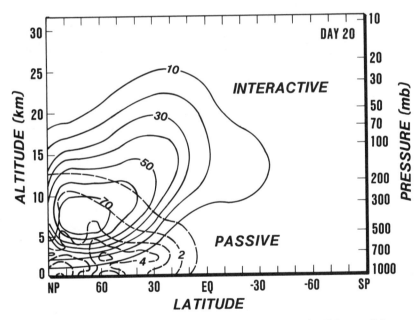

FIGURE 2   Longitudinally averaged mass mixing ratios for July conditions at day 20. The dashed contours apply to a passive tracer, while the solid contours apply to interactive smoke. In each case 170 Tg (1 Tg = 10^{12} g = 1 million metric tons) of material was injected over the Northern Hemisphere continents with a low injection profile (see text). The contours of mixing ratio are labeled in units of 10^{-9} g material/g air. Source: Malone et al. (1986, p. 1044).

are shown with dashed contours. In both calculations the same amount of material (170 Tg) was injected over the Northern Hemisphere continents in July at altitudes between 2 and 5 km (low injections). The contours indicate the concentrations of material (in parts per billion by mass) remaining at day 20 in the calculations, averaged over all longitudes. The display extends from the North Pole to the South Pole and from the surface of the earth up to about 30 km, which is in the lower stratosphere. (I will explain a little more about the normal atmospheric structure in connection with Figure 3.) These contours tell us how much of the material is left at day 20 and how it is distributed over latitude and altitude.

Most of the passive tracer remains at low altitudes, where it was injected, because the passive tracer and surrounding air are not heated by sunlight. Since scavenging by rainfall is fastest in the lower atmosphere, the passive tracer is rapidly removed, as indicated by the relatively small concentrations (Figure 2).

In the interactive case, on the other hand, the smoke does absorb sunlight. The heating drives vertical motions that carry smoke-filled air upward from the region of injection in the lower atmosphere. This takes some smoke up higher, completely out of reach of removal by precipitation. Also, the heating of the atmosphere inhibits the formation of precipitation. This allows more smoke to remain, as can be seen by the larger concentrations on the solid contours.

Before showing how the structure of the atmosphere is changed by the heated smoke, let me first describe the atmosphere as it normally exists. Figure 3A displays the longitudinally averaged temperature in the atmosphere for normal July conditions. The temperature contours are labeled in degrees Kelvin (273°K = 0°C). The structure of the atmosphere in its normal state is such that the temperature is warmest at the surface and decreases upward with height to an altitude of about 10 km. This region is called the troposphere. At about 10–15 km, the temperature becomes relatively constant with height and then increases with height in the stratosphere because of the absorption of sunlight by ozone. The heavy dashed line in Figure 3A shows the approximate position of what is called the tropopause, which is the boundary between the troposphere and the stratosphere.

For the purpose of this study, the most important characteristic of the troposphere is that it is the region of the atmosphere in which storms and rainfall occur. Since precipitation is the primary removal mechanism for smoke, this is where smoke removal will take place.

Figure 3B also displays the longitudinally averaged temperature for July conditions, but with the atmosphere being perturbed by the injection of 170 Tg of smoke. The smoke was injected with constant density from the surface up to about 9 km (NAS injection), so that all of it is in the

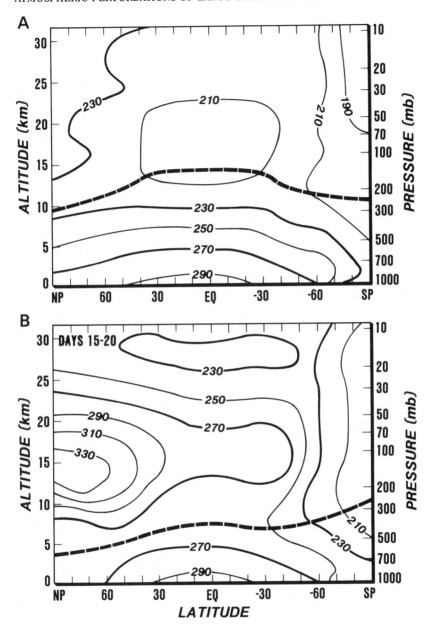

FIGURE 3   The longitudinally averaged temperature (degrees Kelvin) in the simulated unperturbed (A) and perturbed (B) atmospheres for July conditions. The perturbed distribution in (B) is a 5-day average beginning 15 days after the initiation of injection of 170 Tg of smoke with the NAS vertical injection profile. The unperturbed distribution in (A) is a long-term average. In each figure the approximate position of the tropopause is indicated by a heavy dashed line. Source: Malone et al. (1986, p. 1045).

unperturbed troposphere and is initially subject to removal by rainfall. The heating by sunlight of this smoke, some of which is carried higher (Figure 2), is quite intense and changes the vertical thermal structure of the atmosphere significantly. Figure 3B shows a 5-day average of the temperature during the third week after smoke injection began. There is still a region in the lower atmosphere in which temperature decreases with height; that is, there is still a troposphere. However, the top of the troposphere is now at about 5 km, rather than at 10–12 km as in the normal atmosphere.

Higher up the solar heating of smoke has raised the temperatures by as much as 50–80°K above normal. A situation now exists in which the smoke has created its own "stratosphere." Above the lowered tropopause [heavy dashed line in Figure 3B], warm air overlies cooler air, a condition that inhibits convective motions that would bring about precipitation.

Consequently, precipitation is confined below the tropopause and most of the remaining smoke is above it, as illustrated in Figure 4. The heavy dashed line, taken from Figure 3B, again represents the tropopause, the boundary between the troposphere and the heated region. The cross-hatching shows where precipitation is occurring; clearly, it is confined below the tropopause. The black stippling, which indicates various concentrations of smoke, shows that smoke now resides primarily above the tropopause. Smoke that was below the lowered tropopause largely has been removed by precipitation. Because the remaining smoke is now separated physically from its primary removal mechanism, its lifetime in the atmosphere is greatly increased.

This increased lifetime can be seen in Figure 5, which shows the temporal evolution of the total mass of material remaining in the atmosphere. The upper four curves apply to interactive smoke calculations with vertical injection profiles, as indicated, while the lower pair of curves apply to passive tracer calculations with low injection profiles. The vertical axis has a logarithmic scale. The total injection in all of these cases was 170 Tg, a value that is near the top of the diagram. As a result of scavenging by rainfall, none of the curves ever reaches the 170-Tg level. A substantial amount of material is removed while the injection proceeds.

The passive tracer curves in Figure 5 approximately represent normal aerosols in the unperturbed atmosphere. Following the cessation of injection at day 7, these curves fall in almost straight lines, which means that material is removed exponentially in time. These two curves provide a useful validation of our model. They tell us that aerosols in the normal atmosphere, as calculated by the model, have a residence time on the order of one week. This is in good agreement with observations.

Now, contrast that with the behavior of interactive smoke indicated for July by the upper pair of dashed curves. During the first week or two, a

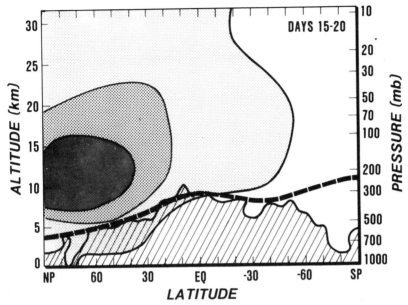

FIGURE 4   The relative positions of the modified tropopause (heavy dashed line) and the precipitation distribution (cross-hatched region below the tropopause), both averaged over days 15–20, and the smoke distribution at day 20 (stippled area above the tropopause) for the 170-Tg NAS case portrayed in Figure 3B. Darker stippling indicates greater smoke loading; the smoke contour intervals correspond to mixing ratios of 10×10^{-9}, 40×10^{-9}, and 70×10^{-9} g smoke/g air. These can be compared with the solid contours in Figure 2, which apply to a low injection July case, also at day 20. Source: Malone et al. (1986, p. 1045).

substantial amount of smoke has been removed from the atmosphere. This is mostly smoke down low that can be easily removed by rain. But because there is strong solar heating in the Northern Hemisphere in July, the rate of removal of smoke is greatly decreased after the first two weeks. As explained above, this occurs because some smoke has been carried higher in the atmosphere and because the atmospheric structure has been modified. Approximately one-third of the mass of smoke initially injected still remains in the model atmosphere after 40 days of the July calculations. This smoke has a very long lifetime in the atmosphere, as indicated by the near constancy after day 15 of the upper pair of dashed curves in Figure 5.

Up to this point, I have only talked about July because it is easier to illustrate the interesting effects for July conditions than for January. The upper pair of solid curves in Figure 5 show the interactive smoke results

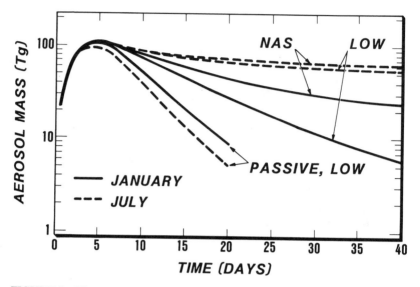

FIGURE 5 The mass of material remaining in the global atmosphere as a function of time. The upper four curves apply to smoke; the lower pair apply to the passive tracer. Solid and dashed curves indicate January and July conditions, respectively. Labels indicate low and NAS injections. The slopes of the passive tracer curves at late times yield 1/*e*-residence times of 5 to 6 days, which agree well with observed residence times of aerosols in the lower troposphere. Source: Malone et al. (1986, p. 1046).

for January. Smoke is removed faster in January than in July simply because there is less sunlight in the Northern Hemisphere to drive the atmospheric perturbations that enhance the lifetime of smoke. By the end of six weeks in our January calculations, the remaining fraction of smoke injected with the low and NAS profiles is about 5 and 15 percent, respectively, compared with 35 percent in the July cases. Nevertheless, solar heating of smoke does have a significant effect even under winter conditions. After three weeks, there is approximately a factor of three more smoke present in the atmosphere in January than would have been the case without the influence of solar heating (compare the passive tracer curve). In July the comparable ratio of smoke to passive tracer mass is about 10 after 3 weeks.

Figure 6 consists of two maps of the world showing the distribution of smoke looking down through the atmosphere at days 20 and 40. Most of the smoke is still concentrated in the Northern Hemisphere. Transport of smoke by the winds has made the geographical distribution of smoke fairly

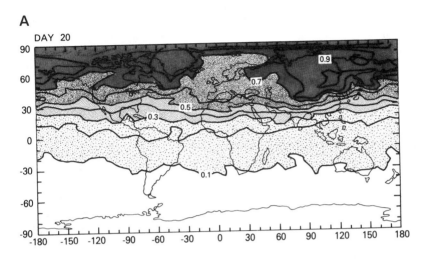

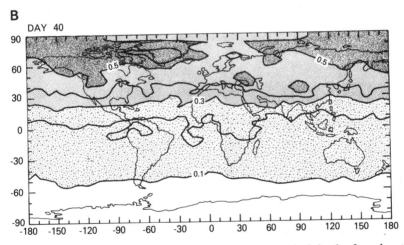

FIGURE 6 The vertically integrated solar absorption optical depth of smoke at day 20 (A) and day 40 (B) of the interactive July simulation with 170 Tg injected with the NAS vertical profile. The contours are presented at intervals of 0.1, with the lowest value being 0.1 on the southernmost contour. If τ is the absorption optical depth, the light reaching the surface from the sun overhead is reduced by a factor of $e^{-\tau}$. For $\tau = 0.1, 0.3, 0.5$, and 0.7, the factor $e^{-\tau}$ is $0.90, 0.74, 0.61$, and 0.50, respectively. Source: Malone et al. (1986, p. 1047).

uniform in longitude, although some nonuniformities remain. Some low-level smoke lingers over the continents. This is possible because the surface cooling (Figure 7) causes evaporation and precipitation to decrease over the continents. Air over the oceans is clearer. Some smoke has reached the Southern Hemisphere. The quantity displayed in Figure 6 is called the *absorption optical depth* and can be used to determine the attenuation at the surface of sunlight coming down through the atmosphere. The fractional attenuation is about 10, 25, 40, and 50 percent for optical depths of 0.1, 0.3, 0.5, and 0.7, respectively.

Figure 7 shows the changes in surface air temperature, relative to normal, predicted by the model when 170 Tg of smoke is injected in July. A 5-day average of the temperature change near the end of the first week is displayed in Figure 7A. It shows cooling by 15°C or more over large areas of the interiors of the North American and Eurasian continents during this period when the smoke clouds are particularly dense over the regions of injection. The long lifetime of smoke under summer conditions causes significant reductions in the surface air temperature to last through the end of the calculation at day 40. Figure 7B shows the simulated temperature changes during week 6; reductions of 5–15°C persist over the northern midlatitude continents. The features in the Southern Hemisphere have nothing to do with what is going on in the Northern Hemisphere; they are due simply to normal weather fluctuations in the winter (Southern) Hemisphere.

For 170 Tg of smoke injected in January, simulated surface air temperature reductions of 5–15°C occur over portions of the northern midlatitude continents during the first few weeks. However, the faster removal of smoke allows the temperatures to recover toward normal more rapidly than in July.

The discussion so far has focused on a baseline value of 170 Tg of injected smoke. However, it was pointed out in connection with Figure 1 that the intensity of heating, the magnitude of the atmospheric perturbations, and the smoke removal rate all depend on the concentration (hence, total mass) of injected smoke. A very small amount of smoke has little impact on the atmosphere, which allows the smoke to be quickly removed from the troposphere, much like the passive tracer results in Figures 2 and 5. As the injected mass is increased in the simulations into the range estimated for a major nuclear exchange, the solar heating of smoke and the atmospheric perturbations increase in magnitude. The fractional mass remaining in the atmosphere at late times also increases, and its rate of removal decreases. This trend continues up to injected masses comparable to the baseline value (170 Tg). With still larger values, another effect comes into play that causes the fractional mass remaining to stop increasing and even to decrease somewhat (Malone et al., 1986).

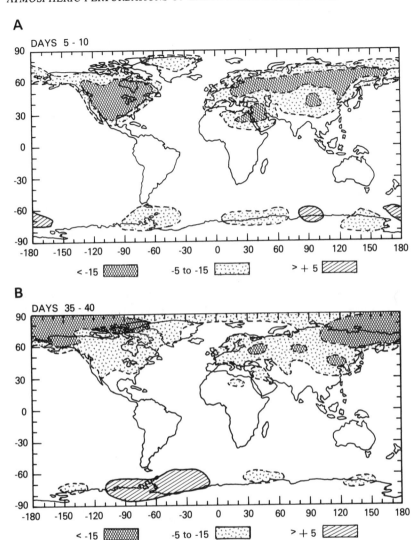

FIGURE 7   The change in surface air temperature relative to the unperturbed atmosphere in July for 170 Tg of smoke injected with the NAS profile. Five-day averages of the perturbed case, minus the long-term average of the unperturbed case, are shown: (A) days 5–10, (B) days 35–40. Only changes larger in magnitude than 5°C are shown. Values are indicated at the bottom of the figure; the designation < − 15 refers to temperature reductions below normal in excess of 15°C. Note that the warm and cool regions near Antarctica are simply manifestations of storms which occur naturally in the wintertime circumpolar flow; they have no connection with the changes occurring in the Northern Hemisphere. Source: Malone et al. (1986, p. 1049).

In summary, solar heating of smoke is a very important factor. It produces two effects. One is that some smoke is carried well above its initial injection height. The second is a modification of the atmospheric structure in which heating pushes the tropopause downward. Both effects contribute to isolation of smoke above the tropopause from precipitation below and cause an increase in the lifetime of that smoke relative to what one would find if solar heating of smoke were neglected. The magnitude of these effects depends on the season of year and the amount of smoke injected into the atmosphere by fires.

There would be substantial cooling of the Northern Hemisphere continents during the first few weeks in both January and July. In the July case only, the prolonged lifetime of smoke suggests that significant temperature reductions could persist for many weeks. Smoke would spread into the Southern Hemisphere in July as a result of the strong circulations driven by the solar heating of smoke. There would be very little spread into the Southern Hemisphere for January conditions; the smoke simply is not heated enough and is removed too fast.

Interested readers should consult the paper of Malone et al. (1986) for a more complete discussion that includes the simulated surface climate impact of various smoke amounts.

REFERENCES

Malone, R. C., L. H. Auer, G. A. Glatzmaier, M. C. Wood, and O. B. Toon. 1985. Influence of solar heating and precipitation scavenging on the simulated lifetime of postnuclear war smoke. Science 230:317–319.

Malone, R. C., L. H. Auer, G. A. Glatzmaier, M. C. Wood, and O. B. Toon. 1986. Nuclear winter: Three-dimensional simulations including interactive transport, scavenging and solar heating of smoke. J. Geophys. Res. 91 (D1):1039–1053.

National Academy of Sciences, Committee on the Atmospheric Effects of Nuclear Explosions. 1985. The Effects on the Atmosphere of a Nuclear Exchange. Washington, D.C.: National Academy Press.

Turco, R. P., O. B. Toon, T. P. Ackerman, J. B. Pollack, and C. Sagan. 1983. Nuclear winter: Global consequences of multiple nuclear explosions. Science 222:1283–1292.

The Medical Implications of Nuclear War, Institute of
Medicine. © 1986 by the National Academy of Sciences.
National Academy Press, Washington, D.C.

Possible Toxic Environments
Following a Nuclear War

JOHN W. BIRKS, PH.D., and SHERRY L. STEPHENS
University of Colorado, Boulder, Colorado

The direct effects of a nuclear war, the killing and maiming effects of
the blast, the thermal pulse, prompt nuclear radiation, and fire storms,
are too horrifying for the human mind to comprehend. Following a major
nuclear war, approximately 1 billion people would be left dead, and
millions more, probably hundreds of millions more, would be injured
(Ambio, 1982, vol. 11, No. 2–3; Ehrlich et al., 1983; Harwell and Grover,
1985). Still, 3 to 4 billion people around the world would find themselves
alive, once the thousands of megatons of nuclear energy had been released.
It is this realization that makes it so important to consider what the long-
term environmental effects of a nuclear war would be—not for the purpose
of planning better bomb shelters and survival techniques, but in the hope
that a clearer picture of life after a nuclear war may help provide the
incentive necessary to bring about the ''aroused understanding and insistence of the peoples of the world'' (Einstein*), to bring nuclear weaponry
under control.

Besides the destruction of shelter, food, means of transportation and
communication, and radioactive contamination, nuclear war survivors would
find their physical environment, particularly the atmosphere, radically

---

*The full text of Einstein's statement of January 22, 1947, reads: ''Through the release
of atomic energy, our generation has brought into the world the most revolutionary force
since prehistoric man's discovery of fire. The basic power of the universe cannot be fitted
into the outmoded concept of narrow nationalism. For there is no secret and there is no
defense; there is no possibility of control of atomic energy except through the aroused
understanding and insistence of the peoples of the world.''

changed. Dust lofted by the clouds generated by atomic bombs and especially smoke from fires in cities, forests, industries, and oil refineries would darken the sky. A simple calculation, in which one takes the total amount of smoke (about 200 million metric tons) that might be introduced into the atmosphere by the nuclear war fires and distributes it uniformly over the middle half of the Northern Hemisphere, indicates that more than 99 percent of the sunlight would be absorbed by the smoke cloud (Crutzen and Birks, 1982; Turco et al., 1983; National Research Council [NRC], 1985). Although smoke highly absorbs the visible region of the solar spectrum, it is relatively transparent to the infrared region. As a result, land surfaces would cool, particularly near the interiors of continents where the buffering action of the oceans would be less effective. This nuclear winter effect is the exact opposite of the greenhouse effect which maintains most of the Earth's surface at above-freezing temperatures during the warmer seasons.

Nuclear winter would have its greatest impact if the nuclear war occurred during the summer, because the incremental change in the amount of sunlight that would reach and warm the Earth's surface would be greatest then. Furthermore, during summer plants are not in their dormant states and would be most vulnerable to subfreezing temperatures. Of course, it is not possible to predict the season in which a nuclear war might break out.

Some of the most sophisticated computer model calculations of the climatic effects of a nuclear war are presented in an accompanying article (Malone, this volume). Temperature perturbations are calculated to be in the tens of degrees Celsius, and in a fully interactive model the atmospheric lifetime of the particulate matter is enhanced so that the duration of nuclear winter would be at least a few months. These qualitative conclusions are also important in helping assess other environmental stresses associated with the atmosphere. These include (1) the distribution and transformation of toxic chemicals released from chemical plants and produced in the nuclear fires; (2) the partial destruction of the protective ozone layer, with a consequent increase in the level of biologically damaging ultraviolet radiation that would impinge on the biosphere once the smoke cloud has subsided; and (3) the possibility of a global photochemical smog. These additional environmental effects propagated by the atmosphere are the focus of this paper.

TOXIC CHEMICALS

A multitude of toxic pollutants would be produced by the pyrolysis and partial combustion of chemicals, petroleum products, and synthetic materials stored in strategic, industrial, and urban areas. Military installations, chemical plants, gas and oil refineries, and urban centers contain vast stores of chemical and petroleum products, as well as the waste products of defense, industry, and everyday life. The tragedy of Bhopal, India, where a ruptured storage tank released methyl isocyanate, killing 5,000 people (Chemical and Engineering News, 1985), is a small indication of what might happen following a nuclear war as the result of explosions near chemical plants. Clearly, in heavily industrialized regions, the kill area for nuclear explosions could be greatly increased by the release of poisonous chemicals into the atmosphere.

The first question that one might logically ask is whether chemical releases would make the atmosphere lethally toxic on a global or semi-global basis. The answer is no. Even if an entire year's production of organic chemicals were released and uniformly mixed over half of the Northern Hemisphere, the total concentration of all chemical compounds would still be a factor of 5,000 times less than the 50 percent lethal dose (LD_{50}) of hydrogen cyanide gas. Of course, most compounds are not nearly so toxic, and probably only 5–10 percent of a year's chemical production is in storage at any one time. Similarly, it is also true that toxic compounds such as carbon monoxide, acrolein, hydrogen chloride, hydrogen cyanide, sulfur dioxide, phosgene, and the oxides of nitrogen produced in urban fires could be significant causes of death only on a local basis. Thus, for the long-term survivors of a nuclear war, the concern with chemical releases would be similar to concern with delayed radioactive fallout, namely, mutations leading to cancers and birth defects. In this sense, we might, by analogy, refer to these effects as arising from the chemical fallout.

Many of the most important mutagens would be nonvolatile compounds and would be associated with particulate matter. Once deposited in the soil and water, many of these compounds would be very stable against chemical and biological degradation and would be subject to bioaccumulation in a manner similar to that of radioactive isotopes. For example, a community of people becomes very concerned when a transformer fire, such as that which occurred in Binghamton, New York, in 1981, contaminates an office building with soot rich in polychlorinated biphenyls (PCBs) (Schecter, 1983). However, as the result of a nuclear war, of the order of 1,000 cities of the Earth would become the equivalent of toxic waste dumps. Also, the lofting of toxic smoke to high altitudes by the fire storms and by the buoyancy of solar heating (Malone, this volume) would ensure that these pyrotoxins would be distributed on a global basis as well.

Any realistic estimates of the levels of chemical contamination is virtually impossible, as thousands of different toxic chemicals would be produced, and the amounts of each would be highly dependent on the types and mixtures of fuels burned (e.g., wood, petroleum, asphalt, rubber, plastics) and the fire conditions, especially temperature and oxygen concentration. Estimates of biological effects are further complicated by the wide range of toxicities exhibited by the various isomers of a given parent compound. Dioxin, for example, is expected to be an important carcinogen introduced into the environment by the pyrolysis of PCBs and possibly other chlorine-containing compounds (Turco et al., 1983; NRC, 1985; Birks et al., 1985). However, the highly toxic compound 2,3,7,8-tetrachlorodibenzodioxin (TCDD) is only one of 75 dioxin isomers. As seen in Table 1, the relative toxicities of these various isomers span more than six orders of magnitude.

While cognizant of the enormity of the uncertainty, it is still useful to make some calculations, however crude, of the increased cancer incidence that might be expected on a semiglobal basis for a few carcinogens, so that the seriousness of chemical contamination can be compared with that of radioactive contamination. To do this for PCBs and TCDD, we have used the average emission factors found in the Binghamton fire (Schecter, 1983). Assume that approximately 30 percent of the current world supply of PCBs (0.3 teragram; 1 Tg = 1 million metric tons) are affected by nuclear fires, that the soot emission factor is 10 percent (by weight), and that 15 percent of the soot is composed of unburned PCBs. If the soot is uniformly deposited over one-half of the Northern Hemisphere and mixed to a depth of 10 cm of soil, the level of contamination is calculated to be 0.1 parts per billion. If the soot fell on one-fourth of the world's freshwater lakes and if it were evenly mixed throughout the water, it would result in a calculated concentration of 0.09 parts per trillion (Birks et al., 1985). In Binghamton, the TCDD isomer of dioxin averaged only about 3.5 parts per million of the soot, so that the calculated TCDD concentrations in soil and water would still be lower by more than four orders of magnitude. Using the same assumptions, the average concentrations of TCDD over half of the Northern Hemisphere are calculated to be 0.008 parts per trillion in soil and 0.01 parts per quadrillion in freshwater.

Using present recommendations for estimating cancer risk for those persons drinking water and eating fish from freshwater lakes (U.S. Environmental Protection Agency, 1984), the added risk of contracting cancer is calculated to be 10^{-8} (one chance in 10^8) for PCBs and 10^{-5} (one chance in 10^5) for the dioxin isomer TCDD.

Considering that the present risk of contracting cancer in one's lifetime is about 1 in 5, these numbers are not all that frightening. Of course, many other chemical carcinogens, about which we know even less, would be produced in the nuclear war fires. Nevertheless, these calculations strongly suggest that on a global or semiglobal basis, chemical carcinogenesis may not be a serious impact of nuclear war. We must realize, however, that the deposition of chemical toxins would be highly irregular.

TABLE 1   Acute Lethality of Dioxin Isomers

Isomeric Cl Positions	LD_{50} (μg/kg) in Guinea Pigs
2,8	300,000
2,3,7	29,000
2,3,7,8	1
1,2,3,7,8	3
1,2,4,7,8	1,125
1,2,3,4,7,8	73
1,2,3,6,7,8	100
1,2,3,7,8,9	100
1,2,3,4,6,7,8	7,200
1,2,3,4,6,7,8,9	4×10^{6}[a]

[a] In mice.

It is possible that a large fraction of the smoke aerosol would be removed within the first few hours by precipitation. For example, an estimated 5 to 10 cm of rain fell in Hiroshima 1 to 3 hours after the blast. Dust, rubble, and large amounts of radioactive matter were concentrated in the black rain that spread over a wide area, creating many secondary victims (The Committee for the Compilation of Materials on Damage Caused by the Atomic Bombs in Hiroshima and Nagasaki, 1981). It has been suggested (Knox, 1983) that under certain meteorological conditions, convective clouds would form over burning cities and effectively scrub out much of the smoke. This remains one of the hotly debated criticisms of the nuclear winter theory. For the lack of any better evidence, it has been common to assume that about half of the smoke produced by nuclear fires would be promptly removed (e.g., NRC, 1985).

The 1985 NRC study assumed that a total urban area of 250,000 km^2 would burn. Assuming that half of the toxic smoke was promptly deposited in an area of 1 million km^2, then the average concentrations of chemical toxins in soil and water within these urban areas would be higher than the concentrations calculated above by a factor of about 60. Of course, these areas would contain a large fraction of the surviving population. Cancer risks from chemical carcinogens would likewise be increased. The average cancer risk because of TCDD, for example, would be increased to 7×10^{-4} for those persons remaining in the urban areas. This is approximately 10 percent of the cancer risk resulting from exposure to 50 rads of ionizing radiation, which has been estimated as the average radiation dose to nuclear war survivors (Turco et al., 1983). Considering that this calculation is based on one specific isomer of one class of compounds and that many other carcinogens would be produced by the nuclear fires, it is not unreasonable to suspect that long-term human and biological effects of the chemical fallout would be as important, if not more important, than that of radioactive fallout. Estimates of the increased cancer incidence because of inhalation of asbestos fibers released to the atmosphere by a nuclear war, for example, is also of the order of 10 percent of that due to radiation exposure (Birks et al., 1985). It is important to note that it is possible that synergisms between chemical exposure and radiation exposure could also increase the cancer incidence following a nuclear war, but insufficient data exist to evaluate such effects.

An important difference between chemical toxins and radionuclides is that radioactive contamination is readily detected by relatively inexpensive Geiger counters, while the TCDD isomer of dioxin, like many other toxic compounds, can only be determined by use of a gas chromatograph coupled to a mass spectrometer; the cost of the latter instruments are in the range of \$100,000 to \$500,000. Thus, an important characteristic of chemical fallout is that living environments, food, and water could not be readily surveyed in order to determine their safety.

ULTRAVIOLET SPRING

It was first recognized in 1972 that oxides of nitrogen produced in nuclear fireballs and lofted to the stratosphere could result in severe ozone depletion (Foley and Ruderman, 1973; Johnston et al., 1973). Ozone in the stratosphere serves as a protective shield against ultraviolet radiation. Particularly significant to the biosphere is radiation in the ultraviolet-B (UV-B) region (280–320 nm). This finding that nuclear explosions could affect stratospheric ozone came as a result of the earlier recognition by Crutzen (1971) and Johnston (1971) that oxides of nitrogen serve as catalysts for ozone destruction according to the now well-known cycle of reactions:

$$NO + O_3 \rightarrow NO_2 + O_2$$
$$NO_2 + O \rightarrow NO + O_2$$
$$O_3 + h\nu \rightarrow O_2 + O$$
$$\text{Net: } 2O_3 \rightarrow 3O_2$$

Note that nitric oxide (NO) initiates the ozone destruction process, but is regenerated, so that no net consumption of nitrogen oxides occurs. In fact, each NO molecule introduced into the stratosphere can destroy about 10^{12} to 10^{13} ozone molecules during its residence time in the stratosphere (Brasseur and Solomon, 1984).

In 1975 the National Academy of Sciences evaluated the effect of a 10,000-megaton (Mt) nuclear war on the stratospheric ozone shield (NRC, 1975). That study estimated a 30 to 70 percent reduction in the ozone column over the Northern Hemisphere and a 20 to 40 percent depletion for the Southern Hemisphere. Since that time, there has been a modernization of the nuclear arsenals; large multimegaton warheads have been replaced by more numerous warheads (due to MIRVing—Multiple, Independently Targetable, Reentry Vehicles), typically having individual yields of 100 to 500 kilotons (kt). The degree of ozone depletion is highly dependent on the height of injection of oxides of nitrogen, and these smaller warheads produce bomb clouds that stabilize at much lower altitudes. The altitude distributions of the nitric oxide injections for the two scenarios evaluated in the recent 1985 study of the National Academy of Sciences (NRC, 1985) are superimposed on the ozone concentration profile in Figure 1. The NRC baseline scenario utilizes exactly half of the strategic warheads of every type in both the U.S. and Soviet arsenals, except for any weapons with yields greater than 1.5 Mt. For this scenario oxides of nitrogen would only be carried to altitudes as high as 18 km, and the maximal ozone depletion in the Northern Hemisphere, as shown in Figure 2, would be 17 percent. An excursion scenario considers that an additional 100 bombs with yields of 20 Mt each would be detonated. (There are

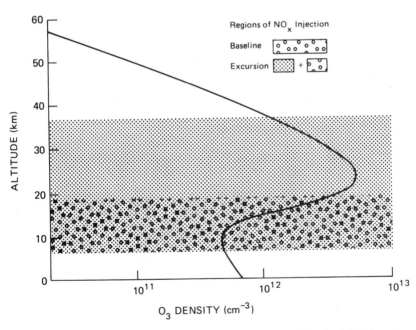

FIGURE 1 Altitudes of injection of oxides of nitrogen for the NRC baseline and excursion nuclear war scenarios. The normal ozone concentration profile is also shown by the solid line. (National Research Council, 1985.)

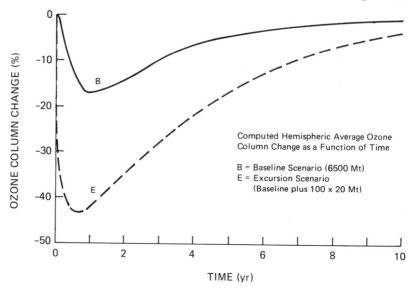

FIGURE 2   Ozone depletion as a function of time following a nuclear war for the NRC baseline and excursion scenarios. (National Research Council, 1985.)

thought to be 300 such warheads in the Soviet arsenal.) For this scenario, oxides of nitrogen would reach an altitude of 37 km, and the maximal ozone depletion would be 43 percent. Note that the maximum in ozone depletion would occur after a period of 8 to 12 months, and it would take on the order of 10 years for ozone concentrations to return to normal. Thus, once most of the smoke and dust was removed from the atmosphere and sunlight began to break through, the biosphere would not receive normal sunlight but, rather, sunlight highly enriched in ultraviolet radiation.

No estimates of ozone depletion have yet taken into account the large perturbations in atmospheric physics and chemistry resulting from the dust and smoke emissions. The recent finding by Malone (this volume) that the solar-heated smoke clouds would rise into the stratosphere is extremely important in this regard. The introduction of smoke aerosol to the stratosphere would be expected to add to ozone destruction in at least three ways: (1) The absorption of short-wavelength radiation by the smoke would reduce the rate of oxygen photolysis, thereby decreasing the rate at which ozone would be produced in the stratosphere. (2) The absorption of solar radiation by the smoke particles would heat the stratosphere and increase the rates of reactions that catalyze ozone destruction (e.g., the $NO + O_3$ reaction given in the cycle above). (3) Reaction of ozone at he particle surfaces would directly destroy ozone. The particle surface could catalyze the conversion of ozone to oxygen ($2O_3 \rightarrow 3O_2$) or be oxidized by ozone to form products such as carbon monoxide [O_3 + C (solid) $\rightarrow O_2$ + CO (gas)]. The latter reaction would act to consume the particles and thereby shorten the duration of the nuclear winter. Although ozone would be destroyed in either case, UV-B radiation would also be strongly absorbed by soot particles, so that the effects on the biosphere would not be felt until most of the soot was either destroyed by ozone or removed from the stratosphere. This is a very important problem that should be treated by model calculations in the near future. We are currently obtaining laboratory data on the reactions of ozone with carbonaceous particles (S. Stephens, M. Rossi, and D. Golden, manuscript in preparation) for input into such models.

An increase in UV-B radiation would affect the already stressed ecosystems of our planet in several ways (Ehrlich et al., 1983). UV-B wavelengths of light are absorbed strongly by peptide bonds and by nucleic and amino acids (National Research Council, 1982), and these energetic photons can cause chemical changes which affect biological structure and function. Productivity of terrestrial plants and marine plankton is known to decrease with even small increases in UV-B levels (Caldwell, 1981; National Research Council, 1982). Immune system suppression (National Research Council, 1982), blindness (Pitts, 1983), and other physiological stress factors caused by UV-B increases would lead to increased incidence of disease in humans and other mammals. Even normal processes of DNA repair in bacteria are suppressed by increased UV-B exposure (National Research Council, 1982).

PHOTOCHEMICAL SMOG FORMATION

The chemistry of the troposphere (the region of the atmosphere between the ground and the stratosphere, 0–12 km) is very complicated and would become even more complicated by the addition of millions of tons of dust, smoke, and gaseous chemicals. A mild example of tropospheric perturbation is seen in a heavily polluted urban center. These population centers are sources of oxides of nitrogen, carbon monoxide, partially combusted hydrocarbons, and particulates; it is the interaction of these species with sunlight that results in the formation of strong oxidants such as ozone. The potential of a severe global photochemical smog following a nuclear war was suggested by Crutzen and Birks (1982). However, a necessary ingredient to photochemical smog formation is sunlight, and it was their concern that the absorption of sunlight by smoke might reduce the levels of oxidant formation that led them to make the first estimates of the amount of smoke produced in nuclear war fires.

The darkness of nuclear winter would certainly prevent a photochemical smog from forming during the early weeks following a nuclear war, and the parallel removal of gaseous pollutants and particulates would tend to ameliorate the rate of oxidant formation at later times (Penner, 1983). Reactions of oxidants with particle surfaces would also tend to prevent a photochemical smog from forming (Birks et al., 1985). However, photochemical smog with high concentrations of ozone could occur near the edges of pollutant clouds for the period of time that the particulate cloud cover is still patchy.

Because of their damaging effects on plants and animals, atmospheric oxidants are generally viewed as undesirable. However, these oxidants particularly the hydroxyl radical (OH) derived from the photolysis of ozone, provide the useful function of cleansing the atmosphere. For example, of the order of 100 million tons of reduced sulfur compounds such as hydrogen sulfide and dimethyl sulfide are emitted to the atmosphere each year by microoganisms in the soil and ocean. The oxidation of these compounds to sulfuric acid in the normal atmosphere is initiated by OH. The highly soluble sulfuric acid is then rapidly removed by rain. Under the dark clouds of nuclear winter, the OH radical and other oxidants would be greatly reduced in concentration, and as a result such biogenic emissions would accumulate to unusually high levels in the atmosphere. Although lethally toxic levels are not expected to be reached, at least for the sulfur compounds it is likely that the concentrations would build up to levels well above the threshold for human smell (Birks et al., 1985).

CONCLUSIONS

Those who would survive the prompt effects of a nuclear war would face a radically altered physical environment. A period of weeks to months of darkened days and subfreezing temperatures would stress the ecosystems, on which mankind ultimately depends, in ways unprecedented in recorded history. Not only would the distribution of existing food stores be interrupted, but the growing of food would become impossible. As the sooty smoke is slowly removed from the atmosphere and the sunshine begins to break through, it is likely that this light would be highly enriched in damaging ultraviolet radiation—adding a further insult to the already injured biosphere. There would always be great uncertainty about the safety of any food eaten, because it could be contaminated by chemical toxins, in addition to radioactivity. With the lack of sophisticated analytical instruments, chemical contamination would be impossible to detect.

That the nuclear winter and other environmental effects of a nuclear war were overlooked for so long should make us wary; the worst effects of a nuclear war may not yet be discovered and, in fact, may be undiscoverable except by the actual experience.

Forty years after Hiroshima we are finally beginning to come to grips with the full consequences of the use of nuclear weapons. The intuition of the average human being since the first use of these weapons against population centers has been that a nuclear war would cause the extinction of our species. In light of recent studies, it appears that this intuition is much closer to the truth than the enlightened understanding of those who have advocated doctrines of the survivability and therefore fightability of a nuclear war.

REFERENCES

Birks, J. W., J. Staehelin, and S. L. Stephens. 1985. Changes in tropospheric composition and chemistry resulting from a nuclear war. Paper presented at the National Meeting of the American Chemical Society, Miami, Florida, April 30.

Brasseur, G., and S. Solomon. 1984. P. 464 in Atmospheric Science Library. Vol. 5: Aeronomy of the Middle Atmosphere. Chemistry and Physics of the Stratosphere and Mesosphere. Dordrecht, Netherlands: Reidel.

Caldwell, M. M. 1981. P. 169 in Encyclopedia of Plant Physiology, 12A, Physiological Plant Ecology, I, Responses to Physical Environment, edited by O. L. Lange, P. S. Nobel, C. B. Osmond, and H. Ziegler. Berlin: Springer-Verlag.

Chemical and Engineering News. 1985. February 11, p. 14.

The Committee for the Compilation of Materials on Damage Caused by the Atomic Bombs in Hiroshima and Nagasaki. 1981. Pp. 87–101 in E. Ishikawa and D. L. Swain (trans.), Hiroshima and Nagasaki: the Physical, Medical, and Social Effects of the Atomic Bombings. New York: Basic Books.

Crutzen, P. J. 1971. Ozone production rate in an oxygen-hydrogen oxide atmosphere. J. Geophys. Res. 76:7311.

Crutzen, P. J., and J. W. Birks. 1982. The atmosphere after a nuclear war: Twilight at noon. Ambio 11:115–125.

Ehrlich, P. R., J. Harte, M. A. Harwell, P. H. Raven, C. Sagan, G. M. Woodwell, J. Berry, E. S. Ayensen, A. H. Ehrlich, T. Eisner, S. J. Gould, H. D. Grover, R. Herrera, R. M. May, E. Mayr, C. P. McKay, H. A. Mooney, N. Meyers, D. Pimentel, and J. M. Teal. 1983. Long-term biological consequences of nuclear war. Science 222: 1293–1300.

Foley, H. M., and M. A. Ruderman. 1973. Stratospheric NO production from past nuclear explosions. J. Geophys. Res. 78:4441.

Harwell, M. A., and H. D. Grover. 1985. Biological effects of nuclear war I: Impact on humans. Bioscience 35:570–575.

Johnston, H. S. 1971. Reduction of stratospheric ozone by nitrogen oxide catalysts from supersonic transport exhaust. Science 173:517.

Johnston, H. S., G. Z. Whitten, and J. W. Birks. 1973. Effects of nuclear explosions on stratospheric nitric oxide and ozone. J. Geophys. Res. 78:6107–6135.

Knox, J. B. 1983. Global Scale Deposition of Radioactivity from a Large Scale Exchange. UCRL-89907. Livermore, Calif.: Lawrence Livermore National Laboratory.

Malone, R. C. 1986. Atmospheric perturbations of large-scale nuclear war. This volume.

National Research Council. 1975. Long-Term Worldwide Effects of Multiple Nuclear

Weapon Detonations. Washington, D.C.: National Academy of Sciences.

National Research Council. 1982. Causes and Effects of Stratospheric Ozone Reduction An Update. Washington, D.C.: National Academy Press.

National Research Council. 1985. The Effects on the Atmosphere of a Major Nuclear Exchange. Washington, D.C.: National Academy Press.

Penner, J. E. 1983. Tropospheric response to a nuclear exchange. UCRL-89956. Livermore Calif.: Lawrence Livermore National Laboratory.

Pitts, D. M. 1983. Hearing on the Consequences of Nuclear War on the Global Environment 97th Cong., 2d session, serial no. 171, pp. 83–101. Washington, D.C.: U.S. Government Printing Office.

Schecter, A. 1983. Contamination of an office building in Binghamton, New York by PCBs, dioxins, furans and biphenyls after an electrical panel and electrical transformer incident. Chemosphere 12:669–680.

Turco, R. P., O. B. Toon, T. P. Ackerman, J. B. Pollack, and C. Sagan. 1983. Nuclear winter: Global consequences of multiple nuclear explosions. Science 222:1283–1292.

U.S. Environmental Protection Agency. 1984. Intermedia Priority Pollutant Guidance Documents. PCBs, March.

The Medical Implications of Nuclear War, Institute of
Medicine. © 1986 by the National Academy of Sciences.
National Academy Press, Washington, D.C.

Radioactive Fallout

CHARLES S. SHAPIRO, PH.D.
San Francisco State University, San Francisco, California
Lawrence Livermore National Laboratory, Livermore, California

TED F. HARVEY, PH.D., and KENDALL R. PETERSON, M.S.
Lawrence Livermore National Laboratory, Livermore, California

OVERVIEW

Potential radiation doses from several scenarios involving nuclear attack
on an unsheltered United States population are calculated for local, intermediate time scale and long-term fallout. Dose estimates are made for
both a normal atmosphere and an atmosphere perturbed by smoke produced
by massive fires. A separate section discusses the additional doses from
nuclear fuel facilities, were they to be targeted in an attack. Finally, in
an appendix the direct effects of fallout on humans are considered. These
include effects of sheltering and biological repair of damage from chronic
doses.

RADIOACTIVITY FROM NUCLEAR WEAPONS

Introduction

In this paper the potential doses associated with the radionuclides created
by nuclear explosions are assessed. Our focus is on the areas outside the
zone of the initial blast and fires. Prompt initial ionizing radiation within
the first minute after the explosion is not considered here, because the
physical range for biological damage from this source for large-yield
weapons is generally smaller than the ranges for blast and thermal effects.
The contributions from local (first 24 hours) and more widely distributed, or global fallout, will be considered separately. Global fallout will

167

be further subdivided into an intermediate time scale, sometimes called tropospheric, of 1 to 30 days, and a long-term (beyond 30 days) stratospheric component. Mainly the dose from gamma-ray emitters external to the body is considered. Contributions from external beta emitters are not estimated because of the limited penetration ability of beta radiation, but there is the possibility that in areas of local fallout, beta radiation can have a significant impact on certain biota directly exposed to the emitters by surface deposition (Svirezhev, 1985). Potential internal doses from ingestion and inhalation of gamma and beta emitters are estimated in only an approximate manner, as these are much more difficult to quantify.

The total amount of gamma-ray radioactivity dispersed in a nuclear exchange is dominated by the weapon fission products whose production is proportional to the total fission yield of the exchange. Exposure to local fallout, which has the greatest potential for producing human casualties, is very sensitive to assumptions about height of burst, winds, time of exposure, protection factor, and other variables. For global fallout, the dose commitments are sensitive to how these fission products are injected into various regions of the atmosphere, which depend on individual warhead yield as well as burst location.

For local fallout, aspects of the baseline scenario outlined in the Scientific Committee on Problems of the Environment-Environmental Effects of Nuclear War (SCOPE-ENUWAR) Study (Pittock et al., 1985) are considered. For global fallout, both the 5,300-megaton (Mt) baseline scenario reported by Knox (1983) and the 5,000-Mt reference nuclear war scenario described by Turco et al. (1983; also known as the TTAPS study) are considered.

Local Fallout

Local fallout is the early deposition of relatively large radioactive particles that are lofted by a nuclear explosion occurring near the surface in which large quantities of debris are drawn into the fireball. For nuclear weapons, the primary early danger from local fallout is due to gamma radiation.

Fresh fission products are highly radioactive and most decay by simultaneous emission of electrons and gamma rays. An approximate rule of thumb for the first 6 months following a weapon detonation is that the gamma radiation will decay by an order of magnitude for every factor of seven in time (Glasstone and Dolan, 1977).

If the implausible assumption is made that all of the radioactivity in the fresh nuclear debris from a 1-Mt, all-fission weapon arrives on the ground 1 hour after detonation and is uniformly spread over grassy ground such that it would just give a 48-hour unshielded dose of 450 rads, then approximately 50,000 km² could be covered. Given such a uniform deposition model, it would require only about 100 such weapons to completely cover Europe. In reality, because of a variety of physical processes, the actual areas affected are much smaller. Most of the radioactivity is airborne for much longer than an hour, thus allowing substantial decay to occur before reaching the ground. Also, the deposition pattern of the radioactivity is uneven, with the heaviest fallout being near the detonation point where extremely high radiation levels occur. When realistic depositional processes are considered, the approximate area covered by a 48-hour unshielded 450-rad dose is about 1,300 km², i.e., nearly a factor of 40 smaller than the area predicted using the simplistic model above. This large factor is partially explained because only about one-half of the radioactivity from ground bursts is on fallout-sized particles (Defense Civil Preparedness Agency [DCPA] 1973). The other portion of the radioactivity is found on smaller particles that have very low settling velocities and therefore contribute to global fallout over longer times. Portions of this radioactivity can remain airborne for years. For airbursts of strategic-sized weapons, virtually no fallout-sized particles are created, and all of the radioactivity contributes to global fallout.

Lofted radioactive fallout particles that have radii exceeding 5 to 10 μm have sufficient fall velocities to contribute to local fallout. Some particles can be as large as several millimeters in radius. Settling velocities range from a few centimeters per second to many tens of meters per second for these particles. They are lofted by the rising nuclear debris cloud and are detrained anywhere from ground level to the top of the stabilized cloud. Horizontal wind speeds usually increase with height up to the tropopause, and frequently, wind directions have large angular shears. Nuclear clouds disperse due to atmospheric shears and turbulence. The arrival of radioactivity at a given location can occur over many hours, with large particles from high in the cloud usually arriving first at a downwind location.

Rainout effects have been suggested as being potentially significant contributors to local fallout effects from strategic nuclear war (Glasstone and Dolan, 1977). The inclusion of rainout processes would probably not significantly affect the answers to generic questions pertaining to large-scale nuclear war phenomena (for example, What percentage of Western Europe would suffer lethal levels of gamma radiation from local fallout in a large-scale nuclear exchange?), especially if a substantial portion of the weapons are surface burst. This is particularly true for strategic weapon yields of greater than 30 kilotons (kt), because the radioactivity on the small particles most affected by rainout rises above all but the largest convective rain cells. Thus potentially lethal doses from rainout should occur only from large convective rain cells, and this should occur only over relatively small areas (i.e., beneath moving convective cells). However, for any given radioactive air parcel, the overall probability of rainout the first day from a convective cell is quite low for yields greater than 30 kt. Rainout also may occur over large areas associated with frontal systems, but in the case of strategic weapons yields, the radioactivity on small particles must diffuse downward from levels that are often above the top of the precipitation system to produce rainout. As a result, radiological doses from debris in precipitation would be substantially lower than early-time doses associated with local fallout. In either case (frontal or convective rainout), for a large-scale multi-burst exchange, the size of the expected lethal-dose rainout areas should typically be small (i.e., well within the range of modeling uncertainty) compared to the size of the fallout areas created by particles with large settling velocities. Thus, to first order rainout areas can be ignored in calculating the radiological hazard from a large-scale nuclear war scenario. However, for lower yield ($\leq$30 kt) tactical war scenarios, or for scenarios at specific locations, rainout could lead to important and dominant radiological effects.

Single-Weapon Fallout Model

For this work the KDFOC2 computer model (Harvey and Serduke, 1979) was used to calculate fallout fields for single bursts, which in turn were used to develop a semiquantitative model for preparing rough estimates of fallout areas for typical strategic weapons. A wind profile (including shear) characteristic of midcontinental Northern Hemisphere summer conditions was selected from observations, and baseline fallout calculations were performed for several explosion yields under the assumption that all-fission weapons were used. As an example of the results, a 1-Mt fallout pattern is shown in Figure 1. Figure 2 gives the area versus minimum dose relationship for several different yields. Fallout areas are shown rather than maximum downwind extents for various doses since areas are less sensitive to variations in wind direction and speed shears and should be more useful for analysis. These areas correspond to unshielded doses associated with external gamma-ray emissions. All of the local fallout estimates given below are based on the KDFOC2 model and the wind pattern used for Figure 1.

To convert from areas for the 48-hour curves shown in Figure 2 to areas for minimum doses over longer times, an area multiplication factor, AMF, is given in Figure 3. For example, if the 2-week, 300-rad area is needed, first the 48-hour, 300-rad area is found from Figure 2 and then the ap-

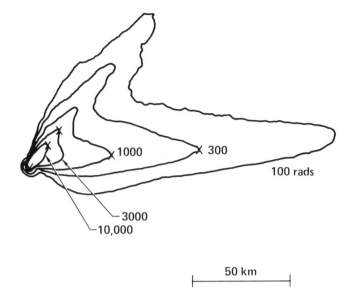

FIGURE 1   48-hour dose predictions for a 1-Mt all-fission weapon detonated at the surface. A midcontinental Northern Hemisphere summer wind profile was used. The double-lobed pattern is due to a strong directional wind shear that is typical during this season. For a 1-Mt weapon, the lofting of radioactivity is so high that topographic features are not expected to play a large role in pattern development; thus, a flat surface has been used. The protection factor is 1. The local terrain is assumed to be a rolling grassy plain. Source: Pittock et al. (1985, p. 242). Reprinted with permission from the Scientific Committee on Problems of the Environment (SCOPE).

propriate AMF is read from Figure 3. The 2-week, 300-rad area is the product of the 300-rad, 48-hour area and the 2-week, 300-rad AMF. For example, a 1-Mt, all-fission weapon, has a 2-week, 300-rad area of

$$\sim 2{,}000 \text{ km}^2 \times 1.30 \simeq 2{,}600 \text{ km}^2.$$

There are two scaling laws that allow weapons design and various sheltering to be factored into dose calculations. The first scaling law permits consideration of weapons that are not all fission. Most large-yield weapons (>100 kt) are combined fission-fusion explosives with approximately equal amounts of fusion and fission (Fetter and Tsipis, 1981). The fission fraction (ρ) is the ratio

$$\rho = \frac{\text{fission yield}}{\text{total yield}} \, .$$

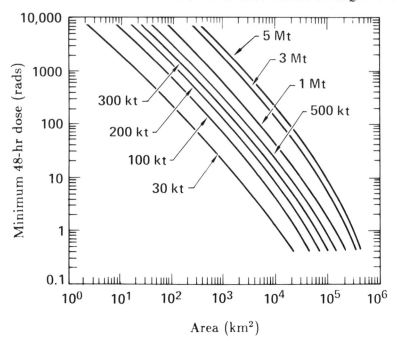

Area (km^2)

FIGURE 2   Fallout areas versus minimum 48-hour doses for selected yields from 30 kt to 5 Mt. The weapons were surface burst and all fission. The wind was that used in the calculation to produce Figure 1. These curves include an instrument shielding factor of about 25 percent (Glasstone and Dolan, 1977). Doses within the area defined would exceed the minimum dose. Source: Pittock et al. (1985, p. 243). Reprinted with permission from the Scientific Committee on Problems of the Environment (SCOPE).

To find a 48-hour minimum dose area for a particular fission fraction using Figures 2 and 3, the dose of interest, D, should be multiplied by $1/\rho$ before reading the values of the area and the area multiplication factor. For example, to obtain the 450-rad, 48-hour dose area for a 50 percent fission weapon, the area for the scaled dose of 900 rads would be obtained from Figure 2. For a 1-Mt, 50 percent fission weapon, the estimated 450-rad dose area is found to be 720 km^2. The rationale for this scaling law is that the thermodynamics and hydrodynamics of fallout development are insensitive to fission fraction because particle characteristics and lofting altitudes are determined predominantly by total energy yield. For yields that are only part fission, each particle has a fraction of the gamma radioactivity that it would otherwise have if the weapon were an all-fission weapon. This scaling law is appropriate for fission fraction ratios above ~0.3; smaller ratios can lead to situations where neutron-induced radioactivity becomes a significant factor. For such cases, careful consideration of surrounding materials may be necessary to produce accurate fallout estimates.

The second scaling law accounts for protection factors (K) against ionizing radiation that would be provided by sheltering. The 48-hour minimum dose areas given in Figure 2 are appropriate for a person or other organism located on a rolling grassy plain. In other configurations, radiation exposure varies according to how much shielding is obtained while a person remains in the area. For example, a person leading a normal lifestyle is likely to achieve an average K of 2 to 3 for gamma radiation from time spent inside buildings and other structures. Basements can provide K values of 10 to 20. Specially constructed shelters can provide K values of 10 to 10,000 (Glasstone and Dolan, 1977).

To determine the radiation area for a dose of D when shielding with a protection factor K is available, the scaled dose KD from Figure 2 should be used. For example, for those in an undamaged basement with $K = 10$ for the first 48 hours, Figure 2 indicates that the effective dose area of 450 rads or more from a 1-Mt, all-fission weapon is about 130 km^2. This is obtained by using a scaled dose of 4,500 rads. For comparison, the

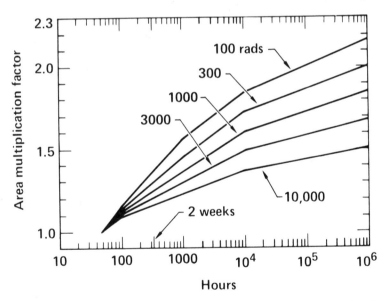

FIGURE 3   Area multiplication factors to extend the dose integration time from 48 hours to longer times. These factors must be used in conjunction with the areas given in Figure 2. Source: Pittock et al. (1985, p. 244). Reprinted with permission from the Scientific Committee on Problems of the Environment (SCOPE).

450-rad minimum dose area is about 1,300 km^2 for people with no shelter, greater by a factor of 10 than the area for those with a K of 10.

Other factors that could reduce the effects of fallout on the population over long time periods (≥ 1 month) include weathering (runoff and soil penetration), cleanup measures, relocation, and the ability of the body to repair itself when the dose is spread over time or occurs at lower rates. These considerations can be taken into account with existing computer models but are not treated here. Several factors that could enhance the effects of fallout are mentioned below.

Dose Estimation from Multiple Explosions

In a major nuclear exchange, thousands of nuclear warheads could be detonated. For such an exchange, realistic wind patterns and targeting scenarios could cause individual weapon fallout patterns to overlap in complicated ways that are difficult to predict and calculate. Even though acute doses are additive, a single-dose pattern calculated for a weapon cannot be used directly to add up doses in a multiweapon scenario, except under limited conditions. For example, if the wind speed and direction are not approximately the same for the detonation of each weapon, then different patterns should be used. In addition, the number of possible fallout scenarios far exceeds the number of targeting scenarios. This is because, for each targeting scenario that exists, the possible meteorological situations are numerous, complex, and varying. Thus, only under limited conditions may a single dose pattern be moved around a dose accumulation grid to obtain the sum of total doses from many weapons.

Two relatively simple multiburst models can be developed for use in conjunction with the semiquantitative model presented here. These cases can provide rough estimates of fallout areas from multiple weapons scenarios; however, their results have an uncertainty of no better than a factor of several, for reasons explained below, and are neither upper nor lower case limits. The no-overlap (NO) case is considered first; this could occur when targets are dispersed, there is one warhead per target and the fallout areas essentially do not overlap. Second, the total-overlap (TO) case is examined where multiple bursts are assumed to be at the same burst location. This approximation would arise when targets are densely packed and warheads of the same size are used against each. A large number of warheads used against, say, a hardened missile field site would be more closely modeled by the TO model than the NO model.

As an example of the use of the NO and TO approximations, a case with 100 1-Mt, 50 percent fission, surface-detonated explosions is considered, and estimates are developed for the 450-rad, 48-hour dose areas for both cases. For the NO case the fallout area can be obtained by determining the area for a single 1-Mt weapon (900-rad scaled dose from Figure 2) and multiplying by 100. This gives 7.2×10^4 km^2 for the 450-rad, 48-hour dose contour. For the TO model, the area is obtained for a single 1-Mt weapon, 9-rad scaled dose from Figure 2. One hundred of these, laid on top of each other, would give 450 rads for 50 percent fission weapons. The area in this case is 3.3×10^4 km^2. These results differ by about a factor of two, with the NO case giving a larger area.

Although these models are extremes in terms of fallout pattern overlap, neither can be taken as a bounding calculation of the extremes in fallout areas for specified doses. It is very possible that a more realistic calculation of overlap would produce a greater area for 100 weapons than either of these models. Such a result is demonstrated by a more sophisticated model prediction that explicitly takes overlap into account (Harvey, 1982). In this study, a scenario was developed for a severe case of fallout in a countervalue attack on the United States where population centers were targeted with surface bursts. Figure 4 shows the contours of a 500-rad minimum 1-week dose where overlap was considered. The 500-rad area

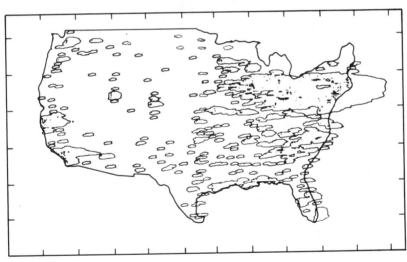

FIGURE 4   A fallout assessment that explicitly takes fallout pattern overlap into account. Shown are 500-rad, 1-week minimum isodose contours. This scenario was intended to emphasize population dose. Approximately 1,000 population centers in the United States were targeted, each with a 1-Mt, 50 percent fission weapon. The assumed winds were westerly with small vertical shear and were nearly constant over the continent (taken from Harvey, 1982). Reprinted with permission from Lawrence Livermore National Laboratory.

is about three times greater than that predicted by the NO model and six times that of the TO model. Note also that the distribution of radioactivity is extremely uneven. About 20 percent of the United States is covered with 500-rad contours, including nearly 100 percent of the northeast, approximately 50 percent of the area east of the Mississippi River, 10 percent of the area west of the Mississippi River, and only a few percent of the area in the Great Plains.

Results of these scenarios, as well as those postulated by others, clearly show that such estimates are very scenario dependent and that detailed estimates should be made with care. For example, the regional results shown in Figure 4 could be significantly different if military targets (e.g., intercontinental ballistic missile [ICBM] silos) were included as well. Although the NO and TO cases presented in this paper are simple to apply, they must be used only to develop rough estimates of total area coverage within regions with relatively uniformly dispersed targets. When the density of targets of one area is as large as that in the northeastern United States and another is as dispersed as that in the western United States, regional models should be used to develop specific regional estimates. Even then, multiple-weapon fallout estimates should be considered to have uncertainties no smaller than a factor of several, with the uncertainty factor increasing as the model sophistication decreases.

Sample Calculation of Multiple-Weapon Fallout

To illustrate the fallout prediction method presented here, an escalating nuclear exchange scenario, which is consistent with that described in the SCOPE-ENUWAR study (Pittock et al., 1985), is used to estimate fallout areas. In this scenario there are four sequential phases of attack against five different regions. The five regions are Europe (both east and west), western USSR (west of the Ural Mountains), eastern USSR, the western United States (west of 96° W latitude), and the eastern United States. The four phases of attack are initial counterforce, extended counterforce, industrial countervalue, and a final phase of mixed military and countervalue targeting. The weapon yields and the number of warheads that are employed for just the surface bursts during each phase are shown in Table 1. Airbursts are omitted since they do not produce appreciable local fallout.

In the first phase, land-based ICBMs are the primary targets. These are assumed to be located in the western United States and the USSR at sites containing 125 to 275 missiles. The geographical distribution of missile silos in the USSR is assumed to be 50 percent east and 50 percent west of the Ural Mountains. Each missile silo is attacked with a surface-burst and an airburst weapon. For a given site, the TO model is used to calculate

TABLE 1   Surface-Burst Warheads in a Phased Nuclear Exchange[a]

Weapon Yield (Mt)	Number of Warheads				
	Initial Counterforce Phase	Extended Counterforce Phase	Industrial Countervalue Phase	Final Phase	Full Baseline Exchange
0.05	0	300	0	250	550
0.1	975	150	50	8	1,183
0.2	0	250	50	121	421
0.3	500	250	0	125	875
0.5	1,000	200	0	25	1,225
1.0	250	495	160	125	1,030
5.0	0	50	15	8	73
Total surface-burst yield	~1,000	~1,000	~250	~250	~2,500

[a]All weapons are assumed to have 50 percent fission yield.

the fallout pattern. All U.S. ICBM sites are attacked with 0.5-Mt weapons. Each of five U.S. ICBM complexes is presumed to have 200 missile silos, while each of six USSR complexes is presumed to have between 125 and 275 missile silos, with a total of 1,300. The Soviet sites are attacked with 1-, 0.3-, and 0.1-Mt weapons. During this phase, each side employs a total of about 1,000 Mt. Besides the attack on Soviet missile silos, 425 0.1-Mt weapons are assumed to be surface-burst against other Soviet military targets, with approximately 28 Mt west of the Urals and 14 Mt to the east. The 425 fallout patterns from these weapons have been modeled with the NO model.

In the second phase of the attack, there are an additional 1,000 Mt of surface-burst weapons employed. These are employed against each region with 20, 40, and 40 percent of the weapons being used against targets in Europe, the United States and the USSR, respectively. Here, Europe includes both the North Atlantic Treaty Organization (NATO) and Warsaw Pact countries. To roughly account for population distribution, the weapons employed against the United States are divided up as two-thirds in the eastern U.S. and one-third in the western United States; for Soviet targets it is assumed that two-thirds are detonated west of and one-third are detonated east of the Ural Mountains.

For all the weapons employed in the second, third, and fourth phases, the fallout pattern is calculated using the NO model. The results, in terms of percent of land covered by at least a 450-rad, 48-hour dose, are shown in Table 2. No shielding has been assumed in calculating these percentages. Similar areas were found for 600 rads over 2 weeks.

Care must be taken in interpreting these results. To begin with, there is an uncertainty factor of several in the NO and TO modeling schemes, as discussed earlier. Another substantial bias is introduced by neglecting the radioactivity that is blown into or out of a region. For example, the western USSR would likely receive substantial amounts of radiation from weapons detonated in eastern Europe because the wind usually blows from Europe toward the Soviet Union. Thus, the area percentages shown in Table 2 for Europe would be expected to decrease since some of the area credited to Europe would actually be in the Soviet sector. Similarly, the percentage of radiation over the western United States is probably overestimated, assuming typical wind conditions. For the eastern United States the area covered would be increased by radioactivity originating in the central United States and decreased as a result of radioactivity blowing out over the Atlantic Ocean.

There are a number of factors that could change these local fallout assessments.

• Shielding is probably the most sensitive parameter in reducing the effective dose to a population. This effect has been ignored in these calculations. Protective measures could substantially reduce the impact of fallout on humans.

• Choosing a scenario that exacerbates local fallout (e.g., surface bursts over cities) could increase lethal areas by factors of several.

• Large differences in doses could arise because of irregularities in fallout patterns in the local fallout zones that could range over orders of magnitude. Relocation could substantially reduce a population's dose.

• Debilitating, but not lethal, radiation doses ($\sim$200 rads or more) would be received over much larger areas than areas receiving lethal doses.

TABLE 2   Percentage of Land Mass Covered by a Minimum 450-rad, 48-hour Dose

Land Mass	Initial Counterforce Phase	Extended Counterforce Phase	Industrial Countervalue Phase	Final Phase	Full Baseline Exchange
Europe	0	2.9	0.6	0.8	4.3
Eastern USSR	0.5	0.5	0.1	0.2	1.3
Western USSR	1.6	2.3	0.7	1.7	6.3
Eastern United States	0	4.7	1.0	1.4	7.1
Western United States	4.4	2.3	0.7	6.6	8.0

• Fission fractions of smaller modern weapons could be twice the baseline assumption of 0.5. Adding these to the scenario mix could increase lethal fallout areas by up to 20 percent of the baseline calculation.

• Tactical weapons, ignored in the baseline scenario, could increase lethal local fallout areas in certain geographical regions, particularly within Europe, by about 20 percent of the baseline calculations.

• Internal radiation exposure could increase the average total doses to humans by about 20 percent of the external dose.

• External beta exposure, not treated here, could add significantly to plant and animal exposures in local fallout areas.

• Targeting of nuclear fuel cycle facilities could contribute to radiation doses.

Global Fallout

Global fallout consists of the radioactivity carried by fine particulate matter and gaseous compounds that are lofted into the atmosphere by nuclear explosions. One may distinguish two components to global fallout—intermediate time scale and long term. Intermediate-time-scale fallout consists of material that is initially injected into the troposphere and is removed principally by precipitation within the first month. The fractional contribution to intermediate-time-scale fallout decreases as the total weapon yield increases above 100 kt. The importance of intermediate-time-scale fallout has grown with reductions in warhead yields. Long-term fallout occurs as a result of deposition of very fine particles that are initially injected into the stratosphere. Because the stratosphere is so stable against vertical mixing and the fine particulate matter has negligible fall velocities, the primary deposition mechanism involves transport of the radioactivity to the troposphere through seasonal changes in stratospheric circulation. Once within the troposphere, these particles would normally be removed within a month by precipitation scavenging.

Given a specific nuclear war scenario, it is possible to use experience gained from atmospheric nuclear tests to estimate the fate of both intermediate-time-scale and long-term fallout particles if the atmosphere is not perturbed by smoke. GLODEP2 (Edwards et al., 1984), an empirical code that was designed to match measurements from atmospheric testing, has been used. The model contains two tropospheric and six stratospheric injection compartments. By following unique tracer material from several atmospheric nuclear tests in the late 1950s, combined with subsequent balloon and aircraft measurements in the stratosphere and upper troposphere and many surface air and precipitation observations, it was possible to estimate the residence time of radioactivity in the various stratospheric compartments and the interhemispheric exchange rate in the stratosphere. Radioactive material that is placed initially into the troposphere is also handled by the GLODEP2 model (Edwards et al., 1984). From this information, surface deposition tables were prepared. The GLODEP2 model has never been tested against atmospheric nuclear tests in middle latitudes since no extensive series of explosions have occurred in this region. As a result, there is some uncertainty in the results of explosions centered around the Northern Hemisphere middle latitudes, but little uncertainty in the Northern Hemisphere subpolar latitude calculations since the stratospheric fallout there would deposit much the same as the global fallout from the polar bursts used to generate the polar deposition tables in the model.

Global Dose in an Unperturbed Atmosphere Using Specific Scenarios

A variety of scenario studies have been performed using GLODEP2 (Knox, 1983; Edwards et al., 1984). Dose calculations for scenarios A and B, which are described in Table 3, are presented in detail in Table 4. The atmospheric compartments in Table 3 refer to those used in the GLODEP2 model.

From a comparison of GLODEP2 results for the A and B scenarios for a Northern Hemisphere winter injection (Table 4, columns A_1 and B_1), it is seen that the Northern Hemisphere averages for scenarios A and B are about 16 and 19 rads, respectively, while Southern Hemisphere averages are more than a factor of 20 smaller. The maximum appears in the 30 to 50°N latitude band, where scenarios A and B yield 33 and 42 rads, respectively. All the doses reported here for global fallout are integrated external gamma-ray exposure over 50 years and assume no sheltering, no weathering, and a smooth plane surface.

For scenario A, 55 percent of the dose emanates from the tropospheric injections. The corresponding value for B is 75 percent. This emphasizes the sensitivity of dose to the yield mix of the scenario. As individual warhead yields decrease, the fractional injections into the troposphere increase, resulting in much larger doses on the ground due to more rapid deposition. Tropospheric radioactivity injections per megaton of fission can produce doses on the ground about a factor of 10 greater than those resulting from lower stratospheric injections, which in turn contribute about 3 to 5 times higher doses compared to upper stratospheric injections (Shapiro, 1984). Injections of radioactivity above the stratosphere as a gas or as extremely fine particles would produce relatively negligible doses at the ground.

TABLE 3 Nuclear War Scenarios

Scenario A (Knox [1983] 5,300-Mt baseline nuclear war)		Scenario B (TTAPS [Turco et al., 1983] 5,000-Mt reference nuclear war)	
Total Yield/Warhead (Mt)	Total Fission Yield Injected (Mt)	Total Yield/Warhead (Mt)	Total Fission Yield Injected (Mt)
20.0	305	10.0	125
9.0	235	5.0	125
1.0–2.0	355	1.0	557
0.9	675	0.5	312
0.75	15	0.3	188
0.55	220	0.2	125
0.3–0.4	115	0.1	87
0.1–0.2	110		
<0.1	1		

Mt of fission products injected into atmosphere

	Scenario A	Scenario B
Polar troposphere	226	369
Lower polar stratosphere	1,234	898
Upper polar stratosphere	571	226
High polar atmosphere	0	25
Total	2,031	1,520
Fraction of yield in surface bursts	0.47	0.57
Fission fraction	0.5	0.5
Total number of explosions	6,235	10,400

Table 4 includes calculated values for the global human population dose. This quantity is calculated by multiplying the dose in each 20°-wide latitude band by the population of the latitude band, and then summing over all latitudes. For a given scenario, this number is one measure of the potential global biological impact. The global population dose as calculated by GLODEP2 for scenarios A and B are 7×10^{10} and 8×10^{10} person-rads, respectively. Essentially all of this dose occurs in the Northern Hemisphere because 90 percent of the world's population and higher doses prevail there.

Figure 5 illustrates the time behavior of the buildup of the dose to the 50-year lifetime value as a function of latitude for scenario A. The bulk of the dose is caused by deposition (mainly from the troposphere) and exposure during the first season after the war, followed by a gradual rise to the 50-year value.

A comparison of the GLODEP2 results for the TTAPS scenario (B) and the results of Turco et al. (1983) (using an entirely different methodology) reveals that GLODEP2 doses are 19 rads for the Northern Hemi-

TABLE 4   Global Fallout Dose Assessments (rads) for an Unperturbed Atmosphere with No Smoke

Latitude Band	A_1	B_1	A_2	B_2	A_3	B_3
70–90°N	4.5	3.7	2.9	2.5	7.8	8.2
50–70°N	27.3	28.8	21.7	22.7	21.3	24.6
30–50°N	32.9	41.7	27.4	33.7	22.3	23.9
10–30°N	6.9	8.3	5.6	6.6	7.6	7.2
10°S–10°N	0.8	0.6	0.5	0.3	1.3	1.0
10–30°S	0.6	0.4	0.4	0.2	0.6	0.4
30–50°S	0.8	0.4	0.6	0.4	0.7	0.4
50–70°S	0.5	0.3	0.5	0.3	0.5	0.3
70–90°S	0.1	0.0	0.2	0.1	0.2	0.1
Area averaged						
Northern Hemisphere	16.2	19.1	13.1	15.2	12.8	13.7
Southern Hemisphere	0.6	0.4	0.5	0.3	0.7	0.4
Global	8.4	9.8	6.8	7.8	6.8	7.1
Global population dose ($\times 10^{10}$) person-rads	6.7	8.2	5.5	6.6	5.3	5.5

A_1 = Winter injection using GLODEP2. B_1 = Winter injection using GLODEP2. A_2 = Summer injection using GLODEP2. B_2 = Summer injection using GLODEP2. A_3 = Summer injection using GRANTOUR with stratospheric contributions from GLODEP2. B_3 = Summer injection using GRANTOUR with stratospheric contributions from GLODEP2.

SOURCE: Pittock et al. (1985, p. 255). Reprinted with permission from the Scientific Committee on Problems of the Environment (SCOPE).

sphere average and 42 rads for the 30–50°N latitude band, while estimates of Turco et al. give corresponding doses of 20 rads and about 40 to 60 rads.

Other studies that have been undertaken using GLODEP2, and the 5,300-Mt scenario A have led to the following conclusions:

Winter versus Summer Injection Because of a decrease in the frequency and intensity of large-scale precipitation systems in summer, the doses from the troposphere and lower polar stratosphere are reduced somewhat in comparison to those in winter, while the upper stratospheric contribution is increased. The total dose differences between summer and winter are not large, and other sources of uncertainty would predominate.

Scenarios with Smaller-Yield Devices The long-term consequences of the shift in the nuclear arsenals from larger- to smaller-yield devices has been assessed. Table 5 presents results comparing the 5,300-Mt baseline scenario with two variations. In scenario Aa, the number of devices in the baseline scenario A is increased from 6,235 to 13,250, while the total yield is held at 5,300 Mt. In scenario Ab, smaller yields have been used, but the number of devices is constant at 6,235 (the total yield consequently

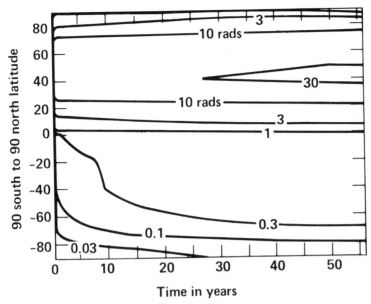

FIGURE 5   Global fallout: accumulated whole-body gamma dose (rads) from 6,235 explosions totaling 2,031 Mt of fission products (scenario A). An 8-day tropospheric deposition decay constant, characteristic of a winter injection, is assumed. Source: Pittock et al. (1985, p. 256). Reprinted with permission from the Scientific Committee on Problems of the Environment (SCOPE).

is reduced by 25 percent, from 5,300 to 4,000 Mt). The figures presented are for the 50-year gamma-ray dose. For the same total yield, it is seen that a shift to smaller weapons in the baseline scenario has approximately doubled the dose (scenario Aa). For Ab, the dose remains about the same even with a 25 percent drop in the total yield.

TABLE 5   Global Fallout: Sensitivity of Dose to Warhead Yield[a]

Scenario	Total Yield (Mt)	Number of Explosions	Average Yield per Warhead	30–50°N Dose (rads)	Global Average Dose per Person (rads)	Global Population Dose (10^{10} person-rads)
A	5,300	6,235	0.85	33	15	6.7
Aa	5,300	13,250	0.40	64	27	12.5
Ab	4,000	6,235	0.64	33	14	6.5

[a]The fission and groundburst fractions are those assumed for scenario A.

SOURCE: Pittock et al. (1985, p. 257). Reprinted with permission from the Scientific Committee on Problems of the Environment (SCOPE).

Global Fallout in a Perturbed Atmosphere

Following a large-scale nuclear exchange, the large quantities of smoke and soot lofted to high altitudes could decrease the incoming solar radiation, resulting in tropospheric and stratospheric circulation changes. Over land in the Northern Hemisphere, the presence of smoke and soot would probably result in less precipitation and a lowering of the tropopause; these changes could decrease the intermediate-time-scale (tropospheric) fallout and, depending on changes in stratospheric circulation, could alter the stratospheric contribution to fallout in the Northern Hemisphere. However, before the stratospheric burden is carried into the troposphere, a sizeable fraction would be transported to the Southern Hemisphere by the accelerated interhemispheric transport, resulting in doses there that are likely to be increased over those calculated for an unperturbed atmosphere.

Both the GLODEP2 and the Turco et al. (1983) models assumed fission product depositions from a normal atmosphere in calculating global fallout. Preliminary studies have been conducted with radionuclides in a perturbed atmosphere using a three-dimensional version of the GRANTOUR model (see MacCracken and Walton, 1984). GRANTOUR is a three-dimensional transport model driven by meteorological data generated by the Oregon State University (OSU) general circulation model (Schlesinger and Gates, 1980). Particulate matter appearing as an initial distribution or generated by sources is advected by wind fields, locally diffused in the horizontal and vertical, moved vertically by convective fluxes and the re-evaporation of precipitation, and removed by precipitation scavenging and dry deposition. It is assumed that the fission products are in the form of particulate material in two size ranges: greater than and less than 1 μm in diameter. Coagulation from small to large particles is not treated in the version of the model used here.

Studies focused on comparisons of radiation dose assessments with smoke in the atmosphere (interactive atmosphere) and without smoke (noninteractive); other relevant parameters were also explored, including consideration of particle size distribution, source location, different initial meteorology, and averaging doses over land areas only. All of the GRANTOUR simulations reported here are for the Northern Hemisphere summer season and use five radioactivity and smoke source locations of equal strength. The locations include two in the United States, two in the USSR, and one in western Europe. This division of sources is similar to that assumed in our earlier discussion on local fallout. Sources were initially injected with a Gaussian distribution whose amplitude was 10 percent of the maximum at a radius of 15° along a great circle. The total amount of smoke injected was 150 teragrams (equivalent to the urban smoke contributions used by Turco et al. [1983] and the National Research Council [NRC, 1985]). MacCracken and Walton (1984) describe the induced climatic perturbations. The vertical distribution of the radioactivity injections were distributed, as was the smoke, with the same vertical distribution as the source term injections calculated using the GLODEP2 injection algorithm. Deposition was followed for 30 days in most calculations. A single 60-day run indicated that 30 days is sufficient to account for 90 percent of the deposition. Results are compared for a 50-year unsheltered, unweathered, external gamma-ray dose.

GRANTOUR treats only the troposphere and splits it into three vertical layers extending from 800 to 1,000, 400 to 800, and 200 to 400 mbar. In a normal atmosphere, these layers reach up to 2.0, 7.1, and 11.8 km. In the comparisons, GLODEP2 was used to estimate the dose contributions from the stratospheric injections, which were added to the doses calculated by GRANTOUR assuming altered climatic conditions.

Scenarios A and B were used in the calculations. Columns A_2 and B_2 in Table 4 display a comparison of the predictions of GLODEP2 for these two scenarios. Columns A_3 and B_3 list the results from GRANTOUR, assuming an unperturbed atmosphere (no smoke; no climatic perturbation) for the same two scenarios. There is reasonable agreement (i.e., generally within about 50 percent) between the GLODEP2 only and GRANTOUR/ GLODEP2 methodologies for an unperturbed atmosphere (scenarios 1 and 3), providing some confidence that the results of GLODEP2 and GRANTOUR can be combined for simulations with a perturbed atmosphere, although the initial accelerated interhemispheric mixing of radionuclides in the stratosphere has not yet been considered. This may lead to a small underestimate of the long-term Southern Hemisphere dose.

Table 6 compares calculations for a perturbed atmosphere (interactive smoke) with estimates for normal July conditions. These results are also shown in Figure 6 and indicate that the perturbed atmosphere lowers the average dose in the Northern Hemisphere by about 15 percent. Because the principal mechanism for radionuclide removal from the troposphere is precipitation, the GRANTOUR calculations are roughly consistent with the thesis that precipitation is inhibited when large amounts of smoke are introduced. The transfer of fission product radionuclides to the Southern Hemisphere is somewhat enhanced by the perturbed climate, resulting in higher doses than for the unperturbed case. The increases in Southern Hemisphere dose, however, are not large, and the resulting doses are still about a factor of 20 lower than those in the Northern Hemisphere. This is because the increased transfer to the Southern Hemisphere is mitigated by the decay in activity during the time before the radionuclides are deposited on the ground.

TABLE 6   Global Fallout Dose Using the Three-Dimensional GRANTOUR Model (summer scenario)[a]

Latitude Band	A_3 (no smoke)	A_4 (smoke)	B_3 (no smoke)	B_4 (smoke)
90–70°N	7.8	6.4	8.2	5.8
70–50°N	21.3	17.2	24.6	18.0
50–30°N	22.3	20.1	23.9	20.4
30–10°N	7.6	7.5	7.2	7.2
10°N–10°S	1.3	1.6	1.0	1.4
10–30°S	0.6	0.8	0.4	0.6
30–50°S	0.7	0.8	0.4	0.5
50–70°S	0.5	0.5	0.3	0.3
70–90°S	0.2	0.2	0.1	0.1
Area averaged				
Northern Hemisphere	12.8	11.5	13.7	11.5
Southern Hemisphere	0.7	0.8	0.4	0.6
Global	6.8	6.1	7.1	6.1
Population average—Global	11.5	10.7	12.0	10.7
Global population dose ($\times 10^{10}$)				
person-rads	5.3	4.9	5.5	4.9

[a]Comparison of perturbed atmosphere (smoke) and unperturbed atmosphere (no smoke). External gamma-ray doses are in rads. Because GRANTOUR only calculates the tropospheric contribution, the doses here include the contributions from the stratosphere as calculated by GLODEP2. A_3 = 5,300 Mt (Knox, 1983), unperturbed atmosphere (no smoke). A_4 = 5,300 Mt (Knox, 1983), perturbed atmosphere (smoke). B_3 = 5,000 Mt (Turco et al., 1983), unperturbed atmosphere (no smoke). B_4 = 5,000 Mt (Turco et al., 1983), perturbed atmosphere (smoke).

SOURCE: Pittock et al. (1985, p. 260). Reprinted with permission from the Scientific Committee on Problems of the Environment (SCOPE).

Figure 6 reveals longitudinal, as well as latitudinal, details that are not apparent in the averages of Table 6. Scenario B is illustrated here since the changes due to smoke-induced effects are more apparent. The five original sources have produced four discernible peaks in the tropospheric dose distribution, and the two U.S. sources have merged in the 30-day dose distribution. The tabulated values presented in Table 6 are averages over 20° latitude bands. The dose in hotspots can be examined by looking at peaks on the 10° × 10° grid. Typically the highest value for a grid square ($\sim 5 \times 10^5$ km^2) is about a factor of 6 to 8 higher than the Northern Hemisphere average dose. There will also be local areas much smaller than the 10° × 10° grid size where the peak doses would be considerably higher.

As GRANTOUR tests only the troposphere and GLODEP2 has been used for the stratospheric contributions (which assumes an unperturbed stratosphere), additional calculations using a computer model that includes the perturbed stratosphere should be undertaken.

Internal Dose Due to Inhalation and the Food Chain

One serious problem following a large-scale nuclear exchange is radioactive contamination of drinking water. Those cities that are damaged would undoubtedly lose their water system due to power loss and ruptured supply pipes. Suburban residents within the local fallout pattern would encounter heavily contaminated water supplies and would have to rely on stored water. Surface water supplies would be directly contaminated by fission products.

During the first few months in areas extending several hundred kilometers downwind of an explosion, the dust, smoke, and radioactivity could cause severe water pollution in surface waters. The dominant fission product during this time would be ^{131}I (iodine-131). Beyond a few months, the dominant fission product in solution would be ^{90}Sr (strontium-90) (Naidu, 1984). Many of the fission products would remain fixed in fallout dust, river and lake sediments, and soils. In rural areas, intermediate- and

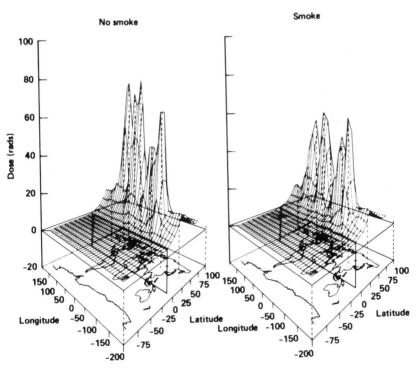

FIGURE 6 Comparison of radionuclide global dose distribution for cases with unperturbed and smoke-perturbed climates (tropospheric contributions only). Source: Pittock et al. (1985, p. 261). Reprinted with permission from the Scientific Committee on Problems of the Environment (SCOPE).

long-term fallout would pollute water supplies to a lesser extent than the city and suburban supplies. In the absence of additional contamination from runoff, lakes, reservoirs, and rivers would gradually become less contaminated as water flowed through the system.

Initially groundwater supplies would remain unpolluted but they may be difficult to tap. Eventually, however, some groundwater could become contaminated, and remain so for some tens of years after a nuclear war. It would take hundreds or thousands of years for an aquifer to become pure (or nearly so) (van der Heijde, 1985). Doses from drinking this water would be small but, nonetheless, possibly above current water quality standards. In the long term, ^{90}Sr and ^{137}Cs (cesium-137) would be the major radionuclides affecting fresh water supplies.

The GLODEP2 fractional deposition rates have been used to calculate ^{90}Sr surface concentrations. The results are given in Table 7 for the Northern Hemisphere winter and summer seasons. The values are based on the Knox (1983) 5,300-Mt baseline scenario A, and are expressed in mCi/km^2 for a 6-year period over 20° latitude bands. The maximum deposition occurs between 30 and 70°N. The concurrent deposition values for ^{137}Cs can be obtained by multiplying the ^{90}Sr values by 1.6. These values assume an unperturbed atmosphere. As stated earlier, introducing smoke and soot into the troposphere and stratosphere would probably slightly reduce Northern Hemisphere values and slightly increase ^{90}Sr deposition in the Southern Hemisphere.

Significant doses to individual human organs can also arise from specific radionuclides via food pathways. Such doses are caused by consumption of radioactively contaminated milk, meat, fish, vegetables, grains, and

TABLE 7　Average Accumulated ^{90}Sr Deposition (mCi/km^2) after 6 Years, as a Function of Latitude

Latitude Band	Season Winter	Summer
70–90°N	271	226
50–70°N	937	946
30–50°N	862	978
10–30°N	234	237
10°S–10°N	39	26
10–30°S	25	19
30–50°S	47	39
50–70°S	26	30
70–90°S	3	10

SOURCE: Pittock et al. (1985, p. 264). Reprinted with permission from the Scientific Committee on Problems of the Environment (SCOPE).

other foods. For a normal atmosphere, various researchers (International Commission on Radiological Protection Publication 30, 1980; Kocher, 1979; Ng, 1982; Lee and Strope, 1974) have provided means to calculate organ doses for a number of radionuclides and food pathways. However, in a post-nuclear-war atmosphere perturbed by large quantities of smoke, the results of the above studies may not be valid since the dose (in rads/Ci) from soil to animal feed to humans are highly variable geographically and depend upon the degree of perturbation of weather and ecosystems.

However, the internal total body dose (the sum of the dose to each organ weighted by the risk factor due to consumption of various foods) has been very roughly estimated by J. Rotblat (private communication) to be about 20 percent of the external dose from local fallout, about equivalent for intermediate-time-scale fallout, and somewhat greater than the external dose from long-term fallout. These estimates are very uncertain.

Summary

For radionuclides, the most important short-term consequence is the downwind fallout during the first few days of relatively large radioactive particles lofted by surface explosions. The deposition of fresh radioactive material in natural and induced precipitation events also could contribute to enhanced surface dose rates over very limited areas (hotspots) both near to and far away from detonation sites. For both local fallout and distant hotspots, dose rates can be high enough to induce major short- and long-term biological and ecological consequences.

Calculations of local fallout fields were performed using the KDFOC2 model and an escalating nuclear exchange scenario. In this illustrative example, where simple assumptions are made about the overlap of fallout plumes, these estimates indicate that about 7 percent of the land surface in the United States, Europe, and the USSR would be covered by external gamma-ray doses exceeding 450 rads in 48 hours, assuming a protection factor of 1 (i.e., no protective action is taken). A similar area estimate is obtained for doses exceeding 600 rads in 2 weeks. More realistic overlap calculations would suggest that these areas could be greater (by a factor of 3 in one specific case). For those survivors protected from radiation by structures, these areas would be considerably reduced. Areas of sublethal debilitating exposure (≥ 200 rads in 48 hours), however, would be larger. A good approximation is that these areas are inversely proportional to the 48-hour dose. In local fallout fields of limited area, the dose from beta rays could be high enough to significantly affect surviving biota. Variations in fallout patterns in the local fallout zones could range over orders of magnitude. If large populations could be mobilized to move from highly radioactive zones or take substantial protective measures, the impact of fallout on humans could be greatly reduced.

The uncertainties in these calculations of local fallout could be factors of several. In addition, the use of different scenarios (e.g., all surface bursting or little surface bursting of weapons) could modify the calculated lethal areas by factors of several. There are a number of other factors that could change these local fallout assessments. Fission fractions of smaller modern weapons could be twice the baseline assumption of 0.5. Adding these to the scenario mix could increase lethal fallout areas by about 20 percent of the baseline calculation. Tactical weapons, ignored in the baseline scenario, could increase lethal local fallout areas in certain geographical regions, particularly within western Europe, by up to 20 percent of the baseline scenario. Internal radiation exposure could increase the average total doses to humans by up to 20 percent of the external dose. Targeting of nuclear fuel cycle facilities could contribute to radiation doses.

For global fallout, different computer models and scenarios have been intercompared. The calculations predict that the 50-year unsheltered, unweathered average external total body gamma-ray dose levels in the Northern Hemisphere would be about 10 to 20 rads, and about 0.5 to 1 rad in the Southern Hemisphere. The peak doses of 20 to 60 rads appear in the 30 to 50°N latitude band. Values predicted for the global population dose using the assumptions made in this study are typically about 6×10^{10} person-rads. The doses in the maxima grid points using a $10° \times 10°$ latitude and longitude mesh size, are a factor of 6 to 8 higher than the Northern Hemisphere averages. From 50 to 75 percent of the global fallout dose would be due to the tropospheric injection of radionuclides that are deposited in the first month. These results were obtained assuming a normal (unperturbed) atmosphere and have an estimated confidence level of a factor of 2 for a given scenario. The most sensitive parameter that affects global fallout levels is the scenario (e.g., total yield, yield mix, surface or airburst, burst locations).

Additional calculations involving a perturbed atmosphere indicate that the above dose assessments would be about 15 percent lower in the Northern Hemisphere and marginally higher (to approximately 1 rad) in the Southern Hemisphere compared to predictions for the unperturbed atmosphere. These results are consistent with the projection that smoke injections can increase vertical stability, inhibit precipitation, and increase interhemispheric transport.

Estimates of dose contributions from food pathways are much more tenuous. Rotblat (private communication) has estimated roughly that internal doses would be about 20 percent of the external dose from local fallout, about equivalent to the external dose from intermediate fallout, and somewhat greater than the external dose from long-term global fallout.

RADIOACTIVITY FROM NUCLEAR FUEL CYCLE FACILITIES

The possible targeting with nuclear warheads of nuclear fuel cycle facilities arouses considerable controversy. There is general agreement that enormous reservoirs of long-lived radionuclides exist in reactor cores, spent fuel rods, fuel reprocessing plants, and radioactive waste storage facilities. Disagreement arises when the feasibility and extent of such a targeting strategy are considered. Even if one adopts the view that "what if" questions must be considered, there is still disagreement over the quantitative treatment of the potential dispersal of the radioactivity contained in these sources. In the present treatment, some of the assumptions regarding radioactivity release are considered highly improbable by a number of researchers. The results, therefore, should not be separated from the assumptions and the large uncertainties associated with these assumptions.

Introduction

A gigawatt nuclear power plant may be a valuable industrial target in a nuclear war. If a targeting rationale is proposed that the largest possible amount of gross national product be destroyed in an attack on a nation's industry (one measure of the worth of a target to a nation), then large (~1000 MW(e)) nuclear power plants could become priority targets for relatively small ($\leq$125 kt) strategic weapons (Chester and Chester, 1976). In the United States there are about 100 such targets, and worldwide there are about 300. There are also military nuclear reactors and weapons facilities that could be targeted. Since these facilities may be targeted, reactor-generated radioactivity should be considered as part of the potential postattack radiological problem.

Whether the radioactivity contained in a reactor vessel can be dispersed in a manner similar to a weapon's radioactivity is debatable. Nuclear reactor cores are typically surrounded by a 1-m-thick reinforced concrete building that has about a 1-cm-thick inner steel lining, many heavy steel structural elements inside the containment building, and an approximately 10-cm-thick reactor vessel. Inside the reactor vessel are fuel rods and cladding capable of withstanding high temperatures and pressures. For the core radioactivity to be dispersed in the same way as the weapon's radioactivity, all of these barriers must be breached. The core itself must be at least fragmented, and possibly vaporized, and then entrained into the rising nuclear cloud column along with possibly hundreds of kilotons of fragmented and vaporized dirt and other materials from the crater and nearby structures, including the thick concrete slab that supports the reactor building. Under certain conditions of damage, there is a possibility of a reactor core meltdown resulting in the release of some of the more volatile radionuclides to the local environment. If this were to occur, however, the area of contamination would be relatively small compared to the contamination by a reactor core if it were to be pulverized and lofted by a nuclear explosion.

The primary contributor to the long-term dose at a nuclear power plant would not be the core. The most hazardous radioactivity, when assessing long-term effects (≥ 1 year after attack), is that held in the spent-fuel ponds, if the reactor has been operating at full power for a few years. Since the spent-fuel storage usually has no containment building nor reactor vessel to be breached, it is much more vulnerable to being lofted by a nuclear weapon than are the core materials. Unless spent fuel is located at sufficient distance from a reactor, it could potentially become part of the local fallout problem.

Other nuclear fuel cycle radioactivity may also be significant. Reprocessing plants, although not as immediately important economically as power plants, contain a great deal of radioactivity that could significantly contribute to the long-term doses. Also, military nuclear reactors developing fissile material and their reprocessing plants might be important wartime targets. They also hold significant amounts of radioactivity in their waste ponds and reactor cores.

Military ships fueled by nuclear power could be prime targets as well. Ships' reactors typically produce less power (~ 60–250 MW(t)) than commercial reactors (Ambio Advisors, 1982). They could, however, have substantially radioactive cores, depending on the megawatt hours of service a shipboard reactor has produced since refueling. A large nuclear-powered ship with more than one reactor, designed for years of service without refueling, can have nearly as much long-lived radioactivity (e.g., ^{90}Sr) on board as an operating commercial reactor (Rickover, 1980). Such shipboard reactors may also be more vulnerable to vaporization than commercial reactors.

Figure 7 shows the gamma radiation dose rate-area integrals from a 1-Mt, all-fission nuclear weapon and from possible commercial fuel cycle facilities. In the first few days, the higher activity of the nuclear weapon debris dominates over the gamma radiation of the reactor. Likewise, gamma-radiation levels from a light water reactor (LWR) are greater than those of 10 years worth of stored spent fuel for about 1 year after the detonation.

Subsequently, the spent fuel would be relatively more radioactive. Similarly, the gamma radiation from 10 years of spent fuel is greater than the radioactivity of a 1-Mt fission weapon after about 2 months because of the greater abundance of long-lived gamma emitters in the spent fuel.

Thus, for doses from a 1-Mt, all-fission weapon detonated on a reactor, the core gamma radiation would be comparable to the weapon's radiation at about 5 days. By 2 months the gamma radioactivity from the weapon would have decayed by a factor of over 1,000 from its value at 1 hour. Beyond about 1 year the gamma radiation from the weapon is insignificant compared to a reactor's radiation; however, the dose levels are no longer acutely life threatening.

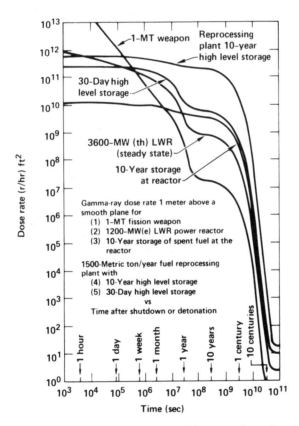

FIGURE 7   Gamma-ray dose rate-area integral versus time after shutdown or detonation (Chester and Chester, 1976, p. 333). Reprinted with permission from the American Nuclear Society.

Local Fallout

For dose estimates from local fallout, two time frames are considered—the short term, where there is acute and potentially lethal radiation, and the long term, when chronic doses become important. In the short term, the gamma radiation is the main hazard. Later, specific radionuclides become important concerns for doses via food pathways.

For doses received within the first 48 hours, the nuclear weapon gamma radiation pathway for a high-yield (~1-Mt) warhead dominates the fuel-cycle gamma radioactivity, even if one assumes a worst case assumption in which all the radioactivity from the attacked nuclear fuel cycle facility is lofted with the weapon products. For lower yields and thermonuclear weapons, the core gamma radiation becomes more important and could be potentially greater than the dose from the nuclear weapons, even at very early times. However, since there are now only approximately 100 nuclear power plants available for targeting in the United States and possibly a few hundred shipboard reactor targets which are dispersed over the globe (Ambio Advisors, 1982), and because there are typically more than 1,000 other U.S. targets in major nuclear-exchange scenarios, the impact of fuel cycle radiation to the total U.S. 48-hour external gamma-ray dose would likely be less than 10 percent.

In the long term, the radioactivity from the core and spent-fuel ponds could be a dominant effect, both around the reactor and at substantial distances downwind. After about 1 year, the products from the nuclear fuel cycle could make a substantial contribution to the total gamma-ray dose fallout patterns over the United States. Certainly, if released, fallout gamma radiation from a large reactor would dominate the dose of a 1-Mt weapon over the long term (see Figure 8).

In terms of radiological effects, individual radionuclides (e.g., ^{90}Sr) become more important over the longer time frame than the whole-body gamma radiation. Assuming 50 percent fission weapons, it is possible to have more ^{90}Sr in a single reactor and its spent-fuel pond than that produced in a 1,000-Mt attack. Most of the ^{90}Sr is in the spent-fuel pond and thus could be more easily lofted as fallout than the ^{90}Sr in the heavily shielded reactor core. Accordingly, in the long term, the fuel cycle ^{90}Sr contribution can dominate over the weapon contribution. For example, Chester and Chester (1976) calculated levels of ^{90}Sr much higher than the current maximum permissible concentration (MPC) over much of the U.S. farmland 1 year after an attack on the projected nuclear power industry of the year 2000. Scaling down their results to an attack on a 100-MW(e) nuclear power industry, they calculated that about 60 percent of the U.S. grain-growing capacity would be in areas that exceed current ^{90}Sr MPC levels.

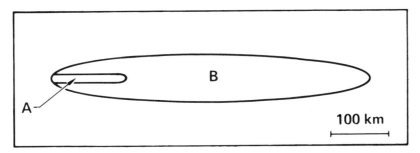

FIGURE 8   Contours of 100-rad fallout dose during 1 year's exposure, starting 1 month after the detonation of a 1-Mt bomb (A) and a 1-Mt bomb on a 1-GW(e) nuclear reactor (B). Source: Rotblat (1981). Reprinted with permission from the Stockholm International Peace Research Institute (SIPRI).

Global Fallout

In calculation of the potential global fallout, assumptions have been made that facilitated calculations and allowed estimation of expected dose. For example, it was assumed that each nuclear facility would be surface targeted by a high-yield, accurately delivered warhead that would completely pulverize and vaporize all of the nuclear materials and that these materials would then follow the same pathways as the weapon materials (a worst-case assumption). It was assumed further that the major nuclear facilities in a 100-GW(e) civilian nuclear power industry would also be attacked. The results should be viewed as providing estimates that approach maximum global fallout for an attack on a commercial nuclear power industry of 100 GW(e). Higher estimates would be obtained, however, using the same assumptions by including military nuclear facilities and a larger civilian industry.

This hypothetical reactor attack scenario assumed that, as part of the 5,300-Mt exchange of Knox (1983), some of the warheads would be targeted on nuclear power facilities. Specifically 0.9-Mt weapons would be surface burst on 100 light water reactors, 100 10-year spent-fuel storage (SFS) facilities, and one fuel reprocessing plant (FRP). With a 0.9-Mt surface burst on each facility, 2 percent of the radioactive fission products would be injected into the troposphere and 48 percent into the stratosphere. The remaining activity (50 percent) would contribute to local fallout. Such large yields were assumed because of the hardness of the nuclear reactor. If smaller-yield weapons were used to target the nuclear facilities, the relative injections of radioactivity into the troposphere would be much greater. While the weapons radioactivity would result in higher doses on

TABLE 8 Fifty-Year External Gamma-Ray Global Fallout Dose, in Rads, for Nine Latitude Bands[a]

Source	Latitude Bands								
	70–90°N	50–70°N	30–50°N	10–30°N	10°N–10°S	10–30°S	30–50°S	50–70°S	70–90°S
Weapons	4.5	27.3	32.9	6.9	0.8	0.6	0.8	0.5	0.09
LWR[b]	1.8	6.3	9.1	3.0	0.6	0.3	0.3	0.1	0.01
SFS[c]	6.7	23.8	32.7	11.3	2.3	1.0	1.0	0.4	0.03
FRP[d]	4.1	14.6	20.1	7.0	1.4	0.6	0.6	0.2	0.02
Total	17.1	72.0	94.8	28.2	5.1	2.5	2.7	1.2	0.15

[a]Assuming a full nuclear attack, including a full-scale, totally effective attack on a 100-GW(e) nuclear power industry. These values do not account for weathering, sheltering, or rainout.
[b]LWR = 100 light water reactors.
[c]SFS = 100 spent-fuel storage facilities.
[d]FRP = fuel reprocessing plant.
SOURCE: Pittock et al. (1985, p. 272). Reprinted with permission from the Scientific Committee on Problems of the Environment (SCOPE).

the ground, this would not be true for the nuclear facility radioactivity. This is because of the relatively slow decay of the facilities' radioactivity. Hence, a faster deposition time would not significantly affect the 50-year dose. The patterns and local concentrations of fallout deposition would, however, be affected.

Using GLODEP2 and a Northern Hemisphere winter scenario, the resulting unsheltered, unweathered doses are shown in Table 8. The largest value of 95 rads for the total of weapons plus the nuclear power industry occurred in the 30–50°N latitude band. The doses obtained for the Southern Hemisphere were about a factor of 30 smaller than in the Northern Hemisphere. The majority of the dose contributions came from the spent-fuel storage facilities and the high level waste in the reprocessing plant.

Figure 9 is a plot of accumulated dose in the 30–50°N latitude band as a function of time to 50 years (200 quarter years) for the 5,300-Mt scenario (Northern Hemisphere winter injection) with and without the targeting of nuclear power facilities. The bulk of the dose from the weapons alone for this scenario resulted from deposition in the first year. The relative contributions of the nuclear facilities were minimal in the first year, but

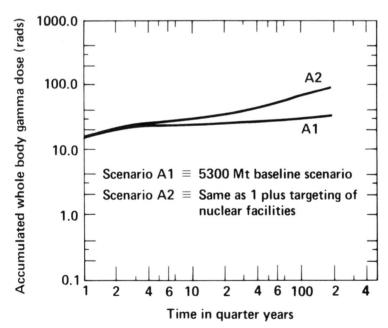

FIGURE 9   Accumulated dose at 30–50°N versus time scenario A, with (A2) and without (A1) an attack on nuclear facilities. Source: Pittock et al. (1985, p. 273). Reprinted with permission from the Scientific Committee on Problems of the Environment (SCOPE).

became larger with time. At 50 years, the contribution of the nuclear facilities would be approximately double that of the weapons alone. In addition, while the weapons-only curve at 50 years is almost flat, the nuclear facilities curve has a positive slope with the radioactivity continuing to directly affect future generations.

An attack on all of the world's civilian nuclear fuel cycle facilities (approximately 300 GW[e]) would scale the above results up by about a factor of 3, although this scenario is even less likely. The potential effect is growing in time; the world's nuclear capacity has been projected to grow to 500 GW(e) by 1995. A significant contribution could also come from the targeting of military nuclear facilities, with results qualitatively similar to those obtained from attacks on power plants.

In summary, using some worst-case assumptions for a speculative nuclear war scenario wherein 100 GW(e) of the nuclear power industry is included in the target list, the 50-year global fallout dose is estimated to increase by a factor of 3 over similar estimates wherein nuclear power facilities are not attacked.

If one adds the internal doses necessarily accompanying the external doses (perhaps doubling or tripling the latter) and considers that localized hotspots can be formed with up to 10 times the average dose, it seems that moderate to heavy attacks on civilian and military nuclear facilities could result in significant long-term radiological problems for humans and ecosystems. Many of these problems involving the radiological assessments associated with nuclear facilities are unresolved and uncertain but deserve more thorough attention.

APPENDIX: THE IMPACT OF FALLOUT ON HUMANS

In the main body of this paper the focus was an estimation of unprotected doses due to fallout. The focus of the SCOPE-ENUWAR fallout calculations (Pittock et al., 1985) was on assessing the impact on nonhuman biota; direct effects on humans was specifically excluded. Hence, the calculations made were predictions of the unprotected dose, and it is these that have been reported on earlier in this paper. Here, we are more concerned with direct effects of fallout on humans. Consequently, this appendix extends our previous discussion of unprotected doses to focus on the latter subject. We begin with a short discussion about the impact of global fallout on humans. The remainder of this appendix discusses the more serious impact of local fallout.

Global Fallout

As we have reported above, our GLODEP2 calculations for strategic nuclear exchanges of about 5,000 to 6,000 Mt predict that the 50-year unsheltered, unweathered, external total body gamma-ray dose levels average about 15 rads in the Northern Hemisphere and about 0.5 rads in the Southern Hemisphere. The maximum longitude-averaged dose of 30 to 40 rads appears in the 30 to 50°N latitude band. Values predicted for the global population (chronic) dose are typically about 6×10^{10} person-rads. The dose in rainout hotspots, obtained by using 10° latitude and longitude areas, are a factor of 6 to 8 higher than the Northern Hemisphere averages, or 90 to 120 rads, respectively. These results have an estimated confidence level of a factor of 2. From 50 to 75 percent of the global fallout dose is due to tropospheric injections of radionuclides that are deposited in the first month.

Additional calculations, utilizing GRANTOUR and assuming a perturbed nuclear winter atmosphere, indicate that the above dose assessments would be about 15 percent lower in the Northern Hemisphere and marginally higher (to approximately 1 rad) in the Southern Hemisphere than in an unperturbed atmosphere.

These calculations have been presented at a number of scientific meetings, including the ICSU-SCOPE workshop on radiation held in Paris, October 1984. There, internationally known radiation experts carefully reviewed this work, which subsequently became the basis of the chapter on radioactivity in the SCOPE-ENUWAR report (Pittock et al., 1985).

For radiation exposure that is protracted in time, biological repair of the resulting damage is significant in mitigating the effects. Dose effectiveness factors from 0.1 to 0.5 for chronic exposures have been suggested (National Council on Radiological Protection Report 64, 1980). This means that a large chronic dose will have an effect equivalent to a much smaller acute dose. This phenomenon has particular relevance here in assessing the impact of global fallout, which is chronic, low-dose-rate irradiation received over many decades.

The effects of the above levels of global fallout, even including the hotspots referred to earlier,were summarized in the Report of the Paris Commission on Radiological Dose Assessments and Biological Effects (SCOPE-ENUWAR Newsletter, 1984). It concluded that "the long-term increase in genetic and carcinogenic effects on humans from global fallout is of the order of 1% of the natural incidence and should be considered a second order effect." No mention was made of prodromal effects on humans because at these lifetime (50 years) dose levels, and assuming biological repair mechanisms, prodromal effects would not be observed. This result is far from that pictured in the *On the Beach* syndrome.

Local Fallout

As we have seen, projections of the intensity and extent of local fallout are highly sensitive to a number of variables, which helps explain why many assessments have produced widely different results. Uncertainties in these projections can be divided into three categories: those due to the targeting scenario, the fallout calculations model, and the selected meteorological conditions.

The targeting scenario contains variables such as the number of weapons and their yield mix, fission fractions, heights of burst, and precise target locations. The height of burst (HOB) is of particular significance because airbursts do not produce significant local fallout, except for rainout of debris from tactical yield weapons. Only when the fireball interacts with the ground (a ground or near-ground burst) does significant local fallout ensue. A widely used and reasonable assumption is that hardened military targets are targeted with ground bursts. For the softer industrial and other military targets, maximum damage is accomplished by airbursts where the HOB can be optimized. The fires hypothesized in urban areas in nuclear winter studies are assumed to be initiated by airbursts since ground bursts are not efficient in initiating large fires. Uncertainties in dose calculations in the best fallout models originate from several sources. These include limited experimental data, whether the modeled radioactivity is rigorously conserved, whether time of arrival is properly accounted for, and other inaccuracies of the model. Assumptions about selected meteorology (e.g., wind velocities, shears, precipitation patterns) affect the results. Hence, local fallout assessments can vary greatly, depending on these many assumptions.

For assessing the impact of local fallout on humans, additional factors must be considered. By far the most sensitive of these is the protection factor afforded by homes, buildings, basements, and other shelters. These structures can dramatically mitigate the unprotected dose assessments normally cited and used previously in this paper. In Table 9, structure protection factors from fallout gamma rays are listed.

An additional important consideration for humans is the assumption of what are the lethal acute external whole-body dose levels (50 percent lethal dose [LD_{50}] values from 220 to 600 rads of external gamma radiation have been reported). Finally, for local fallout delivered over days and weeks, biological repair will reduce the damage from the dose by a significant factor, vis-à-vis an instantaneously delivered dose by a significant amount.

Our calculations of the total fatalities produced by large-scale attacks on the continental United States have produced estimates of fallout fatalities (after subtracting those already killed by blast and thermal effects) that range over almost 2 orders of magnitude. This large variation in fallout fatalities is well understood in terms of variations in the parameters discussed above.

TABLE 9   Fallout Gamma-Ray Dose Protection Factors
for Various Structures

Structure	Protection Factor
Three feet underground	5,000
Frame house	2–3
Basement	10–20
Multistory building (apartment-type)	
Upper stories	100
Lower stories	10
Concrete blockhouse shelter	
9-inch (23-cm) walls	10–150
12-inch (30-cm) walls	30–1,000
24-inch (61-cm) walls	500–10,000
Shelter, partly above grade	
With 2-feet (61-cm) earth cover	50–200
With 3-feet (91-cm) earth cover	200–1,000

SOURCE: Glasstone and Dolan (1977).

In one study, fallout fatalities resulting from a massive countervalue attack of 1,000 Mt against U.S. urban population centers was estimated (Harvey, 1982). The scenario contained 1,000 surface-burst warheads each of 1 Mt, 50 percent fission yield. This population-destroying scenario was not purported to be realistic; rather, it was part of a parameter study to estimate the effects of evacuation and/or sheltering on fatality estimates. In this study, we used realistic overlap of fallout from multiple weapon bursts, the U.S. Census Bureau population distribution, and a probability of death from fallout with 500 rads received in 1 week with no sheltering. The total number of fatalities was estimated at about 160 million, of which 16 million were attributed to fallout. This study illustrated the great sensitivity of fallout fatalities to the choice of parameters.

Physicians are more concerned with nonfatal injuries. Radiation effects become apparent in humans with acute doses greater than about 100 rads. We can estimate the extent of the areas that are covered with a minimum dose by referring to Figure 2. The slope of the 48-hour dose versus area curves for strategic-sized weapons yield are approximately -1, meaning that the minimum dose area contours are inversely proportional to the 48-hour dose. As an example, the SCOPE-ENUWAR study reported that about 7 percent of the land masses of the United States, the USSR, and Europe would receive a minimum of 450 rads within 48 hours. The figure for the continental United States was about 8 percent. This result assumed no shielding and applied to an unsheltered population. Our inverse approximation would then project that the area covered by a minimum dose of 100 rads would be 4.5 times larger, or 36 percent of the total land area of the contiguous United States.

However, minimum dose contours over land areas do not relate in a simple manner to human exposure. Here, both protection factor distributions and population distributions must be considered to make a proper assessment.

In summary, global fallout is not expected to result in prodromal symptoms from radiation exposure because of both the magnitude of exposures and the chronic (long-term) exposure rate. Global fallout would result in a small statistical increase, of the order of 1 or 2 percent, above the current incidence of cancers and genetic mutations in the decades following the occurrence of a nuclear war. Local fallout can produce significant numbers of injuries and fatalities from radiation exposure, but numerical estimates are highly uncertain and are very sensitive to the assumptions made to obtain these estimates. Attempts to make these assessments as realistic as possible by including credible population distributions (relocated and/or sheltered) should be made. Superficial attempts at reality will yield an artificially large spread in the results.

ACKNOWLEDGMENTS

This work was performed under the auspices of the U.S. Department of Energy by the Lawrence Livermore National Laboratory under Contract No. W-7405-Eng-48.

REFERENCES

Ambio Advisors. 1982. Reference scenario: How a nuclear war might be fought. Ambio 11:94–99.

Chester, C. V., and R. O. Chester. 1976. Civil defense implications of the U.S. nuclear power industry during a large nuclear war in the year 2000. Nuclear Technol. 31:326–338.

Defense Civil Preparedness Agency (DCPA). 1973. Response to DCPA questions on fallout. DCPA Research Report No. 20, November 1973. Washington, D.C.: U.S. Defense Civil Preparedness Agency.

Edwards, L. L., T. F. Harvey, and K. R. Peterson. 1984. GLODEP2: A computer model for estimating gamma dose due to worldwide fallout of radioactive debris. Report UCID-20033. Livermore, Calif.: Lawrence Livermore National Laboratory.

Fetter, S. A., and K. Tsipis. 1981. Catastrophic release of radioactivity. Sci. Amer. 244(4): 41.

Glasstone, S., and P. Dolan. 1977. The Effects of Nuclear Weapons. Washington, D.C.: U.S. Department of Defense and U.S. Energy Research and Development Administration.

Harvey, T. F. 1982. Influence of civil defense on strategic countervalue fatalities. Report UCID-19370. Livermore, Calif.: Lawrence Livermore National Laboratory.

Harvey, T. F., and F. J. D. Serduke. 1979. Fallout model for system studies. Report

UCRL-52858. Livermore, Calif.: Lawrence Livermore National Laboratory.

ICRP Publication 30. 1980. Limits for Intakes of Radionuclides by Workers. New York: Pergamon.

Knox, J. B. 1983. Global scale deposition of radioactivity from a large scale exchange. Proceedings of the International Conference on Nuclear War, 3rd Session: The Technical Basis for Peace, Erice, Sicily, Italy, August 19–24, 1983. Servizio Documentazione dei Laboratori Frascati dell'INFN, July 1984, pp. 29–46. Also Report UCRL-89907. Livermore, Calif.: Lawrence Livermore National Laboratory.

Kocher, D. C. 1979. Dose-rate conversion factors for external exposures to photon and electron radiation from radionuclides occurring in routine releases from nuclear fuel cycle facilities. Health Phys. 38:543–621.

Lee, H., and W. E. Strope. 1974. Assessment and control of the transoceanic fallout threat. Report EGU 2981. Menlo Park, Calif.: Stanford Research Institute.

MacCracken, M. C., and J. J. Walton. 1984. The effects of interactive transport and scavenging of smoke on the calculated temperature change resulting from large amounts of smoke. Proceedings of the International Seminar on Nuclear War 4th Session: The Nuclear Winter and the New Defense Systems: Problems and Perspectives, Erice, Italy, August 19–24, 1984. In preparation. Also Report UCRL-91446. Livermore, Calif.: Lawrence Livermore National Laboratory.

Naidu, J. R. 1984. Impact on water supplies—II. SCOPE/ENUWAR meeting, New Delhi, India, February 1984. Draft manuscript.

National Council on Radiation Protection and Measurement. April 1, 1980. Influence of dose and its distribution in time on dose-response relationships for low-LET radiations. Washington, D.C.: U.S. Government Printing Office. (Report No. 64.)

National Research Council (NRC). 1985. The Effects on the Atmosphere of a Major Nuclear Exchange. Washington, D.C.: National Academy Press.

Ng, Y. C., C. S. Colsher, and S. E. Thompson. 1982. Transfer coefficients for assessing the dose to man from radionuclides in meat and eggs. Lawrence Livermore National Laboratory Report NUREG/CR-2976.

Pittock, A. B., T. A. Ackerman, P. Crutzen, M. MacCracken, C. S. Shapiro, and R. P. Turco. 1985. Environmental Consequences of Nuclear War. Volume I. Physical and Atmospheric Effects. SCOPE 28. Chichester, U.K.: John Wiley & Sons.

Rickover, H. G. 1980. Naval nuclear propulsion program—1980. Statement before the Procurement and Military Nuclear Systems Subcommittee, 96th Cong. Washington, D.C.: U.S. Government Printing Office.

Rotblat, J. 1981. Nuclear radiation in warfare. Stockholm International Peace Research Institute (SIPRI). London: Taylor and Francis.

Schlesinger, M. E., and W. L. Gates. 1980. The January and July performance of the OSU two-level atmospheric general circulation model. J. Atmos. Sci. 37:667–670.

SCOPE-ENUWAR Newsletter. 1984. Scientific Committee on Problems of the Environment. University of Essex, England.

Shapiro, C. S. 1984. Scenario and parameter studies on global deposition of radioactivity using the computer model GLODEP2. Lawrence Livermore National Laboratory Report UCLD-20548.

Svirezhev, Y. M. 1985. Long-term ecological consequences of a nuclear war: Global ecological disaster. Moscow: Computer Center of USSR Academy of Sciences. Draft manuscript.

Turco, R. P., O. B. Toon, T. P. Ackerman, J. B. Pollack, and C. Sagan. 1983. Nuclear winter: Global consequences of multiple nuclear explosions. Science 222:1283–1292.

van der Heijde, P. K. M. 1985. Groundwater contamination following a nuclear exchange, SCOPE/ENUWAR Workshop Report. Delft, The Netherlands, October 3–5, 1984.

PART II

Health Consequences of Nuclear War

The Medical Implications of Nuclear War, Institute of
Medicine. © 1986 by the National Academy of Sciences.
National Academy Press, Washington, D.C.

Casualties Due to the Blast, Heat, and Radioactive Fallout from Various Hypothetical Nuclear Attacks on the United States

WILLIAM DAUGHERTY, BARBARA LEVI, PH.D., and
FRANK VON HIPPEL, PH.D.
Princeton University, Princeton, New Jersey

OVERVIEW

We have developed the tools for calculating the deaths and injuries due to blast, thermal effects, and local fallout from hypothetical nuclear attacks on the United States. This is the first time that the capability to do such consequence calculations has existed outside the (mostly classified) government domain.

We have used this capability to explore the sensitivities of the consequences of a nuclear attack to various assumptions. The first was the sensitivity to the types of targets involved. We examined three different hypothetical "limited" nuclear attacks on the United States, each involving a 1-megaton (Mt) airburst over approximately 100 targets of three different types:

- The city centers of the 100 largest U.S. urban areas
- 101 industries rated as the highest-priority targets for an attack on U.S. military-industrial capability
- 99 key strategic nuclear targets.

The calculated ranges of fatalities and casualties (deaths plus severe injuries and illnesses) from blast, burns, and radioactive fallout for these

This paper is based on a much longer technical report that is available from Princeton University's Center for Energy and Environmental Studies as Report #PU/CEES 198.

"100-Megaton" attacks are shown in Table 1. This table indicates that more than 10 million deaths could result from these "limited" attacks even if the targets were industrial or military and not population per se. The results also indicate that even a strategic defense system that was 99 percent effective might not protect the United States against potential catastrophe in a nuclear war with the USSR.

We also explored the sensitivity of these calculations to different models for predicting casualties. Lower numbers result if we use the predictions of the traditional "overpressure" model, which assumes that the same casualty rates will occur as those that occurred at Hiroshima at given levels of peak blast overpressure. Higher numbers result when we use a new "conflagration" model (Postol, 1986), which postulates that much higher fatality rates might be expected in the large "burnout" areas that would be caused by modern weapons than occurred in the burnout area of the much lower yield Hiroshima bomb.

We find, for 1-Mt airbursts, that the numbers of fatalities predicted by the conflagration model are 1.5 to 4 times higher than those predicted by the overpressure model, with the exact factor depending on the population distribution and the assumed scaling of the burnout area with yield. The predicted numbers of injured are significantly smaller for the conflagration model because many of the people injured in the overpressure model die from fire effects in the conflagration model. In view of the plausibility of the conflagration model, we believe that previous estimates of the deaths due to the blast and burn effects of nuclear attacks are very uncertain and probably low by a large factor.

Next, we calculated the consequences from a major "counterforce" attack on U.S. strategic-nuclear forces. We assumed an attack on more than 1,200 targets with almost 3,000 attacking warheads. Because such

TABLE 1   Estimated Deaths and Total Casualties from the "100-Megaton" Attacks

	Deaths (millions)		Total Casualties (millions)	
Attack	Overpressure Model	Conflagration Model*	Overpressure Model	Conflagration Model*
City-centers	14	23, 42, 56	32	40, 51, 61
Military-industrial	11	17, 29, 38	23	27, 35, 41
Strategic-nuclear	3	6, 11, 19	10	13, 16, 21

*The three estimates were obtained using three possible radii (8, 12, and 15 km) for the conflagrations that might be started by a 1-megaton airburst.

an attack would result in a great amount of local fallout from many ground bursts, our casualty models in this case included the effects of radioactive fallout as well as blast and thermal radiation. The estimated number of deaths ranged from 13 to 34 million people. The range reflects the varying predictions associated with different possible winds, the different models for blast and burns, and different assumptions about the susceptibility of the population to death from radiation. The corresponding final estimates made by the Department of Defense (DOD) in 1975 for a similar attack ranged from 3 million to 16 million deaths (U.S. Congress, Senate Foreign Relations Committee, 1975; pp. 12–24).

Our casualty estimates should still be considered as only a partial accounting of the potential human toll due to the attacks discussed here. Nuclear weapons are powerful enough to destroy both our social and environmental support systems, and the numbers of casualties from second-order effects such as exposure, starvation, or disease could be as great as or greater than the numbers presented in this paper for direct casualties.

INTRODUCTION

An all-out nuclear war between the United States and the Soviet Union would destroy the urban areas of both countries and thereby the infrastructure that makes them modern industrial states. This fact makes the deliberate launching of such a war the ultimate act of folly. Nevertheless, military planners have felt that the United States should have "credible strategic nuclear options," and have worried about those credible nuclear options that the Soviets might devise. This concern led to debates in the 1970s over the possibility of "limited" nuclear wars that might produce significant military results but minimal civilian casualties. During this same period, according to Ball (1983; p. 19), U.S. policy was changed to exclude targeting "population per se"—presumably because "collateral" civilian casualties from the targeting of economic or military facilities were expected to be much lower than those from direct attacks on population centers. And recently, the Strategic Defense Initiative has provoked debates over whether strategic defenses could reduce U.S. casualties from an all-out nuclear attack to less than catastrophic levels.

How much would these options and policies actually buy in reduced casualties? Unfortunately, quantitative estimates of these reductions are hardly ever offered. Yet such estimates of casualties—and, just as important, the public disclosure of the assumptions behind them—are essential to the evaluation of these concepts.

In this paper, we describe the results of an exploration of the sensitivities of the estimates of direct casualties from limited nuclear attacks on the

United States to various assumptions concerning the targets and the casualty models used. We have estimated the casualties from four different types of attacks: three involving approximately 100 targets each and the fourth a major counterforce attack on U.S. strategic-nuclear facilities.

CASUALTIES FROM "100-MEGATON" ATTACKS

Blast and Burn Casualty Models

The primary basis for models of the blast and burn effects of nuclear explosions is the casualty data from Hiroshima. The nuclear weapon used on Hiroshima, however, had a yield of only 15 kilotons (kt) (Loewe and Mendelsohn, 1982)—much less than most warheads in the current strategic arsenals of the superpowers. Therefore, casualty models must contain rules for extrapolating the number of casualties at Hiroshima to those caused by explosions of higher yields.

Overpressure Model

The standard method for extrapolation that is, to our knowledge, used in virtually all government calculations is to assume that casualty probabilities are a function of peak blast overpressure. Given the weapon yield and height of burst, the peak overpressure is calculated as a function of the distance from ground zero, and the Hiroshima blast and burn casualty rates for that overpressure are applied to the population at that distance (e.g., U.S. Congress, Office of Technology Assessment, 1979; p. 19). Figure 1 shows the casualties at Hiroshima as a function of distance from ground zero. Figure 2 shows the same data replotted as a function of the peak blast overpressure.

For obvious reasons, we call the standard casualty model the "overpressure" model. The use of blast overpressure as the explanatory variable does not mean that burns are ignored. At Hiroshima, the probability of blast injuries and burn injuries fell off with distance from ground zero in about the same manner (Oughterson and Warren, 1956; p. 43), and the cause of death was not generally known. Under these circumstances, it was natural to choose overpressure as a basis for scaling—especially since the distance corresponding to a given level of overpressure can easily be calculated, given the weapon's yield and height-of-burst.

Postol has recently challenged this "overpressure casualty model." He points out that the fires simultaneously ignited by a megaton-sized explosion over an urban area would merge into a "superfire" of such large extent and intensity, with asphyxiating gases and gale-force winds, that

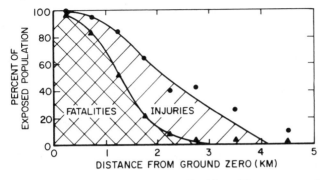

FIGURE 1   Mortality and casualty rates at Hiroshima. The percent probability of total casualties (●) and fatalities (▲) is shown as a function of distance from the hypocenter. (From Oughterson and Warren, 1956, Figure 3.10.)

many more casualties would result than would be predicted by the over-pressure model (Postol, 1986). Postol notes that even those not fatally injured or trapped under collapsed buildings would have insufficient time to escape from the inner regions of superfires before the fire effects became lethal. Therefore, he argues that for higher-yield explosions, casualty rates would depend primarily on the area of the subsequent conflagration.

At Hiroshima, a mass fire, or conflagration, developed approximately

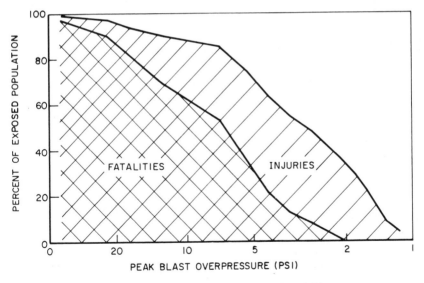

FIGURE 2   Hiroshima casualty rates as a function of peak blast overpressure.

20 minutes after the explosion and ultimately consumed essentially all combustible materials in an area with a radius of about 2 km (see Figure 3). The growth of the area of the conflagration with weapon yield is difficult to predict because a nuclear explosion would cause fires through two mechanisms: (1) direct ignition by heat radiated from the fireball and (2) indirect ignition by blast-caused electrical short circuits, gas line breaks, ruptured fuel tanks, and other sources.

If the radius of the conflagration area were scaled with peak overpressure, then the Hiroshima conflagration area would scale up to have a radius of 8 km for a 1-Mt airburst. There are at least two reasons why the conflagration radius could grow more rapidly than this: (1) the blast effects at a given peak overpressure could be much more damaging at higher weapon yields because the associated winds would last much longer (Wilton et al., 1981); and (2) given a relatively clear atmosphere, the radius of incendiary effects by direct ignition might reach out well beyond 8 km.

Brode and Small (1983; Figure 27 therein) have estimated that the conflagration caused by a 1-Mt airburst over an urban area could have a radius anywhere from 4 to 14 km, depending on the atmospheric conditions and the types of buildings involved. The lower end of the range is not relevant to considerations of conflagrations in ordinary urban areas, since it is associated with extremely blast-resistant, reinforced concrete buildings, while the upper end involves blast-caused fires in building types that are quite common in U.S. cities. Therefore, we have considered conflagrations with radii ranging from a minimum of 8 km to a maximum of 15 km, i.e., from the radius that would be predicted if the conflagration radius occurred at a fixed peak overpressure to a radius almost twice as large. Our medium-radius conflagration model has a fire radius of 12 km.

Given this range of conflagration radii, we have constructed a conflagration casualty model by dividing the distance from ground zero into three zones (see Figure 4):

• An inner conflagration zone—the area further in than 2 km from the edge of the conflagration zone. Here we assume that there would be 100 percent fatalities because the population would not have time to escape before individual fires would merge into a single inferno.

• An outer conflagration zone—the outer 2 km of the conflagration zone. Here we assume that there would be 50 percent fatalities and 33 percent severe injuries. These are approximately the average values observed within the 2-km radius Hiroshima burnout zone.

• An overpressure injury zone—the area outside of the conflagration zone, where there would be blast effects and scattered fires. Here we assume that the fatality and injury rates are the same functions of peak

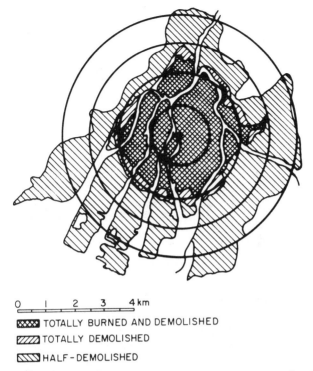

0   1   2   3   4 km

▨ TOTALLY BURNED AND DEMOLISHED

▨ TOTALLY DEMOLISHED

▨ HALF-DEMOLISHED

FIGURE 3   Map of Hiroshima damage areas. (From Committee for the Compilation of Materials on Damage Caused by the Atomic Bomb in Hiroshima and Nagasaki, 1981; pp. 58–59. Reprinted with permission from Basic Books, Inc.)

blast overpressure as were observed outside the conflagration zone at Hiroshima.

In Figures 5a and 5b, we compare the probabilities of death and injuries as a function of distance from ground zero predicted by the overpressure and conflagration models for a 1-Mt airburst at a 2-km altitude. A mid-range conflagration radius of 12 km has been assumed.

Ranges of Casualties Calculated for 100-Mt Attacks on U.S. City Centers, Military-Supporting Industry, or Strategic Nuclear Targets

The calculated results of an all-out attack on the U.S. population or economic targets involving thousands of megatons would be relatively insensitive to the casualty model used. The degree of overkill would be

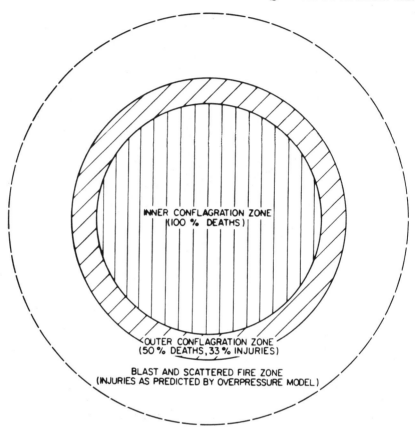

FIGURE 4   Conflagration model.

so high that, regardless of the casualty model assumed, the calculations would find that virtually the entire U.S. urban population would be killed by blast and burns. Much of the rural population would die of fallout-caused radiation illness, and most of the remainder would die of starvation and disease (e.g., Haaland et al., 1976; Harwell, 1984).

Therefore, in order to explore the sensitivity of blast and burn casualty estimates to the choice of casualty model and types of targets involved, we have considered much more limited hypothetical attacks on three different classes of targets in the United States—each containing approximately 100 ground zeros:

- The city centers of the 100 largest U.S. urban areas;
- 101 final-assembly factories selected by a Department of Defense

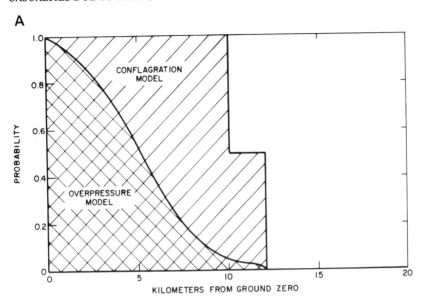

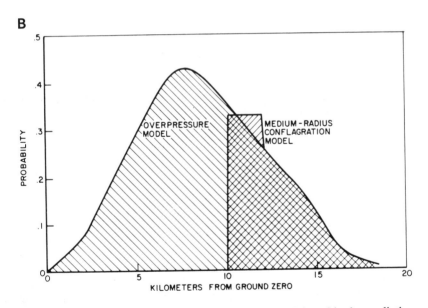

FIGURE 5   A: Fatality rates from a 1-Mt explosion at 2-km altitude: predictions of two casualty models. B: Injury rates from 1-Mt explosion at 2-km altitude: predictions of two casualty models.

contractor as the highest-priority targets for an attack on U.S. military-industrial capability;

• 99 key strategic nuclear targets (34 home bases for nuclear bombers and their associated refueling aircraft; 16 nuclear naval bases; 9 nuclear weapon storage facilities; and 40 command, communication, and early-warning sites).

We have assumed 1-Mt airbursts for all these attacks. This provides a common basis for comparison and is certainly well within Soviet capabilities. More than 1,000 Soviet intercontinental and submarine-based ballistic missiles carry single warheads with estimated yields of approximately 1 Mt (Arkin, Burrows, et al., 1985).

Our data base for the U.S. population distribution was obtained from a tape prepared for the government from 1980 U.S. census data (Federal Emergency Management Agency, 1980). Since the data are for the residential population, our casualty estimates are for nighttime attacks. However, the results should be indicative for daytime attacks as well.

Figure 6a shows the cumulative populations around the ground zeros of the three hypothetical target sets. It will be seen that the populations around the military-industrial sites are almost as high as those around the city centers. This is because most of the military-industrial targets are located in major urban areas, including those around Boston, Detroit, Los Angeles, Minneapolis-St. Paul, Philadelphia, Phoenix, Rochester, Sacramento, St. Louis, San Diego, San Jose, Seattle, Tucson, and Wichita (Science Applications Inc., 1984).

The cumulative population around the 99 strategic nuclear targets is considerably lower than that around the city centers or military-industrial sites but still includes tens of millions of people (see the breakdown by classes of target in Figure 6b). Many of these targets are in urban areas (Table 2). For example,

• Strategic nuclear bombers or their associated aerial refueling groups are based outside Chicago, Milwaukee, Phoenix, Salt Lake City, Sacramento, Wichita, Fort Worth, and Shreveport (Air Force Magazine, 1985).

• Aircraft carriers carrying nuclear-armed fighter bombers are based in San Francisco Bay; and battleships equipped with long-range, nuclear-armed, land-attack cruise missiles are proposed for bases off both Long Beach, Calif., and Staten Island in New York harbor.

• The Pentagon and the White House in the Washington, D.C., urban area and the Strategic Air Command headquarters outside Omaha are among the most important strategic nuclear weapons command posts. And a number of other major urban areas are the sites of key radio transmitters for communicating with ballistic missile submarines, bombers, and mil-

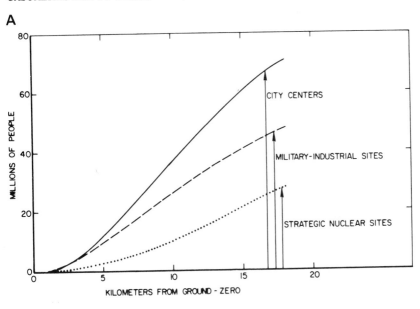

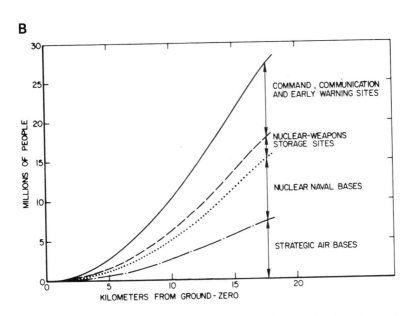

FIGURE 6   A: Cumulative population around ground zeros for 100-Mt attacks.
B: Cumulative population around 99 U.S. strategic nuclear targets.

TABLE 2   Some Major U.S. Urban Areas with Nearby
Strategic Nuclear Facilities

Nuclear Bomber Bases
  Sacramento, Calif.
  Wichita, Kans.
  Fort Worth, Tex.
  Shreveport, La.
Nuclear Bomber Aerial Refueling Groups
  Chicago, Ill.
  Milwaukee, Wis.
  Phoenix, Ariz.
  Salt Lake City, Utah
Nuclear Navy Bases
  San Francisco, Calif.
  Long Beach, Calif.
  New York, N.Y. (proposed)
Command Sites
  Washington, D.C.
  Omaha, Neb.

itary early-warning and communications satellites (Arkin and Fieldhouse, 1985).

The numbers of blast and burn deaths and injuries predicted for attacks involving 1-Mt airbursts over each of these targets are listed in Table 1. Figure 7 shows the results from the overpressure and medium-radius conflagration models. The conflagration model predicts 1.5 to 4.1 times as many deaths as the overpressure model—up to 56 million—depending on the conflagration radius that is assumed.

Figure 7 also shows that the targeting of factories instead of city centers does not greatly reduce the number of deaths, and that there could still be more than 10 million fatalities even if the 100 warheads were targeted solely against strategic military targets. So, if Soviet targeteers were to declare that they did not target cities per se—as their American counterparts have done (Ball, 1983; p. 19)—that statement should not give us a great deal of comfort. Our finding that tens of millions of people might die from just 100 warheads also shows that any strategic defense system would have to reduce an attack to well below this level before the results would be less than catastrophic.

CASUALTIES FROM A MAJOR ATTACK ON
U.S. STRATEGIC NUCLEAR TARGETS

U.S. strategic-nuclear capabilities would be the highest-priority targets for any Soviet attack because they represent by far the greatest threat posed by the United States to the Soviet Union. "Counterforce" attacks, restricted to military bases containing strategic nuclear weapon delivery vehicles and to their command, control, and warning systems, have therefore become a staple of debates over nuclear weapons policy.

During 1974–1975, a series of hearings held by a subcommittee of the U.S. Senate Foreign Relations Committee focused on the potential U.S. casualties that might result from such counterforce attacks on the United States. Even in 1985, a decade later, the record of these hearings represents the fullest open discussion thus far of the U.S. government's views on this subject. We therefore briefly summarize these hearings here.

James R. Schlesinger, then Secretary of Defense, provoked the hearings with a section in the DOD report to Congress on the proposed budget for fiscal year 1975. Schlesinger argued in that report that the United States required additional nuclear options to be able to respond in case of a "limited attack on military targets that caused relatively few civilian casualties." When asked in the first hearing on March 4, 1974, what he meant by "relatively few casualties," Schlesinger responded: "I am talking here about casualties of 15,000, 20,000, 25,000 . . ." (U.S. Congress, Senate Foreign Relations Committee, March, 1974; p. 26). However, he never explained where these low numbers came from.

Schlesinger was recalled by the subcommittee on September 11, 1974 for a "Briefing on Counterforce Attacks." In this hearing, he presented

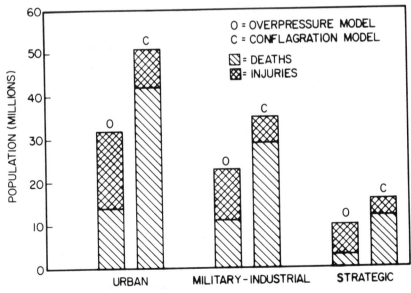

FIGURE 7 Casualties for three target sets, 100-Mt attacks.

the results of DOD calculations of hypothetical Soviet attacks on U.S. missile silos and bomber bases. Although other numbers were mentioned, he summarized the results as follows: "In an attack on the ICBMs alone, the mortalities would run on the order of a million and for SAC [bomber] bases the mortalities would be less than that—on the order of 500,000" (U.S. Congress, Senate Foreign Relations Committee, September, 1974; p. 12). He pointed out that these numbers were much smaller than the 95–100 million U.S. deaths that he believed would result from an all-out Soviet nuclear attack on the United States.

In response to a request from the Senate Foreign Relations Committee, the Congressional Office of Technology Assessment organized a panel of experts, chaired by Jerome Wiesner, then President of the Massachusetts Institute of Technology, to review the DOD casualty estimates. The panel questioned the credibility of the assumed attacks since they "were evidently not designed to maximize destruction of U.S. ICBMs and bombers. . . ." The panel also questioned the DOD assumption that "the urban population is familiar with the shelter areas available [and] that these shelters are all stocked with adequate supplies of essential material for sustaining inhabitants for 30 days." The panel suggested that the DOD analysts do additional calculations to determine the sensitivity of their results to changes in a number of the challenged assumptions. The most significant changes suggested were to assume groundbursts for the weapons attacking the missile silos, to use "pattern attacks" on the bomber bases, and to adopt a more realistic fallout shelter posture (U.S. Congress, Office of Technology Assessment, 1975; pp. 4–9).

The DOD submitted a written response on July 11, 1975. The number of deaths estimated in this report for "comprehensive attacks" on U.S. ICBM, bomber, and ballistic-missile submarine bases believed to be within Soviet capabilities ranged from 3.2 million to 16.3 million (U.S. Congress, Senate Foreign Relations Committee, 1975; p. 14). In the 10 years since this set of hearings, no other Congressional Committee has seen fit to pursue the subject further.

Description of the Attack

Table 3 summarizes our hypothetical attack on 1,215 U.S. strategic-nuclear targets. The attack involves almost 3,000 warheads with a total yield of about 1,340 Mt. This represents perhaps one-third of the warheads and one-quarter of the megatonnage carried by Soviet strategic delivery vehicles (not including reloads) (Arkin, Burrows, et al., 1985).

We have made the usual assumption that each of the 1,116 U.S. missile silos and missile launch-control centers would be struck by two 0.5-Mt warheads—the first, a low-altitude airburst, and the second, a groundburst

TABLE 3   Targets for Full Attack on U.S. Strategic Nuclear Forces[a]

Target Type	Number	Level of Attack on Each
Missile silos	1,016	0.5-Mt low airburst + 0.5-Mt groundburst
Strategic bomber and tanker bases	17 17	1-Mt groundburst + 14 0.2-Mt airbursts (pattern attack)
Nuclear navy bases	16	1-Mt airburst + 1-Mt groundburst
Nuclear weapon storage facilities	9	1-Mt airburst + 1-Mt groundburst
Missile launch control facilities	100	0.5-Mt low airburst + 0.5-Mt groundburst
National command posts (including alternate headquarters)	7	1-Mt airburst + 1-Mt groundburst (5 sites)
Early-warning radars	5	1-Mt airburst
Navy radio transmitters	10	1-Mt airburst
Strategic Air Command radio transmitters	9	1-Mt airburst + 1-Mt groundburst (2 sites)
Satellite command transmitters	9	1-Mt airburst

[a]Totals: 1,215 targets, 2,839 warheads, 1,342 Mt.

(e.g., U.S. Congress, Senate Foreign Relations Committee, 1975; p. 7). About 3,000 such warheads are carried by Soviet SS-18 intercontinental ballistic missiles (e.g., Arkin, Burrows, et al., 1985). We have assumed that the low-altitude airburst would produce one-half as much local fallout as the groundburst.

In the case of the attacks on the 34 U.S. strategic bomber and aerial refueling tanker bases, we have assumed "pattern attacks" with a number of nuclear warheads exploding in the air around the base in an effort to destroy any aircraft that have just taken off (Quanbeck and Wood, 1976; U.S. Congress, Senate Foreign Relations Committee, 1975; p. 23). We have assumed that each air base would be attacked by a 1-Mt groundburst, to destroy the runway and stored nuclear weapons, and by a pattern attack of 14 0.2-Mt airbursts. This attack would require only 102 of the Soviets' 966 submarine-based ballistic missiles (Arkin, Burrows, et al., 1985). We estimate that everyone within 13–17 km of the center of an air base under such an attack would be killed and those out to a radius of 18–19 km would be injured.

We have not included in our target set the many bases to which U.S. bombers and aerial refueling tankers would be dispersed during a crisis. During the Cuban missile crisis, U.S. strategic bombers were dispersed to 40 civilian airports—many of them near major cities (Allison, 1971;

p. 139). Inclusion of such dispersal bases on our target list would have greatly increased the number of deaths calculated for this attack.

In the case of the attacks on the 16 nuclear navy bases, we have assumed that, because of their importance, they would be targeted with two warheads each. Since submarines are quite hard targets (U.S. Defense Intelligence Agency, 1969) and some of the port facilities might be also, we have assumed a 1-Mt airburst and a 1-Mt groundburst per port. Since the nuclear weapons at the nine major nuclear weapon storage depots are stored in hardened bunkers, we have assumed that they would be subjected to the same type of attack.

The highest-priority targets for a Soviet attack on U.S. strategic nuclear forces would be their early-warning radars, their command posts, the communications links between the command posts, and the ballistic missile submarines and bombers. According to Blair (1985; p. 182), the United States has about 400 primary and secondary command communication and control targets. Of these, 100 are the missile silo launch control centers and 10 are Minuteman missiles in silos at the Whiteman missile field that are equipped with emergency radio transmitters that would be fired aloft if all other forms of communication between the command posts and the missile fields and bombers failed (Arkin and Fieldhouse, 1985). These 110 targets have already been included in the countermissile silo attack component described above. Still other targets are located at bomber bases that have also been included in the bomber targets described above. We have therefore included in our attack on U.S. strategic nuclear forces only 40 additional key command, communication, and early-warning targets:

- Seven major headquarter and alternate headquarter installations;
- Five early-warning radar installations;
- Ten key naval radio transmitters for communicating to submarines;
- Nine key Strategic Air Command (SAC) transmitters for communicating to bombers;
- Nine key terminals for communication with and control of satellites.

We assume that these 40 targets would be attacked with 1-Mt airbursts with seven exceptions:

- The White House, the Pentagon, SAC headquarters at Offut Air Base, Nebraska; Cheyenne Mountain, Colorado; and the Alternate National Military Command Center near Fort Ritchie, Md. All of these are high-priority targets, and at least three have underground command posts.
- SAC's two survivable low-frequency transmitters.

It is assumed that each of these seven targets would be attacked by a 1-Mt groundburst as well as by a 1-Mt airburst.

Fallout Casualty Model

Nuclear explosions create a great deal of short-lived radioactivity—mostly associated with fission products. We have made the standard assumption in our calculations that one-half of the yield from the attacking weapons would be from fission. In the case of airbursts, the fireball would carry this radioactivity into the upper atmosphere, from which it would slowly filter down as a rather diffuse distribution called "global fallout" over a period of months to years. In the case of an attack on so-called "hard" targets such as missile silos, which can withstand high overpressures, the nuclear weapons would have to be exploded so close to the ground that surface material would be sucked into the fireball, mixed with the vaporized bomb products, and carried by the buoyancy of the fireball into the upper atmosphere. There, much of the bomb material and surface material would condense into particles, a large fraction of which would descend to the surface again within 24 hours in an intense swath of "local fallout" downwind from the target.

Various models have been developed to describe the effect of winds in distributing this early fallout. Our calculations were done using the WSEG-10 model developed by the Weapons System Evaluation Group of the Department of Defense (Schmidt, 1975).

Our wind data base, which also comes from the Department of Defense, contains the wind speed and direction at five different altitudes on a 2-degree latitude-longitude grid for the entire Northern Hemisphere for a "typical day" of each month of the year (U.S. Defense Communications Agency, 1981).

Radiation Protection Factors

The WSEG-10 model predicts the doses that would be received by a population standing fully exposed on a perfectly flat surface. These doses must be reduced by dividing by the protection factors that account for the shielding effects of the shelters in which the population would take refuge. Wooden and brick residences have average protection factors of about 2.5 and 5, respectively (U.N. Scientific Committee on the Effects of Atomic Radiation, 1982; p. 62), and below-ground residential basements typically offer protection factors of 10–20 (Glasstone and Dolan, 1977; p. 441). We have assumed in our calculations that one-half of the population would be in shelters with effective protection factors of 3, and one-half would be in shelters with protection factors of 10.

Protection factors of more than 100 are often discussed by those who argue that the USSR (or the United States) could effectively shelter its populations from radioactive fallout in improvised shelters (e.g., Nitze,

1979; p. S10080). Such protection factors are unrealistic, however, because they assume implicitly that it would be possible for the sheltered population to stay in shelters without interruption for several weeks. Even staying inside a *perfect* radiation shield for the first 2 days and coming out thereafter for only 2 hours a day would result in a decrease in the shelter's effective protection factor from infinity to about 20. Additional radiation doses would be absorbed because, within a relatively short time, most of the population would be drinking water and eating food contaminated with radioactivity.

Population Radiation Sensitivity

The WSEG-10 model takes into account the well-known fact that mammals can survive larger cumulative doses of radiation if these doses are delivered over a longer period of time. This is done by assuming that 90 percent of the radiation damage is repairable and that this repair proceeds exponentially at a rate of 3.3 percent of the remaining unrepaired damage per day (30-day average repair time). Making this assumption, we can calculate the total unrepaired radiation dose as a function of time. At some time, as the intensity of the fallout radiation declines, the rate of biological repair will exceed that of accumulation of new damage and the total radiation damage will peak. The level of this "peak equivalent residual radiation dose" determines the probability of death. If no biological repair were assumed, the total absorbed dose out to 6 months would be 30–60 percent higher than the peak residual dose calculated by the WSEG-10 model, depending on the fallout arrival time.

Since the end of World War II, the standard assumption used in official U.S. estimates of deaths from radiation has been that, in the absence of intensive medical treatment, a 450-rad peak residual dose would cause a 50 percent fatality rate from radiation sickness within 60 days (LD_{50} = 450 rads) (Lushbaugh, 1982; pp. 46–57). However, this number is near the top of the current range of uncertainty (Lushbaugh, 1982). In 1960, Cronkite and Bond estimated that, in the absence of treatment with antibiotics and blood transfusions, the LD_{50} would be 350 rads. Their estimates were based principally on a comparison of the hematological effects of radiation on a group of Marshall Islanders, after the fallout from a U.S. nuclear test in 1954 accidentally exposed them to 175 rads, with similar hematological effects in dogs subject to radiation exposures in the laboratory. Cronkite and Bond assumed that the lethality curve for humans would be parallel to that of the dogs and estimated that human fatalities would begin at about 200 rads (Cronkite and Bond, 1958; p. 249).

Recently Rotblat analyzed the recalculated doses from Hiroshima and estimated an LD_{50} for Hiroshima of 220 rads (Rotblat, 1986). This is much lower than that estimated for the Marshallese by Cronkite and Bond. Rotblat's lower value for the people of Hiroshima may reflect synergistic effects of radiation dosage with the traumatic effects of the explosion and its aftermath. The population surviving the immediate effects of a large-scale nuclear attack on the United States would certainly also find itself under multiple stresses, including emotional shock, hunger, unsanitary conditions, and possibly exposure to cold weather. We have therefore estimated fallout deaths for an LD_{50} of 250 rads as well as for 350 and 450 rads. We approximated the associated lethality curves as straight lines parallel to the Cronkite-Bond curve (see Figure 8). Numbers of cases of severe radiation illness were estimated by assuming that *everyone* would get seriously ill from radiation sickness at radiation doses where *anyone* died.

Cancers

In addition to the short-term radiation illnesses and deaths from fallout, there would also be a large number of radiation-caused cancers in the longer term. In calculating these cancers, we use the "linear hypothesis" that the probability of developing a radiation-caused cancer is proportional to the radiation dose. According to the linear dose-effect model in the

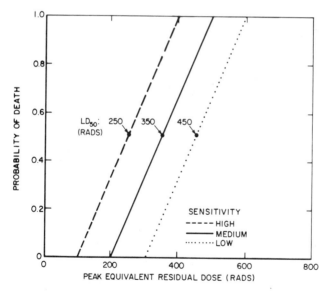

FIGURE 8   Three possible population sensitivities to ionizing radiation.

1980 report of the National Academy of Sciences' Committee on the Biological Effects of Ionizing Radiation, a radiation dose of 10^9 person-rads would result in 0.4–1.25 million extra cancers in the general population, of which 0.17–0.5 million would be fatal. (National Academy of Sciences, Committee on the Biological Effects of Ionizing Radiation, 1980.)

The cancer dose is calculated assuming no biological repair. This means that the population cancer dose would continue to increase even after radiation levels had fallen to the point where the population sheltered below ground felt that they could emerge without risk of short-term radiation illness. We assume that they might emerge at 2 weeks and that the average protection factor would be 3 thereafter for the entire population.

Ranges of Casualties Calculated for Attack on U.S. Strategic Nuclear Targets

We have calculated the fallout patterns for the attack on U.S. strategic nuclear forces described in Table 3, assuming typical February, May, August, and October winds. Figure 9 shows, as an example, the calculated pattern for typical February winds.

The large fallout patterns originate at the six Minuteman-MX missile fields, each of which would absorb the equivalent of hundreds of 0.5-Mt groundbursts. The long fallout pattern originating in mid-California is due to an attack on the 16 missile silos at Vandenburg AFB. The other smaller fallout patterns are each associated with a 1-Mt groundburst on a total of 66 bomber, aerial tanker, nuclear-navy, nuclear-weapons storage, and command and communications facilities. Three contours for the un-shielded, peak residual air-dose are shown:

- *3,500 rads.* Within this region, given an LD_{50} of 350 rads and our assumed sheltering posture (half the population with a protection factor of 10 and half with a protection factor of 3), more than three-quarters of the population would die.
- *1,050 rads.* Within this region, given an LD_{50} of 350 rads, more than half of that part of the population with an effective protection factor of 3 (i.e., one-quarter of the total population) would die.
- *300 rads.* Outside this region, given a protection factor of 3 or more, few deaths would occur from radiation illness.

To get an adequate idea of the sensitivity of our results to the monthly winds, we have also done casualty calculations for May, August, and October winds.

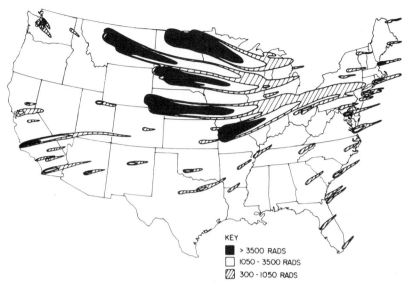

KEY
- ■ > 3500 RADS
- □ 1050 - 3500 RADS
- ▨ 300 - 1050 RADS

FIGURE 9   Fallout pattern in a February attack on U.S. strategic nuclear targets.

Table 4 shows our estimated ranges of deaths and total casualties due to blast, fire, radiation sickness, and cancer. Shown explicitly is the sensitivity of these results to the choice of blast-burn casualty model, radiation sickness LD_{50}, and cancer-risk coefficient. The ranges in each subcategory show the variation associated with the choice of winds. The range shown for the total deaths reflects the combined effect of the variability associated with the winds, the LD_{50}s, and the cancer dose-risk coefficients. Table 5 shows ranges of deaths from blast and burn and from fallout for the components of the attack. The summed total of the upper ends of the ranges of casualties calculated for these component attacks exceeds the maxima given for the total attack in Table 4. In part, this is because some of the same people would be killed by different subattacks and in part because the winds that maximize the fallout casualties from the counter-silo attack tend to minimize the fallout casualties from the other component attacks.

Overall, taking into account the different estimates associated with the two blast-burn casualty models, we find that there would be 13–34 million deaths and 25–64 million total casualties from this "counterforce" attack. Figure 10 shows how these estimates vary with low and high assumptions about casualty rates and with different months of the year.

How do we explain the fact that the lower end of our range of estimated

TABLE 4   Deaths and Total Casualties from Large-Scale Attack on U.S. Strategic-Nuclear Targets (in millions)

Blast and Fire	Radiation Illness LD$_{50}$ (rads)			Cancer Risk[a]		Total[b]
	450	350	250	Low	High	
Deaths						
Overpressure Model 7	5–6	7–8	9–14	1–3	4–8	13–28
Conflagration Model 16	4–5	6–7	8–12	1–3	3–7	20–34
Total Casualties						
Overpressure Model 14	7–9	11–16	17–29	3–6	10–20	25–63
Conflagration Model 19	7–8	10–15	15–27	2–6	9–19	28–64

[a]For the survivors of the short-term effects of blast, fire, and radiation sickness, assuming an LD$_{50}$ for radiation sickness of 350 rads. "Low" ("high") cancer risk means a probability of 0.17 (0.5) million extra cancer deaths and 0.4 (1.25) million total extra cancer cases for each 10^9 person-rads absorbed dose.

[b]The totals were added before rounding so they may differ from the sum of the individual rounded subtotals.

TABLE 5   Deaths and Total Casualties from Subcomponents of the Large-Scale Attack on U.S. Strategic-Nuclear Targets (in millions)

	Blast and Fire	Fallout[a]	Total[b]
Deaths			
Class of Target			
Missile Silos	0.1–0.2	2.2–14.9	2.4–15.0
Bomber Bases	4.2–6.7	0.5– 3.6	4.7– 9.9
Naval Bases	1.0–3.3	0.4– 4.5	1.4– 7.4
Command and Control	1.4–4.0	0.1– 2.4	1.5– 5.9
Weapons Storage	0.3–0.9	0.2– 2.3	0.5– 3.1
Total Casualties			
Class of Target			
Missile Silos	0.3–0.3	3.7–31.5	4.0–31.8
Bomber Bases	7.4–8.1	1.3– 8.6	8.9–16.0
Naval Bases	2.8–4.6	1.1–10.0	3.9–13.8
Command and Control	3.5–5.3	0.2– 4.7	3.9– 9.1
Weapons Storage	0.7–1.4	0.5– 5.8	1.2– 6.5

[a]Fallout deaths and total casualties are those from both immediate illness and long-term cancers. The low value occurs in August and the high value in February for attacks on missile silos. The reverse is true for the other target types. The results for May and October were always between these two extremes.

[b]The low and high values for the totals are not simply the sum of low and high values in the columns labeled "Blast and Fire" and "Fallout." The totals are sums of numbers corresponding to the same input assumptions.

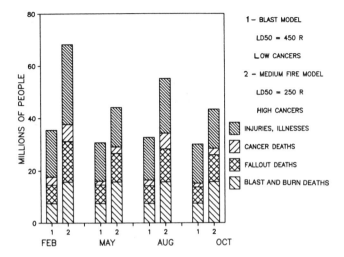

FIGURE 10   Major attack on counterforce targets. The bars labeled "1" correspond to assumptions that would cause the fewest deaths; bars labeled "2" correspond to the assumptions causing the most deaths.

deaths is approximately equal to the upper end of the range of 3.2–16.3 million deaths calculated by the DOD in 1975 for a major counterforce attack on the United States (U.S. Congress, Senate Foreign Relations Committee, 1975; pp. 12–24)?

The low end of the DOD's range of deaths is apparently associated with the optimistic sheltering posture that was criticized by the Office of Technology Assessment review panel. Using a less optimistic sheltering posture, somewhat like that used in this paper, and assuming a 550-kiloton airburst and groundburst over each silo, the DOD analysts estimated 5.6 million deaths resulting from an attack on U.S. missile silos alone (assuming March winds). This is quite close to the 4.9 million deaths that we find for February winds if we, like the DOD analysts, assume an LD_{50} of 450 rads and neglect cancer deaths.

The upper end of the DOD range of estimated deaths is associated with a sheltering posture similar to that we have used. However, the DOD analysts made a number of other assumptions that correspond roughly to those that characterize the *lower* end of our uncertainty range:

• The overpressure model was used to calculate blast and burn casualties.

• An LD_{50} of 450 rads was used for calculating the number of deaths from radiation sickness.

• Cancer deaths were ignored.

The DOD analysts *did* assume March winds for their calculations—an assumption that would tend to maximize the fallout casualties from the attacks on the missile silos. This assumption was offset, however, by their omission of most of the targets in three of the five subsets of targets considered in our attack: strategic command, communication, and early-warning facilities; nuclear storage sites; and the ports for naval ships that have recently been assigned a strategic role with the deployment of long-range, sea-launched cruise missiles. As may be seen from Table 5, these target sets account for a large fraction of the total number of deaths calculated for our counterforce attack.

As has already been noted, our own range of 13–34 million deaths and 25–64 million total casualties would be higher if we included other likely targets, such as potential bomber dispersal bases. Our casualty numbers would climb higher still if we added estimates of the numbers of deaths and illnesses from the economic and social collapse that could be expected following such an attack.

CONCLUSIONS

Some of our results show clearly the enormous casualties that only 1 percent of the current Soviet strategic arsenal could inflict on the United States, even if the targets were military-industrial or strategic rather than population per se. We have also found that, as counterforce attacks become more comprehensive, the distinction (in terms of casualties) between "counterforce" and "counterpopulation" targeting becomes increasingly blurred. We expect to find similar results for U.S. counterforce attacks on the USSR.

These casualty estimates have a critical bearing on the debate over the possibility of "limited nuclear options" as part of a strategic doctrine. Either superpower contemplating such an attack should be well aware of the fact that such attacks—even if limited to military targets—could cause casualties that approach those from all-out attacks. We emphasize this point especially because the significant underestimates in the published DOD casualty estimates for counterforce attacks suggest that U.S. policy concerning counterforce attacks is not fully realistic. Certainly this appeared to be the case during the recent debate of the "window of vulnerability" of U.S. ICBMs. Virtually no attention was given to the casualties that would result from an attack on U.S. missile silos.

Other work has shown that, even after such a devastating attack, either superpower would retain a residual capability to destroy the cities and economic infrastructure of the other many times over (e.g., Feiveson and von Hippel, 1983). And it seems likely that the other superpower—after suffering tens of millions of deaths—would launch at least as horrendous an attack in response. Therefore, the only conceivable rationale that theoretically could be used to justify a strategic counterforce attack would be the certainty that the other side had already committed itself to a major nuclear attack—a certainty that could not be achieved in the real world. It is our hope that national decision makers will develop a better understanding of the "collateral" consequences of hypothetical first strikes and of the enormous destructive capacity of the weapons that would survive. That understanding should make them less likely to seek counterforce capabilities or to fear such attacks from the other side.

REFERENCES

Air Force Magazine. May 1985. Guide to USAF Bases at Home and Abroad, pp. 170–181.

Allison, G. T. 1971. Essence of Decision: Explaining the Cuban Missile Crisis. Boston: Little, Brown.

Arkin, W. M., A. A. Burrows, R. W. Fieldhouse, T. B. Cochran, R. S. Norris, and J. I. Sands. 1985. Nuclear weapons. Pp. 41–74 in World Armaments and Disarmament: SIPRI Yearbook 1985. London and Philadelphia: Taylor and Francis.

Arkin, W. M., and R. W. Fieldhouse, 1985. Nuclear Battlefields: Global Links in the Arms Race. Appendix A. Cambridge, Mass.: Ballinger.

Ball, D. 1983. Targeting for Strategic Deterrence. Adelphi Paper no. 185. London: International Institute for Strategic Studies.

Bennett, B. 1977. Fatality Uncertainties in Limited Nuclear War. Report no. R-2218-AF. Santa Monica, Calif.: The Rand Corporation.

Blair, B. G. 1985. Strategic Command and Control. Washington, D.C.: The Brookings Institution.

Brode, H. L., and R. D. Small. 1983. Fire Damage and Strategic Targeting. Note 567. Los Angeles, Calif.: Pacific-Sierra Research Corp.

Committee for the Compilation of Materials on Damage Caused by the Atomic Bomb in Hiroshima and Nagasaki. 1981. Hiroshima and Nagasaki: The Physical, Medical, and Social Effects of the Atomic Bombings. New York: Basic Books.

Cronkite, E. P., and V. P. Bond. 1958. Acute Radiation Syndrome in Man. U.S. Armed Forces Med. J. 9:313–324.

Duffield, J., and F. von Hippel. 1984. The short-term consequences of nuclear war for civilians. Pp. 19–64 in The Environmental Effects of Nuclear War, J. London and G. F. White, eds. Boulder, Colo.: Westview Press.

Federal Emergency Management Agency. 1980. Population Grid File Tape based on 1980 Census Data (1 minute grid). Washington, D.C.: Federal Emergency Management Agency.

Feiveson, H., and F. von Hippel. 1983. The freeze and the counterforce race. Physics Today, January, p. 37.

Glasstone, S., and P. J. Dolan. 1977. The Effects of Nuclear Weapons. Washington D.C.: U.S. Departments of Defense and Energy.

Greer, D. S., and L. S. Rifkin. 1986. The Immunological Impact of Nuclear Warfare. This volume.

Haaland, C. M., C. V. Chester, and E. P. Wigner. 1976. Survival of the Relocated Population of the U.S. after a Nuclear Attack. Report no. ORNL-5041. Oak Ridge, Tenn.: Oak Ridge National Laboratory.

Harwell, M. A. 1984. Nuclear Winter: The Human and Environmental Consequences of Nuclear War. New York: Springer-Verlag.

Loewe, W. E., and E. Mendelsohn. 1982. Neutron and gamma doses at Hiroshima and Nagasaki. Nuclear Science and Engineering 81:325. See also a preliminary Los Alamos reestimate of the yield of the Hiroshima bomb as 14–16 kt. quoted in W.J. Broad, 1985.

Lushbaugh, C. C. 1982. The impact of estimates of human radiation tolerance upon radiation emergency management. Pp. 46–57 in The Control of Exposure of the Public to Ionizing Radiation in the Event of Accident or Attack. Bethesda, Md.: National Council on Radiation Protection and Measurement.

National Academy of Sciences, Committee on the Biological Effects of Ionizing Radiation. 1980. The Effects on Populations of Exposure to Low Levels of Ionizing Radiation. Washington, D.C.: National Academy Press.

Nitze, P. H. 1979. A Method for Dealing With Certain Fallout Questions. Attachment to a Prepared Statement for Presentation before the Senate Foreign Relations Committee. P. S10080. Congressional Record, July 20.

Oughterson, A. W., and S. Warren. 1956. Medical Effects of the Atomic Bomb in Japan. National Nuclear Energy Series. Atomic Energy Commission. New York: McGraw-Hill.

Postol, T. 1986. Possible Fatalities from Superfires following Nuclear Attacks in or Near Urban Areas. This volume.

Quanbeck, A. H., and A. L. Wood. 1976. Modernizing the Strategic Bomber Force: Why and How. Washington, D.C.: The Brookings Institution.

Rotblat, J. 1986. Acute Radiation Mortality in a Nuclear War. This volume.

Schmidt, L. A., Jr. 1975. Methodology of Fallout-Risk Assessment. Paper P-1065. Arlington, Va.: Institute for Defense Analyses.

Science Applications Inc. 1984. Assessment of Potential Military-Industrial Targets in CONUS (Continental United States) for Soviet Nuclear Attack.

U.N. Scientific Committee on the Effects of Atomic Radiation. 1982. Ionizing Radiation: Sources and Biological Effects. New York: United Nations.

U.S. Congress, Office of Technology Assessment. 1975. Response of the Ad Hoc Panel on Nuclear Effects, in U.S. Congress, Senate Foreign Relations Committee, Analyses of Effects of Limited Nuclear Warfare. Washington, D.C.: U.S. Government Printing Office.

U.S. Congress, Office of Technology Assessment. 1979. The Effects of Nuclear War. Washington, D.C.: U.S. Government Printing Office.

U.S. Congress, Senate Foreign Relations Committee. March 1974. J. R. Schlesinger in U.S.-U.S.S.R. Strategic Policies. Hearing before the Subcommittee on Arms Control, International Law and Organization of the U.S. Senate Committee on Foreign Relations, March 4, 1974. Washington, D.C.: U.S. Government Printing Office, 1974.

U.S. Congress, Senate Foreign Relations Committee. September 1974. J. R. Schlesinger in Briefing on Counterforce Attacks. Hearing before the Subcommittee on Arms Control, International Law and Organization of the US Senate Committee on Foreign Relations, September 11, 1974. Washington, D.C.: U.S. Government Printing Office, 1974.

U.S. Congress, Senate Foreign Relations Committee. 1975. Sensitivity of collateral damage calculations to limited nuclear war scenarios. In Analyses of Effects of Limited Nuclear Warfare. Washington, D.C.: U.S. Government Printing Office.

U.S. Defense Communications Agency. 1981. Unclassified tapes EA 275 and EB 275. Washington, D.C.: U.S. Defense Communications Agency.

U.S. Defense Intelligence Agency. 1969. Physical Vulnerability Handbook: Nuclear Weapons (AP-550-1-2-69-INT). Washington, D.C.: U.S. Defense Intelligence Agency.

Wilton, W., D. J. Myronuk, and J. V. Zaccor. 1981. Secondary Fire Analysis. Report #8084-6. Redwood City, Calif.: Scientific Service Inc.

The Medical Implications of Nuclear War, Institute of
Medicine. © 1986 by the National Academy of Sciences.
National Academy Press, Washington, D.C.

Acute Radiation Mortality in a Nuclear War

JOSEPH ROTBLAT, PH.D.
University of London, London, England

OVERVIEW

Estimates of radiation casualties in a nuclear war depend on assumptions made about the LD_{50} value in humans. In the absence of direct evidence, this value has been deduced partly from animal data and partly from a few radiation accidents, many victims of which have been receiving extensive medical treatment. The LD_{50} value thus deduced was very high, 600-rad bone marrow dose. The largest amount of data for humans—the 1945 inhabitants of Hiroshima and Nagasaki—has been rejected for a variety of reasons.

The recent reassessment of the dosimetry in the Japanese cities for long-term effects has provided an opportunity for the assessment of acute radiation effects as well. A survey carried out on a large number of people in Hiroshima, who were inside their houses during the explosion, contains information about dates of deaths at various distances from the hypocenter. It is suggested in the paper that this survey is highly suitable material for an estimate of radiation casualties under wartime conditions.

A detailed analysis of the mortality as a function of time of death and distance from the hypocenter has been carried out with the aim of proving that, after the first day, the mortality was due predominantly to radiation exposure. The distance at which 50 percent mortality occurred has been deduced from this analysis and found to be 892 ± 11 meters.

To convert this to an LD_{50} one needs to know the intensity of the radiation field as a function of distance, the transmission factors for Japanese-style houses, and the organ factor. All these quantities have been the subject of detailed studies by a U.S.-Japan Workshop. Although the final values are yet to be agreed upon, it is unlikely that they will differ significantly from those presented so far. Using these data, a probit of mortality versus bone marrow dose was obtained, which showed that the bone marrow LD_{50} for the Hiroshima survey was only 154 rads (220 rads at body surface). The slope of the line is several times smaller for humans than for animals.

The implications of these findings on the number of radiation casualties in a nuclear war are discussed.

*   *   *

In this paper the basis for calculations of casualties from acute effects of radiation in a nuclear war, which may result in death within 60 days after exposure, is discussed. The time of death after whole body exposure is a function of dose; the general trend of this function, compiled mainly from mammalian data,[1] is shown in Figure 1.

At very high doses death may occur within hours, but with decreasing dose, the time of death is extended to weeks. Down to a dose of the order of 1,000 rads mortality is 100 percent. At lower doses, where the hemopoietic syndrome is relevant, there is an increasing chance of survival. In this dose range the probability of death is a sigmoid function of the dose that reaches the bone marrow, and is best examined by probit analysis or by using special probability paper (Figure 2) with the dose plotted logarithmically. (This particular curve is the result of experiments with SAS/4 mice, carried out over many years by Lindop and Rotblat.[2] I will make frequent use of these results when comparing various effects in mice with those in humans.) The sigmoid curve is then transformed into a linear relation, yielding two characteristic values: the LD_{50} (the dose that causes 50 percent mortality in the population exposed to it) and the slope. The remarkable steepness of the line means that estimates of radiation casualties are very sensitive to the LD_{50}. An error of 30 percent in the LD_{50} can make all the difference between practically 100 percent survival and practically 100 percent mortality. It will be shown later that for humans the line is less steep, but the LD_{50} is still the best statistic for an estimate of casualties.

The problem is that while there are plenty of such data for animals, there are practically none for humans. Early data from a group of patients with cancer,[3] which indicated an LD_{50} in bone marrow of about 250 rads, were dismissed as not being applicable to the general population. The estimate of the LD_{50} in humans is based mainly on the very small number of people exposed to radiation in accidents. Most of these victims received

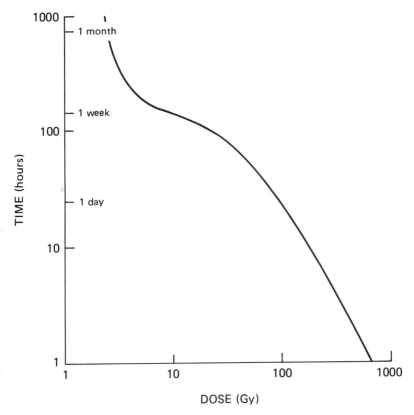

FIGURE 1   Time of occurrence of death from acute radiation effects. Note that both axes have logarithmic scales (1 Gy = 100 rad).

intensive medical treatment, including barrier nursing, antibiotics, platelet and red blood cell concentrates, and bone marrow transplants.[4] Although it is well known that such treatment enables people to survive very high doses, nevertheless, it is being assumed that this does not affect the LD_{50}. In the United Kingdom an effective LD_{50} of 600 rads to bone marrow— deduced mainly from the people exposed to radiation in accidents—is being used to estimate radiation casualties in a nuclear war.[5]

In Hiroshima and Nagasaki a large number of people were exposed to radiation under wartime conditions, but these data have not been used because of the alleged difficulty in separating mortalities caused by radiation from those caused by blast or heat.[6] However, recent surveys carried out in Japan in connection with the reassessment of the dosimetry for long-term effects provided an opportunity for another look at the acute effects of radiation. The World Health Organization—which carried out

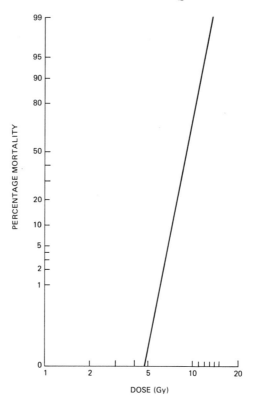

FIGURE 2   Probability of death as a function of dose, for SAS/4 mice.

a study of the effects of thermonuclear war[7]—has requested that two Japanese teams undertake such studies. These are still in progress, but the team directed by T. Ohkita has produced data which form the basis for this paper. I should stress that while the data are those of Ohkita and coworkers, they are not responsible for the analysis that I have carried out.

The data come from a survey of people in Hiroshima (to my knowledge no such survey is as yet available for Nagasaki) who were shielded inside Japanese-style houses during the atom bomb explosion. The houses were at distances from the hypocenter that varied from less than 600 meters to 1,300 meters. There were a total of 1,216 people in the houses that were surveyed, of whom 451 died during the first day and 201 (26 percent of those surviving the first day) died during the following 2 months. The tabulated data give the number of people that died each day at various distances, in 100-meter intervals.

My thesis is that the deaths that occurred after the first day were predominantly due to radiation exposure and, therefore, that the data obtained from this survey are suitable for an estimate of the LD_{50} in humans under conditions of a nuclear war. The evidence for this is based on an analysis of mortality as a function of time and distance, which shows that the observed mortality is in much better accord with radiation exposure than with other causes of death.

First, the time factor will be examined. Figure 3 shows the mortality in 4-day intervals as a function of time after the explosion. It is expressed as the percentage of the total number of people in the survey who died during 2 months, starting from the second day after the explosion. The histogram shows that there was initially an increase in mortality, which—after peaking at about 10 days—gradually decreased. This is not the result that would be expected for deaths from blast injuries or burns. A survey by Masuyama[8] has shown that after the first day, the cumulative mortality—mostly in people caught in the open—was increasing according to an exponential law, with a half-value of 6 days. From Masuyama's

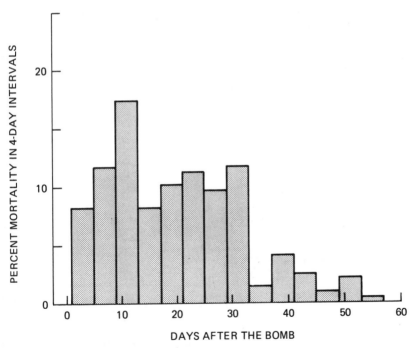

FIGURE 3   Percent mortality, in 4-day intervals, as a function of time after the Hiroshima explosion, starting from the second day.

curve, it can be calculated how the percent mortality, in 4-day intervals, would vary with time. As the curve in Figure 4 shows, this variation is quite different from the findings in the survey of the people in houses (histogram). By contrast, closer agreement is obtained with radiation exposures. In the absence of data from humans, data from animal experiments must be used. The histogram in Figure 5 shows the percent mortality observed in mice exposed to a range of doses on both sides of the LD_{50}. Here the time interval is 2 days instead of 4, because in small mammals

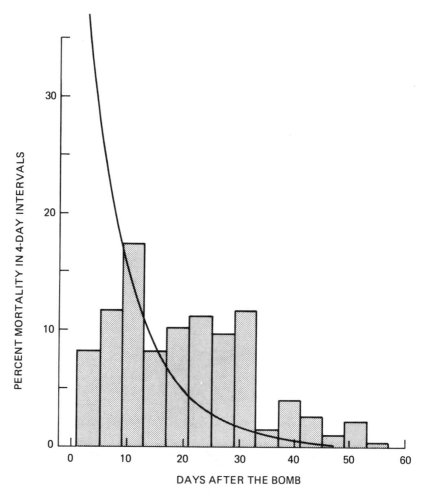

FIGURE 4 Calculated percent mortality, in 4-day intervals, starting from the second day, for all victims of the Hiroshima explosion. The histogram is for the survey group (the same as in Figure 3).

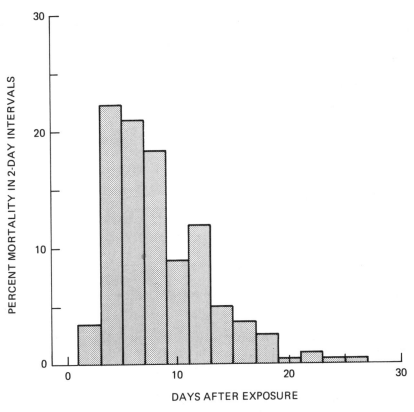

FIGURE 5   Percent mortality in 2-day intervals, for SAS/4 mice, exposed to a range of doses on both sides of the LD_{50}.

death occurs over 30 days, instead of over 60 days as in larger mammals. The resemblance of the data to those from the Hiroshima survey (Figure 3) is quite good.

Another way of looking at the time distribution is to calculate the mean survival time of a population exposed to a given dose. As shown in Figure 1, at high doses the time of death depends very much on the dose, but such dependence—albeit smaller—also occurs in the LD_{50} region. The lower line in Figure 6 shows the variation of the mean survival time, in days, as a function of dose, for mice. In order to compare the data obtained from mice with those from humans, the dose is expressed as the proportion of the LD_{50}. The upper line shows this dependence for the Hiroshima survey. Taking into account the difference in time of death, as explained above, the similarity between the results is striking.

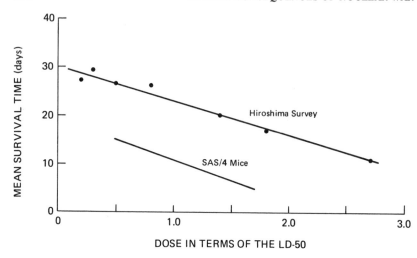

FIGURE 6   Mean survival time as a function of dose expressed in terms of the LD_{50}. The upper line is for the Hiroshima survey group. (The doses at the relevant distances were taken from Figure 13.) The lower line is for SAS/4 mice.

Yet another time dependence of interest is the LD_{50} calculated for a population surviving a given time. In Figure 7 the distance at which 50 percent of the exposed people died is plotted against the day in August 1945 from which the calculation of the mortality was started. For example, the first point (50 percent mortality distance = 1,022 meters) was calculated for all 1,216 people in the survey. For the second point, on August 7, the 50 percent mortality distance of 892 meters was obtained from the 765 people who survived after the first day, and so on. The notable feature of this graph is the very steep drop after the first day, after which the 50 percent mortality distance remains practically steady and then decreases gradually (indicating a gradual increase in the LD_{50}). The shape of the curve after the first day is as would be expected for radiation mortality. Indeed, the top graph, obtained from the data from mice, shows exactly the same behavior: the LD_{50}, calculated for consecutive days, changes little initially and then gradually increases.

The second evidence for the suitability of the survey data to calculate the LD_{50} comes from the analysis of mortality versus distance. In a recent paper, Ohkita[9] presented data (Figure 8) for the whole population in Hiroshima (both in the open and inside houses during the explosion) in terms of the daily mortality rate against distance at various time periods after the explosion. The earlier time periods show a two-component decrease, which Ohkita interprets to be due to the difference between radiation and other fatal casualties. The smaller slope must be due to the latter because the mortality extends beyond the distance at which the gamma rays from the bomb were significant. In Figure 9, line A is a reproduction of Ohkita's data for the period from 7 to 14 days after the bomb. Line B shows the data from the survey group. The notable difference between the two lines is to be expected, if it is assumed that line B gives the mortality predominantly due to radiation and that line A represents deaths from a mixture of radiation and other causes, with the latter being predominant.

A similar but more direct result is obtained by plotting the probit of mortality found in the survey group against the distance from the hypocenter. Figure 10 shows the probit for mortality during day 1, and Figure

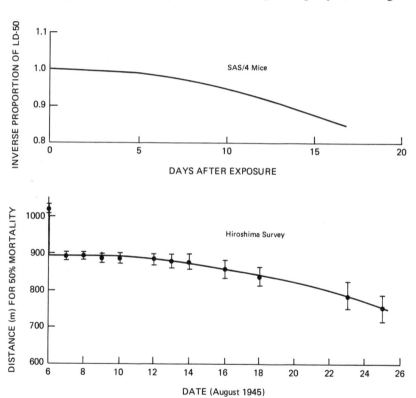

FIGURE 7 Lower curve: Distance from the hypocenter at which a 50 percent mortality occurred in the people from the Hiroshima survey group who were alive on the date shown on the horizontal scale. Upper curve: Similar plot for SAS/4 mice, but with the vertical scale giving the LD_{50} in terms of its value for the initial population. Note that the relative dose increases downward.

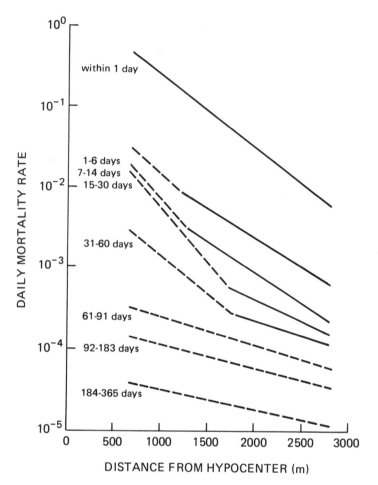

FIGURE 8   Average daily mortality rates for various periods as a function of distance from the hypocenter based on a 1946 survey in Hiroshima (data from T. Ohkita[9]).

11 shows the probit for mortality during the subsequent 2 months. The slope of the latter is 2.2 times greater; therefore, I submit that Figure 11 represents a true regression line for radiation exposure in Hiroshima. The good fit enables the determination, with great accuracy, of the distance from the hypocenter at which there was a 50 percent mortality. This distance is 892 ± 11 meters.

The next step is to convert this distance to dose, and here there is a snag. The necessary parameters for the conversion are: the variation of

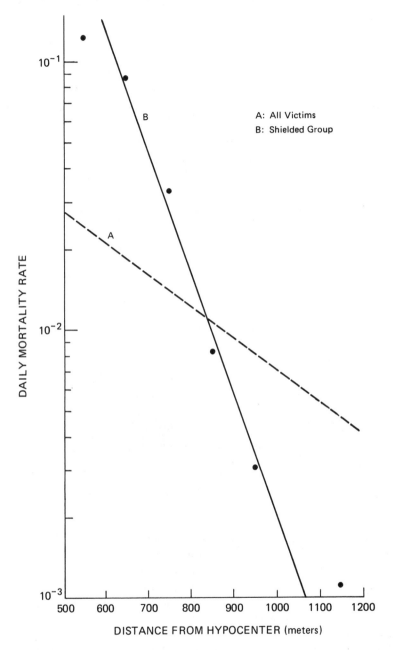

FIGURE 9   Line A: Data from Figure 8 for the interval from 7 to 14 days after the bomb. Line B: The same data for the group in the Hiroshima survey.

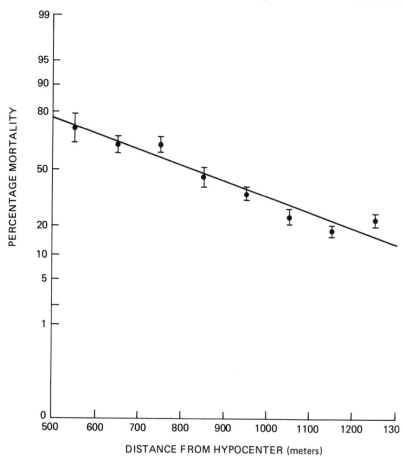

FIGURE 10   Probability of death as a function of distance from the hypocenter for the people in the survey group who died on the first day. The bars denote ± 1 standard deviation.

tissue kerma in air (a measure of the intensity of a radiation field, in rads) with distance; the transmission factor for buildings; and the organ factor, that is, the fraction of the dose that reaches the bone marrow. All these parameters have undergone considerable revision recently in the U.S.-Japan Joint Workshop for the Reassessment of Atomic Bomb Radiation Dosimetry. The last workshop meeting, held in Pasadena, California, in March 1985, was supposed to come up with final figures, but they will not be available until the end of 1986. However, the calculations yet to be made are not likely to bring significant changes. Therefore, I will use the most recent data available. The data by Kerr et al.[10] from Oak Ridge

National Laboratory on tissue kerma are reproduced in Figure 12. It shows the different gamma-ray components, as well as the neutron component. The greatly reduced neutron contribution resulted in a large reduction of the transmission factors for Japanese-style houses.

By applying the appropriate values,[11] one can calculate the contribution of the various components to the LD_{50}. As is seen from Table 1, the LD_{50} turns out to be 154 rads. (In this calculation the relative biological effectiveness of neutrons was assumed to be 1.)

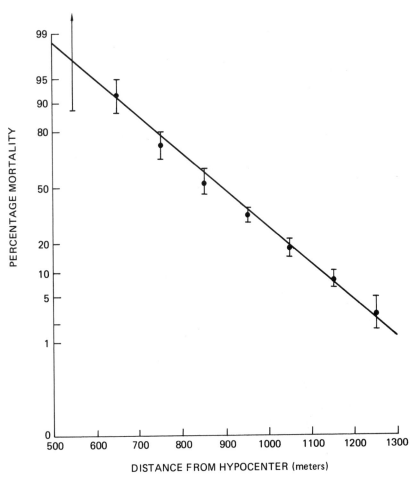

FIGURE 11   Probability of death as a function of distance from the hypocenter for people in the Hiroshima survey group who died from day 2 to 2 months after the explosion.

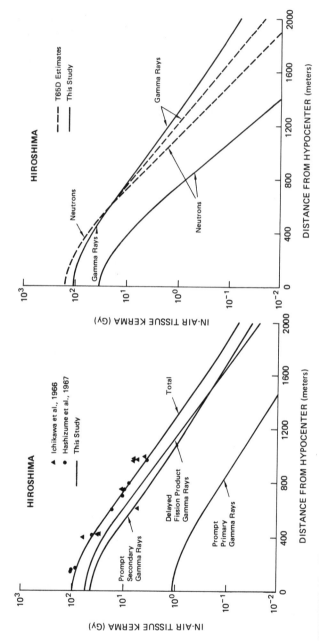

FIGURE 12   Kerma versus distance for the various components of the radiation in Hiroshima (data from Kerr et al.[10]). Note that the doses are in grays (1 Gy = 100 rad).

TABLE 1   Calculation of the LD_{50} for a distance of 892 meters

Radiation	Kerma (rad)	Dose (rad) after Transmission through Buildings	Organ Dose (rad)[a]
Delayed gamma rays	294	106	74
Prompt gamma rays	200	92	74
Primary gamma rays	9	4	3
Neutrons	33	12	3

[a]Total, 154 rad.

Similar calculations for other distances establish the relationship between dose and distance (Figure 13). It fits excellently a straight line on a logarithmic scale of dose. By using this graph, the regression line can be redrawn to give the probit as a function of dose (Figure 14).

Apart from the very low LD_{50}, another interesting feature is the small slope of the line obtained for humans, compared with that obtained for mice (Figure 2). The coefficient of variation, i.e., the ratio of the gradient of the probit line to the LD_{50} value, is nearly 5 times smaller for humans than for mice. This coefficient depends on several factors, including the homogeneity of the population. A smaller coefficient is to be expected when a highly homogeneous population, like the purebred strain of mice, is compared with a highly heterogeneous population, like humans.

Before the LD_{50} can be applied to an estimate of radiation casualties in a nuclear war, two more points must be considered. One is that the exposure to radiation in Hiroshima was practically instantaneous, while that from fallout is spread out over hours or days. Since there are no directly relevant data from humans, data from animal experiments must be used. From data presented in the literature[12] it can be inferred that, in larger mammals, if the same dose were delivered at a constant dose rate over 24 hours, the LD_{50} would be increased by about 40 percent. However, in the case of fallout the dose rate is not constant; it decreases rapidly. Calculations show that for a fallout dose received in 24 hours, the LD_{50} would be increased by about 10 percent.

The second point is that in fallout calculations, the dose at the surface of the body and not to the bone marrow is usually calculated, as was the LD_{50} of 154 rads presented above. Therefore, this value must be divided by the organ factor, which probably lies between 0.75 and 0.8. This would give an LD_{50} at the surface of the body of about 220 rads.

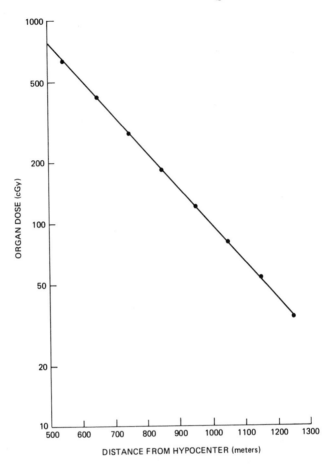

FIGURE 13   Bone marrow dose versus distance from hypocenter in the Hiro-shima survey group.

How many radiation casualties would result from such a low LD_{50}? In a recent paper, Lindop et al.[13] investigated the sensitivity of radiation casualty estimates to the assumed value of the LD_{50}. For a single 1-megaton bomb over London, the number of fatalities was calculated for LD_{50}'s that varied from 300 to 800 rads and for protection factors (the ratios of the doses received in the open to those received inside buildings or in shelters) between 1 and 20. Although these calculations covered a large range of doses, the number of fatalities (N) can be expressed by the following simple empirical formula: $N = 4 \times 10^6 (PD)^{-2/3}$, where P is the protection factor and D is the LD_{50}. According to this formula, a reduction of the LD_{50} from 600 rads to 150 rads would increase the number of fatalities by a factor of 2.5. At an average protection factor of 5, this would mean an increase in the number of radiation deaths by more than half a million—just from one bomb.

However, as we pointed out in that paper,[13] under wartime conditions, even exposure to sublethal doses could give rise to fatalities, because the suppression of the immune system would reduce the chance of recovery from other normally nonlethal injuries; indeed, the interactions may be synergistic. It has been suggested[13] that any exposure above 100 rads should be considered a radiation injury. This would make the total fatalities, direct and indirect, less dependent on the LD_{50}.

In another paper presented in this volume, Greer and Rifkin listed several conditions that may impair the immune response. Apart from exposure to radiation, they include physical trauma, burns, and malnutrition. This last condition may explain the low LD_{50} in Hiroshima, since there is evidence that the people in Hiroshima were undernourished both

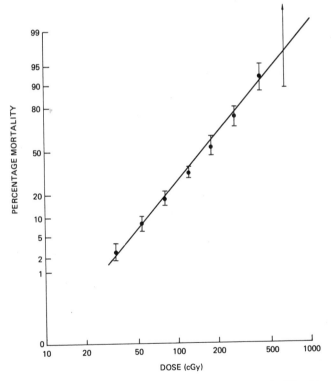

FIGURE 14   Percent mortality versus bone marrow dose in the Hiroshima survey group.

before and after the bomb.[14] By the same token, the other conditions mentioned by Greer and Rifkin—if confirmed—would reduce the LD_{50} in wartime, even without the malnutrition factor.

In conclusion, it must be stressed that although it is now fairly certain that the LD_{50} in humans is considerably lower than was thought before, at least under wartime conditions, the actual values, and therefore the estimates of radiation casualties in a nuclear war, are still uncertain. While final calculations must be deferred until the new dosimetry has been firmly established, it is fair to conclude that estimates of radiation casualties previously thought to lie at the upper end of the range have now shifted to the region of probable.

NOTES

[1]Bond, V. P., T. M. Fliedner, and J. O. Archambeau. 1965. Mammalian Radiation Lethality: A Disturbance in Cellular Kinetics. New York: Academic Press.

[2]Lindop, P. J., and J. Rotblat. 1960. Protection against acute effects of radiation by hypoxia. Nature 185:593–594 (and unpublished data from subsequent experiments).

[3]Lushbaugh, C. C. 1974. Human radiation tolerance. Pp. 475–522 in Space Radiation Biology and Related Topics, C. A. Tobias and P. Todd, eds. New York: Academic Press.

[4]Hübner, K. F., and S. A. Fry. 1980. The Medical Basis for Radiation Accident Preparedness. New York: Elsevier.

[5]Martin, J. H. 1983. Human survival-radiation exposure levels. J. Soc. Radiol. Prot. 3:15–23.

[6]Adams, G. E. 1984. Lethality from acute and protracted radiation exposure in man. Int. J. Rad. Biol. 46:209–217.

[7]World Health Organization. 1984. Effects of Nuclear War on Health and Health Services. Geneva: World Health Organization.

[8]Masuyama, M. 1953. Statistical study of human casualties of the atomic bomb, especially of the death rate in the acute stage (quoted by T. Ohkita in Immediate Effects, 1985, Hiroshima ENUWAR Workshop).

[9]Ohkita, T. 1985. Immediate Effects, in Lessons from Hiroshima and Nagasaki. Hiroshima ENUWAR Workshop.

[10]Kerr, G. D., J. V. Pace, and W. H. Scott. 1983. Tissue kerma vs. distance relationship for initial nuclear radiation from the atomic bombs Hiroshima and Nagasaki. Pp. 57–103 in U.S.-Japan Joint Workshop for Reassessment of Atomic Bomb Radiation Dosimetry in Hiroshima and Nagasaki. Radiation Effects Research Foundation. February 1983.

[11]Ellett, W. H., and T. Maruyama. 1983. Shielding and organ dosimetry. Pp. 83–101 in U.S.-Japan Joint Workshop for Reassessment of Atomic Bomb Radiation Dosimetry in Hiroshima and Nagasaki. Radiation Effects Research Foundation. November 1983.

[12]Page, N. P. 1968. The effect of dose-protraction on radiation lethality of large animals. Pp. 12.1–12.23 in Proceedings of a Symposium on Dose Rate in Mammalian Radiation Biology. USAEC CONF 680410.

[13]Lindop, P. J., J. Rotblat, and P. Webber. 1985. Radiation casualties in a nuclear war. Nature 313:345–346.

[14]Committee for the Compilation of Materials on Damage Caused by the Bombs in Hiroshima and Nagasaki. 1981. Hiroshima and Nagasaki: The Physical, Medical and Social Effects of the Atomic Bombing. Hutchinson: London.

The Medical Implications of Nuclear War, Institute of
Medicine. © 1986 by the National Academy of Sciences.
National Academy Press, Washington, D.C.

Burn and Blast Casualties:
Triage in Nuclear War

JENNIFER LEANING, M.D.
Harvard Community Health Plan, Boston, Massachusetts

THE CONCEPT OF TRIAGE

During the last century, events creating large numbers of casualties
have, with infrequent but depressing repetition, absorbed the attention of
the world community. In these years, nations have increased to sufficient
population densities and have developed technologies of sufficient power
to create the conditions for sudden catastrophe, whereby in a relatively
brief time span an enormous number of people may be killed or injured.
When discussing nuclear war, reference to precedent may admit sources
of serious error, since in terms of scale of effects, this disaster would
depart fundamentally from anything the world has yet experienced. Yet
people still struggle to comprehend what nuclear war might mean, if only
to give better warning now. As part of this attempt to make real the
unimaginable, it is instructive to inquire into how massive numbers of
casualties have been managed in the past. The perspective taken here is
the organization of medical response. Wars and major civilian disasters
provide the context and the time frame dates from the U.S. Civil War.

The current theory of mass casualty management rests on the concept
of triage, according to which casualties are sorted into categories by
severity of injury and treatment plans assigned to each based on assessment
of transport availability and resources. The word is said to derive from
the French *triage*, meaning the process of sorting by quality, and its use
in the wool and coffee trades during the eighteenth and nineteenth centuries
carried the distinct connotation of separating higher from lower quality.[1]
Although the process of prioritizing military casualties on the basis of

251

wound severity has been traced to Baron Dominique Jean Larrey, surgeon in chief of Napoleon's Russian Campaign,[2] the term *triage* was first applied in this context during World War I.[3] The British Expeditionary Force used *triage* to mean *division into three*: those who could withstand travel back from the front, those who required immediate surgery, and those whose injuries were so severe that they would be left to die.[4] The U.S. military command currently prefers the term *sorting*, but in all other respects relies on the concept of triage in its protocols for mass casualty management.[5]

The principle of sorting casualties into categories carries both technical and ethical complexities. To sort is to assign value, according to a system that may or may not be explicit. In modern casualty medicine, this system must also respect the issue of time. Medical understanding and skill have advanced to the point at which salvage of the severely injured can be accomplished if intervention proceeds within 6 to 8 hours.[6] In settings in which resources are ample and accessible, the act of triage devolves into a straightforward organizing technique. For the sake of clarity and efficiency, the most severely injured get treated first, and the less severely injured get treated second. All casualties are assured of rapid assessment and appropriate disposition; all are assured of receiving the best care in adequate time. The triage technique requires experience and skill, and consequently, in well-designed mass casualty systems, it is the most seasoned medical officer who takes on this task.[7]

Ethical issues intrude in settings of relative resource scarcity, which often pertain to mass casualty situations. The code of ethics for physicians, which has evolved over centuries, squarely assigns to the physician the responsibility of protecting the interests of the individual patient in all situations. The physician is enjoined to refrain from a calculus that incorporates any consideration other than the patient's well-being.[8] When resources are perceived as scarce, however, other social or institutional values weigh in and attempt to influence physician choice and behavior. In peacetime, as technology has offered technically feasible but expensive possibilities for individual salvage, society has begun to debate cost-benefit ratios in health care, a discussion fraught with ethical complexity for physicians as practitioners and for society as a whole.[9] In mass casualty situations, triage decisions provide ample opportunities for ethical analyses that lie outside the scope of this discussion. In the absence of an explicit ethical code for physicians in settings in which need has far outstripped the available capacity to respond, it has become accepted practice to assign top priority to those who, without intervention, would otherwise die.[10] All other casualties, who would live despite initial delay in transport or treatment, are relegated to lower-priority categories. Those who would die regardless of treatment are assigned to the category of lowest priority.[11]

The underlying principle at work is to provide the greatest good, defined as life, for the greatest number, defined as all casualties.[12] According to this principle, it is unsound medical practice to devote time and resources to someone whose chances of living in any case are minimal, at the cost of losing the lives of some who could very well be salvaged.

The principle of maximizing the number of lives that can be saved, although axiomatic to those in emergency and trauma medicine, in actual situations translates into some exceedingly difficult ethical decisions. The process can succinctly be illustrated as follows:

Typically, a hospital with only a limited supply of blood on hand and with little likelihood of more becoming available in the near future will use that blood so as to aid in the recovery of the largest number of injured. On this basis, the critically wounded man who would require all of the only 10 units of blood available in order to aid in his possible recovery would drop in priority to a position below that of the five casualties whose recovery would be assured by the receipt of 2 units each. Conversely, where only 2 units of blood are on hand to treat the shock of 10 casualties, the best utilization of this item would entail using it in the resuscitation of no more than one or two of these casualties rather than wasting it by giving each only 1/5 unit.[13]

The process of sorting according to this principle of extending life to the largest number of people, as much as it is at a variance with the ethical approach of the individual physician to his or her individual patient, has come to be accepted by both the profession and society in general when it is invoked in settings of plenty, to sort for the sake of efficiency, and in settings of scarcity, to sort so that the greatest number of casualties may survive.

Triage during wartime conforms to a different principle. As a particular and relatively modern aspect of military medicine, the concept of triage reflects the interest of the military leadership in maximizing the fighting capacity of the force.[14] Sorting of casualties appears to date from the era of standing armies, during which, from the perspective of military efficiency, casualties were seen, first, as encumbrances.[15] During the wars of the seventeenth and eighteenth centuries, this interest of the military command extended to identifying those too injured to continue fighting and removing them from the path of the advancing or retreating armies.[16] Although over the centuries the record abounds with examples of the ways in which military administrators and individuals and groups within the physician and religious communities participated in preventive and rehabilitative care of the soldier,[17] the injection of a more humane spirit in the systematic approach to casualties took the influence of several factors that were at work in the nineteenth century.

During this period, significant sections of civilian elites witnessed the battlefield horrors at the Crimean and U.S. Civil wars. Their outcry and subsequent efforts contributed greatly to the transport and resource systems that supported military medicine in World War I.[18] Second, developments in weapons technology began to inflict an increasingly high proportion of injuries at a time when engagements were still decided by how many soldiers were on the field. The military began to place a premium on returning the maximum number of soldiers to active duty as soon as possible. For all conventional wars in the twentieth century and in current North Atlantic Treaty Organization (NATO) protocols for nuclear war, this same instruction has been given to military physicians.[19] The third factor in the shift from getting rid of the wounded to returning them to battle has been progress in medical skill and knowledge. Especially since the latter part of World War II, military physicians have had at their command a significant range of techniques and interventions that can markedly alter the morbidity and mortality of casualties from conventional war.[20] It has been precisely during this time frame that the dilemma for military physicians has been the most intense: equipped with the skills to save the severely injured, in the setting of resource scarcity physicians are constrained by military guidelines not to carry out triage according to salvage of life but according to salvage of fighting capacity. As General Patton is said to have enjoined a group of medical officers in Casablanca in 1943:

If you have two wounded soldiers, one with a gunshot wound of the lung, and the other with an arm or leg blown off, you save the s.o.b. with the lung wound and let the g.d.s.o.b. with an amputated arm or leg go to hell. He is no g.d. use to us anymore.[21]

The dilemmas for the military physician in a mass casualty situation, in which he or she is asked to function as a triage officer, structured according to the military principle of maximizing the fighting force, are not directly addressed in the Geneva Conventions of 1949, which affirm even in time of war the physician's personal responsibility for the care of the individual patient and define the limits within which a military or political bureaucracy can intrude upon that obligation.[22] The World Medical Association in 1956 prepared a statement on the code of ethics for physicians in wartime, referring obliquely to this triage dilemma, by rejecting all forms of distinction among patients ''except those justified by medical urgency. . . .''[23]

The ethical questions involved in military triage become even more complex as weapons of mass destruction threaten to engulf the civilian noncombatant population as well as the military force. The military, with some support from civilians within the medical ethics community,[24] has a clear point of view. In mass casualty settings involving both civilians and soldiers, the role of the military medical officer is to concentrate first on the combatant military force.[25] The NATO field manual on emergency war surgery devotes several pages to careful explication of this principle, concluding:

Even in the thermonuclear age, however, the basic principle of military medicine remains unchanged. It is, as it has always been, the salvage of the greatest possible number of lives for the support of the military mission.[26]

In this regard the Geneva Conventions are also silent, perhaps not anticipating the extent to which military war might extend to mass civilian catastrophe.

EXPERIENCE WITH MASS CASUALTY MANAGEMENT

Triage protocols have defined the organization of medical management of mass casualties by framing the problem in terms of where to do what to whom when. The actual details of how medical response is mobilized and how the outcome is achieved have always had to conform to two key variables defined by the existing situation: available modes of transportation and relative reserves of resources. A brief account of military management of mass casualty medicine during the last 150 years demonstrates the increasing capacity of the medical profession to manage the care of large numbers of injured people and illuminates the ways in which the variables of field conditions and resources have always imposed limits on medical response and shaped triage protocols.

The record also reveals the paradoxical effects of technology. As the weapons of war have been perfected to inflict a wider variety and proportionately greater number of battlefield casualties, the innovations in response (transport, facilities, understanding, skill) have not only more than kept pace but have in fact occurred in large part because of the challenge of war. The management of complex medical and surgical problems has taken quantum leaps during and after each war of the twentieth century, and the tenets of civilian mass casualty medicine derive directly from this military experience. Since the last world conflict, the technology of war has taken another quantum leap, raising again the question of medical response. The medical community has evolved, as will be discussed, a serviceable system for what has been encountered in the past. The issue is how it would fare in the setting of nuclear war. In tracing the development of mass casualty medicine, I outline here a history that may or may not prepare us to meet the possible near future.

The U.S. Civil War

In the early years of the U.S. Civil War, a principal problem in treating the wounded was getting to them. Neither the North nor the South had developed transport systems for the retrieval of battle casualties, yet the new rifles and artillery used during this war exacted an unprecedented toll.[27] Contributing to the increased destructive power of the infantry on both sides were the breech-loading magazine rifles and the Minié rifled bullet, accurate to 500 yards (which replaced muzzle-loading flintlock rifles with accuracy only up to 200 yards), and the widespread heavy use of artillery batteries comprised of 6-pounder bronze guns and 12-pounder bronze howitzers. Cavalry charges and bayonet warfare slipped into the past.[28]

After the Second Battle of Bull Run (August 29–30, 1862), the fields were strewn with the dead and injured: 1,747 killed and 8,452 wounded on the Union side; 1,481 killed and 7,627 wounded on the Confederate side.[29] Despite substantial improvement in transport services since the First Battle of Bull Run almost a year earlier, the casualties from this engagement lay on the field for days. At both these battles, outraged civilians organized cavalcades of volunteers from adjacent towns to go in with wagon trains, gather up the wounded who were still alive, and bring them to whatever hospitals were available. In response to public pressure, Dr. Jonathan Letterman was appointed Medical Director of the Army of the Potomac and by 1864 had organized an ambulance corps for the entire Union Army, providing each regiment with four horse-drawn wagon ambulances and drivers. The South could not marshall the resources to support such a system, which, even at its best, was routed or overwhelmed by the heaviest battles of the war.[30]

Delivery of care was also impeded by available resources. Organizing an effective medical response during the Civil War was complicated by the fact that the lines of battle moved rapidly and unpredictably. The establishment of a secure forward medical station was fraught with hazard. Yet it was found that carrying casualties by horse-drawn wagon or cart to field hospitals 5 to 10 miles distant from the front inflicted great hardship on all casualties and increased morbidity and mortality.[31] In this setting, the heroic battlefield interventions attributed to Clara Barton and others make much medical sense.[32] It has become a standard of mass casualty medicine that the more distant and inaccessible the site for definitive care, the more extensive must be the on-site treatment.

It was apparent even to the medical providers at the time that although it was important to remove casualties from the battlefield in order to be able to care for them, and although it was prudent to remove them beyond the reach of the next day's front line, subsequent questions about where to do what had no clear answers. The field hospitals were poorly equipped, the physicians lacked knowledge, if not experience, and the rear hospitals, whether Union or Confederate, offered little more technological or material support than whatever the armies could drag with them.[33] The role of the military physician in the Civil War, and in other wars waged with similar technologies and supported by similar levels of medical understanding, acquired at best a humanitarian function. There were so few technically effective interventions known to physicians that removing the wounded from cold damp fields and placing them in bed, giving them food and water, and administering whiskey and morphine constituted the essence of appropriate treatment. Whatever else physicians attempted (amputations, applications of poultices and liniments, experimental explorations under ether or chloroform) were as likely to add to patient morbidity as to detract from it. Deep wounds of the thigh with fracture of the femur carried fatality rates of 50 percent if not treated, and 34–70 percent if treated.[34] Abdominal wounds were usually fatal and were found in about one-tenth of those dying on the field.[35] Those with upper limb and superficial scalp wounds were most likely to survive, perhaps chiefly because they could walk off the battlefield and seek help on their own.[36] An authoritative summary of military casualties from the Civil War suggests that on both sides as many soldiers died from their wounds as were killed outright,[37] a ratio that is difficult to compare with modern statistics because of the delay that transport conditions introduced between the time of injury and the time of treatment. The Civil War data do show, however, that death from disease was more than double the overall mortality from battlefield wounds.[38] Inpatient mortality from local wound infection ranged from 40 to 60 percent; if bacteremia ensued, mortality was virtually assured.[39] Of those who developed tetanus in the hospital, 89 percent died.[40] Poor water, inadequate hygiene, overcrowding, and malnutrition, all of which are factors that defined the hospital environments at field and rear echelons, also proved major determinants of outcome among hospitalized casualties.[41]

World War I

During World War I, innovations in transport and treatment at a forward medical station created conditions for developing distinct stages in the management of battle casualties. The advent of motorized ambulances (drawn out of the Letterman tradition and used first by the British during the Boer War) permitted the rapid removal of casualties from the initial triage site, the Regimental Aid Post, to the casualty clearing station (CCS). Situated within a few miles of the front line, the CCS afforded medical personnel an enclosed, moderately well-equipped, rudimentary hospital which, by design, could be swiftly packed up and moved if the tactical situation required immediate retreat.[42] As it turned out, however, this mobility was unnecessary because the front lines in World War I proved relentlessly stable. Innovations in artillery (quick-firing, nonrecoiling cartridges with ranges up to 3,000 yards) inflicted enormous numbers of casualties[43] (60,000 British were killed or wounded in the first day of the Battle of the Somme).[44] These weapons were supplemented by the perfected magazine rifle, which was accurate up to 2,000 yards, and the water-cooled, hand-held machine gun.[45]

The fixed forward lines on the European front allowed for detailed stratification of care by geographic location. The CCS was initially set up to handle 200 casualties per day. The work consisted primarily of sorting, bandaging, and returning to the field those who could still fight or sending the more seriously wounded by ambulance back to the rear. Facilities were available to hold casualties at the site for 1 to 3 days. As evidence began to accumulate about the morbidity of casualties handled in this way, however, and as physicians became more experienced in the treatment of traumatic injury, the techniques used at the CCS evolved into a more complex and almost comprehensive approach to care. The CCS became, in effect, a semipermanent triage and treatment center, with facilities that allowed postoperative cases to stay for 1 to 3 weeks.[46]

The relative stability of the front, the extensive supply lines that could thus be set up and maintained, and the motorized transport services allowed physicians at the CCS to develop increasingly aggressive techniques and test out increasingly explicit treatment guidelines. By the end of the war, wound care consisted of wide debridement and excision (the risk of gas gangrene from wounds incurred in the Belgian and French countryside had become well recognized) and local application of antiseptic wound packs. The patients were then sent back from the front for more definitive care (delayed primary closure) at the rear hospitals. Those arriving off the field with impending shock were wrapped in warm blankets, given oral fluids if they could still swallow and intravenous gum acacia solutions if necessary and if available, and rushed by ambulance back to the field hospital. Many died in transit, and others arrived at the field hospital profoundly hypovolemic as they faced immediate surgery. Casualties arriving at the CCS who were already in frank shock were given fluid resuscitation (the widespread use of blood and plasma awaited collection and storage methods not developed until the latter part of World War II), and thoracic and abdominal explorations might have been attempted. The issue of when, then, to transport the postoperative survivors remained unresolved. Burn cases were wrapped in gauze and sent back from the front; at the field hospital the dressings were changed and the patients were put to bed. The incidence of shock in burn patients was underestimated, although by the end of the war it became general practice to refrain from frequent dressing changes in order to reduce the risk of infection.[47]

Organized to manage casualties by these guidelines, the CCS at its peak could accommodate over 1,000 admissions per day. Data from the Battle of the Somme in July 1916 indicate that on the first day 14,400 men were admitted to 13 clearing stations; on the second day, 13,806 were admitted, and on the third day 8,793 were admitted.[48] This influx stretched medical capacities to their limits, and the experience has been cited later by senior medical officers as reflecting the utmost in medical organization and discipline.[49]

Despite the advances in surgical assessment and technique forged during this war, the initial delay in retrieving the wounded from the field and bringing them to the Regimental Aid Post often stretched for hours, occasionally days. Many of the most seriously injured died before they were reached by the stretcher-bearers, whose round trip from field to aid post and back averaged 1 hour. Each battalion had 32 stretcher-bearers, but in some of the heavier battles of this war, every battalion suffered hundreds of casualties.[50]

World War II

The improved motor vehicle technology that sustained the mobility of all armies in World War II made the Allied front fluctuate far more swiftly and dramatically than it had in World War I.[51] These fluid field conditions also made forward placement of complex medical response units much more problematic. The technological innovations in offensive military vehicles had not yet extended to the transport systems for removing the injured from the scene of battle, so that paradoxically the imbalance between fighting mobility and speed of medical retrieval paralleled the situation in the U.S. Civil War more than that in World War I. The major new weapons of World War II were the tank and the tactical airplane, overpowering well-equipped infantry and rendering distinctions between land and sea warfare obsolete.[52]

Forward clearing stations were far flung and forced by rapid shifts in battle lines to curtail capacities for intervention. Yet at the same time medical knowledge had advanced to the point at which it was becoming increasingly apparent how much could be done during the first 6 to 8 hours of resuscitation if the resources were at hand. The lifesaving potential of fluid replacement in the treatment of burns and the use of plasma and blood transfusions preoperatively in the stabilization of those with serious traumatic injury had become extensively appreciated techniques. Penicillin was first widely used in the treatment of battle wounds during the early part of 1943 at the start of the Italian campaign and heralded the enormous importance of antibiotics in determining medical outcome. The practice of exploring penetrating wounds of the thorax and abdomen had become routine, and much discussion surrounded the management of bowel injuries.[53]

The combination of increased medical understanding about how to salvage the severely injured with the difficulties in securing a stable forward treatment base forced World War II physicians into finely developed assessments of when to time critical interventions. The morbidity attached to the postoperative transport of patients with bowel injuries and the high incidence of hypotension in seriously burned patients presented particularly acute dilemmas to a medical service that could not, owing to the tactical situation, count on being in one place for more than 12 hours. Senior medical officers began to devise tight and detailed triage protocols and undertook systematic evaluations of front line casualty experiences. Their memoranda provide a terse and intense record of how informed, observant, and pragmatic physicians attempted to construct from their daily practice a manual of military medicine that could promise the injured the best care possible in circumstances that were constantly shifting.[54]

The Vietnam War

The helicopter revolutionized military medical care.[55] Developed during the latter years of the Korean War and introduced gradually during the Vietnam War, the helicopter permitted the immediate extrication of the injured and the rapid transit over insecure territory to a field hospital where major stabilization and, often, definitive care could be delivered. Over the years of this war, the field hospital structure increasingly conformed to the geography of the battlefield. In Vietnam there were no front lines. Pockets of intense engagement riddled the countryside, and areas of relatively permanent safety were located within 30 to 40 miles (about 48 to 64 km) of these war zones. The concept of the field hospital supported by the full-service hospital in the rear secure zone telescoped into a flexible system of clearing stations, hospitals and the MUST (Medical Unit, Self-Contained, Transportable) unit. First deployed in 1966, the MUST unit evolved into the site for the delivery of much definitive care. Soldiers injured in the field were picked up by medical evacuation teams assigned to helicopters, carried by helicopter to the semipermanent MUST hospitals, and given whatever treatment they required. If their injuries were sufficiently severe as to eliminate the possibility of return to combat or if convalescence were to extend beyond 30 days, soldiers would be sent by C-141 transport plane to major offshore hospitals. This combination of secure bases in transport proximity to the war zones and rapid retrieval afforded by the helicopter transformed the concept of casualty sorting at the front into a process less fraught with hard decisions.[56]

The new weapons used in Vietnam (high-velocity, lightweight rounds from the M16 and AK47 rifles, claymore mines, fragmentation grenades, varieties of cluster bombs and booby traps, phosphorus and napalm chemicals) inflicted particularly severe and dirty wounds.[57] Casualties in the Vietnam War experienced an increased incidence of small fire injuries with a relatively higher proportion of trunk wounds.[58] As the medical capacity to intervene improved during these years, the question of resource availability at the front might have been expected to move into increasingly sharp focus. During the Vietnam War, however, the medical resource systems and the casualty transport systems kept pace with each other and with the pace of medical technology. U.S. military hospitals never lacked blood, receiving shipments of more than 350,000 units during the peak year of 1968.[59] Sophisticated radiology and operating suites relied on plumbing and generator systems installed on site at the MUST units; and the most complex cardiac, vascular, and neurosurgical procedures could be accomplished within a 30-minute helicopter ride from the combat zone.[60]

The hospitalized mortality rate for wounded casualties in Vietnam during the 5-year period from 1965 to 1970 was 2.6 percent, compared with 4.5 percent in World War II, 8.1 percent in World War I, and 14.1 percent in the U.S. Civil War.[61] This decline in mortality occurred despite the successful helicopter evacuation to hospitals of those so severely injured that, in earlier wars, they would have died on the field or in transit. This decline is due in part to the speed with which the injured were transported to the source of care. Since the U.S. Civil War, the delay from time of injury to time of first aid has been much reduced, compressed from several days in the early years of that war to within 1 day during World War I, to a few hours in World War II, and a matter of 15 to 45 minutes during the Vietnam War.[62]

This decline in mortality is also due to the resources available at the site of care. As an index of medical effectiveness, the U.S. Army employs the concept of ''deaths as a percent of hits,'' or the ratio of deaths to deaths plus surviving wounded. For World War II, the ratio was 29.3 percent, and for the Vietnam War, the ratio was 19 percent.[63] The average inpatient length of stay was reduced from 80 to 63 days, and, reflecting progress in vascular surgical practice, the amputation rate for those with significant arterial and venous injury was 13 percent during the Vietnam War, compared with 49 percent during World War II.[64]

Summary of Experience from Conventional War

Although the course of military medicine in the last century has been characterized by significant discontinuities, as one generation of military physicians faded back into civilian life and another saw practice only as the new war erupted, bringing with it conditions, casualties, and technologies for which the old lessons were no longer applicable, a few salient principles of mass casualty care have begun to emerge as relative constants.

1. With an increasing medical capacity to salvage and save the severely injured, the factor of timing becomes paramount. The sooner that advanced resuscitation can reach the victim, the more likely are the chances of success. For all injuries that affect the respiratory and circulatory systems (which means for all serious head, neck, thoracic, abdominal, extremity, and vascular wounds and for all second-degree burns involving greater than 20 percent of the body surface area), fluid replacement and airway support must be initiated within 6 to 8 hours. The more serious the injury in any of these conditions, the more compressed that time frame becomes. The response of the human organism to injury sets this clock; trauma medicine has learned how absolute it is and how to accommodate to its needs.

2. All transport and resource systems must be organized to conform to this time frame. Their actual conformation will directly depend on field conditions. Where the combat zone shifts frequently and dramatically or where delivery of resources presents substantial logistic difficulties, priority must be placed on early and rapid extrication and transport of the injured to the nearest appropriate facility.

3. The principle of triage persists as the active sorting method in all mass casualty situations. By definition, such situations create the potential for the volume of casualties to overwhelm the transport and resource systems and force delays in the ministration of care. Where transport is primitive and resources scarce, this potential can be realized at low numbers. All of medicine during the U.S. Civil War was practiced in this margin; the absence of medical knowledge served in part to shield physicians of both sides from that recognition. There was no standard triage protocol; physicians and health providers of all kinds simply did what they could, serially, with each patient they encountered. Subsequent U. S. experience with wartime triage varied with each war. Perhaps the most firm triage posture was taken during World War II, during which the tension between the recognized need to intervene quickly and the occasional incapacity to do so forced military physicians into difficult decisions. In Vietnam, the capacities of an entire industrialized society could be directed to the transport and care of 300,000 casualties over 15 years.[65] This ratio of casualty to resource allocation was so favorable that the harsh aspects of medical triage rarely intruded. Current U.S. civilian understanding of the concept of triage derives from disasters that have occurred in distant regions, where geographic inaccessibility can impose severe

constraints on the delivery of care and can re-create historical dilemmas in which what is there is inadequate and what is elsewhere effectively does not exist.

BURN AND BLAST INJURIES IN NUCLEAR WAR

The current approach to mass casualty incidents, developed with much insight and perseverance from the experience of several wars, has been applied with excellent results to civilian disasters and has formed the basis for all medical emergency units that respond to the daily crises of modern life.[66] The central question is whether anything that has been learned can be applied to managing the casualties from the disaster of a nuclear war. The NATO field manuals and handbooks for medical officers, published by the U.S. Department of Defense, discuss at some length the management of mass casualties from nuclear war. The approach used derives directly from military medical practice in the two world wars. What is presented would serve well for a war waged within similar parameters. Its inapplicability to the disaster of a nuclear war arises from a failure to recognize the limits of our past experience and a failure to imagine what the next war might be.

Triage in Nuclear War

According to NATO guidelines, the medical response is to be organized by echelon: the battle aid station and field hospital would be in the combat zone, the full service hospital in the communications zone, and the rehabilitative facilities at some distant undefined site. Ground and air transportation would be mobilized to serve strict protocols and carry the injured to and through the echelons appropriate for each category of care. The sense of place implied by this scheme conveys an American view of a European conventional war. Nuclear war on the U.S. mainland is not discussed, nor is the possibility that a nuclear war in Europe might eclipse life on the entire continent.

The NATO triage protocols recognize four categories of injured: those requiring minimal attention; those in need of immediate care; those for whom delayed treatment is acceptable; and expectant, or those for whom death is assessed as being inevitable. Some variation of these four categories is found in all triage systems; the guiding principle behind the NATO sorting method is the imperative to maximize the military capacity.

In two respects the NATO guidelines acknowledge that nuclear war may be different from other wars. Radiation injury receives substantial attention, including a qualitative assessment of synergism with burn and blast. The triage protocol also makes explicit that in nuclear war the category of expectant may extend over a wide range of injury, including many who might in other, less-stressed circumstances be assigned greater chances of survival.[67]

What is not discussed in the NATO guidelines is the problem of numbers. Without direct attention to the fact that in nuclear war the word *many* may mean millions, protocols derived from wars in which *many* meant thousands may prove irrelevant and, prospectively, misleading. The reference cases prepared for use in the studies presented in this volume contribute data on infrastructure loss, geographic extent, and numbers and types of casualties for a series of possible nuclear attacks on the U.S. mainland. This data range permits an assessment of potential medical response from the perspective of mass casualty management.

Medical Management

The medical management of massive numbers of casualties requires, in addition to attention to the demands of individual patient care, recognition of the constraints imposed by numbers. Conventional war, disasters, and peacetime disturbances have provided the medical profession with much experience in managing both aspects of the care of burn and blast casualties. The burn and blast casualties of a nuclear war would be similar in essential respects to what has been seen in the past, with the significant exceptions that these injuries would be created in enormous numbers and would be potentially complicated by the additional factor of radiation. Here I will focus on the nature of these burn and blast injuries, paying particular attention to the ways in which the magnitude of the need may determine the structure and content of triage decisions.

Blast Injury

The blast wave created by nuclear explosions inflicts injuries on people through a number of phenomena:[68]

1. the massive shift in environmental pressure as the air front hits the human body (primary effect);

2. the projection of missiles into the human body (causing either penetrating or nonpenetrating injury);

3. the sudden displacement of the human body against a standing rigid surface;

4. the collapse of structures on people either contained within or adjacent to them.

The extent and nature of human injury in this context depend on the biomechanical parameters of the explosion, whether caused by nuclear weapons or other means. Experimental literature has defined in detail the physical characteristics of the blast wave (peak overpressure, overpressure duration, wind velocities, negative displacement forces), but injury correlates are confined to animal models.[69] The medical literature describes the injuries seen in settings ranging from conventional war to terrorist bombings but cannot retrospectively establish precisely the physical characteristics of the explosions.[70]

A few general conclusions emerge from this experience and apply to a taxonomy of injuries to be expected in the vicinity of all cities hit by the airburst of a 1-megaton (Mt) nuclear weapon.

Head injuries. Skull fractures, intra- or extracerebral hemorrhage, and cervical spine injuries occur at high overpressures, which create peak wind velocities that could drive people into a rigid surface or drive a blunt object against the skull.[71] At an overpressure of 5.3 psi an adult might achieve maximum acceleration of 21 ft/s (6.1 m/s), which, as impact velocity, would produce lethal injury in approximately 50 percent of cases and, if the head were struck at this force, a 100 percent incidence of skull fracture. At much lower overpressures (1–2 psi), buildings may still collapse and cause severe head injury to those trapped within or nearby.[72]

Thoracic injuries. A particular entity called blast lung has been identified among soldiers killed by explosions during World Wars I and II and among experimental animals.[73] The lesion appears to be caused by the primary effect of the overpressure as it produces a shock front that initially compresses the chest wall against the spinal column and then, in its displacement phase, releases it. Human body displacement and blunt projectiles can also create this injury. Physical structures within the thoracic cage most prone to damage in this context are those at tissue interfaces and hollow viscera.[74] Acute deaths can arise from the sudden propagation of air emboli into the cerebral and cardiac circulation. Pulmonary hemorrhage and pulmonary edema can lead to delayed mortality. The incidence of blast lung appears to be higher in the military setting than among the survivors of civilian bombings, prompting speculation that civilian fatalities attributed to other causes may have incurred pulmonary damage as well.[75]

Tympanic membrane rupture. The tympanic membrane (eardrum) is very susceptible to rupture from the primary effect of the blast wave, and such injury was found in approximately 36 percent of hospitalized casualties from a series of bombings in Northern Ireland and among 45 percent of those who died, indicating its association with severe injury.[76] Data on threshold incidence range from 2 to 5 psi.[77] In the Texas City disaster of 1947 (in which a ship containing fertilizer exploded and caused approximately 3,000 casualties), eardrum rupture was found among 10 percent of the survivors.[78]

Long-Bone Fractures. Long-bone fractures arise from displacement phenomena or from the trauma inflicted by external structures. Fractures constituted approximately 35 percent of the injuries among hospitalized casualties from the Northern Ireland series and occurred with unspecified frequency among those casualties that were treated and released.[79] In the Texas City disaster, approximately 7 percent of survivors experienced fractures.[80]

Soft Tissue Injuries. Lacerations, abrasions, and contusions form the majority of wounds encountered among survivors of blast injury and are caused primarily by the effects of penetrating missiles accelerated to high velocities by the blast wave.[81] In the winds created by the blast of nuclear explosions, almost any object can be transformed into a penetrating missile; in conventional war and terrorist bombings, the examples range from shards of glass to table legs.[82] Lacerations causing extensive soft tissue destruction or wounds penetrating deeply create ideal conditions for serious infections such as gas gangrene; damage to major vessels or organs can also prove life threatening. Many victims of blast injury suffer numerous minor cuts and abrasions, causing them to face a major long-term risk of infection from retained fragments of glass, wood, or other contaminated material.[83] Among the survivors of the bombings in Northern Ireland, approximately 36 percent of all injuries were lacerations, abrasions, or bruises; and 44 percent of these were sufficiently serious to require hospitalization.[84]

Abdominal Injuries. Abdominal injuries are relatively uncommon among survivors of blast injuries that occur on land. Abdominal injuries were found in only 4 percent of the Texas City survivors[85] and in 3 percent of survivors of another series of bombings in Northern Ireland.[86] It is postulated that the patients with the most serious abdominal injuries do not survive to reach the hospital.[87]

The current approach to blast injuries can be illustrated by summarizing the treatment protocols developed by the Royal Victorian Hospital in Belfast:

1. Triage at site of arrival

   —Assess severity of wounds (in bombings, experience indicates 15 percent will be severe injuries and 85 percent will be minor)

      —For severe cases, resuscitate (airway, chest tubes, intravenous fluids and blood); this often requires two or three senior medical officers per patient

      —For minor cases, assign to house officers and medical students

2. Sort by priority for operating room time and direct specialty teams to appropriate patients

   —This is the role of the chief casualty officer

   —Available surgical teams must include ophthalmology; ear, nose, and throat; vascular; neurosurgical; orthopedic, pediatric surgical; plastics; urogenital; chest; and general

3. Treatment of individual injuries

   —On site, with operating room, lab, x-ray, and blood bank capacities

   —Standard operations include thoracotomies, abdominal explorations, cleaning and wide debridement of wounds with delayed primary closure and intravenous antibiotics, and stabilization and early fixation of fractures

With extensive organization, a new facility, and years of practice, the surgical teams at the Royal Victoria Hospital were prepared to handle, on a one-time basis only, the sudden arrival within 1 hour of 50 to 100 casualties.[88]

Burn Injury

The thermal energy released from nuclear weapons explosions can cause human burns by direct radiation or by igniting clothing or other materials that secondarily engulf people in flames. Over 90 percent of burns seen among survivors of Hiroshima and Nagasaki were from direct thermal radiation, termed *flash* burns.[89] *Flame* burns, resulting from exposure to secondary fires or contact with ignited clothing, are identical to the burns seen in conventional war or peacetime disasters.[90] From the standpoint of patient management, flash burns, although limited to exposed surfaces and tending, perhaps, to give rise to slightly less tissue swelling and fluid loss, can be seen as resembling first- and second-degree burns along the continuum routinely used in burn classification.[91]

First-degree burns, affecting only the epidermis, can cause transient dehydration and pain but require no emergency treatment. Second-degree burns (or partial-thickness burns) result in blistering of the skin and, in severe cases, can resemble clinically and in terms of complexity of management full-thickness or third-degree burns. This last category, if extensive at all, will heal only with skin grafts; partial-thickness burns heal by slow regrowth of skin from the wound base.

At the thermal energy levels delivered by the explosion of a 1-Mt bomb, measured in calories per centimeter squared (cal/cm^2), the range for flash burns is extensive. At 9–10 miles (about 14.5–16 km) from ground zero, assuming that 25 percent of the population is exposed, approximately 82 percent of that population might be expected to receive first-degree flash burns on exposed surfaces and 18 percent would suffer second-degree burns. The thermal flux in that area would be approximately 5 cal/cm^2.[92]

A particular aspect of flash burns is their propensity to affect the eyes. The intensity of the brief light flash is sufficient to cause transient blindness (from the bleaching of retinal rods and cones) to all those looking in the general area of the explosion. This effect lasts for a matter of minutes to several hours and was reported among many survivors in Hiroshima. The risk of flash blindness extends for approximately 20 miles (about 32 km) from ground zero for a 1-Mt explosion. True burns of the retina, which may cause permanent blindness depending on the extent and position of the burns, are caused by the heat of the thermal pulse hitting the eyes of someone who happens to look and focus on the flash of light from the explosion.

Serious burns requiring emergency intervention and 3 to 6 weeks of intensive care are second- or third-degree burns extending beyond 20 percent of the body surface area (BSA); second- or third-degree burns in critical locations (from the viewpoint of infection and function), such as the face, neck, perineum, and hands; and pulmonary or airway burns (either thermal or toxic).[93] Failure to recognize that people with these injuries will require early and significant intravenous fluid and electrolyte replacement, scrupulous treatment of infection, and possibly aggressive airway support has led in the past to significant mortality among initial survivors of major burn disasters. Only well into World War II and after the analysis of deaths from the Cocoanut Grove Fire in Boston in 1943 did the risks of shock and hypoxia or airway obstruction from pulmonary injury become fully appreciated.[94]

Other factors contributing to increased mortality from burns include extremes of age and combined traumatic and burn injury. The interaction of either burn or blast with radiation injury has also enhanced mortality in all settings, clinical and experimental. Marked delay in wound healing, extending to immunological collapse and overwhelming sepsis, have been observed in both blast and burn subjects suffering acute radiation exposures.[95]

The resources that must be marshalled to manage successfully the care of one seriously burned patient have been extensively detailed elsewhere.[96] In sum, the services of an intensive care unit, several physicians and nurses, hundreds of units of blood products, and scores of operations may be required. Still, with the utmost skill, perseverance, and capacity, only marginal chances of survival can be promised to those over middle age with a greater than 50 percent BSA burn.[97]

Casualty Assessment

The Princeton group's studies presented in this volume contribute casualty data for a series of hypothetical nuclear attacks on the continental United States. In attempting to construct a medical response to this kind of catastrophe, the reference case that describes 100 Mt exploding over 100 major cities (1 Mt per city) has been examined from the perspective of three individual cities. For these cities, projections have been made of the key parameters defining any triage system that might be invoked: the number of injured, the kind of injuries, the number of health care providers, and the geographical relationship between the injured and the providers. The question of available transport and resource delivery systems has been addressed in general terms, insofar as it affects decisions about patient management. The case of 100 Mt exploding over 100 major cities is referred to for analytical purposes only; no comment on its strategic relevance is implied.

In developing these projections, the data on the number of injured and the number killed for each of these three city cases have been modified in this discussion to be in accord with a reanalysis of the casualty data from Hiroshima and Nagasaki.

Review of Hiroshima and Nagasaki Data

To evaluate the role of medical triage at the site of a disaster, it is necessary to have some grasp of the number of injured people alive at the time the triage intervention is applied. The reference cases rely on the standard partition of killed and injured developed from the Hiroshima casualty data compiled previously.[98] Based on surveys of hospitalized survivors who were alive after 20 days, this data base counts as dead both those who had died immediately in the bombing and those who had died from their injuries during the intervening 20 days.[99] Given the chaos and destruction that reigned during those first few weeks, it is remarkable that the record is as precise as it is: the medical relief stations did not begin recording casualty data at Hiroshima until August 11, five days after the bombing.[100] The other main data sources derive from surveys of hospitalized patients conducted in September, October, and November 1945.[101] As important and informative as the existing sources are, for the purposes of evaluating triage postures they present a distorted picture of the actual casualty mix during the first week after the bombing, let alone during the first few hours.

Records from police and aid stations located on the periphery of the 2-km damage zone yield some information about this early period. A deluge of injured people was reported, most of whom were described as "arriving," without a reliable accounting of the proportion who required assistance in making the trip. Overwhelmed by the influx, officials called for help from throughout the country. Had relief not poured in within the next week, the consequences for these initial survivors would probably have been more severe than those that actually occurred.[102]

As it was, the imbalance between need and resources remained marked. It is axiomatic in medical triage that in settings in which severe injuries occur, treatment delays will result in increased mortality.[103] The most comprehensive compilation of casualty data from Hiroshima and Nagasaki estimates that 90–100 percent of all deaths occurred within the first 2 weeks; another source estimates that the 2-week mortality rate was 61.2 percent of the total recorded deaths.[104] A Japanese source, relying on police records of people seeking help from the station about 15 km from the hypocenter, reports that 50 percent of those severely injured had died by day 6; another 25 percent died by day 12, and 90 percent of all deaths had occurred by day 40 after the bombing.[104]

The Hiroshima data present cumulative mortality under circumstances in which intensive medical care or organized response could not and did not take place until several days had lapsed. Included among those counted, in later surveys, as dead at the end of 1 week were many who were in fact survivors of the first few hours and perhaps the first few days.

From the perspective of initial medical management and the role that triage might have played, it is difficult to extrapolate from this data base the numbers and kinds of injuries that, with immediate intervention other than what took place, might have resulted in further salvage. The casualty statistics from Hiroshima and Nagasaki instead describe what happened at the given level of medical care that was then possible to administer.

Projections of Number of Injured and Number of Providers

The conflagration model of Daugherty et al.[105] assumes that all people within the 10-km radius of ground zero would be killed by the immediate blast and superfire effects of the 1-Mt explosion and that the injured would be clustered in the next two circumferential zones of 10–12 and 12–15 km from the epicenter. Because the number of dead and injured derived by this model is based on the casualty data from Hiroshima and Nagasaki, it represents what might apply 20 days after the bombing. To develop the situation that might actually pertain during the first few hours and days, the following modifications were employed (see Tables 1 and 2):

1. Twenty percent of those located within the 10–12-km zone were estimated to be able to flee the fires and winds and, though injured, make it into the 12–15-km area. These people would have sustained injuries primarily to the upper torso, still allowing them some mobility. Those with more severe injuries in this zone would be trapped and would die from one of the several possible causes discussed by Postol.[106]

2. These moderately injured people would join those in the 12–15-km zone, of whom slightly over one-third would be severely injured. This proportion is in accord with the hypothetical injury profile recently constructed from an analysis of the mix of burn and blast casualties found at Hiroshima and Nagasaki and among the survivors of the Texas City fertilizer explosion.[107] These people with severe injuries in the 12–15-km zone would be truly incapacitated and would have to rely on the help of others to get to sources of care.

3. The number of people killed in this revision of the reference case is reduced by the number of severely injured assumed to be among the initial survivors. Over the subsequent 20-day period, as cumulative mortality took its toll, the mix of dead and injured estimated here approaches that predicted by the model of Daugherty et al.[105]

4. The number of physicians (used as a rough indicator of health care providers) available to treat the injured in the 12–15-km area was derived by assuming a uniform distribution of physicians within the circle defined by the 18-km radius around each city and by assuming that all those located in the unaffected 15–18-km area would converge to join those physicians in the 12–15-km zone.[108] Only the surviving physicians within this 18-km area are assumed to be available, since the 100-Mt reference case postulates that 99 other cities would be in similar distress. Whatever medical response these local providers could present and sustain would constitute the sum total of care delivered—in an attack that hits this many cities with this force, no reliance can be placed on a full service base in a rear echelon.

Medical Response

According to the above assumptions, the injured would either be in or flee into the area 12–15 km from ground zero in a narrow band of territory

TABLE 1 Number of Injured and Providers after 100-Mt Explosion over Selected Cities from the 100-Mt City Reference Case

Selected Metropolitan Area	Total Population in 18-km Radius (398 mi²)	No. Killed in 0–12 km Radius	No. of People/mi²	No. Injured in 10–12 km Radius Able to Flee to 12–15 km Zone[a]	No. Injured Located in 12–15 km Radius	Total No. Injured in 12–15 km Radius	Total No. of Physicians in 12–18 km Radius (1/508)[b]	No. Physicians/No. Injured
New York	15,500,000	3,000,000	38,945	420,606	800,000	1,220,606	16,963	1/72
Washington, D.C.	2,800,000	800,000	7,035	75,978	200,000	275,798	3,100	1/89
Omaha	512,000	360,000	1,286	13,889	59,000	72,889	554	1/132

[a]Number of people/mile²; this assumes a uniform population density for the calculation of the data in this column. Twenty percent were assumed to flee to the 12–15 km zone.

[b]The number of physicians in the United States is 371,000[107] 87 percent of whom are urban (323,000); the urban United States has 73 percent of the overall population; hence the ratio of urban physicians to urban population is 1/508. This assumes that the survival rate of physicians is the same as that of general urban population. A uniform distribution of physicians was assumed for the calculation of the data in this column.

TABLE 2 Cumulative Mortality and Net Survival Among Those Injured in Selected Cities in the 100-Mt Reference Case[a]

Selected Metropolitan Area	Day 1	Day 2[b]	Days 2 to 20[c]	Triage Model (Overall Casualties on Day 20)	Reference Case Model (Overall Casualties on Day 20)
New York					
0–12 km radius (injured flee to 12–15 km zone)	2,579,394/420,606	0/420,606	58,885/361,721		
12–15 km radius	0/800,000	296,000/504,000	70,560/433,440		
Total	2,579,394/1,220,606	296,000/924,606	129,445/795,161	3,004,839/795,161	3,000,000/800,000
Washington, D.C.					
0–12 km radius (injured flee to 12–15 km zone)	724,022/75,978	0/75,978	10,637/65,341		
12–15 km radius	0/200,000	74,000/126,000	17,640/108,360		
Total	724,022/275,978	74,000/201,978	28,277/173,701	826,299/173,701	800,000/200,000
Omaha					
0–12 km radius (injured flee to 12–15 km zone)	346,111/13,889	0/13,889	1,944/11,945		
12–15 km radius	0/59,000	21,830/37,170	5,204/31,966		
Total	346,111/72,889	21,830/51,059	7,148/43,911	375,089/43,911	360,000/59,000

[a]Data in columns are presented as the number of dead/the number of surviving injured.
[b]Mortality rate is 37 percent among those in the 12–15 km radius.
[c]Mortality rate is 14 percent among those in the 0–12 km radius (with the injured fleeing to the 12–15 km zone) and those in the 12–15 km radius.

approximately 1.6 miles (about 2.6 km) wide and 62 miles (about 100 km) around the zone of total destruction. This site, the area of several fronts in World Wars I and II, would constitute the triage location—adjacent to the devastation, it would be the first stop for all seeking help. In terms of infrastructure damage and social regrouping, it corresponds rough-ly to the 2–4-km zone around ground zero in Hiroshima.

The terrain would have sustained blast waves of 1.5 to 2 psi, which is sufficient to destroy much of the building stock and disrupt roads and bridges throughout. (The model of Daugherty et al.[105] discusses the pos-sibility of scattered secondary fires in this zone.) During the first day, the winds would probably be in the range of 30- to 50-mile per hour (about 48 to 80 km per hour). These winds would be filled with hot and toxic fumes from the central fire zone.

From the standpoint of setting up a medical triage system in this setting, the first issue to determine is that of timing. Can transport or medical resources be marshalled sufficiently to make it possible to intervene during the critical 6 to 8 hours during which all salvage of the seriously injured must take place? Timing will cease to exist as the critical variable when lack of transportation or resources, relative to numbers of casualties, precludes complex medical intervention. At that point the triage protocols for mass casualties would be reduced to a most austere mode, and medical management, if the term can still be used, would revert to that of another era. In the reference case used here, both factors (overwhelming numbers and resource scarcity) apply in full force even at the relatively constrained end of the spectrum of possible attack parameters. Here the example of New York City is discussed.

In the first few hours, at a rate dependent at least in part on road and fire conditions, physicians would begin to congregate at whatever health facilities remained standing. Including those physicians in the 12–15-km zone and those from the 15–18-km zone, in New York City there would be approximately 1 physician for every 72 people injured from the bomb-ing. In the U.S. Civil War, approximately 16,500 physicians enrolled on both sides were involved in treating 318,200 wounded, yielding a ratio of 1 physician for every 19 injured people.[109]

Each physician would have to choose between two strategies: one of rapid triage and one that essentially abandons triage and treats each patient in order, a serial pattern described among Japanese physicians during the first several days after the bombings. In rapid triage, the physician would move quickly from one casualty to the next, assigning each to a treatment category, carrying out the role of labeling victims, but not treating them. In the reference case setting, in which the capacity to deliver advanced care would be problematic, a large number of casualties would be placed in the expectant category.[110] In serial treatment, the physician would move from one casualty to the next, spending whatever time may be necessary to stabilize or support the patient. This strategy might well result in the physician failing to see or treat some of the most severely injured; yet these, even if seen, might present problems too complex for resolution in this context.

Every square mile (about 2.62 km^2) of this triage area in New York City would contain 12,274 injured people. Statistically, there would be one casualty every 19–20 yards (about 17–18 m). The majority of the casualties would have sustained first- and second-degree burns of the upper body, covering less than 20 percent of their body surface area, fractures of the upper limbs and torso, contusions and lacerations of all kinds, and head and face injuries. They might well be mobile and would constitute the population that would flock to sites of care. Approximately 37 percent of those who would be injured in the 12–15-km zone, or 296,000 people, would be severely injured (see Table 3). Some of these people would be trapped in collapsed buildings, pinned under heavy wreckage, and unable to move on their own. Their injuries would include blunt and penetrating chest and abdominal trauma, major long-bone and pelvic fractures with significant hemorrhage, and extensive second- and third-degree burns. Even under the best of circumstances, for people with these injuries to survive, they would have to be found, assessed, and treated within 6 to 8 hours.

In the first 2 days, each physician might be able to encounter 72 casualties, but, in these postattack conditions, advanced intervention would be very difficult to carry out or sustain. The situation would present two insuperable obstacles: no transport or access to the victims and scarce resources. The skills and experience of the teams that assembled would be relatively random. It is likely that no power or water would be available for the first several days. Equipment and supplies would be limited to what remained on site at standing health facilities. Extricating victims is a time-consuming and arduous task: it took several heavy construction cranes, 10 hydraulic rescue tools, and scores of fire department members and emergency medical technicians a total of 13 hours to remove 301 people (113 of them dead) from the wreckage of the Hyatt Hotel in Kansas City in 1981.[111] Transporting these severely injured from where they were found to a site of care might prove impossible. Treating these patients would require intravenous fluids, blood transfusions, intravenous antibiotics, airway resuscitation and maintenance, debridement and excision of contaminated wounds, fracture stabilization, and operative intervention for those with penetrating injuries or ongoing internal bleeding. Unless circumstances permitted an intense and focused allocation of medical

TABLE 3 Number and Kind of Injuries Among Casualties in Selected Cities from 100-Mt City Reference Case[a]

Selected Metropolitan Area	No. Injured (in 12–15 km Zone)	No. with Blast/Burn (35% of Total)	No. with Severe Blast/Burn[b]	No. with Burns (30% of Total)	No. With >20% BSA[c]	No. Injured by Blast (35% of Total)	No. Injured by Severe Blast[d]	No. Dying if Not Hospitalized in 8 h[e]
New York	800,000	280,000	140,000	240,000	72,000	280,000	84,000	296,000
Washington, D.C.	200,000	70,000	35,000	60,000	18,000	70,000	21,000	74,000
Omaha	59,000	20,650	10,325	17,700	5,310	20,650	6,195	21,830

[a]See text for details.
[b]Values are 50 percent of blast/burn casualties.
[c]Values are 30 percent of burn casualties.
[d]Values are 30 percent of blast casualties.
[e]Values are 37 percent of the total number injured, or the sum of severe blast/burn, >20 percent BSA burn, and severe blast casualties.

SOURCE: Distribution of burn/blast casualties published previously.[68,99,107]

resources on systems of support and intervention, the mortality rate among these severely injured would approach 100 percent within 2 days.

The majority of the injured (assumed here to be the thousands who fled the 10–12-km zone and those in the 12–15-km zone) would confront a much lower ongoing mortality rate, due primarily to hypovolemia from dehydration or hemorrhage, the effects of exposure and exhaustion, and the impact of infection. In the 1-Mt scenario for one city, radiation would not be a significant factor, but the medical care available to these survivors might well not match the resources marshalled by the Japanese in the early postattack period.

The pattern of medical management this data base implies mirrors what took place during the U.S. Civil War, in which those listed as wounded were those who had survived the privation of days of lying in fields before being picked up or, for the bulk of them, those who had walked to sites of care. Whether or not these reference case casualties would survive their injuries would depend, as it did in the U.S. Civil War, on whatever food and water could be obtained, the subsequent risk of infection in an effectively preantibiotic era, and the local incidence of disease. Mortality rates among those hospitalized in the U.S. Civil War were approximately 14 percent; it is unlikely that the prevailing rate for the moderately and mildly injured survivors of a nuclear war could be less. A most conservative estimate of early mortality among each group of 72 initial survivors thus approximates 100 percent for all severely injured and 14 percent for all others, resulting, among those not killed outright at the time of the bombing, in an overall death rate, 20 days later, of 46 percent, or 33 of every 72 injured.

This figure results from what might grimly be termed best case analysis, in which the population casualty rates are the lowest of all instances prepared in the 100-Mt urban reference attack, in which systematic reversion to an austere triage posture is assumed and in which the care of the moderately injured is estimated to be in accord with the hospital experience of the U.S. Civil War.

A number of assumptions were made in evaluating the New York City 1-Mt nuclear attack example; these assumptions will certainly not hold in progressively more comprehensive reference cases.

1. All surviving physicians were assumed to possess some knowledge of acute care medicine, to behave professionally, and to maintain a triage discipline not previously demanded of any U.S. physician, civilian or member of the military. The inadequacy of this assumption is profound. The disaster of nuclear war, even as narrowly defined as it is in this reference case, would create an enormous stress on those attempting to function in the role of health care provider. The literature on coping

behavior among disaster victims does not support facile assumptions in this regard.[112] Pushed to his limits, Sasaki, a physician in Hiroshima, roamed among the injured aimlessly "wiping, daubing, winding, wiping, daubing, winding."[113] Behavior in the postattack world may well reach extremes of fragmentation, terror, and involution we have not yet seen.[114] Nothing in the training of a physician confers protection against the psychological ravages of this environment.

2. Those with moderate and minor injuries were assumed to suffer the same mortality rates as hospitalized casualties in the U.S. Civil War, a cohort composed predominantly of patients with blast injuries, subject to high rates of infection and disease, yet of young and vigorous constitution and sustained by a system of medical supply and nursing care incomparably superior to that which the injured survivors of nuclear war would face. There is no basis, aside from common sense, for extrapolating a higher mortality rate: data from later wars increase the disparity in support system comparability; data from earlier wars or disasters yield less reliable information on early and delayed mortality. As an underestimate, it contributes a cautious level of magnitude to the dimensions of mass casualty management in this circumstance.

3. By limiting the discussion to the 100-Mt airburst reference case, the factor of radioactive fallout was excluded. In the more extensive cases, involving surface as well as air explosions, radiation injury would contribute seriously to all subsequent mortality rates for those injured by burn and blast. Estimates of excess mortality in this setting of mixed trauma might serve to increase to 50 percent the proportion of those classified as severely injured (and thus expected to die) and might well double the 14 percent mortality rate among those with moderate and minor injuries.

CONCLUSION

The methodical approach to such dimensions is to recognize the limits of possible intervention. Modern triage protocols apply to conditions in which the mix of transport and resource availability allows physicians to make early headway against the high mortality of the severely injured. From World War I on, the knowledge that complex support delivered within a matter of hours could save lives once thought lost has driven the development and design of the response to mass casualties. If it is acknowledged at the outset that no galvanization of effort can contribute to the salvage of the severely injured, the problem becomes less complex. The choices then revolve around how much time and material should be expended on humanitarian support of those who are probably going to die and how much should be devoted to the care of those with moderate injuries who might live. Those with minor injuries, in this setting, could not receive care.

The reference case employed here, and all those developed by Daugherty et al.,[105] refrain from a discussion of a massive nuclear war. Population losses in such a catastrophe lie outside our experience and defy the human and technological systems we have so far devised to attempt to mitigate disaster and alleviate suffering. On the global scale of nuclear war, as described in the scenario of Harwell and Grover,[115] people would face a picture of such devastation and death that the concept of mass casualty management loses all meaning. Historically, such medical management has constituted a highly complex human enterprise. In the bleakness of a post-war world, virtually every survivor would be a casualty, and social organization could well prove unsustainable. Mass casualty medicine, crafted and practiced in war, is a product of the process that may eventually drive it, and everything we know, into oblivion.

ACKNOWLEDGMENT

The author would like to thank Robert Mascola for his contribution as research assistant in the preparation of this paper.

NOTES

[1]The Shorter Oxford English Dictionary, Third Edition, Vol. 2. Pp. 2358, 2375. Oxford: Clarendon Press; Rund, D. A., and T. S. Rausch. 1981. Triage. P. 3. St. Louis: C. V. Mosby.

[2]Richardson, R. G. 1974. Larrey: Surgeon to Napoleon's Guard. Pp. 1–6, 158–168. London: John Murray.

[3]Tuttle, A. D. 1927. Handbook for the Medical Soldier. Pp. 84–85. New York: William Wood and Co.

[4]Keegan, J. 1976. The Face of Battle. Pp. 267–269. New York: Viking Press.

[5]U.S. Armed Forces. 1958. Emergency War Surgery, NATO Handbook, Pp. 163–173. Washington, D.C.: U.S. Department of Defense, U.S. Government Printing Office.

[6]Baker, S. P., B. O'Neill, W. Haddon, Jr., and W. B. Long. 1974. The injury severity score: A method for describing patients with multiple injuries and evaluating emergency care. J. Trauma 14:187–196; Ebskov, B. 1981. Initial hospital care of the multitraumatized patient. Ann. Chir. Gyn. 70:233–236; Melsom, M. A., M. D. Farrar, and R. C. Volkers. 1975. Battle casualties. Ann. R. Coll. Surg. 56:289–303; Ryan, J. M. 1984. The Falklands War—Triage. Ann. R. Coll. Surg. 66:195–196.

[7]Cowley, R. A., ed. 1982. Mass Casualties: A Lessons Learned Approach. Pp. 141–145. Washington, D.C.: U.S. Department of Transportation, U.S. Government Printing Office.

[8]Goldwyn, M., and V. W. Sidel. 1968. The Physician and War. Pp. 325–346 in E. F. Torrey, ed., Ethical Decisions in Medicine. Boston: Little, Brown.

⁹Zawacki, B. E. 1985. ICU physician's ethical role in distributing scarce resources. Crit. Care Med. 13:57–60.

¹⁰Morton, J. H., L. M. Cramer, and S. I. Schwartz. 1964. Emergency management of a major civilian disaster. Arch. Surg. 89:105–113.

¹¹Yates, D. W. 1979. Major disasters: Surgical triage. Br. J. Hosp. Med. 22(4):323–328.

¹²Winslow, G. R. 1982. Triage and Justice. Pp. 1–23. Berkeley, Calif.: University of California Press.

¹³Ziperman, H. H. 1959. Sorting for Disaster Survival. J. Am. Med. Assoc. 171:202.

¹⁴Straub, P. F. 1912. Medical Service in Campaign: A Handbook for Medical Officers in the Field. Pp. 5–6. Surgeon General's Office, War Department. Philadelphia: P. Blakiston's Son & Co.; Tuttle, Handbook, p. 84; Spencer, J. H. 1963. Mass casualties in the civilian hospital. Bull. Am. Coll. Surg. 48:342–361.

¹⁵Keegan, Face of Battle, pp. 112–113, 197–203; Winslow, Triage and Justice, pp. 1–3.

¹⁶Richardson, Larrey, pp. 2–4.

¹⁷Garrison, F. H. 1922. Notes on the History of Military Medicine. Pp. 5, 41–46, 84–95, 133–134. Washington, D.C.: Association of Military Surgeons.

¹⁸Brooks, S. 1966. Civil War Medicine. Pp. 50–62. Springfield, Ill.: Charles C Thomas; Woodham-Smith, C. 1960. The Reason Why. Pp. 258–271. New York: E. P. Dutton.

¹⁹U.S. Army. 1959. Medical Service Theater of Operations, Field Manual FM8-10. P. 17. Washington, D.C.: Department of the Army. As cited in Goldwyn and Sidel, Ethical Decisions, p. 346.

²⁰Fulton, J. F. 1953. Medicine, warfare, and history. J. Am. Med. Assoc. 153:482–488.

²¹Churchill, E. D. 1972. Surgeon to Soldiers: Diary and Records of the Surgical Consultant, Allied Force Headquarters, World War II. P. 89. Philadelphia: J. B. Lippincott.

²²Goldwyn and Sidel, Ethical Decisions, pp. 335–336.

²³World Medical Association. 1956. Code of Ethics in Wartime. World Medical Association: New York. As cited in Goldwyn and Sidel, Ethical Decisions, p. 346.

²⁴O'Donnell, T. J. 1960. The morality of triage. Georgetown Med. Bull. 14:68–71.

²⁵U.S. Armed Forces, Emergency War Surgery, pp. 1–6.

²⁶Ibid., p. 7.

²⁷Brooks, Civil War Medicine, pp. 3–40; Cunningham, H. H. 1968. Field Medical Services at the Battles of Manassas. Pp. 1–22. Athens, Ga.: University of Georgia Press.

²⁸Fuller, J. F. C. 1961. The Conduct of War 1789–1961. Pp. 105–106. London: Methuen; Millis, W. 1956. Arms and Men. Pp. 114–116. New York: New American Library.

²⁹Cunningham, Field Medical Services, p. 61, 90.

³⁰Maxwell, W. Q. 1956. Lincoln's Fifth Wheel: The Political History of the United States Sanitary Commission. Pp. 70–92. New York: Longmans, Green; Brooks, Civil War Medicine, pp. 36–37.

³¹Brooks, Civil War Medicine, pp. 22–40; Cunningham, Field Medical Services, pp. 1–41.

³²Adams, G. W. 1952. Doctors in Blue: The Medical History of the Union Army in the Civil War. Pp. 67–70. New York: Henry Schuman.

³³Ibid., pp. 112–129.

³⁴Diffenbough, W. G. 1965. Military surgery in the Civil War. Military Med. 130:492–493.

³⁵Ibid., p. 493.

³⁶Brooks, Civil War Medicine, pp. 1–10.

[37]Commager, H. S., ed. 1950. The Blue and the Gray. New York: Bobbs-Merrill.
[38]Ibid., p. 769; Steiner, P. E. 1968. Disease in the Civil War. Pp. 3–45. Springfield, Ill.: Charles C Thomas.
[39]Diffenbough, Military Surgery, pp. 491–492.
[40]Ibid., p. 492.
[41]Adams, Doctors in Blue, pp. 130–173; Brooks, Civil War Medicine, pp. 106–121.
[42]Wallace, C., and J. Fraser. 1918. Surgery at a Casualty Clearing Station. Pp. 1–6. London: A.&C. Black.
[43]Millis, Arms and Men, p. 185; Fuller, Conduct of War, pp. 134–45, 166–67, 171.
[44]Keegan, Face of Battle, p. 255.
[45]Fuller, Conduct of War, p. 135.
[46]Wallace and Fraser, Casualty Clearing Station, p. 2.
[47]Ibid., pp. 1–320.
[48]Churchill, Surgeon to Soldiers, pp. 272–274.
[49]Ibid.
[50]Keegan, Face of Battle, p. 268.
[51]Millis, Arms and Men, pp. 252–254.
[52]Ibid.
[53]Beebe, G. W., and M. E. DeBakey. 1952. Battle Casualties: Incidence, Mortality and Logistic Considerations. Pp. 74–147. Springfield, Ill.: Charles C Thomas.
[54]Churchill, Surgeon to Soldiers, pp. 12–25, 36–70, 456–466, 475; Simeone, F. A. 1984. Studies of trauma and shock in man: William S. Stone's role in the military effort. J. Trauma 24:281–287.
[55]Neel, S. 1973. Medical Support of the U.S. Army in Vietnam 1965–1970. P. 59. Washington, D.C.: Department of the Army; Whelan, T. J., Jr., W. E. Burkhalter, and A. Gomez. 1968. Management of war wounds. Adv. Surg. 3:338–349.
[56]Neel, Medical Support, pp. 59–79.
[57]Ibid., pp. 49, 53.
[58]Bellamy, R. F. 1984. The causes of death in conventional land warfare: Implications for combat casualty care research. Military Med. 148:55–62.
[59]Neel, Medical Support, p. 119.
[60]Neel, Medical Support, pp. 46–58; Whelan et al., Management of war wounds, Adv. Surg., pp. 229–257.
[61]Neel, Medical Support, pp. 50–51.
[62]Keegan, Face of Battle, pp. 269–270.
[63]Neel, Medical Support, p. 52.
[64]Ibid.
[65]Department of Defense. 1976. In Connection with the Conflict in Vietnam, fact sheet January 1976, Washington, D.C.: U.S. Government Printing Office. As cited in G. Emerson. 1976. Winners and Losers. Pp. 58–59. New York: Harcourt Brace Jovanovich.
[66]Rund and Rausch, Triage, pp. 3–10.
[67]U.S. Armed Forces, Emergency War Surgery, pp. 172–173; Department of the Army. 1973. NATO Handbook on the Medical Aspects of NBC Defensive Operations, AMedP-6. Pp. 6-1–6-11. Washington, D.C.: Department of the Army.
[68]Glasstone, S., and P. J. Dolan. 1977. The Effects of Nuclear Weapons. Pp. 80–86, 132–153. Washington, D.C.: U.S. Department of Defense, U. S. Government Printing Office; Cooper, J., R. L. Maynard, N. L. Cross, and J. F. Hill. 1983. Casualties from terrorist bombings. J. Trauma 23:955–967; Stapczynski, J. S. 1982. Blast injuries. Ann. Emerg. Med. 11:687–694.
[69]Glasstone and Dolan, Nuclear Weapons, pp. 548–559.

[70]Cooper, Terrorist Bombings, p. 959.

[71]Kennedy, T. L., and G. W. Johnston. 1975. Civilian bomb injuries. Br. Med. J. Vol. I, February 15, p. 383.

[72]Glasstone and Dolan, Nuclear Weapons, pp. 553–557, 175–189.

[73]Keegan, Face of Battle, p. 264.

[74]Cooper, G. J., B. P. Pearce, M. C. Stainer, and R. L. Maynard. 1982. The biomechanical response of the thorax to nonpenetrating impact with particular reference to cardiac injuries. J. Trauma 22:994–1008.

[75]Coppel, D. L. 1976. Blast injuries of the lungs. Br. J. Surg. 63:735–737.

[76]Cooper, Terrorist Bombings, p. 961.

[77]Ibid; Glasstone and Dolan, Nuclear Weapons, p. 552.

[78]Blocker, V., and T. G. Blocker, Jr. 1949. The Texas City disaster: A survey of 3000 casualties. Am. J. Surg. 78:756–771.

[79]Cooper, Terrorist Bombings, pp. 960–961.

[80]Blocker and Blocker, Texas City Disaster, pp. 756–771.

[81]Kennedy and Johnston, Civilian Bomb Injuries, p. 382; Stapczynski, Blast Injuries, p. 690.

[82]Cooper, Terrorist Bombings, pp. 955–967.

[83]Ibid., pp. 959–960; Kennedy and Johnston, Civilian Bomb Injuries, pp. 382–383.

[84]Cooper, Terrorist Bombings, pp. 959–961.

[85]Blocker and Blocker, Texas City Disaster, pp. 756–771.

[86]Coppel, Blast Injuries of the Lungs, pp. 735–736.

[87]Kennedy and Johnston, Civilian Bomb Injuries, p. 383.

[88]Rodgers, H. W., and J. D. A. Robb. 1973. Surgery of civil violence. Pp. 321–331 in Selwyn Taylor, ed., Recent Advances in Surgery, no. 8, Edinburgh: Churchill Livingstone.

[89]Glasstone and Dolan, Nuclear Weapons, p. 566.

[90]Constable, J. D. 1982. Burn injuries among survivors. Pp. 202–210 in E. Chivian et al., eds., Last Aid. San Francisco: W. H. Freeman.

[91]Cooper, Terrorist Bombings, pp. 961–962; Glasstone and Dolan, Nuclear Weapons, pp. 568–570; Committee for the Compilation of Materials. 1981. Hiroshima and Nagasaki. Pp. 118–121. New York: Basic Books.

[92]Glasstone and Dolan, Nuclear Weapons, pp. 563–565.

[93]Glasstone and Dolan, Nuclear Weapons, pp. 568–574; Constable, Burn Injuries among Survivors, pp. 202–210.

[94]Beecher, H. K. 1943. Resuscitation and sedation of patients with burns which include the airway. Ann. Surg. 117:825–833; Churchill, Surgeon to Soldiers, pp. 12–25.

[95]Dimick, A. R. 1981. Triage of Burn Patients. Pp. 17–20 in Thermal Injuries, Topics in Emergency Medicine. Gaithersburg, Md.: Aspen Systems Corp.; Glasstone and Dolan, Nuclear Weapons, pp. 558–559; Committee for the Compilation of Materials, Hiroshima and Nagasaki, pp. 120–121.

[96]Constable, Burn Injuries among Survivors, pp. 202–210.

[97]Artz, C. P., and D. R. Yarbrough III. 1972. Burns. Pp. 272–293 in D. C. Sabiston, Jr., ed., Textbook of Surgery. Philadelphia: W. B. Saunders.

[98]Daugherty, W., B. Levi, and F. von Hippel. 1986. Casualties Due to the Blast, Heat, and Radioactive Fallout from Various Hypothetical Nuclear Attacks on the U.S. This volume.

[99]Oughterson, A. W., and S. Warren. 1956. Medical Effects of the Atomic Bomb in Japan. Pp. 6–8, 90–93, 437–443. New York: McGraw-Hill.

[100]Committee for the Compilation of Materials, Hiroshima and Nagasaki, p. 523.

[101]Committee for the Compilation of Materials, Hiroshima and Nagasaki, pp. 107–114.

[102]Committee for the Compilation of Materials, Hiroshima and Nagasaki, pp. 503–510.

[103]Rund and Rausch, Triage, pp. 84–96.

[104]Committee for the Compilation of Materials, Hiroshima and Nagasaki, pp. 107–114.

[105]Daugherty et al. This volume.

[106]Postol, T. A. 1986. Possible fatalities from superfires following nuclear attacks in or near urban areas. This volume.

[107]Abrams, H. L. 1984. Medical resources after nuclear war. J. Am. Med. Assoc. 252:653–658.

[108]These assumptions overstate the number available by (a) ignoring the probability that the physicians might be more densely settled in the central areas of the cities, and (b) by not accounting for injuries among those physicians in the 12–15 km area. This latter effect is somewhat offset by assuming that all physicians among the injured who fled the 10–12 km zone would be considered in the category of casualty and not provider.

[109]Diffenbough, Military Surgery, pp. 490–491.

[110]Sheedy, J. A. 1962. The role of forward medical support in handling masses of casualties in active nuclear warfare. Military Med. 127:147–154; Warren, R., and J. H. Jackson. 1950. Suggestions for first-aid treatment of casualties from atomic bombing. N. Engl. J. Med. 243:696–698.

[111]Orr, S. M., and W. A. Robinson. 1983. The Hyatt Regency skywalk collapse: An EMS-based disaster response. Ann. Emerg. Med. 12:601–605.

[112]Lifton, R. J., et al. 1984. The second death: Psychological survival after nuclear war. Pp. 285–400 in J. Leaning and L. Keyes, eds., The Counterfeit Ark. Cambridge, Mass.: Ballinger.

[113]Hersey, J. 1977. Hiroshima. Pp. 33–34. New York: Bantam Books.

[114]Sorokin, P. A. 1942. Man and Society in Calamity. New York: E. P. Dutton; Lifton, Second Death, pp. 285–400; Kinston, W., and R. Rosser. 1974. Disaster: Effects on mental and physical state. J. Psychosomat. Res. 18:437–456.

[115]Harwell, M. A., and H. D. Grover. 1985. Biological effects of nuclear war I: Impact on humans. Bioscience 35:570–583.

The Medical Implications of Nuclear War, Institute of
Medicine. © 1986 by the National Academy of Sciences.
National Academy Press, Washington, D.C.

Food and Nutrition in
the Aftermath of Nuclear War

ALEXANDER LEAF, M.D.
Massachusetts General Hospital and Harvard Medical School
Boston, Massachusetts

Hunger and starvation would plague the survivors of a nuclear war.
Millions of people would starve to death in the first few years following
an all-out nuclear war. This statement has a high probability of being
accurate as indicated by the following considerations:

1. World food reserves, as measured by total cereal stores at any given
time, are frighteningly small should production fail. They have amounted
in recent years to about 2 months' supply of cereals at present consumption
rates.[1] In the United States food stores would feed the population for about
a year.[2] Portions of the stores, however, would be destroyed by blast or
fire or would be contaminated by radioactivity.[3,4] Crops in the field would
be damaged to an unpredictable extent.[4,5]

2. More important, the means to transport the food from sites of harvest
or storage to the consumers would no longer exist. Transportation centers
would be prime targets of an aggressor intent on destroying the industrial
competence of an opponent to sustain a war. Roads, bridges, and rail and
port facilities would be likely targets. Foods that appear in our markets
are not grown locally. In Massachusetts, for example, more than three-
quarters of the food arrives from out of state by truck or rail, and supplies
on hand would last for only a few days. In a nuclear attack most of these
supplies in urban areas would be destroyed.

In the United States and other developed countries, food no longer is
carried by farmers to nearby markets. The northeastern United States is
particularly vulnerable to a breakdown in transportation of foods since

some 80 percent of its food is imported, but other sections of the country would fare only little better. Eighty-five percent of U.S. corn is grown in 11 Midwestern states. One-sixth of the wheat is grown in Kansas alone, and most of the rest is grown from Texas north to Minnesota, North Dakota, and Montana, with some being grown in Michigan, the Pacific Northwest, and New York State, but only a negligible amount is grown in the Northeast. Two-thirds of the soybeans are grown in the Great Lakes States and the Corn Belt. Rice is grown mainly in Arkansas, Louisiana, Texas, Mississippi, and California. Fruit and vegetable production is nearly as regionally concentrated.[2] With key railway links and highways destroyed and gasoline and diesel fuels unavailable, whatever crops survived could not be moved to places where they would be needed.

3. Food is supplied today in the United States and developed countries by a complex network of enterprises that involves not only farming, animal husbandry, and fishing but also farm machinery, pesticides, fertilizers, petroleum products, and commercial seeds. This network utilizes sophisticated techniques and technology to handle the food that is produced. These include grain elevators, slaughterhouses, cold-storage plants, flour mills, canning factories, and other packaging plants. It also includes the transportation, the storage, and the marketing and distribution of foods through both wholesale and retail outlets. A breakdown in this vast agribusiness would be an inevitable consequence of a nuclear war. Without the means to harvest, process, and distribute those crops that survived, there would be much spoilage.

4. So much of the social and economic structure of society as we know it would be destroyed that relationships that we take for granted would disappear. Money would have little or no value. Food and other necessities would be obtained, when available, by barter. More likely, as people became desperate with hunger, survival instincts would take over, and armed individuals or marauding bands would raid and pilfer whatever supplies and stores still existed. Those fortunate individuals who had stores would hoard their resources and soon become the victims of the crazed behavior of starving and desperate survivors who would ransack warehouses and attack individual homes. Law enforcement would not exist, and many would be killed in the fighting between those trying forcefully to obtain possession of food stores and those trying to protect their own homes, families, and food supplies.

5. The early death of millions of humans and animals following a major nuclear war would not sufficiently compensate for the reduced available food supplies. Stocks of fuels, fertilizers, agricultural chemicals, and seed would soon be exhausted. Not only functioning tractors but also beasts of burden would be in short supply, and food production would become

very labor intensive—a throwback to the primitive farming methods of the Middle Ages or earlier. The resistance of insects to radiation and the lack of pesticides would further reduce the yield of crops. Fields downwind from targeted sites are likely to be made unusable by radioactive fallout for weeks to years.

6. A reduction in average temperature by even 1°C at the Earth's surface because of the absorption of solar energy by soot and dust in the atmosphere would shorten the growing season in northern latitudes and markedly reduce or prevent maturation and ripening of grains that are the staple of human diets. But the debates that have been heard are not of whether a "nuclear winter" would occur but how many tens of degrees the temperature would be reduced and for how long. During most of the growing season, a sharp decline in temperature for only a few days may be sufficient to destroy crops. The lack of rain that has been predicted after a nuclear war would contribute to crop failures. Since most of the wheat and coarse grains are grown in the temperate regions of the Northern Hemisphere, which would be the zones most affected by a "nuclear winter," it is evident that a nuclear war, especially during the spring or summer, would have a devastating effect on crop production and food supplies for at least that year. The United States and Canada are literally the breadbasket for the world; total cereal production in North America in 1982 was 387 million metric tons, of which 123 million metric tons or nearly one-third was exported.

7. After the atmospheric soot and dust finally clear, the destruction of the stratospheric ozone would allow an increase in hard ultraviolet-B (UV-B) rays to reach the Earth's surface. In addition to the direct harmful effects to the skin and eyes of humans and animals, these hard ultraviolet rays would be damaging to plant life and would interfere with agricultural production. If the oxides of nitrogen increase in the troposphere, there may occur an actual increase of ozone at the lower levels of the atmosphere.[6] Ozone is directly toxic to plants.

8. There would likely be a deterioration of the quality of the soil following a nuclear war. The death of plant and forest coverage because of fire, radiation, the lack of fertilizers, and the probable primitive slash-and-burn agricultural practices of survivors would leave the soil vulnerable to erosion by wind and rain. Desertification and coarse grasses and shrubs would render agriculture and animal husbandry less productive.

9. Water supplies may be seriously reduced after a nuclear war. Dams and large irrigation projects may well be targets, especially in a counter-value attack. Reduced rainfall, which is predicted in some models of the climatic effects of a nuclear war, would interfere with agricultural pro-

ductivity. If freezing temperatures actually were to occur during the warm season, surface waters would be frozen and unavailable. Radioactive fallout would contaminate reservoirs and surface waters with long-lived radioactive isotopes, primarily strontium-90, which has a half-life of 28 years, and cesium-137, which has a half-life of 33 years. These elements in the groundwater would soon be taken up by plants and would enter the food chain. Eventually they would become concentrated in humans; the strontium would accumulate in bones and the cesium in cytoplasm, where they would contribute to the long-term burden of radioactivity in survivors.

10. Not only would food be scarce but it would likely be unsanitary as well. The destruction of sanitation, refrigeration, and food-processing methods, especially in the remaining urban areas or population centers, would result in the contamination of food by bacteria, particularly by enteric pathogens. Spoiled meat, carrion of domestic animals and even of human corpses, are likely to be eaten by starving persons, as has happened in major famines in the past.[2] Pathogens to which civilized man has lost resistance would be acquired from foods and water contaminated by excreta and flies, other insects, and rodents, which would likely proliferate in the aftermath of nuclear war.

11. But the hunger and starvation would not be limited to the combatant countries alone, or even to just the Northern Hemisphere. It would truly be a global occurrence. Even without the spread of the possible climatic effects of a "nuclear winter" to the Southern Hemisphere, millions would die of starvation in noncombatant countries. Today a large portion of food exports goes to parts of the world where, even with the grain imports shown in Table 1, millions of people suffer from undernutrition and hunger.[2,3,7]

The number of undernourished persons in developing countries is staggering, approaching one-quarter of all mankind.[2] On the basis of 1980 data, the World Bank estimated that some 800 million persons in developing countries—from 61 to 71 percent of their population—have deficient diets.[7] The U.N. Food and Agriculture Organization, using slightly more stringent criteria, estimate that some 16 to 23 percent of the global population, or 436 million persons, have food intake levels that permit little more than survival (1.2 times the basal metabolic rate, a level of caloric intake below which survival is not possible and which is incompatible with productive work).[8,9] In addition, the World Health Organization identifies at least 450 million children that suffer from varying degrees of protein malnutrition.[10] A large number of these persons are dependent on the food supply and price structure made possible by the

TABLE 1   Total Cereal Exports and Imports[a]

| Country | Total Cereals ($\times$ 10^6 metric tons) | | |
	Exported/ Imported	Produced	Percent of Production
Exports			
United States[b]	95	333	29
Canada	28	54	52
European Economic Community	18	133	14
Argentina	18	34	53
Australia	11	14	79
Total	170	568	30
Imports			
Africa	24	74	32
South America	11	80	14
Asia (except People's Republic of China)	64	363	18
Europe	31	271	11
Total	130	788	16
United States	2	333	0
USSR	33	173	19

[a]Cereals comprise wheat, coarse grains, and rice.

[b]The United States, with 5 percent of the world's population, grows 20 percent of the world's cereals and imports only 0.7 percent of the world's total cereal imports.

SOURCE: U.N. Food and Agriculture Organization (1985).[1]

food exports of North America, so a disruption of these supplies would have grave consequences for most of the populations of developing countries.[2]

In the past decade an increasing interdependence of countries on their food supplies has occurred.[11-13] In 1982, as shown in Table 1, the major grain-exporting countries, the United States, Canada, the European Economic Community, and Australia, exported 170 million metric tons of cereals.[1] The developing countries were the major recipients of these exports. Africa imported 24 million metric tons of cereals in 1982, which is equal to one-third of its own total grain production for that year. In South America cereal imports equaled 11 percent of total cereal production, and in Asia, excluding the People's Republic of China, this figure equaled 18 percent of total cereal production. By 1990 the situation in the countries with a food production deficit will worsen and the food shortages will increase, despite their efforts to increase production and contain populations.[9,14] Of this deficit, 40 percent will occur in Asia, 25 percent in North Africa and the Middle East, 22 percent in Sub-Sahara Africa, and 12 percent in Latin America.[14]

In conclusion, it is evident from the considerations listed above that hunger and starvation would decimate the survivors of a major nuclear war. Millions of deaths would result not only among survivors in combatant countries but throughout the world. The developing countries, in fact, would possibly be the main victims of this famine, as their populations may not be reduced as immediately as would those in the combatant countries. Starvation would be essentially global—a consequence of nuclear war that would not have been predictable from a simple extrapolation from the experiences in Hiroshima and Nagasaki.

NOTES

[1]U.N. Food and Agriculture Organization. 1985. Food outlook No. 6, 1985. Rome: Food and Agriculture Organization.

[2]Scrimshaw, N. 1984. Food, nutrition, and nuclear war. N. Engl. J. Med. 311:272–276.

[3]Hjort, H. W. 1982. The impact on global food supplies. Ambio 11:153–157.

[4]Bensen, D. W. et al., eds. 1971. Proceedings of a Symposium. Survival of food crops and livestock in the event of nuclear war. Conf-700929. Springfield, Va.: National Technical Information Service.

[5]Bondietti, E. A. 1982. Effect on agriculture. Ambio 11:138–142.

[6]Crutzen, P. J., and J. W. Birks. 1982. The atmosphere after a nuclear war: Twilight at noon. Ambio 11:114–125.

[7]Reutlinger, S., and H. Alderman. 1980. Prevalence of calorie deficiency diets in developing countries. World Bank Staff Working Paper No. 374. Washington, D.C: World Bank.

[8]World Health Organization Food and Nutrition. 1975. Energy and protein requirements; recommendations by a joint FAO/WHO informal gathering of experts. Vol. 1(2):11–19.

[9]U.N. Food and Agriculture Organization. 1981. Agriculture toward 2000. Rome: Food and Agriculture Organization.

[10]Infant and young child nutrition. 1983. Report by the Director General to the World Health Assembly, March 15, 1983. Document WHA 36/1983/7.

[11]International Food Policy Research Institute. 1977. Recent and prospective developments in food consumption: Some policy issues. IFPRI Research Report No. 2, Revised Edition. Washington, D.C.: International Food Policy Research Institute.

[12]Josling, T. 1980. Developed-country agricultural policies and developing-country supplies: The case of wheat. International Food Policy Research Institute, Research Report No. 17. Washington, D.C.: International Food Policy Research Institute.

[13]U.S. Department of Agriculture. 1970. World demand prospects for wheat in 1980 (With emphasis on trade by less developed countries). Foreign Agricultural Economic Report No. 62, U.S. Department of Agriculture, U.S. Economic Research Service. Washington, D.C.: U.S. Government Printing Office.

[14]International Food Policy Research Institute. 1977. Food needs of developing countries: Projections of production and consumption to 1990. Research Report No. 3. Washington, D.C.: International Food Policy Research Institute.

The Medical Implications of Nuclear War, Institute of
Medicine. © 1986 by the National Academy of Sciences
National Academy Press, Washington, D.C.

Psychological Consequences of Disaster: Analogies for the Nuclear Case

JAMES THOMPSON, PH.D.
Middlesex Hospital, London, England

INTRODUCTION

No disaster experienced in recorded history resembles the potential destruction of major nuclear war. Nonetheless, past disasters can give us pointers to the likely responses of those who survive the immediate effects, though it will always be necessary to interpret the findings carefully with due allowance for the differences that restrict the applicability of the comparison.

Localized disasters such as explosions and fires give a partial view of likely reactions, which, in the case of nuclear war, would be repeated across whole continents. Earthquakes and floods give a better understanding of large-scale and generalized destruction, though it is correspondingly more difficult to comprehensively evaluate how everyone reacted. All these disasters differ from the nuclear case in that there is always an undamaged outside world able to offer some help and assistance. Furthermore, the imponderable effects of radiation will impose a delay on rescue attempts, since most people will be unable to establish when it is safe to come out from what remains of their shelters. The electromagnetic pulse is likely to have severely damaged the communication networks on which all effective relief operations depend. Most of all, the probable extent of the physical destruction to civilization would be so extensive as to make unlikely any concerted rescue operation, even if it could be mounted. Most people would be concerned with their own survival, and the *illusion of centrality* that is held by disaster victims would, for many, be more of a reality than an illusion.

Classification of Disasters as Analogies for the Nuclear Case

It is a matter of considerable relief that, as yet, there are no references to how people have reacted to a major nuclear war. Therefore, in order to provide some illustrative guidance, data about other catastrophes have had to be used as analogies for the nuclear case.

Disaster Agents

A descriptive system first put forward by Hewitt and Burton (1971), and later adapted by Leivesley (1979), can be used to divide disaster agents into five categories:

Atmospheric: cyclone and hurricane, tornado, drought, snow, fire
Hydrologic: flood, storm surge, Tsunami
Geologic: earthquake, landslide, volcano
Biologic: epidemics, crop diseases, and biological warfare
Technologic: Accident (engineered structures, transport, chemicals, nuclear reactors, nuclear weapons, nuclear weapons testing, radioactive materials, fire), war (conventional bombing, nuclear weapons)

Disasters can also be categorized by the extent of energy release, frequency of occurrence, and period of duration. An earthquake can last for a few seconds, an avalanche for a few minutes, a blizzard for several hours, a flood for days or even weeks, and a drought for months or even years.

In general, the disasters that cause most casualties, earthquakes, floods, and cyclones, occur with the lowest frequencies. This means that such terrible events tend to be rare in most people's experience, and thus it is hard to learn how to predict them and protect people against their worst effects. The power of these natural events may also make it seem futile to take many protective steps.

In a more general sense, there are a wide variety of hazards which may lead to disaster. The perception of these hazards has an important impact on whether precautionary steps are taken. Hazards can be classified into the following categories:

Natural—tornado, earthquake, flood
Quasinatural—air and water pollution

Social—epidemic and riot
Man-made—building collapse, fire, car accident, boat accident

People's perceptions of hazard have been studied by factor analytic methods (Kates, et al., 1976), and it has been found that they can be organized into two factors. The first factor, which accounts for most of the variation in perceptions, is orderly, relaxed, and peaceful versus chaotic, tense, and ferocious. The second factor is natural, uncontrollable, and fair versus artificial, controllable, and unfair. From this it will be evident that wars are seen as chaotic, tense, and ferocious and also artificial, controllable, and unfair.

Turning now from the disasters themselves to the impact that they have on humans, differences exist between the levels at which the response of victims to the disaster can be studied. Individuals can be studied, or the level of analysis could be raised to that of the family, the community, and society as a whole.

Appropriateness of Analogies

The problem with the approach by analogy is that no single disaster approximates all the features of a nuclear war. Although Hiroshima and Nagasaki represent the only examples of nuclear bombing, the weapons used there were very much smaller in their explosive power than those that are available today. The bombings occurred without any warning, the construction of housing was very different from that of modern European cities, and the population had no knowledge of nuclear explosions or radioactivity. In terms of psychological reactions, Japanese culture was very different from that of present-day Europe, with there being a high degree of group identification and respect for authority.

Most of all, the surrounding areas were not under nuclear attack and were able and willing to give some assistance. Communications were maintained at a national level, so that radio and telegraph, roads, and railways in the surrounding countryside were all functioning. Despite this, the basic effect of the blast was the same.

A modern nuclear war could involve the detonation of large numbers of far more powerful weapons, with or without any warning, over large sections of the Northern Hemisphere. Such a nuclear war might last hours, weeks, or months and the electromagnetic pulse could serve to disable most electronic communications.

In terms of sheer physical destruction, earthquakes give an indication of the effects of massive blast damage, but not even these physical effects are really comparable. Depending on the intensity and waveform of the quake, different types and degrees of damage occur, but they are different in form from blast damage. In some cases the tremors preceding the major event serve as a warning, particularly in areas where earthquakes have already been experienced by the population. Although earthquake damage can be widespread, radio communications are generally still possible and there is no fear of immediate contamination, as would be the case with radioactivity.

Massive fires resemble the effects of postnuclear firestorms, but, once again, present data are based on the fact that there is an undamaged outside world to come to the assistance of those in the fire zone. Hurricanes and tornadoes replicate many features of blast damage, but they generally come with some warning and do not leave immediately contaminated ground. Floods cause widespread damage, generally come with some warning, and often lead to fears of health risks. Major epidemics leave the physical world undamaged, but they replicate the immense depletion of population that would follow a major nuclear war and come closest to revealing attitudes to radioactive contamination.

Table 1 summarizes the major features of disasters as analogies for a major nuclear war and gives very rough, and highly debatable, estimates of impact for illustrative purposes only. It serves not so much to tie down each disaster into a rigid system of measurement, but simply to summarize some of their major features to make comparisons possible.

ANALYSIS OF HUMAN REACTIONS TO DISASTERS

Although past disasters are imperfect guides to the future, they must be studied if likely future reactions are to be understood. Leivesley (1979), in a study on disasters and welfare planning, gives over 400 references and Kinston and Rosser (1974) give 117. Quarantelli (1980) has worked extensively in this area, and Churcher et al. (1981) have reviewed the literature with reference to nuclear war. Kinston and Rosser (1974) reviewed the psychological effects of disasters, which they define as situations of massive, collective stress, in an attempt to draw some conclusions from the extensive but unsystematized literature on human reactions to catastrophes. They note that there has often been a reluctance to fully investigate these reactions, as if researchers were averting their eyes from what they found. It was 17 years before any attempt was made to study the psychological consequences of the bombings of Hiroshima and Nagasaki. Even civil defense exercises set up to deal with simulated disasters fail to meet the pressing psychological needs of the supposed victims, and reveal an apparent unwillingness to confront the misery of personal tragedy.

TABLE 1 Categorization of Disasters by Nature of Their Impact[a]

Disaster	Features					Communication
	Frequency	Suddenness	Power	Extent	Contamination	Disruption
Plague	1	3	0	9	10	0
Hurricane	3	9	8	4	1	4
Fires	3	8	4	4	0	4
Floods	3	6	5	4	3	4
Earthquake	3	10	10	5	3	7
Conventional war	2	4	2	5	3	4
Nuclear	<1	10	10	9	9	9

[a]Estimates are given on a 10-point scale. Features are frequency, suddenness of impact, destructive power, geographic extent of damage, degree of contamination of environment, and extent to which communications are disrupted.

Even when prompt and effective treatment is available, as in the burns victims described by Cobb and Lindemann (1944), and despite excellent planning and precautions to minimize psychological stress, 43 percent of the survivors showed evidence of psychiatric illness. This indicates the pressing need to investigate as fully as possible how people react to disasters and to be aware of the psychological impairment which usually results.

Despite a measure of reluctance to investigate the consequences of catastrophes, some features have been identified. Kinston and Rosser (1974) use a classification system based on the work of Tyhurst (1951) and Glass (1959), who categorize the phases of disaster as threat, warning, impact, recoil, and postimpact. Although these categories merely represent points along a continuum and describe average reactions which may not occur in all people, they help us understand the course of events.

Threat

All life is subject to potential hazards, but some hazards are more evident and dangerous than others. Earthquake belts, volcanic slopes, war zones, and floodplains all carry particular risks. In terms of the risk of nuclear war, countries that themselves deploy nuclear weapons are especially at risk, and within those countries missile bases and possibly urban centers are likely targets. The evaluation of risk is a problematic subject, involving subjective estimates and attempts at calculated probabilities.

Slovic and Fischoff (1980) have looked at public perceptions of a variety of hazards and have shown that perceived risks are often at variance with actual risks. These differences may be partly accounted for by the prominence that the media gives to dramatic events, thus increasing their salience over less newsworthy occurrences. But Slovic et al. (1982) have shown that when both experts and members of the public are asked to rate hazards by other perceived characteristics such as whether the risk is voluntary and what the extent of catastrophic potential might be, much of the difference between the two groups disappears.

Threat is the condition under which we live at present. It is evident that a pressing danger exists, but the perceived salience of the threat varies from person to person and from time to time. Chivian (1983) has reviewed children's sense of nuclear threat, and argues that this is more widespread and substantial than generally realized. Escalona (1963, 1965, 1982) has extensively studied children's and adolescents' fears about nuclear war, which she feels threatens their belief in the future and the trustworthiness of their parents. Schwebel (1982) suggests that the nuclear threat is a contributing factor in anxiety and other disorders noted among teenagers.

Beardslee and Mack (1982) conclude that children are deeply disturbed by the threat of nuclear war and have doubts about their own survival. In the United Kingdom, 52 percent of teenagers feel that nuclear war will occur in their lifetime, and 70 percent feel that it is inevitable one day (Business Decisions, 1983). Tizard (1984) reviewed the literature on children's fears about nuclear war. She found that many of the studies were unsystematic, but that methodologically sound studies, which had asked large representative samples of graduating high school students in the United States neutral questions about the future, found increasing levels of alarm about the nuclear threat. Bachman (1984), in a study of the sort described above, found that the proportion of adolescents who often worried about the nuclear threat rose from 7 percent in 1976 to 31 percent in 1982, and the feeling that nuclear or biological annihilation would occur in their lifetimes rose from 23 percent in 1976 to 35 percent in 1982.

Solantous et al. (1984), in a survey of 5,000 Finnish 12- to 18-year-olds, found that even in this nonnuclear, neutral country, 79 percent of the 12-year-olds and 48 percent of the 18-year-olds named a probable future war as their major fear.

Adults share this concern and show a general perception that they are at risk because of nuclear weapons, though this is rarely stated as the most pressing worry people face. A 1982 Gallup Poll found that 72 percent of an adult sample was worried about nuclear war, and 38 percent thought that nuclear war would occur.

In general, there is no consistent relationship between such anxieties and attitudes to nuclear weapons policies. Despite evidence of anxiety in many people, the most consistent reaction appears to be some form of denial, which Lifton (1967) describes as "consistent human adaptation." Some people avoid the subject totally. Other reactions are resignation, helplessness (Seligman, 1975), fatalism, and unquestioning trust. The myth of personal invulnerability, that necessary fiction of everyday life, holds strong and allows people to continue the necessary tasks of living. All authority tends to be displaced onto leaders and authorities, and people tend to feel helpless and unable to influence events through their actions.

Warnings

To understand the way that people respond to warnings of impending catastrophes, it is necessary to review the accounts that have been given of those disasters in which warnings were possible. A few points must be considered about the relationships among warnings, stress, and behavior. For a warning to be effective it must have a reliable association with the threat, and there must be a credible action to take in response to it.

However, humans have considerable shortcomings as estimators of the probabilities of future hazards (Slovic et al., 1974; Kahneman et al., 1982). Even when a hazard is acknowledged, people may perceive it in many different ways, seeing it as improbable or, on the other hand, so inevitable as to vitiate any human actions.

Research on responses to stressors indicates that appraisal of threat is a psychological process, and knowledge about a stressor tends to improve coping responses in any situation in which coping responses are possible. In general, having something to do that reduces the threat, or even simply appears to do so, reduces the impact of stressors. In studies of experimental stress on animals, the least affected groups are those that receive warnings of impending shocks and can reduce the probability of receiving them by carrying out avoidance behaviors, however onerous. The groups that suffer most stress, as measured by the rate of stomach ulceration, are those that suffer an equal number of shocks without benefit of warning and cannot reduce their frequency by any instrumental means (Weiss, 1973). Without a warning these animals can never relax, since they have no safety signal and could experience a shock at any time. A reliable warning, on the other hand, does cause temporary high levels of anxiety, but once the danger is over, safety can be assumed by the absence of danger warnings. Such helpless animals suffer considerably, and their helpless behavior has many similarities to human depression (Seligman, 1975), which is characterized by a failure to initiate responses, even when these might lead to the avoidance of further stresses. The safety signal hypothesis should explain why the conventional bombing attacks on London appeared to cause less psychological stress than those of the V-bombs later in the war. In the first case the air raid sirens and the eventual all clear provided reasonably reliable signals of safety, but with the rockets no such indication was possible.

Studies of Disaster Warnings

Simply because a warning has been given does not mean that it will be heeded. Denial can continue in some individuals up to the moment of impact itself. During the Hawaiian tidal wave of May 1960, evacuation was minimal (Lachman et al., 1961); and on the banks of the Rio Grande, festive crowds watched and cheered the rising floodwaters (Wolfenstein, 1957). These active denials of danger have their place in everyday life, but when they are carried over in the face of a real threat, they constitute a danger in themselves, since they obstruct preventative action. The myth of personal invulnerability still holds. A measure of this delusion can be gauged by the finding that the majority of people believe that they are more likely than average to live past 80 years of age (Britten, 1983). Once the danger is admitted, people who are very trusting may overrely on official pronouncements. Those who lack faith in parental establishment figures may be susceptible to rumor. Precautionary activity depends on the adequacy of information as to what needs to be done and whether a group effect begins to take place once people take the warning seriously. Conflicting advice is usual (Churcher et al., 1981), and many people may be unable to decide on a consistent response.

Some studies have looked at the warning process in detail, and these will be considered as analogies for likely reactions to warnings of an attack with nuclear weapons.

Short Warning Times

Drabek and Stephenson (1971) have given a detailed account of the behavior of 278 families randomly selected from approximately 3,700 families who had been evacuated from their homes prior to a flood in Denver, Colorado. At 5:30 p.m. one cloudy afternoon, in which there had been occasional showers throughout much of the day, police cars cruised past suburban houses with the following announcement: "A 20-foot wall of water is approaching this area. You have 5 to 15 minutes to evacuate. Leave for high ground immediately."

The events leading to this announcement need a brief summary. After a tornado earlier in the day, a wall of water was seen sweeping down one of the tributaries of the South Platte River, which flows through Denver. The local sheriff raised the alarm at 3 p.m., and this was received with some incredulity, since a major flood had not occurred on the river for 100 years. By 4 p.m. police began evacuating those closest to the river, and by 5 p.m. they broadened the area of evacuation. Throughout the warning period radio and television responded in a sporadic fashion. Some stations carried on with normal programs, while others gradually shifted to increased flood coverage. This led many people to switch from one station to another in an attempt to confirm conflicting stories which seemed impossible to believe. The wide area of television coverage meant that people in safe areas converged on the danger zone to contact friends and relatives or, in the largest number of cases, simply because of curiosity. From the viewpoint of the families in the danger area, their many attempts to confirm the warnings frequently yielded contradictory information, and of those who evacuated immediately, as many as one-third returned home, often infiltrating through police lines which had been set up to prevent looting. At 8:15 p.m. the floodwaters arrived, causing considerable damage but no loss of life because of the evacuation.

Drabek and Stephenson argue that five analytical characteristics are especially important. In contrast to more typical slowly developing floods this one was (1) sudden, (2) unexpected, (3) unfamiliar to the populace, and (4) highly localized in its danger area; and (5) warnings were received in quite varied social contexts.

Response to warnings suggests that individual responses are affected greatly by group memberships, with the most important being the family unit. Most people responded to the flood as family members, not as isolated individuals; and of those families that were together at the time of warning, 92 percent evacuated together. When family members were separated at the time of the initial warnings, which happened for 41 percent of the total sample, their immediate concerns were making contact with each other.

Although 52 percent received their warnings from mass media (as opposed to 28 percent from peers and relatives and 19 percent directly from the authorities) these people were far more likely to ignore the message or spend time attempting to confirm it than those who got more direct warnings. For example, see the results in Table 2.

Although mass media sources often urged evacuation of very specific areas, these warnings tended to be viewed as background information, while a direct request from the authorities was far more likely to get people moving. Mass media seemed to generate the behavior of further information seeking—people stayed "glued" to their sets rather than leave as advised.

Mass media and peer recommendations to evacuate were received with skepticism by 60 percent of respondents, but when the authorities were the source, such skepticism occurred in only 22 percent of cases. Even in this case one police officer recounted an experience in which a woman casually approached the car from which he was broadcasting the evacuation

TABLE 2   Response of Denver Residents to Flood Warnings

Message Content	Continued Routine Activity (percent)	Attempted Confirmation (percent)	Evacuated (percent)
"Some areas flooding or evacuating"	36	38	26
"River rising"	38	33	29
"Flood water coming down River Platte"	29	25	46
"Evacuate"	22	18	60

SOURCE: Drabek and Stephenson (1971:Table 2).

warning over a loudspeaker and calmly asked "What theater is it at?" Several exchanges were required before the woman was willing to accept that it was not a publicity stunt.

The overwhelming bias was to interpret the warnings as nonthreatening and then search for other clues with which to discount or confirm them. Rather than being sterile receptacles of news, people actively worked on what they had been told, and even when they came to accept that a flood was imminent, they still maintained a feeling of personal invulnerability and thought that their own house would not be hit.

Another study of short warning times, in this case of about 1.5 hours, was conducted by Hodler (1982), who surveyed residents in the path of a tornado which had passed through Kalamazoo, Michigan, killing 5 people, injuring 79, and leaving 1,200 homeless. The storm had first been spotted and tracked at 2:30 p.m. and was routinely handled by the mass media, which at 3:45 issued a severe thunderstorm warning. A tornado was seen 15 miles to the west of the city, and the civil defense sirens sounded at 3:56, with the mass media by that time making near continuous emergency broadcasts. By 4:10 the tornado struck. A random sample led to 263 personal half-hour interviews. Two-thirds of the subjects had heard the warning sirens, but 17 percent of those did not know what they meant. Safety was sought by 48 percent, the warnings were disregarded by 18 percent, and 22 percent tried to confirm the warning by looking outside or turning on their radios and televisions. This means that in total 40 percent did not try to evacuate. Michigan had experienced 306 tornados between 1953 and 1975, so this lethargic response was not based on ignorance.

Longer Warning Times

Perry et al. (1982) investigated the level of perceived risk, the warnings received, and the extent to which these were believed by residents near the Mount St. Helens volcano about 16 days after moderate earthquakes indicated that it had come to the end of a 123-year dormant period. At the time when the telephone survey started on a sample of 173 respondents, a state of emergency had been declared for the surrounding area, and when data collection was completed two days later, the news media reported that the immediate crisis was over. The study thus affords a quick look at a crucial phase in the disaster warning process. Residents monitored news media avidly, with a majority of 55 percent even hearing four or more volcano reports per day, while only 10 percent heard only one per day. Television was the most common source of news at 98 percent, with newspapers at 91 percent and radios at 87 percent following close behind. Interpersonal contact was a somewhat less frequent source, though 70 percent received hazard information from friends and relatives and 21 percent had direct contact with officials. A majority of 52 percent were very confident that they had all the information they needed, 32 percent were moderately certain, and only 16 percent remained very uncertain. Confidence was not related to how near respondents were to the volcano, to the source of the information, or to the frequency with which news reports were heard. Although the authors do not comment on this, the question could be conceived of as a measure of anxiety. Despite the high level of news monitoring, only two respondents had evacuated from their homes at the time of the survey.

Janis and Mann (1977) proposed a conflict model of decision making, in which they outlined five patterns of response to warnings of impending danger:

1. Unconflicted inertia is the decision to continue with routine activities because of the belief that there is no serious threat.
2. Unconflicted change is the decision to take the most available protective action.
3. Defensive avoidance results when even the most available protective action will not ensure safety and there is no hope of a better means of escape.
4. Hypervigilance, or panic, occurs when there is not enough time to think what best to do.
5. Vigilance results from realizing that there is time to think what to do.

Perry et al. (1982) conclude from their survey that the situation around Mount St. Helens was sufficiently threatening to make people attend to the danger, but there appeared to be enough time to evaluate the options for action without any pressing need for immediate evacuation. Therefore, in terms of the Janis and Mann (1977) model, vigilance was the most prevalent response, with both hypervigilance and unconflicted change being a rarity. However, it must be said that the model is so general and all-inclusive that these observations constitute only weak validation of its tenets. By way of a general summary, the authors conclude that the intensive dissemination of hazard information during a short period of imminent threat of disaster sensitized people to the impending event.

Effects of Warnings, and Features That Lead People to Heed Them

Hansson et al. (1982) distributed questionnaires to 300 residents of a large floodplain in Oklahoma and got a response rate of 59 percent to a series of questions about knowledge of floods and flood warnings and a wide range of stress indicators. The respondents were people who had lived in their homes for 8 years on average, and 40 percent of them had been flooded before, generally 2.5 years before. Only 10 percent of respondents had ever rehearsed a family plan of action, and only a third had taken any action whatsoever to protect their homes from flooding. Knowledge of the variables affecting urban flooding was associated with reports of actions during the last flood, which reflected greater calm and perceived control. Warning was associated with intensified trauma, as measured by most of the stress indicators. The nature of the 4-hour flood warnings tended to generate anxiety rather than effective defensive activities. Those with personal experience of flooding paid greater attention to the reality and immediacy of the threat, and they did so with increased dread. The more often they had been flooded, the higher their scores on measures of depression and family health stress. The more recent the flooding, the stronger the support for community intervention plans.

Miller (1981) conducted a telephone survey of 248 heads of household living within 10 miles of Three Mile Island to find out which factors determined whether people evacuated during the accident at the nuclear plant. Measures of coping style showed little effect, but situational variables such as proximity to the plant, disruption of telephone service, and specific directives to evacuate were significantly related to the decision to leave.

Jackson (1981) surveyed 302 residents of earthquake zones on the west coast of the United States and found that there was a preference for crisis response. Even though 80 percent had experienced an earthquake and 96 percent expected earthquakes to occur in the future, few believed that they themselves would sustain damage. Only 7.5 percent had taken out insurance or made structural improvements to their homes. When asked to list the disadvantages of their city, only 1.7 percent mentioned earthquakes, as opposed to the 18.2 percent who mentioned air pollution, suggesting that more immediate social and environmental concerns take precedence over the earthquake hazard for the majority of respondents.

When people's views about the likelihood of future earthquakes were sought, it was found that 23.2 percent denied that they would experience an earthquake, 8.9 percent expected that they would, and 67.9 percent were uncertain. An interesting relationship was found with the extent of the loss that had been experienced in previous earthquakes. Those who had suffered the most damage showed the least uncertainty and polarized into those who denied that there would be any further earthquakes and those who expected further damage. The reasons for this finding may lie in the notion of a just world, in which those who have been punished will be spared further castigation.

Summary

A full explanation for people's failure to respond to well-founded threats and warnings is required. The theory of bounded rationality is a possible explanation. As described by Slovic et al. (1974) a very narrow range of adjustments is perceived and adopted. Most people do nothing, or very little. People show a preference for crisis response, saying that they will respond when disaster strikes, foregoing precautions in the absence of personal experience and making changes only in the aftermath of the disaster. People tend to misperceive risks and deny the uncertainty inherent in nature, or they show an unshakable faith in protective devices such as flood control dams or earthquake building codes. They may sometimes flatly deny that a recurrence of a disaster is possible, or misperceive such events as coming in cycles.

The heavy casualties in the Bangladesh cyclone of 1985 were ascribed to an unwillingness to heed warnings which had proved unreliable in the past. The Bradford, England, football fire occurred in a stadium which was known to be a fire hazard 4 years previously, but no action was taken to clear the stand of inflammable material. The Bhopal, India, chemical gassing tragedy was similar in conceptual terms to the accident at Three Mile Island, in that the back-up safety systems designed to cope with an event that the planners could not really believe would ever happen were unable to properly cope with the rare event when it did occur. The conceptual failures that cause major technological accidents have been well described by Perrow (1984) and do not bode well for a tightly coupled and time-sensitive system like the global nuclear weapons machine.

POSTDISASTER BEHAVIOR: IMPACT, RECOIL, AND POSTIMPACT

Impact

When disasters are sudden and severe, most people feel that they are at the very center of the catastrophe. This illusion of centrality, though understandable, may prevent optimum responses since most people will concern themselves with their own local problems. In a tornado people believe that only their house has been hit. The myth of personal invulnerability, which is so strong in the threat phase, is now called into question. Faced with the reality of death, usual assumptions disintegrate, and mood and beliefs oscillate wildly. As the full extent of the destruction becomes apparent and help fails to materialize, there is the second shock effect of dismay at abandonment. Intense emotions are felt, and these fluctuate, making later recall of events problematic. Feelings fluctuate between terror and elation, invulnerability and helplessness, catastrophic abandonment and miraculous escape. All survivors must attempt to make sense of the fact that they could have died, and nearly died, but managed to come through alive. They show not only the exhilaration of massive anxiety relief but also the vulnerability to disappointment which is the longer-term effect of the massive fear that they have experienced. Joy at having survived may be mixed with colossal optimism that the worst is over. Life itself seems sufficient reward, and in particular, joining up with loved ones who were feared lost brings intense happiness. The quite random fact of survival may be rationalized by a feeling of personal invulnerability and mission. Those who have had a brush with death are left in a heightened state of emotional turmoil. This effect is short-lived and soon gives way to the *disaster syndrome.* Victims appear dazed, stunned, and bewildered (Wallace, 1956). Contrary to popular belief, their reactions are not the ones associated with panic. Quarantelli (1954) describes panic as an acute fear reaction, developing as a result of a feeling of entrapment, powerlessness, and isolation, leading to nonsensical and irrational flight behavior. Such frenzied activity is only found when people are trapped and when escape is thought possible only for a limited period of time. Then, contagious panic can indeed occur, but it is not the norm in disasters.

After a disaster, victims are apathetic, docile, indecisive, and unemotional; they behave mechanically. They are still in a state of high autonomic arousal but appear to be paying for their period of terror by emotional and behavioral exhaustion. Various explanations have been put forward for this passive response. It may be a protective reaction, cutting people off from further stimuli which would only cause them anxiety and pain. In an account of the Tokyo earthquake of 1894, Balz noted that he observed the terrible event "with the same cold attention with which one follows an absorbing physical experiment . . . all the higher affective life was extinguished" (cited in Anderson, 1942). Again, it could be a form of wishful fantasy—"if I don't react then nothing has happened." Or it could be that people feel helpless in the face of the massive damage and the impossibility of repairing their shattered world. Whatever the reason, the survivor is left in a diminished condition and is highly vulnerable. Guilt feelings are common, since the catastrophe will have released unacceptable egotistical feelings, including excitement at the deaths of others. Fear will have prevented people from helping others, leaving survivors with only the fantasy of the heroism that they would have liked to have shown in the emergency. Even within families, some will have put their own safety above those of other family members.

Popovic and Petrovic (1964) arrived on the scene of the Skoplje, Yugoslovia, earthquake 22 hours after the event, and in the following 5 days, together with a team of local psychiatrists, they toured the evacuation camps. They found that much of the population was in a mild stupor, depressed, congregating in small unstable groups, and prone to rumors of doom. Prompt outside help, responsible and informative reporting by the press, and the speedy evacuation of the more disturbed victims all contributed to an eventual return to apparent psychological normality. By way of comparison with nuclear war, it should be noted that only 1 in 200 of the people died, and 3 in 200 were injured, far less than would be expected in a nuclear explosion.

In any disaster, according to Kinston and Rosser's (1974) estimates, although roughly three-quarters of the population are likely to show the disaster syndrome, anywhere from 12 to 25 percent will be tense and excited but able to cope by concentrating on appropriate preparatory activities. They will be capable of making themselves too busy to worry, though their activities may often be of only marginal relevance to the threat they face. At times of stress, overlearned familiar routines can serve as a solace. Equally, 12 to 25 percent will fare far worse and will show grossly inappropriate behavior, with anxiety symptoms predominating. There will be an immediate increase in psychological distress as those already vulnerable are triggered into breakdown. Such effects are more likely for reactive disorders than those that are psychotic in origin. Those whose behavior is contained only by social pressure are likely to behave in psychopathic ways. The crisis will provide an opportunity that some will be willing to exploit.

Recoil

If the cause of the disaster is seen to pass and some sort of "all clear" can be announced, there will be an opportunity for a return to something approximating a normal psychological state. About 90 percent of subjects show a return of awareness and recall. They are highly dependent, talkative, and childlike, seeking safety and forming unstable social groups. In this state they remain highly vulnerable and emotionally labile. Some respond with totally psychopathic behavior; and looting, rape, and heavy drinking may occur. People show a return of energy with a commensurate return of reason. They behave hyperactively and often irrationally. They become obsessed with communicating their experiences to others and the need to work through the events in order to give them some meaning. The need for explanation is part of dependency and leads to rumor and absurd gullibility. People will be anxious to obtain reliable news, and will expect their own experiences to be news. The monitoring of the news serves as an attempt to reconstruct a comprehensible set of explanations and to reduce the uncertainty brought about by uncontrollability. For example, following the assassination of President Kennedy the average U.S. adult spent 8 hours per day for the next 4 days listening to the radio or watching television, behavior which Janis (1971) interpreted as an attempt to work through the cultural damage. In this dependent and vulnerable state, chance factors can have a disproportionate effect on the interpretation of the event and the view as to what must be done in the future. Scapegoats may need to be found, and chance may provide them. Scientists, militarists, and politicians may escape initial attention, while those involved in bringing relief may be the target of frustration and feelings of betrayal (Lacey, 1972).

Once the immediate danger is past, some survivors will begin to take steps to cope with the consequences. Even as the warning of danger is announced people will find themselves in conflicting roles. They will have to decide whether they should continue with their jobs, take up civic and emergency duties, or return to look after their families. Killian (1952) found that conflicting group loyalties and contradictory roles were significant factors affecting individual behavior in critical situations. Typically, it is the person without family ties who leads rescue work, while the others generally run to their homes to discover if their families are in danger. Even so, Killian reported that some who were searching for their families, after a tornado had struck, were capable of helping others they found on the way. Those whose occupational roles bore little relationship to the needs created by the disaster, such as shopkeepers, disregarded their jobs more easily and came to the assistance of the community.

Faced with an overwhelming catastrophe, family bonds are likely to predominate over civic duties, because everyday tasks and responsibilities will be seen as irrelevant and futile by most people. It should be noted that natural disasters generally come without warning, and rarely require emergency workers to leave their families unprotected while moving themselves to places of relative safety, as would apparently be required of them in the event of nuclear war.

Postimpact

Gradually, individual reactions become coordinated into an organized social response. The form this will take depends very much on cultural norms. Many of the victims will be coping with the consequences of loss and bereavement. This will diminish their capacity to interact socially in a productive manner. Victims need some form of acknowledgment of their suffering, but social norms may deny them the right to express their grief and hopelessness. Fear and apprehension persist, and many may feel that the catastrophe will recur. Aftershocks of an earthquake commonly cause more fear than the initial shock itself. People develop a conditioned fear response, and their capacity to maintain control of their emotions is diminished. Disaster persists as a tormenting memory, and is relived again and again.

CONVENTIONAL BOMBING

Although conventional bombing campaigns involve far less explosive power and far longer time courses than would be likely to be the case in a nuclear war, they should be given some attention for two main reasons. First, the mass raids on cities in some instances approach the extent of destruction caused by small nuclear weapons. Second, facts and fictions about the Blitz influence both popular and official perceptions of the way Londoners would react to a future bombing campaign.

Many accounts have been given of World War II bombing raids (Titmus, 1950; Ilke, 1958; Janis, 1951; Harrison, 1978), and in this instance, it would be most informative to collate data from many different sources to highlight the common features that have emerged.

Preparations

The Blitz raids were preceded by a long period of international tension, which gave the public and the authorities time to make practical and psychological preparations. The previous data on urban bombing were sparse, and the predictions were that there would be massive casualties and considerable panic, and that if deep shelters were provided this would lead to a shelter mentality in which people would refuse to come out to work. As a projection of the reports from Guernica, Spain, this was an understandable view, as was the overriding fear of a gas attack.

The very long conditioning period of the phony war served to give the population time to develop coping responses. Duties were allocated which served to give key community members an important role in air raid preparations, thus providing them with something to do and setting a coping example for others to follow.

Effects

When the bombing began, however, social cohesion and morale broke down very quickly in the worst-affected areas, though censorship ensured that this was not widely known at the time. Badly damaged zones had to be cordoned off by the police, and emergency services were unable to cope. All this occurred despite the fact that there was warning of attack and pauses between attacks and that 1.5 million women and children had been evacuated. The fact that the bombing could not be maintained without pause gave the population time to make some adjustments, and the fortuitous fact that a bomb fell near Buckingham Palace while the East End was receiving the brunt of the attack defused an explosive social divide and made Londoners feel that they were all in it together. The shelter policy resulted in fewer casualties than had been calculated, but the extent of damage to housing and infrastructure had been severely underestimated, as had been the problems of dealing with large numbers of displaced homeless people. Nearly a quarter of a million homes were damaged beyond repair, while 3.5 million suffered repairable damage, though these losses could not be made good during the war period. Emergency services adapted to the new demands, but in many areas of London fires raged uncontrollably. The authorities had prepared for massive casualties and panic. Instead they got a dazed but functioning population that required food, clean water, shelter, and new forms of social organization. Titmus (1950) observed: "The authorities knew little about the homeless who in turn knew less about the authorities."

The speed with which the large number of people in a dazed and bewildered condition could be organized and rehabilitated determined the rate at which the damage could be repaired, production returned to full capacity, and further demoralization in surrounding areas avoided. What was needed, the observers of that time agreed, was a "much more powerful and imaginative organization" to deal with "the purely psychological and social effects of violent air attack" (mass observation of 1940, cited in Harrison, 1978). This organization should have brought a wave of social help, hot tea, and sympathy to snatch people out of their introversion and to link them up again with the outside world.

The impact of World War II bombing on the United Kingdom population was twofold. First, there were the direct casualties (about 60,000 deaths plus injuries); but second, and more numerous, were those who suffered disruption and loss because of damage to the structure of society itself. Children and old people suffered disproportionately through neglect, such that their wartime mortality figures were elevated and accounted for another 6,000 deaths through indirect effects.

The raid on Coventry on the night of November 14–15, 1940, caused such damage to the infrastructure of that city that in the aftermath there was close to being a breakdown of social organization. Food had to be brought in from Birmingham and Stoke on Trent, and entry into the damaged areas was prevented by armed troops.

In the Southampton raids, large sectors of the population ignored official instructions and began *trecking*, moving out into the country and sleeping in hedges during the night, and then some of them trecked back in to work the next day. The stresses of long periods of deprivation and uncertainty caused deep rifts in society that were also noted in Japan and Germany during the air war.

Toward the end of the war the V-bomb campaign imposed new stresses on London's population, and this was particularly the case for the V2 rocket, which fell without warning. Stress levels were very high, and a new evacuation began again. No all clear was ever possible until the launch bases themselves were destroyed.

The raids on Hamburg in 1943 caused heavy casualties and mass evacuation. Only because of the evacuation were there sufficient undamaged houses (only about 50 percent of the housing stock remained) for the very much smaller population that returned to the city to live in cramped quarters.

Summary

The findings from conventional bombing offer only a very partial view of reactions to nuclear war. The power of nuclear weapons is so great that massive destruction can be caused virtually without warning on a society which is now even more interdependent and tightly coupled as an industrial system. It is thus more fragile and will have to absorb more damage without time to recover. However, conventional bombing does provide an analogy. The aftermath of a major nuclear war would be like Coventry trying to get help from Hamburg, while Dresden seeks help from both.

NUCLEAR BOMBING: HIROSHIMA AND NAGASAKI

The bombings of Hiroshima and Nagasaki offer a partial view of the effects of a potential future nuclear war. The weapons were very small by present-day standards, the culture and the era were different, and there was neither warning nor any knowledge of radiation. The Hiroshima bomb, at about the equivalent of 12,500 tons of TNT, would now be regarded as a small battlefield weapon or merely as the detonator of a 1-megaton strategic bomb. However, these bombings are still the closest examples of what would occur in a contemporary nuclear war, with larger explosions occurring on a potential 18,500 strategic targets (SIPRI, 1984).

Considering the importance of these events for our era, the bombings of Hiroshima and Nagasaki have been underreported. Some accounts have been repeated often, but much of the film material collected at the time has only recently been released, and the work done with the survivors was incomplete and often exaggeratedly technical, avoiding personal accounts and bypassing a mass readership. The account here is taken from Thompson (1985).

Lifton (1967) picked 33 survivors at random from lists kept by local Hiroshima research institutes, plus 42 survivors who were particularly articulate or prominent with regard to the atom bomb. A structured interview explored the individual's recollection of the original experience and its meaning in the present, as well as residual concerns and fears, and the meaning of his or her identity as a survivor.

No account can hope to capture what the survivors experienced. They were submitted without warning to an explosion so vast that it seemed that the world itself was coming to an end. At 8:15 a.m. on August 6, 1945, most people in Hiroshima were in a relaxed state, since the all clear had just sounded. Few people could recall their initial perceptions. Some saw the *pika*—a flash of light—or felt a wave of heat, and some heard the *don*—the thunder of the explosion—depending on where they were at the moment of impact. Everyone assumed that a bomb had fallen out of a clear sky directly on them, and they were suddenly and absolutely shifted from normal existence to an overwhelming encounter with death, a theme which stayed with each survivor indefinitely (Lifton, 1963). Those far from the city were shocked to see that Hiroshima had ceased to exist. A young university professor, 2,500 meters from the hypocenter at the time, summed up those feelings of weird, awesome unreality in a frequently expressed image of hell:

Everything I saw made a deep impression—a park nearby covered with dead bodies waiting to be cremated . . . very badly injured people evacuated in my direction . . . Perhaps the most impressive thing I saw were girls, very young girls, not only with their clothes torn off but their skin peeled off as well . . . My immediate thought was that this was like the hell I had always read about. . . . I had never seen anything which resembled it before, but I thought that should there be a hell, this was it.

In Nagasaki a young doctor Akizuki (1981) was preparing to treat a patient when the atom bomb exploded. After pulling himself from the debris of his Urakami hospital consulting room, he was eventually able to look out of where the window had been to the world outside.

The sky was dark as pitch, covered with dense clouds of smoke; under that blackness, over the earth, hung a yellow-brown fog. Gradually the veiled ground became visible, and the view beyond rooted me to the spot with horror. All the buildings I could see were on fire. . . . Electricity poles were wrapped in flame like so many pieces of kindling. Trees on the near-by hills were smoking, as were the leaves of sweet potatoes in the fields. To say that everything burned is not enough. The sky was dark, the ground was scarlet, and in between hung clouds of yellowish smoke. Three kinds of color—black, yellow and scarlet—loomed ominously over the people, who ran about like so many ants seeking to escape. What had happened? Urakami hospital had not been bombed—I understood that much. But that ocean of fire, that sky of smoke! It seemed like the end of the world (Akizuki, 1981).

After encountering so much horror, survivors found that they were incapable of emotion. They behaved mechanically, felt emotionally numb, and at the same time knew they were partly trying to pretend to be unaffected in a vain attempt to protect themselves from the trauma of what they were witnessing.

I went to look for my family. Somehow I became a pitiless person, because if I had pity I would not have been able to walk through the city, to walk over those dead bodies. The most impressive thing was the expression in people's eyes— bodies badly injured which had turned black—their eyes looking for someone to come and help them. They looked at me and knew I was stronger than they. . . . I was looking for my family and looking carefully at everyone I met to see if he or she was a family member—but the eyes—the emptiness—the helpless expression—were something I will never forget (Lifton, 1963).

A businessman who had hastily semirepaired his son's shoe before he went to work in the city center was overcome with guilt that this same shoe had prevented his child from fleeing the fire. The man fruitlessly searched for his child's body and was left in a state of perpetual self-accusation.

Most survivors focused on one ultimate horror which had left them with a profound sense of pity, guilt, or shame. A baby still half-alive on his dead mother's breast, loved ones abandoned in the fire, pathetic requests for help which had to be ignored—each survivor carried a burning memory.

In Nagasaki, Akizuki was swamped by burnt survivors clamoring for water and medical attention.

Half naked or stark naked, they walked with strange, slow steps, groaning from deep inside themselves as if they had travelled from the depths of hell. They looked whitish; their faces were like masks. I felt as if I were dreaming, watching pallid ghosts processing slowly in one direction—as in a dream I had once dreamt in my childhood.

Severely injured people cried out for help. Parents refused to leave dead children, still requesting that they be attended by the doctor. Passing planes caused panic, and victims tried to hide till they passed. Most survivors had witnessed terrible scenes, piles of dead bodies heaped up in streams, mothers and children locked in each other's arms, a mother and her fetus still connected by its umbilical cord, all dead (Akizuki, 1981).

These survivors were so profoundly affected by what they had experienced that all aspects of their subsequent lives were marked by it, and they felt that they had come into contact with death but remained alive. Survivors attempt to make sense of the fact that they have survived while others have perished. Unable to accept that this was a chance occurrence, survivors are convinced that their survival was made possible by the deaths of others, and this conviction caused them terrible guilt. Guilt and shame developed very quickly in Hiroshima survivors, as it did in those who escaped concentration camps, and in both cases it has been intense and persistent. Lifton set out the train of thought of Hiroshima survivors thus:

I was almost dead . . . I should have died . . . I did die or at least am not alive . . . or if I am alive it is impure of me to be so . . . anything which I do which affirms life is also impure and an insult to the dead who alone are pure . . . and by living as if dead, I take the place of the dead and give them life.

This is the painful accommodation that the Holocaust survivor makes to the joyless fact of having survived. It is grief made the more keen by there being no bodies to be buried and mourned, nor any familiar landmarks to show that life continues, and thus aid the adjustment to loss. Person, body, house, street, city, and even nature itself have been consumed.

Summary

Although proper follow-up studies of psychological effects do not appear to have been done, psychotic disorder is uncommon; but depression and anxiety about cancer; fears of death and dying; and generalized complaints of fatigue, dizziness, irritability, and difficulty in coping are usual. This pattern is similar to that found after major civil disturbances and can be conceptualized as an understandable concentration of the attention on possible danger signals to the exclusion of long-term plans. The absence of proper follow-up studies is itself a psychological phenomenon worthy of note, since it suggests that the scientific community itself averted its eyes from the long-term consequences of the disaster.

In Lifton's view the experience of the atomic bombings differed from other disasters in that it plunged the survivors into an interminable and unresolvable encounter with death. The immediate horrifying carnage was followed by long-term delayed effects, thus breaking the myth of personal invulnerability in a permanent way. In experiential terms, every victim saw his secure sunlit world destroyed in an instant. It felt like the end of the world, not just the end of one city. It is not hard to understand why they should distrust the apparent "all clear."

REFERENCES AND BIBLIOGRAPHY

Akizuki, T. 1981. Nagasaki 1945. London: Quartet.

Anderson, C. R. 1977. Locus of control, coping behaviours, and performance in a stress setting: A longitudinal study. J. Appl. Psychol. 62(4):446–451.

Anderson, E. W. 1942. Psychiatric syndrome following blast. J. Mental Sci. 88:328.

Anderson, W. A. 1969. Disaster warning and communication processes in two communities. J. Comm. 19(2):92–104.

Bachman, G. G. 1984. How American high school seniors view the military: 1976–1982. Armed Forces and Society 10(1):86–94.

Baker, E. J., J. C. Brigham, J. A. Paredes, and D. D. Smith. 1976. The Social Impact of Hurricane Eloise on Panama City. Tallahassee, Florida: The Florida State University.

Baum, A., R. Fleming, and J. E. Singer. 1983. Coping with victimisation by technological disaster. J. Social Issues 39(2):117–138.

Beardslee, W., and J. Mack. 1982. The impact on children and adolescents of nuclear developments. American Psychiatric Association Task Force Report No. 20. Pp. 64–93 in Psychosocial Aspects of Nuclear Developments. Washington, D.C.: American Psychiatric Association.

Britten, S. 1983. The Invisible Event: An Assessment of the Risk of Accidental or Unauthorized Detonation of Nuclear Weapons and of War by Miscalculation. London: Menard Press.

Business Decisions. 1983. Nuclear Weapons Study—Summary Report, Survey conducted for the TV Times.

Chivian, E. 1983. Adverse effects on children. Pp. 105–118 in S. Farrow, and A. Chown, eds., The Human Cost of Nuclear War. Medical Campaign against Nuclear War. Cardiff, England: Titan Press.

Churcher, J., J. Gleisner, E. Lieven, and R. Pushkin. 1981. Nuclear war and civil defence: some psychological and social implications. Paper presented at British Psychological Society Annual Conference.

Churcher, J., and E. Lieven. 1983. Images of nuclear war and the public in British civil defence. J. Social Issues 39:117.

Cobb, S., and E. Lindemann. 1944. Neuropsychiatric observations during the Cocoanut Grove fire. Ann. Surg. 117:814.

Cutter, S., and K. Barnes. 1982. Evacuation behaviour and Three-Mile Island. Disasters 6(2):116–124.

Dawes, R. M. 1980. Social dilemmas. Annu. Rev. Psychol. 31:169–193.

Drabek, T., and J. Stephenson. 1971. When disaster strikes. J. Appl. Social Psychol. 1(2):187–203.

Drabek, T. E., W. H. Key, P. E. Erikson, and J. L. Crowe. 1975. The impact of disaster on kin relationships. J. Marriage & The Family 37(3):481–494.

Escalona, S. K. 1963. Children's responses to the nuclear war threat. Children 10:137–142.

Escalona, S. K. 1965. Children and the threat of nuclear war. In M. Schwebe, ed., Behavioural Science and Human Survival. California: Behavioral Science Press.

Escalona, S. K. 1982. Growing up with the threat of nuclear war: Some indirect effects on personality development. Am. J. Orthopsych. 52:600–607.

Fischoff, B., P. Slovic, and S. Lichtenstein. 1978. Fault trees: Sensitivity of estimated failure probabilities to problem representation. J. Exp. Psychol. Human Percep. Perform. 4:342–355.

Glass, A. J. 1959. Psychological aspects of disaster. J. Am. Med. Assoc. 171:222.

Greene, M. R., R. W. Perry, and M. K. Lindell. 1981. The March 1980 eruptions of Mt. St. Helens: Citizen perceptions of volcano threat. Disasters 5(1):49–66.

Greenson, R., and T. Mintz. 1972. California Earthquake 1971: Some psychoanalytic observations. Int. J. Psychoanalyt. Psychother. 1(2):7–23.

Gunter, B., and M. Wober. 1982. Television viewing and public perceptions of hazards to life. Report of the Independent Broadcasting Authority.

Haas, J. E. 1978. The Philippine earthquake and tsunami disaster: A reexamination of behavioural propositions. Disasters 2(1):3–11.

Halpern, E., and H. Schleifer. 1978. Volunteer deployment during community crisis: A view within Caplan's concept of support systems. Crisis Intervention 9(1):2–11.

Hansson, R. O., D. Noulles, and S. J. Bellovich. 1982. Knowledge, warning and stress: A study of comparative roles in an urban floodplain. Environ. Behav. 14(2):171–185.

Harrison, T. 1978. Living Through the Blitz. London: Penguin.

Hewitt, K., and I. Burton. 1971. The Hazardousness of a Place: A Regional Ecology of Damaging Events. Toronto: University of Toronto Press.

Hodler, T. W. 1982. Residents' preparedness and response to the Kalamazoo tornado. Disasters 6(1):44–49.

Ilke, F. C. 1958. The Social Impact of Bomb Destruction. Norman, Okla.: University of Oklahoma Press.

Jackson, E. L. 1981. Response to earthquake hazard: The west coast of North America. Environ. Behav. 13(4):387–416.

Janis, I. 1951. Air War and Emotional Stress. New York: McGraw-Hill.

Janis, I., and L. Mann. 1977. Emergency decision making: A theoretical analysis of responses to disaster warnings. J. Human Stress 3(2):35–48.

Janis, I. L. 1971. Stress and Frustration. New York: Harcourt Brace.

Kahneman, D., P. Slovic, and A. Tversky. 1982. Judgement under Uncertainty: Heuristics and Biases. Cambridge: Cambridge University Press.

Kates, R. W. 1976. Experiencing the Environment, S. Wapner, S. B. Cohen, and B. Kaplan, eds. New York: Plenum Press.

Killian, L. M. 1952. The significance of multiple group membership in disaster. Am. J. Sociol. 57(4):310.

Kinston, W., and R. Rosser. 1974. Disaster: Effects on mental and physical state. J. Psychosomat. Res. 18:437–456.

Lacey, G. N. 1972. Observations on Abervan. J. Psychosomat. Res. 16:257.

Lachman, R., M. Tatsuoka, and W. J. Bank. 1961. Human behaviour during the tsunami of May 1960. Science 133:1405.

Laube, J. 1973. Psychological reactions of nurses in disaster. Nursing Research 22(4):343–347.

Leivesley, S. 1977. Toowoomba: Victims and helpers in an Australian hailstorm disaster. Disasters 1(3):205–216.

Leivesley, S. 1979. A study of disasters and the welfare planning response in Australia and the UK. Unpublished Ph.D. thesis, University of London.

Leivesley, S. 1984. Disasters, disaster agents, and response: A bibliography. Disasters 8:288–308.

Lifton, R. J. 1963. Psychological effects of the atomic bomb in Hiroshima: The theme of death. Daedalus, J. Am. Acad. Arts Sci. 93(3).

Lifton, R. J. 1967. Death in Life: Survivors of Hiroshima. New York: Random House.

Lifton, R. J., and E. Olsen. 1976. Human meaning of total disaster. The Buffalo Creek experience. Psychiatry 39:1–18.

Lindy, J., and J. Tichener. 1983. "Acts of God and man": Long-term character change in survivors of disasters and the law. Behav. Sci. Law 1(3):85–96.

Milburn, T. W. 1972. A comparison of the effects of crises and disasters on values. P. 9 in R. S. Parker, ed., The Emotional Stress of War, Violence and Peace. Pittsburgh, Pa.: Stanwix House.

Miller, I. 1981. Dispositional and situational variables related to evacuation at Three Mile Island. Dissertation Abstracts International 42(5-B):2071.

Okura, K. P. 1975. Mobilising in response to a major disaster. Community Mental Health J. 11(2):136–144.

Openshaw, S., P. Steadman, and O. Green. 1983. Doomsday: Britain after a nuclear attack. London: Blackwell.

Parker, G. 1977. Cyclone Tracy and Darwin evacuees: On the restoration of the species. Br. J. Psych. 130:548–555.

Pennebaker, J., and D. Newtson. 1983. Observation of a unique event: The psychological impact of the Mount Saint Helens volcano. New Directions for Methodology of Social and Behavioural Science 15:93–109.

Perrow, C. 1984. Normal Accidents: Living with High-Risk Technologies. New York: Basic Books.

Perry, R. W., M. K. Lindell, and M. R. Greene. 1982. Threat perception and public response to volcano hazard. J. Social Psychol. 116(2):199–204.

Popovic, M., and D. Petrovic. 1964. After the earthquake. Lancet ii:1169.

Quarantelli, E. L. 1954. Am. J. Sociol. 60:267.

Quarantelli, E. L. 1980. Disasters: Theory and Research. London: Sage.

Rangell, L. 1976. Discussion of the Buffalo Creek disaster: The course of psychic trauma. Am. J. Psych. 133(3):313–316.

Schwebel, M. 1982. Effects of the nuclear threat on children and teenagers: Implications for professionals. Am. J. Orthopsych. 52:608–618.

Seligman, M. P. 1975. Helplessness: On Depression, Development and Death. San Francisco: Freeman.

SIPRI (Stockholm International Peace Research Institute). 1984. World armaments and disarmament. In Yearbook 1984. London: Taylor and Francis.

Slovic, P., H. Kunreuther, and G. F. White. 1974. Decision processes, rationality, and adjustment to natural hazards. In Natural Hazards: Local, National, and Global, G. F. White, ed. New York: Oxford University Press.

Slovic, P., and B. Fischoff. 1980. How safe is safe enough? In J. Dowie, and P. Lefrere, eds., Risk and Chance. Milton Keynes: Open University Press.

Slovic, P., B. Fischoff, and S. Lichtenstein. 1982. Facts versus fears: Understanding perceived risk. In D. Kahneman, P. Slovic, and A. Tversky, eds., Judgement under Uncertainty: Heuristics and Biases. Cambridge: Cambridge University Press.

Solantous, T., M. Kimpela, and V. Taipale. 1984. The threat of war in the minds of 12–18 year olds in Finland. Lancet 1(8380):784–785.

Taylor, A., and A. Frazer. 1982. The stress of post-disaster body handling and victim identification work. J. Human Stress 8(4):4–12.

Thompson, J. 1985. Psychological Aspects of Nuclear War. Chichester, England: British Psychological Society and John Wiley and Sons.

Tichener, J., and F. Kapp. 1976. Family and character change at Buffalo Creek. Am. J. Psych. 133(3):295–299.

Titmus, R. M. 1950. Problems of Social Policy. London: Longmans Green.

Tizard, B. 1984. The impact of the nuclear threat on child development: Problematic issues. Harvard Ed. Rev. 54(3):271–281.

Tversky, A., and D. Kahneman. 1974. Judgement under uncertainty: Heuristics and biases. Science 185:1124–1131.

Tyhurst, J. S. 1951. Individual reactions to community disaster. Am. J. Psych. 107:764.

Wallace, A. F. 1956. Tornado in Worcester. National Academy of Sciences Disaster Study No. 3, Washington, D.C.

Weiss, J. 1973. Effects of coping behavior in different warning signal conditions on stress pathology in rats. J. Compar. Physiol. Psychol. 77(1):1–13.

Wolfenstein, M. 1957. Disaster: A Psychological Essay. London: Routledge and Kegan Paul.

The Medical Implications of Nuclear War, Institute of
Medicine. © 1986 by the National Academy of Sciences.
National Academy Press, Washington, D.C.

The Immunological Impact of
Nuclear Warfare

DAVID S. GREER, M.D., and LAWRENCE S. RIFKIN
*Brown University Program in Medicine,
Providence, Rhode Island*

Medical interest in nuclear warfare initially was focused on the immediate effects in human populations of blast, heat, and radiation and the
futility of civil defense measures. Recently, the concept of nuclear winter
has called attention to intermediate and long-term outcomes. The biological impact of a major exchange of nuclear weapons has been addressed
in general terms, but little attention has been given to the specific elements
of potential biological injury. With this paper, we hope to carry biomedical
interest in nuclear warfare to another level of detail and specificity by
postulating, from a review of relevant literature, that there would be major
immunological damage to surviving human populations. We also speculate
on the likelihood of additive or synergistic deleterious effects that would
arise from exposure to multiple toxic agents.

BACKGROUND

Human lymphocytes are classified on the basis of differing developmental pathways as B lymphocytes and T lymphocytes, which display
different immunological functions. B lymphocytes are precursors of antibody-secreting cells. T lymphocytes control cellular immune responses
and are the effectors of cell-mediated immune reactions; they protect
against certain bacterial infections and many viral and fungal infections,
and they provide resistance to malignant tumors.

There are several distinct functional T lymphocyte subpopulations (Table 1). *Effector T lymphocytes* respond specifically to target antigens in

TABLE 1   Functional Subpopulations of Lymphocytes

I. T lymphocytes
  A. Regulatory T lymphocytes
    1. Helper lymphocytes
    2. Suppressor lymphocytes
  B. Effector T lymphocytes
    1. Delayed-type hypersensitivity (DTH)
    2. Mixed lymphocyte reactivity
    3. Cytotoxic T lymphocyte (CTL or killer cells)

II. B lymphocytes
  A. Precursors of antibody-forming cells
  B. Memory cells
  C. Regulatory B lymphocytes

cell-mediated immune responses, such as the rejection of foreign tumors and the elimination of virus-infected cells. *Helper T lymphocytes* stimulate the differentiation of B lymphocytes into mature antibody-secreting plasma cells and regulate the activation of effector T lymphocytes. *Suppressor T lymphocytes* actively suppress the initiation of specific immune responses by preventing the activation of helper T lymphocytes, hindering helper T lymphocyte interactions with B lymphocytes and directly inhibiting B lymphocyte differentiation.

IONIZING RADIATION

Numerous studies in animals have demonstrated that ionizing radiation produces significant impairment of the immune system. Whole-body x irradiation with 400 rads in albino rabbits completely eliminates antibody response to an antigen presented 48 hours after exposure.[1] Mice exposed to 450 rads of total body x irradiation exhibit suppressed intracellular digestion of foreign erythrocytes.[2] Sublethal x irradiation in mice results in an increased incidence of neoplastic diseases.[3]

There is much clinical evidence of immunosuppression by x irradiation in humans. Patients receiving extensive radiotherapy for Hodgkin's disease experience an increased incidence of viral infections (herpes zoster and varicella-zoster virus).[4] The antibody response to pneumococcal vaccine is profoundly impaired in patients receiving total lymphatic irradiation. The ability of these patients to respond to immunization may not return to normal for as long as four years following therapy.[5] Impaired T lymphocyte-mediated immunity has been noted in Japanese atom bomb survivors 30 years after exposure.[6]

Studies of human radiation injuries resulting from laboratory accidents, the Pacific Testing Ground accidents, and medical whole-body radiation therapy and in Hiroshima and Nagaski victims reveal an almost 100 percent fatality rate in individuals exposed to 500-600 rads or more of whole-body irradiation.[7] At the other extreme, recovery and survival is virtually certain in whole-body exposures of less than 100 rads in healthy humans. Infections are prominent among individuals exposed to 200-450 rads. Although there may be some increase in infections 2 to 4 weeks after human exposure in the 100-200 rad range, there are usually no serious long-term clinical consequences.[7] However, hematopoietic suppression is observed in the 150-200 rad range.[8] Various studies suggest, therefore, that the vulnerability of the human immune system begins at levels of about 150-200 rads of x irradiation. Rotblat's studies[9] suggest that under wartime conditions these levels of vulnerability may be lowered by other deleterious factors, e.g., malnutrition, stress, and exposure.

Much of our knowledge of radioimmunology in humans comes from clinical experience with total lymphoid irradiation (TLI) therapy, in which suppression of undesirable immune reactions is attempted by delivering ionizing radiation in multiple doses to lymphoid tissue over a period of weeks.[10] TLI produces marked and prolonged humoral and cell-mediated immunosuppressive effects in humans. TLI in patients with Hodgkin's disease results in a decrease of helper T lymphocytes for up to 12 months, while the fraction of suppressor T lymphocytes remains constant.[11] Similar effects have been observed in rheumatoid arthritis patients treated with TLI.[12] TLI induces potent nonspecific suppressor lymphocytes which inhibit the cytotoxic T lymphocyte response.[10] In a variety of clinical situations, TLI produces lasting reductions in the ratio of helper to suppressor T lymphocytes.

The mechanism of immune suppression by x irradiation appears to be a reduction in T lymphocyte function associated with a reduced ratio of helper to suppressor T lymphocytes. The calculations of Harwell,[13] Ehrlich et al.,[14] Daugherty,[15] and others indicate that millions of people in the Northern Hemisphere would be exposed to sublethal x irradiation in this range in a 5,000-10,000 megaton (Mt) nuclear exchange. They would be susceptible, therefore, to a wide range of immunodeficiency diseases.

ULTRAVIOLET RADIATION

Studies in animals have confirmed that ultraviolet-B (UV-B) exposure results in a state of T lymphocyte-mediated immune suppression attributable to a predominance of suppressor T lymphocyte.[16] In mice, for example, UV-B irradiation results in an impairment of antigen-presenting cell function[17] and a relative excess of suppressor T lymphocytes.[18]

The suppressor T lymphocytes generated following exposure to UV-B inhibit the antitumor response. UV-irradiated mice are unable to reject UV-B-induced tumors.[19] This inability to reject tumors is mediated by suppressor cell activity, which persists in UV-B-exposed animals long after termination of UV-B exposure.[20,21] UV-irradiated mice are more susceptible to leukemias and lymphomas[22] and to tumors induced by chemical carcinogens.[23] UV-induced suppressor lymphocytes appear to be the agents that predispose the host to the premature development of cancer.

In studies of the effect of UV irradiation on humans, it has been noted that helper T lymphocytes are more sensitive to UV than are B lymphocytes.[24] Normal human subjects exposed to UV irradiation, both in commercial solaria and in natural sunlight, exhibit increases in suppressor T lymphocyte activity sufficient to impair defense against tumors.[25,26] The pathophysiologic mechanism appears to differ for UV-A and UV-B exposure, but relative predominance of suppressor T lymphocytes results in both instances.[27]

Clinical data on the effect of UV irradiation on humans also are available from studies of long-term psoralen plus UV-A (PUVA) radiation therapy for psoriasis. PUVA photochemotherapy causes a reduction in helper T lymphocytes and a reduction in the lymphocytic response to the mitogen phytohemagglutinin.[28] The abnormally low response to mitogens is associated with a decrease in the percentage of helper lymphocytes.[29]

If the predominant nuclear winter scenarios prove accurate, the increased UV-B exposure of human populations can be expected to impair immune function in a manner similar to the effects of ionizing radiation; i.e., it would result in a reduction of the helper-to-suppressor T lymphocyte ratios in many survivors. Crutzen and Birks[30] estimate a 37–70 percent average ozone reduction in a nuclear exchange ranging from 5,000 to 10,000 Mt and predict that a 10,000-Mt nuclear war would result in increases in UV-B radiation by a factor greater than 5 throughout most of the Northern Hemisphere. Turco et al.[31] and Ehrlich et al.[14] estimate UV-B doses of roughly twice the normal level in the Northern Hemisphere after a 5,000-Mt exchange and an increase by a factor of 4 following a 10,000-Mt exchange. Such increases in UV radiation exposure would be in the range expected to affect T lymphocyte populations in the survivors. Based on the assumption that skin cancer incidence is proportional to lifetime UV radiation dose, a National Academy of Sciences committee has estimated that a 50 percent reduction in global ozone would cause an increase in skin cancer of approximately 10 percent that would be maintained for 40 years.[32]

BURNS AND TRAUMA

Severe immunosuppression occurs after major burns and traumatic injuries. Burn patients often show altered cellular immune responses, such as impaired skin test reactivity to antigens and delayed graft rejection. Burns and wounds in the skin also serve as portals of entry for infection. The resultant increase in the incidence and severity of infection in trauma and burn patients is well known. Gram-negative bacilli are the most common wound pathogens, and sepsis is the most common cause of death in survivors of the shock phase of thermal injury.[33,34]

Several recent studies support the concept that reduced T lymphocyte activity is largely responsible for burn-induced immunosuppression.[35,36] Clinical evidence suggests that depressed T lymphocyte function is caused by a shift in the balance of suppressor and helper T lymphocyte subpopulations following thermal injuries. Sepsis is most likely to occur when suppressor cell populations are at a maximum, 7 to 14 days after the injury.[37] A high suppressor-to-helper T lymphocyte ratio has been noted in patients soon after burn injuries of greater than 30 percent of body surface area, and high levels of postburn suppressor T lymphocyte activity accurately predict the incidence of mortality from sepsis.[38] T lymphocyte function is significantly depressed in burn injuries covering more than 25 percent of the body surface area,[36] accompanied by a reduction in helper and an increase in suppressor T lymphocytes.[39] Reduced helper-to-suppressor ratios are a predictor of mortality from sepsis.

Thus, blast and burn injuries in nuclear war survivors can be expected to reduce immune competence in a manner similar to the effect of ionizing and ultraviolet radiation. The T lymphocytes would primarily be affected, and, specifically, a decrease in the ratio of helper-to-suppressor T lymphocytes would be anticipated.

PSYCHOLOGICAL FACTORS: STRESS, DEPRESSION, AND BEREAVEMENT

Chazov and Vartanian[40] have estimated that at least one-third of the population surviving a nuclear war would suffer from severe emotional and behavioral disturbances. Stress, depression, and bereavement have all been reported to alter the immune system and increase the risk of infection.

Studies in animals under stress have shown an increased susceptibility to infection by coxsackie B, polio, herpes, and vesicular stomatitis viruses.[41] Rats given a graded series of stressors manifest progressive suppression of lymphocyte function.[42]

Clinical studies suggest that psychological variables influence susceptibility to infection and delay recovery from upper respiratory diseases, influenza, herpes simplex lesions, and tuberculosis.[43] These psychologically induced altered immune states are probably mediated by changes in lymphocytes. T lymphocyte function is significantly depressed in bereaved spouses.[44] Marked decreases in lymphocyte mitogenic activity have been noted among patients with primary depressive illness.[45,46] Suppression of mitogen-induced lymphocyte stimulation in widowers has been associated with bereavement.[47] Clinically depressed patients have been shown to have an increased mortality rate, cancer rate, and incidence of certain viral infections.[46,48]

The mechanisms by which stress influences the immune system are largely unknown. Neuroendocrine mediation has been suggested. Once again, T lymphocytes appear to mediate the abnormal immunological state.

MALNUTRITION

It has long been recognized that nuclear war would have a major impact on agriculture and world food supplies. More recently, Harwell[13] has written that nuclear winter could result in termination of agricultural production and distribution systems and that widespread starvation might ensue. Specifically, he predicted that surviving populations would be deprived of vitamins A, B_{12}, and C; riboflavin; and iron.

Each of these nutrients is important in maintaining a healthy immune response. Studies in rats and mice indicate that vitamin B_{12} may be highly important to T lymphocyte immune reactions.[49] Riboflavin-deficient animals are more susceptible to infection.[50] Vitamin A deficiency in animals leads to depleted numbers of T lymphocytes; depressed lymphocyte response to certain mitogens; and an increased frequency and severity of bacterial, viral, and protozoan infections.[50] Iron deficiency is also accompanied by impaired in vitro lymphocyte responsiveness to mitogenic stimulation.[50] Abnormalities of T lymphocyte function have also been noted in pyridoxine and zinc deficiency.[51] Based on epidemiologic observations, the World Health Organization report on interactions between nutrition and infection[52] noted that severe ascorbic acid (vitamin C) deficiency tends regularly to lower resistance to most infectious diseases.

There is epidemiological and clinical evidence that the cell-mediated immune response is defective in protein-calorie malnutrition.[53] Individuals with protein-calorie malnutrition have a high incidence of infection, particularly by mycobacteria, viruses, and fungi; and they develop lymphopenia with decreased cutaneous hypersensitivity to several antigens.[54] In communities where protein-calorie malnutrition is prevalent, there is a high mortality from infections which cause only minor illnesses in well-nourished individuals.[55]

The diminished cellular immunity of protein-calorie malnutrition is associated with a marked decrease in the number of T lymphocytes.[56] Almost every conceivable alteration of the T lymphocyte subpopulation and its function (as well as the B lymphocyte population and its function) can be evoked through nutritional, protein, or caloric manipulation.[57] In severe protein-calorie deprivation, the entire lymphocyte population and T lymphocyte immunity can virtually be eliminated. The cellular immune deficits associated with protein-calorie malnutrition correlate with the frequency and severity of infections with *Candida albicans*, measles, and tuberculosis, all of which are T lymphocyte-mediated infections.

DISCUSSION

Sublethal injuries in combination can prove lethal. Since the five major injurious agents associated with nuclear warfare attack the same component of the immune system, the T lymphocyte, and generally do so in a similar manner by decreasing the helper-to-suppressor T lymphocyte ratio, additive influences can be anticipated. Impairment of immunity to a variety of infectious diseases and tumors is likely. Infections associated clinically with depressed cell-mediated immunity have been those with intracellular pathogens like tuberculosis, leprosy, and histoplasmosis;[57] DNA-type virus infections (e.g., varicella-zoster virus, cytomegalovirus); and a variety of rarer pathogens (e.g., *Legionella*, *Pneumocystis*, and *Toxoplasma*). Abrams and Von Kaenel[33] have suggested that in the post-nuclear-war world, surviving populations would be particularly susceptible to tuberculosis.

A striking similarity exists between acquired immunodeficiency syndrome (AIDS) and the anticipated immunosuppressed condition of survivors of a nuclear war: both are characterized by absolute depression of the helper T lymphocyte population, reduced helper-to-suppressor T lymphocyte ratios, reduced lymphocytic response to mitogens and antigens, and reduced to absent antibody response following immunization. In AIDS, the T lymphocyte abnormalities appear to be induced by infection with the human T lymphocyte virus type III (HTLV-III), which kills helper T lymphocytes. The resulting profound immunosuppression apparently produces enhanced susceptibility to other infections. These are listed in Table 2.

Patients with AIDS also experience increased incidences of malignancies, especially Kaposi's sarcoma, which is thought to be caused by the cytomegalovirus. AIDS patients frequently develop non-Hodgkins lymphomas, oral squamous cell carcinoma, and cloacogenic carcinomas.

Since large numbers of the survivors of nuclear war can be expected to have immunologic deficits like those in individuals with AIDS, an increase in the incidence of AIDS-related diseases should be anticipated. The data of von Hippel[15] and others suggest an immediate at-risk popu-

TABLE 2 Principal Agents of Infection in Patients with Acquired Immunodeficiency Syndrome (AIDS)

Viruses	Mycobacteria
Herpesvirus (types 1 and 2)	*Mycobacterium tuberculosis*
Cytomegalovirus	*Mycobacterium avium-*
Varicella-zoster	*intracellulare*
Adenovirus	*Mycobacterium kansasii*
Epstein-Barr	*Legionella* sp.
Retrovirus (HTLV-I, -III)	
	Spirochetes
Fungi	*Treponema* sp. (including
Candida albicans	*Treponema pallidum*)
Cryptococcus neoformans	
Nocardia	Bacteria
	Campylobacter sp.
Protozoa	*Neisseria* sp. (including
Pneumocystis carinii	*Neisseria gonorrhoeae*)
Toxoplasma gondii	*Shigella* sp.
Isospora sp.	*Salmonella* sp.
Cryptosporidium	*Chlamydia*
Giardia iamblia	
Entamoeba histolytica	

SOURCE: Ammann (1984: Table 22-10).[58] Reproduced with permission, from Stites, D.P., et al. (editors): Basic and Clinical Immunology, 5th ed. © 1984 by Lange Medical Publications, Los Altos, California.

lation of at least 10 million Americans in an attack directed at strategic targets only. Exposure to UV radiation, malnutrition, and stress could increase this in the months and years following an attack.

SUMMARY AND CONCLUSIONS

Survivors of a nuclear attack would suffer from injuries caused by ionizing and UV radiation, physical trauma, burns, malnutrition, and psychosocial stress. Several independent lines of research have indicated that these separate agents converge on the T lymphocyte component of the immune system, generally causing a reduction in T lymphocytes and a decrease in the ratio of helper-to-suppressor T lymphocytes.

T lymphocyte defects are associated with some of the most disabling immunodeficiencies. T lymphocytes are essential in the defense against a variety of bacterial diseases and are vital in resistance to many viral and fungal diseases. Patients with AIDS show depression of T lymphocyte populations and reduced helper-to-suppressor T lymphocyte ratios similar to those anticipated in millions of nuclear war survivors. There is considerable experimental evidence that T lymphocytes provide immune surveillance against cancer. T lymphocyte functional abnormalities may explain some of the susceptibility to malignancy which is clinically associated with exposure to ionizing and UV radiation.

Multiple factors converging on a single element of the immune system, the T lymphocyte, can be expected to be additive. The possibility of synergy has been raised by several observers,[33,59] and this could magnify the impact. Severe immunodeficiencies of the T lymphocyte variety are to be anticipated after exposure of human populations to nuclear war. Epidemics of diseases in which T lymphocytes mediate the immune response would be likely in the months and years following a nuclear attack.

NOTES

[1]Dixon, F. J., D. W. Galmage, and P.H. Mauren. 1952. Radiosensitive and radioresistant phases in the antibody response. J. Immunol. 68:693–700.

[2]Donaldson, D. M., S. Marcus, K. K. Gyi, and E. H. Perkins. 1956. The influence of immunization and total body x-irradiation on intracellular digestion by peritoneal phagocytes. J. Immunol. 76:192–199.

[3]Peter, C. P., E. H. Perkins, W. J. Peterson, H. E. Walburg, and T. Makinodan. 1975. The late effects of selected immunosuppressants on immunocompetence, disease incidence, and mean life expectancy. Mechanisms of Ageing and Development 4:251–261.

[4]Reboul, F., C. Donaldson, and H. Kaplan. 1978. Herpes zoster and varicella infections in children with Hodgkin's disease. Cancer 41:95–99.

[5]Siber, G. R., S. A. Weitzman, A. C. Aisenberg, H. J. Weinstein, and G. Schiffman. 1978. Impaired antibody response to pneumococcal vaccine after treatment for Hodgkin's disease. N. Eng. J. Med. 299:442–448.

[6]Akiyama, M., M. Yamakido, K. Kobuke, D. S. Dock, H. B. Hamilton, A. A. Awa, and H. Kato. 1983. Peripheral lymphocyte response to PHA and T cell population among atomic bomb survivors. Radiat. Res. 93:572–580.

[7]Bond, V., T. Fliedner, and J. Archambeua. 1965. Mammalian Radiation Lethality. New York: Academic Press.

[8]Cronkite, E. P. 1981. The effects of dose, dose rate, and depth dose upon radiation mortality. Proceedings from a Symposium of the National Council of Radiation and Protection Measurements, Reston, Va., April 27–29. The Control of Exposure of the Public to Ionizing Radiation in the Event of Accident War Attack. Bethesda, Md.: National Council of Radiation and Protection Measurements.

[9]Rotblat, J. 1986. Acute Radiation Mortality in a Nuclear War. This volume.

[10]Strober, S. 1984. Managing the immune system with total lymphoid irradiation. Pp. 369–378 in The Biology of Immunologic Diseases, F. J. Dixon and D. W. Fisher, eds. Sunderland, Mass.: Sinauer Associates.

[11]Posner, M., E. Reinherz, H. Lane, P. Mauch, S. Hellman, and S. F. Schlossman. 1983. Circulating lymphocyte populations in Hodgkin's disease after mantle and paraaortic irradiation. Blood 64:705–708.

[12]Field, E. H., E. G. Engelman, C. P. Terrell, and S. Strober. 1984. Reduced in vitro immune responses of purified human leu-3 (helper/inducer phenotype) cells after lymphoid irradiation. J. Immunol. 132:1031–1035.

[13]Harwell, M. A. 1984. Nuclear Winter. New York: Springer-Verlag.

[14]Ehrlich, P., et al. 1983. Long-term biological consequences of nuclear war. Science. 222:1293–1300.

[15]Daugherty, W., B. Levi, and F. von Hippel. 1986. Casualties due to the blast, heat, and radioactive fallout from various hypothetical nuclear attacks on the United States. This volume.

[16]Harm, W. 1980. Biological Effects of Ultraviolet Radiation. Cambridge: Cambridge University Press.

[17]Greene, M., M. I. Greene, M. S. Sy, M. Kripke, and B. Benacerraf. 1979. Impairment of antigen-presenting cell function by ultraviolet radiation. Proc. Natl. Acad. Sci. USA 76:6591–6595.

[18]Elmets, C. A., et al., 1983. In vivo low dose UVB irradiation induces suppressor cells to contact sensitizing agents. Pp. 317–336 in The Effect of Ultraviolet Radiation on the Immune System, J. A. Parrish, ed. Johnson & Johnson Baby Products Co., Skillman, N.J.

[19]Kripke, M. L., and M. S. Fisher. 1976. Immunologic parameters of ultraviolet carcinogenesis. J. Natl. Cancer Inst. 57:211–215.

[20]Spellman, C. W., and R. A. Daynes. 1977. Modification of immunological potential by ultraviolet radiation. Transplantation 24:120–126.

[21]Parrish, J. A. 1983. P. 213 in The Effect of Ultraviolet Radiation on the Immune System. Johnson & Johnson Baby Products Co., Skillman, N.J.

[22]Ebbesen, P. 1981. Enhanced lymphoma incidence in BALB/c mice after ultraviolet light treatment. J. Natl. Cancer Inst. 67:1077.

[23]Roberts, L. K., and R. A. Daynes. 1980. Modification of the immunogenic properties of chemically induced tumors arising in hosts treated concomitantly with ultraviolet light. J. Immunol. 125:438–447.

[24]Cripps, D., S. Horowitz, and R. Hong. 1974. Selective T cell killing of human lymphocytes of ultraviolet radiation. Cell. Immunol. 14:80–86.

[25]Hersey, P., et al. 1983. Alteration of T cell subsets and induction of suppressor T cell activity in normal subjects after exposure to sunlight. J. Immunol. 31 (1):171–174.

[26]Hersey, P., et al. 1983. Immunological effects of solarium exposure. Lancet i:545–548.

[27]Sober, A., and T. Fitzpatrick. 1984. Yearbook of Dermatology. Chicago, Ill: Year Book Medical Publishers.

[28]Moscicki, R. A., M. L. Morison, J. A. Parrish, K. J. Bloch, and R. B. Colvin. 1982. Reduction in the fraction of circulating helper:inducer T cells identified by monoclonal antibodies in psoriatic patients treated with psoralen/ultraviolet A radiation (PUVA). J. Invest. Dermatol. 79:205–208.

[29]Morison, W. L., et al. 1981. Abnormal lymphocyte function following long-term PUVA therapy for psoriasis. J. Invest. Dermatol. 76:303.

[30]Crutzen, P. J., and J. W. Birks. 1982. The atmosphere after a nuclear war: Twilight at noon. Ambio 11:114–125.

[31]Turco, R. P., O. B. Toon, T. P. Ackerman, J. B. Pollack, and C. Sagan. 1983. Nuclear winter: Global consequences of multiple nuclear explosions. Science 222(4630):1283–1292.

[32]National Academy of Sciences. 1975. Long Term Worldwide Effects of Multiple Nuclear Weapons Detonations. National Research Council. Publication 2418. Washington, D.C.: National Academy of Sciences.

[33]Abrams, H., and W. Von Kaenel. 1981. Medical problems of survivors in nuclear war. N. Eng. J. Med. 305:1226–1232.

[34]Gelfand, J. A. 1984. Infections in burn patients: A paradigm for cutaneous infection in the patient at risk. Am J. Med. 76:158–165.

[35]McIrvine, A. J., J. H. N. Wolfe, K. Collins, and J. A. Mannick. 1983. Fatal injections in mice after injections of immunosuppressive serum factors from surgical patients. Br. J. Surg. 70:558–561.

[36]Menon, T., T. Sundararaj, S. Subramanian, R. Murugesan, and C. R. Sunderarajan. 1984. Kinetics of peripheral blood T cell numbers and functions in patients with burns. J. Trauma 24:220–223.

[37]Munster, A. M. 1984. Immunologic response of trauma and burns. Am. J. Med. 143–145.

[38]McIrvine, A. J., J. B. O'Mahony, I. Saporoschetz, and J. A. Mannick. 1982. Depressed immune response in burn patients: use of monoclonal antibodies and functional assays to define the role of suppressor cells. Annals of Surgery 196(3):297–304.

[39]Antonacci, A., R. Good, and S. Gupta. 1982. T-cell subpopulations following thermal injury. Surgery 55:1–8.

[40]Chazov, E., and M. Vartanian. 1982. Effects on human behavior. Ambio 11:158–160.

[41]Amkraut, A., and G. F. Solomon. 1975. From the symbolic stimulus to the pathophysiologic response: Immune mechanism. Int. J. Psych. Med. 5(1):541–563.

[42]Keller, S. E., J. M. Weiss, S. J. Schliefer, N. E. Miller, and M. Stein. 1981. Suppression of immunity by stress: Effect of a graded series of stressors on lymphocyte stimulation in the rat. Science 213:1397–1400.

[43]Kaplan, H., A. Freedman, and B. Sadock. 1980. Comprehensive Textbook of Psychiatry/III. P. 1965. Baltimore: Williams & Wilkins.

[44]Bartrop, R. W., E. Luckhurst, L. Lazarus, L. G. Kiloh, and R. Penny. 1977. Depressed lymphocyte function after bereavement. Lancet i:834–836.

[45]Kronfol, Z., J. Silva, J. Greden, S. Dembinski, R. Gardner, and B. Carroll. 1983. Impaired lymphocyte function in depressive illness. Life Sci. 33:241–247.

[46]Schleifer, S. J., S. E. Keller, A. T. Meyerson, M. J. Raskin, K. L. Davis, and M. Stein. 1984. Lymphocyte function in major depressive disorder. Arch. Gen. Psych. 41:484–486.

[47]Schleifer, S., S. E. Keller, M. Camerino, J. C. Thornton, and M. Stein. 1983. Suppression of lymphocyte stimulation following bereavement. J. Am. Med. Assoc. 250:373–377.

[48]Shekelle, R. B., W. J. Raynor, A. M. Ostfeld, D.C. Garron, L. A. Bieliauskas, S. C. Liu, C. Maliza, and O. Paul. 1981. Psychological depression and 17-year risk of death from cancer. Psychosomat. Med. 43:117–125.

[49]Newberne, P. M. 1977. Effect of folic acid, B_{12}, choline, and methionine on immunocompetence and cell-mediated immunity. Pp. 373–386 in Malnutrition and the Immune Response, R. Suskind, ed. New York: Raven Press.

[50]Neumann, C. G. 1977. Nonspecific host factors and infection in malnutrition—A review. Pp. 366 in Malnutrition and the Immune Response, R. Suskind, ed. New York: Raven Press.

[51]Beisel, W. R. 1981. Single-nutrient effects of immunologic functions. J. Am. Med. Assoc. 245:53–58.

[52]WHO Monograph Series 1968. Interactions of Nutrition and Infection, Vol. 57; P. 100. Geneva: World Health Organization.

[53]Edelman, R. 1977. Cell-mediated immune response in protein-calorie malnutrition—A review. Pp. 47–75 in Malnutrition and the Immune Response, R. Suskind, ed. New York: Raven Press.

[54]Levy, J. A. 1984. Nutrition & the Immune System. Pp. 293–298 in Basic and Clinical Immunology, 5th ed., D. P. Stites, J. D. Stobo, H. H. Fudenberg, and J. V. Wells, eds. Los Altos, Calif.: Lange Medical Publications.

[55]Smith, N. J., S. Khadrovi, V. Lopez, and B. Hamza. 1977. Cellular immune response in Tunisian children with severe infantile malnutrition. Pp. 105–109 in Malnutrition and the Immune Response, R. Suskind, ed. New York: Raven Press.

[56]Neumann, C. G., E. R. Stiehm, M. Swenseid, A. C. Ferguson, and G. Lawlor. 1977.

Cell-mediated immune response in Ghanaian children with protein-calorie malnutrition. Pp. 77–89 in Malnutrition and the Immune Response, R. Suskind, ed. New York: Raven Press.

[57]Good, R. A. 1977. Biology of the cell-mediated immune response—A review. Pp. 29–46 in Malnutrition and the Immune Response, R. Suskind, ed. New York: Raven Press.

[58]Ammann, A. J. 1984. Immunodeficiency diseases. In Basic and Clinical Immunology, D. P. Stites, J. D. Stobo, H. H. Fudenberg, and J. V. Wells, eds. Los Altos, Calif.: Lange Medical Publications.

[59]Chandra, R. M., and Newberne P. M. 1977. Nutrition, Immunity, and Infection. P. 2. New York: Plenum Press.

Expected Incidence of Cancer Following Nuclear War

NIKOLAI P. BOCHKOV, M.D., and PER OFTEDAL, PH.D.
*Soviet Academy of Medical Sciences, USSR, and University of
Oslo, Oslo, Norway*

The carcinogenicity of ionizing radiation has been investigated in some
detail both under experimental conditions and through direct observations
of irradiated persons. The high incidence of occupational cancer in roent-
genologists who did not suspect the treacherous properties of ionizing
radiation has been well known since the 1920s. The data on radiation-
induced cancer have been systematically examined by the United Nations
Scientific Committee on the Effects of Atomic Radiation (UNSCEAR),
by the National Research Council Committee on Biological Effects of
Ionizing Radiation (BEIR), and by the International Commission on Radiological Protection (ICRP).

The calculation of expected incidence of cancer following nuclear war
can be based on experimental data on radiation-induced cancer, observations of occupational cancer, and the data from Hiroshima and Nagasaki.

Data on cancer incidence in populations of Hiroshima and Nagasaki
obtained during checkups of survivors of A-bombs, from analysis of case
histories, and from pathological certificates allow one to draw objective
conclusions on the cancer rate induced by radiation. The following results
were obtained.[1-3]

An increase in leukemia incidence began in both cities about 3 years
after exposure and reached a peak around 1951-1952. Later the leukemia
rate among exposed persons declined. The rate in the Nagasaki-exposed
survivors has not exceeded that of the control population since the early
1970s. There is still evidence of continuation of a slightly increased leukemia rate in Hiroshima among exposed survivors. There are complex

329

differences between the types of leukemia in relation to age at the time of the bombing, city of exposure, and duration of the latent period following exposure. Through 1978, total excess incidence of leukemia deaths due to radiation among all A-bomb survivors is estimated to be about 95 percent of the leukemia deaths not associated with radiation—that is, the overall rate is nearly twice as high as it would have been without atomic radiation exposure. It is revealed that the younger the age at the time of the bomb, the greater the risk of leukemia during the early period and the more rapid the decline thereafter.

A clear relationship between the incidence of leukemia and radiation dose is present for both cities, but the effect is more pronounced in Hiroshima than in Nagasaki. The lowest doses with a demonstrable leukemogenic effect appear to be in the 0.2-0.4 gray (Gy) (20-40 rads) range in Hiroshima.

The marked difference between the Hiroshima and Nagasaki experiences has been attributed to the neutron component of the ionizing radiation in Hiroshima. However, the doses are now in the process of being reevaluated.

In regard to malignant solid tumors, the following conclusions can be made. Analyses of mortality have shown a significant excess of deaths from malignant solid tumors. The relative risk for various malignant tumors to be induced by radiation (2 versus 0 Gy) varies considerably by site. A significant increase is evident for leukemia; cancers of the lung, breast, and stomach; and multiple myeloma. It is also suggested, though not yet confirmed, that there is an increase in risk for cancers of the esophagus, colon, urinary tract, and salivary glands. Incidence data suggest that breast and thyroid tissues are especially sensitive to the carcinogenic effect of ionizing radiation.

Death rates from all malignant tumors increased with dose in both Hiroshima and Nagasaki, but the increase with dose was higher in Hiroshima than in Nagasaki. In most cases the relative risks for various organs are not significantly different from one another at the level of age of mortality.

Radiation-induced solid tumors appear only after a latency period. The length of the latency period seems to decrease with dose increases. Malignancies other than leukemia exhibit different latency patterns over time. Radiation-induced cancers do not become apparent until the usual cancer age is reached. For example, even for those individuals who had already reached the age for lung cancer at the time of the bombing, the shortest latency period was 10-15 years, and in this case, no shortening of the latency period was evident in the high-dose group.

The process of radiation carcinogenesis could be modified by factors such as age at the time of the bombing; attained age; sex; and exposure to tobacco smoke, hormones, and the like. If age at death is fixed, the absolute risk is clearly greater for those who were younger at the time of exposure.

The strongest effect among women has been an excess risk of breast cancer. The effect appears strongest for those exposed before the age of 20 years and less among women aged 20-39 at exposure, and it may not exist among women exposed at older ages. For women aged 20-30 at exposure, the minimal induction period appears to have been between 5 and 10 years.

The increase in cancer mortality appears to be fairly general, including cancers of the lung, esophagus, stomach, colon, and urinary organs and multiple myeloma. The magnitude of the radiation effect varies by site. The excess risk of radiogenic breast cancer begins at ages when cancer rates normally become appreciable, and after 5-10 years among persons already at or near ages of appreciable cancer risk when exposed. Most solid tumors differ from breast cancer, however, in that an excess risk is seen among the oldest survivors as well as among those exposed at younger ages.

The total excess cancer mortality from radiation-induced cancer through 1978 among all survivors is estimated to be 3.4 percent (340 excess deaths from radiation-induced cancers, compared with more than 10,000 not associated with radiation).

The calculation of expected cancer incidence is based on the main conclusions of UNSCEAR, BEIR, and ICRP, which prognosticated the cancer incidence in case of nuclear war. According to these recommendations, radiation-induced carcinogenesis does not have a dose threshold, but the incidence dose rate is linear or linear-quadratic. It is necessary to stress that radiation exposure does not induce any specific "radiation-type" of cancer but just enhances the incidence of spontaneous malignant tumors.

The principle of calculating the expected cancer incidence following nuclear war is not based on specific scenarios of nuclear war but draws on more general approaches based on radiation dose and the age structure of the population.

The expected cancer rate in a nuclear war depends on the irradiation dose. In the case of modern nuclear war, the doses of gamma- and neutron-irradiation will be substantially greater than those in Hiroshima and Nagasaki. A number of scenarios of nuclear wars have been published (from 1 to 10,000 megatons [Mt]) and respective levels of irradiation have been calculated for different explosions and heights above certain localities.[4]

The main conclusion from all scenarios is the following. The survivors near the target areas of a conflict involving 10,000 Mt of nuclear explosives will be exposed at least to doses of 0.5 to 1.0 Gy (50-100 rads) and greater, which by far exceeds those to which the inhabitants of Hiroshima and Nagasaki were exposed. Naturally, the proportion of exposed persons will be a great deal higher. Practically all the nuclear war survivors throughout the world will be irradiated. Even in territories distant from the explosion sites the people will be exposed to radiation from radioactive fallout at doses up to 0.1 Gy (10 rads) and higher.

Complex interacting radiation factors and limited understanding of the operative dose-effect relations preclude exact predictions of the postwar incidence of cancer.

The calculation of cancer risk following nuclear war was made for target areas and for areas exposed to global fallout.[3]

First, with regard to target areas, the cancer frequencies have been calculated by making assumptions about the distribution function of the exposure rates, the survival from the blast, and the distribution of shelters.

In Table 1, one can see a calculated distribution, by dose, of the surviving population. After attenuation for death from acute symptoms, the assumptions yield a 43 percent total survival rate. A reduction factor of 0.55 has been applied to convert average surface exposure to average organ dose. The mean dose among survivors is in this way calculated to be 0.58 Gy. Obviously, choosing other values for the various parameters would change the estimates to some extent. It is possible to modify the function affected according to new information and thus increase the reliability of the estimates.

TABLE 1   Calculated Exposure Distribution of Survivors of Blast and Acute Radiation Effects

Exposure (R)	Percentage	Average exposure (R)	Bone marrow and organ dose	
			rad	Gy
0– 9	21	2.7	1.5	0.015
10– 49	27	22	16	0.16
50– 99	14	77	42	0.42
100–199	18	140	75	0.75
200–299	13	240	131	1.31
300–399	1.5	310	173	1.73
>400	5.5	470	256	2.56
Total	100.0	105	58	0.58

TABLE 2   Estimated Cancer Deaths per Million Survivors, Using 1980 BEIR Risk Equations and Projection Models (all ages combined)

		Projection Model			
		Absolute Risk		Relative Risk	
		Males	Females	Males	Females
Total expected, all cancers		180,000	147,000		
Leukemia					
Expected		9,860	8,018		
Estimated excess					
Linear model	No.	3,280	2,180		
	(% increase)	(33)	(27)		
Linear quadr.	No.	3,120	2,070		
	(% increase)	(39)	(26)		
All other cancers					
Expected		170,400	139,400	170,400	139,400
Estimated excess:					
Linear model	No.	5,330	8,530	24,500	28,200
	(% increase)	(3.1)	(6.1)	(14)	(20)
	mean	5		17	
Linear quadr.	No.	4,790	7,430	21,900	24,300
	(% increase)	(2.8)	(5.3)	(13)	(17)
	mean	4		15	

SOURCE: World Health Organization (1984, p. 157).[3] Reprinted with permission.

Table 2 indicates that cancer mortality owing to local fallout would be greatly increased among the survivors of a nuclear war.[3] The increased risk of cancer would be far from being the most horrible consequence of the disaster. Depending on the risk model used and the method of projection beyond the 30 years of present follow-up, the excess mortality would be around 5 percent, or 17 percent of the normal cancer burden. In other words, if 15 percent of some present populations today could normally be expected to die of cancer, taking into consideration a 10-year latency period, about 16-18 percent of the surviving population would die of cancer.

The most noticeable oncological effect would be that of leukemia. The excess risk would be relatively high compared with the normal risk, and it would occur within 2-30 years after nuclear war. However, the total number of deaths from radiation-induced leukemia would be large.

Radiation-induced solid tumors tend to occur at ages at which such cancers normally occur; that is, radiation causes more cancer deaths to occur, but not at earlier ages than usual. Because most cancer deaths occur among the elderly, the effect of a 5 percent excess mortality or 17 percent increase in cancer mortality would not have a marked effect on the average life span.[3]

Much less refined calculations (based on the risk factor estimated by UNSCEAR, 1.25 x 10^{-4} per rad) give practically the same increase in cancer risk, namely 4.3 percent excess mortality.

This calculation was made for the oncological effects of local fallout on the population. Other scenarios for other areas would produce different values. However, in view of the generalized character of the assumptions, it seems that there would be no major modifications in the conclusions drawn.

As far as the global fallout is concerned, the estimates have been based on the general assumption of a total bomb yield of 10,000 Mt. The mean effective dose equivalent to the population of the world would be 0.1 Gy per person. The collective dose could be found by multiplying the number of individuals exposed by the mean dose. The distribution of the fission products would be nonuniform and would result in the following doses: bone marrow, 17 rad; bone cells, 19 rad; lung, 16 rad; other sensitive organs, 10 rad.

The risk of cancer according to the ICRP data for an individual would be as follows: leukemias 3.5 x 10^{-4}; osteosarcomas, 1.5 x 10^{-4}; lung cancer, 3.0 x 10^{-4}; cancer of other organs, 20.5 x 10^{-4}.

The rate of natural occurrence of cancer in the population of an industrialized country is 15 percent. The global fallout of fission products from blasts of 10,000 Mt would increase the cancer rate in the surviving world population by slightly more than 1 percent.

Chazov and colleagues[4] presented the estimates of late radiation consequences for the population in the form of the expected incidence of malignant tumors developed in various organs and tissues with a fatal outcome. As one can see from Table 3, local radioactive fallout can give rise to malignant tumors induced by ionizing radiation that is expected to kill 21 million; of these, approximately 3 million will die of leukemia, 3.6 million of mammary gland cancer, and more than 4.6 million of thyroid gland cancer.

The risk factors normally used by the ICRP are based on fatal cancers only. In view of the reduction in the efficiency of health services to be expected in a postwar world, the inclusion of normally nonfatal cancers might be relevant. This leads to an approximate doubling of the risk, owing mainly to the large contribution from thyroid cancer. Note, however, that if the risk factors are used that include the normally nonfatal component—which might to some extent become fatal under postwar

TABLE 3   Expected Incidence of Malignant Tumors with Fatal Outcome as a Result of the Effect of Local and Tropospheric Fallout

Type of Late Consequences	Risk Factor of Development of Tumor per rem	Number of Cases, million
Leukemia	$2.0 \cdot 10^{-6}$	2.83
Mammary gland cancer	$2.5 \cdot 10^{-6}$	3.60
Thyroid gland cancer	$5.0 \cdot 10^{-6}$	4.62
Lung cancer	$2.0 \cdot 10^{-6}$	2.88
Malignant tumors in other organs and tissues	$5.0 \cdot 10^{-6}$	7.20

SOURCE: Chazov et al. (1984, p. 202).[4] Reprinted with permission.

conditions—this is then at variance with the usual definition of effective dose, which refers to the induction of fatal cancer.

In summary, a general nuclear war would presumably expose populations of industrial and densely populated areas around the world to levels not less than 1.0 Gy.[3] The rest of the world would be exposed to delayed fallout. Based on a total explosive force of 10,000 Mt, survival in the target areas would be about 50 percent. It might be expected that there would be 100 million survivors in each of the target areas of North America, Western Europe, the USSR, and various scattered smaller areas. About 400 million survivors would be irradiated with doses leading to a 17 percent increase of the present cancer incidence, from 15 percent to about 18 percent. This means that about 12 million cases of cancer due to radiation would arise in target areas. In the rest of the world an increase of about 1 percent from 15 percent to about 15.2 percent might lead to some 7 million extra cases. Cancer induction would thus add to the suffering of the postwar world. The general health detriment implicit in such an increase in cancer frequency would, under ordinary circumstances, be regarded as gravely significant.

In conclusion, we would like to stress the following. When cancer develops in new victims, life becomes very difficult for all survivors. They begin to fear the fatal end. Naturally, immediate casualties after nuclear attack will be much greater than oncological consequences, but if even one child develops cancer or leukemia, this will not lighten the burden of responsibility on those who might want to launch a nuclear war. As the great Russian humanist Fydor Dostoyevsky said, "No goods of civilization are worth the tears of a single tortured child."

NOTES

[1]Committee for the Compilation of Materials on Damage Caused by the Atomic Bombs in Hiroshima and Nagasaki. 1981. Hiroshima and Nagasaki: The Physical, Medical and Social Effects of the Atomic Bombings. Tokyo: Iwanami Shoten. (London: Hutchinson; New York: Basic Books).

[2]Kato, H., and W. J. Schull. 1982. Studies of the mortality of A-bomb survivors. Mortality, 1950-1978: Part I. Cancer mortality. Radiation Res. 90:395-432.

[3]World Health Organization. 1984. Effects of Nuclear War on Health and Health Services. Geneva: World Health Organization.

[4]Chazov, Y. I., L. A. Ilyin, A. K. Guskova. 1984. Nuclear War: The Medical and Biological Consequences. Moscow: Novesti Press.

The Medical Implications of Nuclear War, Institute of
Medicine. © 1986 by the National Academy of Sciences.
National Academy Press, Washington, D.C.

Genetic Consequences of Nuclear War

PER OFTEDAL, PH.D.
University of Oslo, Oslo, Norway

INTRODUCTION

In the aftermath of a nuclear war, genetic effects may appear trivial in comparison with the enormity of the catastrophic development in the survivors' health and the environment.[1] Gross effects are immediately or subtly demonstrable on the basis of diverse war scenarios. On the other hand, in a great number of organisms, genetic effects of radiation have been shown to occur according to a no-threshold dose-effect curve, thus implying that effects may be found even in situations and population groups where other direct effects are small. When I tried to quantitate these effects the first time—in the working papers for the World Health Organization (WHO) expert committee 3–4 years ago—there was also the possibility that an analysis might uncover unexpected aspects, in addition to those at least qualitatively obvious.[2] The discussions on the effects of nuclear war have indicated that whatever sector of effects is focused on, closer examination has, in each case—be it treatment of casualties, effects on climate, or effects on world trade—led to a picture of possible and often probable catastrophic collapse.[3]

It is not easy to think differently, especially in an analysis that projects beyond a tragedy for which more and more occluding consequences are found. This paper is therefore basically a summary of my calculations for the WHO paper, with marginal additional reflections inspired by views and information that have appeared during the past 2 years.

RADIATION DOSE TO SURVIVORS

Radiation is the only mutagen considered in this discussion, and doses of genetic consequence are only those of nonsterilizing magnitude and absorbed by survivors with present or future reproductive capacity.

Figure 1 shows schematically the elements of the situation to be considered in the target areas.

With bombs bigger than 10–100 kilotons (kt), the radiation lethal area may be smaller than the blast and heat lethal areas, as can be seen in Table 1.[4] Transmissible genetic damage is then induced in survivors beyond the blast and heat lethal zones as well as the radiation lethal zone.

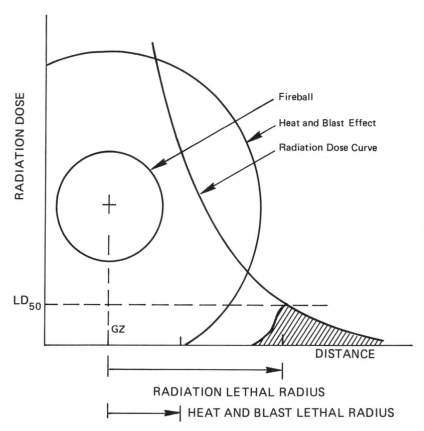

FIGURE 1   Genetically effective exposure to radiation would occur mainly outside the radiation lethal area, with dose distribution as determined by the dose-distance curve.

TABLE 1   Areas of Lethal Damage from Various Effects (km^2)

Type of Damage	Explosive Yield				
	1 kt	10 kt	100 kt	1 Mt	10 Mt
Blast	1.5	4.9	22	104	480
Heat	1.1	10.5	60	350	1,300
Initial radiation	2.9	5.7	11	22	54

SOURCE: Based on Rotblat.[4]

If the blast and heat lethal zones extend beyond the radiation lethal zone, the mean radiation dose to the survivors will be relatively smaller.

In Hiroshima and Nagasaki, the mean dose to parents of the 19,000 children born to parents of whom one or both had been irradiated is estimated to be somewhat over 100 rem (subject to ongoing revisions).[5,6] I have used this as a measure of the prompt radiation dose received by the reproducing fraction of a surviving population after an isolated bomb. If several small bombs are exploded near each other, there will be more irradiated survivors (because the collective lethal zone perimeter will be longer), but the mean genetically significant dose may be taken to remain the same. With bombs bigger than 50 kt, the blast and temperature lethal areas will to some extent cover the genetically significant irradiated survivor zone, thus leading to fewer irradiated survivors and to a lower mean radiation dose in those that do survive.

With low-altitude and groundbursts, exposure to local fallout downwind from the target will lead to genetically significant doses in the survivors. Using arguments similar to those applied to the prompt radiation exposure, one may assume that there is a lethal area in the central portion of the plume path and survival zones on the periphery.[4]

To the extent that fallout is massive and fresh and few countermeasures have been instituted beforehand, one may take the mean genetically significant dose to parents to be of the same order of magnitude as for radiation from the bomb itself (100 rem) and to be of sufficiently high dose rate to have the same mutagenic efficiency as acute exposures.

In areas with uniformly heavy fallout, those in good shelters may survive. It has been calculated that in the most heavily contaminated areas of the United States, following a 5,000-megaton (Mt) attack, it might be necessary to spend some 6–7 weeks totally in shelter, thereafter making excursions timed so as to limit daily exposures to 3 rem.[7] After about 8 months, it may be possible to spend a full 16-hour day outside the shelter. Over a period of 20 years, a total external radiation dose of about 1,500 rem may accumulate.[7] Half of this is possibly genetically significant, but additional exposure will stem from radioactive contamination. So maybe one can assume a genetically effective dose of 1,000 rem absorbed at a low dose rate and thus probably only one-third as effective a mutagen as the corresponding acute dose.[8] It is highly uncertain how many survivors would belong to this category. In heavily contaminated areas, the number would no doubt be large, but the efficiency of shelters; protective actions; cleanup of local areas; and selective protection of the pregnant, the young, and the potentially reproductive will all influence the genetically significant exposure. On the other hand, with large and contiguous areas being contaminated, the probability of both parents being equally exposed is higher than that in the Hiroshima/Nagasaki model calculation; thus the genetically significant dose may be expected to be somewhat higher than that proposed above.

The rest of the world would be exposed to delayed global fallout, which would reenter the biosphere after weeks to years in the upper atmosphere. The United Nations Scientific Committee on Effects of Atomic Radiation (UNSCEAR) has calculated that the fallout from the atmospheric tests during 1954–1962 led to dose commitments for the first generation of about 1 rad per megaton of fission yield.[9] On the simplified assumption that a war with a total of 10,000 Mt of fission took place, a total mean dose of 10 rem to each person in the world would result. Because a large fraction of the energy would be fusion, not fission, this calculated dose is probably on the high side, but not by as much as an order of magnitude. On the other hand, special circumstances—such as direct hits on nuclear power plants—may lead to major contaminations with long-lived radioactive isotopes, increasing the mean survivor population dose in the less contaminated areas.[3,4] In those localities where the lethal dose or dose rate is already closely approached, a further increase would lead to more deaths, but, as expected, it would influence the reproducing survivor dose to a lesser extent.

It seems to be a significant feature of the situation that the variation in the genetically effective dose between individuals of the three categories discussed—bomb exposure, local fallout exposure, and global fallout exposure—may vary within little more than 2 orders of magnitude, including mutagenic efficiency variation due to dose rate. This compression of the range is caused on the upper side by the limits determined by the lethal effect of radiation and on the lower side by the wide distribution of the global fallout. Concurrently, there may be 2 orders of magnitude of variation in terms of individual dose and effect, depending on local fallout conditions and variation in radiation sensitivity.

GENETIC RADIATION EFFECTS

Genetic damage as a result of radiation exposure is generally believed to consist of the same elements found in so-called spontaneous mutations. This view may change as knowledge of the molecular mechanisms of heritable mutations in higher organisms develops.

Effects to be expected after a given dose may be calculated by a doubling dose method or by a direct method. With the doubling dose method, estimates of effects in humans are based on the spontaneous mutation rate seen in humans and in an experimental animal (usually the laboratory mouse) and on the dose needed to double the rate in the experimental animal.[10,11] Difficulties are due mainly to the paucity of knowledge about the normal situation in human populations and to the problems involved in drawing parallels between two different biological species. The direct method is based on the observed sensitivity of certain types of genes in the experimental animal (e.g., those having to do with normal skeletal development or with cataracts) and an estimate of the corresponding number of genes in humans.[12] Subsequently, the calculation is extended to encompass all known conditions in humans with similar genetic mechanisms. The principal difficulties are again the transition from one species to another and the extension of the estimates from one type of anomaly to the whole spectrum of damage.

The International Commission on Radiological Protection (ICRP) takes genetic damage seen in the first two generations to constitute one-quarter of the stochastic risk induced, following occupational exposure (age 18–30) to low-dose, low-dose-rate radiation, with the remaining risk being various forms of cancer exposure (age 18–65).[13,25] On the assumption of constant sensitivities, it may be calculated that for population exposures, the corresponding fractions are about 0.4 for genetic risks (age 0–30) for each child born and 0.6 for cancer risk (age 0–65) for lifetime cancer.

In Hiroshima/Nagasaki, it has not been possible to demonstrate genetic effects in children born to parents, one or both of whom were exposed to bomb radiation.[14] The question may be discussed whether the effect might be too small to be registered, or if circumstances limit the possibility of insight, or if the findings really demonstrate that humans are less sensitive to genetic harm from radiation than are, for instance, laboratory mice.[14,15] Types and numbers of genetic anomalies expected after exposure to 1 million manrem (which appears to correspond to the genetically significant dose in Hiroshima/Nagasaki) are shown in Table 2. (All these calculations are made by the doubling dose method, except for Ehling's,[16] which uses a direct method.)

TABLE 2   Genetic Effects of One Million Manrem of Radiation to a
Population of Constant Size: Types and Numbers of Anomalies

Damage Category	Acute First Generation	Acute Equilibrium	Chronic First Generation	Chronic Equilibrium
Unbalanced translocation → malformed liveborn	46	60	23	30
Trisomics, XO	90	90	30	30
Simple dominants	60	300	20	100
Complex dominants, multifactorial disease mutationally maintained	45	450	16	160
Multifactorial disease non-mutationally maintained	0	0	0	0
Recessive mutations	(2,400)		(900)	
Total (excluding recessive)	240	900	89	320
Total UNSCEAR'77 [5]			63	185
Total UNSCEAR'82 [9]			22	144
Ehling 1984[16]				
Simple dominants	25			
Recessives	(250)			

NOTE: The upper part of this table is based on the material and arguments presented in Oftedal and Searle.[25]

During the next few years, it is expected that improved data on spontaneous mutation rates will be available, in particular from Hungary (A. Czeizl, personal communication). It is also hoped that an international collaborative effort sponsored by the International Commission for the Protection Against Environmental Mutagens and Carcinogens (ICPEMC) and organized in collaboration with John Mulvihill from the National Cancer Institute may yield data on the sensitivity of man's genetic material, based on mutation rates observed in children born to surviving cancer patients treated with radiation or cytostatics.[17]

POPULATIONS AND EFFECTS

In view of the many uncertainties involved in estimating the genetic effects, it seems unwarranted to try to differentiate between different scenarios. However, let us again look at the three categories of exposure: direct bomb radiation, local fallout, and global fallout.

On the perimeter of one or several smaller bombs, survival conditions similar to those in Hiroshima and Nagasaki may be expected, and mean genetically significant doses of just over 100 rad may be experienced. On the basis of ICRP's sensitivity figures, one would expect about 240 extra cases of genetic ill health among the 19,000 children born to exposed parents, but none were found.[13,15] If one assumes that the populations involved are 10 times that of Hiroshima/Nagasaki, about 200,000 children would be born to exposed parents. Some 2,000–3,000 cases of genetically determined ill health might appear, in addition to the 10,000–20,000 normally expected. So in this category of population, genetic ill health might increase by a quarter in the first two generations postexposure, subsequently decreasing over a period of several generations.

Areas of heavy local fallout would, according to several scenarios, cover extensive areas and involve large populations. In my WHO paper, I suggested a total world population of 2×10^8 reproducing survivors in this category.[2] With a mean genetically significant dose of 1,000 rem, but delivered at a low dose rate, the amount of genetically defective offspring would be about doubled. Obviously, this estimate is very tentative, there being uncertainties at all levels of calculation, from the bombing scenario details to the normal incidence of genetic ill health. The implications of a doubling of the present mutation rate are not easy to foresee, keeping in mind the speculative nature of our picture of society in the ravaged areas of large portions of the earth. If the present family pattern is retained, if generally both parents are exposed, and if the number of children per couple is elevated in order to compensate for the population lost in the war, the majority of families would experience one or several genetically determined cases of ill health.

The third element discussed—global fallout—would imply that the genetically determined ill health would be increased by a small fraction.[2] Calculations can be performed to show that the absolute numbers may become very large, but it would probably take a refined epidemiologic analysis to prove that the increase had in reality taken place.[14,18] However, due to regional differences in climatic conditions, quite significant variations in amounts of fallout would occur, with a corresponding variation in exposure.[19]

OTHER EFFECTS ON FUTURE GENERATIONS

Two other aspects deserve to be mentioned in order to make the picture complete.

In experimental work with the mouse it has been demonstrated that recessive mutations may be induced by radiation about seven times more frequently than dominant mutations.[20] In an outbreeding large population, recessive mutations are ordinarily expressed only in the distant future and

with low predictability. They are therefore generally disregarded in estimating harmful genetic effects of radiation. However, in small, isolated,
and inbreeding populations, recessive mutations might come to expression
earlier and in significant numbers and add to the detriment resulting from
radiation exposure. It is conceivable that situations of this type might
develop after a nuclear war, if small bands of survivors were to live in
isolation for several generations. Modern man probably experienced this
kind of breeding pattern in his early history, and many racial characteristics
may have become established in this way.

Another aspect that concerns the next generation, although not genetic,
is the teratogenic effect of radiation. Some stages of embryogenesis are
particularly sensitive to radiation, but in general the defects lead to spontaneous abortion and so may be regarded as a category of limited consequence.[21,22] However, it has been shown recently in Hiroshima and
Nagasaki that fetuses irradiated during the third and fourth months of
development are particularly prone to brain damage, with a relatively large
frequency of mentally retarded children born in this group.[23] In any normally reproducing population, a small fraction of the population under 30
years of age—about 1.0 percent—will be pregnant with a child at this
stage of development. Among the children born to survivors some 5–7
months after exposure to bomb radiation, mental retardation may thus be
expected to be a dose-dependent characteristic. To the extent that protracted irradiation is equally efficient in this respect, even those exposed
to fallout radiation and contamination may show this type of damage. On
the basis of the dose calculations referred to above, a prevalence of some
additional 2–3 percent of retarded children might be the result in the target
areas.

It also appears from the Hiroshima/Nagasaki data that the intelligence
quotient of children exposed during the sensitive fetal period may be
reduced, even if it remains in the normal range (W. J. Schull, personal
communication). The reduction is dose dependent. Generally speaking,
then, fetal exposure may conceivably lead to a lower level of intelligence
in large portions of the generation born during the first years after war.

There is a possibility that material on hand in Norway might give some
information on whether the fallout from atmospheric bomb tests has had,
to a corresponding degree, the same kind of effect. A project to investigate
this is being planned.

GENETIC HANDICAPS IN THE POSTWAR WORLD

If, under given circumstances, the radiation and genetic load would
appear to threaten the survival of a group, a number of practices might

be instituted to reduce the load and to conserve the material resources available. These practices could range from selective shielding of reproducing individuals, to infanticide and euthanasia, to selective or, indeed, compulsory breeding by those individuals showing indications of least genetic damage. In animal husbandry, this principle is known as progeny testing.

THE WORSE, THE BETTER: A TRAGIC PARADOX

As is apparent from this discussion, the upper limit of the genetically significant radiation exposure is determined by the lethal and sterilizing effects of radiation. To the extent that postwar adverse conditions reduce survival, it may be presumed that those suffering greater radiation insults will succumb before those that have a lighter radiation load.[24] Thus, adverse conditions, whether societal (e.g., lack of care for the disabled), physical (e.g., nuclear winter), or biological (e.g., plagues or pests), all serve to reduce genetic damage by selective mechanisms that are tragically unspecific, inefficient, and harsh. The wanton and meaningless destructiveness of the nuclear holocaust is illustrated even in this detail.

NOTES

[1]World Health Organization. 1984. Effects of Nuclear War on Health and Health Services. Geneva: World Health Organization.

[2]Oftedal, P. 1984. Genetic damage following nuclear war. Pp 163–174 in Effects of Nuclear War on Health and Health Services. Geneva: World Health Organization.

[3]World Health Organization. 1985. Effects of Nuclear War on Health and Health Services. A38/Inf. DOC/5 Thirty-Eighth World Health Assembly. Geneva: World Health Organization.

[4]Rotblat, J. 1984. Physical effects of nuclear weapons. Pp. 41–64 in Effects of Nuclear War on Health and Health Services. Geneva: World Health Organization.

[5]United Nations Scientific Committee on the Effects of Atomic Radiation. 1977. Sources and Effects of Ionizing Radiation. New York: United Nations.

[6]Loewe, W. E., and E. Mendelsohn. 1981. Revised dose estimates at Hiroshima and Nagasaki. Health Phys. 41:663–666.

[7]Gant, K. S., and C. V. Chester. 1981. Minimizing excess radiogenic cancer deaths after a nuclear attack. Health Phys. 41:455–463.

[8]Russell, W. L. 1972. The genetic effects of radiation. Pp. 487–500 in Peaceful Uses of Atomic Energy, Vol. 13. Vienna: International Atomic Energy Agency.

[9]United Nations Scientific Committee on the Effects of Atomic Radiation. 1982. Ionizing Radiation: Sources and Biological Effects. New York: United Nations.

[10]Luning, K. G., and A. G. Searle. 1971. Estimates of genetic risks from ionizing radiation. Mutat. Res. 12:291–304.

[11]Searle, A. G. 1974. Mutation induction in mice. Pp. 131–207 in Advances in Radiation Biology, Vol. 4, J. T. Lett, H. I. Adler, and M. Zelle, eds. New York: Academic Press.

[12]Ehling, U. H. 1984. Methods to estimate the genetic risk. Pp. 292–318 in Mutations in Man, G. Obe, ed. Berlin: Springer.

[13]International Commission on Radiological Protection. 1977. Recommendations of the International Commission on Radiological Protection. ICRP Publication 26. Oxford: Pergamon.

[14]Schull, W. J., M. Otake, and J. V. Neel. 1981. Genetic effects of the atomic bombs: A reappraisal. Science 213:1220–1227.

[15]Oftedal, P. 1984. On the lack of genetic damage in Hiroshima and Nagasaki. Or, is the mouse a good model for man? Health Phys. 46:1152–1154.

[16]Ehling, U. H. 1984. Quantifizierung des genetischen Risikos. Pp. 103–104 in Jahresberifht 1983 Gesellschaft für Strahlen- und Umweltsforschung, Munchen. 8042 Oberschleissheim: Gesellschaft für Strahlen- und Umweltsforschung.

[17]Oftedal, P., and J. Mulvihill. In press. Possible genetic effects of cancer therapy, seen in surviving cancer patients' offspring. Fourth International Conference on Environmental Mutagens, Stockholm, 1985. New York: Alan R. Liss.

[18]International Commission for the Protection Against Environmental Mutagens and Carcinogens. 1984. Mutation Epidemiology: Review and Recommendations. Committee 5 Reports. Amsterdam: Elsevier.

[19]Oftedal, P., and E. Lund. 1983. Cancer of the thyroid and ^{131}I fallout in Norway. Pp. 231–239 in Biological Effects of Low-Level Radiation. Vienna: International Atomic Energy Agency.

[20]Ehling, U. H., and J. Favor. 1984. Recessive and dominant mutations in mice. Pp. 389–428 in Mutation, Cancer and Malformation, E. H. Y. Chu and W. M. Generoso, eds. New York: Plenum.

[21]Russell, L. B. 1954. The effects of radiation on mammalian prenatal development. Pp. 861–918 in Radiation Biology, A. Hoellaender, ed. New York: McGraw-Hill.

[22]Rugh, R. 1958. X-irradiation effects on the human fetus. J. Pediatrics 52:521–538.

[23]Otake, M., and W. J. Schull. 1984. *In utero* exposure to A-bomb radiation and mental retardation: A reassessment. Br. J. Radiology 57:409–416.

[24]Lechat, M. F. 1984. Short term and medium term health effects of thermonuclear weapons and war on individuals and health services. Pp. 77–100 in Effects of Nuclear War on Health and Health Services. Geneva: World Health Organization.

[25]Oftedal, P., and A. G. Searle. 1980. An overall genetic risk assessment for radiological protection purposes. J. Med. Genetics 17:15–20.

PART III

Medical Resource Needs and Availability Following Nuclear War

The Medical Implications of Nuclear War, Institute of
Medicine. © 1986 by the National Academy of Sciences.
National Academy Press, Washington, D.C.

Medical Supply and Demand in a Post-Nuclear-War World*

HERBERT L. ABRAMS, M.D.
Stanford University, Stanford, California

Any analysis of our capacity to survive a nuclear war must view the
medical problems that survivors will confront[1] in the context of the health
care system's capacity to provide a meaningful response.

A *system* has been defined as a group of diverse units combined to
form an integral whole and to function in unison, usually under some
form of control. The health care system is surely one of the most complex
aggregations of people and things that characterize modern society. Its
annual cost of greater than $300 billion is equivalent to that of the entire
U.S. Defense Department. In England, it is the largest single employer
of labor.

The problems of medical supply and demand in the post-nuclear-war
world are too numerous and too complex to be dealt with fully here.
Instead, this analysis will focus on the most acute needs of the injured
population and the most obvious tools of the medical profession—those
without which it could not begin to handle the casualties that will follow
a massive exchange. Only the most obvious elements of a system with
many points of vulnerability will be considered. Even within the hospital
sector—less than half the system at best—the beds, doctors, nurses, blood
products, and drugs required for the injured may represent less severe
constraints than the fuel, power, transportation, communication, food,

---

*From the Center for International Security and Arms Control, Stanford University, and
the Departments of Radiology, Stanford University School of Medicine and Harvard Medical School.

water, and waste disposal (Figure 1) needed to make the entire system work.

This paper will deal with three aspects of need versus availability:

1. A massive exchange between the United States and the Soviet Union. The needs engendered by thermal, blast, and radiation injury will be related to specific resources for acute and urgent care.

2. The effects of a single one-megaton airburst on a densely populated city such as Detroit. Casualty data from the U.S. Office of Technology Assessment (OTA)[2] will be used to determine the degree to which the local and the national systems are stressed by such an event.

3. The impact of a major exchange (in which the United States, Europe, and the Soviet Union are involved) on the developing world's needs for pharmaceuticals, medical equipment, supplies, and food.

SUPPLY VERSUS DEMAND: A MASSIVE EXCHANGE*

How will the supply of medical resources match the demand in a post-nuclear-war world?

To explore this issue, a scenario (referred to as CRP-2B) of massive nuclear war designed by the Federal Emergency Management Agency (FEMA) was used as the basis for projecting the type and number of casualties.[4] The resources considered in this analysis included health personnel, hospital beds, blood and blood products, intravenous fluids, pharmaceuticals, and medical supplies.

Number and Types of Injuries

CRP-2B assumes that the United States is exposed to 6,559 megatons of nuclear explosives. The targets of attack are, in order of priority, military bases and equipment, industrial centers, and population concentrations of 50,000 or more.[4] A worst-case situation has been considered—that is, the same kinds of conditions that existed in Japan in 1945.

In 1981, 73 percent of the population of the United States lived in or near cities with more than 50,000 inhabitants[5] and were prime targets for attack. Approximately 80 percent of the country's medical resources (hospital beds and personnel, blood, drugs, and medical supplies) were also located in these vulnerable areas.

---

*Much of the material in this section was previously published in the *Journal of the American Medical Association*,[3] vol. 252, no. 5, pp. 653–658, © 1984, American Medical Association, and is used here with permission.

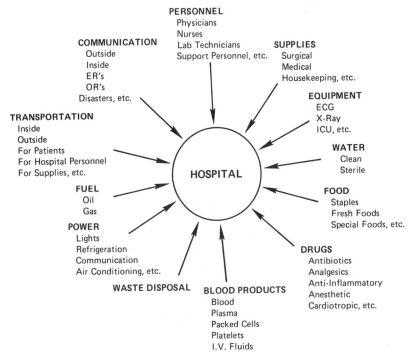

FIGURE 1   Factors on which the proper functioning of a hospital depend.

The numbers and types of injuries in the surviving population were derived from FEMA estimates of casualties.[6]* Accounts of the nuclear attacks on Hiroshima and Nagasaki[7,8] provided additional data, as did those of the Texas City disaster (a dockside explosion of a ship carrying ammonium nitrate fertilizer, which caused more than 3,000 casualties, most of them trauma related).[9,10]

Estimates based on these sources suggest that there will be 93 million survivors, of whom approximately 32 million will have been injured (Table 1). A total of 23 million Americans will have varying degrees of radiation sickness, while 14 million will have suffered trauma, burns, or both. The percentage of moderate and severe injuries in the three major categories was derived from the tables of Oughterson and Warren.[8] The breakdown

---

*The casualties estimated by FEMA used conventional assumptions about nuclear weapons' effects. These do not take into account the "superfires" and the conflagration model described elsewhere in this volume (see Postol; Brode and Small; Daugherty, Levi, and von Hippel).

of FEMA's estimate of 14 million survivors with trauma, burn injuries, or both was extrapolated from Glasstone's table of distribution of injuries among survivors in Japan (70 percent blast and 65 percent burns).[7] A 35 percent overlap of injuries can be estimated by summing the blast and burn injuries. Thus, there would be a total of 9.1 million burn injuries (65 percent of 14 million) and 9.8 million blast injuries (70 percent), of which 4.9 million (35 percent of 14 million) would be combined trauma and burn. Among the 9.8 million blast victims, it is probable that 6 million will have open wounds. There will be hundreds of thousands of head, thorax, abdomen, and extremity injuries (Table 2).[9,10]

Compounding the problem of multiple and combination injuries (e.g., trauma and burns) will be that of nonfatal radiation exposure, which extends the healing time while it increases susceptibility to infection and mortality.[11] (A study of combined burn and radiation injuries in dogs showed that animals with 100-rad exposure alone had a 0 percent mortality rate; with a 20 percent burn, the mortality rate was 12 percent. When the animals were exposed both to a 100-rad exposure and a 20 percent burn, the mortality rate was 75 percent[12]).

Burns and burn-related needs will pose an acute dilemma during the immediate postattack period. Hospital care is most critical for those with burns over 20 percent of the body surface; all of the 5.3 million classified

TABLE 1   Casualty Estimates (in millions)[a]

Radiation sickness (total)	23
Only	5
With trauma, burns, or both	18
Severe	13
Moderate	10
Trauma (total)	9.8
Only	4.9
With burns	4.9
Severe	5
Moderate	4.8
Burns (total)	9.1
Only	4.2
With trauma	4.9
Severe	5.3
Moderate	3.8

[a]Estimates indicate that there would be 93 million survivors, 32 million of whom would be injured. There would be a total of 41.9 million single and combined injuries.

SOURCE: Notes 4 and 6–9.

TABLE 2   Breakdown of Trauma Injuries

Injury	Number
Open wounds	5,791,800
Head	823,200
Thoracic	539,000
Abdominal	392,000
Pelvic and genitourinary	147,000
Extremities	705,600
Upper extremity fractures	264,600
Hand	78,400
Upper leg	78,000
Lower leg and foot	284,200
Maxillofacial	58,800
Eye	400,800
Vertebral or spinal cord	58,800
Ruptured eardrums	891,800
Total	9,800,000

SOURCE: Notes 9 and 10.

as severely burned would most likely be hospitalized in peacetime. A civil defense estimate[6] is that 60 percent of the patients hospitalized in a mass disaster would have lesser burns, leaving 40 percent—or, in this case, 2.12 million survivors—with burns in the critical category.*

Trauma will pose a problem of similar dimensions. In 1978, 20.8 million operations were performed in the United States.[5] Nearly a quarter of that number would have to be performed within the first few days after the attack if the 5 million survivors with severe trauma injuries received surgical treatment at least once. Furthermore, most x-ray film would have been exposed to radiation and thus made useless, so that it would be difficult to identify the precise anatomy of fractures, ruptured viscera, and penetrating wounds before surgery.

The amount of time that elapses before treatment is an important factor in burn and trauma injuries. In one study of severe burn patients (burns over 25 to 64 percent of the body), the mortality rate rose from 63 percent

---

*One 60-bed burn ward in a military hospital requires 8,200 square feet of space (about 762 square meters).[13] Thus, a facility for the 2.12 million most acutely burned survivors of CRP-2B would require 290 million square feet (about 27 million square meters) of space, or 10.4 square miles (about 27 square kilometers)—an area approximately the size of Berkeley, California.[14]

for those admitted to the hospital 2 hours postburn to 88 percent for patients who had treatment delayed from 6 to 23 hours.[12] In addition, use of available resources requires some sort of effective transport: of supplies to the injured and of the injured to an appropriate site for therapy. This may be unlikely or impossible after the attack, when transportation will be disrupted, radiation levels will be high, and the critically injured will be in need of immediate care. Approximately 33 percent of the population of the United States will receive initial fallout levels of 3,000–10,000 rads (R)/hour, 23 percent will receive 1,000–3,000 R/hour, and 22 percent will receive 300–1,000 R/hour.[4] In large cities, the radiation may be more intense; initial fallout in New York City may be at a rate of 32,000 R/hour.[4] Radiation intensity will decrease by a factor of 10 after 7 hours, of 100 after 49 hours, and of 1,000 after 2 weeks.[2] Initially, however, prohibitively high radiation levels would prevent outside help from entering areas where most of the injured would be. For this reason, an individual in an area that initially received 3,000 R/hour may have to wait weeks before outdoor activity is tolerable "up to a few hours per day."[4] Large numbers of injured survivors will be unable to reach care of any kind.

Current Versus Postattack Resources and Requirements

Medical Personnel

Physicians Physicians, nurses, and allied health personnel are more concentrated in urban areas than is the general population. While 73 percent of U.S. inhabitants live in urban areas, the percentage of physicians in cities is 87 percent.[14] Most city dwellers will become casualties, since cities are high-priority targets. In 1979 there were 371,000 active physicians in the United States.[15] The death or incapacitation of 87 percent of these would leave only 48,000 to treat the 32 million injured estimated by FEMA—one doctor for every 663 patients (Table 2). (Viewed in a different perspective, 1.3 million physicians would be required to see each of the 32 million patients for a half hour on the first day, provided that all of the former were able to work a 12-hour shift. If each patient were seen once during the first two days, only 666,667 physicians would be required—still more than 15 times the number available.)

Specialties Certain specialists would be more in demand than others. Most of the population with severe blast injuries (5 million) would presumably require surgery; less than one-third of professionally active physicians are in surgical specialties.[15] If 87 percent became casualties, there would therefore be one surgeon for every 410 patients with serious blast injuries. For the 800,000 head injuries (Table 2), only 399 qualified brain surgeons would be available to treat them. There are only 2,610 plastic surgeons in the country; 339 would remain to treat the 5.3 million severely burned patients—that is, one plastic surgeon for every 15,634 patients.

Nurses   The same critical shortages would occur among nurses and allied health personnel, since they are generally located in the same areas as physicians (Table 3). In 1979 there were 1,223,000 registered nurses and 376,000 practical nurses in the United States.[15] Casualty losses would leave a total of 207,870 nurses, or one for every 154 patients.

In 1976, the average ratio of hospital nurses to patients was about 1 to 3;[16] in intensive care or burn units it is 1 to 1. For the postattack period, data from Hiroshima can be used to estimate a group of 6.7 million patients that will need intensive care—that portion of the most severely injured who would be likely to die between the days 2 and 20 following the attack.[8] Only one registered nurse would be available for every 42 patients in this group.

If the nurse-patient ratio is modified to one nurse for every three of the 6.7 million patients needing intensive care and one nurse for every seven of the 10.9 million regularly hospitalized patients; and if a nurse visits the 14.4 million ambulatory patients at a rate of 10 patients per hour, or 120 patients in a 12-hour shift; and if we assume that ambulatory patients are all seen the first day, 7.7 million nurses would be required on the first day after the attack.

Allied Health Personnel   The work of physicians and nurses would be seriously hampered, if not impossible, without the help of a varied and

TABLE 3   Number of Hospital Beds and Medical Personnel

Resource	Preattack	Postattack	Postattack Needs
Hospital Beds[a]	1,350,000	273,000	17,600,000
Burn beds	1,346	0	2,100,000
Intensive care beds	62,000	14,880	6,700,000
Physicians	371,343	48,275	666,667
Registered nurses	1,200,000	158,990	7,700,000
Licensed practical nurses	387,000	48,880	2,464,000
Medical technologists	129,600	16,770	231,594
Pharmacists	121,500	30,375	419,479
Radiologic technologists	96,790	12,583	173,771

[a]Number of hospital beds minus psychiatric beds.

SOURCE: Notes 15 and 23.

complex group of associated personnel. Medical technologists, pharmacists, and radiological technologists would play an important role. There were 129,000 medical technologists and 97,000 radiological technologists in 1976.[16] Even if the equipment were still available to perform the necessary tests, it would take the 17,000 surviving medical technologists 30 16-hour days to perform one 15-minute test on each patient. A normal type and cross match under peacetime hospital conditions takes 45 minutes. If each medical technologist worked only on typing and cross matching for 16 hours a day, it would take them 49 days to cross match blood for the 17.6 million hospitalized injured.

Similarly, the 9.8 million survivors with blast injuries would need x-rays performed by the 12,600 radiologic technicians who would survive uninjured. Apart from the staggering deficiency of numbers, radiation exposure, as noted above, would render much of the x-ray film unusable and equipment would be largely unavailable.

In 1975, there were 121,500 active pharmacists in the United States.[16] Pharmacists are more widely dispersed than other medical personnel. Most of them work in community pharmacies, not hospitals. Their casualty rate has been figured from the percentage of retail pharmacies located in urban centers with a population over 50,000.* Seventy-five percent work in such areas, so that 30,375 pharmacists will remain uninjured.

In 1979, there was a daily average of 379 full-time employees per 100 patients in community hospitals[15]—a ratio of nearly 4 to 1. If this ratio were to be preserved, 66 million hospital workers would be required after the attack in order to treat the 17.6 million injured at preattack levels of hospital care. This represents a number greater than the 61 million uninjured survivors.

There would also be a vast number of ambulatory and chronically ill patients in need of medical attention following the attack. Burns of less than 20 percent of the body surface are more easily managed,[17] and burns of 15 percent or less may be treated in an ambulatory setting.[18] On the basis of our casualty estimates and FEMA's breakdown of injuries, this group would number about 7 million. The area of the body burned is of great importance, however. Smaller burns involving the face, hands, feet, or genitalia are more serious because they affect airway, vision, excretion, locomotion, or the patient's ability to care for himself.[19] In an exposed population, a large number of facial and hand burns must be anticipated. One military burn unit reported that 66 percent of their patient population had facial burns, even under ordinary conditions.[13]

---

*Data from Pharmaceutical Data Services, Division of Pharmaceutical Care Systems, Subsidiary of Foremost-McKesson, Phoenix, Arizona.

Finally, there are well over 20 million people with diabetes, hypertension, or heart disease in the United States.[20] Without appropriate drugs, many who survive will require health care and hospital beds.

Hospital Beds

In 1978, the United States had 1,137,666 short- and long-stay hospital beds, excluding those set aside for psychiatric patients.[15] Seventy-six percent of all hospital beds are located in urban areas.[14] It is assumed that all of these hospitals would be destroyed or rendered useless, leaving 273,000 beds available following the attack (Table 3).

With an average community hospital occupancy rate of 73 percent,[15] many of these beds will already be occupied by seriously ill patients. During a tense war situation, it is possible that all but the most seriously ill would be removed from hospitals. Hence, a preattack occupancy rate of 20 percent has been assumed.

About 55 percent of the injured with trauma and burns would require hospitalization.[4] The FEMA figures fail to grapple with radiation injury. Those receiving large doses of radiation will require hospitalization, particularly since the exposure level will be uncertain. In patients who have been exposed to 300–1,000 rads, hospital care with antibiotic therapy, blood transfusions, fluid replacement, or bone marrow transplants will frequently make the difference between death and survival.[7,10,21] If 55 percent of the total 32 million injured require hospitalization, there would be 17.6 million patients—64 for each available hospital bed. A 20 percent preattack occupancy rate would leave one bed for every 81 patients.

Burn Beds   A high proportion of the injured will have suffered severe or extensive burns and will require special care. These injuries are the most difficult to treat, since they require a specialized environment as well as more medical supplies and personnel than any other injury category. One estimate, based on the known effects of the bomb in Japan, is that 5.3 million survivors will be classified as severely burned[8]—that is, individuals who would most likely be hospitalized in peacetime.[12] About 60 percent of this group would have burns over less than 20 percent of the body surface.* Even if these patients were excluded, the number requiring burn beds will be 2.12 million—almost eight times the total number of remaining hospital beds (Table 3).

---

*The breakdown is as follows: after a mass disaster 60 percent of hospitalized patients would have burns of less than 20 percent; 30 percent would have burns of 20–40 percent; and 10 percent would have burns of over 40 percent. A study of burn patients at Massachusetts General Hospital over a 19-year period reported a similar distribution of burns.[22]

Burn care is prolonged. In the burn unit of one military hospital, in which the average patient had a 30 percent body burn, the average length of hospitalization was 60.8 days—73.5 days for survivors. Each patient had an average of 4.3 operations.[13] After the initial hospitalization, years of skin grafting operations were needed. A severe burn may require as many as 30–50 operations, both immediate and delayed.[17]

Burn care facilities are scarce even in peacetime. In the United States, there are 135 such units, with a total of 1,346 beds.[23] Their availability is especially crucial for children and for those burned over 60 percent of their bodies. Burn units tend to be in the largest, most centrally located hospitals; Massachusetts has three, all of which are in Boston.[24] All burn beds will probably be destroyed in an attack targeted at urban areas.

Intensive Care Beds   There are 62,000 intensive care beds in the United States (including pediatric and cardiac beds and excluding neonatal beds).[23] The same percentage of intensive care beds as general hospital beds is likely to be destroyed (76 percent), since they are more evenly distributed among hospitals than burn units. This leaves about 15,000 remaining intensive care beds. If the 2.12 million survivors with burns of over 20 percent of the body surface are moved to intensive care beds, there will be a ratio of 142 burn patients for every one intensive care bed.

In Hiroshima, 21 percent of the injured died between days 2 and 20 after the attack.[7] In the attack under consideration,[4] these most severely injured survivors would number 6.7 million—450 patients for every remaining bed. Assuming a 20 percent preattack occupancy rate, there would be one bed for every 563 patients.

Blood and Blood Products

In 1979 11.1 million units of blood were collected in the United States.[25] Nearly all the blood used directly for transfusion is collected from voluntary donors in community blood centers and hospital blood banks; the 213 community and regional centers collect 88 percent of the nation's blood supplies.[25] These centers are generally near the hospitals they service; the same percentage (76 percent) of the national blood supply as of hospitals would therefore be destroyed.

In the last decade, there has been increasing use of blood components, such as red cells and platelets, rather than of whole blood. In 1979, for example, of the 13.4 million units transfused, 54.6 percent were transfused as red blood cells, 16.6 percent as platelet concentrate, 16.2 percent as whole blood, 9.6 percent as plasma, and 3.1 percent as cryoprecipitated antihemophilic factor.[26]

Similarly, whole plasma is now largely transfused into patients for its coagulation factors[26] and collected chiefly for its derivatives—albumin, antihemophilic factor concentrate, and immune serum globulin.[27] Volume expansion is achieved either with balanced electrolyte solutions such as Ringer's lactate or with plasma proteins, such as albumin, which draw several times their weight of fluid into the circulation.[28]

The blood and blood components that are relevant to burn, blast, and radiation injuries are whole blood, red blood cells, platelets, plasma, albumin, and white blood cells. Synthetic volume expanders such as Ringer's lactate and various intravenous fluids must be considered as well.

The following formula was used to estimate the daily inventory of blood and blood components:

$$[(amount\ produced\ daily) - (amount\ transfused\ daily)]$$
$$\times\ (shelf\ life\ of\ product)$$
$$+\ (amount\ produced\ daily) = daily\ inventory.*$$

Throughout most of the country, the shelf life of whole blood is now 35 days[25]—with a few exceptions, such as Massachusetts, where it is still 21 days. Following the above formula, 57,895 units would be available on any given day. This is a 10-day supply under normal rates of usage. If 76 percent of it is destroyed, 13,895 units will remain (Table 4). This estimate is substantiated by the fact that on a random day in January 1981, the American Red Cross—which collects approximately half the blood collected in the United States—had an 8.7-day supply of blood on hand in its New England Region.

White Blood Cells   Since antibiotics are widely available, there is little need to transfuse white blood cells except in patients who are not producing them and who are threatened with infection despite the use of antibiotics. This would include those exposed to whole body radiation as well as patients on immunosuppression or cytotoxic drugs. In peacetime, the use

---

*The amount produced daily was derived from the fact that, on average, there was a yield of approximately 150 percent of blood products from the 11.1 million units of whole blood collected in 1979.[25] Thus, there were actually 16.7 million units of blood products produced, although only 13.4 million units were transfused. Daily production and transfusion were estimated by dividing 16.7 and 13.4 million units by 365 days in a year (45,753 units produced and 36,712 units transfused per day). For example, the daily inventory figure for whole blood was determined as follows: 16.2 percent of the blood supply is transfused as whole blood; 16.2 percent of daily production (45,753) is 7,412; 16.2 percent of daily transfusion (36,712) is 5,947.

TABLE 4   Blood and Resuscitative Fluid Inventories[a]

Inventory[a]	Preattack		Postattack		Postattack Needs
Whole blood	57,895	U	13,895	U	64 MU
Red blood cells	195,041	U	46,810	U	64 MU
Platelets	12,006	U	2,881	U	781 MU
Plasma	105,720	U	25,373	U	85 MU
Albumin	3.4	MU	680,000	U	85 MU
Ringer's lactate	6.4	Ml	1.3	Ml	96 Ml
Intravenous solutions (dextrose and saline)	101	Ml	17	Ml	379 Ml

[a]Unit abbreviations are as follows: U, units; MU, million units; Ml, million liters.

SOURCE: Notes 25–40.

of white blood cells is limited both because demand is not great and because the collection of the cells is a difficult process, presenting some hazard to the donor.[29]

In 1976, 13,433 units of granulocytes were collected.[30] Since they have a shelf life of only 24 hours and are difficult to harvest, it will be assumed that no granulocytes will be on hand for the radiation casualties.

Albumin   Albumin is the most commonly used plasma protein in cases in which volume expansion is required.[31] Nine million units of albumin were produced for domestic use in 1978 (another three million were produced for export).[32] Because of its long shelf life—3 years at room temperature—it is unlikely that consumption exceeds production by a significant amount. Albumin is fractionated from plasma by the pharmaceutical companies. Eighty percent of the pharmaceutical industry is located in urban areas;[33] this percentage of the albumin supply will most likely be destroyed. It has been estimated that approximately 38 percent of yearly pharmaceutical production will be inventory at any one time.[33] Thus 3.4 million units would be on hand on a given day. After the attack, 680,000 units would remain.

Ringer's Lactate and Intravenous Solutions   Intravenous dextrose solution and saline solutions and Ringer's lactate are widely used for plasma volume expansion and fluid replacement in patients with shock, severe trauma, and burns.[34] Both are commercially produced by pharmaceutical companies and have an approximate daily inventory of 7 million liters.[35,36] After the attack, 1.4 million liters would be available (Table 4).

Postattack Requirements for Blood and Fluids

The amount of blood and fluids actually transfused depends on their availability, on the individual responses of patients to injury, and on the therapy that is required. The best estimates are derived from data concerning actual requirements for those who have experienced similar injuries in the past.

Trauma

Trauma creates a strong demand for blood replacement. Data from Vietnam and from the 1973 Arab-Israeli War constitute an appropriate source for estimates of trauma-related blood requirements. An average of 4.4 units of blood were transfused per casualty in Vietnam; in 1970 military planning guidelines allowed for 8 liters of Ringer's lactate per hospitalized casualty.[37,38] In a study of 548 casualties (mainly trauma, with a few burn patients) in an Israeli rear army hospital, an average of 0.25 units of platelet concentrate, 2.74 liters of 5 percent dextrose, 4.34 liters of 5 percent dextrose in saline solution, and 8.76 liters of 0.9 percent sodium chloride solution were used per patient.[39]

Approximately one-third of the 5 million patients with severe trauma will have suffered burns as well (Table 1). These patients with combination injuries will require much higher levels of fluids. The remaining 3.4 million with trauma alone or with trauma and radiation sickness will also need transfusions. Using the data from Vietnam and Israel, this latter group would require the following:

15.0   million units of red blood cells or whole blood
27.2   million liters of Ringer's lactate
0.85   million units of platelets
9.3   million liters of 5 percent dextrose
14.8   million liters of 5 percent dextrose–0.9 percent sodium chloride
29.8   million liters of 0.9 percent sodium chloride solution

Burns

Fluid replacement in massive amounts is an absolute requirement for burn patients, especially during the early hours and days following injury. As judged from available sources[40] (R. Kirkman, personal communication, 1983), the requirements for the first week postinjury of a hypothetical adult of average size (65 kilograms, 1.78 square meters) with a 35 percent body burn approximate the following:

Ringer's lactate, 9.1 liters
Albumin or plasma, 11–17 units
Electrolyte solution, 13 liters
Dextrose (5 percent), 16 liters

For the 2.1 million survivors with burns over 20 percent of their body surface that would require 10–20 units of whole blood or red blood cells during initial skin grafting procedures, total requirements would be as follows:

19.3 million liters of Ringer's lactate
29.7 million units of albumin or plasma (700,000 units)
27.6 million liters of electrolyte solution
33.9 million liters of 5 percent dextrose solution
31.8 million units of red blood cells or whole blood

Radiation

Radiation damage and its accompanying symptoms—severe nausea, vomiting, and diarrhea—will necessitate replacement fluids for another large group of patients. In Hiroshima, 15 percent of the victims with radiation sickness died between days 2 and 20 postattack.[8] Those who died had the most severe radiation sickness—a group that would number 3.5 million in the CRP-2B scenario. Survivors of large, accidental exposures* required 5 liters of fluid daily for about three weeks.[21] This group of survivors will probably also require an average 105 liters of fluid per person, or a total of 367.5 million liters. By extrapolating from Japanese data,[8] it can be seen that 780 million units of platelets and 390 million units of white blood cells would be necessary to handle the radiation-injured group. Since both of these components have very short shelf lives and would not be required until a couple of weeks after the attack,[11] neither one would be available for use.

It should be noted that refrigeration is an essential factor in the availability of blood. Plasma is frozen, for example, and red blood cells must be kept at 4°C–6°C.[28] If no refrigeration is available, the availability of blood products would be drastically altered.

---

*Accounts of the limited number of peacetime radiation accidents are the only sources of information about medical therapy for radiation injuries. One account describes a man who suffered hematological symptoms after being exposed to an estimated 410 rads. He received 60 units of platelets and 30 units of white blood cells during his hospitalization. He survived.[41]

Drugs and Medical Supplies: Preattack and Postattack Resources Versus Need

Resources

Data on the entire range of essential pharmaceuticals are difficult to obtain; a current national inventory is not available.* The difficulties arise not only from the reluctance of pharmaceutical companies to furnish appropriate figures—which they consider proprietary—but also from the steps in the pipeline: manufacturers, warehousers, exporters, and institutional and retail users.[33] Therefore, two drug categories essential to a proper medical response have been emphasized: antibiotics and anesthetics.

The medical supply industry is more diverse than pharmaceuticals, providing products ranging from bandages to computed tomography scanners. The basic information on drugs and medical supplies has been obtained from two reports published in 1970.[35,36] They were derived from data compiled by the Division of Emergency Health Services of the Public Health Service. The quantities per 1,000 population have been used as a basis for calculating the total inventory, using updated population data from the 1980 census (226.5 million people). For example, the inventory of a few important medical supply items would amount to approximately 30 million square yards (about 25 million square meters) of absorbent gauze bandage (132 square yards [about 110 square meters] per 1,000 × 226 million people), 32 million hypodermic needles, and 426,000 general operating scissors.

In estimating the post-nuclear attack inventory, it was assumed that 80 percent of the drug industry had been destroyed—the approximate percentage of the industry located in standard metropolitan statistical areas. Drug production is concentrated in a few states, largely on the Eastern seaboard.[33] Eighty percent was also applied to the medical supply industry, since it is distributed across the country in much the same pattern as hospital beds, health manpower, and the drug industry.

Using these assumptions, a national inventory of 43,000 kilograms of a specific antibiotic (tetracyclines) would be reduced to 8,600 kilograms. Quantities of anesthetics would be similarly reduced. Absorbent gauze bandage would be decreased from 30 million to 6 million square yards

---

*There are about 800 prescription drug companies in the United States, of which 100 account for about 95 percent of all prescription drugs.

(about 25 million to 5 million square meters), hypodermic needles from 32 million to 6.4 million, and surgical scissors from 426,000 to 85,000. Similar data are available for other types of medical supplies (Table 5).

Needs

Drug and medical supply needs of the injured can be compiled by matching CRP-2B casualty estimates to the best figures on requirements for specific injuries.[18] These figures are based on the assumptions that functioning hospitals exist; that treatment is simplified to provide as much definitive medical care as possible in an emergency situation; and that all casualties of the attack will be treated, either as inpatients or outpatients.

In each category of injury—radiation, blast, burn—antibiotics are the most crucial drugs because infection is the most dangerous complication. In peacetime, burn patients combat infection with various surface antiseptic agents and topical antibiotics, systemic antibiotics, and elaborate isolation techniques.[17] The enormous number of casualties after a nuclear war would probably require prophylactic antibiotics as a primary medical strategy.[18] It would be particularly important during the first 24–48 hours after the disaster. In the next days or weeks, established infections would become the dominant problem.[1,18] Measures against existing infections with organism-specific antibiotics require a functioning bacteriological laboratory and a stockpile of assorted antibiotics of varying capabilities. In general, the antibiotics essential for these casualties would be penicillins, tetracyclines, cephalosporins, aminoglycosides, and sulfa drugs. Since it is difficult to predict how much of these antibiotics would be required, the figures on need have been based largely on prophylaxis.

Such an analysis indicates a need for 314,000 kilograms (kg) of tetracyclines when only 8,600 kg would be available.* A total of 1.5 million pounds (680,400 kg) of anesthetic would be required, while 137,000 pounds (about 62,000 kg) would remain. Applied to medical supplies, 193 million square yards (about 161 million square meters) of gauze absorbent bandage would be needed when only 6 million would be available; 76 million hypodermic needles with only 6.4 million available; and 5.2 million general operating scissors with only 85,000 available (Table 5).

This analysis rests on assumptions about the nuclear megatonnage involved in a war and the destruction that would follow. Given the use of a model developed by federal agencies, it is feasible to couple informed

---

*See Table 5, footnote *a*, for a description of the method by which figures on need were derived.

TABLE 5 Availability and Need, Drugs and Medical Supplies[a]

Resource	Preattack Inventory		Postattack Inventory	Postattack Need
	Per 1,000 Population	Total		
Antibiotics (tetracyclines)	190 g	43,000 kg	8,600 kg	314,000 kg
Anesthetics	3 lb (1.4 kg)	688,000 lb (312,077 kg)	137,000 lb (62,143 kg)	1,500,000 lb (680,400 kg)
Bandage, gauze absorbent (all grades and meshes)	132 sq yd (110 sq m)	30,000,000 sq yd (25,084,000 sq m)	6,000,000 sq yd (5,016,722 sq m)	193,000,000 sq yd (161,370,000 sq m)
Needles, hypodermic	140	32,000,000	6,400,000	76,000,000
Intravenous injection sets	10	2,290,000	458,000	36,000,000
Scissors, general operating	1.9	425,000	85,000	5,202,000

[a]The data in this table were derived as follows. For the preattack inventory, the quantities per 1,000 population were obtained from studies by Pyecha et al.[36] and Anderson.[35] Their data, in turn, were based on figures compiled by the Division of Emergency Health Services of the U.S. Public Health Service. The total national inventory was then derived on the basis of updated population data from the 1980 census (226.5 million people). For the postattack inventory, estimates were based on destruction of 80 percent of the drug industry and drug stores, which is the approximate percentage located in standard metropolitan statistical areas.[33] A similar assumption of 80 percent destruction of medical supplies was employed; destruction of the medical supply industry and stores follows the patterns of the drug industry and of hospital beds and health manpower. For postattack need, the figures were the casualty estimates listed in Tables 1 and 2, which were based on the CRP-2B scenario of the Federal Emergency Management Agency.[4,6] The requirements for each type of injury, as described by McCarroll and Skudder[18] and Moncrief,[13] were developed into a series of tables in which the number of patients requiring the supply, the units of supply required per patient, the total units of supply needed, and the size of each supply unit were multiplied to provide a total quantity of needed supply. These quantities for each category of injury were then added to provide the figures on postattack need in this table. The tables containing the precise breakdown of all categories of necessary supplies cover 32 pages and are too detailed to be included in this paper. The choice of the limited number of items listed above provides a representative statement of the degree of disparity between need and available supply.

estimates and prior experience on the likelihood of damage with data about the medical requirements of specific injuries to arrive at acceptable approximations. Of greatest importance is the fact that such figures—even if the projections are subject to some error—provide a perspective from which the magnitude and scale of the disparities can readily be appreciated.

The disparities are large. If there are 14,000 units of whole blood available and 64 million units required, 47,000 units of red blood cells when 64 million are needed, and 1.3 million liters of Ringer's lactate when 96 million liters could be used, then the problems of developing a credible medical response for the millions of surviving injured are readily grasped. The data on drugs and medical supplies are similar, and the disparities are parallel.

It is possible that the most urgent question about resource need versus availability goes beyond all of the foregoing estimates. Access to those resources that remain is a problem that cannot readily be resolved. The hospital beds, health personnel, and supplies located in outlying areas may be unavailable to the injured in populous centers of heavy destruction—not only because transportation systems may be destroyed, but also because intolerably high radiation levels may exist in or adjacent to the areas of most intense need.

SUPPLY VERSUS DEMAND:
A ONE-MEGATON AIRBURST OVER AN URBAN CENTER

The stresses placed on the medical care system following a massive nuclear attack have been described above.

What would be the impact of an event on a much smaller scale—a one-megaton explosion on an urban center? Such an attack—while remote from a massive exchange—would nevertheless represent explosive power approximately 75 times that of the bomb that was dropped on Hiroshima.

The OTA has depicted the damage anticipated in such a scenario using the city of Detroit as the target.[2] Their analysis assumed that the attack took place at night, with the detonation at an altitude of 6,000 feet, no warning, and clear weather. No other cities were attacked. Their calculations suggested that 470,000 of a population of 4.3 million would be killed, while 630,000 would be injured. Among the injured survivors, blast and burn effects would dominate, with radiation effects being far less prominent. Unlike the figures in the massive exchange scenario described by FEMA,[6] an approximate breakdown of 70 percent blast, 65 percent thermal, and at most 20 percent radiation injuries might be expected.[42] This implies that there would be 440,000 blast injuries, 409,000 thermal injuries, and 157,000 exposed to moderate or marked radiation. (Many would have more than one type of injury, bringing the total well above the 630,000 people injured.) The uncertainties of the foregoing breakdown must be recognized, but the total number of injured represents the best estimate of the OTA study.[2]

The figure of 630,000 injured approximates 2 percent of the total number of injuries (32 million) calculated for the massive exchange described above. Even with the larger number of burns and blast injuries, it has been conservatively assumed, in the interest of simplicity, that the medical resources required will be 2 percent of those needed for the larger attack. Thus, 352,000 is the projected number of hospital beds needed after a one-megaton airburst, representing 2 percent of the 17.6 million required in the aftermath of a major exchange (Table 3). Postattack needs for personnel, blood products, and fluids were similarly generated (Tables 6 and 7).

The figures on pre- and postattack inventories have been prepared under two different assumptions. The first embodied all national resources, even though timely access to those in outlying areas cannot be ensured. (The destruction of the transportation system in and around Detroit, the difficulty of getting the injured to distant areas, and the need to use medical resources in other parts of the country for the nearby sick and injured make it unlikely that the resources outside the region will be fully available for the acutely injured.) In the first calculation, the preattack resources were assumed to equal the national inventory (Tables 6 and 7).

TABLE 6   Hospital Beds and Medical Personnel (Case 1: National Resources)[a]

Resource	Preattack	Postattack	Postattack Needs
Hospital beds	1,350,000	1,336,500	352,000
Burn beds	1,346	1,333	42,000
Intensive care beds	62,000	61,380	134,000
Physicians	371,343	367,630	13,333
Registered nurses	1,200,000	1,188,000	154,000
Licensed practical nurses	387,000	383,130	49,280
Medical technologists	129,600	128,304	4,632
Pharmacists	121,500	120,285	8,390
Radiologic technologists	96,790	95,822	3,475

[a]Assuming a one-megaton airburst.

The postattack inventory was derived by considering hospital beds destroyed in Detroit (as indicated by the OTA) as a percentage of the national pool of beds (13,000 destroyed of a national total of 1.35 million, or 1 percent). This percentage was then applied to the preattack inventory of beds, personnel, blood products, and supplies. The resultant data (Tables 6 and 7) demonstrated a considerable disparity between availability and need in important areas: 1,333 burn beds compared with 42,000 needed, for example, or 61,000 intensive care beds with a demand for 134,000 (Table 6). Additionally, blood products would be in urgent demand, yet there would only be 57,000 units of whole blood with 1.28 million needed; 191,000 units of red blood cells with 1.28 million needed; and 12,000 units of platelets with 15 million needed. Adequate numbers of personnel would be available if they could be transported to the stricken area.

A second, more conservative, and perhaps more accurate set of statistics was generated by relying solely on the resources available in the state of Michigan and comparing them with the expected need. Michigan's population—4 percent of the entire country (8.8 million compared with 220 million)—was used as a simplifying basis for assuming a preattack state inventory at 4 percent of the national resources (Tables 8 and 9). As an

TABLE 7   Blood, Fluids, Drugs, and Supply Inventory (Case 1: National Resources)[a]

Type	Preattack	Postattack	Postattack Need
Whole blood (U)	57,865	57,286	1,280,000
Red blood cells (U)	195,041	193,091	1,280,000
Platelets	12,006	11,886	15,620,000
Plasma	105,720	104,663	1,700,000
Albumin	3,400,000	3,366,000	1,700,000
Ringer's lactate (liters)	6,400,000	6,336,000	1,920,000
Intravenous solutions (liters)	101,000,000	99,990,000	7,580,000
Antibiotics (tetracyclines) (kg)	43,000	42,570	6,280
Anesthetics (lbs)[b]	688,000	681,000	300,000
	(312,077)	(308,902)	(136,080)
Bandages (sq yd)[c]	30,000,000	29,700,000	3,860,000
	(25,083,612)	(24,832,775)	(3,227,424)
Needles (no.)	32,000,000	31,700,000	1,520,000
Intravenous injection sets (no.)	2,290,000	21,267,000	720,000

[a]Assuming a one-megaton airburst.
[b]Values in parentheses are metric equivalents, in kilograms.
[c]Values in parentheses are metric equivalents, in square meters.

TABLE 8   Hospital Beds and Medical Personnel (Case 2: Michigan Resources)[a]

Resource	Preattack	Postattack	Postattack Needs
Hospital Beds	48,328[b]	36,729	352,000
Burn beds	54	41	42,000
Intensive care beds	2,480	1,885	134,000
Physicians	15,758[b]	11,975	13,333
Registered nurses	48,000	36,480	154,000
Licensed practical nurses	15,480	11,765	49,280
Medical technologists	5,184	3,940	4,632
Pharmacists	4,860	3,694	8,390
Radiologic technologists	3,872	2,942	3,475

[a]Assuming a one-megaton airburst.
[b]Figures are actual, based on American Hospital Association[43] and American Medical Association[44] statistics. They are close to the 4 percent figure used for all other state inventory estimates.

example, because the national inventory of hospital beds is 1.35 million, it was assumed that the state of Michigan had 54,000, or 4 percent.*

The estimate of the medical resources that might survive a one-megaton strike was based on the OTA calculation that 13,000 hospital beds would be destroyed[2]—or 24 percent of the state total of 54,000. This left 76 percent of the resources available, which was the figure then applied to beds, personnel, and supplies in determining the postattack inventories (Tables 8 and 9).

Postattack need, as noted above, was calculated at 2 percent of that following the massive nuclear exchange. The disparities are considerable: 41 burn beds with 42,000 needed, 1,900 intensive care beds compared with 134,000, and 41,000 hospital beds when 352,000 are required. In terms of blood and resuscitative fluids, 1,800 units of whole blood will be available with 1.28 million needed; 6,000 units of red blood cells will be available with 1.28 million needed; and 350 units of platelets will be available, but over 15 million units could be used. The disparity between supply and demand for medical personnel, drugs, and supplies is also large (Tables 8 and 9).

This assessment of specific medical resources following a one-megaton attack omits entirely such problems as the provision of clean water in light

---

*There are somewhat fewer hospital beds in Michigan than 4 percent of the national total, according to the American Hospital Association,[43] and somewhat more physicians, according to the American Medical Association.[44] On balance, the 4 percent figure seemed a reasonable simplifying approximation.

of pump and power failure and pipe rupture. A significant electromagnetic pulse could be generated by a one-megaton weapon and would disrupt power sources and electronic equipment over a wide area.[45] In the absence of power, no life support instruments would be operative. As noted above, the medical response will be influenced by a host of factors that go well beyond beds, personnel, and supplies.

SUPPLY VERSUS DEMAND: THE DEVELOPING WORLD

Need Versus Availability

The two most important sources of illness in the developing world are malnutrition and infection. In analyzing the impact of nuclear war on the health care of this huge segment of the world's population, it will be assumed that North America, Europe, and the Soviet Union are no longer able to export food, drugs, medical equipment, and supplies to their former markets.

A brief analysis of three areas of central importance to health care— pharmaceuticals, medical equipment, and grain supplies—may help establish the dimensions of the problem.

TABLE 9   Blood, Fluids, Drugs, and Supply Inventory (Case 2: Michigan Resources)[a]

Type	Preattack	Postattack	Postattack Need
Whole blood (U)	2,315	1,759	1,280,000
Red blood cells (U)	7,802	5,929	1,280,000
Platelets (U)	480	365	15,620,000
Plasma (U)	4,229	3,214	1,700,000
Albumin (U)	136,000	103,360	1,700,000
Ringer's lactate (liters)	256,000	194,560	1,920,000
Intravenous solutions			
(dextrose and saline) (liters)	4,040,000	3,070,400	7,580,000
Antibiotics (tetracyclines) (kg)	1,700	1,290	6,280
Anesthetics (lb)[b]	27,500	20,500	300,000
	(12,474)	(9,299)	(136,080)
Bandages (sq yd)[c]	1,200,000	912,000	3,860,000
	(1,003,344)	(762,542)	(3,227,425)
Needles (no.)	1,280,000	973,000	1,520,000
Intravenous injection sets (no.)	91,600	69,616	720,000

[a]Assuming a one-megaton airburst.

[b]Values in parentheses are metric equivalents, in kilograms.

[c]Values in parentheses are metric equivalents, in square meters.

TABLE 10   World Pharmaceutical Production, 1980

Countries	Production Million U.S. Dollars	Percent
Developed countries		
Market economies		
North America	18,600	22.1
Western Europe	27,440	33.0
Others	11,970	14.3
Centrally planned economies		
Eastern Europe	15,960	19.1
Total, developed countries	73,970	88.5
Developing countries		
Africa	470	0.6
Asia*a*	4,690	5.6
Latin America	4,400	5.3
Total, developing countries	9,560	11.5
Total, world market	83,530	100.0

*a*Excluding China.

SOURCE: Derived from note 46.

Drugs

The value of worldwide drug production amounted to US$84 billion in 1980. Developed market economies accounted for 70 percent of total output. Centrally planned economies (Soviet Union, China, and Eastern Europe) followed with 19 percent, while the share for developing countries was just over 11 percent (Asia produced 5.6 percent; Latin America, 5.3 percent; and Africa, 0.6 percent) (Table 10).[46]

A few nations control the bulk of pharmaceutical production. The United States, Japan, and West Germany together represent half of the world's total output. In the developing world, more than two-thirds of the drugs manufactured come from a half dozen countries: India, Brazil, Mexico, Argentina, Egypt, and South Korea. In the other countries, there are few indigenous sources.[47]

Consumption is uneven. Developing countries, with nearly two-thirds of the world's population, consume only 14 percent of the pharmaceuticals produced.* Furthermore, they depend heavily on imports to satisfy their

---

*Developed market economies accounted for 70 percent of world consumption, and the centrally planned economies accounted for the remaining 14 percent.

needs. The international pharmaceutical trade approximates US$14 billion. Of this, developing nations imported 32 percent and exported only 4 percent, whereas developed countries as a whole exported 96 percent and imported 68 percent.[46]

Most developing nations do not have a strong chemical industry. They import finished or semifinished drugs rather than basic or intermediate chemicals that require extensive local processing. The imports come largely from transnational pharmaceutical firms based in the developed market economy countries.[46] An analysis of a sample of 10 developing countries confirms their reliance on foreign firms for maintenance of their health care systems (Table 11).[48] On average, foreign firms held 75 percent of the market share of pharmaceutical products of the sampled developing nations, with the vast bulk coming from the United States and Europe. Of the top 50 firms, U.S. companies are responsible for almost 50 percent of sales; and together the United States, West Germany, and Switzerland house 33 of the 50 largest drug firms. These account for almost 80 percent of the pharmaceutical sales of the top 50 companies. A major nuclear exchange would cut off this critical source of pharmaceuticals for the developing world.

Medical Equipment

Like the pharmaceutical industry, the medical equipment market in developing countries is dominated in large part by foreign suppliers, no-

TABLE 11   Pharmaceutical Market Shares Held by Domestic and Foreign Firms in 10 Selected Countries (percent)

Country	Domestic Share	Foreign Share
Saudi Arabia	0	100
Nigeria	3	97
Venezuela	12	88
Brazil	15	85
Indonesia	15	85
Mexico	18	82
India	25	75
Iran	25	75
Argentina	30	70
Philippines	35	65
Average of 10 countries	25	75

SOURCE: Note 48. Reprinted with permission from the author.

TABLE 12   Imports of Medical Equipment in Developing Countries

Country	Year	Total	From the United States	From Europe	From Europe and the United States
Algeria	1985	100	4	85	89
Argentina	1981	75	41	35	76
Brazil	1985	34	36	50	86
Chile	1983	100	40	45	85
Colombia	1983	72	36	48	84
Ecuador	1978	100	25	60	85
Guatemala	1978	100	58	27	85
Honduras	1978	100	38	18	56
Korea	1983	90	43	16	59
Mexico	1980	80	56	39	95
Philippines	1980	99	56	20	76
Singapore	1980	100	37	50	87
Thailand	1981	90	23	45	68
Venezuela	1980	100	50	25	75

Percent Imported

SOURCE: Notes 49–62.

tably those in the United States and Western Europe. A random sample of developing countries* showed that they imported 89 percent of their medical equipment, 79 percent of it from the United States and Western Europe (Tables 12 and 13).[49-62] Reliance of these developing countries on outside sources has remained constant over the past 7 years. In 1980, Mexico imported 56 percent of its medical equipment from the United States and 39 percent from Western Europe—a combined total of 95 percent.[58] Singapore received 87 percent of its health supplies and instrumentation from the Western developed nations,[60] while Venezuela and the Philippines imported 75 and 76 percent, respectively.[59,62] In 1983 Chile and Colombia acquired 85 percent of their medical equipment from American and European suppliers.[52,53] In 1985, Algeria is projected to import 89 percent and Brazil 86 percent.[49]

As in the drug industry, the United States and Western Europe assume roughly three-quarters of the foreign market share in medical equipment. The destruction of the industrial apparatus of these two areas would cripple

---

*Fourteen countries were selected for this sample: Algeria, Argentina, Brazil, Chili, Colombia, Ecuador, Guatemala, Honduras, Korea, Mexico, the Philippines, Singapore, Thailand, and Venezuela.[49-62] These countries varied markedly in their level of development and the per capita income. The sample is not fully satisfactory because of the difficulty of obtaining data on some of the African countries, whose level of dependence is even higher.

TABLE 13   Imports of Medical Equipment in Developing Countries[a]

		Imports		
	Average of 14 Countries	Total	From the United States	From Europe	From the United States and Europe
Percent		89	39	40	79
Millions of U.S. dollars	42.9	38.3	16.8	17.2	34.0

[a]Totals are from a sample of 14 developing countries, including Algeria, Argentina, Brazil, Chile, Colombia, Ecuador, Guatemala, Honduras, Korea, Mexico, Philippines, Singapore, Thailand, and Venezuela.

SOURCE: Notes 49–62.

the health care systems of the developing world and deprive them of much of the equipment essential for acute and chronic health care.

Food

Food production is powerfully connected to the international economy. While there have been major studies of the effects of a nuclear war on plants, animals, and ecosystems, only a few have addressed the problems of international subsistence from a macrolevel. Some authors have focused on the rebuilding of the U.S. economy without adequate recognition of our dependence on foreign markets for goods, imported raw materials, and sources of energy.[63] Regions that trade with the developed countries are reciprocally dependent on them and would be profoundly affected by their collapse. The effects of a massive nuclear exchange between the United States and Soviet Union, therefore, would spread far beyond the borders of the countries directly involved. Atmospheric changes might limit the agricultural growth of smaller economies, which could no longer depend on the developed nations for either money or materials.

The total gross domestic product (GDP) for the world's market economies in 1977, in millions of U.S. dollars, was 6,161,000. Including estimates for centrally planned economies, that figure was roughly US$7,977,500 million in 1977. (Market economies do not include the centrally planned economies of the USSR, China, Bulgaria, Romania, Poland, Hungary, Czechoslovakia, German Democratic Republic, and Cuba.) To the figure for world market GDP, the United States contributed 31 percent, and the countries of Europe contributed 33 percent. Together with Canada, the United States and Europe account for over one-half (51 percent) of the GDP of the world economy.[64] Estimates indicate that the

Soviet Union generated 13 percent of the total in 1977.[65] Thus, if the economies of North America, the USSR, and Europe were destroyed, almost two-thirds (64 percent) of the world's economic strength would vanish. By contrast, the combined economies of Africa in 1977 produced only 3 percent of the world total. Caribbean and Latin American nations contributed 6 percent. Asian nations, including Japan and the Middle East, added another 20 percent.

These figures contrast sharply with population statistics. The 1979 population of North America and Europe was 17.7 percent of the world total, while that of Africa, Asia, and Latin America amounted to 76.6 percent. The population for India and China alone totals roughly 1.6 billion, over a third of the world's people.[66]

Disparities between world population and production of the basic agricultural staples are equally striking. In 1980 the world production of wheat totaled 444,534 thousand metric tons. North America produced 86,319 thousand tons, or 19 percent, a figure 3.5 times greater than its proportion of the world population. In contrast, Africa produced 8,634 thousand metric tons (2 percent) but had 10 percent of the world population. With nearly 58 percent of the world's inhabitants, Asian countries produced only 29 percent. The Soviet Union produces 98,000 metric tons, yet it must import substantial amounts each year from the United States, Argentina, Canada, Australia, and Western Europe. Europe produces 22 percent of the world's wheat which, as with North America, far exceeds its consumption (Table 14).

Other coarse grains also show an imbalance between level of production and population. The United States produces 43 percent of the world's

TABLE 14 Percentage of World Population and Agriculture Production

	United States	Europe	USSR	Total
Percent of world population	5	11	6	22
Percent of agriculture production				
Oats	16	35	33	84
Barley	5	45	27	77
Soybeans	59	1	1	61
Potatoes	6	41	30	77
Corn	43	14	2	59
Wheat	15	22	22	59
Tractors	21	40	10	71
Harvesters-threshers	18	24	20	62

SOURCE: Note 66.

maize (corn); Canada produces 48 percent (188,077 of 392,249 thousand metric tons in 1980); and Europe produces over 60 percent. Asia produces only 83,139 thousand metric tons (21 percent), yet it has 10 times the population of North America. Corn is a staple not necessarily for the human diet but for animal feed.

Similar considerations apply to barley and oats. North America produces 23 percent, Europe produces 35 percent, and the USSR produces 33 percent of oats (Table 14). Africa produces only 0.6 percent and Asia, 3.5 percent. Europe produces 45 percent of the barley, the USSR produces 27 percent, and North America produces 12 percent. Africa grows only 3 percent.[67]

Different countries have varied demands for such agricultural staples. For example, the Soviet Union, despite its relatively high production figures, in 1979–1980 imported 16 percent of the world's wheat and coarse grain exports.[68] Yet for every major crop, the same pattern is evident: North America, the Soviet Union, and Europe harvest the vast majority of the world's produce for their relatively small societies. Together, their people make up 22 percent of the world's population (Table 14), yet they produce 63 percent of the wheat, 65 percent of the corn, 91 percent of the oats, and 84 percent of the barley.

Three-quarters of all tractors and two-thirds of all harvester-threshers are currently in inventories throughout North America, Europe, and the Soviet Union (Table 14). A total of 68 percent of nitrogenous fertilizers in 1979–1980 were produced in the same three regions, along with 97 percent of potash fertilizers and 75 percent of phosphate fertilizers. Consumption figures are revealing here. The major economies all produce fertilizer in excess of their consumption, but Asia and particularly Africa consume far more than they can produce. Elimination of the supplier nations would not only diminish food supplies but would also strip the world of resources necessary to produce new crops over the long term.

One group of manufactured chemicals that would be lost are herbicides. In 1980 the world's developed market economies were responsible for 98.1 percent of all herbicide exports. North America exported 25 percent and Western Europe exported 70 percent, with West Germany being the largest supplier. Compounding this problem is the fact that a similar situation exists for insecticides. Developed world market economies export almost all the chemicals that noncentrally planned societies require. In 1980 the figure was 96 percent. The United States exported 21 percent, while Europe's share was almost 69 percent.[69]

In the wake of a massive nuclear war, farming methods may well revert to a primitive level, with the lack of access to modern machinery, fertilizers, and insecticides. The impact on the developing world will be pro-

A "SUBSISTENCE LOOP"

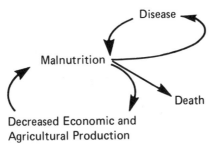

FIGURE 2   Impact of food deprivation. Weakness and increased susceptibility to infection and disease impede the capacity to work, further decreasing agricultural production with a worsening of malnutrition in a theoretical subsistence loop.[63]

found. While it will augment the disparity between food supplies and population need that now exists, it will surely limit the capacity to handle many of the problems of disease and medical care. Like the Northern Hemisphere, the Southern Hemisphere may find itself constrained by a subsistence loop, in which malnutrition begets disease, disease impairs the ability to produce, and decreased production impedes the cycle of recovery (Figure 2).[63]

ACKNOWLEDGMENT

The research presented herein was supported by grants from the Carnegie Corporation, the John D. and Catherine T. MacArthur Foundation, the W. Alton Jones Foundation, and the New Prospect Foundation.

Ruth Chasek played a major role in organizing much of the data on which this article was based. Margaret Sullivan was involved and helpful in the research on the second and third sections. Mrs. Jeffery Stoia contributed importantly in reviewing and shaping the manuscript. Margaret Mariscal typed the manuscript with skill and grace. To all, I am deeply indebted.

NOTES

[1]Abrams, H. L., and W. E. Von Kaenel. 1981. Medical problems of survivors of nuclear war: Infection and the spread of communicable disease. N. Engl. J. Med. 305:1226–1332.

[2]U.S. Office of Technology Assessment. 1979. The effects of nuclear war. Washington, D.C.: Office of Technology Assessment.

[3]Abrams, H. L. 1984. Medical resources after nuclear war: availability vs. need. J. Am. Med. Assoc. 252(5):653–658.

[4]Haaland, C. M., C. V. Chester, and E. P. Wigner. 1976. Survival of the Relocated Population of the U.S. After a Nuclear Attack. Defense Civil Preparedness Agency Report No. ORNL-5041. Springfield, Va.: National Technical Information Service.

[5]U.S. Department of Commerce. 1980. Statistical Abstract of the United States, 1980, p. 17. Washington, D.C.: U.S. Department of Commerce, Bureau of the Census.

[6]Federal Emergency Management Agency. 1980. Material for the Record, Short- and Long-Term Health Effects of the Surviving Population of a Nuclear War. Washington, D.C.: U.S. Government Printing Office.

[7]Glasstone, K. S., and P. Dolan, eds. 1977. The Effects of Nuclear Weapons. Washington, D.C.: U.S. Department of Defense and U.S. Department of Energy.

[8]Oughterson, A. W., and S. Warren. 1956. Medical Effects of the Atomic Bomb in Japan. New York: McGraw-Hill.

[9]Blocker, V., and T. G. Blocker, Jr. 1949. The Texas City disaster: A survey of 3,000 casualties. Am. J. Surg. 78:764–766.

[10]Lyday, R. O., Jr., J. N. Pyecha, and E. L. Hill. 1976. Post-Attack Medical Care Impact on Survivors' Work Force. Final Report 44U-896, p. a.5. Research Triangle Park, N.C.: The Research Triangle Institute. Prepared for the Defense Civil Preparedness Agency.

[11]Andrews, G. A. 1980. Medical Management of Accidental Total-Body Irradiation. In K. F. Hubner and S. A. Fry, eds., The Medical Basis for Radiation Accident Preparedness. New York: Elsevier-North Holland.

[12]Brooks, J. W., E. I. Evans, W. T. Ham, and J. D. Reid. 1952. The influence of external body radiation on mortality from thermal burns. Ann. Surg. 136:535.

[13]Moncrief, J. A. 1969. Logistics of Burn Therapy—Personnel, Supplies, and Space: Military Experience. In A. W. Phillips and C. W. Walters, eds., Workshop on Mass Burns, Proceedings. Washington, D.C.: National Academy of Sciences.

[14]U.S. Department of Commerce, Bureau of the Census. 1978. County and City Data Book, 1977. Washington, D.C.: U.S. Government Printing Office.

[15]National Center for Health Statistics. 1980. Health United States, 1980. Hyattsville, Md.: U.S. Public Health Service.

[16]National Center for Health Statistics. 1976–1977. Health Resources Statistics. Health Manpower and Health Facilities. Hyattsville, Md.: U.S. Public Health Service.

[17]Constable, J. D. 1982. Burn Injuries Among Survivors. P. 208 in E. Chivian, ed., Last Aid: The Medical Dimensions of Nuclear War. San Francisco: W. H. Freeman and Co.

[18]McCarroll, J. R., and P. A. Skudder, eds. 1968. Treatment of Mass Civilian Casualties. U.S. Public Health Service Publication 1071-C-5. Washington, D.C.: U.S. Government Printing Office.

[19]Mason, A. D., and E. G. Bowles. 1969. The Effect of Topical Chemotherapy and Use of Homograft Skin as a Biological Dressing on Burn Mortality. In A. W. Phillips and C. W. Walter, eds., Workshop on Mass Burns, Proceedings. Washington, D.C.: National Academy of Sciences.

[20]National Center for Health Statistics. 1973. Prevalence of Chronic Conditions of the Genitourinary, Nervous, Endocrine, Metabolic, and Blood and Blood-Forming Systems and of Other Selected Chronic Conditions. Series 10, No. 109. Hyattsville, Md.: U.S. Public Health Service.

[21]Jammet, H., R. Gorgora, P. Poullard, R. Le Go, and N. Parmentier. 1980. The 1978 Algerian Accident: Four Cases of Protracted Whole-Body Irradiation. In K. F. Hubner and S. A. Fry, eds., The Medical Basis for Radiation Accident Preparedness. New York: Elsevier-North Holland.

[22]Phillips, A. W. 1968. Burn therapy. V. Disaster management—to treat or not to treat? Who should receive intravenous fluids? Ann. Surg. 168:260.

[23]Hospital Statistics. 1981. Chicago: American Hospital Association.

[24]Katz, A. 1982. Life After Nuclear War. Cambridge, Mass.: Ballinger Publishing Co.

[25]American Blood Commission. 1981. Annual Report of the American Blood Commission, 1980–1981. Arlington, Va.: American Blood Commission.

[26]American Blood Commission. 1981. Blood Facts: Answers to Some Often Asked Questions. Arlington, Va.: American Blood Commission.

[27]American Red Cross. 1981. 1981 Annual Report. Washington, D.C.: American Red Cross.

[28]Rutman, R. C., and W. V. Miller. 1982. Transfusion Therapy. Rockville, Md.: Aspen Systems Corporation.

[29]Nusbacher, J. 1979. White Cell Transfusion. In R. G. Hubbel, ed., Advances in Blood Transfusion. Arlington, Va.: American Blood Commission.

[30]Hemphill, B. M. 1979. Blood collection and use by AABB institutional members (1976). Transfusion 19:365–366.

[31]Petz, L. D., and S. N. Swisher. 1981. Clinical Practice of Blood Transfusion. New York: Churchill-Livingstone.

[32]Tullis, J. L. 1979. The Impact of Advances in Blood Transfusion. In R. G. Hubbel, ed., Advances in Blood Transfusion. Arlington, Va.: American Blood Commission.

[33]Staackman, M., W. H. Van Horn, and C. R. Foget. 1970. Damage to the Drug Industry from Nuclear Attack and Resulting Requirements for Repair and Reclamation. Washington, D.C.: Office of Civil Defense.

[34]Papper, S. 1979. Lactated Ringer's solution—A perspective. Okla. State Med. Assoc. J. 72:327.

[35]Anderson, C. G. 1970. Assessment of Postattack Health Resources. Prepared for the Office of Civil Defense, Office of the Secretary of the Army. OCD Work Unit No 2421 E. Bethesda, Md.: System Sciences, Inc.

[36]Pyecha, J. N., et al. 1970. Alternative Designs for Systems for Providing Postattack Medical Care, Vol.1. Research Triangle Park, N.C.: Research Triangle Institute for the Office of Civil Defense.

[37]Camp, F. R., N. F. Conte, and J. R. Brewer. 1973. Military Blood Banking 1941–1973. Fort Knox, Ky.: The Blood Bank Center, U.S. Army Medical Research Laboratory.

[38]Mendelson, J. 1974. The selection of plasma volume expanders for mass casualty planning. J. Trauma 14:987.

[39]Sandler, S. G., D. Hermoni, R. Sharon, and E. Superstine. 1977. Blood transfusion therapy in the rear hospital during the Yom Kippur War (October 1973). Military Med. 142:51–52.

[40]Macmillan, B. G. 1982. Initial Replacement Therapy. In R. P. Hummel, ed., Clinical Burn Therapy. Boston, Mass.: John Wright-PSG, Inc.

[41]Barlotta, F. M. 1980. The New Jersey Radiation Accidents of 1974 and 1977. In K. F. Hubner and S. A. Fry, eds., The Medical Basis for Radiation Accident Preparedness. New York: Elsevier-North Holland.

[42]Mark, J. C. 1981. Nuclear weapons: Character and capabilities. Pp. 93–109 in The Final Epidemic. Chicago: Educational Foundation for Nuclear Science.

[43]Hospital Statistics. 1983. P 87. Chicago: American Hospital Association.

[44]Physician Characteristics and Distribution in the United States. 1982. P. 133. Chicago: American Medical Association.

[45]Stein, D. L. 1983. Electromagnetic pulse—the uncertain certainty. Bull. Atomic Sci. 39:52–56.

[46]Pan American Health Organization. 1984. Policies for the Production and Marketing of Essential Drugs, Technical Discussions of the XXIX Meeting of the Directing Council of PAHO, No. 462. Washington, D.C.: Pan American Health Organization.

[47]Gereffi, G. 1983. The Pharmaceutical Industry and Dependency in the Third World. Princeton, N.J.: Princeton University Press.

[48]Schaumann, L. 1976. Pharmaceutical Industry Dynamics and Outlook to 1985. Menlo Park, Calif.: Stanford Research Institute.

[49]U.S. Department of Commerce, Industry and Trade Administration. 1983. Country Market Survey: Medical Equipment—Algeria. Washington, D.C.

[50]U.S. Department of Commerce, Industry and Trade Administration. 1984. Country Market Survey: Medical Equipment—Argentina. Washington, D.C.

[51]U.S. Department of Commerce, Industry and Trade Administration. 1984. Country Market Survey: Medical Equipment—Brazil. Washington, D.C.

[52]U.S. Department of Commerce, Industry and Trade Administration. 1981. Country Market Survey: Medical Equipment—Chile. Washington, D.C.

[53]U.S. Department of Commerce, Industry and Trade Administration. 1980. Country Market Survey: Medical Equipment—Colombia. Washington, D.C.

[54]U.S. Department of Commerce, Industry and Trade Administration. 1979. Country Market Survey: Medical Equipment—Ecuador. Washington, D.C.

[55]U.S. Department of Commerce, Industry and Trade Administration. 1981. Country Market Survey: Medical Equipment—Guatemala. Washington, D.C.

[56]U.S. Department of Commerce, Industry and Trade Administration. 1981. Country Market Survey: Medical Equipment—Honduras. Washington, D.C.

[57]U.S. Department of Commerce, Industry and Trade Administration. 1979. Country Market Survey: Medical Equipment—Korea. Washington, D.C.

[58]U.S. Department of Commerce, Industry and Trade Administration. 1979. Country Market Survey: Medical Equipment—Mexico. Washington, D.C.

[59]U.S. Department of Commerce, Industry and Trade Administration. 1977. Country Market Survey: Medical Equipment—Philippines. Washington, D.C.

[60]U.S. Department of Commerce, Industry and Trade Administration. 1977. Country Market Survey: Medical Equipment—Singapore. Washington, D.C.

[61]U.S. Department of Commerce, Industry and Trade Administration. 1979. Country Market Survey: Medical Equipment—Thailand. Washington, D.C.

[62]U.S. Department of Commerce, Industry and Trade Administration. 1978. Country Market Survey: Medical Equipment—Venezuela. Washington, D.C.

[63]Winter, S. G. 1963. Economic Viability After Thermonuclear War, Memorandum RM-3436-PR, Prepared for the U.S. Air Force Project Rand. Santa Monica, Calif.: Rand Corporation.

[64]Statistical Yearbook, 1979–80. 1981. Pp. 693–697. New York: United Nations.

[65]Shoup, P. S. 1981. The East European and Soviet Data Handbook. New York: Columbia University Press.

[66]Statistical Yearbook, 1979–1980. 1981. P. 2. New York: United Nations.

[67]Statistical Yearbook, 1979–1980. 1981. Pp. 106–107, 134–136, 151, and 161–162. New York: United Nations.

[68]USSR Facts and Figures Annual, Vol. 6. 1982. J. L. Schereer, ed. Gulf Breeze, Fla.: American International Press.

[69]Yearbook of International Trade Statistics, Vol. 2. 1980. Pp. 466, 467. New York: United Nations Department of International Economic and Social Affairs, Statistical Office.

The Medical Implications of Nuclear War, Institute of
Medicine. © 1986 by the National Academy of Sciences.
National Academy Press, Washington, D.C.

The Consequences of Nuclear War:
An Economic and Social Perspective

HAL COCHRANE, PH.D., and DENNIS MILETI, PH.D.
Colorado State University, Fort Collins, Colorado

INTRODUCTION

The original purpose of this paper was to assess the systemic effects of
a limited nuclear war and offer some thoughts regarding the potential
health care complications that might result. As work progressed, it became
increasingly apparent that research into the direct and immediate impact
of war has been, and continues to be, the subject of considerable effort.
However, a review of the literature on the consequences of nuclear war
revealed few references to social science research. The citations that were
uncovered appeared to be confined almost entirely to the application of
economic theory to problems of reconstruction. Much of the work was
performed in the mid-1960s to mid-1970s and is therefore dated. To our
knowledge, little has been done on such subjects as social response to a
warning of nuclear attack; willingness of health care organizations to
administer aid under postattack conditions; ability of a moneyless economy
to rebuild without the aid of other nations and without a heavy reliance
on fuel oils. There is, on the other hand, no shortage of assumptions
regarding the nation's institutions, individual behavior, and the likelihood
of social change, none of which have been seriously questioned. As a
result, published projections that implicitly adopt current economic and
social arrangements should be questioned as well.

In such a short paper, we cannot pretend to cover the subject of socioeconomic consequences in any depth. However, we do not apologize for
raising a wide variety of issues that may frustrate even the most patient

reader. We view this as an opportunity to question, speculate, and entertain possibilities that may not have been previously considered.

WARNINGS OF WAR

Mutual assured destruction (MAD) is founded on the condition that each side's offensive weaponry surpasses the defensive capability of the other. Deterrence is thought by some to be stable so long as populations and industry remain vulnerable to the destructive capacity of the other side. If one subscribes to MAD, then it must follow that any movement to reduce vulnerability or enhance offensive capacity heightens the risk of war. Accordingly civil defense could play a dual role. Under ideal circumstances it might reduce casualties, but if thought to be too effective it could also destabilize the arms race, and under certain conditions heighten the potential for misinterpreting intentions.

It is well known that the Soviet Union has invested considerable effort to develop an effective civil defense system. The Central Intelligence Agency (CIA) notes that there is sufficient blast-resistant shelter space for the Soviet leadership at all levels (Weinstein, 1981). The Federal Emergency Management Agency (FEMA) assumes that the Soviet Union would not launch a preemptive strike without first protecting its own citizens (or at least reducing the number of anticipated casualties to tolerable levels), by evacuating the larger cities and population centers proximate to major industrial plants. It is estimated that it would take from 3 to 5 days to complete the process. Such large-scale population movements would be readily detected by U.S. intelligence sources interpreted as a warning of an impending nuclear strike. One response to this message, albeit an unlikely one, would be for the U.S. to launch a first strike directed at the highly vulnerable evacuees. A second, which was favored for some time by FEMA, would take advantage of the lead time afforded by the observed movements to relocate 145 million of our own citizens.

This so-called crisis relocation strategy has been roundly criticized for its lack of realism and the fact that only meager resources were devoted to its preplanning. Despite the apparent lack of support at the federal level for crisis relocation, unplanned evacuations may still be an important factor in determining the number and types of casualties that might be sustained as a direct result of war or indirectly as a product of the evacuation itself. It is interesting to note that the debate over crisis relocation presumes that evacuations are orchestrated primarily by FEMA. However, a spontaneous flight from areas thought to be targeted cannot be precluded, in the event of a sudden escalation in tension between the world's superpowers. It is highly unlikely, for example, that Soviet population movements, of the scale indicated above, would escape the attention of the news media. The question which then must be answered is how will U.S. citizens react? This is an area where lessons learned as a result of studying societal response to natural hazards and warnings, particularly earthquake prediction, may provide insights.

How people in general and people with disaster response roles respond to information about impending catastrophe has been the target of research for three decades. The findings have been summarized (cf. Mileti, 1975; Williams, 1964) and suggest several principles that would affect the vulnerability of medical and health care systems to nuclear war.

People respond to situations of impending danger on the basis of their situationally defined perceptions of risk, and what they then believe to be appropriate response to those perceptions. Even without official government evacuation plans or sanctioned warnings of an impending nuclear exchange, news regarding related events could lead some people to perceive risk and evacuate to areas thought to be safe. Persons who are responsible for providing postimpact aid, such as health care professionals, might be motivated to evacuate personnel and supporting materiel in order to preserve their ability to provide assistance after the attack (cf. Mileti et al., 1981). Given Abrams' (1984) estimates of medical requirements, it is doubtful whether such behavior would alter the outcome.

THE DIRECT AND IMMEDIATE IMPACT OF WAR

The immediate effects of nuclear war, the completeness of the devastation it brings, and the detailed accounting of the expected human suffering have all been the subject of numerous studies. We begin with a war scenario which provides the basis for estimating the demands placed on the medical system, and sets the parameters for determining the direct and indirect economic impacts. The results are then reexamined in the context of what is known about organizational behavior and transformation.

Damage to Cities

Other papers in this volume have touched on many of the direct effects of a limited nuclear war. In order to avoid repetition we will briefly describe the scenario which is used as a point of departure for the issues raised in this paper. The following calculations are based on the Federal Emergency Management Agency's CRP-2B scenario which assumes that the United States is exposed to 6,559 megatons (Mt) of nuclear explosives targeted primarily at military installations and 250 centers of population exceeding 50,000.

In the absence of warning and any subsequent evacuation, about 125 million people would be caught within the 2-psi circles (geographic areas which sustain a blast overpressure of 2 pounds per square inch); nearly 58 million would be inside the 15-psi region (Haaland et al., 1976; p. 20). In preparing the scenario, defense planners anticipated the delivery of 843 1-Mt warheads. It is estimated that each ground burst would leave a crater 1,000 feet (about 305 m) in diameter and 200 feet (about 61 m) deep. All structures from the point of detonation to a distance of 0.6 miles (about 1 km) would be leveled. Within the band between 1.7 and 2.7 miles (about 2.7 and 4.3 km) (5 psi) only skeletal remains of commercial and residential multistory structures would be observed. The 2-psi circle, characterized by moderately damaged structures (cracked load-bearing walls, windowless, contents blown into the streets), would reach 4.7 miles (about 7.6 km) (Office of Technology Assessment, 1979; pp. 27-31).

Damage to Electronic Systems: Effects of Electromagnetic Pulse

In contrast to the effects of blast and fire, the electromagnetic pulses (EMP), generated as a result of airbursts, leave no visible signs. Nonetheless, in theory such pulses could be highly damaging to microcircuitry. Because of the partial test ban treaty (1963) and the highly sensitive nature of EMP to national security, there is little hard evidence to conclude just how much damage might be incurred. However, recent military interest in new communications technology, such as the $10 billion MILSTAR project, to protect against the effects of EMP suggests how serious the problem may prove to be. Although much of what is known about EMP either is classified as secret information or is highly speculative, the danger the phenomenon poses is very real. Telecommunications networks, information processing equipment, and highly sophisticated medical technology would be vulnerable and could be irreparably harmed by such a blast.[1] The problems this pulse poses for electronic equipment are twofold. Electrical power grids would pick up the EMP and transmit a transient spike in voltage to equipment drawing power at the time of the detonation. The rapid rise in voltage would damage microprocessors in a way similar to that resulting from lightning strikes. However, the rise in voltage would be typically 100 times faster, thereby rendering common surge protectors ineffective. Second, the electronic component itself could pick up the pulse and generate internally induced currents. The result could produce physical damage to the equipment.

High-altitude bursts (above 21 km) produce EMP, which could blanket hundreds of thousands of square kilometers (Office of Technology Assessment, 1979; p. 22). A high-yield weapon detonated 200 miles (about 322 km) above Kansas would generate a pulse which would affect the entire country plus parts of Canada and Mexico. Furthermore, the entire region would be blacked out simultaneously, since the radiation produced by the explosion travels at the speed of light (p. 519). The economic and social ramifications of disrupting a highly developed electronic network would be staggering. Not a single facet of the economy would escape the effects of an interruption to the normal flow of communications, data retrieval, and the accompanying capacity to process vast amounts of information. Concern about the potential effects of EMP is new, and as a result little is yet known about the social and economic consequences which might be triggered.

Most large corporations have taken at least minimal steps to prepare disaster plans permitting them to carry on data processing functions in the event of sabotage or fire. Such plans normally involve securing the rights to utilize an alternative facility (e.g., sharing systems) and duplicating records on magnetic tape. Of course, this strategy will succeed only if the backup system is spared, an assumption which may be appropriate in the event of fire but less so given a nuclear exchange. Few corporations and governmental agencies, however, have actually taken steps to protect sensitive data processing equipment. These exceptions appear to be concentrated primarily in the financial sector and are prompted by considerations of liability as much as concern about social and economic impacts.[2] Such protection is likely to fail, however, even in cases where an extreme amount of caution is exercised. For example, the Federal Reserve System, charged with the important task of tracking and controlling the nation's money supply, maintains a bombproof backup facility. However, this is the strongest link in the network. Few other banks or their corporate clients can boast of such a capability. Hence, despite the fact that the Federal Reserve's computers would most likely survive the war, little data would be available for them to process. The viability of the nation's electronic funds transfer and recordkeeping system turns on the degree of protection afforded by all its participants.

The sensitivity of the nation's credit system to computer failure was demonstrated recently when Paul Volcker, Federal Reserve Board Chairman, revealed that "something in the nature of a computer glitch" left the Bank of New York $30 billion overdrawn (November 20, 1985). To quell fears, the Fed was forced to make an unprecedented loan of $22.6 billion to the New York bank, the interest on which amounted to more than $5 million per day. The loan, according to Volcker, was made amid "increasing evidence of potential problems at other institutions around the country," all part of the computer network involved in the purchase and sales of government securities. This is, of course, a rather mild event in contrast to the prospects of disruption due to a nuclear exchange. It does, however, underscore the sensitivity of these financial systems, inviting speculation as to how economic recovery might proceed in the event of a total collapse.

Direct Consequences for Medical Care

Abrams (1984), in pulling together a plausible set of projections regarding the direct effects of such an attack, provides a sobering view of the situation. Abrams' calculations are based on the assumption that the attack is sudden, leaving the victims no time to take protective actions. Furthermore, the need for health care assistance is based on preattack medical procedures. Beginning with the fact that 73 percent of the nation's populace resides in areas assumed to be attacked, along with 80 percent of the country's medical supplies, it quickly becomes evident that the need for care would far outpace the medical resources which survive the attack. However, it is the extent of the imbalance which is so startling. He concludes that of the 93 million survivors, 32 million would require medical care.[3]

It is difficult to imagine how the estimated 48,000 physicians surviving the attack could cope with a workload which would tax 1.3 million (Abrams, 1984; p. 657). How long medical care organizations could continue to function effectively under such conditions is open to question. There is, however, a body of research regarding the sociology of organizations which suggests that cohesiveness and the will to carry on in such an overwhelmingly stressful environment would be a limiting factor in delivering care. This perspective is developed more fully below.

THE LINGERING EFFECTS OF NUCLEAR WAR

The longer-term effects of war would pose an altogether different set of challenges for the medical care system. Maintenance of a reasonable standard of health may be impossible without the rapid recovery of the economy's critical industries: petroleum, petrochemicals, electronics, agriculture, and pharmaceuticals. Without these it is difficult to imagine how the potential for the transmission of disease could be controlled.

Leaning (1983; p. 424) has forcefully argued that some of the greatest risks to health lie in the postattack period. The prolonged period of crowding in makeshift fallout shelters, which are likely to be poorly ventilated and ill equipped to treat or dispose of wastes, would create the conditions for the rapid spread of disease. Providing that the survivors endure this period, they would face similar difficulties outside. The lack of sanitary systems, the absence of power for refrigeration, the presence of millions of unburied dead, and a disturbed ecological balance fostering the rapid growth in insect populations would combine to produce an environment fertile for the contraction and transmission of disease. The complex interactive effects of stress, malnutrition, and an immune system damaged by radiation would tend to weaken the physiological defenses to a point where people may succumb to diseases presently considered to be only moderately virulent.[4]

It might not be unreasonable to anticipate postwar pandemics similar to those just described. Survivors weakened by malnutrition could not expect to be vaccinated nor would antibiotics be available in sufficient quantities to prevent complications.

The focus of health care therefore shifts from the immediate problems of administering postattack aid to the longer-term issues surrounding reconstruction. The number of casualties produced by hunger and exposure would not be significantly altered by the availability of trained medical personnel and pharmaceuticals. Access to food and energy would prove to be the key to survival. The prospects for avoiding catastrophe are tied inextricably to the prospects for reconstruction.

Prospects for a General Economic Recovery

The economic infrastructure which is left intact after the attack would play a key role in determining the length of time during which such life-threatening conditions might persist. The survivors would face the critical task of rebuilding a viable economy capable of rapidly reallocating undamaged capital and distributing uncontaminated foodstuffs. The few studies which have dealt with the issue of economic recovery are sobering. Potential Vulnerability Affecting National Survival (PVANS), a study prepared in 1970 for the Office of Civil Defense by the Stanford Research Institute (SRI) (Goen et al., 1970), estimated the fewest number of nuclear detonations required to ''prevent economic recovery.'' The attack which SRI found to be most effective in achieving this end combined the destruction of the industrial capacity located in 71 of the nation's largest standard metropolitan statistical areas,[5] and SRI concluded that a crippling blow could be delivered by a combination of 500 1-Mt and 200 to 300 additional 100-kiloton (kt) weapons. This number is only 10 percent of that posed by the formulators of the FEMA CRP-2B scenario. The direct effects of the PVANS attack, in terms of health care delivery, would not differ significantly from the projections sketched above. However, the economic dislocations resulting from the attack may create a whole new set of health issues.

The SRI results have been subjected to refinements by Katz (1982; p. 115) and others (Sassen and Willis, 1974). These studies suggest that an even lower exchange threshold (100 to 300 Mt) would result in unacceptable economic disruptions and bottlenecks.

Reasons for Doubting Economic Projections

The picture, grim as it is, may understate the impacts. The tools available to researchers are based on historic patterns of production and institutional arrangements. However, these are likely to change during the period of reconstruction. It is highly unlikely that the social order, for example, would remain static. There are a number of other reasons for doubting the economic projections. The methodology should be questioned. There may be insufficient reserves of domestic oil and gas to meet the needs of both reconstruction and production of essential consumer items. Trading patterns may not return to their prewar state. The destruction of data processing and retrieval facilities would make it difficult to conduct monetary reform or reestablish property rights, both of which have, in past wars, been instrumental preconditions for a rapid recovery.

Naturally, there are a large number of other issues which could have been addressed. The few we have chosen to include offer a perspective which is somewhat different from that of previously published works. They also reflect some highly speculative thoughts regarding the extent to which recent trends in the economy might affect the speed and nature of recovery.

Methodological Concerns

Input-output models, which are the foundation for many of the economic recovery studies, utilize a static matrix of technical coefficients.[6] The fact that these coefficients are computed based on statistics collected while the economy is in a balanced state leads one to wonder about the reliability of the approach when applied to the analysis of catastrophic shocks.

As an alternative to this static model, Cochrane (1984) simulated a market economy which permitted industries to substitute labor for capital and consumers to substitute more abundant commodities for those in limited supply. It was found that the destruction of a portion of an economy's capital stock results in a new matrix of trade flows and hence in a new set of input-output coefficients which adjust throughout the reconstruction period. In addition the model produced

1. new price ratios;
2. new mix of consumer and producer goods;
3. new import-export balance;
4. a pattern of recovery which depends on the elasticity of substitution (labor for capital), the competitiveness of producers in other regions, and the amount of external aid flowing to the victims;
5. new government budget deficit.

Most noteworthy for the issue of postwar reconstruction, the model shows that under certain conditions[7] the economy would never reattain its prewar prominence. It appears that the conditions which led the Japanese and German economies to rapidly rebound from World War II bombing raids are not likely to be repeated.

Systems models (Pugh-Roberts Associates, Inc., 1981) have been conceived as a means of assessing the combined effects of environmental and climatic change on the survivor's health and material well-being. However, here too, the functions (in this case differential equations) are drawn from past experiences which reflect a unique pattern of prices, capital and labor productivity, health, and legal and political institutions. Once again, the accuracy of these dynamic models in portraying the consequences of an event, which is likely to alter the very foundation of man's relationship to nature as well as to his fellow man, should be seriously questioned.

Perhaps the most serious shortcoming we have found in the works cited above is the lack of social science input. Except for Katz (1982), economic projections are made without even a passing reference to behavioral and institutional considerations. One thing is clear. A nuclear exchange of the magnitude reported in these studies would cause a rapid collapse of the nation's social and economic infrastructure. The speed with which a new system could be erected is an open question, and one which may never be answered. However, there are a number of issues worth noting that have been skirted thus far and to which we now turn our attention.

The Social Aspects of Recovery

The results of sociological research suggest that a CRP-2B level of nuclear weapon exchange would alter the social order and, consequently, human behavior in ways which may not have been captured by the analyses just cited. What might the postwar social order look like and what would contribute to its formation?

Conceptual Framework   The social "glue" that holds complex industrialized societies together is efficient but impersonal. In the course of a typical day, an individual is expected to play a variety of highly segmented roles. Adherence to these roles creates an image which often masks the underlying personality. It is only rarely that the true persona, the whole person, is revealed to others. When this happens it is normally to a close intimate. Most human interaction in complex industrialized nations is impersonal and limited role playing. This impersonal social glue serves an important function in that differentiation and objectification are essential to efficiently carrying out the task of provisioning society and caring for unmet needs. For example, once the role of customer is learned, a person can buy almost anything in almost any store in the nation without going through the more personal but time-consuming task of getting to know the salesclerk. Role playing is of lesser importance to small rural communities, agrarian societies, and tradition-bound cultures which are bonded instead by personal relationships. In such a setting, individuals are more apt to get to know each other and interact personally (cf. Tonnies, 1957; pp. 31–102).

The impersonal social glue dissolves quickly under the stress of national or community emergency. Disasters that result in significant loss of life and property will serve to transform the order which bonds social life (cf. Mileti et al., 1975; Dynes, 1970; Barton, 1969), eliciting an intense identification with the community (Barton, 1969), guilt over being a survivor (Lifton, 1967), an energetic response to provide help to those who need it (Dynes, 1970), and the development of an emergency consensus (Barton, 1969) which focuses human attention on the few acts directed toward the sole values of preserving life and helping others. A disaster-induced shift in social order and behavior triggers a temporary suspension of providing aid and comfort to the disaster victims. This pattern has been observed time and again (cf. Mileti et al., 1975; Dynes, 1970). However, these findings are drawn from experiences where communities were capable of rebuilding both their physical capital and social relationships in a form which reflect their predisaster states. In almost every instance, ample resources, information, and relief personnel were funneled from unaffected regions to the disaster-stricken community (cf. Fritz, 1961), making it possible for it to return to the predisaster form of social organization. Localized, community-wide disasters, therefore, would undoubtedly see the social order change, albeit temporarily, to enhance the ability and stamina of medical and health care system personnel to perform their work.

The first order of routine social life is thus impersonal but efficient. The second order of social life is personal and typifies life and behavior in both communities impacted by localized disasters and life in agrarian and traditional societies; it, too, is efficient for it focuses attention on disaster relief goals, temporarily abandoning less-important priorities. The second order soon reverts back to the first as immediate emergency needs are met.

Application to CRP-2B The finding that disasters experienced see the first order of social life replaced temporarily with a second order that reverts back to the first order when emergency needs are met and after outside assistance converges on the stricken area is not likely to hold given the magnitude of disruption and depravation accompanying a nuclear exchange. In this case the second order would give rise to a new third order rather than revert back to the first order; in other words, nuclear exchange would produce changes leading to a permanent social reorganization rather than a temporary change as characterizes most other disasters.

Sociological research has documented the emergence of second orders replacing first orders in hundreds of studied disasters (cf. Mileti et al., 1975; Dynes, 1970; Barton, 1969). These second orders contain the seeds of new third social orders including new group leadership (e.g., Dynes, 1970), new bases for the distribution and use of power (e.g., Quarantelli, 1970), less complex systems of social stratification and status (e.g., Barton, 1969), and the abandonment of traditional societal priorities (cf. Mileti et al., 1975). These changes have been detected in cataclysms of all types ranging from snow storms (Frtiz et al., 1958) and mine disasters (Lucas, 1969) to natural and technological emergencies in general (cf., Mileti et al., 1975; Quarantelli, 1970; Form and Loomis, 1956). These seeds and the second order are only abandoned when the inevitable demise of the second order is triggered by the convergence of outside help and when the goals of meeting emergency impact needs and the restoration of that which was destroyed are met.

It is unlikely that the two factors that trigger the demise of second orders would occur after nuclear exchange; the seeds of a new social order contained in second orders would not be blocked from emerging into a new and permanent third order. The first of these factors is the convergence of nonvictims on the affected area. It is unlikely that outside assistance would reach the surviving victims of destroyed cities in the CRP-2B scenario for months, if at all. The second of these factors is meeting impact needs and the restoration of that which was destroyed. It is also not likely that survivors could, on their own, restore the destroyed physical environment and meet impact needs. The CRP-2B scenario surpasses the threshold needed for a permanent social reorganization into a new third order: surviving human collectives would be isolated from the others, no outside aid could be expected, and survivors could not meet all the needs required to restore their community to its preattack states.

It is not likely that the temporary disaster-response norms that characterize a typical second order would prevail for long. They would produce a permanent social reorganization—a third order—with new leadership, values, systems of stratification and status, power relationships, and societal priorities to guide behavior. The actual shape that the third order takes would be determined by personalities and a mix of individual characteristics (e.g., knowledge of survival skills, emergent leadership qualities, and so on), as well as the ownership of scarce resources that survive the disaster. These are difficult to predict; consequently it is difficult to predict the character of the third order that would emerge. It is not unlikely, however, that new, localized, small, nonnational and self-contained emerging societies would replace the national state and that these would vie for uncontaminated food, fuel, and other resources deemed to have survival value. It is not likely, therefore, that medical resources would be shared between these community-like "societies." Medical and health care systems would be constrained to function within emerging neighborhood societies until international aid is received and equitably distributed.

Critical Industries: Prospects for Recovery

Detailed studies of how quickly critical industries might rebound are clearly lacking. What does exist is either outdated or based on questionable assumptions. No one is likely to question the inclusion of pharmaceuticals, agriculture, and energy in a list of industries crucial to the direct delivery of care or to the maintenance of health over the longer term. However, technological advancements, occurring over the past two decades, have increased the economy's sensitivity to the effects of war. Banking, data processing, telecommunications, and international trade have taken on increased importance. The brief discussion which follows is designed to highlight the potential effects these industries may have on the pace of reconstruction.

Pharmaceutical Industry   The highly concentrated production of pharmaceuticals in the Philadelphia area contributes in no small way to the problem of vulnerability. Programs of cost containment have forced hospitals to cut inventories to the point where, if not resupplied within 3 days, they would be forced to implement rationing. It appears that no significant stocks of critical drugs exist anywhere within the public or private sector. The nation's current state of drug dependence speaks to the importance of this single industry. It is surprising, therefore, that it is the least-studied component of the medical care system. Reports identifying the vulnerability of its production processes, the location of manufacturing plants, and the nature of its distribution networks are out-of-date or classified (Anderson, 1982), or the data have yet to be collected.

The sensitivity of this industry to disruption is changing as a result of the combined effects of technology and international competition. The pharmaceutical industry in the United States, although still a significant contributor to worldwide production, has lost ground in recent years to its foreign competitors. Nearly 150 firms currently conduct research and produce patented drugs in the United States. Only 20 percent of these, however, represent significant U.S.-based multinational operations. An equal number are foreign-owned firms which have chosen to locate facilities in the United States. The following quote from a National Academy of Sciences study (1983, p. 34) of the pharmaceutical industry aptly describes the complicated ties that have evolved within this highly internationalized industry.

The extensive and increasing multi national diffusion of individual pharmaceutical firms has rendered "U.S. pharmaceutical industry" a term of unclear meaning. The larger pharmaceutical houses found in America have long since developed extensive facilities in dozens of foreign markets. Conversely, foreign based firms have established operations in the United States; in fact, the largest U.S. firm in the mid-1970's in terms of pharmaceutical sales to American consumers was Roche Laboratories, a subsidiary of the Swiss based firm Hoffman LaRoche. The widespread practices of licensing innovations, marketing agreements, and joint ventures among firms of many nationalities further complicates the assignment of specific products to individual nations.

It is clear from the statistics that U.S. dominance in pharmaceutical production and research and development (R&D) has declined over the past two decades. The U.S. share of world R&D expenditures has fallen from greater than 60 percent during the 1950s to less than 30 percent in 1982. The percentage of world pharmaceutical production occurring in the United States has declined from 50 percent in 1962 to 38 percent in 1978.[8]

It is still too early to tell exactly what these statistics portend for the U.S. producers. However, if the number of new drugs[9] entering U.S. clinical trials continues to decline, one might expect the profit position of U.S. producers to follow suit and the U.S. position in the world marketplace to further erode. One must conclude, therefore, that world dependence on an undisrupted flow of pharmaceuticals from U.S. firms has been exaggerated.

In recent years, generic drug producers have posed a growing threat to the industry's profit position since technological advances have made it possible to imitate patented drugs by slightly altering a compound's molecular structure. These so-called multisource drugs accounted for 45 percent of licit drug sales within the United States in 1979, 7 percent of which (or 3 percent of all sales) were achieved by smaller firms. Most of the 600 generic producers distribute their product almost exclusively to the domestic market, oftentimes restricting their efforts to a particular region. The scale of operation is typically $10 million or less in annual sales (Egan et al., 1982; p. 37).

How quickly might the pharmaceutical industry be rebuilt and sufficient production of pharmaceuticals and biologicals be resumed? There is, of course, no definitive answer to such a question; however, some indicators are worth noting. Most industry analysts would agree that a nuclear attack on the Northeast would devastate pharmaceutical research and development. The high concentration of skilled lab technicians and scientists in the region would be difficult to replace, given that many of the nation's prestigious institutions of higher learning would perish in the same attack. Such losses would have an incalculable impact on the nation's ability to advance pharmacological research, one which may take decades to recover. The impact such a loss would have on a global scale may, however, be less significant since the Swiss and Japanese have made great strides to advance their own capacity to carry on independent research.

It is clear from Abrams' (1984) work that drug shortages would materialize quickly after the attack and might continue for years as a result of the potential immunological impacts reported by Greer and Rifkin (this volume). However, there are several factors which could work to boost supply in the months after the exchange. Offshore production could be expanded, providing, of course, that the effects of the war are limited to the United States and the Soviet Union. How climatic change may alter production and distribution from these facilities is not at all clear. Second, the technical challenge of producing critical drugs varies widely. The fact that the manufacturers of generic drugs tend to be small suggests that sophisticated training and equipment may not be necessary in all instances. How quickly an onshore drug industry might be reconstructed is open to debate, since to our knowledge the resilience of this important health care sector has never been subjected to careful scrutiny. However, it is quite possible that production of certain antibiotics, volume expanders, and technically less challenging pharmaceuticals might rebound rapidly.

This possibility was confirmed by a reconnaissance study of a representative pharmaceutical firm conducted in preparation for the symposium on which this paper is based. When faced with the questions regarding communications, supplies, or personnel, the managers revealed that automation would play a key role, permitting the firm to continue production. It was agreed that the most threatening aspect of the problem would be the availability of supplies in the desired quantity and quality required by U.S. Food and Drug Administration (FDA) standards. The high cost of carrying raw material inventories (in terms of both product and warehouse space) has induced manufacturers to rely heavily on their suppliers. This has placed firms in a vulnerable position with regard to disruptions of the distribution network. The required ingredients are furnished by suppliers that have either been approved directly by the FDA or indirectly as a result of having a U.S. Pharmaceutical Standards designation.

It should be pointed out that in the absence of the FDA, the purity of supplies might deteriorate rapidly. Furthermore, it is unclear how these small producers would seek out new sources of raw ingredients or adjust production to account for the expected variability in raw ingredients. These two factors, more than almost any other, could act to restrict the speed with which pharmaceutical production might rebound.

The production process, in contrast to quality assurance, is dependent upon durable electromechanical equipment. Providing that power is available, production could be carried on with as few as 20 percent of the workforce reporting. Surprisingly, it was suggested that producing units could continue for at least short periods of time without the involvement of upper-level management. Microprocessors and communications equipment are currently more heavily utilized in the testing laboratory and the marketing and sales departments than in production. It is, therefore, unlikely that EMP-induced damage to electronic testing equipment would force production to be terminated, since mixtures and processes are well established. Operations could continue so long as electrical power and raw ingredients of sufficient quality and quantity are available.

Energy Industry   A secure supply of energy is, without question, one of the two most important ingredients determining the speed with which a viable economy could be reconstituted. Katz (1982) and Sassen and Willis (1974), among others, have pointed out the extent to which the nation's capacity to provide food and shelter is tied to the various facets of energy production, processing, and distribution. It is well known that the nation's largest petroleum refineries are concentrated along the Gulf coast, inviting speculation as to how few warheads would be required in order to deliver the economy a crippling blow. Katz (1982; p. 115) concludes that as few as 100 to 300 Mt could produce unacceptable economic disruption and bottlenecks. In our opinion, it is doubtful whether such a limited exchange would create hardships which would last more than several years. Furthermore, we believe that it is unlikely that significant longer-term health effects would result. The nation's agricultural heartland would be spared, as would be a sizable proportion of the nation's housing stock and productive capital. In contrast, the CRP-2B scenario poses a level of destruction from which the economy might never recover and which could produce a state of chronic malnutrition and health problems similar to those observed in the Third World. It is questionable whether the nation's stock of liquid fossil fuels would be sufficient to replace the vast investment in housing, plant, equipment, and the supporting public infrastructure lost due to such a large-scale nuclear exchange. The importance of energy to the economy has already been noted; however, one must also ask whether rebuilding would so deplete the nation's proven oil, gas, and coal reserves that economic recovery would be a painful process drawn out over several decades. It is noteworthy, however, that both Japan and Germany were able to reestablish viable economies within 5 years after the armistice ending World War II. How were they, especially Japan, able to overcome a heavy dependence on external suppliers of energy and raw materials? If, in the process of rebuilding, the United States is forced to exhaust its liquid fossil fuel reserves, might it still count on repeating the Japanese experience?

Capital as Embodied Energy   The complexity of modern production techniques belies the simple fact that energy, predominantly in the form of fossil fuels, is an essential ingredient. It is easy to conceive of manufacturing processes which are fully automated and therefore require little or no labor. Such methods may even appear to economize on the use of energy. However, robotic machines are little more than common tools controlled by microprocessors. They are fashioned primarily from materials such as steel forgings and wire harnesses which involve the use of furnaces, drop hammers, and similar energy-intensive processes. It is, therefore, misleading to focus solely on the direct energy used in projecting fossil fuel requirements to rebuild a war-shattered economy. Barring the obvious exceptions of transportation and space heating, most energy is consumed by the intermediate goods and primary metals industries.

   Sorting out what might appear to be an infinite number of interactions continuously taking place in a sophisticated economy is less of a problem than one would first anticipate. Economists have learned that by normalizing the shipment of goods and resources from one industry to another, the direct and indirect effects of any change in product demand can be forecast. The resultant multipliers are readily modified to determine the amount of energy, measured in Watt years (a unit of energy equivalent to the energy expended in one year by one watt of power), for example, that would be required per dollars worth of shelter produced. Table 1 shows a range of energy intensiveness for a sample of industries. As of 1977, the average energy intensiveness of the U.S. economy was 2 Watt years; radio and telecommunications required only 0.46, while buildings, public utilities, and highways absorb 1.61, 1.99, and 3.32, respectively (Krenz, 1977; p. 122). The shift from a predominantly service-based economy characteristic of the prenuclear war U.S. pattern of production to one designed to emphasize construction would result in a potential doubling of direct and indirect energy demand per dollar worth of product.

TABLE 1   Energy Intensiveness by Selected Sectors of the National Economy

Sector of the Economy	Watt year/$ GNP^a (1967)
Products	
Food and kindred products	1.57
Apparel	1.17
Transportation and warehousing	2.64
Communications and radio	0.46
Wholesale and retail trade	0.95
Finance and insurance	0.61
Medical and educational	1.05
New construction	
Residential	0.93
Nonresidential buildings	1.61
Public utilities	1.99
Highways	3.32
Average of all sectors (approximate)	2.00

^{a}Gross national product.

Do We Have Enough Oil and Gas to Rebuild?   Since plant, equipment, shelter, and public facilities are to some extent the embodiment of fossil fuels, nuclear war would not only destroy cities and communities but the process of rebuilding would deplete the nation's stock of natural resources. Estimates of how much are open to heated debate. However, given certain simplifying assumptions regarding the magnitude of losses and the postwar availability of fuel from abroad, a reasonably accurate picture can be developed.

The U.S. stock of capital is currently worth nearly \$9 trillion (1985 dollars).[10] Assuming that 60 percent of this stock is destroyed in the wake of the CRP-2B 6,559-Mt exchange, and given the simplifying conditions shown in Table 2, a total of 3.7×10^{13} Watt years would have to be expended to restore the capital stock to its prewar state. At present, however, the nation's demand for fossil fuels far outpaces domestic supply. Hence, energy required for reconstruction can only be obtained by cutting into the prewar pattern of use or by boosting imports significantly. For reasons discussed under the topic of trade relationships and underscored in Table 2, the process of rebuilding may have to rely on domestic reserves alone.

TABLE 2   Assumptions Used to Compute Energy Requirements

Energy Requirements—2 Watt years of direct and indirect energy is needed to recreate the lost capital (measured in 1967 dollars).

Unchanging Composition of Fossil Fuel Supplies—The composition of fossil fuels consumed during the period of reconstruction, i.e., the percentage provided by oil, gas, and coal, would remain unchanged. As of 1985, oil, gas, and coal comprised a respective 45, 22, and 25 percent of the nation's annual energy needs. The combination of hydropower, nuclear thermal plants, and other minor sources made up the remaining 8 percent.

Proven Reserves—The ultimate postwar supply of recoverable oil, gas, and coal are assumed to be equivalent to the current proven reserves, which are 29.5 billion barrels, 5.9 trillion cubic meters, and 292 billion metric tons, respectively. It is assumed that nuclear detonations would not significantly diminish these reserves, but no additions could be anticipated.

Termination of Energy Imports—The decimated U.S. economy would not produce sufficient foreign exchange in order to import energy supplies.

Energy Refining Transportation and Distribution Unaffected—All facets of the energy industry would be spared. This is, of course, an overly optimistic assumption since most defense strategists believe that the nation's refineries would be a high priority target.

Capital Goods Industry Could Meet Demands—Sufficient capacity exists to produce replacement housing, plant, equipment, and necessary public facilities. This too may exaggerate the speed with which rebuilding might proceed. As in the case of the energy sector, it is unlikely that domestic manufacturers would be able to meet such demands. Primary industries, which have comprised a declining proportion of national production over the past two decades, would certainly be targeted.

Energy Production Is Limited to 10 Percent of Remaining Reserves—As a rule of thumb, the volume of oil extracted from a pool is maximized so long as the ratio of production to reserves is less than 10 percent. Since a more rapid rate of depletion results in larger volume of oil left unrecovered, petroleum engineers ensure that production is managed accordingly.

The Destroyed Capital Is Not Salvageable

The Production of Oil, Coal, and Gas Is Dictated by the Ability to Produce from Reserves—Economic factors are assumed to play a secondary role.

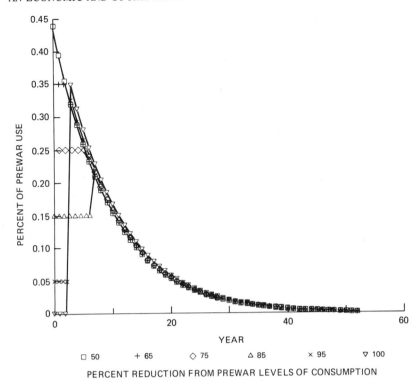

FIGURE 1   Oil for consumption.

Provided that these assumptions hold, one might expect a pattern of production and exhaustion such as that shown in Figures 1 through 4. The results indicate that the nation's stock of shelter and productive facilities can only be reestablished if other energy uses are drastically curtailed. For example, the reconstruction process would take 8 years to complete if the annual supply of petroleum allocated to activities other than rebuilding was cut to 15 percent of that observed prior to the war. In the event that these petroleum demands can only be reduced to 25 percent of the prewar level, total reconstruction would never occur; slightly more than 40 percent of the capital stock could be replaced.

These results are dependent on a rather restrictive set of assumptions which, if anything, exaggerate the speed with which rebuilding might occur. The only factors which hold the potential to brighten the picture is a dramatic jump in the level of energy imports or a rapid growth in U.S. coal production. Both would be subject to a variety of bottlenecks

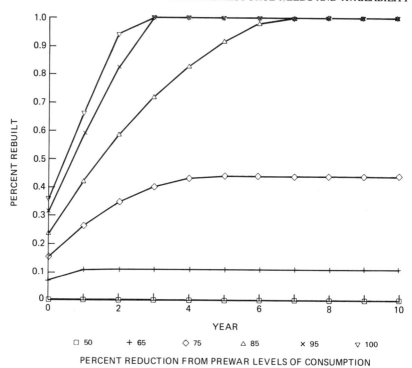

PERCENT REDUCTION FROM PREWAR LEVELS OF CONSUMPTION

FIGURE 2   Percent of capital stock rebuilt as a percentage of prewar oil consumption.

and economic considerations, reducing the likelihood that such simplifying assumptions would significantly alter the conclusions.

Agriculture   A point which seems self-evident but has not been the subject of systematic research is the effect of the postattack weather on the economy. Without question, the combination of colder temperatures, envisioned by Sagan (Ehrlich et al., 1985), and radiation would reduce agricultural yields. One might also expect that increased variance in rainfall accompanying the new environmental conditions would induce surviving farmers to abandon specialized crops. Diversification might be the only option available for coping with fluctuating temperature and moisture. It is clear that abandoning specialization would depress production. Lastly, the effects of nuclear winter on soil losses have yet to be addressed. It is not implausible to expect significant amounts of wind erosion for several years after the war. The magnitude of such losses and their subsequent impact on agriculture have not yet been established.

Money, Credit, and Banking   The wholesale destruction of physical capital envisioned by the formulators of the CRP-2B scenario would result in a sudden and dramatic flight from money to real assets. To the extent that a postwar voluntary exchange economy is permitted to function, a rapid acceleration in the price of essential goods could be anticipated. Based on the experience of German monetary reform after World War II, it may be possible to quickly reissue currency in amounts which are tied to the reduced scale of economic activity (Stanford Research Institute, 1969). However, the fact that modern banking is highly dependent on electronic funds transfer systems, which have been pointed out above to be highly vulnerable to EMP, may complicate matters. Money is no longer a tangible commodity but is a complex combination of bits stored in electronic memory banks. Who will step forward to conduct monetary reform, and how it would be accomplished in an equitable fashion, is without question one of the most important aspects of economic recovery. Without a means of exchange, the survivors would be forced to resort to barter or simply implement a command economy where production and

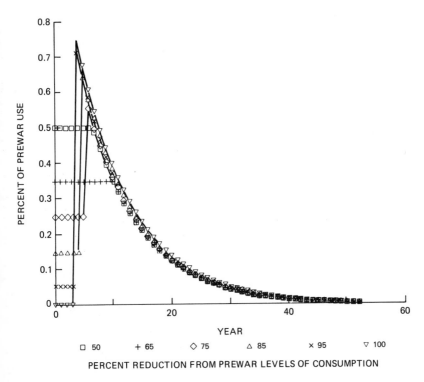

FIGURE 3   Gas for consumption.

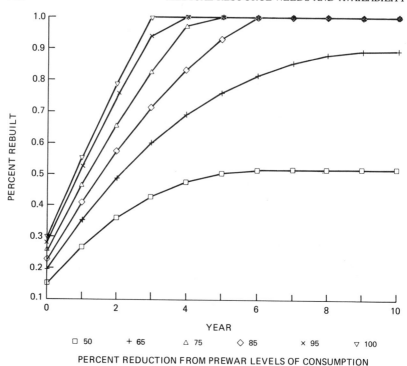

FIGURE 4   Percent of capital stock rebuilt as a percentage of prewar gas consumption.

resource allocation is dictated. In any case, it is clear that the projected period of economic recovery reported in the literature takes no account of this important consideration, and we believe, therefore, that the resultant estimates are overly optimistic. The postwar economy would be more inefficient and grow slower than might appear to be the case given current statistics.

Trade Relationships   International trade would suffer for similar reasons. It is unlikely that our current trading partners would be willing to sustain the balance of payments deficits which have been recorded in recent years. Such has been made possible by the fact that many other areas of the world are politically less stable than the United States. As a result the U.S. dollar has served as a hedge against a sudden reevaluation of other currencies (due to revolutions or monetary mismanagement). Nuclear war would not only wipe out foreign claims on U.S. assets but would eliminate the very reason for the dollar's prominence as an international medium of exchange. Postwar international trading would most likely be conducted on a quid pro quo basis. Both U.S. and foreign economic recovery would suffer as a result.

Treatment of Surviving Capital   One can only wonder how the ownership of property will be settled and what ingenious mechanisms survivors might invent to distribute that which is still economically viable. Records would be difficult to retrieve. In some cases capital would be rendered useless as a result of raw material shortages. At the other extreme, the owners of uncontaminated land located in more favorable climatic zones could reap substantial gains, providing of course that property rights are respected. An unprecedented reduction and transfer of wealth could take place within a relatively short time period. How would the legal and political systems respond?

Why Would the U.S. Experience Differ from that of Germany and Japan?

A recovery period lasting a decade or more contrasts sharply with the recorded postwar economic performance of both Germany and Japan. Each sustained heavy losses but were able to reestablish viable economies within 5 years after the cessation of hostilities. What forces led both of these nations to their current economic prominence? Could such factors be repeated to produce a rapid economic recovery in the United States?

The factors which coalesced to create a favorable climate for both the Japanese and German economies are unlikely to reoccur. Fossil fuels during the postwar period were both plentiful and inexpensive. Contrary to popular belief, Germany sustained relatively minor damage to its productive capital. "It must be emphasized that bomb damage to industry, as opposed to transport and housing, was relatively negligible. Germany's . . . post-war industrial potential was roughly equivalent to that which had existed in 1938." (Owen-Smith, 1983; p. 13). Reconstruction during the war with technically more advanced equipment meant that Germany emerged from fighting with a superior industrial base. Bomber raids simply obliterated housing and commercial establishments in the cities' centers, leaving the industrial plants situated in the outskirts virtually untouched. It has been estimated that industrial losses amounted to between 10 and 20 percent for metallurgical, chemical, engineering, and textile firms.

Japan's losses were more telling. Its index of industrial production dropped from a prewar high 149 (in 1940) to 31 in 1946 (Allen, 1963, pp. 200–209). The previous high was not reachieved until 1953, although it grew steadily throughout the intervening period.

Both Japan and Germany benefited greatly from external aid, primarily from the United States. Assistance to Germany alone amounted to $3.6 billion between 1946 and 1953, a sizable amount, especially when measured in current dollars. Approximately half the aid was in the form of Government and Relief in Occupied Areas (GARIOA), an emergency program to alleviate starvation (Owen-Smith, 1983; p. 29). The foodstuffs provided by both the GARIOA and the Marshall Plan, which succeeded it, permitted Germany to economize on scarce foreign exchange so it could afford to import ingredients essential to its manufacturing operations. Japan's economy benefited equally from the aid it received. The Korean War served to stimulate demand for Japanese products at a point when U.S. aid was dwindling. That, plus a postwar economic boom which fueled demand for vessels fabricated in Japanese shipyards, all provided a sound platform for recovery.

Even though a plentiful supply of cheap energy throughout the 1950s and 1960s provided both countries the opportunity to maintain a sound long-term growth path, energy shortages which materialized immediately after the war were a source of hardship and suffering. Germany was forced to relinquish territories amounting to 25 percent of the Third Reich's land area. The expulsion of German nationals from these areas caused a rapid rise in population which resulted in a homeless rate of nearly one family in three. The loss of 17 percent of Germany's coal-producing capacity to Poland and the imposition of mandatory coal exports as part of reparations contributed to an energy crisis. In the particularly bad 1946–1947 winter deaths per 1,000 of the population were 10 percent higher than in the following years (Owen-Smith, 1983; p. 29).

Despite the short-term hardships both countries benefited greatly from a fortuitous combination of factors which are unlikely to be repeated. No nation would have the resources or possibly the will to come to the aid of a United States devastated by a nuclear exchange. Foodstuffs would be hoarded rather than shared. No worldwide economic boom would ensue. Without an external source of demand for its products, the U.S. economy would languish.

CONCLUSIONS

The medical consequences of nuclear war have proven more elusive than first thought. The number of immediate casualties anticipated and the potential for the spread of disease over the long term hinge on more than the number of warheads targeted at American cities. How the populace responds to the warnings of war cannot be ignored. It is difficult to believe that an attack would occur without foreknowledge, either provided by FEMA or otherwise. Nonetheless, it is safe to say that the medical consequences of an attack depend on whether warnings/rumors of war produce an orderly exodus from cities to rural host communities (as FEMA may have planned it), trigger a spontaneous flight from areas thought to be vulnerable, or are ignored altogether. To our knowledge the required research to answer this question has yet to be initiated.

Abrams (1984) has shown that the administration of aid to the survivors of a CRP-2B attack (assuming minimal evacuation) would be an enormous task, far exceeding available manpower and stockpiles of pharmaceuticals. How health care organizations might respond to the challenge is open to debate, since even the lessons learned from Nagasaki and Hiroshima may not apply to attacks of the CRP-2B magnitude. The totality of the destruction would make it virtually impossible for local health care units to receive external assistance within a reasonable time span.

The longer-term prospects for maintaining the health of the survivors are just as grim. Malnutrition, an immune system weakened by the effects of radiation, and poor sanitary conditions would combine to boost the death toll. Contrary to first impressions, the availability of pharmaceuticals may not be as important a factor as initially expected. The fact that manufacturing facilities located abroad contribute an increasing proportion of world drug supplies should alleviate concern about persistent shortages. One might even expect a relatively rapid rebound of domestic production. U.S. pharmaceutical research, on the other hand, might never reattain its prewar status.

How long survivors must endure such deprivation depends on the speed with which a viable economy can be rebuilt. Without an adequate means of mobilizing manpower to distribute food and other necessities, the health of the survivors would remain in jeopardy. There is sufficient reason to believe that the period of reconstruction would far exceed the 3 to 5 years often reported by economic analysts. The vast quantities of fossil fuel required to reconstitute the nation's destroyed stock of shelter and industrial capital may be the single most important limiting factor. The United States should expect little in the way of international assistance, and trade would most certainly be conducted on a quid pro quo basis. Aid on the scale of that provided to Japan and Germany at the conclusion of World War II would amount to only a minuscule fraction of the estimated $3 trillion to $5 trillion in losses resulting from a CRP-2B exchange.

The pace of rebuilding would also be inhibited by the destruction of the nation's data banks and information processing centers. No one seems to know at this point how electronic networks and equipment may function as a result of EMP. Nor has anyone asked the more general questions regarding information processing failures—how records would be recreated, how money and credit would be tracked, how economic sectors would be coordinated, and how essential information regarding prices and production would be generated and transmitted to the surviving firms. Research into the role that telecommunications and information processing plays in the economy seems vital.

Finally, much of what has been written regarding nuclear war inadvertently assumes that institutions and behavioral norms would remain unaltered. It is not uncommon, for example, to read economists' assessments of reconstruction which assume that property rights would be respected or that government fiscal and monetary policy would be implemented to alleviate the effects of war on the economy. These, of course, are foolish bases upon which to build realistic projections. The tools currently available to economists and sociologists tend to paint a picture which is overly optimistic. Experience gained from the study of past disasters provides little insight as to how society may cope with the aftermath of nuclear war. Certainly snowstorms, floods, and even earthquakes pose sufficiently different problems than those upon which the papers in this volume have centered, and the social response to natural hazards may be an unsound basis for extrapolation.

It is clear that knowledge about the physical and biological aspects of nuclear war have advanced significantly in recent years. Even the climatological and environmental issues have attained greater focus, despite the controversy surrounding the prospects of nuclear winter. The same cannot be said about the state of socioeconomic knowledge. We know that nuclear war will change the foundation of man's relationship to man and to nature, but we are either unwilling or unable to imagine what forms these new social arrangements will take and how they relate to the well-being of the surviving population. A significant change in the extent and direction of socioeconomic research appears warranted.

ACKNOWLEDGMENTS

The authors acknowledge the assistance of Laurie Walters, Jung Soo Kim, and Marjorie Muench, who assisted in the preparation of this paper.

NOTES

[1]At high altitudes, gamma rays are produced in the first nanoseconds of a nuclear explosion, which can travel hundreds of kilometers before encountering electrons in atmospheric molecules. After being knocked out of their original molecular configuration, these electrons would be deflected toward Earth in a downward rotating motion along the Earth's magnetic field lines. These high-energy electrons would be picked up by any metal object. The resultant pulse would peak rapidly (within 10 nanoseconds) to a level of 50,000 to 100,000 V/m. The greater the surface area, the greater the amount of EMP absorbed.

[2]In passing the Electronic Funds Transfer Act (1978), Congress attempted to assign liabilities, rights, and responsibilities to both the consumer and the financial institutions. Interest in backup facilities was spurred by the requirement that transactions be processed within a reasonable length of time. The legal consequences of not fulfilling this obligation were felt to be more than sufficient reason to take protective measures.

[3]The scale would change with the attack scenario, however; even given a very limited war involving 10 major cities, the imbalances Abrams points out would still prevail, albeit to a lesser extent. The approach may in fact understate the effects, since no account is taken of the location of surviving resources relative to where they are needed. Nor is any consideration given to the mix of resources available. The ratios Abrams utilizes are based on normal conditions, wherein personnel, equipment, and pharmaceuticals are available in desired proportions. How effective will a medical staff be in the event that equipment is rendered inoperable?

[4]Contrary to what one might first think, cholera, typhoid, plague, and small pox contributed in only a minor way to the world's morbidity and mortality rate this century. Surprisingly, the influenza virus proved to be the most lethal. Over the 2-year period between 1918 and 1919 flu resulted in nearly 21.6 million deaths worldwide. In the United States alone nearly 20 percent of the population was infected, producing nearly 400,000 deaths in a single month (Ayres, 1965; p. 411). Most of the fatalities were the result of complications such as pneumonia.

[5]The attack was assumed to reduce industrial output to less than 3 percent of the preattack level. The industries considered critical are (1) petroleum refining; (2) iron and steel works; (3) primary smelting and refining of zinc, copper, lead, and aluminum; (4) engines; (5) electrical distribution products; (6) drugs; (7) office mechanisms; and (8) mechanical measuring devices.

[6]This methodology establishes a normalized pattern of trade which weaves the industrial sectors together. A technical coefficient is simply the percentage of one industry's output that another industry comprises.

[7]The most important is that the disaster-stricken region exhibits a cost of production equal to or in excess of its competitors.

[8]These trends can be explained in part by the following: (a) U.S. Food and Drug Administration regulations which impose significantly greater costs and delays on U.S. research efforts; (b) liability regimes for consumer product claims which are more cumbersome and risky in the United States than in competitor nations; (c) antitrust legislation which prevents the achievement of scale economies in terms of pharmaceutical research and development; (d) foreign nontariff trade barriers such as discriminatory safety regulations and pricing.

[9]An average of 60 new drugs were subjected to clinical trials in the mid 1960s. The number has declined to 25 per year in 1982. In contrast, the number of trials conducted by foreign-owned companies has remained constant (at 20 per year).

[10]Statistical Abstract of the United States, 1985. The total comprises the following: $1.4 trillion (nonresidential equipment); $1.6 trillion (nonresidential structures); $2.8 trillion (residential structures); $2.0 (government); and $1.2 trillion (household durables).

REFERENCES

Abrams, H. L. 1984. Medical resources after nuclear war: availability vs. need. J. Am. Med. Assoc. 252:653–658.

Abrams, H. L., and W. E. Von Kaenel. 1981. Medical problems of survivors of nuclear war: infection and the spread of communicable disease. N. Engl. J. Med. 305:1226–1332.

Allen, G. C. 1963. A Short Economic History of Modern Japan. New York: Praeger.

Allen, G. C. 1981. The Japanese Economy. New York: St. Martins Press.

Anderson, C. G. 1982. Emergency Medical Response Capability Analysis. Fairfax, Va.: Associated Research Analysis Corporation.

Ayres, R. U. 1965. Environmental Effects of Nuclear Weapons, Vol. I, HI-418-RR. The Hudson Institute, Harmon-On-Hudson, New York.

Barton, A. H. 1969. Communities in Disaster: A Sociological Analysis of Collective Stress Situations. New York: Doubleday.

Cochrane, H. 1984. Knowledge of loss and the efficiency of public/private protection. Paper presented at the Economics of Natural Hazards Conference, University of Florida, December 14–15.

Dynes, R. 1970. Organized behavior in disasters. Lexington, Mass.: D. C. Heath.

Egan, J. W., H. N. Higinbotham, and J. F. Watson. 1982. Economics of the Pharmaceutical Industry. P. 205. New York: Praeger Publishers.

Ehrlich, P., C. Sagan, D. Kennedy, and W. Roberts. 1985. The Cold and the Dark: The World After Nuclear War. New York: Norton.

Form, W. H., and C. P. Loomis. 1956. The persistence and emergence of social and cultural systems in disaster. Am. Soc. Rev. 21(April):180–185.

Fritz, C. E. 1961. Disaster. Pp. 651–694 in R. Merton and C. Nislet, eds., Contemporary Social Problems, New York: Harcourt.

Fritz, C. E., J. F. Rayner, and S. L. Guskin. 1958. Behavior in an Emergency Shelter: A Field Study of 800 Persons Stranded in a Highway Restaurant During a Heavy Snowstorm. Washington, D.C.: National Academy of Sciences.

Fuchs, V. R. 1974. Who Shall Live? New York: Basic Books.

Goen, R. L., R. B. Rothun, and F. E. Walker. 1970. Potential Vulnerability Affecting National Survival. Menlo Park, Calif.: Stanford Research Institute.

Greer, D. S., and L. S. Rifkin. 1986. The Immunological Impact of Nuclear Warfare. This volume.

Haaland, C. M., C. V. Chester, and E. P. Wigner. 1976. Survival of the Relocated Population of the U.S. After Nuclear Attack. Oak Ridge, Tenn.: Oak Ridge National Laboratory.

Katz, A. M. 1982. Life After Nuclear War. Cambridge, Mass.: Ballinger.

Keller, B. G., and M. C. Smith. 1969. Pharmaceutic Marketing. Baltimore: The Williams & Wilkins Co.

Krenz, J. H. 1977. Energy and the economy: an interrelated perspective. Energy 2:115–130.

Leaning, J. 1983. Civil Defense in the Nuclear Age: What Purpose Does It Serve and What Survival Does It Promise?

Leaning-Link, J., M. Klig, and M. E. Lord. 1983. Disaster Medicine. Vol. I (Fall):386.

Lifton, R. J. 1967. Death in Life—Survivors of Hiroshima. New York: Random House.

Lucas, R. A. 1969. Men in Crisis: A Study of a Mine Disaster. New York: Basic Books.

Mileti, D. S. 1975. Natural Hazard Warning Systems in the United States. Boulder: University of Colorado.

Mileti, D. S., J. E. Haas, and T. E. Drabek. 1975. Human Systems in Extreme Environments. Boulder: University of Colorado.

Mileti, D. S., J. R. Hutton, and J. A. Sorensen. 1981. Earthquake Prediction Response and Options for Public Policy. Boulder: University of Colorado.

National Academy of Sciences. 1983. The Competitive Status of the U.S. Pharmaceutical Industry. Prepared by the Pharmaceutical Panel, Committee on Technology and International Economics and Trade Issues. P. 102. Washington, D.C.: National Academy Press.

Office of Technology Assessment. 1979. The Effects of Nuclear War. Washington, D.C.: U.S. Government Printing Office.

Owen-Smith, E. 1983. The West German Economy. New York: St. Martins Press.

Pugh-Roberts Associates, Inc. 1981. Development of a Dynamic Model to Evaluate the Effect of Natural Resource Policies on Recovery Following Nuclear Attack—Final Report—Vol. I: Description and Simulations. Cambridge, Mass.: Pugh-Roberts Associates, Inc.

Quarantelli, E. L. 1970. Emergent accommodation groups: beyond current collective behavior typologies. Pp. 111–123 in T. Shilretani, ed., Human Nature and Collective Behavior. Englewood Cliffs, N.J.: Prentice Hall.

Sassen, J., and K. Willis. 1974. Data Base and Damage Criteria for Measurement of Arms Limitation Effects on War Supporting Industry. ACDA/WEC-242. Alexandria, Va.: Metis Corporation.

Southwest Research Institute. 1969. Final Report. Evaluation of Industrial Systems Interrelationships and Vulnerability to Nuclear Attack. San Antonio-Houston: Southwest Research Institute.

Stanford Research Institute. 1969. Postwar Monetary Reform in Severely Damaged Economies: Its Role in Recovery from Nuclear Attack. For Office of Civil Defense, Office of the Secretary of the Army. Contract DAHC 20-67-C-0136, Work Unit 3331D. Menlo Park, Calif.: Stanford Research Institute.

Tonnies, F. 1957. Gemeinschaft and Gesellschaft. New York: Harper and Row.

U.S. Department of Congress, Bureau of the Census. 1985. Statistical Abstract of the United States. 105th Edition. Washington, D.C.: U.S. Government Printing Office.

Weinstein, J. M. 1981. Soviet Civil Defense and the Credibility of the U.S. Deterrent: An End to This M.A.D.ness? U.S. Army War College, Carlisle Barracks, Pa.

Williams, H. B. 1964. Human factors in warning and response systems. Pp. 79–104 in G. Grosser, H. Wechsler, and M. Greenblatt, eds., The Threat of Impending Disaster. Cambridge, Mass.: MIT Press.

PART IV

Images and Risks of Nuclear War: Psychosocial Perspectives

The Medical Implications of Nuclear War, Institute of
Medicine. © 1986 by the National Academy of Sciences.
National Academy Press, Washington, D.C.

Children's and Adolescents' Perceptions of the Threat of Nuclear War: Implications of Recent Studies

WILLIAM R. BEARDSLEE, M.D.
Harvard Medical School, Boston, Massachusetts

OVERVIEW

Substantive findings on the attitudes of children and adolescents toward
the threat of nuclear war are reviewed. The evidence indicates that many
youngsters are bewildered and perplexed by the threat of nuclear war.
Some are frankly troubled or frightened. They often find out about it
alone, through the media, or from their peers, without help or guidance
from their usual circle of caring adults. Helplessness and a sense of powerlessness, as well as a profound sense of fear about the future, may
accompany the realization. The methodological issues in the findings to
date are discussed, and the implications of these findings are explored.

INTRODUCTION

Increasing concern has been expressed by educators, parents, mental
health professionals, and children themselves about what effects the threat
of nuclear war may have on children. The considerable attention in the
media, the formation of such groups as Educators for Social Responsibility, the development of curricula and programs in response to the need
to educate high school and junior high school students about the nuclear
threat, and the development of children's groups opposed to nuclear war
reflect this concern.

Surprisingly, most work on this question appeared either in the early
1960s[1-6] or after 1980. The first recent studies started in the late 1970s

and indicated that there was concern about the threat of nuclear war in a substantial number of those high-school-aged youngsters that were surveyed. John Mack and I conducted the first of these studies.[7] Our initial study was an in-depth questionnaire study, partially qualitative, partially quantitative, that eventually involved 1,100 youngsters from various parts of the country. It was undertaken to see whether this was an issue for youngsters at all. The results strongly indicated that it was.

Most striking were the qualitative responses of youngsters in the Boston area to open-ended questions administered in 1978. A few of their verbatim responses indicate the depth of the youngsters' concern.

For example, in response to the question "What does the word nuclear bring to mind?" some students gave the following answers:

"Big grey clouds, pipes and smokestacks, red warning lights, dead wildlife and humans, unnecessary death and violence."

"Danger, death, sadness, corruption, explosion, cancer, children, waste, bombs, pollution, terrible devaluation of human life . . ."

"Stars, planets, space, darkness . . ."

"All that comes to mind is the world's final demise, final kind of holocaust."

In response to the question "When did you first become aware of the nuclear threat?" a student said,

"I believe I was in junior high when I first became aware. Of course I found it terrifying that every human being in my whole world could be destroyed by one bomb that our nation had first discovered. The bomb that every advanced civilization has sought to obtain. To destroy our race, to destroy people, culture, life on the earth, is essentially the outcome of the A bomb."

In response to the question "What effects has the threat of nuclear war had on you?" two students answered as follows:

"I think that unless we do something about nuclear weapons, the world and the human race may not have much time left."

"In a way it has. It has shown me how stupid some adults can be. If they know it could easily kill them I have no idea why they support it. Once in a while it makes me start to think that the end of my life, my time in life, may not be as far off as I would like it to be, or want."

Altogether, three samples totaling 1,143 students from public and private high schools in three cities across the country were given the questionnaire. The three samples were collected in 1978, 1979, and 1980. Most of those studied were adolescents and all were in school when questioned. The initial 1978 questionnaire elicited open-ended essay responses, while the subsequent two questionnaires had a quantitative format.

The sampling was not systematic in any standard sociological sense, but an effort was made to obtain urban and suburban schools and to have all children in the classroom fill out a questionnaire when any one child in that classroom was asked to.

Quantitative analysis revealed that there was no uniformity of political opinion and that very few young people had taken an active position. However, the responses reflected a profound dis-ease and uncertainty about the future and a considerable amount of general pessimism. The majority of youngsters were concerned about at least some aspect of the threat of nuclear war, and a number were afraid. The respondents were relatively alone with their fears and not certain what to do. Their primary informants were the media and schools, not their parents. Other nonsystematic opinion surveys yielded similar findings.[8]

The results of the study described above must be viewed as preliminary and hypothesis generating for several reasons. There was no systematic sampling. The questionnaire focused solely on the nuclear issue rather than being a more general inquiry about youngsters' attitudes about various matters, so that the respondents knew specifically what the investigators were interested in, and this may have affected their responses. There was no attempt, other than in a qualitative way, to rank order or address the relative degree of their concern about the nuclear issue to other concerns.

Since 1978, a large number of studies have been conducted. These address some of the methodological shortcomings of nonsystematic surveys, while they also leave some areas unexplored. In a broad sense, four different kinds of studies exist which address not only the question of how many youngsters voice some concern about the issues but also how important this concern is in their lives. The four kinds of studies are as follows: (1) systematic survey research, using standard techniques conducted in the United States; (2) in-depth questionnaires which attempt to address the relative weight of concerns about this issue, as opposed to other concerns; (3) international studies; (4) in-depth qualitative studies. Representative studies from each area will be reviewed in order to highlight the findings, although this review is not intended to be a complete or exhaustive one of all studies.

SYSTEMATIC SAMPLING

The best evidence about the importance of this issue from a study using rigorous sampling techniques has been conducted by Jerald Bachman and associates. He has presented findings about the threat of nuclear war as it relates to youths as a part of a study of adolescent attitudes toward the military and the draft.[9]

Recently Bachman presented findings from surveys of students in seven consecutive graduating high school classes—1976–1982. Each yearly survey was conducted during the spring. In order to sample representatively, a three-stage probability sampling approach was employed, and through this approximately 130 public and private high schools from 48 states were selected from a much larger pool of schools. Between 77 and 85 percent of all the students in the classes selected were studied, and the total sample size (by year) ranged from 16,662 to 18,924. A series of questions were asked in the area of monitoring the future. One question asked was: "Of all the problems facing the nation today, how often do you worry about each of the following?" One possible choice was chance of nuclear war. There has been a steady rise in the percentage of those who worried about the nuclear threat. In 1976, 19.9 percent of male seniors never worried about it, while in 1982, only 4.6 percent of the males never worried. Similarly, in 1976, 7.2 percent of the male seniors said they worried about it often, while in 1982, 31.2 percent did. Female high school seniors showed a similar dramatic change over the seven-year period. Another statement in the series was: "Nuclear or biological annihilation will probably be the fate of all mankind within my lifetime." There was a steadily increasing trend for both boys (from 23.1 to 35.3 percent over the seven-year interval) and girls (from 20.2 to 36.0 percent) to agree or mostly agree with this statement.

It is important to understand these findings in the context of the Michigan Survey data* as a whole.[10] While there is an increase in those who agree with the statement about nuclear or biological annihilation, nonetheless, in 1982, for example, slightly more than 15 percent of all high school seniors indicated that they disagreed with this statement. Similarly, the majority of seniors surveyed in 1982 responded that they agreed or mostly agreed with the statement: "The human race has come through tough times before and will do so again."

The larger study provides clear evidence on another point of interest. Are youngsters from less affluent homes or of minority group status concerned about the threat of nuclear war? In the 1982 data, seniors in high school not planning to attend college had consistently more pessimistic responses than those planning to attend college. As those who attend college, in part, come from families with higher social status, this argues

---

*I am indebted to David Beardslee, Oakland University, Rochester, Mich., for a review of and insight into the Michigan Survey data.

against the notion that this is a class-bound phenomenon. In terms of race in this survey, 46 percent of the black seniors agreed or mostly agreed with the statement, "nuclear or biological annihilation will probably be the fate of all mankind within my lifetime," as compared with only 34 percent of the white seniors. Fundamentally, these survey research data show few class differences in response to worrying about a variety of problems and no evidence that less affluent youngsters are less concerned.

Standard opinion survey research involving adolescent populations has also confirmed that this is a significant issue for a large number of youngsters. As one example from a number of surveys, Gallup[11] reported on a representative national cross section of 514 teenagers, age 13–18, conducted from April to June in 1984. About half (51 percent) indicated that it is somewhat likely that a nuclear war will be started during their lifetimes, and 15 percent of the group reported that it is very likely to happen during their lifetimes. Of this group of teenagers, 49 percent said that the possibility of nuclear war has had some influence on how they plan for the future, and 25 percent described this influence as serious, in terms of thinking or planning about the future.

As another example, Offer and colleagues interviewed 356 high school juniors from the Chicago area during 1983–1984 as part of an ongoing comprehensive study of adolescent development. Respondents were both white and black and covered the range of the middle class: lower, middle, and upper. When asked a general question about problems facing the world, about one-fifth of the students voiced concern about nuclear issues (war and energy). Those who worried about nuclear issues did not have a specific profile—that is, they were not different from the rest of the sample with respect to gender, race, or socioeconomic status; nor did this group differ on measures of idealism, coping abilities, drug abuse, or delinquency.[12]

RELATIVE WEIGHT OF NUCLEAR WAR VERSUS OTHER ISSUES

John Goldenring and Ronald Doctor[13,14] have studied a large group of adolescents in southern California with a questionnaire which they developed to address the question of the relative weight of concern about the threat of nuclear war. Questions about the threat of nuclear war were embedded among questions about other representative worries of adolescents. Youngsters were asked to rank each of 20 main possible worries in terms of four degrees of worry: not worried at all, worried a little, moderately worried, very worried. In a separate, later section of the questionnaire, there were direct inquiries about the threat of nuclear war and the possibility of survival. This questionnaire was administered to 913 students in May 1983 in the San Jose and Los Angeles areas (ages 11–19) representing grades 7 to 12 with a wide range of ethnic backgrounds. The sample was largely middle and lower income families. The highest rated worry was about parents' death, and the second highest rated worry was getting bad grades. The third overall worry was the possibility of nuclear war, with 58 percent responding that they were worried or very worried about the possibility. When the students were to indicate their top 5 worries out of a list of 20, concern about parental death remained highest, and concern about nuclear war moved up to second.

Of those surveyed, 33 percent considered nuclear war often, and more than half thought a nuclear war between the United States and the USSR would occur in their lifetimes. Despite the high levels of concern, 51 percent admitted they never spoke to their parents about nuclear war, and 39.4 percent had talked with them about it only a few times. The chief sources of information were television, school, and newspapers, with parents much less frequently being a fourth source. Surprisingly, 42 percent reported that they felt they had not been given sufficient information about nuclear issues in school. Youths who were most worried in the sample showed significantly better scores on a series of statements that measured self-esteem and adjustment. This group had also talked more often with their parents about nuclear war, and despite their increased levels of concern, they were more hopeful that nuclear war could be prevented than were their less overtly worried peers. These findings were replicated with a sample of 250 southern California suburban adolescents. Although not based on a national sample, Goldenring and Doctor's findings substantiate the earlier nonsystematic observations.

INTERNATIONAL STUDIES

The last few years have witnessed a remarkable growth in the study of young people's attitudes in a variety of countries. This review is not exhaustive but will indicate the breadth of studies conducted.

Finland

In a methodologically carefully conducted study in Finland, Solantaus and colleagues,[15,16] using standard sampling techniques, surveyed 6,851 youngsters, age 12–18 years. The study was carried out as part of a larger study of health habits, and the youngsters were thus not questioned only on war and peace. A questionnaire was administered by mail, and the response rate was 81 percent. A total of 108 items formed the questionnaire and concerned living conditions, family, school, health, health habits, exercise, and psychosomatic symptoms. Respondents were asked for the three main hopes that they had for their own lives and their futures and also the three main fears that they had, and then the experience of war was investigated by eight structured questions.

Of all fears, fear of war was by far the most frequent, with 81 percent listing war as one of their three main fears. In terms of the corresponding question about hopes, hopes concerning work and employment were ranked first, and hopes for peace were expressed by about a third of the respondents. Solantaus remarked that it is paradoxical that while as many as four out of five respondents expressed fear of war, hope for peace was expressed by only a third. She offered the speculation that peace may be an empty concept for young people, meaning mostly an absence of war. Solantaus noted that girls' reactions to the threat of war seemed stronger than boys' and speculated that boys are socialized to expect to see not the whole picture but only the positive aspects of combat. In terms of social class, the threat of war was in the minds of respondents of all social classes. Young people who were confident about their own contribution to the prevention of war had more anxiety about war than those who did not see the possibility of change. A small group reported that it had an effect on their daily functioning.

Canada

Sommers and associates[17] completed a questionnaire survey in Toronto, Canada, in 1984. They used a questionnaire with 103 items in which the nuclear questions were embedded in other questions about other areas of concern in order to minimize bias. It was administered to over a thousand students in six public schools in metropolitan Toronto. A wide range of ages and sexes were represented, as well as a wide range of social classes. The students were equally distributed over grades 9 to 13. The authors caution that this sample is urban in nature, has somewhat of a representation of high social class and educational level in two sections of the sample, and has a large representation of immigrants. Students were asked to state their three strongest hopes and their three greatest worries. These were then coded into 11 categories following the scheme developed by Solantaus[14,15] in Finland. Students were then asked to rate nine possible hopes and nine possible worries in terms of how important they were, and then they were asked about three future-oriented domains: unemployment, job and career plans, and threat of nuclear war.

In terms of the open-ended questions, the highest percentage of students mentioned work and employment first (41 percent) and war and peace second (29 percent). A total of 51 percent mentioned war and peace as one of their three major worries, the highest rating of any category. On multichoice questioning, 63 percent of the students indicated that nuclear war was a very important issue or worry for them, as it was ranked second out of the nine possible worries, the first being parents' death.

Ten percent of the sample reported thoughts about nuclear war daily. Thirty percent reported having some thoughts at least twice a week. Similarly, 8 percent reported fear or anxiety about nuclear war almost every day and 24 percent reported these feelings once or twice a week or every day. The majority of students reported that they had no influence in preventing a nuclear attack, which contrasted with their attitudes on job and career plans. They further perceived that their parents had little influence on preventing a nuclear war. In comparing unemployment, job plans, and threat of nuclear war, in terms of being discussed at home, nuclear war was talked about least. Television and newspapers were the primary source of information on this topic for those surveyed. Faced with the threat of nuclear war, 24 percent admit some or a lot of desire to live only for today and forget about the future. Surprisingly, 16 percent had sought counseling or advice for worries about nuclear war at school, and 9 percent sought counseling or advice for worries about nuclear war outside of school.

The authors compared the groups who reported daily fear with the group identified as "all others." The groups did not differ in terms of sex, Canadian birth, or whether their parents had been active. They did differ in being younger and having lower social economic status. Interestingly, students who were more anxious and fearful about nuclear war also thought more about their personal future. In addition, they felt that they were more likely to have some personal influence on the political process. The fears thus were not associated with feelings of helplessness, but with a greater sense of personal efficacy. Surprisingly, the authors conclude, "The data further suggests that those who say they are not fearful and anxious at all, may also be at high risk for difficulties. It is in this group that the students express the most helplessness and show the least interest in planning for their own future."[6]

New Zealand

Gray and Valentine[18] have reported about the knowledge and attitudes of New Zealand's secondary school children toward nuclear war based on a survey of 876 fifth, sixth, and seventh form students. This questionnaire dealt solely with the nuclear issue. A number of questions dealt with factual information, and others dealt with attitudes about it. Altogether, 90 percent of the sample had seen, heard, or read something about nuclear weapons, largely from television and other forms of the media. Half (50 percent) of the sample thought that the situation at present would deteriorate through more armaments or world war in the future; very few were hopeful about disarmament as a realistic possibility. Students said that they did not feel they knew enough about nuclear weapons.

Sweden

In Sweden, Holmborg and Bergstrom[19] have studied a sample of 917 adolescents, age 13 to 15, with the help of the Swedish Institute for Opinion. They used an instrument that was adapted from Goldenring and Doctor's[13,14] questionnaire, as the questions about nuclear war were embedded in general concerns about teens' worries. The number one worry, both in mean score and percentile ranking, was nuclear war, with 42 percent listing it as their greatest worry. This was higher than the score in the study of American youth by Goldenring and Doctor.[13,14] The death of a parent was listed second. A total of 24 percent reported thinking about a nuclear war between once a week and daily, and 26 percent thought a nuclear war would definitely or probably occur during their lifetime. Only 17 percent of the sample felt that adults were very worried, and 46 percent thought that adults were very little concerned. Of the teenagers surveyed, 67 percent stated that they received insufficient information or none at all, and 63 percent of those sampled seldom or never talked to anyone about their worries. Two-thirds of the sample thought that the USSR, the United States, and Europe would not survive a nuclear war. There was some optimism in that three-fourths of the teenagers showed faith that various actions could do something to prevent a nuclear war.

International Survey Research

The findings of these more detailed studies are supplemented by standard survey research findings. For example, in 1981 the Institute of Peace Research at the University of Groningen in The Netherlands[20] surveyed 13- and 14-year-olds in Groningen. The majority of the children believed a nuclear war would occur and would destroy their city, and almost half thought that they would not survive. In West Germany, public opinion polls show that approximately 50 percent of the young people between the ages of 18 and 24 expect the world to be destroyed by nuclear war.[21] Similarly, in Britain, in 1983, a representative sample of teenagers, age 15–18, was surveyed, and 52 percent thought it was either extremely or quite likely that nuclear war would occur within their lifetimes.[22]

USSR-United States

Eric Chivian and associates[23] have, in collaboration with Russian physicians, studied Soviet youth with a questionnaire very similar to that used by Goldenring and Doctor[13,14] and compared the findings to their findings in the United States. Studies were conducted in 1983 in two pioneer camps for youngsters. One was a camp for children whose parents worked at a domestic airport, and the other was a camp for children who had been selected as outstanding in one or another respect, such as academic performance, athletics, or citizenship. The youngsters were interviewed, singly or in groups, and were also surveyed with a questionnaire. Approximately 50 young people were interviewed, and 293 youngsters completed the questionnaire. In terms of questionnaire responses, the greatest worry of the Soviet sample of youngsters was nuclear war, as almost 90 percent of the Soviet children regarded the prospect of nuclear war as disturbing or very disturbing. The Soviet sample was significantly more concerned about global issues, such as world overpopulation, world hunger, and pollution, while the American sample had significantly more concern about family and personal matters. Strikingly, the Soviet youth were more optimistic than the American youth that a nuclear war would not occur during their lifetimes. In the Soviet group, three times as many youngsters felt positive about the possibility of preventing nuclear war than the American students did (75 compared with 25 percent). In general, Chivian and associates observed from their data that Soviet children reported that they learned about the facts of nuclear war earlier than American children and appeared to have consistently more detailed and accurate information than their American counterparts. There also appeared to be more discussion in families than in the United States. The Soviet youngsters were more pessimistic about the possibilities of survival if war occurred. Virtually all the Soviet children had taken part in officially organized peace education activities.

QUALITATIVE STUDIES

While quantitative published reports of relatively large numbers of subjects provide important evidence, so do qualitative studies.

There is increasing anecdotal evidence that at least some children under the age of 11 are seriously concerned about the possibility of nuclear war. Such evidence consists of videotaped discussions with children in public schools, as carried out by Chivian and Snow;[24] anecdotal case reports from clinical material, as reported by Stoddard and Mack;[25] and an increasing body of work from primary school teachers who have dealt with these subjects with their students.[26,27] These qualitative investigations have established that at least some children under age 11 are concerned. It is undoubtedly true that this group represents a smaller percentage than those adolescents who are concerned. The meaning of this is even less well known than the meaning of results with adolescents. No data from a developmental point of view exist.

In terms of qualitative interview studies, Goodman et al.[28] conducted a pilot interview study with adolescents in the metropolitan Boston area. While such a small sample in no sense can be called representative, and although the youngsters were not selected because of their view of the nuclear question, interviews with these youngsters give an even more vivid and detailed sense of the meaning of the threat of nuclear war in their lives.

Although some students reported that they try not to dwell on it, while others claimed that they worry about it constantly, all of the 31 adolescents asserted that the existence of nuclear weapons impinges on their lives on a daily basis. They reported that they are reminded of the arms race when they read the papers or watch television and that there is a constant worry in the back of their minds. These teenagers say they are afraid every day that nuclear annihilation will come, if not right away, then in a relatively short time. Some have planned to move away from the cities because of the threat; a few have decided not to have children, and they say that the threat of nuclear war has forced them to live more in the present.

Most of these youngsters do not advocate unilateral disarmament and, given the current international political situation, feel that some nuclear weapons are necessary. However, a deep discouragement, a sense of things being out of control, pervades their perceptions of the arms race; they draw no sense of security or safety from the presence of the weapons. One student explained his helplessness this way:

I don't have the power to control, to say whether to have bombs or not, I don't have the control to say whether we make nuclear weapons or not . . . I don't know what kind of thing would happen, but at any minute there goes the bomb. It scares me a lot, this kind of emptiness, this kind of hollowness, like being in a tunnel and having to fight and nothing is around you and you're clawing at everything trying to find something. That's the kind of feeling.

From quite a different perspective, Robert Coles[29] has reported some in-depth interviews with youngsters about the threat of nuclear war. These lasted several sessions over a period of time, as opposed to the interviews of Goodman and associates, which were one session each. His descriptions are eloquent; his conclusions are that it is largely, if not entirely, young people whose parents are upper class and who are involved in the nuclear movement who are deeply concerned about this. He specifically argues that lower class youth are not concerned and gives several anecdotal illustrations. He also raises the question that some youngsters may be putting on or pretending to be concerned about this issue and that, in any case, youngsters keep on with their usual activities in spite of this worry.

No description is given in Coles' report of how these youngsters were selected, how many were interviewed, and, from the number interviewed, how many were selected to be reported. Neither the length of the relationship nor the way that the interviews were described to the children is given. Nonetheless, Coles' work emphasizes the importance of in-depth interviews over time and of understanding the full context of the child's experience in trying to understand the impact of the threat of nuclear war.

DISCUSSION

All of the quantitative studies discussed above concur in demonstrating that a significant number of youngsters report serious concern about the threat of nuclear war. Estimates of the percentage of those seriously concerned in the United States vary. Evidence from Bachman[9] and others suggests that many more young people are seriously concerned about this threat than they were a few years ago. It is clear that young people in a number of different countries in several parts of the world share these concerns.

Youngsters are primarily made aware of the threat of nuclear war through the media; this is sometimes supplemented by information in school. They report that they do not discuss these matters with their parents for the most part and often are alone with their fears.

The meaning of these attitudes in the context of the youngsters' lives has been much less well investigated, and some critiques of the work have appeared.[29-31] Qualitative studies, such as the initial study by Mack and myself,[7] our interview study,[28] videotapes of youngsters,[24] family interviews,[32] and educators who have talked with classes about this issue,[27,33] all suggest that the concerns for some young people are serious, and major, and are talked about with eloquence. Coles' interviews present a different picture, with much more class-limited areas of concern. However, the survey research of Bachman and associates[9,10] argues strongly against the fact that concern about the future or worries about the fate of the world are class-bound phenomena. The reported seriousness of the youngsters' concerns is substantiated by studies such as those of Goldenring and Doctor.[13,14]

Methodological Issues

The study and understanding of the impact of the threat of nuclear war on the lives of children and adolescents is in an initial stage. This must be expected given the fact that so little work has been done over the last 20 years in this area and that so little research time and funding have been directed to it. Perhaps most telling is the fact that there are no clear analogous areas of inquiry from other studies in social science that can serve as models. We have not begun to fully understand the impact on young people of attitudes and beliefs about the current society, or about their future in it in general, and so at this point it is impossible to parcel out and describe quantitatively and definitively the effect on young people of these attitudes toward the threat of nuclear war alone. Moreover, there are unique characteristics of this issue that make it difficult to study, as will be discussed below. Understanding these difficulties should assist further research, but it should also give a broader perspective on why so little work has been done.[8]

In terms of the specific limitations of the current studies that have been described above, while questions about the representativeness of the samples have been adequately addressed in the survey studies, for example in Bachman's efforts,[9] they have been less well addressed in some of the international studies. Goldenring and Doctor's impressive findings[13,14] are based on systematic sampling, but in a very limited number of school systems in one area of the country, and thus require replication in other areas. The use of in-depth interviews and questionnaires in the United States and elsewhere have not yet been done on any serious systematic sampling basis.

Given the difficulties of translation and the immense cultural differences between countries, quantitative comparison of youngsters in different, non-English-speaking countries to English-speaking youngsters, or to one another, must be viewed at this point as hypothesis generating rather than as definitive. However, the finding of serious concern in a substantial percentage of children in all countries surveyed is not called into question.

As yet, no study of the impact of nuclear war on children and adolescents has demonstrated any serious psychopathological effects that have resulted from the threat, nor has any serious large-scale study even attempted that. There are a number of compelling individual anecdotal reports about distress[25,34] resulting from the threat of nuclear war, but there is no quantitative evidence on this question. More broadly, there is little evidence about the effects of the attitudes of these youngsters on actual behavior. They do, indeed, report that they are worried and that such worry has an effect, but studies of the effect have not been conducted.

Little is known about the development over time of attitudes of children and adolescents toward the nuclear threat, although some data are available about the development of attitudes by youngsters toward war in general.[35] There is evidence of differing perspectives when college students are compared with older adults.[36] Recent studies of the responses of youngsters to war situations and extreme environmental stress[37] may offer some relevant analogies to approaches to understanding these impacts in general.

From a research perspective, understanding the impact of the nuclear threat is complicated by the fact that the issue is only one of several complex, rapidly changing forces operating in our modern industrial society. Some of the attitudes and concerns that have emerged from interviews questioning young people about the threat of nuclear war are pessimism about the future, fear, hopelessness, and the need to live in the present. These psychological phenomena probably are related to other factors as well. Such factors are the growth of technology itself, the changing patterns of family structure, broad disillusionment with the political system as evidenced by decreasing rates of voter participation, declining American prestige at home and abroad, and economic woes. It is difficult in studies to separate the role of the nuclear threat from these other social problems, but it is important to do so insofar as it is possible.

Thus more research is needed. It should build on the existing research and be specifically addressed to defining the areas in which the impact of nuclear war influences the youngsters' attitudes and behavior and should be informed by the need to attempt to separate out the complexity of the factors involved. There is a need for detailed longitudinal prospective studies in systematically chosen samples, including evaluation of the influence of the development, the vicissitudes, the changes, and the effects at various developmental epochs of awareness of the threat of nuclear war and concern about it on youngsters. Similarly, as Coles has suggested,[29] attention to the context of the children's and adolescents' lives in relation to this concern is necessary. Related to this, surely, is the investigation of the development of possible differences between young women and young men in their attitudes. It would be especially useful to have in-depth interviews and questionnaires in the same samples followed over time.

Surprisingly, almost no attention has been directed to studying what enables youngsters to cope well with the threat of nuclear war, perhaps because it is difficult to define what successful coping is. However, at the least, in two areas related to successful coping much more work is needed. The first of these is a more detailed description of how parents and children interact about this issue and what effects, if any, such interactions have on the youngsters. Initial work indicates that this is a rich and potentially rewarding area for exploration.[32] The second is the systematic evaluation of educational efforts to date, particularly the various curricula that have been developed. The intriguing initial findings of Goldenring and Doctor,[13,14] Sommers and associates,[17] and others[38] suggest that being better informed and aware is in no sense maladaptive and may be associated with good functioning. This also should be replicated, and then efforts should be directed to understanding it further. Zweigenhaft[39] has presented preliminary evidence indicating a positive response to an educational program. This also needs much fuller investigation.

It would be incorrect to conclude, however, that all that is needed is more research, or that we do not know much about this area because there are some methodological limitations in what we do know or because more systematic research is needed. In a few years, we have learned a substantial amount in several areas, and that process is important and has implications both for research and for dealing with youth about this issue. These areas are the characteristics of the nuclear issue, the feelings engendered in those who become involved, and the implications for education.

Characteristics of the Nuclear Issue

The nuclear issue is an issue which reflects intense conflict among experts. It has provoked a polarization of political viewpoints. From a research perspective, this makes it difficult to obtain the necessary distance and objectivity to evaluate its effect fully and to understand young people's concerns. In terms of dealing with young people, it is also important to recognize that there are distinct characteristics of this issue that set it apart from other social and political problems. It is important to be aware of these in conceptualizing the task young people face in understanding this issue.

The nature of the threat of nuclear war is at the same time abstract, outside of the personal experience of adolescents, and yet overwhelming in its horror and scale. Only twice has a nuclear weapon actually been used, on Hiroshima and Nagasaki. At no time has a large-scale nuclear war taken place. There is substantial disagreement among experts on what the consequences of such a war would be. To contemplate the threat of nuclear war requires an act of the imagination which is difficult, if not impossible, for most adults. It requires young people to venture into an unknown and uncertain territory, into which many of the adults around them will not travel.

There has been an understandable though unfortunate tendency on the part of adults and society as a whole to keep these matters secret.[40] Nuclear weapons were initially developed during World War II, when debate was not possible. The prevailing attitude since then has been that further weapon development was largely a matter best left to scientific experts. It is not correct simply to attribute this silence to governmental policy. The subject is so painful, frightening, and seemingly technically impenetrable that

most adults have chosen to deal with it by denial and avoidance.[41–43] Until
recently there has been virtually a total lack of public discussion of nuclear
weapons issues.

Feelings Engendered in Those Who Become Involved: A Painful Awareness

To work with the subject of nuclear annihilation is painful and difficult
for everyone—researcher, clinician, parent, or child. To consider seriously the possibility of nuclear war is to contemplate the destruction of
life as it exists on the earth. It means the end not only of one's own life,
but of the lives of everyone we love, indeed of all relationships which
exist, possibly forever. It is a horrifying idea, the vision of a holocaust
unlike anything the planet has known. Moreover, it is not clear that any
one citizen can do very much by him- or herself about the problem, so
that there is an attendant helplessness as one confronts its reality. Thinking
that a nuclear war will occur obviates thinking about the future.

For adults, thinking about children and nuclear war is a particularly
difficult task. Children—one's own or anyone else's—are far more vulnerable than adults to the effects of nuclear war. Their futures are potentially longer; their own children are yet to be born. Their genes, bones,
and other tissues are more susceptible to the effects of radiation.

For all of us, another part of the difficulty in achieving full awareness
of the nuclear issue is the pain of realizing that one is potentially both
victim and perpetrator of nuclear violence: victim because there is so little
control over the weapons; perpetrator because those of us who are U.S.
or Soviet citizens are members of countries that are spending huge amounts
in tax dollars to build instruments of destruction whose sole possible use
is to annihilate large portions of the human race. It is difficult for anyone
to think about these matters, let alone know how to talk to or deal with
young people about them. Beyond this, it is disturbing to think that the
threat of nuclear war in and of itself might be having an impact on our
children's development. Furthermore, the subject itself, precisely because
it is so painful and yet so politically controversial, is inherently divisive.

I do not wish to overdramatize the problem but to raise an issue which
is something like countertransference in psychotherapy and psychoanal-
ysis, the deeper thoughts and feelings which are evoked in the clinician
by the case material before him. Special attention to these feelings has
proved necessary in certain situations, such as dealing with patients with
cancer or survivors of the Holocaust.[44–46] Such troubling emotions provide
one of the major reasons that so little work has been done in this area,

but also provide experience in determining the need for the kind of help and education that young people need.

IMPLICATIONS

The Nature of Young People's Experience and the Need for Education

The presence of nuclear weapons and the threat of nuclear war are major realities in our society today and will continue to be so in the future. Regardless of whether the percentage of youngsters seriously concerned at present is 30 or 40 or 60 percent, this represents a very large number of youngsters. That number is likely to increase. The data to date strongly indicate that young people are not receiving systematic education and open discussion about this immensely complex and difficult issue. Those that are concerned primarily find out about it through the media, and they are deeply troubled by what they find out. They are alone with their fears.

It is certainly true that this issue of the immense destructiveness of nuclear weapons and the possibility of the destruction of the entire world is a crucial issue and must remain in the forefront of the issues considered in our democratic society. As yet, such full consideration generally has not taken place in the United States.

In order for the democratic process to operate with regard to this issue, or any other, it is essential that citizens be informed and express their opinions. This issue has not drawn citizen participation, unlike many other issues, because it is so painful and difficult and because of the sense of powerlessness and helplessness it engenders. It is necessary to educate young people about this issue so that they can participate fully in the political process.

The usual media presentation, whether print or visual, is a partial and incomplete way for youngsters to become educated about this issue. Most media presentations are not systematic or general discussions but are news items, focused on the particular subject of the day. They are often visually dramatic. This does not provide any systematic overview of the problems of nuclear issues; nor does it transmit to young people any sense of how to deal with nuclear issues, how to discuss them with others, or how to understand them. The exception to this are media presentations specifically focused on education, and some of these have been quite helpful. Beyond the media, most areas in which the nuclear area is touched upon in fiction, television drama, videogames of destruction, and so forth, are also partial and incomplete presentations at best. The way youngsters become aware of the nuclear issues contributes to their helplessness and hopelessness.

I have dwelt at length on the complexities of the issue and on the feelings engendered in those concerned with it because I think these are the issues that any citizen must wrestle with in coming to grips with the nuclear issue. I also believe that any young person in adolescence who is coming to grips with the nuclear issue must also wrestle with these matters, and they cannot be expected to do so alone. Youngsters must have help in doing so. As a psychiatrist, I am particularly aware of the workings of the mind, or inner processes, that accompany outward actions and changes in behavior. It is essential that some attention be made to these inner processes or that people work through the fears and implications of the threat of nuclear war so that we can deal with young people about this threat.

There is a great need for more systematic education. The work carried out to date gives us a clear idea of what kind of education is needed. I think there are two issues in education: what the content should be and to whom it should be directed. This education should be directed to those young people who have become aware of the issue and who are worried about it. I think, more broadly, there is a need for all adolescents to have some education about this issue so that they can be introduced to it. With regard to the content, education for youth should be systematic, not partial or incomplete. Partial accounts are frightening and may turn youth away.

It is essential that young people not be left alone with their fears. It is essential that they make contact with others who are willing to hear them and to share their concerns. Education must take place in a context, that is, in a relationship which allows back and forth questioning and which also takes place over time. The context may be provided by school, media presentations with follow-up discussions, parents, doctors, educators, or others. What is necessary for those providing the education is knowledge of the issue, sensitivity to the inner processes of working through the painful feelings engendered, and a willingness to try to come to grips with what the youngsters are voicing.

This means that people doing the educating must have learned to deal with the issue themselves to some extent. It is no accident that the Educators for Social Responsibility program, under the leadership of Roberta Snow in Boston, was developed from a program in the Brookline Public Schools for Teaching History in Ourselves, which dealt with the question of the Holocaust.[33] Teachers found that they could not teach students about the Holocaust, without some preparation and support for themselves, because it is so horrifying an historical subject. Likewise, teachers have found that such preparation is necessary for teaching students about the threat of nuclear war. Similarly, it has been recommended to parents and mental health professionals that it is necessary for them to work on their own feelings about the issue before they deal with it with others. [8,47] These are examples of how those who have worked in the area have had to deal with the issue themselves first.

The most important component of education is making youngsters aware that they are not powerless, that their actions are important and that they do make a difference on this issue, as on other issues in a democracy. From a psychological point of view, the central psychological concomitants of partial and incomplete awareness of the nuclear issue are helplessness and hopelessness, which often lead to inactivity, to paralysis. It is essential to counteract these feelings through education to help young people become aware that they are not powerless. Indeed, from a psychological point of view, some corrective focus is necessary for the sense of helplessness engendered by this issue, and action can be very beneficial. By action, of course, I do not mean getting involved in political action per se, but rather being educated, talking with others, coming to grips with the issue in an inner sense.

Concern with young people's attitudes is not an idle, speculative, or irrelevant matter. I believe it is likely that the declining involvement of youth in the political process is in part related to the perception that the threat of nuclear war is frightening and that little can be done about it, so involvement is useless. Yankelovich,[48] Offer,[49] and others have argued that the current generation of adolescents is considerably less hopeful and more pessimistic than previous ones and that this is not confined to any one social class. While it is difficult to quantify and neatly parcel out the relative effects of these various forces that lead to this pessimism, the nuclear threat and the immense amounts of energy and money expended on the nuclear arms race is a fundamental part of our society and surely contributes substantially to an overall sense of hopelessness and pessimism.

HOPE AND THE FUTURE

Nuclear war is not inevitable. The actions of individuals and groups are not insignificant or unimportant in trying to prevent a nuclear war. While we may differ enormously about whether more weapons or fewer will more successfully prevent a nuclear war, we agree on the need for its prevention.

As M. B. Smith has commented,[50] it is the responsibility of one generation to be able to transmit a vision of the future to the next. I am deeply concerned that our understanding of the nuclear issue and its impact on youth suggest that it weakens or diminishes the vision of hope for the future of a substantial number of youngsters. It is, after all, true that the prevention of nuclear war rests not only on our current generation, on ourselves, but also on our children's generation, on them. They will have to make this a central issue of their lives. This can only occur when they are fully informed and carefully introduced to the issue, supported in their understanding of it, and then willing to take action. This can occur only when they have a vision, a hope for the future, which includes the belief that nuclear war can be prevented and that their actions have an effect. This must be the central aim of our educational efforts.

NOTES

[1]Escalona, S. 1965. Children and the threat of nuclear war. In Behavioral Science and Human Survival, M. Schwebel, ed. Palo Alto, Calif.: Science and Behavior Books Inc.

[2]Schwebel, M. 1965. Nuclear cold war: Student opinions and professional responsibility. Pp. 210–223 in Behavioral Science and Human Survival, M. Schwebel, ed. Palo Alto, Calif.: Science and Behavior Books Inc.

[3]Adams J. F. 1963. Adolescent opinion on national problems. Personnel Guidance J. 42(4):397–400.

[4]Allerhand, M. E. 1965. Children's reactions to societal crises: Cold war crisis. Am. J. Orthopsych. 35:124–130.

[5]Wrightsman, L. 1964. Parental attitudes and behaviors as determinants of children's responses to the threat of nuclear war. Vita Humana 7:178–185.

[6]Darr, J. M. 1963. The impact of the nuclear threat on children. Am. J. Orthopsych. 33:203–204.

[7]Beardslee, W., and J. E. Mack. 1982. The impact on children and adolescents of nuclear developments. In Psychosocial Aspects of Nuclear Developments, Task Force Report Number 20. Washington, D.C.: American Psychiatric Association.

[8]Beardslee, W. R., and J. E. Mack. 1983. Adolescents and the threat of nuclear war: The evolution of the perspective. Yale J. Biol. Med. 56:79–91.

[9]Bachman, J. 1983. American high school seniors view the military, 1976–1982. Armed Forces and Society 16(1):86–94.

[10]Johnston, L., J. Bachman, and P. O'Malley. Monitoring the future: Questionnaire responses from the nation's high school seniors 1975–83 (annual volumes). Ann Arbor: Institute for Social Research.

[11]Gallup, G. 1984. The Gallup youth survey, released October 17, 1984, Associated Press.

[12]Offer, D., E. Ostrov, and K. I. Howard. 1986. Normal adolescents' concern with nuclear issues. Unpublished manuscript. Michael Reese Hospital and Medical Center, Chicago, Illinois.

[13]Goldenring, J. M., and R. M. Doctor. 1983. Adolescent concerns about the threat of nuclear war. Testimony for the House of Representatives Select Committee on Children, Youth and Families, U.S. Congress, September 20, 1983.

[14]Goldenring, J. M., and R. Doctor. 1981. California adolescents' concerns about the threat of nuclear war. Pp. 112–133 in Impact of the Threat of Nuclear War on Children and Adolescents, T. Solantaus, E. Chivian, M. Vartanyan, and S. Chivian, eds. Boston: International Physicians for the Prevention of Nuclear War.

[15]Solantaus, T., M. Rimpela, V. Taipale, and O. Rahkomen. 1981. Young people and the threat of war: Overview of a national survey in Finland. Pp. 94–103 in Impact of the Threat of Nuclear War on Children and Adolescents, T. Solantaus, E. Chivian, M. Vartanyan, and S. Chivian, eds. Boston: International Physicians for the Prevention of Nuclear War.

[16]Solantaus, T., M. Rimpela, and V. Taipale. 1984. The threat of war in the minds of 12–18 year olds in Finland. Lancet 8380(1):784.

[17]Sommers, E., S. Goldberg, D. Levinson, C. Ross, and S. LaCarbe. 1981. Children's mental health and the threat of nuclear war: A Canadian pilot study. Pp. 61–93 in Impact of the Threat of Nuclear War on Children and Adolescents, T. Solantaus, E. Chivian, M. Vartanyan, and S. Chivian, eds. Boston: International Physicians for the Prevention of Nuclear War.

[18]Gray, B., and J. J. Valentine. 1981. Nuclear war: The knowledge and attitudes of New Zealand secondary school children. In Impact of the Threat of Nuclear War on Children and Adolescents, T. Solantaus, E. Chivian, M. Vartanyan, and S. Chivian, eds. Boston: International Physicians for the Prevention of Nuclear War.

[19]Holmborg, P. O., and A. Bergstrom. 1981. How Swedish teenagers think and feel concerning the nuclear threat. Pp. 170–180 in Impact of the Threat of Nuclear War on Children and Adolescents, T. Solantaus, E. Chivian, M. Vartanyan, and S. Chivian, eds. Boston: International Physicians for the Prevention of Nuclear War.

[20]DeJong, J. 1981. Teaching about nuclear weapons. Presented at Institute of Polemology, University of Groningen, Groningen, The Netherlands, June.

[21]Richter, H. E. 1982. Psychological effects of living under the threat of nuclear war. J. Royal Coll. Gen. Practitioners June:377.

[22]Tizard, B. 1984. Problematic aspects of nuclear education. In A special issue: Education and the threat of nuclear war. Harvard Ed. Rev. 54(3):271–281.

[23]Chivian, E., J. E. Mack, J. P. Waletsky, C. L. Lazaroff, R. Doctor, and J. Goldenring. In press. Soviet children and the threat of nuclear war: A preliminary study. Am. J. Orthopsych.

[24]Chivian, E., and R. Snow. 1983. There's a nuclear war going on inside me (a videotape of interviews with 6–16 year olds). Boston: International Physicians for the Prevention of Nuclear War.

[25]Stoddard, F. J., and J. E. Mack. 1985. Children, adolescents and the threat of nuclear war. In Basic Handbook of Child Psychiatry, Vol. V, J. Noshpitz, ed. New York: Basic Books.

[26]Friedman, B. 1984. Preschoolers' awareness of the nuclear threat. Calif. Assoc. Ed. Young Children Newsl. 12(2).

[27]Engel, B. S. 1984. Between feeling and fact: Listening to children. Harvard Ed. Rev. 54(3):304–314.

[28]Goodman, L., J. E. Mack, W. R. Beardslee, and R. Snow. 1983. The threat of nuclear war and the nuclear arms race: Adolescent experience and perceptions. Polit. Psychol. 64(3):901–930.

[29]Coles, R. 1985. The Moral Lives of Children. Boston: Atlantic Monthly Press.

[30]Smith, M. B. 1982. The threat of nuclear war: Psychological impact. Address at the Physicians for Social Responsibility Symposium, Eugene, Oregon, October 9.

[31]Bower, B. 1985. Kids and the bomb: Apocalyptic anxieties. Science News 128:106–107.

[32]Zeitlin, S. 1984. What do we tell mom and dad? The Family Therapy Networker 8(2):31ff.

[33]Snow, R. S., and L. Goodman. 1984. A decision making approach to nuclear education. Harvard Ed. Rev. 54(3)321–328.

[34]Koupernick, C. 1967. Refusal of an adolescent to accept the modern world. J. Child Psychol. Psych. Allied Disciplines 8:233–240.

[35]Kahnert, M., D. Pitt, and V. Taipale, eds. 1983. Children and war. Geneva, Switzerland: Geneva International Peace Research Institute.

[36]Van Hoorn, J., and P. French. 1985. Facing the nuclear threat: A cross-age comparison. Presented at American Educational Researchers Association, April.

[37]Garmezy, N., and M. Rutter. 1985. Acute reactions to stress. Pp. 152–176 in Child and Adolescent Psychiatry: Modern Approaches, M. Rutter and L. Hersov, eds. Boston: Blackwell Scientific Publications.

[38]Eisenbud, M. B., J. Van Hoorn, and B. B. Gould. In press. Children, adolescents, and the threat of nuclear war: An international perspective. In Advances in International Maternal and Child Health, Vol. 6.

[39]Zweigenhaft, R. L. The psychological effects of living in the nuclear age. Report of the War Planning Evaluation Committee, Greensboro-Guilford County, Greensboro, N.C.

[40]Carson, D. I. 1982. Nuclear weapons and secrecy. In Psychosocial Aspects of Nuclear Developments, Task Force Report Number 20. Washington, D.C.: American Psychiatric Association.

[41]Bernard, V. W., P. Ottenberg, and F. Redl. 1965. Dehumanization: A composite psychological defense in relation to modern war. Pp. 64–82 in Behavioral Science and Human Survival, M. Schwebel, ed. Palo Alto, Calif.: Behavioral Science Press.

[42]Mack, J. E. 1984. Resistances to knowing in the nuclear age. Harvard Ed. Rev. 54(3):260–270.

[43]Frank, J. 1967. Sanity and Survival: Psychological Aspects of War and Peace. New York: Vantage Books.

[44]Weisman, A. D. 1972. On dying and denying: A psychiatric study of terminality. New York: Behavioral Publications.

[45]Kubler-Ross, E. 1970. On Death and Dying. New York: MacMillan.

[46]Bergmann, M. 1982. Recurrent problems in the treatment of survivors and their children. In Generations of the Holocaust, M. Bergmann, ed. New York: Basic Books.

[47]Schwebel, M. 1982. Effects of the nuclear war threat on children and teenagers: Implications for professionals. Am. J. Orthopsych. 52(4):608–618.

[48]Yankelovich, D. 1982. Changing social values. Research Workshop in Preventive Aspects of Suicide and Affective Disorder in Young Adults. Harvard Medical School and Harvard School of Public Health, Boston, December 3.

[49]Offer, D. 1982. Adolescent self-image: Empirical studies and theoretical implications. Cambridge Hospital Symposium on Self-Esteem, Boston, December 10.

[50]Smith, M. B. 1983. Hope and despair: Keys to the sociopsychodynamics of youth. Am. J. Orthopsych. 53:388–399.

The Medical Implications of Nuclear War, Institute of
Medicine. © 1986 by the National Academy of Sciences.
National Academy Press, Washington, D.C.

Scandinavian Youth View the Future: A Preliminary Report of a Large Questionnaire Survey

MAGNE RAUNDALEN, PH.D., and OLE JOHAN FINNOY
University of Bergen, Bergen, Norway

Several recent studies have asked children to rank the most pressing
problems of the world and to list their feelings about the future. Data from
these surveys indicate the percentages of children who are pessimistic or
optimistic about the future and how many think about nuclear war daily,
twice a week, twice a month, and so on. But multiple-choice questionnaires alone cannot elicit the spontaneous thoughts or feelings of children
or describe their perceptions of how future problems may color their daily
lives and affect their psychological functioning.

In 1984 and 1985, we also asked students—3,000 Norwegian and 1,000
Swedish boys and girls between the ages of 12 and 19—to rank the world's
problems in order of importance to them. Among a given list of 10
problems, the study group ranked the threat of nuclear war first. (Unemployment was ranked second, with older youths giving more weight
to this problem than younger group members.)

In addition to the ranking, we requested that the youths write essays
on what they thought the future might be like. From their extensive writings
we tried to classify or systematize their attitudes. We are sorry to report
that 44 percent of those surveyed were pessimistic about the world—an

---

This survey took place in cooperation with the Norwegian Save the Children Fund.

For a more comprehensive description of research methods used in this study, see
Raundalen, M., and O. J. Finnoy, in press, Children's and teenagers' views of the future,
International Journal of Mental Health.

attitude we defined as a profound hopelessness toward the possibilities of peace and future life on earth, including their own survival.

Other attitudes were more complex to categorize. For example, we rated about 13 percent of the group as having "forced" optimism. These children and adolescents seemed to shift gears, punctuating a long list of the world's problems with a sudden declaration of a hopeful outlook.

Another 12 percent had an attitude we classified as powerlessness. This group passively listed future problems, emphasizing that solutions were beyond their control. But they did not indicate whether they were optimistic or pessimistic about the fate of the world.

Ten percent of the respondents had "active denial," refusing to answer and declaring that they could not bear to think about future world conflicts or problems. This group repressed all feelings and reactions to the bomb and other threats. Even within this group there were differences: Some easily shut out thoughts about the future, and others said they were compelled to ignore such thoughts in order to avoid mental distress.

The last and fifth group we called "active hope." Fourteen percent of the youths surveyed were in this category. They not only expressed an optimistic attitude about the world, but could tell us why (unlike those with "forced optimism"). Their main sources of hope, they said, were international organizations working in poor (third world) countries. These youths viewed efforts of the United Nations, UNICEF, Red Cross, and Save the Children Fund as peace work with which they felt a bond. Generally, children who were active or whose parents were active with international organizations such as these expressed more optimistic attitudes about the future. This group felt strongly that the threat of nuclear war and other global problems could be solved.

Less quantitatively, we also tried to grasp main themes within the writings of the youths. We believe that these themes can guide future research.

One of the central themes that emerged from the essays was concern about planning for the future. Here, we selected all writings about personal aspirations, including education, work, and family. Only about 20 percent had high expectations for the next 12 to 15 years.

Many of the youngsters felt it was meaningless to plan for these pursuits at all, especially long-term education and vocational training. We believe that combating this personal pessimism will be a primary challenge to the entire education system in the future. Allowing and encouraging pupils to participate in work for a better world and constantly emphasizing what is being done around the globe to prevent ecological disaster and poverty and to halt the arms race may be one solution.

Another theme was anger, which was expressed by many of the youths toward the bomb and other threats that they believed were taking the future out of their hands. Still others expressed depression, and some said they were living under such a heavy burden that it was an effort to decide whether to live another year.

Some young people said they were tempted to use drugs to relieve their pain about the future. Others commented that it was pointless to avoid alcohol and narcotics, since the world might soon be destroyed anyway. Relating to these feelings, a number of the youths wanted immediate rewards for their accomplishments. It appeared that they were seeking instant gratification in a world where there may be no future.

Many of the youngsters commented on the upsetting news they receive from the media. They see in the news a tidal wave of rising problems— the global hurricane that could very well destroy, with no potential for saving or rebuilding. It seems that some young people have developed a "news phobia." Unfortunately, this closes off a channel of communication that might lessen their fears—to the extent that the media do report on positive actions for peace and justice.

The pessimism encountered in our survey raises questions about how the media, schools, and parents present the world to children. The survey also suggests that working with international organizations to promote peace and justice is one strategy for allaying fears and increasing optimism among children. In the youngsters' own words, becoming involved with such groups is an important source of relief and comfort for those who are depressed about the future of the world.

STUDY METHODS

In our survey we used the following methods. Three sheets of paper containing questions were distributed during a school lesson. The front page listed 10 problems about the future, which the students were asked to rank according to importance. (The problems had been selected after surveying a previous group of approximately 200 children and adolescents.)

After ranking the 10 problems, the students were asked to comment on the problem that they cited as most threatening. They were also asked to write what they thought could be done about the world's problems and to indicate whether their view of the future was optimistic. Lastly, we asked the youngsters what they thought about the nuclear bomb. It was emphasized that no answer was right or wrong and that it was their own thoughts in which we were interested.

These open questions were especially attractive to the students. They wrote lengthy descriptions about their concerns and perspectives on the world's future. The problems that they described were both of a global character—such as the nuclear bomb, food shortages, and pollution—and a more local character, such as drugs, unemployment, and bringing up children.

Regarding our methodology, we acknowledge the following: The contents of the entire survey form were directed at problems about the future; that is, they were focused so that we expected that many students would voice considerations specifically on the subject of nuclear war. We did this because we believed that the threat of nuclear war was already of great concern to them. There may have been other answers to the survey had we asked different questions about the future or used a different format; but this does not mean that the statements are not significant. Rather, we must interpret their pessimistic responses from the perspective that they were asked to focus on a few of the world's problems in a relatively short amount of time.

The children in the survey were selected to yield a broad distribution in age and geographic location. We also wanted children that lived in the north, close to the Soviet border, to participate in the survey. To some extent we had to abandon the principle of random selection because some school authorities reacted so strongly to the theme of the survey that under no circumstances would they have allowed it to be conducted in their schools. So far, we have not focused on an analysis of attitudes in different parts of the country.

The data were analyzed as follows: The structured part of the survey, in which the children were asked to rank the future problems from 1 to 10, was registered, punched, and analyzed with a program that will be described thoroughly in a later article. Systematization of the written material took place in several phases. After reading through all the answers, we worked out score categories that we found were representative of the children's main responses. We started with the category "optimism" at one end of the spectrum and the category "pessimism" at the other.

TABLE 1   Ranking of Problems About the Future

Rank	Problem	Average Ranking
1	Nuclear Weapons	2.31
2	Unemployment	3.84
3	Drugs	4.08
4	Pollution	4.87
5	Scarcity of food	4.88
6	Russia	5.48
7	World population growth	6.44
8	United States	6.71
9	Genetic and medical experimentation	7.55
10	Bringing up children	8.18

TABLE 2   Future Problems that Students Ranked Number One

Rank	Problem	Number of Students	Percent of Students
1	Nuclear weapons	935	52.7
2	Unemployment	357	20.1
3	Drugs	166	9.4
4	Pollution	103	5.8
5	Scarcity of food	89	5.0
6	Russia	55	3.1
7	World population growth	33	1.9
8	Bringing up children	16	0.9
9	United States	14	0.8
10	Genetic and medical experimentation	5	0.3

Gradually it became clear that the optimists could be divided into two categories: those who said that they chose to be optimists, in spite of the dark future outlook they expressed, and those who had a supported hope, who believed that what is being done is of some use and something that they could actually take part in. Furthermore, it became clear that pessimism had several nuances of powerlessness and escape. As a result of the analysis, we broke down the responses into groups of active hope, forced optimism, powerlessness, repression (active denial), and pessimism.

RESULTS*

Page one of the survey, which contained the ranking of the 10 problems about the future, was used for several analyses. First, we calculated the average ranking of all 10 problems (Table 1).

The nuclear weapons issue was clearly given the lowest numerical value, indicating that it generally was ranked high as a problem. Next were unemployment and drugs, which are local concerns—that is, problems that may concern youths more directly in their private lives. The fourth and fifth concerns, however, were the global threats of pollution and scarcity of food.

The ranking may also be analyzed according to how often a single problem area was ranked first, as shown in Table 2.

The results presented in Table 2 show that, according to this method of analysis as well, the threat of nuclear weapons is the future problem

---

*The findings of the analysis of the first 1,800 responses are reported here. The results from the full 4,000 show no significant changes in these trends; they are described in Raundalen, M., and O. J. Finnoy, in press, Children's and teenagers' views of the future, International Journal of Mental Health.

TABLE 3   Differences in Ranking the Number One Future Problem, by Age

Age (years)	Nuclear Weapons (%)	Unemployment (%)	Drugs (%)
12	64.6	5.7	16.6
13	66.9	9.9	11.9
14	56.5	21.4	10.0
15	49.1	26.6	5.6
16	52.5	14.8	10.9
17	41.9	25.2	8.1
18	38.0	32.7	4.7
19	38.9	27.8	7.4

that the children most often considered to be number one, but the analysis reveals the distance between the ranking of the problems, for example, between nuclear weapons and unemployment.

There were only modest differences in the ranking between sexes. Girls ranked nuclear weapons, unemployment, and bringing up children as the number one future problems slightly more often than did boys.

Table 3 shows differences by age in the ranking of the number one future problems of nuclear weapons, unemployment, and drugs. Evident age-related factors are shown by the fact that the ranking of nuclear weapons as the number one problem decreases with age. The importance of unemployment increases in ranking with age, while the importance of drugs decreases.

Table 4 shows that pessimism is the dominant attitude group, whereas the other groups are about equally distributed. In an analysis of all the data, the negative group consisting of attitudes of pessimism, powerlessness, and repression constitutes nearly 70 percent of the study population, whereas the two groups with optimistic attitudes represent 26 percent.

We found that the attitudes of boys and girls were distributed differently among the categories of optimism and pessimism. Girls were slightly less

TABLE 4   Attitudes About the Future

Attitude	Number of Students	Percent of Students	
Forced optimism	239	13.3	25.8
Active hope	224	12.5	
Pessimism	794	44.2	69.3
Powerlessness	220	12.2	
Repression (active denial)	232	12.9	
Impossible to code	89	4.9	

pessimistic but expressed a higher degree of powerlessness. The percentage of boys with active hope was considerably lower than the percentage of girls, but forced optimism was twice as common among boys than among girls.

We also found that attitudes toward the future changed across the age span of the study group. Pessimism tended to decrease with age. More significantly, forced optimism tended to be replaced by active hope in the older children.

DISCUSSION AND SUMMARY

Currently, several surveys can be found in which children and adolescents have been asked to rank and write about problems of the future. They vary in specificity—that is, some only use the word "future," whereas others also use formulations about problems and threats. Furthermore, there are more specific surveys in which children are asked their views about local problems and especially the use of nuclear weapons or the risk of comprehensive nuclear war.

Within this framework, the questions we asked the youngsters to write about were directed toward their feelings. We wanted to know how much or how often they were bothered by thoughts of the world's future problems, whether they shared their feelings with someone, and what their perspective was on the future according to their age. In response, approximately one-half of the students answered that the world is going to be destroyed by one or several of the future threats during their lifetime.

When the youngsters were asked how much they were bothered by these threats, great variations in response, especially among age groups, were found, but the answers did not point in a particular direction. However, children and adolescents agreed that they did not talk to adults about future threats, especially about nuclear war. We also got the impression that they do not frequently share these thoughts with their companions.

Data from other surveys are primarily quantitative and do not address issues of feelings. Our method, a more problem-oriented approach, was aimed at providing more insight into how children express themselves and what they say when concerned about the future. It appears that our questionnaire-essay format was attractive to the respondents, especially those over 14 years of age. They enjoyed the ability to freely express their thoughts, and a majority provided answers that were detailed and personal.

An analysis of the responses to such a questionnaire, which was only partially structured according to how the problems were presented to the children, is of course difficult to systematize. Our analysis is not finished, and currently we are classifying the data into certain theme areas. We are doing this by re-reading the material and noting the themes that occur throughout and then discussing the structure and essence of these themes. The method is very exciting, but it is necessary to compare many statements and to avoid interjecting our own biases into what we read. It is therefore very important that two people do the analysis and have a continuous discussion during the work. So far we have chosen to examine the following theme areas:

1. *Psychological reaction.* Many youths described their feelings in detail as they faced the future threats. So far we can say that they usually described their situation as stressful: It is heavy, they live under the burden of the threats, and so on.

2. *Long-term planning.* We gathered together all those who wrote about looking far ahead into the future and planning their lives. A marked trait was the large number of youths (more than 20 percent) who found it meaningless to invest in long-term educational and vocational training because the future of the world was uncertain.

3. *Politicians and democracy.* About 1 in 10 wrote that they can no longer trust democratic processes, politicians, and government officials or international alliances in any way. They are looking for strong leaders, and if there are none, then it is better to have the world end. Some young people combined this outlook with contempt for weakness and suggestions that insane persons should be institutionalized so that they cannot come near "the button" and destroy the world. We were concerned to find such intensity of antidemocratic attitudes.

4. *Aggression.* This group comprises those who express strong aggression in the description of their future perspective. The aggression is directed toward the destruction of nuclear weapons and against the generation who they say is "playing with our future."

5. *Belief in the good forces.* This group comprises those who express belief in the good powers and in the possibility of action and peace for the world. Many have similar attitudes to those who were placed in the active hope group in the analysis discussed above.

In summary, 7 out of 10 children and adolescents between 12 and 19 years of age fall into the negative response category. This includes those who either express directly that they are pessimists or note that they do not want or cannot bear to write about future world problems. The pessimism is attached to nuclear war and unemployment and to the fact that soil, air, and water may be damaged by other threats in the near future.

The actively hopeful view of the future that we found in a sizable minority of young people typically is connected with the fact that they or their parents have taken part in actions against the proliferation of nuclear weapons or to improve the conditions of the world. The young people often equate peace work with aid to developing countries. They associated the spread of nuclear weapons with the risk of revenge and terrorism being directed against us from the third world. These children also tend to be knowledgeable about the United Nations and the disarmament talks.

The Medical Implications of Nuclear War, Institute of Medicine. © 1986 by the National Academy of Sciences. National Academy Press, Washington, D.C.

Adult Beliefs, Feelings, and Actions Regarding Nuclear War: Evidence from Surveys and Experiments

SUSAN T. FISKE, PH.D.
University of Massachusetts, Amherst, Massachusetts

I would like to begin with a story. I have a friend who has cancer, and she has reason to believe that she has a one-third chance of dying from it. She understands this diagnosis, but her possible death remains somewhat hypothetical to her. She imagines it mostly in the abstract, and she talks about missing the city and her occasional trips into the country. She does not talk so much about missing the people in her life. She believes she cannot do anything to change her odds. She does not worry about it very often; it mostly is not salient to her. If asked about it, she reports fear and worry, and certainly she prefers effective treatment to nothing. But she does not change her life with regard to her cancer. She does not seek support. She does not join organizations. She does not discuss her situation publicly. She goes on about her normal life. Some people say she is marvelous, remarkable, life-affirming, brave, and adaptable. Other people say she is suppressing her fear, denying reality, and desensitized to her own death.

My friend is the average American citizen. Her cancer is the possibility of a nuclear war. This portrait of her reactions resembles the portrait I will draw of the ordinary person's reactions to the possibility of nuclear war. I have described it this way initially because it is becoming difficult to have a fresh perspective on this issue. I will come back to this point at the end, but it may be useful to keep the story in mind while reading this paper.

This paper addresses three issues. First, it describes the average citizen's response to the possibility of nuclear war. Second, it describes possible sources of that response. And, third, it contrasts the average citizen with the antinuclear activist and the survivalist.

In describing adult response to nuclear war, I use a three-part distinction that is standard in social psychology. As the title indicates, this paper separately examines people's beliefs, feelings, and actions. Beliefs include conceptions of the likelihood of nuclear war, images of mushroom clouds and utter destruction, and expectations about one's own survival. People's feelings, for these purposes, consist of their reported emotional reactions and their nuclear policy preferences. People's activity regarding the possibility of nuclear war includes political activity and survival activity.

With respect to most issues, people's beliefs, feelings, and actions are fairly consistent; such consistency enables psychological equilibrium. In the context of nuclear war, however, there are major discrepancies between the ordinary person's beliefs, on the one hand, and the ordinary person's feelings and actions, on the other hand. Although this observation is not entirely new, there has been little effort to review the hard data concerning the modal person's beliefs, feelings, and actions.[1] The sources of data include more than 50 studies from social and behavioral science: mainly surveys of adults, with preference given to national findings, where available, over local findings; some questionnaire studies of college students; and a few experimental studies with college students. The data span a period from 1945 to the present, and they lend some new insights into the discrepancies among people's beliefs, feelings, and actions.

MODAL BELIEFS ABOUT NUCLEAR WAR

People think of nuclear war as somewhat unlikely, imagining mainly complete material destruction, in the abstract, with themselves definitely not surviving.

Psychologists have long attempted to document people's beliefs about nuclear war, primarily using survey interviews and questionnaires, but also drawing on the in-depth relationship of the clinical setting (for historical overviews, see Klineberg [1984] and Morowski and Goldstein [1985]). Immediately following the bombings of Hiroshima and Nagasaki, the first surveys began to examine people's attitudes toward the bomb and its use. Attitude surveys ebbed and flowed over the next four decades, peaking after the Russians' first atomic test, the creation of the hydrogen bomb, the Bay of Pigs and Cuban Missile Crisis, the Nuclear Test Ban Treaty, the Strategic Arms Limitation Treaty (SALT) initiatives, and during the present unprecedented level of worldwide concern over nuclear weapons (Kramer et al., 1983). The number of surveys reflects variations in levels of public interest, as indicated by citation frequencies in the *Reader's Guide to Periodical Literature* (Polyson et al., 1985). Complementing the survey efforts, some clinical psychologists and psychiatrists have lately begun to note the intrusion of concerns about nuclear war within the therapy hour.

This review of the survey data will suggest that ordinary people's nuclear war beliefs have changed remarkably little over the four eventful decades since the bombings of Hiroshima and Nagasaki. Despite massive technological change in the power of the weapons and in their delivery time, despite their considerable proliferation, and despite dramatic fluctuations in the geopolitical situation, we will see that the adult American's response has endured with remarkable consistency. Moreover, people's responses differ surprisingly little across age, gender, race, education, income, and political ideology. Apparently this is one thing on which ordinary citizens agree, and have agreed, for decades.

Most important, people view nuclear war as not very probable, a hypothetical event. The average person views nuclear war as fairly unlikely within the next 10 years.[2] A local survey in Pittsburgh found that, on average, people estimated a one-third chance of a nuclear war within their lifetimes (Fiske et al., 1983), and a local sample in Chicago put the estimate at one-half (Tyler and McGraw, 1983). Three decades ago, people were asked about the likelihood of another world war, which they overwhelmingly believed would be nuclear; they viewed such a war as somewhat more likely than people do now, but the average person still estimated the chances as 50/50 (Withey, 1954). People are considerably more pessimistic about the possibility of nuclear war if a conventional war should erupt. Since 1946, between 63 and 79 percent of Americans have believed that any subsequent major war would necessarily be nuclear (Kramer et al., 1983). Overall, however, the indications are that people now view nuclear war as unlikely, on balance.

If the hypothetical were to occur, people expect it would be horrific. As early as 1954 and as recently as 1982, survey respondents described similar images of the event and its aftermath (Fiske et al., 1983; Withey, 1954).[3] Two features of these descriptions are notable. First, material destruction is described more than human destruction, and second, abstract content outweighs concrete content. This primary emphasis on the material and abstract, rather than on concrete human devastation, is in marked contrast to the descriptions of Hiroshima survivors, who focus almost entirely on the human misery (e.g., Lifton, 1968; Thurlow, 1982; *Time,* 1985a).

In describing what is hypothetical to them, American citizens report images involving material damage, mostly in the abstract as complete ruin or sometimes in the concrete as a blinding light; as buildings on fire; and, subsequently, as dust, barren land, and no cities. References to death and injury also occur, mostly in the abstract, but also sometimes as concrete references to the death of family and friends; to charred bodies; and to injuries such as mutilation, burns, bleeding, hair loss, sores, vomiting, and diarrhea. Some typical, but longer than average, responses to our telephone survey (Fiske et al., 1983, p. 55) include three relatively abstract ones:

- Nobody left. We'll just all be blown up. The loser will be gone completely.
- It would destroy people. Everything in the world. All the beautiful things will be gone.
- Death. Destruction. Chaos. Survival. Hiroshima.

And two relatively concrete ones:

- I hope I die with everyone else. I can't see planning for it. Utter destruction, desolation, ruin.
- Death. Buildings on fire. Screaming. Wondering what to do. Being scared. Take cover. Wondering what to do next.

The typical images elicited in this survey setting contain about twice as much abstract content as concrete content. People report general impressions more than specific, sensory, proximate, personal impressions. And, as noted, they focus more on material damage than on human damage. One naturally wonders whether the telephone survey context determines the abstractness and material focus of these reports.

Turning to the highly personal, in-depth setting of a clinical approach, some observers report that they, their patients, or both have vivid images of nuclear holocaust (e.g., Nelson, 1985; Pilisuk, 1985; Wolman, 1984, cited in Wagner, 1985). Lifton (1983) describes end-of-the-world imagery in literature and in some individuals. For example, a "vision of crashing skyscrapers under a flaming sky," was reported by nuclear physicist and activist Eugene Rabinowitch and "dreams of doom" were reported by United Nations Secretary General Dag Hammarskjöld. Artists have depicted their visions of the bomb and nuclear catastrophe (Boyer, 1985; Time, 1985b). For example, James Agee created a fragment of a novel depicting official celebrations of the bomb above ground, with twisted, menacing events below ground (as described in Boyer [1985]).

Of course, although these data provide an intimate view of a few people's concrete images, it is not clear that these people are typical of the larger public who are not artists, or who do not seek out a therapist known to be a peace activist, or who are not themselves prominent peace activists. People with nuclear war images oriented toward the concrete and the human may well be exceptional. Indeed, Lifton (1983) argues that vivid end-of-the-world imagery involves "an anticipatory imagination capable of sensitivity to a trend of events which other people have become numb to'' (p. 131). For the present purposes, survey documentation of the modal citizen's image seems the most reliable indicator of how most people understand nuclear war. By this evidence, the images are more abstract than concrete, more oriented toward material ruin than human misery. At the same time, people expect complete annihilation.

Included in that annihilation is the self. The ordinary person does not expect to survive a nuclear holocaust. Even abstract references are clear in that respect (utter destruction, nobody left, annihilation). Moreover, when specifically asked whether they personally would expect to survive, people on average rate their chances as poor (The Gallup Poll, 1983; cf. Kramer et al., 1983). People's perception that they would not survive a nuclear war represents the only major change from people's earlier beliefs. The number of people rating their chances as poor has steadily increased over the decades from about 40 percent in the 1950s to about 70 percent today (The Gallup Poll, 1983). In the early 1950s, survey respondents commented about the quality of life after an atomic attack, describing the possible psychological and economic aftermath (Withey, 1954). They described the possibilities of panic, low or high morale, scarcity of food, production problems, and failed transportation systems. In describing these long-term effects of an atomic attack, the clear majority of people (68 percent) thought that the military would provide complete protection or at least prevent heavy damage. Today, people no longer believe that the U.S. military has the capacity to prevent heavy damage, probably because they perceive the Soviet Union to be ahead in the arms race and because they believe that a nuclear war cannot be limited (Kramer et al., 1983). Thus, people used to comment about the quality of life in a post-nuclear-war world; now they do not expect to see it.

To summarize, people report horrific images consisting of mostly abstract content related to extreme material destruction, along with content that is concrete and content related to terrible human destruction. Most people now do not expect to survive a nuclear confrontation, in contrast to earlier expectations. However, people's modal belief about a nuclear war includes a relatively moderate expectation of its occurrence. Finally, these beliefs do not differ dramatically across identifiable sectors of the adult population.

MODAL FEELINGS ABOUT NUCLEAR WAR
People worry seldom, but they overwhelmingly
favor a mutual nuclear freeze.

The beliefs people commonly report about a nuclear holocaust are bleak, which implies that people should also report some concomitant emotional reactions. When asked directly what emotions come to mind regarding a nuclear war, the typical person does report fear, terror, and worry (Fiske et al., 1983) or fear and sadness (Skovholt et al., 1985). On the whole, however, most people do not frequently think about nuclear war (Fiske et al., 1983; Hamilton et al., 1985a). The typical adult apparently worries seldom or relatively little about the possibility (Kramer et al., 1983). And such emotional responses do not vary dramatically as a function of social class or overall political ideology.

Women sometimes report more anxiety than do men (e.g., Hamilton et al., 1985d; Newcomb, 1985a), but this may be due to reporting biases caused by gender role differences in the perceived appropriateness of revealing one's feelings (e.g., Ruble and Ruble, 1982). Many studies of children also report higher levels of concern (e.g., Escalona, 1982; Goodman et al., 1983; Schwebel, 1982; see also W. R. Beardslee, this volume, for a review of representative sample surveys). Similarly, college students report more distress than do their parents (Hamilton et al., 1985d). Again, however, it is not clear how much this difference is due to reporting biases, as opposed to actual levels of felt worry. Quite possibly, many of the same factors that determine one's willingness to report worry publicly also determine one's willingness to admit worry privately, but it would be difficult to evaluate this premise empirically. The available evidence indicates, on the whole, that the modal level of reported worry is not high.

The relatively low level of worry is puzzling to many observers, given people's consensual horrific images and their low estimates of personal survival. If one combines people's estimated probability of nuclear war and their estimated probability of dying, should a nuclear war occur, people are essentially saying that they have about one chance in three of dying from a nuclear attack. Returning to the analogy used at the beginning of the paper, if most people received a cancer diagnosis giving comparable odds, they would doubtless be considerably upset. Why is there this discrepancy between people's understanding and their feelings?

One commonly suggested possibility is that people cope emotionally with the threat of nuclear war in different ways. Some preliminary survey evidence indicates that people take distinct cognitive and emotional stances that range from romanticist to hedonist to fatalist to deterrentist to disarmist and that their emotional reactions vary accordingly (Hamilton et al., 1985a). For example, romanticists believe that fundamental human goodness will prevent nuclear war, and they report little anxiety, worry, and thought about the issue. Hedonists believe that the prospect of nuclear war justifies immediate gratification, and they report a high degree of personal impact, a high probability of nuclear war, but only moderate worry and moderate anxiety. Altruistic fatalists believe nuclear war is quite possible but not preventable, so in the meantime they should work for the good of humanity, and they report low levels of personal impact and anxiety. Deterrentists report some worry and anxiety and they estimate a moderate probability of nuclear war. Disarmists report the highest levels of thought, worry, and anxiety.

More generally, people's level of nuclear anxiety is related to nonconforming attitudes, felt vulnerability, drug use, low self-esteem, and perceived lack of social support (Newcomb, 1985b). Similarly, nuclear anxiety is related to death anxiety (Hamilton et al., 1985b). Of course, the direction of causality is not clear. People who experience nuclear anxiety may therefore be more vulnerable socially and emotionally (e.g., Escalona, 1982), but the reverse is equally possible: people who are vulnerable for other reasons may then focus disproportionately on the nuclear threat. These are promising lines of inquiry, but the data on these matters are only beginning to come in.

Clinical interviews—with less representative samples but with more depth—indicate deep-seated worry, fear, and anxiety on the part of some individuals (Nelson, 1985; Wolman, 1984, cited in Wagner, 1985). These individuals are not typical of the larger population, however, so unfortunately, we do not know whether the interviews uncovered something about those particular people or a deeper truth about all of us.

The essential research requires both in-depth interviews *and* representative samples; it apparently remains to be done. Nevertheless, the best current evidence indicates that, although people report concern when asked, for most people, most of the time, the issue is not emotionally central.

People's feelings about nuclear war emerge more dramatically, however, in their policy preferences. The typical person clearly supports a mutual freeze on nuclear arms, although not a unilateral freeze (The Gallup Poll, 1983; Kramer et al., 1983). Support for a mutual freeze is remarkably consensual (77 percent agree); it is unusually broad based, showing few differences across gender, age, income, and education (Milburn et al., 1984); and it has held firm over the decades since 1945 (Ladd, 1982). The typical person believes that the use of atomic weapons in Japan was necessary and proper but does not accept their use any longer (Kramer et al., 1983).

Some group differences in attitudes do occur regarding the use of nuclear force, with men and older generations being more supportive. Men and women have differed consistently, although not dramatically, in their acceptance of the use and risks of nuclear weapons since 1949, with women being less favorable. This fits with the 5 to 10 percent gender gap on other foreign policy issues related to force (e.g., *Public Opinion,* 1985). Political generations also differ in their approval of the use of force generally and in the nuclear case specifically (Jeffries, 1974; Pavelchak and Schofield, 1985); there is a nuclear generation gap, with younger generations being somewhat less accepting of the use of force. Income and education can influence nuclear force attitudes (Jeffries, 1974), with increases in either leading to decreased support, although this is not found consistently (Milburn et al., 1984). Note that the gender, age, and class differences do not occur in nuclear freeze support (Milburn et al., 1984), but only in the use of nuclear force, should the occasion arise.

MODAL ACTIONS REGARDING NUCLEAR WAR
Most people do nothing.

The typical person does not act in any way that goes beyond voicing support for the policy of a nuclear freeze. Age, gender, and social class are not reliable predictors of activism, although political ideology may be. Most people simply do not write antinuclear letters to the editor or to their elected representatives, they do not join or financially support the relevant organizations, and they do not sign petitions (Fiske et al., 1983; Milburn and Watanabe, 1985; Pavelchak and Schofield, 1985; Tyler and McGraw, 1983). From one perspective, given people's nuclear war beliefs, including the low likelihood of personal survival and their at least minimal worry, they might be expected to be more active. What is especially surprising, to some observers, is that people are inactive in a matter of such literally earth-shattering consequence. From another perspective, however, the inaction of ordinary citizens is not at all surprising, for most people most of the time pay scant attention to politics and almost never engage in political activity beyond voting, if that (Kinder and Sears, 1985; Milbrath and Goel, 1977). Moreover, with regard to this particular issue, there is no evidence that people expect their actions to have consequences; that is, they have a low sense of political efficacy. I will come back to this point.

To summarize, the modal person has strong beliefs about nuclear war. Although it seems to them fairly unlikely that it will occur and people describe it mostly in the abstract, the modal person imagines total material and human destruction and emphatically does not expect to survive. People's feelings are elusive; they do not worry about nuclear war very often, but when asked, they report that the possibility of nuclear war is fearsome and they overwhelmingly favor a mutual nuclear freeze. Most people do not act in support of their beliefs and feelings.

SOURCES OF THE CONSENSUAL BELIEFS, FEELINGS, AND (IN)ACTION
Family, friends, and the media

Most aspects of the typical person's response are remarkably consistent across different sectors of the population. One naturally wonders about the sources of such a powerful consensus. There are two especially plausible sources.

It seems evident that people's significant others would fashion their responses to the possibility of nuclear war. Unfortunately, on this point the hard data are sparse. Moreover, they are limited to nuclear policy attitudes, so the data do not describe the sources of people's more emotional responses, their beliefs, or their actions. As with most political attitudes, one might expect that the parents primarily socialize the child (Kinder and Sears, 1985), but the data on children's responses to nuclear war suggest that this may not be the case (W. R. Beardslee, this volume). In one study, college students' stance toward nuclear war resembled the perceived but not actual stance of their parents (Hamilton et al., 1985a,c). Thus, although they think they share their parents' perspective, perhaps they often do not. As noted earlier, young people are less accepting of the use of force, including nuclear force. This discrepancy is preserved by most families' reported failure to discuss nuclear issues (Hamilton et al., 1985c). One possible explanation for the actual but not perceived discrepancy between the attitudes of young people and their parents is that major political events can powerfully influence people's political attitudes, especially if they occur around adolescence. Such events account for generational shifts in people's attitudes toward the use of force, for example (Jeffries, 1974). Hence, postadolescents can experience cross pressures between family ties and world events. Perhaps the nuclear generation gap results from this.

Moving outside the family, it is well documented that people tend to have friends whose attitudes resemble their own, both because similarities attract and because friends influence each other (Berscheid, 1985). Moreover, people perceive that their friends' attitudes are similar, to an even greater extent than they actually are (Levinger and Breedlove, 1966; Newcomb, 1961). Hence, people probably perceive that their nuclear war attitudes are shared by their friends. Although the relevant evidence is slim, college students do perceive their friends to have similar attitudes (Hamilton et al., 1985a)—whether they do or not is another question. More data are needed to investigate how family and friends influence nuclear war attitudes in older adults as well as in college students.

The media are also plausible sources for the powerful consensus in people's nuclear beliefs, feelings, and actions. When directly asked the source of their responses to the possibility of nuclear war, people often cite media coverage (Fiske et al., 1983; Milburn et al., 1984). A recent media event allowed social researchers to investigate whether people's intuitions are right about this. Dozens of efforts examined the impact of the docudrama *The Day After,* which was televised in November 1983.

will devote considerable attention in this paper to that event, for several reasons. One is that it is a diagnostic example or case study of media effects. Another is that it allows me to make a point about motivating the average citizen to express an opinion based on his or her perceptions. Also, there are scores of studies on *The Day After;* it was the single major source of data available for this review. Finally, the conclusions are intriguingly well substantiated by research done a dozen years ago on the effects of the film *Hiroshima-Nagasaki: 1945.*

The single major impact of *The Day After* was to increase the salience of nuclear war as an issue. In 1970, a study examined the impact of the film *Hiroshima-Nagasaki: 1945* (Granberg and Faye, 1972). Results of this study were strikingly parallel to those of *The Day After* studies. Like the recent film, the earlier film makes the abstract concrete and brings the unthinkable into awareness. And like the recent film, the earlier one demonstrates the specific ways that the media can influence people: by making certain issues salient and by reinforcing people's prior reactions. Consider each effect in turn.[4]

The *Hiroshima-Nagasaki: 1945* study concluded that the film sensitized people to the issues of nuclear war. *The Day After* studies concluded similarly that the movie made nuclear war issues highly salient. People consistently reported that they spent more time thinking about nuclear war after watching the movie (Brown, 1984; Cross and Saxe, 1984; Feldman and Sigelman, in press; Reser, 1984; Schofield and Pavelchak, 1984), and they were far less likely to report that they put out of mind the threat of nuclear war (Warner-Amex Qube, 1983, cited in Schofield and Pavelchak, 1985). This salience effect was especially true of less-educated viewers (Feldman and Sigelman, in press). However, the heightened salience of nuclear war was short-lived, fading after several weeks (Reser, 1984; Schofield and Pavelchak, 1984). The temporary effect of *The Day After* on salience apparently was due to overall media hoopla rather than to the movie itself (Oskamp et al., 1984). Viewers and nonviewers alike reported more nuclear war-related thoughts after the movie (Schofield and Pavelchak, 1984). People also spent more time thinking about the issue if they had read newspaper articles about it or discussed it with others (Feldman and Sigelman, in press). The single clearest impact of *The Day After* was an increase in the salience of nuclear war in the media and, consequently, in people's minds. This was a temporary but widespread phenomenon.

If increased salience was the major impact of the movie (and other media events), what are the most likely effects of salience? Existing research indicates a general principle. Making an issue salient polarizes the individual's thoughts, feelings, and actions; that is, however the person would respond to a stimulus, the response becomes more extreme as a result of the salience of the issue (Taylor and Fiske, 1978). As people dwell on their thoughts, they become more focused (Tesser, 1978). As people think about their feelings, they become stronger, and as people focus on an issue, they are more likely to act on it. Salience exaggerates their response in whatever direction it would have tended to go anyway.

The effects of *The Day After* and *Hiroshima-Nagasaki: 1945* are entirely consistent with these standard effects of salience. People's beliefs, which were bleak originally, became even more pessimistic. Two studies of *The Day After* directly examined changes in people's images of nuclear war, and the results confirm the potential influence of the media on people's concrete images. After the movie, people were considerably more pessimistic about the availability of shelters, the adequacy of medical care, the sufficiency of food supplies, the possibility of social chaos, the proportion of survivors, the likelihood of their own survival, and the possibility of rebuilding the country afterward (Feldman and Sigelman, in press; Oskamp et al., 1984). The politically inexperienced and the young were especially likely to report that they learned a lot from the movie (Oskamp et al., 1984). Considering the focus of *The Day After,* which concretely depicted the aftermath of nuclear war, the movie was effective in influencing people's images. Presumably, the movie was designed primarily to increase the salience of people's concrete images, as are other persuasive attempts to bring nuclear war home to people.

Many observers also expected the movie to influence people's feelings—their emotions and nuclear policy preferences. Consistent with the usual effects of salience, *The Day After* not only worsened people's images of nuclear war, it also seems to have made people's emotional reactions somewhat more extreme. Notably, the earlier movie *Hiroshima-Nagasaki: 1945* had increased people's reported anxiety and decreased their desire to survive a nuclear war (Granberg and Faye, 1972). The effects of *The Day After* apparently were similar. People reported that the film was disturbing, frightening, depressing, and numbing (Reser, 1984). Some people reported feeling more worried after watching the movie, and this was especially true for less-educated people (Feldman and Sigelman, in press). After the movie aired, watchers and nonwatchers alike reported more hopelessness regarding nuclear war and decreased desire to survive a nuclear war (Schofield and Pavelchak, 1984). Not all researchers found effects on all the relevant emotions, however; the data are somewhat uneven on these points. Nevertheless, there is some evidence that the movie increased people's prior emotional reactions to the prospect of nuclear war. According to one experimental study, widespread public expectations that the movie would be upsetting probably enhanced its emotional impact (Baumann et al., 1984; but see Schofield and Pavelchak, 1984). Moreover, the self-selected audience may have especially expected the movie to have great impact, creating a self-fulfilling prophecy (Cross and Saxe, 1984). Regardless of why the movie enhanced people's worries, its emotional impact lasted for at least a couple of weeks (Oskamp et al., 1984). Given that most people report at least moderate worry over nuclear war, emotional responses to *The Day After* seemed to be exaggerations of those prior feelings, caused by the temporary salience of nuclear war in all the media. Social science research indicates that the media chiefly serve to reinforce people's existing feelings, by bringing certain issues into public salience (Kinder and Sears, 1985). These conclusions fit media coverage of nuclear issues well.

In addition to its effects on people's emotions, some observers expected *The Day After* to change people's policy preferences, as if to make them instant pacifists. Despite unprecedented preshowing fuss by the network, administration officials, news magazines, antinuclear groups, prodefense groups, therapists, and educators, the movie had no measurable impact on people's nuclear policy preferences. Study after study—which together asked varied questions, used samples that ranged from national to local to classroom, at times that ranged from minutes to days to months after the show—found no effects on nuclear policy preferences (Adams et al., 1984; Baumann et al., 1984; Brown, 1984; Cross and Saxe, 1984; Feldman and Sigelman, in press; Gutierres et al., 1984; Kelly, 1983; Mayton, 1984; McFadden, 1983; Oskamp et al., 1984; Reser, 1984; Schofield and Pavelchak, 1984, 1985; Wolf et al., in press). The movie had essentially no impact on people's attitudes toward arms control, defense spending, perceived likelihood of nuclear war, trust in government leaders' handling of war and peace, or personal political efficacy regarding war and peace issues. Similarly, the earlier film *Hiroshima-Nagasaki: 1945* had no effects on nuclear policy preferences.

In retrospect, none of this is surprising. The media provide information to people, especially to the young and the less educated, but they do not typically change people's attitudes. This is not what most people think the media do, but social scientists have long studied the impact of the media on people's policy preferences. For quite a while, research has shown little or no impact of the media on people's political attitudes (Kinder and Sears, 1985), creating the law of minimal effects. There are several reasons for this. People's policy preferences are long-standing predispositions, reinforced by others in their environment and by their own inattention to political inputs. People's political preferences come from their enduring memberships in particular social groups, from their lifelong values, and from traumatic historical events. People's political preferences regarding nuclear war and other policy issues do not come from persuasion by the media.

Also, in this case, people's policy preferences, at least with regard to the mutual freeze, are fairly strong already, so it would be difficult for them to become more strong than they already are. Finally, *The Day After* was not addressing policy issues (cf. Schofield and Pavelchak, 1984), nor was it addressing the efficacy of political action (cf. Wolf et al., in press).

In sum, with respect to people's beliefs and feelings, people's prior reactions to nuclear war were not substantially changed; their images, emotions, and policy preferences were not transformed to be opposite from what they had been before. Few, if any, were converted to pacifism. But conversion to the opposite is not the only way for people to change. The movie enhanced people's bleak images. It had some impact on the extremity of people's reported emotions, which were stronger after the movie. Both probably resulted from the overall media coverage that dramatically heightened the salience of nuclear war.

Some observers also expected *The Day After* to have a galvanizing effect on nuclear protest activities. However, single media events do not typically influence people's political action. Consistent with this standard research result, people did not register protests with the government or the public media. The movie did not create a flood of mail or calls to the White House, Congress, the networks, or the newspapers (Schofield and Pavelchak, 1985). However, the salience of the nuclear war issue did affect people's behavior in very particular ways. Salience typically catalyzes people to action (Taylor and Fiske, 1978) because people are more likely to act on their attitudes when they are held in awareness (Kiesler et al., 1969). Consistent with this usual effect of salience, *The Day After* motivated people's intent to act on their feelings, although in limited ways. People called an antinuclear toll-free number given on television, they contacted Physicians for Social Responsibility, and they contacted other antinuclear groups (King, 1985; Oskamp et al., 1984; Schofield and Pavelchak, 1985; cf. Wolf et al., in press). People contacted these sources mainly to seek information rather than to engage in antinuclear action. Thus, *The Day After* changed the salience of nuclear war, thereby spotlighting people's prior concerns and enhancing their intent to act on their existing attitudes. Presumably, the movie did this by increasing the salience of people's concrete images. Consistent with the aims of antinuclear groups' efforts to make people's images of nuclear war concrete, salient concrete images were indeed associated with antinuclear action, in this event, as is true in general (Fiske et al., 1983; Milburn and Watanabe, 1985; note that the latter researchers suggest that both concrete and abstract images may be associated with antinuclear action).

To summarize, the movie had a remarkably clear impact on people's beliefs, emotions, and information-seeking behavior; it had remarkably little impact on their policy preferences and political behavior. A movie such as *The Day After* can change the images of the inexperienced. And the salience of people's prior worries about nuclear war can be enhanced by massive media events, such as this one, presumably by increasing the amount of thought people give to their feelings and to their concrete images. Salience also motivates people's behavioral intentions to act on their existing feelings, at least in terms of gathering information. These effects may be especially true of the politically inexperienced, the young, and the less educated. Apart from the media, people's overall attitudes toward nuclear war may well be shaped by significant others in their lives, as are other political attitudes, but the data are sparse on this point.

PREDISPOSITIONS TO ACTION
Antinuclear activists and survivalists both think a lot about nuclear war and believe they can do something about it.

Despite media events such as *The Day After*, for most people, most of the time, nuclear war is not a salient concern. But it is for a tiny fraction of the population. The tiny fraction for whom the issue is chronically salient is an important fraction: they tend to be active, and they create events that the media cover, so they potentially make the issue more salient for everyone. Salience exaggerates people's propensity to act in whatever direction they already would tend to act. Hence, two types of action can be spurred by salience: antinuclear action and prodefense action. This section will portray the typical antinuclear activist and the typical prodefense activist because they provide some clues to the discrepancy between people's bleak beliefs and their usual inaction.

The antinuclear activist may have engaged in only a few modest behaviors, such as writing congressional representatives and donating money to antinuclear groups. Nevertheless, this is far more than the average person does, and far more than people's usual levels of political activity. Even this humble degree of antinuclear action is worth examining. Factors that motivate antinuclear protest centrally include an extreme chronic salience of the issue and an unusual sense of political efficacy, as well as some attitudinal and demographic factors.

Chronic personal salience clearly distinguishes the activist. Antinuclear activists report that they frequently think about the issue (Fiske et al., 1983; Hamilton et al., 1985a; Pavelchak and Schofield, 1985), on the order of several minutes a day. Having the issue on their minds apparently creates detailed and concrete images of nuclear war (Fiske et al., 1983;

Milburn and Watanabe, 1985). The examples given earlier are also illustrative here: images of dismembered bodies, people screaming, buildings on fire, miles of rubble, and a barren landscape. Presumably, these uniquely salient concrete images are motivating for these people. Moreover, the combination of high perceived severity and high perceived likelihood of nuclear war is a good predictor of intent to become involved in antinuclear activity (Wolf et al., in press).

The activist also has a strong sense of political efficacy (Flamenbaum et al., 1985; Garrett, 1985; Hamilton et al., 1985d; Milburn and Watanabe, 1985; Oskamp et al., 1984; Tyler and McGraw, 1983). The antinuclear activist believes that nuclear war is preventable, not inevitable, and that citizens working together can influence government action to decrease the chance of a nuclear war. The antinuclear activist is specifically motivated by a sense of personal political capability, combined with a belief in the efficacy of political action (Wolf et al., in press). The correlation between political efficacy and behavioral intent is substantial by social science standards (Schofield and Pavelchak, 1984; Wolf et al., in press). Moreover, although activists believe that governments create the risk of nuclear war, they also believe that citizens can and should be responsible for preventing it (Tyler and McGraw, 1983). Not surprisingly, considering their strong sense of political efficacy, antinuclear activists tend to participate in other types of political activities as well (Fiske et al., 1983; Milburn and Watanabe, 1985; Oskamp et al., 1984).

Note that although activists believe nuclear war is preventable, they do not believe it is survivable (Tyler and McGraw, 1983). Hence, their sense of efficacy is limited to political activity, not to their own ability to live through the holocaust should they fail.

How do people develop a strong sense of political efficacy? Doubtless there are complex personal and social causes (Kinder and Sears, 1985). The activist's sense of political efficacy is linked to a broad sense of personal, rather than external, control over life events in general (Tyler and McGraw, 1983). Moreover, antinuclear activists perceive social support for their actions from role models, family, friends, and people who are important to them (Flamenbaum et al., 1985; Garrett, 1985; McClenny and Allbright, 1985; Pavelchak and Schofield, 1985). Antinuclear activists, then, are people who think about nuclear war a lot and think they can help prevent its occurrence, and they are fortified by a sense of personal control and social support for their activity.

In addition to heightened salience and efficacy, antinuclear activists differ from the modal person in some less clear-cut and less interesting ways. They of course have even stronger antinuclear attitudes than does the average citizen (Fiske et al., 1983; Flamenbaum et al., 1985). They sometimes report more worry, more anxiety, more anger, more outrage, and less hopelessness (Garrett, 1985; Hamilton et al., 1985b,d; Milburn and Watanabe, 1985; Oskamp et al., 1984; Tyler and McGraw, 1983).[5] Antinuclear activists may be more likely to be liberals and Democrats (Oskamp et al., 1984; Tyler and McGraw, 1983; Werner and Roy, 1985), although this result is not always found (Fiske et al., 1983; Pavelchak and Schofield, 1985). They may be more likely to be educated and well-off (Tyler and McGraw, 1983), although, again, not all researchers find this (Fiske et al., 1983; Flamenbaum et al., 1985; Milburn and Watanabe, 1985).

Finally, the activists' view of the likelihood of nuclear war is still unclear. One might expect that frequently imagining the event would make it seem more likely (Carroll, 1978). On the other hand, activity by oneself and others might be viewed as decreasing the odds of nuclear war, especially for people with a strong sense of efficacy. Some research indicates that antinuclear activists indeed do estimate a higher probability of nuclear war (Milburn and Watanabe, 1985; Tyler and McGraw, 1983; but cf. Fiske et al., 1983). More data are clearly needed on all these points.

To summarize, antinuclear activists are distinguished by the chronic salience of the issue and their consequently concrete, detailed images. They are also distinctive by virtue of their political efficacy, in the sense that they believe nuclear war is preventable but not survivable. Antinuclear activists do not, however, differ dramatically from the majority of Americans in their attitudes toward nuclear war; they express only somewhat more extreme attitudes and feelings than does the ordinary American. Hence, it is mainly their activity, not their thoughts and feelings, that requires explanation. Issue salience and political efficacy go some distance toward doing this.

Less is known about the prodefense activist. In a sense, such people are doubly puzzling, for they are likely not only to oppose a nuclear freeze and favor a defense buildup, which puts them in a minority of Americans, but also to be active in the service of their attitudes, which also makes them unusual. One form of prodefense activism is survivalist activity that includes building a shelter, storing food and water, making family evacuation plans, and the like. Survivalists rate nuclear war as relatively probable (Tyler and McGraw, 1983; but see Hamilton et al., 1985a). Accordingly, nuclear war may well be a chronically salient issue for them, as it is for the antinuclear activist. In this case, however, salience catalyzes an entirely different sort of activity, which is in line with different preexisting attitudes. How they acquired those attitudes is unclear, but long-standing predispositions grounded in family, peer, and group identification are likely influences.

Survivalists' type of efficacy differs too from those of ordinary people and antinuclear activists. Survivalists believe that nuclear war is not preventable, but that it is survivable (Tyler and McGraw, 1983). Hence, although survivalists believe nuclear war is likely, they do not report being worried about it (Hamilton et al., 1985a; Tyler and McGraw, 1983). Consistent with their belief that nuclear war is not preventable, survivalists are low on political efficacy. Surprisingly, they are also low on what psychologists call internal locus of control; that is, they do not believe they have much effect on their lives in general. Perhaps this is consistent with their belief that responsibility for nuclear war lies with historical forces, not with the ordinary citizen or the government (Tyler and McGraw, 1983). More data are needed to describe not only the survivalist but also other types of more obviously prodefense activists.

To summarize, action first depends on people's sense of efficacy, that is, their perception of whether action might make a difference to the prevention of nuclear war and to their own survival. Action also depends on the salience of people's beliefs, that is, how often they think about nuclear war. Political efficacy and issue salience matter both to people who act to prevent nuclear war and to people who act to survive nuclear war if it occurs.

CONCLUSION

Decades ago psychologists anticipated people's fears about the bomb; they initially worked to assuage these fears, to promote public trust in the atomic experts, and to examine civil defense from a psychological perspective (Morowski and Goldstein, 1985). But these efforts soon tapered off as it became clear that, surprisingly, the ordinary person was apparently less concerned than the researchers expected. Despite high levels of reported awareness about the issues, people report relatively little fear or worry, at least in survey interviews, and most people take no action to prevent nuclear war. Many observers have wondered publicly about the ordinary citizen's apparent indifference when confronted with the potential annihilation of humankind (e.g., Goldman and Greenberg, 1982; Lifton, 1982; Mack, 1981, 1982). These contrasts have prompted the enduring puzzle variously called fear suppression, psychic numbing, denial, and apathy, which are attributed to people's feelings of impotence, helplessness, inefficacy, and the like. The discrepancy between people's nuclear understanding and their elusive emotional and behavioral concern continues to be a puzzle.

Most participants in the symposium on which this proceedings volume is based and most readers of this book probably agree that nuclear war is an important issue, as shown by their involvement. But our personal and professional involvement in this issue has a risk. It creates a danger of what social psychologists call a false consensus bias (Ross et al., 1977); that is, it is too easy to believe that the average citizen shares a sense of urgency, shares a sense that something must be done. The false consensus biases us to believe that others share our attitudes. Becoming aware of the false consensus bias means realizing that, for the average citizen, the issue is not all that salient. We must not overestimate the degree of disturbance in the average person. Although they are clearly aware and deeply concerned, nuclear war, for the most part, is not on their minds. The average person is also low on political efficacy, which is probably in contrast to the majority of readers and symposium participants. But most people's inaction is consistent with their understanding of political reality. We must not judge people by our own values.

Remaining relatively unworried and inactive, despite the horrific possibility of nuclear war, is not irrational if people are correct in judging that their activism would have no consequences. The ordinary person does not possess the antinuclear activist's sense of political efficacy, does not believe that nuclear war is preventable by citizen actions. And, according to some analysts, people are right about this: the activity of one ordinary person hardly makes a difference. Some observers argue that even collective public opinion rarely influences foreign policy; they rank public opinion far behind perceived geopolitical realities in influencing government leaders' decisions in this realm (Rosenau, 1967). Some experts even argue that the public is not competent to judge in these matters anyway. If one accepts all these premises, then ordinary people's relative lack of worry and complete inaction, despite their horrific beliefs and clear expectation that they would die in a nuclear war, are not irrational. Viewed this way, one can come to the defense of the ordinary person, and there is no massive problem revealed by the discrepancy in beliefs, feelings, and action about nuclear war.

Many readers and symposium participants would resist this conclusion. Given the unbelievable magnitude of the potential event and the fact that most people understand this magnitude to a great extent, the discrepancy between their beliefs and their relatively unworried inaction might seem intolerable. Some would call it irrational, or at least a major mental health issue (e.g., Goldman and Greenberg, 1982). Caution dictates, however, that one not confuse the magnitude of the event with the realistic possibility of affecting its occurrence. No one really knows whether citizen action will help to prevent a nuclear war. It is not an empirical question, and informed opinions differ about the effectiveness of citizen action.

Hence, those who are worried cannot take it for granted that everyone shares their urgency, but that everyone has somehow suppressed it. One sees this in some psychologists' claims that the average person is dramatically disturbed about the possibility of nuclear war. Unfortunately, it is admittedly possible that researchers overestimate the ordinary person's concerns because they themselves are professionally concerned with nuclear war; the researchers' own values and concerns may lead to inadvertent exaggeration of the psychological disruption in the ordinary person (cf. Fischhoff et al., 1983; Hamilton et al., 1985a).

Similarly, the politically active participants cannot take it for granted that everyone shares their sense of efficacy. Most people believe, rightly or wrongly, that they can do nothing with regard to nuclear war. Nevertheless, some people, not many, do share the active participants' sense of political efficacy. These are likely to be people who have been politically active before, and they can be mobilized to be active again. One role that the active few serve is to keep the issue salient for everyone.

There is a final lesson from the data reviewed here. People do have feelings and beliefs about nuclear war, and these are not inappropriate, given what is known. Granted, the issue of nuclear war is not central for most people, most of the time. When it is salient, however, people do respond to it. Because most people in the United States report that nuclear war creates worry, fear, and sadness when they think about it, and because most people support a mutual freeze, it seems likely that the effect of continued activity, on the part of some, makes the issue salient for everyone. Keeping the issue salient is likely to accentuate people's existing worry and their preference for a mutual nuclear freeze. For those inclined to be active in the service of their beliefs, there are two key tasks to give citizens a voice based on their perceptions of this horrific possibility.

First, we must find a way to give people a sense of political efficacy or hope through action. This is not easy, but one clear message of existing data is that one must pair fear-arousing communications with possible action solutions for people (cf. Skovholt et al., 1985; Wolf et al., in press). The solutions must be perceived to be politically effective and something the ordinary person is capable of doing.

Second, we must keep the issue salient by public events such as this symposium and by media coverage of those events, which, ironically, is even more important. Keeping the issue alive may help to keep us all alive.

ACKNOWLEDGMENTS

I wish to thank William Beardslee, Michael Milburn, Steven Neuberg, Mark Pavelchak, and Janet Schofield for comments on an earlier draft of this paper.

NOTES

[1]This is partly because much of the relevant hard data are only now being generated. Hence, this article, of necessity, cites several unpublished papers and convention presentations.

[2]Roughly a quarter of the population view it as very unlikely, a quarter as fairly unlikely, and a quarter as fairly likely; the remainder say it is very likely or express no opinion (The Gallup Poll, 1983).

[3]An image, for these purposes, is a conception, an impression, or an understanding; it is a mental picture, but not necessarily visual. Readers familiar with the concept of a cognitive *schema* may wish to substitute that term for *image*. Image is used here to minimize jargon and because of its connotations of something gleaned through public channels such as the media. See Fiske et al. (1983) for a fuller discussion of these issues.

[4]Readers familiar with the social psychological concepts of vividness (e.g., making the abstract concrete) and salience (e.g., bringing the issue into awareness) will note that the most likely relationship of the two concepts here is that increasing the vividness of people's concrete images apparently contributed to the salience of the nuclear war issue; see Fiske and Taylor (1984) for further discussion of these two concepts.

[5]Similarly, worry sometimes predicts antinuclear attitudes (Feshbach, 1982; Hamilton et al., 1985a).

REFERENCES

Adams, W. C., D. J. Smith, A. Salzman, R. Crossen, S. Hieber, T. Naccarato, R. Valenzuela, W. Vantine, and N. Weisbroth. 1984. Before and After *The Day After:* A Nationwide Study of a Movie's Political Impact. Paper presented at the International Communication Association meeting, San Francisco.

Baumann, D. J., L. L. Bettor, S. M. Curtis, L. S. Heller, N. F. Lamb, B. E. Ritter, C. M. Roberts, D. G. Wessels, and A. Wiebe. 1984. *The Day After:* An Experimental Investigation of Media Impact. Paper presented at the 92nd annual meeting of the American Psychological Association, Toronto, Ontario, Canada.

Berscheid, E. 1985. Interpersonal attraction. Pp. 413–483 in G. Lindzey and E. Aronson, eds., The Handbook of Social Psychology, 3rd ed. Reading, Mass.: Addison-Wesley.

Boyer, P. August 12 and 19, 1985. How Americans imagined the bomb they dropped. The cloud over the culture. The New Republic, pp. 26–31.

Brown, J. M. 1984. Attitudes Toward Violence and the Film *The Day After*. Unpublished manuscript, Lafayette College, Easton, Pa.

Carroll, J. S. 1978. The effect of imagining an event on expectations for the event: An interpretation in terms of the availability heuristic. J. Exp. Social Psychol. 14:88–96.

Cross, T. P., and L. Saxe. 1984. *The Day After:* Report of a Survey of Effects of Viewing and Beliefs About Nuclear War. Paper presented at the 92nd annual meeting of the American Psychological Association, Toronto, Ontario, Canada.

Escalona, S. K. 1982. Growing up with the threat of nuclear war: Some indirect effects on personality development. Am. J. Orthopsych. 52:600–607.

Feldman, S., and L. Sigelman. In press. The political impact of prime-time television: *The Day After*. J. Politics.

Feshbach, S. 1982. Resistance to Nuclear Disarmament: A Psychological Perspective. Paper presented at the 90th annual meeting of the American Psychological Association, Washington, D.C.

Fischhoff, B., N. Pidgeon, and S. T. Fiske. 1983. Social science and the politics of the arms race. J. Social Issues 39:161–180.

Fiske, S. T., F. Pratto, and M. A. Pavelchak. 1983. Citizens' images of nuclear war: Contents and consequences. J. Social Issues 39:41–65.

Fiske, S. T., and S. E. Taylor. 1984. Social Cognition. Reading, Mass.: Addison-Wesley.

Flamenbaum, C., A. Hunter, B. Silverstein, and C. Yatani. 1985. Demographic and Social Psychological Predictors of Nuclear Disarmament Activism. Paper presented at the meeting of the Eastern Psychological Association, Boston.

The Gallup Poll. 1983. Public opinion, pp. 265–267. Wilmington, Del.: Scholarly Resources.

Garrett, M. 1985. Psychological Differences Between Student Activists and Nonactivists in Response to the Nuclear Threat. Paper presented at the meeting of the Eastern Psychological Association, Boston.

Goldman, D. S., and W. M. Greenberg. 1982. Preparing for nuclear war: The psychological effects. Am. J. Orthopsych. 52:580–581.

Goodman, L. A., J. E. Mack, W. R. Beardslee, and R. M. Snow. 1983. The threat of nuclear war and the nuclear arms race: Adolescent experience and perceptions. Political Psychology 4:501–530.

Granberg, D., and N. Faye. 1972. Sensitizing people by making the abstract concrete: Study of the effect of "Hiroshima-Nagasaki." Am. J. Orthopsych. 42:811–815.

Gutierres, S. E., G. W. McCullough, R. Marney-Hay, R. Petty, D. J. Baumann, and M. Trost. 1984. Impact of *The Day After* on those closest to it. Paper presented at the 92nd annual meeting of the American Psychological Association, Toronto, Ontario, Canada.

Hamilton, S. B., E. L. Chavez, and W. G. Keilin. 1985a. Thoughts of Armageddon: The Relationship Between Nuclear Threat Attitudes and Cognitive/Emotional Responses. Unpublished manuscript, Colorado State University, Fort Collins, Colo.

Hamilton, S. B., W. G. Keilin, and T. A. Knox. 1985b. Thinking About the Unthinkable: The Relationship Between Death Anxiety and Cognitive/Emotional Responses to the Threat of Nuclear War. Unpublished manuscript, Colorado State University, Fort Collins, Colo.

Hamilton, S. B., T. A. Knox, and W. G. Keilin. 1985c. The Nuclear Family: Correspondence in Cognitive and Affective Reactions to the Threat of Nuclear War Between College Students and Their Parents. Unpublished manuscript, Colorado State University, Fort Collins, Colo.

Hamilton, S. B., T. A. Knox, W. G. Keilin, and E. L. Chavez. 1985d. Reactions Toward the Threat of Nuclear War: A Study of Four Subject Characteristics. Paper presented at the 93rd annual meeting of the American Psychological Association, Los Angeles.

Jeffries, V. 1974. Political generations and the acceptance or rejection of nuclear warfare. J. Social Issues 30:119–136.

Kelly, J. December 5, 1983. Fallout from a TV attack. Time, pp. 38–40.

Kiesler, C. A., R. E. Nisbett, and M. P. Zanna. 1969. On inferring one's beliefs from one's behavior. J. Personality Social Psychol. 11:321–327.

Kinder, D. R., and D. O. Sears. 1985. Public opinion and political action. Pp. 659–741 in G. Lindzey and E. Aronson, eds., The Handbook of Social Psychology, 3rd ed. Reading, Mass.: Addison-Wesley.

King, J. C. 1985. The Impact of *The Day After* on Anti-Nuclear War Behavior. Paper presented at the 93rd annual meeting of the American Psychological Association, Los Angeles.

Klineberg, O. 1984. Public opinion and nuclear war. Am. Psychol. 39:1245–1253.

Kramer, B. M., S. M. Kalick, and M. A. Milburn. 1983. Attitudes toward nuclear weapons and nuclear war: 1945–1982. J. Social Issues 39:7–24.

Ladd, E. 1982. The freeze framework. Public Opinion 5:20–41.

Levinger, G., and J. Breedlove. 1966. Interpersonal attraction and agreement: A study of marriage partners. J. Personality Social Psychol. 2:367–372.

Lifton, R. J. 1968. Death in Life: Survivors of Hiroshima. New York: Random House.

Lifton, R. J. 1982. Beyond psychic numbing: A call to awareness. Am. J. Orthopsych. 52:619–629.

Lifton, R. J. 1983. The Life of the Self: Toward a New Psychology. New York: Basic Books.

Mack, J. E. 1981. Psychosocial effects of the nuclear arms race. Bull. Atomic Sci. 37:18–23.

Mack, J. E. 1982. The perception of U.S.–Soviet intentions and other psychological dimensions of the arms race. Am. J. Orthopsych. 52:590–599.

Mayton, D. M. 1984. *The Day After:* A Quasi-Experimental Study of Its Impact. Paper presented at the 92nd annual meeting of the American Psychological Association, Toronto, Ontario, Canada.

McClenny, J. T., and L. Allbright. 1985. Psychological Responses to the Threat of Nuclear War: Structural Modeling of the Relationships Between Attitudes and Behavior. Unpublished manuscript, University of Connecticut, Storrs.

McFadden, R. D. November 22, 1983. TV atom war spurs vast discussion. New York Times, p. Y11.

Milbrath, L. W., and M. L. Goel. 1977. Political Participation, 2nd ed. Chicago: Rand McNally.

Milburn, M. A., B. M. Kramer, and P. Y. Watanabe. 1984. The Nature and Sources of Attitudes Toward a Nuclear Freeze. Paper presented at the 92nd annual meeting of the American Psychological Association, Toronto, Ontario, Canada.

Milburn, M. A., and P. Y. Watanabe. 1985. Nuclear Attitudes, Images and Behavior. Paper presented at the International Studies Association meeting, Washington, D.C.

Morowski, J. G., and S. E. Goldstein. 1985. Psychology and nuclear war: A chapter in our legacy of social responsibility. Am. Psychol. 40:276–284.

Nelson, A. 1985. Psychological equivalence: Awareness and response-ability in our nuclear age. Am. Psychol. 40:549–556.

Newcomb, M. D. 1985a. Dynamics of Nuclear Denial and Psychic Numbing: An Empirical Consideration of the Impediments to Peace. Unpublished manuscript, University of California, Los Angeles.

Newcomb, M. D. 1985b. Living with the Bomb: Nuclear Anxiety and Emotional Health. Paper presented at the 93rd annual meeting of the American Psychological Association, Los Angeles.

Newcomb, T. M. 1943. Personality and social change. New York: Dryden.

Newcomb, T. M. 1961. The Acquaintance Process. New York: Holt, Rinehart & Winston.

Oskamp, S., V. Dunwoody-Miller, J. King, L. Macbride, J. Pollard, M. White, S. Burn, and A. Konrad. 1984. The Media and Nuclear War: Reactions to Viewing *The Day After*. Paper presented at the 92nd annual meeting of the American Psychological Association, Toronto, Ontario, Canada.

Pavelchak, M., and J. Schofield. 1985. Some Determinants of Anti-Nuclear Behavior. Paper presented at the meeting of the Eastern Psychological Association, Boston.

Pilisuk, M. 1985. Psychological Accommodations to the Potential Extinction of All Life. Paper presented at the meeting of the Western Psychological Association, San Jose, Calif.

Polyson, J., J. Hillmar, and D. Kriek. 1985. Levels of Public Interest in Nuclear War: "Reader's Guide" Citations 1945–1985. Paper presented at the 93rd annual meeting of the American Psychological Association, Los Angeles.

Public Opinion. 1982. Women and men: Is a realignment under way? 5(2):21–30.

Reser, J. P. 1984. Thinking the Unthinkable: Impact of the Film, *The Day After* on the Imageability of a Nuclear Holocaust. Unpublished manuscript, James Cook University of North Queensland, Queensland, Australia.

Rosenau, J. N. 1967. Introduction. Pp. 1–10 in J. N. Rosenau, ed., Domestic Sources of Foreign Policy. New York: Free Press.

Ross, L., D. Greene, and P. House. 1977. The "false consensus effect": An egocentric bias in social perception and attribution processes. J. Exp. Social Psychol. 13:279–301.

Ruble, D. N., and T. L. Ruble. 1982. Sex stereotypes. Pp. 188–252 in A. G. Miller, ed., In the Eye of the Beholder: Contemporary Issues in Stereotyping. New York: Praeger.

Schofield, J. W., and M. A. Pavelchak. 1984. Fallout from *The Day After:* Content-Relevant Effects. Paper presented at the 92nd annual meeting of the American Psychological Association, Toronto, Ontario, Canada.

Schofield, J., and M. A. Pavelchak. 1985. *The Day After:* The impact of a media event. Am. Psychol. 40:542–548.

Schwebel, M. 1982. Effects of the nuclear war threat on children and teenagers: Implications for professionals. Am. J. Orthopsych. 52:608–618.

Skovholt, T. M., D. Moore, R. Williams, and C. Steffen. 1985. Psychological Reactions to the Nuclear War Threat. Unpublished manuscript, University of Minnesota, Minneapolis, Minn.

Taylor, S. E., and S. T. Fiske. 1978. Salience, attention, and attribution: Top of the head phenomena. Pp. 249–288 in L. Berkowitz, ed., Advances in Experimental Social Psychology, Vol. 11. New York: Academic Press.

Tesser, A. 1978. Self-generated attitude change. Pp. 289–338 in L. Berkowitz, ed., Advances in Experimental Social Psychology, Vol. 11. New York: Academic Press.

Thurlow, S. 1982. Nuclear war in human perspective: A survivor's report. Am. J. Orthopsych. 52:638–645.

Time. July 29, 1985a. What the boy saw: A fire in the sky, pp. 34–39.

Time. July 29, 1985b. What the people saw: A vision of ourselves, pp. 54–57.

Tyler, T. R., and K. M. McGraw. 1983. The threat of nuclear war: Risk interpretation and behavioral response. J. Social Issues 39:25–40.

Wagner, R. V. 1985. Psychology and the threat of nuclear war. Am. Psychol. 40:531–535.

Werner, P. D., and P. J. Roy. 1985. Measuring activism regarding the nuclear arms race. J. Personality Assess. 49:181–186.

Withey, S. B. 1954. Survey of Public Knowledge and Attitudes Concerning Civil Defense. Ann Arbor: Survey Research Center, Institute for Social Research, University of Michigan.

Wolf, S., W. L. Gregory, and W. G. Stephan. In press. Protection motivation theory: Prediction of intentions to engage in anti-nuclear war behaviors. J. Appl. Social Psychol.

Wolman, C. S. 1984. Current Consciousness About Nuclear Weapons in the United States. Unpublished manuscript.

The Medical Implications of Nuclear War, Institute of
Medicine. © 1986 by the National Academy of Sciences.
National Academy Press, Washington, D.C.

Hope and the Denial of
Stress in the Nuclear Age

SHLOMO BREZNITZ, PH.D.
Haifa University, Haifa, Israel

It must be with a shared sense of frustration that we try to comprehend
all the incredible things that are in store for us if nuclear war breaks out,
and at the same time, to hear about the minimal level of involvement with
the issues by the general population.

This discrepancy, which was the focus that Susan Fiske took in her
paper on adults' images of nuclear war (this volume), is very frustrating
because one has the sense that not much more can be said or done to
increase our awareness or stimulate action. I would like to discuss some
of the key findings that have been reported, and to suggest some explanations for some of these disturbing discrepancies.

Unfortunately, there are very few in-depth data which go beyond self-
report and paper and pencil tasks, whether with children, adolescents, or
adults; consequently, some of the ideas are extrapolations and speculations.

From the papers presented in this volume I have uncovered five points
that I found to be particularly important: (1) Children and adolescents do
seem to be quite seriously worried. (2) They claim that they receive little
information about nuclear war and the nuclear threat. (3) Adults appear
to be less concerned than adolescents. (4) Considering the problem and
the understanding of the information, there appears to be relatively little
fear and emotion and much less action. (5) Parents and children apparently
do not spend much time talking about these problems together.

Let me start by making a distinction, which is a very problematic one,
between the lack of concern on the one hand and active denial on the

467

other. If somebody claims that he or she does understand what is at stake and at the same time does not often feel very worried or anxious about it, does this suggest that a person is not truly concerned or that there is some active denial taking place that suppresses these worries so that the person can maintain his or her life-style? This is not an easy question to answer, but it is very important because it holds very different implications. Most of the findings about adults suggest that there is at least some extent of denial of a particular kind that I will describe below. The evidence presented in the papers in this volume suggests that something happens between adolescence and adulthood that makes people less worried.

What can it be that makes people less worried? Did they find out something about the world that justifies their being less worried? This is unlikely. If there is evidence that up to some point there is awareness and worry and then the worry is reduced, it cannot be claimed that the person was never exposed to the information and did not reach the point of feeling worry. Something active must take place to reduce it. Among several psychological processes that can accomplish this, a particular kind of denial is probably the best candidate.

There are some other ''symptoms'' that suggest that denial is at work, in addition to the data presented about children from both Norway and the United States.

It is of some interest to note that adults exaggerate the risks of disasters from nuclear power plants, as compared with the risks of living under a dam, which could break and cause flooding, even though objective analysis of the risks suggests that the second threat is much more serious than the first one.

One wonders whether people are not displacing some of their worries to something that is related to nuclear war, like nuclear power plants, and expressing their fears by focusing on a less-devastating aspect.

Denial is often useful and sometimes lifesaving. There is some medical evidence that suggests that people in great trouble sometimes have a better chance of survival if they deny the enormity of what is happening to them during crises. Thus results of studies by Hackett and Cassem (1975) in a Boston hospital of patients in the intensive care unit just shortly after they have had a heart attack suggest that those patients who actively deny what is happening to them have a better chance of coming out of the hospital alive than those whose evaluations of their situation are more realistic.

But denial can also be dangerous. The obvious danger is that in some situations it can lead to procrastination in seeking help or to avoidance of action that might prevent harm. Two simple illustrations can help exemplify this. Studies suggest that between 40 and 50 percent of patients who are subsequently diagnosed as having cancer seek medical attention much too late, not because they were not aware of any symptoms but because they were fearful to find out that it might be a serious problem. Another illustration that is quite dramatic is the story of a person who, in the midst of very severe chest pain, starts to do push-ups or to run up and down stairs to convince himself that if he can still do that, it obviously cannot be a heart attack. There is no limit to what one can do in order to achieve temporary relief from major anxiety.

It used to be thought that denial is a very simple and primitive defense, but more and more it has been determined that there are many different kinds of denial, each of which serves different purposes at different stages. Forms of denial go all the way from some minor changes in perceptions to perhaps what is the most extreme form of denial, fainting. One hears some terrible news and faints; losing consciousness is a perfect time-out from threatening information.

Denial cannot ever be complete, because one must process the information in order to decide whether to deny it. Thus at some level the information must infiltrate the consciousness; otherwise, denial would be totally indiscriminate.

One way to look at the different kinds of denial is to view them like different stages of defense. One starts with the simple forms, and if they do not work, because there is evidence to the contrary, then there is the second level of defense, and the third, and the fourth, and so on. I believe that in the sphere of nuclear threats people are now stuck at a level of defense that is particularly difficult to alter. Research suggests that the first and easiest form of denial is the *denial of personal relevance* (Breznitz, 1983). People think, ''Sure, there are problems, but they really don't concern me. I don't have to worry.'' When there is evidence to the contrary, such as in the case of the threat of nuclear holocaust, it is impossible to maintain this particular posture for long. The second type of denial is often the *denial of urgency*: ''Yes, I, too, am under danger, but there is time and there is no reason to worry now.'' Because emotion, particularly fear and anxiety, are always affected by temporal considerations, when there is time, there is no need to be anxious.

One has the illusion that a lot can be done in a short time. As T. S. Eliot said, ''In a minute there is time for a thousand decisions and revisions which a minute will reverse,'' which gives us some hope, perhaps. At the same time, one wonders whether, if T. S. Eliot knew that the warning time would be so short, he would still have made this point.

The third level of denial is the *denial of vulnerability*. One can still maintain the belief: ''Yes, it is dangerous; it is dangerous to me; it is very close, but when it comes I will be able to deal with it. I will be able to handle it.''

Often, there is the hyperbolic reasoning (like the person who does the push-ups in order to convince himself that the chest pains cannot be a heart attack): "The very fact that I still don't do anything about it suggests that it is not so dangerous, that I can deal with it when the time comes."

When denial of vulnerability is also removed, as the evidence presented in this volume clearly suggests, there comes the fourth kind of denial, and that is a particularly difficult one. This kind of denial, which is very prevalent, is the *denial of responsibility*. It is almost the opposite of the denial of vulnerability. Not that, "When the time comes, I will be able to deal with it," but "It doesn't matter what I do, because it wouldn't change anything." I submit that this is the stage at which most of the world's enlightened citizens really are, i.e., the stage of denial of responsibility. They know the facts and are able to give information about how horrible a nuclear holocaust could be, and they estimate as one-third the probability that in their lifetime it will happen and believe that there is nothing that they can do about it.

This is different from what Lifton called "resignation," a point that I will discuss below.

If this analysis is true, then additional information about how terrible it is going to be is not going to overcome denial. It is only going to push people into more extreme forms of denial, and indeed there are more extreme forms of denial, like denial of information. There has been information presented about some children who do not want to hear or think about it, which is a more extreme form of denial, since it implies that the filter has already been placed at the point of information input.

Therefore, I do not think that more information about how important it is to consider the nuclear threat is going to change much. Also, consideration should be made about how easy it is to deny the information in the case of the nuclear threat. First, there is no direct experience and there is nothing concrete on which to build one's images of subjective probability. What is it that is going to happen when there is a nuclear war? We have heard about how abstract these images are, how important a television program of a particular kind can be, precisely because it provides common images that become more concrete. On television people see faces, not numbers. It is not abstract anymore, but it is a particular family that is involved.

There are other reasons that denial is very easy to maintain; one of them is that the nuclear threat is so big that it does not make sense. Even the experiences in Hiroshima and Nagasaki, which could have provided a focus for our images, are irrelevant considering that whatever could happen in a nuclear war would be on a totally different scale of magnitude. Thus, even the few images that people can still perhaps muster from a real occurrence are irrelevant.

Finally, one of the main reasons that it is so easy to deny the nuclear threat and not be concerned about it on a day-to-day basis is that the world is too much with us. People have other things on their minds. People are worried about interest rates and about diet. I discovered a short quotation that I found to be very illuminating. It is taken from the *Beverly Hills Diet*, by Judy Mazel, and it talks about the use of a scale in the morning to measure one's weight: "The scale, that little mechanical device that has more effect on us than an atom bomb. It can literally make or break our day. I have seen the most gorgeous, the most powerful, the most secure, and the most self-assured, crumble beneath its force."

The nuclear threat has little social relevance, because we are all in the same boat. If some people were more threatened than others, then it could have been translated into a motivational force, but it is a great equalizer, and therefore it has very little social, interactional relevance to everyday life.

At this point I would like to make a distinction between denial and its very close cousin hope. There are two ways to defend against terrible images of the future. One is to concentrate on the negative aspects and try not to see them, not to hear them, and not to think about them, resorting to the various forms of denial; the other defense consists of locating whatever positive elements are there and amplifying them. This is hope.

There are different combinations of hope and denial. It is possible to have hope based on denial; this is an illusory hope that is continuously challenged by new information because it is based on false information.

There is also hope that can be called mature hope, in which case a person is aware of the danger and yet maintains a level of hope. This, I believe, is related to the findings reported by Dr. Beardslee (this volume), in that those children who are more worried also have a greater sense of efficacy and think that there is greater hope to prevent the nuclear holocaust.

One must be worried in order to have hope, because by denying that which causes worry, one cannot think about it, and there is no such thing as hoping without thinking.

The worst combination is when there is neither denial nor hope, which implies resignation and depression. Denial can be viewed as a vital psychological sign. It suggests that a person is putting up a defense, trying to protect him- or herself from something terrible. Once that is given up, there is no denial and no hope.

Without hope there cannot be any action or involvement, and denial prevents that action because of anxiety-inducing reminders. Reminders often are very painful; therefore, denial prevents action that would remind a person of that which is being denied.

The impact of reminders can be illustrated by patients who have had a heart attack. During recovery they must maintain a strict regimen to keep physically fit. One of the problems that often comes up in this regimen is that even though the patients feel that they are in good shape, the various things that they must do constantly remind them that they are potentially at risk. This is one of the reasons that there is backsliding and a lack of adherence to their therapeutic regimen: they do not want to face these reminders all the time.

I want to suggest two possible ways out of this discrepancy between action and understanding. People can be encouraged to engage in protective behavior and increase the level of involvement of the general population with regard to the nuclear threat.

One point refers to what is called desynchrony between action and emotion. One often finds that fear and protective behavior do not go together. At first it was thought that if people are scared, then they do something to protect themselves; this in turn reduces fear, which reduces the motivation to protect themselves. The danger then grows and fear goes up again, leading to a continuous dynamic flow between action and emotion. That, however, is not what seems to be the case. There is a desynchrony between the two. Sometimes fear does not lead to action, and sometimes action can be taken without being under the control of fear. That is the only reason that people sometimes have courage; namely, they do something in spite of their fear.

There appears to be two distinct reasons for self-protection. The usual one is to reduce danger, and the other one is to reduce present worry. Nobody would be able to sell insurance if the only motivation to buy insurance would be that if something terrible happens, the family will get the money. People do not want to think about anything happening to them. They are willing to buy insurance because it makes them feel better now, not because something is going to happen tomorrow or a few years later.

Therefore, if there is interest in motivating large groups of people, youngsters, adolescents, and young adults in being more concerned and more active about the nuclear threat, they cannot be motivated by the belief that they can prevent a nuclear holocaust. The only motivation that makes sense is the motivation that can work on a day-to-day basis; that is, to do something for this cause is part of a definition of being a better person today.

Let me mention briefly some things about home and family. It has been stated in some of the papers in this volume that there is a problem in that children do not often speak with their parents about the nuclear threat, and in turn the parents apparently do not speak often with their children. One can understand that part of the shift from adolescence to adulthood, which has been seen in the data reported in this volume, is due to the fact that as adolescents grow up, they need to stabilize their images of the world. The image of inevitable doom does not allow one to make long-term commitments in terms of a career, a family, and raising children; so perhaps it can be understood why young adults must invest more in this denial process in order to be able to move into their new roles. In addition, there might be yet another problem, which is hinted at in Beardslee's (1986) report. The problem is that adolescents might take advantage of the nuclear threat issue as something that serves as a rationale for a particular life-style. We have heard about the drugs. We have heard *carpe diem*, live for today, because there is no tomorrow. There is then a distinct possibility that the parents challenge this, pushing their feelings in the opposite direction from those of their children. They try to minimize the danger of the nuclear threat and actually lose the ability to honestly discuss the issue with them. I believe that it is of tremendous importance that this one issue be removed from the intergenerational conflict. There are enough other conflicts to deal with.

REFERENCES

Beardslee, W. R. 1986. Children's and adolescents' perceptions of the threat of nuclear war: implications of recent studies. This volume.

Breznitz, S. 1983. The Denial of Stress. New York: International Universities Press.

Hackett, T. P., and N. Cassem. 1975. Psychological management of the myocardial infarction patient. J. Human Stress 1:25–38.

The Medical Implications of Nuclear War, Institute of
Medicine. © 1986 by the National Academy of Sciences.
National Academy Press, Washington, D.C.

The Nuclear Arms Race and
the Psychology of Power

JEROME D. FRANK, M.D., PH.D.
*The Johns Hopkins University School of Medicine
Baltimore, Maryland*

INTRODUCTION

The information presented in this volume on the reactions of children,
adolescents, and the general public to the threat of a nuclear holocaust
has been most illuminating. This paper shifts the focus from the potential
victims of such a disaster to its creators, the national decision makers of
the nuclear powers.

Leaders of the national security establishments throughout the world
are remarkably impervious to outside pressures. Marches, rallies, and
demonstrations attracting millions of participants; numerous writings in
medical and academic journals; and many conferences have had no appreciable impact on the nuclear arms race. There are reasons for the
ineffectiveness of such activities. Probably the most important is the rapid
formation of vast technological, scientific, economic, bureaucratic, and
military constituencies behind every new weapon system. Often the only
decision involving a new weapon system is the first one. Once a bureaucratic unit has been set up and money has been allocated, the process
unrolls virtually automatically from research to testing and then to development and deployment.

This paper examines a psychological feature of national leaders that
contributes to their resistance to public pressure for nuclear disarmament
and is probably the chief psychological instigator of the nuclear arms
race—the will to power. The Roman historian Tacitus has called this drive
the most flagrant of all the passions, and the contemporary military his-

torian Michael Howard has written, "The causes of war remain rooted in perceptions by statesmen of the growth of hostile power and the fears for the restriction . . . of their own" (Howard, 1984).

The counterpart of the drive for power is the equally strong propensity to obey (Milgram, 1974). Were there not a drive to obey orders, leaders would be powerless, and this drive seems to be as powerful as any other human propensity. In recognition of this fact, instillation of automatic obedience to command is a major function of all military training. In response to a leader's commands, human groups perform incredible acts of both heroism and destruction, including perpetrating massacres and committing mass suicide.

Examined in this paper are some psychological aspects of the exercise of power in the anarchic and dangerous international environment with special reference to pursuit of the nuclear arms competition. The presentation therefore inevitably emphasizes the aspects of power that are socially destructive. Obviously the power drive accounts for ambition, competitiveness, and other characteristics of members of a healthy society. The prevalence of such qualities is necessary for the emergence of leaders who are essential for the organization and functioning of any group. Without people willing to give orders and others willing to obey them, societies could not organize themselves or protect themselves against the external threats.

In organized, cohesive societies, moreover, the drive for power generally expresses itself constructively. Leaders seek to enhance the welfare of their followers, and rules, social customs, and shared values inhibit the use of violence to resolve conflicts. Only in the absence of such constraints is violence the final arbiter of power struggles (Schmookler, 1983).

PERSONAL CHARACTERISTICS OF LEADERS

All successful leaders have certain psychological characteristics that, in varying degrees, are essential to the exercise of power. Among these characteristics are practicality, a low threshold for suspiciousness, optimism, and strength of will.

Successful exercise of leadership requires that leaders acquire and control the means of exerting power, whether these means be weaponry or mastery of the structure and finances of the organizations they lead. As a result, leaders are characteristically men of action who seek to master practical problems as they arise. Most are impatient of abstractions and theoretical considerations.

To advance in the hierarchy of leadership, it is helpful, perhaps essential, for an aspiring leader to have a low threshold of suspicion of the intentions of others. All leaders at times must conceal information from others, even if this requires dissembling or deceit. An example was President Kennedy's concealment from the Russian ambassador of his knowledge of the Russian missile bases being constructed in Cuba. In their rise to power, furthermore, leaders are likely to encounter some superiors who wish to hold them back, rivals who seek to displace them, and subordinates who seek to curry favor. The recognition of leaders that they themselves sometimes dissemble and their experiences in thwarting machinations of those around them may facilitate the formation of the image of the enemy discussed below.

Leaders' optimism contributes to their ability to persevere in the face of disappointments and defeats. Leaders who have reached the top have typically experienced more victories than defeats, sometimes despite prophecies of defeat by their advisers, so such leaders develop high confidence in their judgment and ability to prevail.

Optimism contributes finally to strength of will, probably the most important single psychological attribute of the successful leader. Strength of will involves not only the ability to persist in spite of obstacles but also to endure physical suffering as well as unpleasant emotions such as fear. Moreover the effective use of power involves the infliction of as much suffering on the opponent as is necessary to prevail.

In this connection a major psychological reason for the failure of antinuclear activists to influence national policies may be that their major appeals are to fear and compassion. Appeals to these emotions have been implicit throughout this symposium in the delineations of the many and varied horrors of a nuclear holocaust, and the distressing feelings the prospect of such an event arouses in children and the general public.

Fear powerfully motivates most people, and appeals to compassion resonate particularly with physicians and other members of the helping professions. Yet it is hard to imagine two emotions less likely to influence those with a strong power drive. In fact, for members of the national security establishment, appeals to such emotions are counterproductive because those who make them are readily dismissed as cowards and sentimentalists.

EMOTIONAL INSTIGATORS OF VIOLENCE

International struggles differ primarily from domestic ones in that there are no enforceable rules for guiding the course of conflict into nonviolent channels, and opportunities for mutual accommodation are restricted by the fact that two rival groups may be operating under different rules and with different values. In such an anarchic situation, victory goes to the side that can bring to bear superior means of violence.

The proclivity to resort to violence is deeply rooted in the human psyche. At an emotional level the two main instigators of violent behavior are fear and anger. Fear instigates violence in an animal only when it feels cornered; that is, when it is unable to flee. Because of their symbolic powers, humans often feel cornered even when physically they are not. The recognition of a warrior that flight would mark him as a coward and expose him to the contempt of his fellows is often a more powerful obstacle to flight than any physical barrier could be, leaving the warrior no alternative but to fight. Similarly, a national leader might well feel cornered by the prospect of loss of his domestic power base if he yielded to an enemy's threat.

Anger, which is the typical response to frustration, evokes the urge to harm or destroy its source. Since under the goad of the drive to power groups seek continually to expand, inevitably they eventually collide and thus frustrate each other. So the international arena never lacks for stimuli to fear and anger.

The role of emotions in influencing decisions of national leaders is hard to evaluate. Historically emotions have influenced leaders' behavior in crises where rapid decisions had to be made under conditions of extreme tension (George, 1986). By and large, however, leaders are among the most emotionally stable members of their societies, because in order to reach the top they must have weathered many emotionally stressful situations.

Although fear and anger are prime instigators of violence in hand-to-hand combat, the major destructiveness of modern war is inflicted on invisible targets by bombs and shells launched by soldiers who are simply obeying orders. Moreover, decisions of heads of state to go to war are usually based ostensibly on highly rational calculations. On the other hand, emotions can influence ostensibly rational decisions of national leaders in subtle ways (Janis, in press). Emotional reactions almost certainly contribute to the frequent misinterpretations by leaders of antagonistic groups of each other's capabilities and intentions.

THE IMAGE OF THE ENEMY

The major psychological instigator of the accumulation of weaponry and the major target for its use has always been another group perceived as an enemy (Frank, 1982). Humans, like all social creatures, are programmed to fear and mistrust members of groups other than their own.

When two such groups find themselves in conflict this mutual distrust escalates to what has been termed the image of the enemy. No matter who the conflicting groups are, each sees the other as warlike, cruel, and treacherous. This perception was correct for those societies, from the Assyrians to the Nazis, whose values glorified military conquest and death in battle.

Fortunately, according to the dominant values of the two leading international antagonists today, the United States and the Soviet Union, war is an evil, justified only in the service of the highest moral goals or in self-defense. Groups that hold these values see themselves as peaceful, honorable, and humane, while portraying their opponents as treacherous, warlike, and cruel. As a result, each group attributes its own violent acts to irresistible environmental forces, while similar actions by the other are attributed to their innate evil qualities, a phenomenon psychologists have termed the attribution error (Jones and Davis, 1965). Each antagonist attributes the atrocious acts of an enemy to the enemy's viciousness, while attributing those committed by itself to regrettable necessities.

Unfortunately the evil image of the enemy is a self-fulfilling prophecy. Whatever the characteristics of warring groups initially, each group, in its effort to combat what it perceives as the treacherousness and warlikeness of the other, becomes treacherous and warlike itself. Enemies that do not recognize each other to be treacherous and warlike would not long survive. So each antagonist can legitimately justify its own accumulation of weaponry as being necessary for self-defense.

VIOLENCE AND NUCLEAR WEAPONS

In an anarchic world the ultimate means of controlling the behavior of an enemy has been the threat or actual use of violence. Efforts to resolve international conflicts by negotiation have always been conducted in this context. The creditability of the threat of violence depended on the ability to maintain the tightest control possible over the course of battle should negotiations break down. Control was sought through battle plans based primarily on experience with previous wars. Even when based on extensive previous experience, these plans have often failed to work under battle conditions. Scenarios for waging limited or controlled nuclear war are based only on extrapolations from Hiroshima and Nagasaki and the results of underground tests. Most of the creators of these scenarios have never been in combat or even witnessed a nuclear explosion, and none, of course, has experienced a nuclear holocaust. To quote a high-ranking military expert: "In a very literal use of the language, they do not know what they are talking about" (T. L. Davies, Rear Admiral, U.S. Navy, personal communication, 1982). If battle plans based on extensive experience so often failed under conditions of actual combat, what are the chances of success for these computerized nuclear fantasies?

In addition to the unfamiliarity of nuclear weapons, their unprecedented destructiveness coupled with such phenomena as electromagnetic pulses hamper the ability to maintain the tight command and control that would be required to assure the successful use of nuclear weapons in battle. Breakdowns of command and control leading to serious errors have frequently occurred under the stress and confusion of combat. Nuclear weapons allow virtually no margin for error. As the historian Henry Steele Commager puts it, "Technologically for the first time we've reached the stage of the irretrievable mistake."

National leaders are well aware of these considerations. They nevertheless continue to place their faith in weaponry because no alternative means of exercising power is in sight. They continue to create ever more elaborate and sophisticated nuclear weapon systems in hopes of acquiring meaningful superiority over their rivals.

NUCLEAR WEAPONS AND CONCEPTUAL INERTIA

To be able to pursue this goal, leaders must psychologically assimilate nuclear weapons to conventional weapons, with which relative power had meaning. The view of nuclear weapons as simply bigger conventional ones is a manifestation of what has been called conceptual inertia or the force of habit. Whenever humans are faced with a brand new problem they try to make it look like an old, familiar one and then attempt to solve it by the same means that succeeded with the familiar one.

The assimilation of nuclear weapons to conventional ones is abetted by the misuse of language. Words used to describe arms races and nuclear weapons are still almost exclusively those used for conventional weapons. Concepts such as superiority, inferiority, defense, margin of safety, and so on, dominate the language of military affairs. As semanticists have pointed out, in the absence of actual experience reality is what we tell ourselves it is, so if we use the wrong words to describe a situation, we are off on the wrong foot before we even know we have started to think (Rapoport, 1984).

To cite one example, every speaker in this symposium has used the terms nuclear war to refer to a nuclear holocaust, while simultaneously providing abundant evidence that a nuclear holocaust differs fundamentally from war in at least two crucial respects: it cannot be won in any meaningful sense of the term, and its destructiveness continues and probably increases long after hostilities have ceased. The mere use of the word war, by evoking images of the possibilities of victory and of survival of an intact society, can subtly distort one's thinking about the nuclear threat.

The pursuit of greater security through technology is strikingly exemplified by the Strategic Defense Initiative. Proponents justify research on this program by citing the solutions of many problems long thought to be insoluble, examples being human flight, the splitting of the atom, and the cracking of the genetic code. Moreover, an effective defense, it has been said, has been developed against every weapon in the past. This statement is probably true, but only because a considerably less than perfect defense was adequate against even the most powerful prenuclear weapon. Adequate protection against nuclear warheads would require a virtually perfect defense. This has never been achieved against any weapon because the same mental processes that devise the defense are simultaneously thinking of ways of circumventing it.

The triumphs of technology in mastering inanimate nature depend on the fact that the physical world does not fight back. The problem remains stationary during attempts to solve it. The real problem posed by an enemy's weapons, however, lies not in their physical properties but in the mental processes of the enemy's weapons experts. Since the mental processes of all humans are similar, although one side may achieve a temporary technological advantage, the other inevitably catches up.

The optimism of national leaders seems to prevent them from drawing this obvious conclusion, creating what has been termed the fallacy of the last move. Leaders of each side apparently believe that its latest technological solution to threats created by an enemy's weapons will assure final victory, while actually both are pursuing an ever-receding goal.

NUCLEAR WEAPONS AND DEMONSTRATION OF RESOLVE

As mentioned earlier, the successful exercise of power depends on both possession of the means of power and demonstration of the will to use it. Stronger will has often been a more important determinant of the victory than arms—witness Hitler's successful invasion of the Rhineland in the face of vastly stronger French military power and the victory of the North Vietnamese over the United States.

The more conventional weapons a nation had the more powerful it appeared to be and, indeed, the more powerful it really was. The accumulation of nuclear weapons, beyond the level where each nuclear opponent can destroy the other many times over, no matter how large or sophisticated the other's nuclear arsenal (a level long since exceeded by the United States and the Soviet Union), conveys only the appearance of security and power. As a result, the main function of nuclear weapons has become to demonstrate determination to prevail. For example, President Reagan has argued for the support of the MX and other weapons systems of dubious military value on this ground: "Indeed should Congress delay or eliminate the Peacekeeper program, it would send an unmistakable signal to the Soviet Union that we do not possess the resolve required . . . to maintain . . . the policy of deterrence" (Reagan, 1985).

To put it bluntly, with nuclear weapons appearance is really all that counts: ". . . objective reality, whatever that may be, is simply irrelevant: only the subjective phenomena of perception and value-judgment count" (Luttwak, 1977). Furthermore, an arsenal that is continually innovating is a more convincing demonstration of will than one that is static: "A growing and innovative arsenal will be perceived as more powerful than one which is static—even if the latter retains an advantage in purely technical terms" (Kline, 1975).

These arguments, incidentally, provide intellectual justification for the pursuit of an endless arms race not only with the military establishments of other nations but also within the military establishment of each of them. Under the spur of the drive for power each of the military services competes with the other for a larger share of the military budget, and each goes to great length to justify its need for ever new and more sophisticated weaponry.

A possibly hopeful consequence of the universal recognition that the use of nuclear weapons in combat carries an inordinately high risk is that, in contrast to previous arms races, the major purpose of both nuclear superpowers is not to win a nuclear war but to avoid or prevent one. Unfortunately, this goal itself becomes a justification for pursuit of the nuclear arms race.

The justification goes something like this: Prudence requires that military policy be based on the worst case assessment, the worst case in this instance being that the opponents believe they can win a nuclear war. Each side can quote ample evidence for this possibility in the form of public statements by military and political leaders, military directives, elaborate preparations to enable essential leaders to function during a prolonged nuclear war, and the like. Should the opponents come to believe that they could prevail in a nuclear war, the argument continues, they might threaten to attack. Our side would then be faced with the dread alternatives of yielding to this nuclear blackmail or launching a nuclear holocaust. Therefore our side must maintain escalation dominance—that is, sufficient superiority at every level of armaments and in all nuclear weapon systems, so that the opponents could not possibly believe blackmail would succeed.

In short, there seems to be no limit to the intellectual gymnastics leaders of national security establishments will perform to avoid confronting the realization that weapons—chemical and biological as well as nuclear— are becoming too destructive to be usable as instruments of power.

GROUNDS FOR HOPE CREATED BY NEW TECHNOLOGIES

The analysis I have presented implies a bleak future for humankind. In searching for crumbs of hope, I recollect that violence is the ultimate source of power only in an anarchic world. As already mentioned, within an orderly community resort to violence is inhibited by customs and rules, and leaders are free to devote their talents to socially desirable goals. Fortunately, technological innovations as radical as nuclear weaponry for the first time in human history have created a possibility that the psychological grounds for a world order, namely a worldwide sense of community, could be achieved.

A hopeful consideration in this respect is that nations can change from enemies to friends with remarkable rapidity when they discover that cooperation can yield vastly greater benefits than antagonism to both. Witness the evolution of relationships between the People's Republic of China and the United States. In 1976, according to public opinion polls, about 75 percent of Americans saw China as a hostile power. Only 6 years later, in 1982, the same percentage saw China as a friendly power or close ally (Kalven, 1982), even though the Chinese leaders, like the Russian ones, were still atheists and had treated their own people as ruthlessly as the Soviet leaders did theirs.

The most immediate task is to reduce mutual fear and mistrust among the nations of the world. Technological advances as revolutionary as nuclear weaponry are now available to promote this goal. Modern communication equipment is already being used in the hot line and to reduce the probability of incidents at sea, two important steps to reducing the mutual fear of nuclear war starting by inadvertence or accident.

At the public level, a major technological advance is worldwide electronic communication by satellite. Electronic communications could be used with great effectiveness to increase mutual understanding among the peoples of the world. Millions of international voice channels will soon be available (Ahmad and Hashmi, 1983), and already it is possible to reach almost everyone on earth simultaneously. Even many of the very poor possess transistor radios, and television receivers are set up in many village squares. Audiovisual communication circumvents the literacy barrier and has considerably more effect on behavior than the written word.

A more potent method for reducing international mistrust than increased communication is international cooperation toward goals that all nations want but none can achieve alone. The modern world provides many new opportunities and incentives for cooperation in the pursuit of such superordinate goals. Successful examples are the Antarctic Treaty based on the International Geophysical Year, the program devised by the nations bordering the Mediterranean to clean it up, and the elimination of smallpox. There is good experimental evidence that although no one episode of cooperation has much effect on group antagonisms, repeated experiences of this sort do gradually build a sense of mutual trust (Sherif and Sherif, 1966).

CONCLUSION

The emergence of nuclear, biological, and chemical weapons of unimaginable destructiveness will eventually force national leaders to recognize that continued reliance on these instruments of power is incompatible with survival of their own nations if not civilization itself.

To put it bluntly, these weapons are making war obsolete as an arbiter of international conflict. As a result, national leaders will be forced to find other means of satisfying the will to power. Concomitantly many new technologies are emerging that for the first time could enable the peoples of all nations, through cooperative activities, to achieve heights of well-being that our ancestors could not even imagine.

Perhaps it is not too much to hope that the threat of annihilation by violent conflict on the one hand and the prospect of unprecedented benefits through international cooperation on the other will yet persuade the world's leaders to use their power for constructive rather than destructive ends.

REFERENCES

Ahmad, I., and J. Hashmi. 1983. World peace through improved perception and understanding. Pp. 1–3 in Proceedings of the Thirty-Second Pugwash Conference on Science and World Affairs. London: Pugwash Conference on Science and World Affairs.

Frank, J. D. 1982. The image of the enemy. Pp. 115–136 in Sanity and Survival in the Nuclear Age. New York: Random House.

George, A. L. 1986. The impact of crisis-induced stress on decision making. This volume.

Howard, M. 1984. The causes of wars. Wilson Quarterly, Summer, 99.

Janis, I. In press. Problems of international crisis management in the nuclear age. J. Social Issues.

Jones, E. E., and K. E. Davis. 1965. From acts to dispositions: the attribution process in person perception. In L. Berkowitz (ed.), Advances in Experimental Social Psychology, Vol. 2. New York: Academic Press.

Kalven, J. 1982. A talk with Louis Harris. Bull. Atomic Sci. September, 3–5.

Kline, R. 1975. World power assessment. Washington, D.C.: Center for Strategic and International Studies.

Luttwak, E. N. 1977. Perceptions of military force and U.S. policy. Survival, January-February, 4.

Milgram, S. 1974. Obedience to Authority. New York: Harper & Row.

Rapoport, A. 1984. Preparation for nuclear war: The final madness. Am. J. Orthopsych. 54:524–529.

Reagan, R. R. 1985. Message to the Congress, March 4.

Schmookler, A. B. 1983. The Parable of the Tribes: The Problem of Power in Social Evolution. Berkeley, Calif.: University of California Press.

Sherif, M., and C. W. Sherif. 1966. In Common Predicament: Social Psychology of Intergroup Conflict and Cooperation. Boston: Houghton Mifflin.

The Medical Implications of Nuclear War, Institute of
Medicine. © 1986 by the National Academy of Sciences.
National Academy Press, Washington, D.C.

Managerial Demands of
Modern Weapons Systems

JOHN D. STEINBRUNER, PH.D.
The Brookings Institution, Washington, D.C.

Other papers presented in this volume discussed the psychology of
individual decision makers. As a complement to this analysis, I would
like to examine the context in which decision makers must operate. I will
focus on the burdens that modern military forces impose upon decision
makers and on some of the very predictable difficulties that individual
decision makers are likely to have in dealing with them, particularly
decision makers in the American political system.

Not the least of these burdens is the uniqueness of the current situation.
Contemporary military forces have a combination of properties that make
them much more difficult to manage under crisis circumstances than were
their historical counterparts: the extreme destructiveness of individual
weapons, the rapid timing of the delivery vehicles, the technical complexity of weapons that imposes very intricate operational requirements
on the forces that manage and operate them, and the worldwide scale of
deployment.

It is not frequently realized that the full maturation of the military
situation has taken considerable time, and it probably has only been in
the last decade that both sides have really had fully integrated and developed forces. This means that any experience before this time can be
drawn upon for evidence only by using very uncertain extrapolations.

Fortunately, the world has survived this condition for at least a decade,
and that fact has to do with the success of modern management techniques
for military forces in peacetime. Advanced communications and automated
information processing have made safe and coherent management of these

arsenals feasible under normal circumstances, but by extrapolation it can be ascertained that in all probability this coherent management could not be sustained under the conditions of a nuclear war. Though individual weapons probably could survive a dedicated attack in fairly substantial numbers, the military organizations necessary for strategic management could not. If explicitly directed to that purpose, for example, only a small fraction of the current U.S. or Soviet nuclear arsenals would be required to incapacitate the opponent's command system. That fraction, depending on which estimates are used, varies from 1 to 5 percent of the current nuclear arms inventories, and 1 percent is likely enough. Managerial coherence is at once the most critical and the most vulnerable aspect of contemporary military forces.

Under peacetime circumstances the dominant objective of the managerial system is that of preventing any unauthorized use of even an individual nuclear weapon. This objective has been labeled by outside observers as that of negative control, although that is not the standard usage within the military. Elaborate, and so far very successful, procedures have been worked out within all military systems to guarantee that negative control can be exercised under all situations that are normally encountered, and again, for more than 20 years the world has successfully survived under these arrangements.

If negative control procedures were to be preserved unaltered under advanced crisis circumstances, however, they would expose military organizations to decisive defeat by means of destroying their central command authorities. This has been recognized, and for this reason all military forces have established a competing managerial objective of positive control. The essence of positive control is to ensure that authorization to conduct military missions can be provided and that authoritative orders will be carried out. Strategic forces exercise continuously to be sure that they can do just that.

One of the principal effects of crisis is that it would force the military organizations to go through changes of state that in effect would adjust the balance between managerial directives of negative and positive control. To some degree these state changes are explicitly thought out and organized in advance by formalized alert procedures, but they cannot be completely determined or centrally controlled in their entirety. Operational procedures are too complex, too widely dispersed, and too responsive to the immediate circumstances of individual weapons commanders for centralized direction to be feasible. To a significant extent the changes in state in a military organization under crisis are necessarily spontaneous, and their full effects cannot be known in advance by anyone, however wise he might be.

As has become familiar in the long discussion of deterrence, the governing policies of the two major military establishments, those of the United States and the USSR, are disciplined by the conditions of strategic parity. The prevailing balance of military power confers no decisive global advantage on either the United States or the Soviet Union, and there is no serious prospect for changing that fact in the foreseeable future, however strong political aspirations to do so might be. It is a fact that neither side can wish away by political rhetoric. Whatever that rhetoric might be, both superpowers are compelled to act in a crisis to try to avoid global war, and both thoroughly understand that.

At the same time, both superpowers are compelled to acknowledge that a threat to the managerial coherence of their forces gives powerful incentive to initiate war if they judge that the threat can no longer be avoided. There is an inherent tension between this imperative to avoid war on the one hand and that of controlling the circumstances of initiation if war cannot be avoided on the other. There is good reason to believe that this tension would increase dramatically at the point of crisis and would subject both opposing establishments to severely conflicting internal impulses. That fact makes the prevailing circumstances of deterrence prone to sudden catastrophic failure at the point of serious crisis, a point that could not be known about in advance and that would only be experienced as it happened.

The circumstances of the global balance do not apply to all local conditions. Each side enjoys a substantial advantage of conventional military power in certain areas of the world, and that fact does have strong effects on a crisis that is focused on one of those areas. In general, undisputed military dominance of one side makes a localized crisis less dangerous and its management easier, simply because its outcome is determined by those initial local conditions. At some of the more likely sources of crisis, however, most notably in the Middle East and in Eastern Europe, the local balance of military capability is or could readily become inherently ambiguous. When that occurs, the outcome turns upon details of circumstances that the leaders must try to control.

Given these situations, under a severe crisis or under one that is occurring with an ambiguous local balance, the managerial capacities of decision makers, no matter how stable psychologically or skilled politically they may be, are likely to be overwhelmed. There are several basic reasons for this fact.

First, in a serious crisis under current world conditions, the spontaneous interactions of conventional nuclear forces could not be predicted or controlled in all their important details. They are far too extensive and too elaborate for anyone to completely determine.

Second, the rapid timing of these operations would make the discovery and timely correction of the inevitable errors of managerial judgment extremely difficult. It would be very difficult to keep up with the pace of events that would be triggered. The extensive flows of information created by technical sensors directly observing the opponent's military operations would produce interacting perceptions by both military establishments that would tend to dominate the normal channels of diplomacy used to try to produce a constructive resolution.

Finally, the background tension between the objectives that I discussed above would inevitably produce major differences in judgment between the civilian and political leadership on both sides, making it very difficult for completely consistent lines of action to be established.

Problems of this sort have been experienced during the only two crises involving nuclear weapons in the post-World War II period: in Cuba in 1962 and in the Middle East in 1973. It should be noted that neither crisis is directly relevant to the current situation. The Cuban crisis occurred before both sides had fully developed their managerial establishments. The Middle East was a one-sided crisis as far as nuclear weapons are concerned. Nonetheless, there were some significant failures of managerial direction under those circumstances, although the crises obviously were successfully resolved.

In Cuba, despite extraordinary and largely effective measures undertaken to coordinate the American government, some significant features of American actions escaped central control, most of which are well known. There was an unauthorized incursion into Soviet air space by a reconnaissance plane—a strategic aircraft. It was officially described as an accident and clearly was not intended directly, certainly not by the top managers.

Very extensive antisubmarine warfare operations were conducted by the United States, implicitly under U.S. Navy rules of engagement but without the advance knowledge of the executive committee that was attempting to manage the crisis. It is not known explicitly what the executive committee would have done had they thought about it in advance, but it certainly was inconsistent with the tight control that they exercised in other aspects of the crisis.

The tactical air operations in the southern part of the United States anticipated the crisis and extensively developed their capability of dealing with it well in advance of the leaders in Washington. Because the American press was able to discover this preparedness, it is very likely that the Soviets were able to as well. These are inevitable features of a crisis, and they would be far worse under current circumstances.

In the Middle East in 1973, an alert was ordered for the sole purpose of sending a diplomatic signal, a signal that was intended to be secret. The persons ordering the alert thought that they could keep it from being public, which reveals just how little they knew about what they were ordering. There is no way that U.S. forces can be put on alert without it being made public.

None of these episodes had any major negative consequences on the outcome of these crises; indeed, in context they may well have helped their resolution. However, that may be, in part, a product of fortuitous circumstances, and there is no guarantee that fortune will always be so kind. These were not centrally directed or managed actions.

The American political system is particularly susceptible to these kinds of problems. The domains of civilian and military authority are separated fairly sharply, making it difficult for anyone to mesh diplomacy and military operations. The United States has problems with that in peacetime. These problems would intensify in a crisis situation.

Neither civilian nor military leaders are normally granted long tenure in office in the U.S. system, making it virtually impossible for anyone to develop all the types of expertise that the circumstances of crisis would, in fact, demand. The open and adversarial political process of the United States protects against wide deviations from common judgment that make it very difficult to identify and correct mistakes emerging from a consensus of opinion. In order to operate at all in the American system, there is dependence on consensus of opinion; otherwise, no coherence is produced.

In general, then, the pressures that would be created by an intense crisis with military forces at their current state of development appear to be so formidable that prudent security should focus on their prevention rather than any expectation of safe management. That does not mean we should not try to manage crises safely and think about that, but we shouldn't count on it.

Unfortunately, that principle is not widely acknowledged in U.S. foreign policy at the moment. Indeed, the emphasis it appears to deserve would require very substantial change in prevailing assumptions about how foreign policy is conducted.

The Medical Implications of Nuclear War, Institute of Medicine. © 1986 by the National Academy of Sciences. National Academy Press, Washington, D.C.

Sources of Human Instability in the Handling of Nuclear Weapons*

HERBERT L. ABRAMS, M.D.
Stanford University, Stanford, California

All men are liable to error . . .

John Locke

The last error shall be worse than the first.

Matt. 27:64

The resolution of superpower conflict to the point where nuclear war is no longer a threat is a 30- to 50-year project. In the interim, our survival depends on the degree to which we are able to manage short-term risk. No rational leader of the United States or the Soviet Union would embark on a nuclear adventure by design because they understand too well the impact of weapons of annihilation. Nuclear war, if it comes, is far more likely to be unintentional or accidental, based on miscalculation, misunderstanding, or misperception. To focus on the short term is not to accept the nuclear stockpiles as reasonable or desirable avenues to national goals. Instead, it recognizes contemporary reality and attempts to come to grips with the means whereby nuclear peace may be extended for the foreseeable future.

Human errors account for most failures in major weapons and space vehicles, more so than mechanical or technical failure (Dumas, 1980; p. 15). In the first year of a missile test program, 43 percent of all human

*From the Center for International Security and Arms Control, Stanford University, and the Departments of Radiology, Stanford University School of Medicine and Harvard Medical School.

factor errors were due to assembly and installation mistakes (Britten, 1983; p. 17). Errors, accidents, or unintentional launches in the nuclear weapons systems of the great powers represent important potential triggers of hostilities during periods of international tension.

This paper examines the issue of personnel reliability in the handling of nuclear weapons. It explores and summarizes the character of nuclear weapons duty and its impact on behavior; drug use, alcohol abuse, and psychiatric problems in the military and the degree to which they comprise a security risk; efforts to ensure reliability in nuclear weapons personnel; and the weaknesses of the Personnel Reliability Program (PRP). It concludes with suggestions for strengthening the PRP and improving the conditions of PRP personnel.

THE CHARACTER OF THE WORK AND ITS IMPACT

Nuclear weapons duty is known to be conducive to serious behavioral problems. The isolation that is often experienced at sensitive military bases and the boredom that accompanies many tasks tend to induce stress and may degrade job performance. The nature of service life in general has also been thought to encourage drug use.

Over a normal 4-year duty tour, intercontinental ballistic missile (ICBM) launch crew members spend up to a year's time in launch control centers. These underground bunkers, with their attendant inactivity, may come to resemble solitary confinement (Dumas, 1980; p. 28) and induce high levels of anxiety and alienation (Schmidt, 1981).

Crews on long submarine patrols face the stress of leaving family behind for 2 or 3 months at a time (Serxner, 1968; p. 26). They must also cope with the demanding routine of the 1-month refit period, which is when delicate, complicated repairs must sometimes be carried out under deadline pressure (Serxner, 1968). On patrol, isolation, monotony, and confinement affect all but the most stable (Weybrew and Molish, 1979). Depression in the wives of submarine personnel is a problem that places added strains on them when they return home from patrol (Beckman et al., 1979). During emergencies, sleep deprivation and heavy responsibilities may cause inaccuracy in judgment, hostility, or paranoia (Black, 1983). These effects are apparent even in those who appear to be at risk the least. It has been observed that "the most potentially dangerous situations in the navy have involved personnel who demonstrated no sign of psychiatric disturbance at the time of their initial assignment to militarily sensitive duties" (Christy and Rasmussen, 1963).

Among the many efforts to enhance the survivability of nuclear weapons, the air force has apparently considered constructing a deep underground base, 2,500–3,000 feet (about 762–914 meters) below the desert surface, with a 400-mile (about 644-kilometer) network for basing missiles. The base is designed to survive a nuclear attack and to be self-sufficient for at least a year. It would house enough personnel to tunnel their way to the surface and drive out the launchers to fire the missiles if ordered to do so (Halloran, 1984). Such personnel, if confined for long periods, would be particularly prone to behavior changes, especially if all communications were cut off. Prolonged isolation has been found to induce negative social and psychological symptoms among members of a group. One study noted an increase in boredom, irritability, depression, and hostility among military men during 105 days of social isolation (Rockwell et al., 1976). Others have found that group isolation brought out increased territorialism, along with incompatibility and withdrawal from group interaction (Altman and Haythorn, 1967; Altman et al., 1968).

Lack of sleep, coupled with prolonged work, leads to fatigue, thirst, and physical complaints in 24 hours. After 100 hours, visual hallucinations, balance disturbances, slowed movements, and lack of vigilance have been observed (Opstead et al., 1978). In a prolonged nuclear alert, with missile crews working double shifts, bomber crews working on sustained airborne alerts, and submarine crews working beyond their regulated limit, the likelihood of error would surely increase (Morrison, 1983).

Disruptions in internal timing systems and biological clocks are now recognized as a serious public health concern. In industries with round-the-clock work shifts, accidents and errors increase between the hours of 3 and 5 a.m., a time when normal circadian rhythms are at an ebb. Pilots flying aircraft simulators make more errors at this time, and eight times the number of single-vehicle truck accidents take place near 5 a.m. than at other times of the day. The Three Mile Island accident occurred at 4 a.m. with a crew that had just gone on the night shift (Moore-Ede, 1984).

Work schedules themselves may cause degraded job performance. Circadian cycles in humans rotate on a 24- to 25-hour basis. Within a day, people can adjust to time shifts of 1 to 2 hours; beyond this limit, adjustment may take days. Weekly rotations, which force people to adjust to 8-hour time shifts each week, barely give adequate time to settle into a work pattern. The feeling is one of perpetual jet lag (Moore-Ede, 1982).

The duty routines of the navy's nuclear submarine crews are organized around an 18-hour cycle, composed of three 6-hour shifts. Crew members work one shift and then take 12 hours, or two shifts, off before working another shift. Although this would appear to give them ample time for sleep and general rest, the cycle itself is not in keeping with the 24–25-hour circadian system; adjusting daily to a 6-hour change in work shift is humanly impossible. Among naval crews, this constant desynchrony manfests itself in a high incidence of insomnia, emotional disturbance, and impaired coordination. Furthermore, the turnover rate among the U.S. submarine crews is extremely high—up to 33–50 percent per voyage do not return for a second mission (Moore-Ede et al., 1983).

Repetitive tasks may impair job performance because of the physical effects of sensory deprivation or simply because of boredom (Dumas, 1980). We block out sounds after we have grown accustomed to their drone, or we stop seeing the familiar in our daily lives. Military personnel, who sit for hours watching lights bleep across an electronic screen, or guards, who stand watch day after day at a sensitive military post, react similarly. Dissatisfaction in such work may be enhanced by the belief of many who work in missile operations that the military would take no action to have them transferred even if they were placed in the wrong job (Parrott, 1973).

Stress in general, no matter what the source, has been associated with accidents of all types (Alkov and Borowsky, 1980; Connoly, 1981; Padilla et al., 1976). In the air force much attention has been devoted to stress and pilot error (Alkov et al., 1982; Green, 1977; Yanowitch, 1977). Aviators responsible for aircraft mishaps have often been found to cope poorly with stress. The stress itself is commonly associated with difficult life situations and with life-change events (Alkov and Borowsky, 1980).

Crisis situations are among those in which stress is considerably heightened and the chances of operator error are enhanced. Although moderate anxiety may improve performance, the rate of error for a given task is increased when high levels of apprehension or fear are experienced (Lagadec, 1982; p. 343). Events perceived as threatening and uncertain augment stress levels physiologically (Ursin et al., 1978; p. 6), which in turn can impair performance. One study performed on personnel responsible for maintaining Titan II missiles on a 24-hour alert demonstrated that continuous intense stress not only promotes fatigue but may ultimately be associated with collapse of performance (LeBlanc, 1977).

The nuclear reactor accident at Three Mile Island (TMI) is an example of multiple errors associated with a crisis situation. At the onset, the operators in the TMI control room had trouble in correctly interpreting the nature of their problem. They failed to observe that an important valve in the reactor's pressurizer was open when it should have been closed, creating a hidden leak in the primary system. On the basis of this misunderstanding, the operators took several actions that increased the severity of the accident (Lewis, 1980).

Part of the lack of insight has been attributed to an information overload in reading the barrage of emergency signals in the power plant control room. The problem has been described as one of "how to sort out the

100 odd alerts that rang out in a cacophony of hoots and bells'' (Lagadec 1982; p. 111). The ambiguous nature of the warning signals aggravated the quandary. While clues that signaled that the crucial valve was open were available, they were not clear (Perrow, 1980–1981; p. 25).

The operators' training added to their dilemma, rather than helping them cope. Lacking a theoretical background or perspective on their work, they functioned as button pushers instead; they were drilled for an accident in which only one thing went wrong at a time (Kemeny, 1980–1981; p. 5). A multiple failure (common-mode) accident was not anticipated by safety planners or stressed in operator training programs; the operators were not prepared for it.

Information overload exacerbated the Three Mile Island accident, but information underload may have played a role as well. In heavily automated control rooms, the lack of anything but routine work may lead to complacency and inattentiveness. "The burning question of the near future," one expert on aviation safety has said, "will not be how much work a man can do safely, but how little" (Weiner, 1977).

Human error is also responsible for faulty components and systems failure. On June 3 and 6, 1980, false alerts on the air force missile attack warning system were triggered by a bad computer chip. Random failures within the early warning computer systems (EWS) can stem from undetected coding errors in the program software. The possibility of residual software errors is high because the complexity of such programs may prohibit them from ever being fully tested before use (Bereaunu, 1982).

A further limitation in early warning programming lies in the inability of programmers to foresee all future circumstances and combinations of program inputs. It is virtually impossible to write a complete program in such a complex system. Computer errors inevitably result from this inherent shortcoming of the system (Bereaunu, 1982).

The missile alerts of June 3 and 6 did not trigger a nuclear incident because the control room officers correctly evaluated the warnings as false (U.S. Congress, Senate, 1980). The question remains whether human judgment will always be this reliable. If an actual alert occurs in a manner or setting different from a planned alert scenario, will operators be able to act positively or will uncertainty override appropriate action?

Perhaps the most disquieting weakness in command, control, and communication (C^3) lies in its actual transition to nuclear alert. C^3 personnel would face many of the same stresses that arose in the crisis at Three Mile Island. In peacetime, C^3 operators' daily routines include monitoring the worldwide military situation, providing warning information, maintaining continuous communications, and participating in training exercises. Ball has emphasized that "the routine of peacetime operations leads to boredom and carelessness: messages are often filed without having been read, communications are often misrouted, and connections are carelessly interrupted. Most operators are simply not trained to make the rapid transition from indifference to critical awareness that would be required of them in an emergency'' (Ball, 1981, pp. 3–4; Bracken, 1983). Whether in C^3 or in silos or submarines, there are factors other than boredom, inactivity, anxiety, and altered sleep patterns that profoundly affect behavior. Drug and alcohol abuse, a problem that is serious enough in civilian life, takes on a new dimension when it occurs among those who have access to nuclear weapons or military plans.

ALCOHOL, DRUG USE, AND PSYCHIATRIC DISORDERS

While the information base for this paper is for the U.S. armed forces, additional comments on the Soviet and British armed forces are important in recognizing the breadth of the problem.

The U.S. Military

Drug use was not considered an important problem for nuclear weapons personnel until 1970 (Larus, 1970; p. 50), when the military apparently realized that it had become a widespread phenomenon. In 1980, the Department of Defense (DOD) conducted a thorough survey of drug and alcohol use in the U.S. military, questioning over 15,000 randomly selected personnel (Burt, 1981–1982). The study revealed that 27 percent of the respondents had used drugs within the last 30 days (Table 1). Marijuana was used most often; 19 percent smoked it at least once a week (Table 2) (U.S. Congress, House, 1982). The 18–25 age group were most involved, with 50 percent reporting drug use in the last year and nearly 40 percent reporting it in the last 30 days (Table 2 and Figure 1) (U.S. Congress, Senate, 1982; p. 6). The navy had the most severe problem among the four services.

On questions of work impairment and drug use, 10 percent of the 18–25 age group experienced lowered performance, while 19 percent had

TABLE 1   Percentage of Population Using Drugs in the U.S. Military

Drug Use Period Beyond:	Total DOD	Army	Navy	Marine Corps	Air Force
30 days	27	29	33	37	14
12 months	36	38	43	47	23

SOURCE: Derived from Table 3 in Burt (1981–1982, p. 425).

TABLE 2   Percent Prevalence of Drug Use among U.S. Military Personnel and Comparable Civilians (ages 18 to 25)

Drug Use Beyond:	Military (N = 8,224)	Comparable Civilians (N = 2,022)
Marijuana/Hashish		
30 days	40	42
12 months	52	54
Amphetamines or Other Uppers		
30 days	10	4
12 months	21	12
Cocaine		
30 days	7	10
12 months	18	23

SOURCE: Summarized from Table 11 in Burt (1981–1982, p. 432).

been high while working (almost half of these on 40 or more days during the past year). In the navy, 26 percent were high during work (U.S. Congress, House, 1982; p. 259) (Table 3).

In another survey of U.S. military stations in Italy and Germany (June and July 1981), on-duty drug use was described in 43 percent of the army, 17 percent of the air force, 35 percent of the marines, and 49 percent of the navy. On-duty drug use was slightly over 60 percent on the USS *Forrestal*. A total of 27 percent used uppers on duty in the navy, while 24 percent smoked marijuana on duty in the army (U.S. Congress, House, 1982).

The consumption of alcoholic beverages was widespread throughout all services (Table 4). Drinking on duty was also common: 28 percent in the army; 21 percent in the navy; 19 percent in the marines; and 15 percent in the air force (U.S. Congress, House, 1982; pp. 277–278). The highest

TABLE 3   Percentage of Personnel with Work Impairment due to Drug Use

Impairment	Total DOD	Army	Navy	Marine Corps	Air Force
Total	21	22	28	28	9
High while working	19	21	26	25	8
Lowered performance	10	12	15	13	3

SOURCE: Reprinted from Burt (1982, p. 431), by courtesy of Marcel Dekker, Inc.

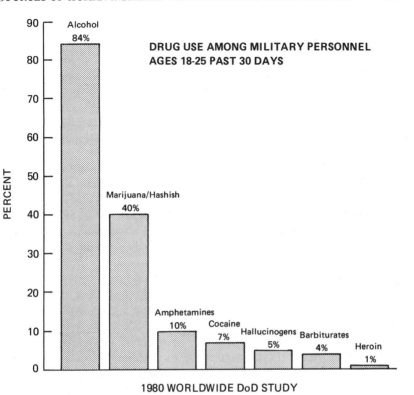

FIGURE 1   Drug use during the previous 30 days among military personnel ages 18–25. Source: U.S. Congress, Senate (1982).

prevalence of drinking was reported by the senior officers (Burt, 1981–1982). Alcohol dependence was found in 7 percent of all military personnel. Another 27 percent suffered some degree of work impairment due to alcohol (U.S. Congress, House, 1982).

An accident aboard the USS *Nimitz* brought at least part of the drug problem to light. On May 26, 1981, a Marine EA-6B aircraft crashed on the deck of the USS *Nimitz*, killing 14 people, injuring 44, and damaging 20 other aircraft. At autopsy, traces of marijuana were found in the blood of six deckhands who died. A House Subcommittee pointed out that "the relevance of this information becomes more pronounced when considered with the fact that the USS Nimitz had been at sea for 11 days prior to the accident" (U.S. Congress, House, 1982; p. 280). The pilot of the plane that crashed was found to have 6–11 times the normal blood level of brompheniramine, an antihistamine, which had not been prescribed by a military physician. Such a level may cause sedation, dizziness, double

TABLE 4   Percentage of Worldwide U.S. Military Population
Using Alcohol During the Previous 30 Days

Total DOD	Army	Navy	Marine Corps	Air Force
83	80	86	86	82

SOURCE: U.S. Congress, House (1982).

vision, and tremors. The naval report concluded that "the presence of this
drug, combined with other stress factors, precipitated the pilot error which
caused this accident" (U.S. Congress, House, 1982; p. 281).

The same investigation also uncovered the regular use of amphetamines
by crew members to sustain themselves during 18-hour workdays. Twenty-
eight percent of navy personnel used amphetamines and did so habitually,
rather than casually or for recreation purposes.

The accident prompted a large-scale test of urine samples of naval
personnel for marijuana, cocaine, opiates, and other drugs; this was followed by a sharp decline in the percentage of those shown to be using
marijuana (New York Times, November 8, 1984).

The Naval Safety Center reported that alcohol and hangover effects
were involved in 15–20 percent of the major aircraft accidents in 1979
(U.S. Congress, House, 1981). In six army accidents during a 5-year
period, drugs were found in the blood samples of military aviators. These
drugs included marijuana, cocaine, methaqualone, and, in one case, in-
sulin prescribed by a civilian physician without knowledge of the military.
The marines also reported eight instances of drug abuse that involved
aviators (U.S. Congress, House, 1982; p. 439).

The official policy of the DOD is to prohibit the induction of drug- or
alcohol-dependent individuals. Each service implements this policy independently, but all "appear flexible enough to enlist anyone except those
convicted of trafficking or declared drug dependent by a medical authority" (U.S. Congress, House, 1982; p. 432).

In recent years, the armed forces have experienced a measurable decrease in drug use, according to the Research Triangle Institute of North
Carolina (New York Times, January 21, 1986). Nevertheless, the problem
remains an urgent one for nuclear forces. In 1982, the House Appropriations Investigative Subcommittee found a large number of drug incidents
and arrests involving personnel working with nuclear weapons. In one
case, four marijuana pushers in an army nuclear missile battalion were
identified. An army husband and wife team managed the enterprise and
indicated that 125 others in the unit were users. Twenty-three were in the

nuclear weapon PRP and remained there because of the lack of hard evidence to deny them security clearances.

At another army nuclear missile site, a company commander disregarded for 3 months a subordinate's request for a drug detection program. He knew that the likelihood of PRP personnel replacements was slim and therefore ignored the army's policies on drug enforcement until some of his soldiers were arrested for drug possession. A nuclear weapons guard on a base in Germany was arrested for smoking hashish while walking his post (U.S. Congress, House, 1982). As recently as last year, 1,400 individuals were decertified from nuclear weapons handling because of drug and alcohol abuse.

The submarine force maintains a zero drug tolerance policy, with offenders being transferred to another post. During 1980, 589 enlisted men— 75 percent of all navy transfers—were removed from the Atlantic submarine force, and for many this was because of drug abuse. "Cost and time to train replacements obviously has a readiness impact when the total submarine force constitutes 32 percent of all navy war ships" (U.S. Congress, House, 1982).

The evidence is compelling that all of the factors associated with drug use in the civilian population and in the military at large are operative— at times in accentuated form—among the forces responsible for nuclear weapons.

PSYCHIATRIC PROBLEMS

The annual incidence of psychosis in the armed forces around the world has been estimated at 3 per 1,000 in peace and war (Group for the Advancement of Psychiatry, 1964). The figures for neurosis and personality disorders are higher. Psychiatric hospitalization rates for navy men from 1966 to 1968 were 689 new cases per 100,000 per year. Thus, nearly 0.7 percent were so obviously unstable that they required in-patient treatment. Of these, 78 per 100,000 were psychotic, 184 were neurotic, 334 suffered from character and behavior disorders, and 93 exhibited "situational maladjustment" (Schuckit and Gunderson, 1973).

Psychiatric disorders can manifest themselves in a number of different ways, including alcoholism or discipline problems. Unstable individuals may be separated from the service through administrative actions, such as general court-martial, without ever being seen by a psychiatrist (Arthur, 1966). Mentally ill crew members may be referred to naval installations far from the home base, creating a care drain (Satloff, 1967). Commanding officers may be unwilling to cite psychiatric disorder as a cause for transfer because of negative attitudes about such a label. All of these factors may render the data base uncertain.

Nevertheless, the magnitude of the problem becomes apparent when the distribution of psychiatric diagnoses in the armed forces is analyzed. During World War II, a total of 160,285 men were discharged from the navy on psychiatric grounds. The psychiatric patients typically came from unstable families, had below average score work performances, and complained of frequent physical illnesses (Arthur, 1966). In a longitudinal study of 11,000 naval enlistees, Plag et al. (1970) found that approximately 1 enlistee in 12 (8.7 percent of the total) was discharged during his first enlistment because of psychiatric illness.

From 1980 to 1984, over 45,000 individuals in the army had psychiatric disorders (Table 5). Approximately 4,500 were schizophrenic, while an additional 3,000 had other psychotic disorders. Dependence on, abuse of, or psychosis from drugs and alcohol accounted for 30,000 cases. Another 4,400 had neurotic disorders and 10,000 had personality disorders (Department of the Army, 1985).

Psychiatric instability, together with the tensions of military life, has been reflected in the number of assaults on officers in the armed forces. From 1968 to 1972, 550 such assaults are said to have occurred, resulting in 86 deaths (Gillooly and Bond, 1976).

The suicide rate in the U.S. Army (10.1 per 100,000 soldiers [Redman and Walter, 1985]) is probably not related only to the stress of military

TABLE 5   Distribution of Psychiatric Diagnoses in U.S. Army (1980–1984)

Diagnosis	1980	1981	1982	1983	1984	Total
Alcoholic psychoses	106	133	158	125	98	620
Alcohol dependence	2,624	2,772	2,573	2,239	2,274	12,482
Drug psychoses	76	62	58	51	22	269
Drug dependence	329	199	144	145	101	918
Drug abuse	1,132	1,051	941	767	1,015	4,906
Schizophrenia	1,465	1,064	873	657	470	4,529
Neurotic disorders	847	621	419	408	385	2,680
Personality disorders	1,223	1,109	698	677	756	4,463
Other psychotic states	525	478	561	511	613	2,688
Mental disorders following organic brain damage	125	116	83	105	121	550
Other diagnoses	2,508	2,185	2,129	2,140	2,223	11,185
Total	10,960	9,790	8,637	7,825	8,078	45,290

SOURCE: U.S. Army Patient Administration Systems and Biostatistics Activity: Disposition and Incidence Rates Active Duty Army Personnel, Psychiatric Cases, Worldwide, CY 80-84.

life, although 40 percent of those who committed suicide were said to have difficulties with their work in the army. A large percentage also have marital or family problems (Rothberg et al., 1984). The rate is slightly lower in the military than in the civilian population (Redman and Walter, 1985). A recent drop in suicide rate has been associated with the shift in the white-black ratio from 3.7 to 2.2 and is probably explained by the lower suicide rate among blacks and their relatively larger number in the armed forces (Datel and Jones, 1982).

The risk of mental illness is especially acute in nuclear armed submarines, in which crews remain for months at a time. In a comparison of submarine crews with a control group of surface fleet personnel subject to the same health screening, the neuropsychiatric illness rate during 1968–1973 was twice as high among those in submarines (Tansey et al., 1979). Up to 5 percent of the crew that were on Polaris submarine patrols for 2 months required treatment for psychological problems, ranging from minor anxiety to acute psychosis (Serxner, 1968). In another study, 3.8 percent of nuclear submarine crews were referred for psychiatric consultation. Of these, 1.9 percent had disorders that were serious enough that they could not return to the submarines. Eight percent of those referred were psychotic (Satloff, 1967).

The Soviet Military

Accurate information on sources of human instability in the Soviet armed forces is not readily available. Emigré accounts often have a strong anti-Soviet bias, and accessible Soviet government sources are generally lacking in objective, quantitative data. Nevertheless, it is clear that Soviet military service may be associated with several kinds of stressful experiences. The very first encounter of the recruit is frequently a shock:

Draftees are packed off in railroad cars to unknown destinations without the slightest ideas of what they will be doing . . . . The abbreviated training course, which puts soldiers under tremendous physical and psychological pressure, is made even more overwhelming by their geographical isolation: they are stationed in faraway places, often in unfamiliar climates (Tarasulo, 1985).

Living conditions in the barracks, or *kazarma*, are a source of constant stress. The chief problem is overcrowding: 50 to 100 men are packed into a room, with an estimated 2 square meters allotted per man. There is no opportunity for privacy. The barracks are often freezing in winter and excessively hot in summer; they tend to be rancid and poorly ventilated. There is a shortage of hot water, and the few toilets are usually outdoors, even in freezing climates.

Food is often inadequate and tasteless. The prevalence of illnesses such as running sores, acne, dental problems, night blindness, oversensitive eyes, or eye infections may at least partially attest to a vitamin-deficient diet. Troops attempt to supplement their military diet by growing produce and raising livestock, especially pigs.

There are differences between services in the quality and quantity of food served, with navy, air force, and border guards generally receiving better rations. In any case, poor nutrition must to some extent undermine soldiers' physical and mental potential (Gabriel, 1980; Cockburn, 1983; Tarasulo, 1985).

Ethnic strains pose another problem. Barely half of the Soviet population is Russian, while the 90 or more ethnic groups speak 130 languages. Not only do non-Russian soldiers experience learning and social difficulties because Russian is the standard language in the military, but they face discrimination in placement and in their dealings with their fellow soldiers. Such tensions are probably less of an issue in the strategic missile forces. These elite positions are more ethnically homogeneous, composed mostly of Russians (R. Anderson, University of California, Berkeley, personal communication, 1985).

Systematic hazing of younger recruits is a feature of Soviet military life. Early in their 2-year term of duty they are forced to give up food rations, exchange new uniforms for older ones, perform unpleasant tasks intended for older recruits, and hand over part of their monthly allowance. This caste system is enforced by older soldiers through physical violence and has even led to death by beating (Myagkov, 1976; Suvorov, 1982). The Soviet military has been described as "an organization riven with hatred and strife to an extent that occasionally borders on anarchy" (Cockburn, 1983; p. 78).

Stress manifests itself in different ways. In a survey of Soviet emigrés, 49 percent felt that soldiers in their unit were absent without leave (AWOL) often or very often. High AWOL rates may be of particular concern as a reflection of low morale and discipline problems.

The frequency with which military leaders are physically assaulted by their own men has also been noted. Of those surveyed, 36 percent had witnessed assaults on officers and 63 percent had direct knowledge of assaults on noncommissioned officers. This kind of insubordination and violence embodies an undue measure both of stress and of disaffection. Suicide is another index and there appears to be a high rate in the Soviet armed forces (Gabriel, 1980; p. 178).

Reliability may also be affected by the way in which Soviet troops are trained. For the most part, this takes place in military academies and training corps. It consists of drills, marching in formation, instruction about their weapons, and field experience with older or cheaper weapons and equipment than would actually be used in combat. Because of the limited amounts of weapons and supplies available, soldiers may fire an average of only three bullets a year (Tarasulo, 1985).

One incident reported in the Soviet military press involved a crew intent on increasing its launching speed for the sake of socialist competition. The men ignored the requirement that ladders be used to mount the mobile launcher and missile and, consequently, damaged the missile. Another account described an antiaircraft unit's eagerness to impress the senior commander with their speed at readying the missile for firing. The launch crew focused so much on speed that they forgot accuracy and coordination (Goldhamer, 1975; pp. 121–122).

While much of the information presented above is based on emigré sources, the problems of alcoholism are treated directly in the Soviet literature. Alcoholism is a health problem of epidemic proportions in the Soviet Union. The high death rate from acute alcohol poisoning indicates the extent of abuse. There are approximately 45,000 deaths annually from acute ethanol poisoning, a figure that is 100 times as high as in the United States (400 per year) (Treml, 1982b). Over the past 20 years the per capita consumption of alcohol has more than doubled (Davis, 1985).

Alcohol abuse throughout the ranks of the Soviet military has also been documented (Gabriel, 1984, p. 119; Goldhamer, 1975, p. 152) and is higher than in the civilian population (Davis, 1985). A typical soldier cannot afford and is not legally allowed to obtain state-produced vodka. Many drink instead surrogate alcohol, such as shaving lotion, varnishes, cleaning fluid, antifreeze, brake fluid, shoe polish, and glue. The toxicity of these home brews, consumed throughout the country, explains in part the high acute alcohol-poisoning rate.

According to one estimate, alcohol dependence affects one-third of the Soviet military (Wimbush, 1981). The effect of this epidemic, combined with extremely poor nourishment and the stress of overcrowding in the barracks, is to undermine Soviet defense capabilities. Furthermore, it is thought that the Soviet officer corps and noncommissioned officers may "account for more than three-quarters of alcoholics and heavy drinkers" (Davis, 1985). Such factors have a definite, though undetermined, impact on the issue of human reliability and nuclear weapons in the Soviet Union.

Little has been written about the abuse of drugs other than alcohol in the Russian military. Hard drugs are probably not a major problem; the annual death rates from these are low in the USSR, far below those in the United States (Treml, 1982a). On the other hand, large numbers of soldiers returning from Afghanistan are said to have used hashish and to have transported it into the Soviet Union in significant quantity (R. Pipes, Harvard University, personal communication, 1984).

Although there is virtually no discussion of nuclear weapons handling in the available Soviet literature, Soviet military doctrine clearly acknowledges the possibility of human error in causing nuclear war. In a July 1982 *Pravda* article, Defense Minister Dimitri Ustinov (1982) stated that one pressing military issue involved

setting up a still more strict framework in the training of troops and staff, the determination of the composition of arms, the organization of still more strict control, for the assured exclusion of the unsanctioned launch of nuclear weapons from the tactical to strategic.

The chain of command in the Soviet military flows from the Politburo through the Defense Council to the main Military Council, which governs the general staff, the direct controlling agent for strategic nuclear forces (Ball, 1981).

If the general staff granted release authority, theater nuclear weapons would fall under the control of the theater command or directly under the control of the front command, which is in turn responsible for dispersing the nuclear weapons to lower commands and authorizing the launch of these weapons. When the lower commands receive authorization, they would have a considerable degree of flexibility in deciding when and whether to use the weapons under their control. One top Soviet military official has observed that

Transfer of nuclear weapons to the disposal of strategic, operational, and tactical command echelons gives each great independence and enables them to choose for themselves the means and methods of military operations within the zones of their responsibility and within the bounds of their authority (Zav'yalov, 1971).

Although strategic and tactical weapons have been fitted with electronic locks to guard against unauthorized launching (Meyer, 1985; p. 188), with the devolution of authority in the field, the issue of human instability requires serious consideration.

The British Military

Alcohol has had a long history in the British military, especially in the navy. Since the seventeenth century, sailors have been able to draw on a daily ration of rum, or *grog*. *Tot-time* was not abolished until 1970, although attempts to control alcohol consumption, such as diluting the grog and reducing rations, were initiated periodically.

Alcohol abuse affects all ages and ranks. One physician has noted that many alcohol users in the military "are highly (and expensively) trained, yet deteriorations in functions are often allowed to continue until a major medical or disciplinary crisis makes avoidance of their recognition impossible" (Blunder, 1981).

While the abolition of the rum ration marked the first major step toward controlling alcoholism in the navy, alcohol treatment units throughout the military have now been established, and preventive education programs are stressed (Hiles, 1980, 1981). In consonance with the U.S. military, the British have identified boredom, underemployment, lack of job satisfaction, lack of group cohesion, and stress among the factors that lead to alcohol abuse. The military's traditional acceptance of alcohol, its ready availability, and its widespread use among the recruiting population add to the problem. For soldiers stationed in northern Europe, alcohol is even more available; there are few licensing restrictions, and it may be purchased cheaply, at duty-free prices (Wood, 1980).

Information on drug abuse is scarce. In a parliamentary response, 73 cases of drug abuse in the British military in 1983 were acknowledged (Thompson, 1985; p. 59). Within a 2-month period at one military hospital, soldiers were observed "abusing heroin intravenously, cannabis, amphetamines, lysergic acid diethylamide (LSD), barbiturates, analgesics, antiparkinsonian agents, benzodiazepine, and glue" (Blunder, 1981). Marijuana is readily available and widely used in the British armed services. (Opiates are rare because they are difficult to conceal.) Barbiturates and amphetamines are not as readily available to soldiers. The abuse of prescribed drugs, which can be purchased legally, is also common.

If the American experience is relevant, the patterns in the British military, in general, are applicable to nuclear weapons personnel as well. Not long ago, the British discovered—and court-martialed—a heroin addict who also used hallucinogenic drugs. He had served on two nuclear submarines and apparently was often stoned while on duty (Boston Globe, October 23, 1981).

No description of the screening procedures for personnel reliability in the British nuclear forces has been made available.

SUBSTANCE ABUSE AND PSYCHIATRIC DISORDERS AS A SECURITY RISK

What kind of security threat is posed by psychiatric and drug-related disorders in the military? The nature of the risk depends on the kind of psychiatric disorder or drug use, the individual's responsibilities, and the extent to which a state of crisis is pending or exists.

"The psychotic individual (manic, depressed, or schizophrenic) represents a severe actual or potential danger to himself, to those around him, and of course to the military mission of his unit" (Kleinmann and Krise, 1957; pp. 1008–1009). Such individuals must be removed from sensitive duties. Because the symptoms of psychosis may appear gradually, it is rare to find an actual breach of security by a psychotic.

Neuroses present another category of psychological disorder that may be damaging to military operations. Although the neurotic may sometimes be unreliable, he is not necessarily a security risk; "frequently, he is a very conscientious worker transferring much of his concern and compulsiveness to his job" (Kleinmann and Krise, 1957; p. 1008). Instances of neurosis are best evaluated individually, on a case-by-case basis. Nevertheless, many feel that the neurotic should be removed from a position that involves highly sensitive duties and transferred to a less critical job.

Character and behavior disorders represent the most common form of psychiatric disability (Arthur, 1966; p. 360). The danger from such individuals may lie in their difficulty in practicing sound judgment, a problem which is especially threatening in times of crisis. Disorders of this nature are difficult to detect and may not be apparent until after some breach of security.

The individual with suicidal tendencies presents a unique threat to security, especially in work with nuclear weapons. Attempted suicide, the air force states, is "particularly significant when attempted through the deliberate detonation of a weapon or crashing of an airplane" (Department of the Air Force, 1983; p. 12).

The impact of drug and alcohol abuse also varies with the substance used and the pattern of use. While the more social drugs such as marijuana or alcohol generally slow reaction time and impair judgment, harder drugs such as LSD, heroin, or PCP may cause more dangerous behavior. The more profound alteration of perceptions presented by these hard drugs probably presents a greater security risk than do the effects of softer drugs. Air force regulations reflect this disparity:

If the investigation [during the decertification process] reveals the use of a hallucinogen either posing the threat of flashback (for example, LSD) or severe behavioral effects (for example, PCP), the certifying official must impose a permanent decertification (Department of the Air Force, 1983; p. 39).

But excessive use of any substance may dangerously diminish reliability. The air force distinguishes between problem drinkers, who are temporarily decertified and entered into a rehabilitation program, and chronic alcoholics with little chance for rehabilitation, who are permanently decertified. The type and pattern of use materially affects the nature of the security threat.

The risk also depends on the individual's responsibilities. Personnel in the nuclear release system are of critical importance in weapons security. Unreliable personnel with immediate access to strategic nuclear weapons, such as launch capsule officers for silo-based ICBMs, are a potential hazard. Checks and safeguards on them are rather tight: once the authorization code is sent, a total of four officers in two separate launch control capsules in the same squadron still need to decide individually to launch the ICBMs before they can be fired. When a launch has been ordered, any other capsule can send out an inhibit command (Senate Armed Services Committee, 1977; p. 6845). While the consequences of an accidental or unauthorized ICBM launch would be disastrous, the likelihood of such a launch is correspondingly low.

Unreliable crew members on ballistic missile submarines also present a security risk. Because the navy maintains no permissive action links (PAL) on its submarine-launched ballistic missiles (SLBMs), the captain and several officers on board can decide to launch a nuclear weapon without higher authorization. A drugged or mentally disturbed individual could not decide to launch a weapon alone; the procedure requires the agreement of several crew members. The navy claims that a minimum of 30 submarine personnel must cast their votes before a weapon can actually be fired, though others contend that the true figure is lower (Meyer, 1984b). PALs are also lacking on aircraft carriers and other vessels that carry nuclear weapons (Center for Defense Information, 1985).

Perhaps the greatest threat to security involves unstable individuals who have access to theater nuclear weapons, including bombs and depth charges on nonstrategic aircraft; air, sea, and land-based cruise missiles; nuclear land mines; artillery projectiles; and short-range ballistic missiles. While short- and medium-range weapons can do less damage than strategic weapons, the controls over these weapons are also looser. During a crisis, such controls are apt to loosen even more as commanders release authorization codes to personnel in order to avoid delay if the weapons are to be used. Such devolution of control would put many in a position to launch theater nuclear weapons. While the two-man rule is applied to theater weapons, the possibility for their unauthorized launch is considerably higher.

In some military services, the small pool of applicants or a high attrition rate may increase the likelihood that suboptimal personnel will be selected—e.g., those with psychiatric disorders or drug habits. For instance, the submarine service in the late 1960s had a selection ratio of 80 to 95 percent, due to an attrition rate of about 20 to 25 percent (Kinsey, 1968).

The service also suffered from a lack of volunteers for long nuclear submarine patrols (D. Morrison, Center for Defense Information, personal communication, 1985). Not only is the training very rigorous, but in times of personnel shortage, individuals may be selected for submarine duty even when it is their last choice (Serxner, 1968).

Line commanders facing a personnel shortage may utilize an individual for short-term duties, even with the knowledge that the person is mentally unstable. "While theoretically this should not occur, in reality it has happened and undoubtedly will in the future" (Christy and Rasmussen, 1963; p. 543). The ultimate decision on whether someone presents a human reliability risk lies not with the physician or psychiatrist but with the line commander.

The possibility of one serviceman "running amuck at the controls" is far less significant than the problem of psychological disorders leading to reduced efficiency and reliability. Similarly, frequent or habitual use of recreational drugs or alcohol takes a toll, with reduced performance while under the influence or hung over and long-term degradation of health and mental alertness.

Although the impact of drugs and alcohol on military readiness has not been formally studied, the Deputy Secretary of Defense stated in June 1981 that a military unit has never been declared noncombat ready because of drug or alcohol abuse. This may be because the DOD reporting system uses the quantity—not the quality—of such items as equipment and personnel to define readiness (U.S. Congress, House, 1982).

In the belief that officers closest to the troops have the most comprehensive view of the drug problem, 167 military commanders in Europe, the United States, and the Pacific were surveyed. Forty-seven percent of the commanders recognized some lowering of combat readiness due to drugs. Nevertheless, only 10 percent believed that drug abuse had a specific or identifiable impact on readiness. Most often it was seen as a casual matter and primarily a discipline problem. "Several commanders felt that the marijuana user posed no problem until he was caught, after which the administrative process began" (U.S. Congress, House, 1982; p. 284).

By strictly employing enforcement measures, a commander may lose necessary personnel. Through frequent drug searches, he risks alienating his troops and lowering morale. There are good reasons to tolerate drugs rather than enforce discipline. Many commanders felt that alcohol abuse posed a larger threat to readiness because senior officials were more likely to be involved.

What seems unassailable is that the navy would have no way of preventing a determined submarine crew from launching its missiles and that t "must rely on the sanity of the skipper and his crew to save us from Armageddon" (Volz, 1983).

THE PERSONNEL RELIABILITY PROGRAM

Approximately 120,000 individuals have access to U.S. nuclear weapons. The military takes special precautions to ensure that these people are suitable for their positions. The heart of the effort is the Personnel Reliability Program (PRP), which is designed to screen out unstable individuals and "to ensure that such weapons are not subject to loss, theft, sabotage, unauthorized use, unauthorized destruction, accidental damage or jettison . . . only those personnel who have demonstrated unswerving loyalty, integrity, trustworthiness, and discretion of the highest order shall be employed in nuclear weapon PRP positions" (Department of Defense, 1981; p. 1).

Among the critical positions that fall under PRP jurisdiction are commanders of nuclear weapons delivery units, pilots and crews of delivery aircraft, and delivery unit personnel with access to and technical knowledge of nuclear weapons. In addition, so-called controlled PRP positions include security guards, storage and supply personnel, and launch personnel in nuclear missile silos.

Qualifying standards for the PRP include the following:

- Physical competence, mental alertness, and technical proficiency
- Evidence of dependability in accepting responsibilities and accomplishing duties, and flexibility in adjusting to changes in the working environment
- Evidence of good social adjustment, emotional stability, and ability to exercise sound judgment in meeting adverse or emergency situations
- Positive attitude toward nuclear weapon duty

The initial screening procedure includes a background investigation and a security clearance. A medical evaluation is also required, to be completed by "competent medical authority or other medical personnel who are specifically trained and designated to perform this function" (Department of Defense, 1981, Enclosure 5, p. 3). It may begin and end with a review of the candidate's medical documents. Only if these are considered inadequate will an actual examination be performed. Although consideration of psychological problems is a part of the basic evaluation, again, no interview is required.

The process also embodies a review of the candidate's personnel files and a personal interview advising the individual as to the nature of the

PRP. The interview is intended to determine the candidate's attitude toward the job. On completion of a course of study relevant to the position, a proficiency certificate is issued.

After certification, medical and personnel records are marked, alerting physicians and others to the sensitive nature of the work. Supervisors are advised that the individual is in the PRP. Factors that might impair performance—medication, for example, or family problems (such as a wife's miscarriage or the death of a close relative)—can then be acted on when recognized, generally by temporary removal of the person from nuclear weapons duties (Department of Defense, 1981, Enclosure 5, p. 3; L. Meyer, 1984a).

There is no formal monitoring system or regular review of PRP members. Those in the program are responsible for reporting any factors that might impair their own performance or that of their peers, while supervisors, managers, and other authorities are expected to observe them daily and continue to assess their reliability (Department of Defense, 1981; Department of the Air Force, 1983, p. 4).

Failure to meet the PRP qualifications theoretically results in temporary or permanent decertification, depending on the situation.

Personnel are disqualified for the following reasons:

• Alcohol abuse
• Drug abuse (isolated or experimental use of marijuana or hashish need not be automatically disqualifying; in each case, the certifying official must judge the impact of the drug use on the individual's reliability)
• Negligence or delinquency in performance of duty
• Court-martial, nonjudicial punishment, serious civil convictions, or behavior indicative of contemptuous attitude toward law or authority
• Aberrant behavior: mental, physical, or character traits that would lead to unreliable performance
• Poor attitude or lack of motivation

Relatively little specific information is available on the Soviet counterpart of the PRP—i.e., individuals involved with nuclear weapons. Presumably, their selection and training procedure produces soldiers of greater reliability and skill than the average draftee. Military schools that train cadets to become lieutenants in the Strategic Rocket Forces have a special entrance requirement: the students' political reliability must be officially certified by a military commissariat officer (Scott and Scott, 1984). Nevertheless, the PVO (Nation Air Defense) suffers from the same kinds of problems as the other services. The Soviet Navy—which carries a special tradition and prestige—has difficulty attracting sufficient numbers to serve on missile submarines. Many are unwilling to endure the strains of long patrols. Consequently, while the U.S. Navy has two rotating crews for each submarine, the Soviet Navy maintains only one crew per boat (Cockburn, 1983).

The Soviet Union is clearly aware of the psychological-physiological stress to which nuclear weapons personnel are subject. Classes on psychological will are given at the training center for officers responsible for launch controls. An article in *Pravda* quotes an officer on the shift: "When an input comes in, in your soul there's an anxiety: is this combat, or is it training?" (Gorokhov, 1985).

A recent article in the Soviet military medical journal emphasizes the importance of psychological testing in an era of complex military technology (Bodrov, 1984). The psychological selection process involves examination of the individual's analytic abilities, motivation, capacity to communicate, leadership qualities, and many other factors. Those who score high are much more successful in completing flight training than those with lower scores. Such tests have been used for many years in the USSR, and they also assess emotional stability, perceptiveness, and attentiveness (Solov'ev et al., 1971). Personnel in whom these psychological measures are less satisfactory often experience tension, confusion, fatigue, and greater tendencies to accidents.

In all likelihood the Soviet screening program for nuclear weapons personnel shares many features with that of the U.S. armed forces. But because of the high degree of secrecy that surrounds the Soviet military, it is impossible to be certain.

WEAKNESSES OF THE PERSONNEL RELIABILITY PROGRAM

A system designed and implemented by humans cannot be 100 percent effective. In 1957–1958, the air force engaged a group of psychologists, psychiatrists, and others specializing in human resources and accident prevention to address the question of human fallibility and nuclear safeguards. The committee concluded that effective screening might reduce the likelihood of an unauthorized launch, but that—because of human fallibility—it was impossible to safeguard all acts involving nuclear weapons (Larus, 1970; p. 25).

Because secrecy surrounds many PRP assignments, medical officers may have little knowledge about the positions for which they interview personnel. Lack of experience with the type of work and the role expected of the applicant may make it difficult for the physician to assess his suitability for the position. Furthermore, the initial screening need not include a medical or psychiatric examination. A record review may suffice.

But in some cases, records give no indication of serious flaws that render an individual unfit for nuclear weapons duty. Psychological problems are a case in point. For reasons of confidentiality, mental health clinic records are kept separate from the rest; thus, unless the main record includes a referral for psychiatric treatment, there may be no indication that an individual ever required or received it. In bases that maintain mental health clinics, the psychiatric records are available for review, but not all bases operate such clinics.

Certain indications of psychological instability may be evident from medical documents. These include frequent appearances on sick call with vague and questionable health complaints; overdependence on medications and tranquilizers; repeated entries reflecting accident proneness or alcohol abuse; and stress-type headaches, chronic diarrhea, or other psychological symptoms of stress (Kentsmith, 1981).

Besides the initial screening, systematic, meaningful follow-up by trained personnel might seem a logical next step. Instead, managers or superiors are relied on to report actions that indicate a lack of dependability (Department of Defense, 1981), and coworkers are expected to evaluate each other (L. Meyer, 1984a). Needless to say, inertia, camaraderie, and peer pressure may hamper honest evaluations of reliability.

The occasional violations of PRP security rules that come to light are not reassuring. In 1969, an air force major allowed three men under his command to continue their nuclear weapons security work even after they were identified as having dangerous psychiatric problems. One of the guards allegedly lost control with a loaded carbine at the base. The major testified that he had known of the men's psychiatric problems, but he had kept them on because he was understaffed (New York Times, August 18, 1969).

The Walker spy case represents a striking example of the problem of ensuring reliability in the military in general and in nuclear weapons personnel in particular. John Walker, Jr., was in the Naval Nuclear Weapons PRP as a petty officer with communications training and a high-level security clearance. He served as a communication specialist on a Polaris submarine. As leader of the espionage ring that sold classified documents to the USSR from 1968 on, he represented one of the most serious security breeches in recent naval history. Clearly, the PRP was unable both to detect and to predict this radical aberration from accepted norms of reliable behavior (Magnuson, 1985; McGrath, 1985).

The data on PRP decertification are disturbing. From 1975 to 1984, an annual average of 112,000 individuals, all screened by the PRP, were employed to handle nuclear weapons (Table 6) (Department of Defense, 1975–1977, 1978–1984). During that period, 51,199 individuals were decertified, which is about 5,100 per year. If the assumed length of service

TABLE 6 Total Number of PRPs and Number Decertified (1975–1984)[a]

Year	Total PRPs	Decertifications
1975	119,625	5,128
1976	115,855	4,966
1977	118,988	4,973
1978	116,253	5,797
1979	119,198	5,712
1980	114,028	5,327
1981	109,025	5,235
1982	105,288	5,210
1983	104,772	5,085
1984	103,832	3,766

[a]Average, 112,686; total, 51,199.

SOURCE: Department of Defense (1975–1977, 1978–1984).

s 1 year, that amounts to 5 percent of the total; if the length of service s 2, 3, or 4 years, it adds up to 9, 14, or 18 percent, respectively (Table 7).

Drugs and alcohol accounted for a large fraction, but psychological problems were also important (Table 8). Over the 10-year period, 33 percent were decertified for drug abuse, and 9 percent were decertified for alcohol abuse (Table 9). This is a larger percentage than in the more loosely screened U.S. Army in Europe, where 27.5 percent were discharged because of excessive drug or alcohol use (Manning and Ingraham, 1981).

If the air force—which is responsible for the major portion of the strategic nuclear arsenal—is looked at separately, the data are similar (Table 10) (Shealy, 1985). To summarize a 7-year period, 26 percent

TABLE 7 Average Annual Rates of PRP Decertifications (1975–1984)[a]

Length of Service (years)	Percent Decertified
1	5
2	9
3	14
4	18

[a]Average annual decertification total, 5,120; average annual PRP total, 112,686.

SOURCE: Department of Defense (1975–1977, 1978–1984).

TABLE 8 Number of PRPs Decertified by Reason (1975–1984)

Reason	1975	1976	1977	1978	1979	1980	1981	1982	1983	1984
Alcohol abuse	169	184	256	378	459	600	662	645	621	545
Drug abuse	1,970	1,474	1,365	1,972	2,043	1,728	1,702	1,846	2,029	1,007
Negligence or delinquency	703	737	828	501	234	236	236	252	220	160
Court-martial or civil conviction	345	388	350							
Behavior contemptuous toward the law	722	945	885	757[a]	747	694	560	605	607	580
Physical, mental, or character trait or aberration	1,219	1,238	1,289	1,367	1,233	941	1,022	882	704	646
Poor attitude				822	996	1,128	1,053	980	904	828
Total no. decertified	5,128	4,966	4,973	5,797	5,712	5,327	5,235	5,210	5,085	3,766

[a]Classification of decertification changed in 1978, and the categories "Court-Martial or Civil Conviction" and "Behavior Contemptuous Toward the Law" were combined.

SOURCE: Department of Defense (1975–1977, 1978–1984).

TABLE 9   Summary: PRP Decertifications (1975–1984)

Reason	Total No. Decertified	Percent
Alcohol abuse	4,519	9
Drug abuse	17,136	33
Negligence or delinquency	4,107	8
Court-martial or civil conviction; behavior contemptuous toward the law	8,185	16
Physical, mental, or character trait or aberration	10,541	21
Poor attitude	6,711[a]	13 (19[a])
Total no. decertified	51,199	

[a]Values are for 1978–1984.

SOURCE: Department of Defense (1975–1977, 1978–1984).

were decertified because of drug abuse and 11 percent because of alcohol abuse (Table 11). For the PRP as a whole and for the air force specifically, 22 percent were separated for psychological, behavioral, or physical traits or aberrations.

The decertified individuals were 5 percent of the total air force PRP, but if a 2-year enlistment on average is assumed, then 11 percent of all PRP personnel were at risk (Table 12).

It is difficult to judge precisely the effectiveness and sensitivity of the PRP. Independent evaluations are not available; it is not even clear whether the military has conducted such studies. A relatively large number of personnel have been permanently decertified from PRP work. This implies not only that the screening process is imperfect but also that at any one time many unstable individuals are charged with the day-to-day responsibility for handling nuclear weapons. Furthermore, among those who are approved for nuclear weapons work, it may be that only the most blatantly unstable or unlucky are later recognized as security risks and are decertified.

STRENGTHENING THE PRP

Analysis of the present structure and function of the PRP suggests a number of discrete measures that could improve the screening process and diminish the number of potentially unstable people handling nuclear weapons.

TABLE 10 Total Number of PRPs in Air Force and Number Decertified (1977–1983)

Reason	1977	1978	1979	1980	1981	1982	1983
Alcohol abuse	52	129	303	415	536	524	452
Drug abuse	340	642	1,020	964	956	848	988
Negligence or delinquency	656	335	81	91	103	111	76
Court-martial or civil conviction; behavior contemptuous toward the law	588	352	417	371	303	290	317
Physical, mental, or character trait or aberration	594	714	809	752	793	699	496
Poor attitude		508	822	908	884	865	764
Total number decertified	2,230	2,680	3,452	3,501	3,575	3,337	3,093
Total number of PRPs	55,751	53,650	53,524	53,353	52,164	52,826	55,481

SOURCE: Shealy (1985).

TABLE 11 Summary: Air Force PRP Decertifications (1977–1983)

Reason	Total No. Decertified	Percent
Alcohol abuse	2,411	11
Drug abuse	5,758	26
Negligence or delinquency	1,453	6
Court-martial or civil conviction; behavior contemptuous toward the law	2,638	12
Physical, mental, or character trait or aberration	4,857	22
Poor attitude	4,751[a]	24
Total no. decertified	21,868	

[a]Value is for 1978–1983.

SOURCE: Shealy (1985).

TABLE 12   Average Annual Rates of
PRP Decertification, Air Force (1977–
1983)[a]

Length of Service (years)	Percent Decertified
1	5
2	11
3	17
4	23

[a]Total number decertified from 1977 to 1983, 21,868;
average annual decertification total, 3,124; average annual PRP total, 53,821.

SOURCE: Shealy (1985).

1. Beyond a review of their medical records, all candidates should be
xamined by a trained physician, without exception.

2. The examining physician should be aware of the individual's re-
ponsibility for nuclear weapons and the exact nature of his work. For
xample, he should be advised if the position will require long periods of
;olation and confinement, in order to assess the candidate's suitability
)r the job.

3. A personal interview should be included that is designed to determine
nd assess the psychiatric or emotional stability of a PRP candidate. Traits
) watch for in such an interview include suspicion, hostility, impulsive-
ess, anxiety, and level of motivation. Such an interview could readily
e combined with the one that advises the individual of the nature of the
'RP and could determine his or her attitude toward nuclear weapons duties.

4. Standardized psychological testing should be incorporated as part of
ie PRP screening procedure. A test such as the Minnesota Multiphasic
ersonality Inventory (MMPI) takes approximately 2.5 hours, can be
asily administered and scored, and is appropriate for group comparisons.
t requires no highly trained professional personnel. It has proved effective
1 identifying rule breakers and those with character disorders in a general
rmy population (Leventhal, 1960). The Recruit Temperament Survey, a
uestionnaire devised for navy enlistees, has been shown to predict not
nly which individuals are likely to be hospitalized for psychiatric reasons
ut also a specific diagnosis of psychosis, neurosis, or personality disorder
Bucky and Edwards, 1974). This survey might effectively be used in
onjunction with or instead of the MMPI.

5. Records of the individual's past emotional, social, and vocational
istory should be available to examiners. Such information "probably is

the best single indicator of his future performance'' (Christy and Rasmussen, 1963; Gunderson and Nelson, 1965; Roff, 1960). To help determine preservice elements that might be indicative of psychological problems, Roff has devised a priority list of sources on a candidate's background. These sources include personnel of schools, camps, and scout organizations; case workers or psychiatrists; family members; and statements by the individual regarding social adjustment (Roff, 1960).

6. The candidate's family records should be reviewed for pertinent information such as psychiatric problems, alcoholism, a tendency toward diabetes or high blood pressure, and a history of drug abuse. Such family data may be important in predicting responses to stress or isolation.

7. Candidates from academically oriented high schools and those with some postsecondary education should be preferentially recruited. An air force study has demonstrated that high-performing nuclear weapons technicians are more likely to come from such an educational background (Sauer et al., 1977).

8. Age limits should be established for admission to particular groups. The 20- to 38-year-olds have been found to have the lowest incidence of ''the kind of serious psychiatric problem which might tend toward accidental or deliberate nuclear detonation'' (Eggertson, 1964; p. 216). This age group was found to have a relatively low frequency of psychosis, with schizophrenia appearing earlier and depressive and paranoid conditions appearing later. Severe behavioral disorders, as well as alcohol problems, occurred both earlier and later. While psychoneurosis increased steadily after the age of 20, this condition appeared to have less bearing on personnel reliability.

9. Periodic evaluations of reliability and work quality currently are not scheduled in the PRP. Systematic monitoring of all personnel should be established. Because of the deficiencies of the screening process itself, such monitoring deserves great emphasis. Surveillance should be performed by outside consultants, especially trained psychiatrists. Commanders may be subject to the same stresses as the individuals they are trying to assess, and therefore, they may make less sound judgments about a person's stability than would outside professionals (Christy and Rasmussen, 1963).

SOURCES OF HUMAN INSTABILITY IN HANDLING NUCLEAR WEAPONS

IMPROVING THE WORKING CONDITIONS OF PRP PERSONNEL

1. In assigning PRP personnel, greater emphasis should be placed on group composition. Team cohesiveness is probably the single most important factor affecting task performance (Sauer et al., 1977; p. 47).

2. The fatigue and boredom involved in nuclear weapons duties should be limited as much as possible. At very low stress levels, when a task is dull and unchallenging, performance tends to be poor; it reaches its peak at a low to medium stress level (U.S. Nuclear Regulatory Commission, 975; p. III–60). Nuclear weapons tasks should therefore include a certain amount of variety and responsibility; in addition, measures such as task rotation or changes in the work schedule can reduce fatigue and boredom.

3. Squadron changes aimed at improving group morale should be employed consistently. This will augment the team cohesiveness that is so essential to performance quality (Sauer et al., 1977; pp. 47 and 54).

4. Further incentives, such as status, financial reward, or employment benefits, should be developed to make certain sensitive jobs more appealing, in order to increase the pool of applicants from which to choose. Work aboard nuclear submarines and missile launch capsules is both sensitive and demanding, and both jobs suffer from a lack of enthusiastic volunteers.

5. Tighter control over drug use and alcohol abuse is required for those already in the PRP program.

6. More thorough data on nuclear weapons task errors should be collected, and additional research on human reliability factors should be undertaken (Sauer et al., 1977; p. 54).

In focusing on the problems of human instability in the microstructure—those involved in day-to-day handling of the nuclear weapons—there is a danger that we may exaggerate their impact. How important are tension, drug and alcohol abuse, psychosis, irrationality, boredom, performance lag, and the other behavioral aberrations observed in nuclear weapons forces? Can such sources of human instability provoke a major nuclear mishap?

Human error is far less critical in times of tranquility than in periods of intense crisis. Given time, even the accidental launching of a nuclear weapon at the city of an adversary can be analyzed and explained. When tensions are high and time for decision making is short, accidents, false alerts, paranoias, misunderstandings, and miscalculations assume different significance and may result in irrevocable actions of grave dimensions.

APPENDIX
NUCLEAR MISSIONS OF EACH MILITARY SERVICE

A brief summary of the nuclear missions and numerical distribution of each military service is useful in understanding the breadth of the problem and in appraising the potential impact of the many factors underlying human instability among the forces. Much of the information that follows is derived from Cochran et al. (1984) and from the Military Balance, 1984–85 (International Institute for Strategic Studies, 1984). When other sources have been used, they are specifically cited.

As of 1980, there were a total of 722 military units with nuclear capability among the various military services. Nuclear units must pass a certification inspection: personnel should know both the capabilities and the safety and control features of the nuclear weapons in their charge.

U.S. Military Services

Air Force Nuclear Role

The air force plays the most pivotal role in U.S. nuclear weapons, with its strategic offensive forces comprising an estimated 90 percent of the United States' total megatonnage strategic capability. Weapons include nuclear-equipped bombers, land-based intercontinental ballistic missiles (ICBMs), and tactical nuclear fighters. As of July 1, 1984, the Strategic Air Command's (SAC) arsenal included 1,037 land-based ICBMs. SAC also maintains some 356 combat aircraft, including long- and medium-range bombers. Many of the air force's 3,700 combat aircraft are equipped as tactical nuclear fighter bombers.

Certified nuclear-capable units usually consist of squadrons which are subordinate to a wing or a group. A squadron includes 15–24 aircraft, 18 Titan missiles, or 50 Minuteman missiles. Nuclear weapons are kept in the custody of the munitions maintenance unit for each wing or group.

The SAC's bomber squadrons each control about 150 nuclear weapons. Strategic bombers are located at 20 air force bases around the United States, with one in Guam. Land-based Titan and Minuteman missiles are deployed in nine underground silo locations, mostly in the Midwest. In addition to these nuclear forces, the air force controls a number of tactical units of the U.S.-based tactical air command, Pacific Air Force, and United States Air Force Europe (USAFE). These are equipped with nuclear weapons and are located primarily in Europe. It is probable that there are nuclear-certified units in the Pacific area and in the United States as well.

In terms of strategic defense, several fighter interceptor squadrons are nuclear certified and equipped. In 1981 there were 6 active squadrons and 10 Air National Guard squadrons with nuclear missions based around the country.

As of December 31, 1984, SAC contained 105,623 personnel of a force of 594,500 in the air force (C. Skill, SAC Public Affairs Headquarters, personal communication, 1985). Among these, there were 53,255 military, federal, and civilian air force personnel in the nuclear weapons Personnel Reliability Program (P. Delaney, SAC Public Affairs Headquarters, personal communication, 1985).

Army Nuclear Role

The nuclear weapons under the control of the army are generally short range and are more integrated into overall military capabilities than they are in the air force. Special ammunition ordnance units have charge of all nuclear weapons until they are needed by a nuclear-certified delivery unit.

The nuclear-capable U.S. forces are responsible for receiving nuclear weapons, maintaining them in a safe and secure environment, and delivering them against specified targets when directed.

Offensive nuclear weapons under army control include the West German-based Pershing 1A missile, targeted at specified Eastern European sites; the Lance missile, intended as general support to U.S. conventional ground forces in Central Europe; and nuclear-capable artillery. Defensive weapons include the Nike-Hercules surface-to-air missile system capable of firing nuclear warheads and nuclear land mines known as atomic demolition munitions (ADMs). These last are extensively deployed, especially in West Germany.

By the end of 1982, there were a total of 16,733 army personnel in the PRP, with 780,000 personnel in the army as a whole.

Navy Nuclear Role

Navy nuclear capabilities consist of strategic warfare through missile-firing submarines, tactical and theater land-attack warfare, defensive anti-air warfare, and antisubmarine warfare. Surface ships, submarines, and ship- and land-based aircraft encompass the navy's nuclear forces.

The navy's strategic capabilities rely on its 35 ballistic missile nuclear submarines (SSBN), which carry Trident or Poseidon missiles. In the tactical realm, most surface ships are nuclear capable and can launch nuclear Terrier surface-to-air weapons or ASROC antisubmarine rockets. Attack submarines are equipped with the short-range SUBROC antisubmarine rocket, while land- and ship-based aircraft are certified to carry nuclear bombs for land attack and antisubmarine warfare.

As of December 31, 1982, there were 34,871 navy (and marine force) PRP personnel of a total of 564,800 (Moore, 1980; p. 613). By December 31, 1984, the navy had a total of approximately 22,000 personnel on 130 SSBN and attack submarines (P. Johnstone, Chief of Information Office of the Navy, personal communication, 1985).

Marine Corps Nuclear Role

The marine corps maintains no nuclear weapons of its own in peacetime. During hostilities, the navy would transfer air-delivered weapons to the Marine Wing Weapons Unit in charge of nuclear weapons. Nuclear artillery and atomic demolition munitions would be delivered to the nuclear ordnance platoon of the Marine Division for use by marine ground forces. The marine corps has two aircraft and several types of amphibious ships which are certified to carry nuclear warheads. As in the army, the marine corps views nuclear weapons as an extension of conventional forces rather than as an independent capability.

Allied Nuclear Roles

Besides the nuclear missions assigned to each service, the United States has nuclear weapons agreements with nine North Atlantic Treaty Organization (NATO) countries, including Belgium, Canada, Greece, Italy, The Netherlands, South Korea, Turkey, the United Kingdom, and West Germany. Bilateral agreements known as programs of cooperation (POCs) address the deployment of nuclear weapons in NATO countries and the transfer and certification of nuclear-capable delivery vehicles. There are over 600 allied dual-capable tactical fighters and medium bombers available for nuclear duties.

The U.S. Air Force, Army, and Navy each operates a custodial unit, composed of U.S. personnel, to maintain nuclear weapons for allied use. No foreign military personnel are in the PRP (U.S. Congress, House, 1978).

Soviet Military Services

The Soviet armed forces consist of five services: the Strategic Rocket Forces (SRF), Ground Forces, Troops of National Air Defense, Air Forces, and Navy. Soviet strategic nuclear forces fall under the command of the trategic Rocket Forces, which are responsible for long-range land-based allistic missiles; the navy, which is in charge of the Soviet ballistic missile ubmarine fleet; and the long-range aviation (LRA) element of the air orces, which operates long- and medium-range bombers. The National ir Defense Troops (Voyska-PVO) are responsible for strategic nuclear efense (Ball, 1981; p. 43).

SRF comprises the most important element of Soviet strategic nuclear apability. With an estimated 415,000 personnel, SRF maintains roughly ,400 ICBMs and some 600 intermediate- (IRBMs) and medium-range allistic missiles (MRBMs). However, ICBMs are kept at a relatively low evel of readiness compared with those in the United States, parallelling ow alert rates of other Soviet strategic forces (Ball, 1981; p. 45). Like ne other five services, its headquarters are located in Moscow. Soviet nissile silos contain four men. Two SRF officers are responsible for aunching a rocket, while two KGB officers would actually arm the nuclear varhead.

Less than 30 percent of Soviet nuclear forces are sea based, compared vith over 50 percent in the United States (Thompson, 1985; p. 68). The oviet navy currently maintains 981 submarine-launched ballistic missiles SLBM) in 79 submarines. KGB officers on board strategic submarines nay perform a function parallel to their role in missile silos; namely, they nay act as a safeguard against inadvertent launch by the military and ssume a key position in the chain of nuclear command. The Soviet navy oes not send more than about 15 percent of its nuclear-capable submarines o sea at any one time (Meyer, 1985; pp. 184–185). This has been said o reflect the higher command's concern over the increased difficulty in naintaining control over the weapons once the submarines are away from ase (Ball, 1981; p. 45). There are 490,000 personnel in the navy (Cock-urn, 1983; p. 295), but no figures are available on the number responsible or handling nuclear weapons.

The strategic elements of the air force maintain 752 combat aircraft, 43 long-range bombers, 475 medium-range bombers, as well as recon-aissance aircraft, tankers, air-to-surface missiles, and electronic coun-ermeasures (ECMs). An estimated 100,000 personnel are involved, with total of 400,000 in the air force.

The National Air Defense Troops, known as Voyska-PVO, were es-ablished as a separate military force in 1948. They number some 370,000 oldiers (Cockburn, 1983; p. 358) and are responsible for a vast antibom-er network of radars, interceptors, and missiles.

These brief descriptions of the matching forces convey some sense of he large number of men that are involved daily in the handling of nuclear veapons. They are spread in various forms throughout the forces, and the tactical weapons, at least, may ultimately be under the control of those in the field if war should come and weapons are threatened with capture or destruction. In the heat of armed conflict, human instability will surely become more pronounced, and whether through fear or anger, the possibility of the use of nuclear weapons will be heightened.

ACKNOWLEDGMENTS

Supported by grants from the Carnegie Corporation, the John D. and Catherine T. MacArthur Foundation, the W. Alton Jones Foundation, and the New Prospect Foundation.

Elizabeth Polin played a major role in organizing much of the data on which this article was based, and did so with perceptiveness, persistence, and wonderful good sense. Annette Makino also made a large contribution to the data-gathering process, working with a keen intelligence and a fine capacity to sift the important signals from the noisy background. Margaret Mariscal and Ann McGrath typed the manuscript at different stages with skill and grace. I am indebted to all of them.

REFERENCES

Alkov, R. A., and M. S. Borowsky. 1980. A questionnaire study of psychological background factors in U.S. Navy aircraft accidents. Aviat. Space Environ. Med. 51(9):860–863.

Alkov, R. A., M. S. Borowsky, and J. A. Gaynor. 1982. Stress coping and the U.S. Navy aircrew factor mishap. Aviat. Space Environ. Med. 53(11):1112–1115.

Altman, I., D. Taylor, and L. Wheeler. 1968. Stress relations in socially isolated groups. J. Personality Soc. Psych. 9(4):369–373.

Altman, I., and W. Haythorn. 1967. The ecology of isolated groups. Behavioral Sci. 12(3):169–182.

Arthur, R. J. 1966. Psychiatric disorders in naval personnel. Military Medicine 131(4):354–360.

Ball, D. 1981. Can nuclear war be controlled? Adelphi Paper 169. London: International Institute for Strategic Studies.

Beckman, K., A. J. Marsella, and R. Finney. 1979. Depression in the wives of nuclear submarine personnel. Am. J. Psych. 136(4B):524–526.

Bereaunu, B. 1982. Self-activation of the world nuclear weapons stockpile. Revue Roumaine de Mathematiques Pures et Appliques 27:652.

Black, A. W. 1983. Psychiatric illness in military aircrew. Aviat. Space Environ. Med. 54(7):594–598.

Blunder, S. 1981. Drugs and the soldier. J. R. Army Med. Corps 127:72–79.

Bodrov, V. A. 1984. Basic principles of the development of a system for the occupational psychological selection of servicemen and its performance. Voenno-Meditsinskii Zhurnal. 9:41–43.

Boston Globe. October 23, 1981. British drug addict served on N-subs.

Bracken, P. 1983. The Command and Control of Nuclear Forces. New Haven, Conn. Yale University Press.

Britten, S. 1983. The Invisible Event. P. 17. London: The Menard Press.

Bucky, S. F., and D. Edwards. 1974. The recruit temperament survey (RTS) as it discriminates between psychoses, neuroses, and personality disorders. J. Clin. Psychol. 30(2):195–199.

Burt, M. R. 1982. Prevalence and consequences of drug abuse among U.S. military personnel: 1980. Am. J. Drug and Alcohol Abuse 8(4):419–439, Marcel Dekker, Inc., New York.

Center for Defense Information. 1985. Who Could Start a Nuclear War? The Defense Monitor. Washington, D.C. 14(3).

Christy, R. L., and J. E. Rasmussen. 1963. Human reliability implications of the U.S. Navy's experience in screening and selection procedures. Am. J. Psych. 120:540–547.

Cochran, T. B., W. M. Arkin, and M. M. Hoenig. 1984. Nuclear Weapons Databook, Vol. 1. U.S. Nuclear Forces and Capabilities. Cambridge, Mass.: Ballinger Publishing.

Cockburn, A. 1983. The Threat: Inside The Soviet Military Machine. New York: Vintage Books.

Connoly, J. 1981. Accident proneness. Br. J. Hosp. 26(5):470–481.

Datel, W. E., and F. D. Jones. 1982. Suicide in United States Army personnel. Military Med. 147:843–847.

Davis, R. B. 1985. Alcohol abuse and the Soviet military. Armed Forces and Society 11(37):399–411.

Department of the Air Force. 1983. Military Personnel: Nuclear Weapon Personnel Reliability Program. AF Regulation 35-99, May 6, 1983. Washington, D.C.

Department of the Army. 1985. Disposition and Incidence Rates, Active Duty Army Personnel, Psychiatric Cases, Worldwide, CY 80-84. U.S. Army Patient Administration Systems and Biostatistics Activity. Washington, D.C.

Department of Defense. 1981. Nuclear Weapon Personnel Reliability Program. Directive Number 5210.42. April 23, 1981. Washington, D.C.

Department of Defense, Office of the Secretary of Defense. Calendar Year Ending December 31, 1975, 1976, 1977. Annual Disqualification Report, Nuclear Weapon Personnel Reliability Program. RCS DD-COMP(A) 1403. Washington, D.C.

Department of Defense, Office of the Secretary of Defense. Year Ending December 31, 1978, 1979, 1980, 1981, 1982, 1983, 1984. Annual Status Report, Nuclear Weapons Personnel Reliability Program. RCS DD-POL(A) 1403. Washington, D.C.

Dumas, L. 1980. Human fallibility and weapons. Bull. Atomic Sci. November 1980.

Eggertson, P. F. 1964. The dilemma of power: Nuclear weapons and human reliability. Psychiatry 27(3):211–218.

Gabriel, R. A. 1980. The New Red Legions: An Attitudinal Portrait of the Soviet Soldier. Westport, Conn.: Greenwood Press.

Gabriel, R. A. 1984. The Antagonists: A Comparative Combat Assessment of the Soviet and American Soldier. Westport, Conn.: Greenwood Press.

Gillooly, D. H., and T. C. Bond. 1976. Assaults with explosive devices on superiors. Military Med. 141:700–702.

Goldhamer, H. 1975. The Soviet Soldier: Soviet Military Management at the Troop Level. New York: Crane, Russak & Company.

Gorokhov, A. 1985. Behind the controls of the strategic missiles. Pravda, May 29, 1985, p. 6.

Green, R. G. 1977. The psychologist and flying accidents. Aviat. Space Environ. Med. 48(10):922–923.

Group for the Advancement of Psychiatry. 1964.

Gunderson, E. K. E., and P. D. Nelson. 1965. Biographical predictors of performance in an extreme environment. J. Psychol. 61:59–67.

Halloran, R. 1984. Air Force seeks missile base deep underground for 1990's. New York Times, October 3, 1984.

Hiles, F. M. J. 1980. The prevention and treatment of alcoholism in the Royal Navy—1. A policy. J. R. Naval Med. Service 3:180–185.

Hiles, F. M. J. 1981. The prevention and treatment of alcoholism in the Royal Navy—3. Preliminary report on a pilot study of naval alcoholics. J. R. Naval Med. Service 2:70–76.

International Institute for Strategic Studies. 1984. The Military Balance 1984–85. London: International Institute for Strategic Studies.

Kemeny, J. 1980–1981. Political fallout. Society 18:5–9.

Kentsmith, D. K. 1981. The physician's determination of personnel reliability in sensitive occupations. Aviat. Space Environ. Med. 52(1):45–49.

Kinsey, J. L. 1968. Selection of personnel for system effectiveness. J. Occupat. Med. 10(5):238–240.

Kleinmann, M. V., Jr., and E. F. Krise. 1957. Mental illness and classified information. U.S. Armed Forces Med. J. 8(7):1007–1016.

Lagadec, P. 1982. Major Technological Risk: An Assessment of Industrial Disasters. New York: Pergamon Press.

Larus, J. 1970. Safing the Nukes: The Human Reliability Problem. Stockholm: Stockholm International Peace Research Institute.

LeBlanc, N. D. 1977. The Measurements of Job Stress on an Operational Unit of the Military. Pp. 45, 46. Technical Report 117, Center for Human Appraisal. Wichita, Kans.: Wichita State University.

Leventhal, A. M. 1960. Character disorders, disciplinary offenders, and the MMPI. U.S. Armed Forces Med. J. 11(6):660–664.

Lewis, H. 1980. The safety of fusion reactors. Sci. Am. 242(3):53–65.

Magnuson, E. 1985. Very serious losses. Time, June 17, 1985, pp. 18–22.

Manning, F. J., and L. H. Ingraham. 1981. Personnel attrition in the U.S. Army in Europe. Armed Forces Soc. 7(2):256–270.

McGrath, P. 1985. A family of spies. Newsweek, June 10, 1985, pp. 32–36.

Meyer, L. 1984a. The men who would finish World War III. The Washington Post Magazine, June 3, 1984.

Meyer, L. 1984b. Fail-safe and subs: Should we trust the Navy to trust itself? The Washington Post Magazine, September 30, 1984.

Meyer, S. M. 1985. Soviet perspectives on the paths to nuclear war. Pp. 167–206 in Hawks, Doves, and Owls: An Agenda for Avoiding Nuclear War. G. T. Allison, A. Carnesale, and J. S. Nye, Jr., eds. New York: W. W. Norton.

Moore, J., ed. 1980. Jane's Fighting Ships 1980–81. London: Jane's Publishing Company United.

Moore-Ede, M. 1982. Sleeping as the world turns. Nat. Hist. 91(10):28–36.

Moore-Ede, M. 1984. The body's inner clocks. P. 173 in Health and Medical Horizons. New York: MacMillan Education Co.

Moore-Ede, M., C. Czeisler, and G. Richardson. 1983. Circadian time keeping in health and disease. Part 2: Clinical implications of Circadian rhythmicity. N. Eng. J. Med. 309(9):534.

Morrison, D. 1983. Weapons wired for war. Nuclear Times.

Myagkov, A. 1976. Inside the KGB. New Rochelle, N.Y.: Arlington House Publishers.

New York Times. August 18, 1969. Three atom guards called unstable; major suspended.

New York Times. November 8, 1984. Navy defends its method in fighting drug abuse.

New York Times. January 21, 1986. Survey finds sharp drop in marijuana use in the military, Pentagon says.

)pstead, P. K., R. Ekanger, M. Nummestad, and N. Raabe. 1978. Performance, mood, and clinical symptoms in men exposed to prolonged, severe physical work and sleep deprivation. Aviat. Space Environ. Med. 49(9):1065–1073.

'adilla, E., D. Rosenow, and A. Bergman. 1976. Predicting accident frequency in children. Pediatrics 58(2):223–226.

'arrott, G. S. 1973. A Career Attitude Survey of Officers Serving on Titan or Minuteman Missile Crews. Technical Report 108. Center for Human Appraisal. Wichita, Kans.: Wichita State University.

'errow, C. 1980–1981. Normal accident at Three Mile Island. Society 18:25.

'lag, J. A., R. J. Arthur, and J. M. Goffmann. 1970. Dimensions of psychiatric illness among first-term enlistees in the United States Navy. Military Med. 135:665–673.

'sychiatric Aspects of Prevention of Nuclear War. 1964. Group for the Advancement of Psychiatry 5(Report 57):223–313.

Redman, R. A., and L. J. Walter, Jr. 1985. Suicide Among Active Duty Military Personnel. Health Studies Task Force, Office of the Assistant Secretary of Defense (Health Affairs). Washington, D.C.: U.S. Department of Defense.

Rockwell, D. A., M. G. Hodgeson, J. R. Beljan, and C. M. Winget. 1976. Psychologic and psychophysiologic response to 105 days of social isolation. Aviat. Space Environ. Med. 47(16):1087–1093.

Roff, M. 1960. Relations between certain preservice factors and psychoneurosis during military duty. U.S. Armed Forces Med. J. 11(1):152–160.

Rothberg, J. M., N. L. Rock, and F. Del Jones. 1984. Suicide in United States Army personnel, 1981–1982. Military Med. 149(10):537–541.

Satloff, A. 1967. Psychiatry and the nuclear submarine. Am. J. Psych. 124(4):547–551.

Sauer, D. W., W. B. Campbell, N. R. Potter, and W. B. Askren. 1977. Human Resource Factors and Performance Relationships in Nuclear Missile Handling Tasks. Advanced Systems Division, Wright-Patterson Air Force Base, Ohio, and Air Force Weapons Laboratory, Kirtland Air Force Base, New Mexico, AFHRL-TR-76-85, AFWL-TR-76-301.

Schmidt, W. E. 1981. Some near Titan base cite strains in crewmen's life. New York Times, June 3, 1981, p. A18.

Schuckit, M. A., and E. K. E. Gunderson. 1973. Job stress and psychiatric illness in the U.S. Navy. J. Occupat. Med. 15(11):884–887.

Scott, H. F., and W. F. Scott. 1984. The Armed Forces of the USSR. Boulder, Colo.: Westview Press.

Senate Armed Services Committee. FY 1978 Authorization Act, Part 10, April 7, 1977.

Serxner, J. L. 1968. An experience in submarine psychiatry. Am. J. Psych. 125(1):25–30.

Shealy, R. W., Lt. Colonel, U.S. Air Force. Chief, Civil Affairs Branch, Community Relations Division, Office of Public Affairs. January 7, 1985. Mimeograph. Washington, D.C.

Solov'ev, A. D., M. S. Liaskovskit, and G. I. Cychev. 1971. Experimental-psychological observations of pilots admitting erroneous actions. Voenno-Meditsinskii Zhurnal 9:66–68.

Suvorov, V. 1982. Inside the Soviet Army. London: Hamish Hamilton Ltd.

Tansey, W. A., J. A. Wilson, and K. E. Schaefer. 1979. Analysis of health data from 10 years of Polaris submarine patrols. Undersea Biomed. Res. 6:S217–S246.

Tarasulo, Y. 1985. A profile of the Soviet soldier. Armed Forces Soc. 11(2):221–234.

Thompson, J. 1985. Psychological Aspects of Nuclear War. Winchester, England: British Psychological Society and John Wiley & Sons.

Treml, V. 1982a. Fatal Poisoning in the USSR. Paper presented at the International Symposium sponsored by Centro Studi sui Sistemi Socio-Economical dell'Esti, Milan, Italy September 1982.

Treml, V. 1982b. Death from alcohol poisoning in the USSR. The Wall Street Journal November 10, 1982, p. 26.

Ursin, H., E. Baade, and L. Seymour. 1978. Psychobiology of Stress. P. 6. New York Academic Press.

U.S. Army Patient Administration Systems and Biostatistics Activity: Disposition and Incidence Rates Active Duty Army Personnel, Psychiatric Cases, Worldwide, CY 80 84.

U.S. Congress, Senate. 1977. Senate Armed Services Committee, FY 1978 Authorization Act, Part 10. April 7, 1977.

U.S. Congress, Senate. 1980. Recent False Alerts from the Nation's Missile Attack Warning System. Committee on Armed Services. U.S. Senate by Senators Barry Goldwater and Gary Hart. October 9, 1980. Washington, D.C.: U.S. Government Printing Office.

U.S. Congress, House. 1978. Military Construction Appropriations for 1979. Section on Security of Nuclear and Chemical Weapons Storage. Hearings before a Subcommittee of the Committee on Appropriations. 95th Cong., 2d sess., Subcommittee on Military Construction Appropriations. Part 2. Washington, D.C.: U.S. Government Printing Office.

U.S. Congress, House. 1981. Drug Abuse in the Military—1981. Hearing before the Select Committee on Narcotics Abuse and Control. 97th Cong., 1st sess. September 17, 1981. Washington, D.C.: U.S. Government Printing Office.

U.S. Congress, House. 1982. Drug Abuse in the Military. Department of Defense Appropriations for 1983. Hearings before the Subcommittee on Appropriations. Part 3. 97th Cong., 2d sess., pp. 253–444. April 1, 1982. Washington, D.C.: U.S. Government Printing Office.

U.S. Congress, Senate. 1982. Drug and Alcohol Abuse in the Armed Services. Joint Hearing before the Subcommittee on Manpower and Personnel and the Subcommittee on Preparedness on the Committee on Armed Services. 97th Cong., May 18, 1982. Washington, D.C.: U.S. Government Printing Office.

U.S. Nuclear Regulatory Commission. 1975. Human Reliability Analysis. Section 6.1 in Appendix III—Failure Data in Reactor Safety Study: An Assessment of Accident Risks in U.S. Commercial Nuclear Power Plants. Wash-1400 (NUREG-75/014). Washington, D.C.: U.S. Government Printing Office.

Ustinov, D. F. 1982. Otvesti ugnozu yadernoy. Pravda, July 12, 1982, p. 4. (As quoted in S. M. Meyer, 1985; p. 185.)

Volz, J. 1983. Living on the nuclear firing line. New York News, October 18, 1983, pp. 8–10F.

Weiner, E. 1977. Controlled flight into terrain accidents: System induced error. Human Factors 19(2).

Weybrew, B. B., and H. B. Molish. 1979. Attitude changes during and after long submarine missions. Undersea Biomed. Res. 6(Submarine Suppl.):S175–S189.

Wimbush, E. 1981. The Red Army. PBS TV documentary. May 6, 1981. (As cited in Cockburn, 1983; p. 62.)

Wood, P. J. 1980. Alcoholism in the Army: A demographic survey of an inpatient population. Br. J. Addict. 75:375–380.

Yanowitch, R. E. 1977. Crew behavior in accident causation. Aviat. Space Environ. Med. 48(10):918–921.

Zav'yalov, I. 1971. The evolution of the correlations of strategy, operational art, and tactics. Military Thought 11:37. (As quoted in S. M. Meyer, 1985; pp. 186–187.)

The Impact of Crisis-Induced Stress on Decision Making

ALEXANDER L. GEORGE, PH.D.
Stanford University, Stanford, California

It is remarkable that all U.S.-Soviet diplomatic confrontations—over Berlin, Korea, the Middle East, Cuba, and the Indian Ocean—have been successfully terminated without any kind of shooting war between U.S. and Soviet forces. The mutual fear of igniting a fuse that could result in thermonuclear holocaust is undoubtedly the major factor that accounts for this success. Moreover, during the 40 years of competing with each other on a global scale, the two superpowers have learned some fundamental rules of prudence for managing their rivalry without becoming embroiled in warfare with each other. At the same time, however, it needs to be recognized that the superpowers have been more successful in managing war-threatening crises than in avoiding them. While the frequency of crises involving the superpowers appears to have declined since the outset of the Cold War and there has been no war-threatening crisis since 1973, it is premature to conclude that the United States and the Soviet Union have learned to manage their rivalry without plunging periodically into dangerous confrontations. We cannot exclude the possibility that the superpowers may again be drawn into dangerous war-threatening crises at some point in the future.

Concern over the danger of nuclear war has mounted in recent years in response to developments in military technology and changes in force postures. Increased missile accuracies, the deployment and forward basing of highly accurate strategic systems that reduce available warning time, and developments in warning and alert systems raise the possibility of so-called decapitation strikes against vulnerable political and military command posts. As a result of these developments in the strategic military environment in which deterrence must operate, both American and Soviet analysts express increasing concern over the heightened danger of crisis instability and the associated possibilities of inadvertent or accidental war.

Given their shared fear of thermonuclear war, American and Soviet leaders can be counted on to be powerfully motivated to manage and terminate any new diplomatic crisis before it erupts into war. Both sides are familiar with the general principles and operational requirements of crisis management. However, mere awareness of crisis management requirements does not guarantee that they will be effectively implemented in a new confrontation. It is a genuinely challenging and difficult task for policymakers to adapt knowledge of these general crisis management principles to the specific, idiosyncratic configuration of each new crisis situation (George, 1984). Moreover, given the above mentioned developments that contribute to crisis instability, it has become more urgent than ever to address the question of whether crisis management concepts are robust and flexible enough to withstand the possibly destabilizing and escalatory potential of the military alerts and actions that each side may feel obliged to take to protect their own interests and hedge against the possibility that crisis management may break down in a new confrontation.*

Detailed studies of past crises and simulations of hypothetical ones have enhanced our understanding of various threats to crisis management. While U.S. and Soviet policymakers have effectively avoided or defused these threats in all of their past confrontations, similar threats are certain to arise in future crises involving the superpowers.

One of these threats to effective crisis management—the possibly harmful effects that psychological stress experienced by policymakers during a tense crisis might have on the performance of critical decision-making tasks—is the subject of this paper.†

---

*This question was the subject of the 8th Conference on New Approaches to Arms Control held by the International Institute of Strategic Studies in England on April 9-11, 1984. For a report on the conference see Survival XXVI (5):200–234, 1984. On the subject of the need for effective crisis management as a safeguard against inadvertent war, see also Roderick (1983).

†In the time available I was able to do little more than to synthesize and summarize material in existing studies which were readily available, including both my own previous publications and those of other investigators (George, 1974, 1980; Holsti, 1972; Holsti and George, 1975; Janis, 1972; Janis and Mann, 1977; Hermann, 1972; Hermann and Hermann, 1975; Suedfeld and Tetlock, 1977). These earlier publications draw on literature produced by psychologists, psychiatrists, political scientists, organizational theorists, sociologists, and historians. To reduce the length of the references for this article, only a few of the sources used in these earlier publications have been cited.

The problem of assessing and dealing with the impact of crisis-induced stress on policymaking may appear at first glance to be reasonably well-defined and sufficiently bounded to permit focused investigation in a direct and straightforward manner. In fact, however, for this purpose one must draw on many of the behavioral sciences and, indeed, the medical sciences as well. A conceptual framework is needed that will permit integration of the many variables that come into play in decision making in crisis situations, variables that determine whether stress will be experienced and how it will be coped with.

Finally, the reader should be aware that despite the effort made in this paper to deal with the many dimensions of the problem, some important matters (the physical and mental health of policymakers) are only touched on, while others (the effects of sleep deprivation and use of drugs and medications during prolonged crises) are not dealt with at all because they require highly specialized competence and knowledge not available for this study.

MENTAL HEALTH

This study does not reject the possibility that gross irrationalities of the type that concern psychiatrists may occur in top-level policymakers. One need only recall the severe mental illness that afflicted the first secretary of defense, James Forrestal, while he was still in office and led to his tragic suicide shortly thereafter (Rogow, 1963). At the same time it is probably the case that the most serious consequences of illnesses, such as Forrestal's, for policy decisions tend to be checked by various built-in safeguards within the organization: "Most key policy decisions are distributed over a number of persons and a variety of agencies," and there is a tendency within the bureaucracy "to remove or reduce the decision-making authority of the sick individual while leaving him in office" (Rogow, 1969, p. 1096).

Although the possibility that major psychiatric impairment in an official may not be detected or controlled in time to prevent a policy disaster or the additional possibility that crisis-induced stress may suddenly activate latent mental illness are matters for legitimate concern, they will not be the focus of this article. In fact, the conventional wisdom that every man has his breaking point obscures from view the fact that few political leaders actually break down under the stress of making difficult decisions. We need to address the broader and murkier question of the adverse effect performance under stress by leaders who are *not* ill may have on public policy.

There is no doubt that most individuals who reach high-level policy-making positions have already acquired relevant experience that provides them with the ingenuity, resiliency, and toughness needed for coping with the stresses of making difficult political decisions. In other words, they have learned to cope with decisional stress. Certainly we would like to know more about the psychological coping mechanisms that help keep political leaders intact and functioning. But the fact that an individual enjoys good mental health does not guarantee that he makes good decisions. A relatively well-adjusted man, after all, may be lazy or have limited imagination and adaptability. Therefore, we cannot be concerned solely with the consequences of a leader's decision making for his own emotional well-being. We must be at least equally concerned with the consequences for others, for the psychological coping mechanisms a decision maker employs to maintain his own equilibrium may be dysfunctional for the group or polity on whose behalf he has acted.

At the same time, we need to recognize that even successful political leaders who have functioned effectively in the past sometimes do suffer breakdowns under the pressure of crisis-induced stress (see below). As Richard Ned Lebow has suggested (personal communication, October 3, 1985), developments during a crisis may generate threats to the individual's self-esteem and activate latent vulnerabilities in his personality structure that undermine his capacity to function effectively.

STRESS AND COPING: IMPACT ON
INFORMATION PROCESSING

It has been found to be necessary in research on stress to distinguish sharply between the properties of a stimulus situation and the characteristics of the behavioral response to it by the individual or group. (Confusion may be generated by the familiar habit of characterizing an event as a stressful situation because this confounds the properties of the stimulus situation with certain kinds of effects it may have on the subject.)

It is customary to regard psychological stress as the anxiety or fear an individual experiences in a situation that he perceives poses a severe threat to one or more of his values. Thus perception of threat in the situation must occur in order for the individual to experience arousal of anxiety or fear. Threat, in other words, is not an attribute of the stimulus situation; it depends on the subject's appraisal of the implications of the situation for his values.

Anxiety and fear, however, do not have a direct impact on decision making; they are mediated by other intervening variables. Research on the effects of situationally induced stress on decision making has increas-

FIGURE 1   Effects of stress on decision making.

ingly focused on coping patterns as an additional intervening variable between the subject's experience (or anticipation) of anxiety and fear and his performance of information-processing tasks that typically precede his decision or choice of policy.

It is important to recognize that a variety of coping patterns can be employed for dealing with psychological stress. Some of these will be discussed below. Coping patterns may have deep roots in personality or they may be learned. Different individuals may favor different modes of coping. Coping includes not merely an individual's resort to ego-defensive maneuvers (e.g., withdrawal, denial, projection, rationalization) to maintain emotional well-being but also the individual's employment of those other ego processes at his disposal that facilitate a reality-oriented approach to dealing with situational and task demands and for effective environmental management.

Moreover, developments in the study of the nature of coping processes (e.g., Murphy, 1962; Janis, 1958; Hamburg and Adams, 1967) indicate that many of the classical ego defense mechanisms can be used constructively by an individual in the total process of coping. An initial resort to defensive operations such as withdrawal, denial, or projection does not preclude that individual from going on to make a timely and reasonable adaptation to a difficult situation.* Defensive operations, in other words, may give the severely stressed individual time to regroup his ego resources and provide him with the immediate tactical ego support that enables him in due course to employ more constructive ego capacities of information seeking, reality appraisal, role rehearsal, planning, and so on. But time must be available to permit recovery of adequate functioning, and one cannot be certain of this in crises that occur suddenly and require immediate responses from decision makers (see below).

Therefore, study of the effects of stress on decision making needs to be conceptualized as a multistage process (Figure 1).

---

*Note, for example, Harry Truman's tendency to resort to projection as his initial method of coping with certain kinds of political stresses before turning to a more constructive, reality-oriented coping strategy. A particularly vivid example is Truman's initial response to the news of the Chinese intervention in the Korean War, for which he impulsively blamed his Republican opponents, before settling down to deal with the crisis (Hersey, 1951).

EFFECTS OF STRESS ON PERFORMANCE:
THE INVERTED U CURVE

Research on the effects of stress on performance of various tasks leads to the general finding of an inverted U-curve relationship between the magnitude of stress and performance of various tasks (Hermann and Hermann, 1975). That is, up to a point situationally induced stress can lead to an improvement in the performance of various tasks. If it increases beyond a certain magnitude and duration, however, stress can begin to markedly impair the ability of decision makers and their staffs to make realistic assessments of the situation and to exercise good judgment in dealing with it (Holsti, 1972). The relationship can be depicted as shown in Figure 2.

It should be kept in mind that the inverted U curve depicts a highly variable general relationship between intensity of stress and level of performance. Its value for practical purposes is limited for a number of reasons: (1) The precise shape of the curve can be expected to differ from one individual to another; (2) for the same individual the threshold, or crossover, point at which increased stress begins to become dysfunctional can be expected to differ for different tasks; (3) for the same individual performing the same task, the threshold crossover point can be expected to vary, depending on circumstances and factors that vary from one trial to another; (4) whether the individual performs in a group and the nature

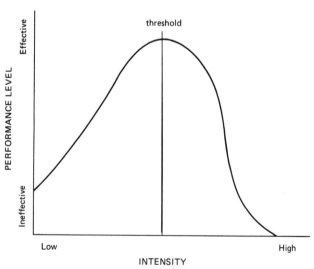

FIGURE 2   Effects of stress on performance.

of the group (composition, structure, decision-making norms, leadership and management, group dynamics) also can be expected to affect the shape of the curve.

For these and other reasons, the vast experimental literature on stress, while highly suggestive, must be used with caution by those who study decision making. As Holsti and George (1975) note: "Relatively few of these laboratory studies have involved more complicated cognitive processes or highly intellectualized tasks that often confront the policymaker. *Subjects* have usually been students, who differ by virtue of age and experience from political leaders. . . . Many experimental studies *isolate the subject*, rather than placing him into the context of groups or organization—both of which may provide the political leaders with supports and/or constraints in performing the required decision making tasks" (p. 258).

INDICATORS OF ACUTE STRESS AND ITS CONSEQUENCES

It would be helpful, of course, if valid and reliable behavioral or physiological indicators that correlate with dysfunctional levels of stress could be identified. Some possible verbal and nonverbal indicators—e.g., flustered speech, increased speech tempo, body tension, irritability, rigidity of speech content, verbal and behavioral withdrawal—have been suggested as candidates for systematic investigation (Hermann and Hermann, 1975).* But the difficulty of establishing valid general indicators that apply to large populations or, somewhat more feasibly, to a single designated individual appears to be formidable; however, this dimension of the problem lies well outside the scope of this paper.

An alternative to seeking physiological and behavioral indicators of acute stress in the individual, however, may be considered. Thus, one may seek to identify the consequences of acute stress experienced by the individual or group as they manifest themselves in the phenomenology of the decision-making process. There are at least two ways in which this can be done. First, the investigator can begin by stating the critical tasks that should be adequately performed in any well-designed, well-managed policymaking system; and then, using these critical tasks as a standard, the investigator can identify possible malfunctions of the process—i.e., the inadequate performance of one or more of these critical tasks. (This approach is elaborated and discussed in some detail by George [1980; see

---

*See also Wiegele (1973) for a discussion of biological factors, and Suedfeld and Tetlock (1977) for the utility of a measure of changes in an individual's integrative complexity in a crisis.

especially Chapter 6].) A limitation of this approach is that it does no
distinguish among the various possible sources, of which acute stress i
only one, of a malfunctioning policy process. (The impact of bureaucratic
politics, for example, may also create malfunctions of the policymaking
process.) On the other hand, this approach does offer the custodian or
manager of the policymaking system a usable basis for undertaking a
variety of preventive and therapeutic interventions to forestall or compensate for malfunctions that could have adverse impacts on the quality
of the decisions to be taken (George, 1980; in particular Part Two: Ways
of Reducing Impediments to Information Processing).

The second approach focuses directly on the possibly adverse consequences of acute stress experienced by the individual or the group for the
performance of cognitive tasks required for effective information processing. Dysfunctional effects of acute stress include impaired attention
and perception, increased cognitive rigidity, shortened and narrowed perspective (see below for a more complete discussion).

These two ways of identifying the effects of acute stress are not mutually
exclusive; in fact, they complement each other. The second approach
focuses specifically and exclusively on stress as a source of cognitive
impairment. (Cognitive impairment, in turn, can lead to one or another
of the malfunctions of the policymaking process identified in the first
approach.) But, as already noted, the first approach focuses on the malfunctions of the process, irrespective of their source or sources. Therefore,
not only is the first approach more comprehensive but it offers a practical
way of identifying and dealing with a variety of threats to information
processing.

THE POLICYMAKING SYSTEM: THE INDIVIDUAL, SMALL GROUP, AND ORGANIZATION SUBSYSTEMS

To study the effects of stress on foreign policymaking requires a conceptual framework that takes into account individual, small group, and
organizational behavior within the executive branch. Efforts at rational
calculation and choice of policy take place in three interrelated contexts
or subsystems: the individual context (e.g., the chief executive, secretary
of state); the small group context of the face-to-face relationships the
executive enters into with a relatively small number of advisers; and the
organizational context of hierarchically organized and coordinated processes involving the various departments and agencies concerned with
foreign policy matters in the executive branch.*

---

*I will not attempt to deal with still other subsystems that interact with the three noted
here—i.e., Congress, public opinion, and allied and neutral governments.

The investigator must take into account the fact that these three sub-systems are interrelated. Thus, the individual-executive, the small decision-making group, and the organizational units often interact with each other in producing foreign policy outputs. Accordingly, a conceptual framework is needed that will incorporate and interrelate these three subsystems, each of which is capable of generating a special set of adaptive and maladaptive ways of coping with the impact of stress on decision making. The research task is to identify the distinctive dynamic processes associated with each of these subsystems and to consider how these processes can have a favorable or adverse impact on the other two subsystems.

The task outlined here is indeed a formidable one. Despite advances in theories of individual psychology, small group dynamics, and organizational behavior, the linkage and synthesis of these three theories is still primitive. In a previous study the author employed information processing as a framework for this purpose (George, 1980). A familiar depiction of information processing identifies three functional tasks: search, evaluation, and choice. Information must be acquired and evaluated to achieve a valid, incisive diagnosis of the situation to which the chief executive must respond. The major values and interests affected by the situation must be identified. If options cannot be invented that promise to further all of the values and interests at stake, trade-offs among competing values must be considered. The expected consequences of alternative options must be assessed prior to the choice of action.

Working with an information-processing framework, the investigator is in a better position to assess the contribution each of the three subsystems makes to the tasks of search, evaluation, and choice; in addition, the investigator is better able to assess the way in which the three subsystems interact in information processing. Each of the subsystems is capable of contributing constructively to the fulfillment of information-processing tasks or generating impediments to those tasks. It is also possible for the workings of one subsystem to block, or compensate for, the impediments to information processing generated by another subsystem. The distinctive dynamic processes associated with each subsystem and the ways in which they can adversely or favorably affect information-processing tasks are described elsewhere (George, 1974; Holsti and George, 1975; George, 1980).

COPING WITH VALUE COMPLEXITY AND UNCERTAINTY

It is important to recognize that cognitive constraints on rational decision making (e.g., March and Simon, 1958) may themselves create stress for the individual who is attempting to judge the utility of alternative courses of action in situations in which important values are engaged. One of the well-known cognitive limits on rationality is the difficulty of formulating a single utility criterion or function that will encompass all the multiple values engaged by the particular problem. If a decision maker lacks a single utility function, he is apt to experience motivational conflict and must cope in some other way with the stressful dilemma of multiple stakes (which will often include personal, political, and organizational values, as well as national interest and ideological values). The decision maker can attempt to cope with this particular type of decisional stress by various psychological and bureaucratic devices for either avoiding or resolving the dilemma of determining how to judge which course of action is best.

The other well-known and equally pervasive cognitive constraints on rational decision making have to do with inadequate information about the situation at hand and inadequate knowledge with which to assess the expected consequences of alternative options. Forced to act in the face of these uncertainties, when so much may be at stake, the decision maker may experience considerable stress. Various ways of coping with the resulting cognitive complexity of the decisional problem have been identified. Thus, the decision maker may resort to defensive avoidance, a device that permits an escape from having to recognize the decisional dilemma. Defensive avoidance can take the form of procrastination: the policymaker seizes on the presumed fact that there is no immediate necessity for a decision to put the problem out of his mind, even foregoing the opportunity for additional information search, appraisal, and realistic contingency planning (for a detailed discussion, see Janis and Mann [1977]).

Another type of defensive avoidance, bolstering, may be resorted to when a decision is difficult to make, when it threatens great loss, or when it cannot be put off because external pressures or a strict deadline demands action. Under these circumstances the policymaker may make the task of choosing an option easier for himself by reevaluating the courses of action before him, increasing in his mind the attractiveness of one option (which he will then select) and doing the opposite for competing options (which he will then reject). Bolstering, also known as spreading the alternatives, can result in distorted information processing and option appraisal. This is particularly likely to occur when the policymaker, acting to cut short the malaise and stress of having to make a difficult decision when much is at stake, needlessly rushes to make his final choice, thereby losing the possibility of using the available time to obtain still additional information and advice. Supportive bolstering by sycophantic (or equally stressed) subordinates to the top decision maker can aggravate this danger of the premature closure of information processing.

In addition to these modes of defensive avoidance, which provide psychological assistance to enable a policymaker to come to a decision, there are a variety of analytical aids and simple decision rules that the policy-maker may rely on to cope with the intellectual task of what to do in the face of the cognitive complexity that clouds the problem. At least seven such analytical aids have been identified as having been employed by political decision makers under these circumstances: (1) the use of a "satisficing"* rather than an "optimizing" decision rule; (2) the strategy of incrementalism; (3) the strategy of sequential decision making; (4) consensus politics—i.e., deciding on the basis of what enough people want and will support rather than by trying to master the complexity of the policy issue; (5) use of historical analogies and lessons of history; (6) reliance on one's ideology and general principles as guides to action; (7) applying one's general beliefs about correct strategy and tactics (George, 1980; see also discussion of Decision-Making Strategies, Chapter 2, in Janis and Mann [1977]).

While these aids to decision making can facilitate the policymaker's choice of action, they can also have adverse consequences for the quality of information processing. The danger is that an executive will resort prematurely to one of his favorite aids to decision or rely too heavily on it in deciding what to do. The result may well be to cut himself off from the possibility of benefiting from a broader or in-depth analysis of the problem that advisers or the organization can provide.†

IMPACT OF CRISIS-INDUCED STRESS ON FOREIGN POLICY DECISION MAKING

Several characteristics of international crises can arouse acute anxiety and other strong emotional feelings, such as fear, shame, anger, and aggressiveness. First, by its very nature an international crisis poses a major threat to national interests that top-level decision makers are responsible for safeguarding. But much is at stake in a crisis also for the political leader: Will he prove equal to the challenge? Will he be able to

---

*The term *satisfice*, coined by Herbert A. Simon, suggests that decision makers will not strive endlessly to reach the optimal position but, instead, will discontinue the search for better solutions after a threshold level of satisfaction has been reached (Simon, Herbert A. February 1955. A behavioral model of rational choice. Quarterly Journal of Economics, Vol. 69).

†This is particularly likely to occur when, under the impact of crisis-induced stress, decision makers attempt to cope via the pattern of what Irving L. Janis (1985) has characterized as *hypervigilance*, i.e., when the decision maker "in a panic-like state searches frantically for a way out of the dilemma, rapidly shifting back and forth between alternatives, and impulsively seizes on a hastily contrived solution that seems to promise immediate relief."

deal with the crisis in ways that will safeguard his sense of personal worth, assure him the esteem and respect of others, and protect his own and his party's political interests?

Second, crises often erupt unexpectedly, and the resulting shock and surprise can have harmful effects on a policymaker's ability to assess the situation calmly and to exercise good judgment. A third stress-inducing characteristic of many crises is that they require (or are perceived by policymakers to require) a quick decision. A short response time can impose an additional psychological burden on decision makers and their advisers. Fourth, there is the factor of cumulative emotional strain and physical fatigue that a prolonged confrontation imposes on policymakers and their staffs. A crisis imposes intense demands on the energies and emotions of the participants, and at the same time, there are limited opportunities for rest and recuperation.

As noted above, moderate amounts of stress may lead to improved performance. Perception of threat may be followed by heightened vigilance that facilitates information search, receptivity to relevant information, and balanced assessments (Janis and Mann, 1977). Detailed case studies of decision making in international crises have provided empirical evidence that, in important respects, the quality of decision making is often improved or remains generally at high or acceptable levels (Brecher and Geist, 1980; Shlaim, 1983; Dowty, 1984; Dawisha, 1985).*

On the other hand, other historical cases provide evidence of the damaging impact of crisis-induced stress. For example, the literature on American policymaking during the Cuban missile crisis offers testimony on the adverse effects crisis-induced stress had on the functioning of several members of the policymaking group. Theodore Sorensen, a participant in President Kennedy's circle of advisers during the crisis, subsequently made the cryptic statement that he had seen at firsthand, ''during the long days and nights of the Cuban crisis, how brutally physical and mental fatigue

---

*These references comprise the first four volumes published thus far in the important collaborative research project on International Crisis Behavior, under the direction of Michael Brecher, that is evaluating the effects of crisis-induced stress on the quality of decision making in a large number of historical cases. A limitation of these studies stems from the difficulty of obtaining a direct measure of the magnitude of stress experienced by individual policymakers; as a result, the investigator cannot easily differentiate moderate stress from acute stress. Earlier, pioneering research on the stress-inducing effects of international crises was done by Robert North and associates at Stanford University. A useful formulation of the findings of the Stanford project is provided by Holsti (1972). Important contributions also appear in several publications by Charles F. Hermann (1969, 1972). A detailed examination of Israeli decision making in the events leading to the Six-Day War of 1967 concludes that its quality was rather mixed (Stein and Tanter, 1980).

can numb the good sense as well as the senses of normally articulate men'' (Sorensen, 1964; p. 76). A similar observation was made by Robert Kennedy in his memoir of the Cuban crisis: ''That kind of crisis-induced pressure does strange things to a human being, even to brilliant, self-confident, mature, experienced men. For some it brings out characteristics and strengths that perhaps even they never knew they had, and for others the pressure is too overwhelming'' (Kennedy, 1969; p. 22). Details of what happened were lacking for many years. In 1984 I was told by a high official in the Kennedy administration that two important members of the president's advisory group (whose names were not revealed) had been unable to cope with the stress, becoming quite passive and unable to fulfill their responsibilities. Their condition was very noticeable, however; others took over their duties, and the performance of the policymaking group during the missile crisis is generally regarded as of a high order.

Inability to cope with crisis-induced stress has been reported for other leaders as well. Stalin evidently suffered a temporary depression after the Nazi invasion of the Soviet Union in 1941. British Prime Minister Eden reacted to the failure of the Suez invasion in 1956 with a near physical and emotional collapse (Thomas, 1967). At one point in the prolonged crisis leading to Israeli initiation of war against Egypt and Syria in June 1967, Israeli Army Chief of Staff Yitzhak Rabin, visibly overstressed or suffering from nicotine poisoning, was temporarily relieved of his duties (Brecher, 1980; Stein and Tanter, 1980; Weizman, 1974; Rabin, 1979). In the aftermath of their countries' military setbacks in 1962 and 1967, respectively, India's Jawaharlal Nehru and Egypt's Gamal Abdel Nasser were mentally and physically incapacitated (Lebow, in press).

In all the cases cited here, the dysfunctional effects of stress on the policymaker were highly visible and could be easily recognized by others, thus providing opportunities for timely intervention and compensatory action. But undue stress can also have less visible but nonetheless insidious effects on the performance of decision making. A great deal is known about the ways in which acute psychological stress degrades performance of cognitive and judgmental tasks of the kind that policymakers must discharge in a crisis. In Table 1 is a brief summary of major types of effects that have been noted.

Evidence of many of these effects of stress was noted in a detailed analysis of historical materials on the origins of World War I. As summarized by Holsti (1972):

Evidence from the 1914 crisis revealed that with increasing stress there was a vast increase in communication; information which did not conform to expectations and preferences was often disregarded or rejected; time pressure became an increasingly salient factor in policy making; attention became focused on the

TABLE 1   Effects of Acute Stress on Performance of Complex Cognitive
Tasks of Decision Making

1. Impaired attention and perception
    a. Important aspects of crisis situation may escape scrutiny
    b. Conflicting values and interests at stake may be overlooked
    c. Range of perceived alternatives is likely to narrow but not necessarily to the best option
    d. Search for relevant options tends to be dominated by past experience; tendency to fall
       back on familiar solutions that have worked in the past, whether or not they are
       appropriate to present situation

2. Increased cognitive rigidity
    a. Impaired ability to improvise; reduced creativity
    b. Reduced receptivity to information that challenges existing beliefs
    c. Increased stereotypic thinking
    d. Reduced tolerance for ambiguity leading to cut off of information search and premature
       decision

3. Shortened and narrowed perspective
    a. Less attention to longer-range considerations and consequences of actions
    b. Less attention to side-effects of options

4. Shifting the burden to the opponent
    a. Belief that one's own options are quite limited
    b. Belief that opponent has it within his power to prevent an impending disaster

immediate rather than the longer-range consequences of actions and one's alternatives and those of allies were viewed as limited and becoming more restricted
with increasing stress, whereas those of the adversary were believed to be relatively
free from constraints. As a consequence European statesmen felt a declining sense
of responsibility for their actions and the consequences to which they might give
rise. These findings clearly deviate rather sharply from some of the common
precepts of calculated decision making (p. 200).

IMPACT OF STRESS ON SMALL GROUP DYNAMICS

The various conformity-inducing dynamics of behavior in small groups
are well-known and need not be recapitulated here (e.g., DeRivera, 1968).
It is useful to distinguish two behavioral patterns that produce conformity
which in turn may create an impediment to the quality of information
processing. The first is the familiar pattern of group pressure on individual
members who raise nettlesome, disturbing questions that undermine the
confidence of the group that it is on the right track, thereby challenging
the emerging consensus. This can occur even in the absence of crisis-
induced decisional stress but may become pronounced under the impact
of a tense international crisis.

The second of the behavioral patterns producing and maintaining conformity within small decision-making groups has been less well articulated and studied, no doubt because the group processes associated with it are more subtle. Without detracting from the importance of the first pattern, we may agree with Marlowe and Gergen (1969) that it is unsatisfactory and "unduly restrictive" to view conformity solely within "the narrow context of a group exerting pressure on individuals, some of whom are susceptible (or suggestible) and consequently conforming" (p. 610). A broader perspective can be gained by observing that small decision-making groups sometimes take on the characteristics of a primary group. Sociologists and psychologists who have studied the remarkable cohesion that develops at times in small combat groups in military organizations have noted the special kinds of mutual identifications and emotional ties that bind members of the primary group together—and sustain individual members in coping with the stresses of combat (e.g., Shils and Janowitz, 1948; Janis, 1963). A number of participant observers, including Bill Moyers and George Reedy, commented on the tendency of President Johnson's top-level policymaking group on the Vietnam War to take on some of the characteristics of an embattled group in order to protect itself from critical views.

Though it may seem farfetched to apply the analogy of a combat group to a small political decision-making group, it is well-known that chief executives often rely on primary group ties with one or more close associates or friends as a means of coping with the stresses of decision making. From membership in the small intimate group, the individual may secure some of the psychological support—esteem, respect, reassurance, affection—needed to sustain him in his efforts to cope with the cognitive complexity, the uncertainty and risks, and the criticism from outsiders that are inevitably a part of political decision making. The chief executive himself may become dependent for emotional support on policy advisers. Some chief executives, however, are evidently aware of the risks of doing so; thus, Woodrow Wilson could accept Colonel House as both a friend and a policy adviser only because House occupied no official position (George and George, 1956). Calvin Coolidge "found it necessary to keep his friend Frank Stearns around him as a kind of buffer-companion-confessor, yet he would not work through him or consult him in any way" (Fenno, 1959, pp. 42–43). Adlai Stevenson noted that Lyndon B. Johnson was very uncomfortable if none of his policy advisers wholly approved of a decision he had just made (Geyelin, 1966).

Janis (1972) hypothesizes that concurrence seeking in small decision-making groups "can best be understood as a mutual effort among the members of a group to maintain self-esteem, especially when they share responsibility for making vital decisions that raise threats of social dis approval and self-disapproval'' (p. 203). This striving for mutual suppor Janis postulates, has functional value for the members insofar as it alle viates distressing emotional states such as feelings of insecurity or anxiet about risks and possible errors, conflicts between different standards c conduct, between ethical ideas and humanitarian values on the one han and the utilitarian demands of national or organization goals.

I noted earlier that one of the major cognitive constraints on rationa decision making arises from the fact that it is often difficult to formulat a single criterion of value to apply in choosing the best course of actior Janis suggests that under these circumstances, and particularly in highl cohesive groups, group concurrence tends to replace reality testing of th morality and efficacy of the policy being chosen or pursued. Earlies Schachter (1960) had postulated that on any issue for which there is n empirical referent, the reality of one's own opinion is established by th fact that other people hold similar opinions.

In Janis's theory, strong cohesion facilitates the emergence of what h calls *groupthink*, a way of coping with stress that is likely to be highl maladaptive for rational decision making. Groupthink is characterized b a shared ''illusion of invulnerability,'' an exaggerated belief in the com petence of the group, a ''shared illusion of unanimity'' within the group and a number of other symptoms. It would appear that under acute stres and other conditions, the existence of strong primary group ties within small decision-making group can encourage regressive forms of thinkin (as well as regressive emotional states), such as the following: (1) globa or undifferentiated thinking, that is, a simplistic cognitive view of th external world and of other political actors; (2) dichotomized modes o thought; (3) oversimplified notions of causation; (4) loss of sense of pro portion; and (5) confusion of means with ends. Regressive forms of think ing are recognizable from time to time in small cliques of fanaticized policy advocates who fight for a certain highly valued policy option in the face of great and persistent difficulties.

Janis deliberately challenges the conventional wisdom that group cohe sion always favors performance of group tasks. Though recognizing the usefulness of strong group cohesion, he warns that it can have an adverse impact on the group's performance: ''The more amiability and esprit de corps among members of an executive group, the greater the danger tha independent critical thinking will be replaced by groupthink.'' The very fact that a group of decision makers enjoys strong cohesion may lead te an erosion of critical intellectual capacities when they resort to concurrence seeking in a stressful decision-making environment. This is a far more ubtle and insidious thing than is the social pressure to conform that is exerted against a member of the group who entertains dissident policy views.

IMPACT OF STRESS ON ORGANIZATIONAL BEHAVIOR*

Many of those who have examined decision making from an organizational perspective note that stressful situations often provide the motivation and means for reducing information pathologies and rigidities associated with the normal bureaucratic behavior familiar in complex organizations characterized by hierarchy, specialization, and centralization. Under circumstances of stress, information search within the organization tends to become more extensive and intensive, although this may not be the case if the time to make the decision is unduly short (as may be the case in some international crises). Similarly, some of the constraints on rational decision making derived from the formal organizational structure, standard operational procedures, and informal bureaucratic political maneuvers may become less potent under the impact of externally stressful events.

On the other hand, negative consequences of stress for search behavior have been noted when an organization is subjected to frequent or perpetual crises. It is important to note, too, that information search and appraisal may be adversely affected by existing organizational mind sets, doctrines, and contingency plans in the various departments and bureaus. Under the pressure of a tense crisis, for example, existing contingency plans may be applied without modification to a situation that, as is often the case, is different in important respects from the contingency that was planned for. The more frequent the crises and the less time available for adaptation of contingency plans and for creative improvisation, the more likely that preplanned, ready-to-go options are applied mechanically. And the more emphasis that is placed on secrecy, the less likely that an organizational subunit's existing, preferred options for dealing with the type of contingency in question will be subjected to searching scrutiny by others on behalf of the top executive before he is called on to approve.

Stress may become dysfunctional also if, as can happen in fast-moving international crises, it is accompanied by an acute information overload that impairs the adaptive capacities of the organization.

---

*This section briefly summarizes and adds to material presented by Holsti and George (1975).

TOWARD PRESCRIPTIVE THEORY*

A broad conceptual framework has been presented for studying th
impact of crisis-induced stress on decision making, and available empiric
findings have been briefly summarized. Opportunities for systematic in
vestigation of this problem in real-life settings are quite limited, and a
noted earlier, the experimental literature on stress, while suggestive, mu
be used with caution by those who study decision making. Despite i
well-known limitations, anecdotal historical case material is useful; th
opportunities for improving the quality and increasing the quantity of suc
raw data have hardly been exhausted. But while the development of a
improved data base and better theory is to be encouraged, one cannot b
sanguine over the prospects for rapid progress. Those who turn to the tas
of developing prescriptive theory and guidelines for reducing the incidenc
and consequences of maladaptive ways of coping with crisis-induced stres
will have to work with the limited data and theories that are available
The challenging task is not merely to find useful measures for stres
reduction and for avoiding possibly damaging effects of acute stress o
policymaking but to find ways of introducing them into the policymakin
system.

It is useful to begin by recognizing that many factors other than stres
can and do affect the quality of foreign policy decisions. These factor
include the intelligence and experience of policymakers, the quality o
information and advice available to them, and the relevance and validit
of the tacit or explicit international relations theories that they employ in
their decision making.

A useful prescriptive theory is unlikely to emerge from a narrow-gaug
search for a single optimal strategy that would minimize stress-induce
impediments to information processing. Top-level policymakers vary greatl
in personality and cognitive style which, in turn, leave them with differen
assets and vulnerabilities in coping with stress. Consider, for example
the freewheeling, extroverted, and often seemingly impulsive decision
making style of Franklin D. Roosevelt and contrast it with the mor
orderly, introverted, and compulsive style of Richard M. Nixon. These
styles of behavior are well-established by the time an individual reaches
top leadership positions. Because each style has its special strengths and
vulnerabilities, a single set of guidelines is unlikely to prove adequate,
even though some procedural norms may apply irrespective of individual
variations in style and personality.

---

*This section reproduces, with some additions and deletions, the discussion of Holst
and George (1975; pp. 304–308). Reprinted with permission from Macmillan Publishing
Company from Political Science Annual: An International Review, Volume 6, edited by
Cornelius P. Cotter. ©1975 by Macmillan Publishing Company.

It is useful to regard the task of avoiding the adverse effects of acute ress as embedded in the larger problem of improving the quality of formation processing. As noted above, this requires attention to the terrelations among the individual, small group, and organizational components of the overall policymaking system. Each of these subsystems is apable of generating impediments to effective information and providing orrections to impediments stemming from the other two subsystems. ecognition of this fact is a useful starting point for the design and management of a complex policymaking system.

Prescriptive approaches will be facilitated by taking into account the levance of two different theories: substantive and process. Substantive eory deals with problems that arise repeatedly in foreign policy—for xample, deterrence, coercive diplomacy, crisis management, alliance anagement, and foreign aid. If policymakers have access to sophisticated bstantive theories, they are likely to diagnose situations more adequately id to choose more effective policy options. The availability and use of a appropriate substantive theory is likely to reduce the policymakers' ulnerability to possibly disruptive stresses that are present in such situions. Thus, for example, the stressful aspects of an intense international isis are more likely to be contained if policymakers guide their actions ith reference to general principles of crisis management and become ensitized to the difficulties of applying these principles in concrete situations. (For a summary of crisis management principles and threats to ffective management of crises, see George [1984].)

Process theory, on the other hand, deals with the question of how to tructure and manage the policymaking process to increase the likelihood f producing quality decisions. The availability of even good substantive eory cannot by itself ensure quality decisions—information must still e acquired and processed to achieve a valid, incisive diagnosis of the ituation; relevant policy options must be identified and properly analyzed o that substantive theory can be employed to sharpen the judgment that nters into the choice of a course of action.

A closer look at process theories identifies two variants: one that focuses n improving the structural design of policymaking systems and one that laces emphasis on the day-to-day management of policymaking systems vithin any given structural design. Despite numerous reorganizations of he machinery and procedures of foreign policymaking in the past, the esulting improvements in policy performance have been marginal and uneven. While structural reorganization can aid in the quest for effective lecision making, there is no single structural formula through which the hief executive and his staff can convert the functional expertise and liversity of viewpoints within and outside the executive branch into consistently effective policies and decisions. This sober observation coincides

with the evaluation of a broader range of experience in many differe
kinds of complex organizations. As a result, organizational theorists ha
increasingly emphasized that efforts to improve policymaking must
beyond the traditional tinkering with organizational structure and stand.
operating procedures to (1) the development of strategies for managi
the policymaking system and (2) the identification of mechanisms 1
timely identification and correction of the kinds of malfunctions to whi
all complex organizations are prone.

Because individual executives vary widely in their tolerance for a
ability to deal with decisional stress, it is not easy to develop a gene:
prescriptive theory on how the individual can help himself cope mc
effectively with such circumstances. Many of the decision-making str.
egies mentioned earlier (e.g., satisficing, incrementalism, use of historic
models, reliance on ideology or principles) that are available to an e
ecutive for coping with the complexity of the cognitive tasks of polic
making carry with them the danger that he will resort to one of the
strategies prematurely, thereby cutting short or misusing the organizatior
search and evaluation activities that should precede choice of policy.

The difficulty an executive experiences in dealing with cognitive co
plexity and other stresses of policymaking also makes him more vulnerab
to certain types of small group dynamics that emerge within his circle
advisers. The criterion of what these significant others will approve m.
easily fill in the vacuum created for him by the difficulty he encounte
in trying to make a good cognitive appraisal of the policy issue. The
are some useful things an executive can do to safeguard against his a
his associates' tendency to allow this pervasive and deep-seated tenden
for concurrence seeking to warp the reality testing needed for developi
sound policies (Janis, 1972). But one must also recognize the possibili
that an executive who is highly sensitive to the danger of becoming over
dependent on his advisers may overcompensate in order to safegua
against the possibility that his judgment will be unduly affected by advise
whom he has accepted as significant others. An executive may there
deprive himself of the full contribution that competent advisers might
able to make to improve the quality of his decisions. Political scientis
need to give more attention to the ways in which executives with differe
cognitive styles and personalities can structure role relations with advise
in order to preserve autonomy needs (or indulge dependency needs) wit
out distorting the intellectual contribution competent advisers can mał
to policy analysis.

We need to understand better the ways in which an executive's late
capacity for good reality testing and effective problem solving might
reinforced by certain kinds of benign small group processes. How c.

ch processes be encouraged and protected against other small group
ynamics that block rational policymaking? What kinds of interventions
ill effectively improve the quality of decision making? The norms that
imprise the problem-solving culture of the small group of policy advisers
ound the executive seem to be critical here. To assist the executive,
ere are procedural norms that regulate the performance of the many
ibtasks undertaken when a small group engages in policy analysis.

Various devices have been considered for structuring the small poli-
ymaking group to strengthen its capacity for rational decision making in
ressful situations. In this connection, a strong case has been made for
e use of a devil's advocate. But one cannot be sanguine about the efficacy
: devil's advocates in foreign policymaking on the basis of some recent
xperience (Thomson, 1968; Reedy, 1970). There is reason to believe that
ie treatment of dissidents is more complicated in real-life decision-making
roups and admits to a wider variation in consequences for group per-
irmance than theories of group conformity pressures based on laboratory
search seem to envisage (George, 1980).

It is often emphasized that the organizational subsystem has latent re-
iurces which, if properly utilized, could enhance the ability of the ex-
:utive and the small group of top-level advisers around him to cope more
ffectively with the difficulties and stresses of policymaking. For example,
i stressful situations they may be inclined to reduce the range of values
insidered or to order the priorities among them incorrectly, thereby
istorting the evaluation and choice of alternative policy options. The
rganization subsystem provides a possible correction to this tendency. A
ider range of relevant values and interests is likely to be surfaced by the
lash over policy on the part of officials identified with different subunits
rithin the organizational subsystem. However, internal competition and
isagreement over policy within the organization—i.e., bureaucratic pol-
ics—also can have dysfunctional effects on policymaking. Prescriptive
ieory at this level therefore must include the task of identifying man-
gement strategies for curbing the harmful dynamics of bureaucratic pol-
ics (George, 1980).

Finally, it should be noted that the required capabilities and preparations
ir crisis management cover a broad gamut, extending all the way from
nowledge of the political and operational requirements for crisis man-
gement to the ability of top-level civilian leaders to direct and control,
s necessary, the actions of tactical military units in the field without
ngaging in harmful micromanagement of military operations. A great
eal of essential knowledge and relevant experience bearing on these
natters should have been gained from managing past crises. But the
earning experience and the acquired know-how must somehow be codified

and institutionalized; it must be transmitted quickly and effectively to ne
incumbents of top-level policymaking positions in each administratio
and it must be internalized by them so that they will do well the first tir
they are called on to manage a crisis. In this connection, consideratic
should be given to developing sophisticated training and rehearsal exe
cises to better acquaint policymakers with the kinds of difficult tasks
crisis management they will encounter in future U.S.-Soviet confront
tions. Finally, as suggested earlier in this paper, the medical suppc
system available to top-level policymakers should be reviewed and u
graded, if necessary, to provide effective monitoring and guidance
matters of stress reduction, avoidance of debilitating fatigue from ove
work and inadequate sleep, and appropriate advice on the use of sleepii
pills and amphetamines during prolonged, intense crises.

ACKNOWLEDGMENTS

I am pleased to acknowledge support from The Carnegie Corporatic
of New York and the Center for International Security and Arms Contr
at Stanford University which made the preparation of this paper possibl
For much help and encouragement over a period of many years in n
efforts to understand the effects of psychological stress on political decisic
making, I express appreciation particularly to David A. Hamburg, Charl
Hermann, Margaret Hermann, Ole Holsti, and Irving L. Janis. For helpf
comments on an earlier draft of this paper, I am indebted to Ole Holst
Irving Janis, Steven Kull, and Richard Ned Lebow.

REFERENCES

Brecher, M., with B. Geist. 1980. Decisions in Crisis: Israel, 1967 and 1973. Berkele
    University of California Press.
Dawisha, K. 1985. The Kremlin and the Prague Spring. Berkeley: University of Californ
    Press.
DeRivera, J. 1968. The Psychological Dimension of Foreign Policy. Columbus, Ohi
    Merrill.
Dowty, A. 1984. Middle East Crisis: U.S. Decisionmaking in 1958, 1970, and 197
    Berkeley: University of California Press.
Fenno, R. F. 1959. The President's Cabinet. Cambridge, Mass.: Harvard University Pres
George, A. L. 1974. Adaptation to stress in political decision making: the individual, sma
    group, and organizational contexts. Pp. 176–245 in Coping and Adaptation, G. V. Coelh
    D. A. Hamburg, and J. E. Adams, eds. New York: Basic Books.
George, A. L. 1980. Presidential Decisionmaking in Foreign Policy: The Effective Use
    Information and Advice. Boulder, Colo.: Westview Press.
George, A. L. 1984. Crisis Management: The Interaction of Political and Military Co
    siderations. Survival XXVI (5):200–234.

George, A. L., and Associates. 1975. Towards a More Soundly Based Foreign Policy: Making Better Use of Information, Appendix D. Commission on the Organization of the Government for the Conduct of Foreign Policy, June 1975. Washington, D.C.: U.S. Government Printing Office.

George, A. L., and J. L. George. 1956. Woodrow Wilson and Colonel House: A Personality Study. New York: John Day.

Geyelin, P. 1966. Lyndon B. Johnson and the World. New York: Praeger.

Hamburg, D. A., and J. E. Adams. 1967. A Perspective on Coping Behavior: Seeking and Utilizing Information in Major Transitions. Archives of General Psychiatry 17:277–284.

Hermann, C. F. 1969. Crises in Foreign Policy. Indianapolis: Bobbs-Merrill.

Hermann, C. F., ed. 1972. International Crises: Insights from Behavioral Research. New York: Free Press.

Hermann, M. G., and C. F. Hermann. 1975. Maintaining the quality of decision-making in foreign policy crises: a proposal. Pp. 124–136 in Towards a More Soundly Based Foreign Policy: Making Better Use of Information, Appendix D, A. L. George, ed. Commission on the Organization of the Government for the Conduct of Foreign Policy, June 1975. Washington, D.C.: U.S. Government Printing Office.

Hersey, J. 1951. Profiles: Mr. President, II-Ten O'clock Meeting. The New Yorker. April 14:38–55.

Holsti, O. R. 1972. Crisis Escalation War. Montreal and London: McGill-Queens University Press.

Holsti, O. R., and A. L. George. 1975. The effects of stress on the performance of foreign policy-makers. Pp. 255–319 in Political Science Annual: An International Review, Vol. 6, C. P. Cotter, ed. Indianapolis: Bobbs-Merrill.

Janis, I. L. 1958. Psychological Stress. New York: John Wiley & Sons.

Janis, I. L. 1963. Group identification under conditions of external danger. British J. Med. Psychol. 36:227–238.

Janis, I. L. 1972. Victims of Groupthink: A Psychological Study of Foreign-Policy Decisions and Fiascoes. Boston: Houghton Mifflin.

Janis, I. L. 1985. International crisis management in the nuclear age. Pp. 63–86 in International Conflict and National Policy Issues, Applied Social Psychology Annual 6, S. Oskamp, ed. Beverly Hills: Sage.

Janis, I. L., and L. Mann. 1977. Decision Making: A Psychological Analysis of Conflict, Choice, and Commitment. New York: Free Press.

Kennedy, R. F. 1969. Thirteen Days: A Memoir of the Cuban Missile Crisis. New York: W. W. Norton.

Lebow, R. N. In press. Leadership in crisis. Science 85.

March, J. G., and H. Simon. 1958. Organizations. New York: John Wiley & Sons.

Marlowe, D., and K. G. Gergen. 1969. Personality and social interaction. Pp. 590–665 in Handbook of Social Psychology, 2nd edition, Vol. 3, G. Lindzey and E. Aronson, eds. Reading, Mass.: Addison-Wesley.

Murphy, L. B. 1962. The Widening World of Childhood: Paths Towards Mastery. New York: Basic Books.

Rabin, Y. 1979. The Rabin Memoirs. Boston: Little, Brown.

Reedy, G. E. 1970. The Twilight of the Presidency. New York: World.

Roderick, H., ed. 1983. Avoiding Inadvertent War: Crisis Management. Austin, Tex: The Lyndon B. Johnson School of Public Affairs, The University of Texas at Austin.

Rogow, A. A. 1963. James Forrestal: A Study of Personality, Politics, and Policy. New York: Macmillan.

Rogow, A. A. 1969. Private Illness and Public Policy: The Cases of James Forrestal and John Winant. Am. J. Psych. CXXV (February).

Schachter, S. 1960. Deviation, rejection, and communication. Reprinted in Group Dynamics, 3rd edition, D. C. Cartwright and A. Zander, eds. New York: Harper & Row.

Shils, E. A., and M. Janowitz. 1948. Cohesion and disintegration in the Wehrmacht. Public Opinion Quarterly 12:280–315.

Shlaim, A. 1983. The United States and the Berlin Blockade, 1948–1949. Berkeley: University of California Press.

Sorensen, T. C. 1964. Decision-Making in the White House. New York: Columbia University Press.

Suedfeld, P., and P. E. Tetlock. 1977. Integrative complexity of communications in international crises. Journal of Conflict Resolution 21:169–184.

Stein, J. G., and R. Tanter. 1980. Rational Decision-Making: Israel's Security Choices, 1967. Columbus: Ohio State University Press.

Thomas, H. 1967. The Suez War. Middlesex, England: Penguin Books.

Thomson, J. C., Jr. 1968. How could Vietnam happen? An autopsy. Atlantic Monthly 221(4):47–53.

Weizman, E. 1974. Aide-Memoire written after the Six Day War. Jerusalem Post, 23 April.

Wiegele, T. C. 1973. Decision-making in an international crisis: Some biological factors. Int. Studies Quart. 17(September):295–335.

PART V

Long-Term Consequences of
and Prospects for
Recovery from Nuclear War:
Two Views

The Medical Implications of Nuclear War, Institute of
Medicine. © 1986 by the National Academy of Sciences.
National Academy Press, Washington, D.C.

LONG-TERM CONSEQUENCES OF AND PROSPECTS FOR RECOVERY FROM NUCLEAR WAR: TWO VIEWS

View I

CARL SAGAN, PH.D.
Cornell University, Ithaca, New York

I have tried to read all the papers presented in this remarkable volume
nd have been impressed with the diversity of topics covered: targeting
nd prompt effects of nuclear explosions, atmospheric physics and chem-
stry, biological consequences, and the wide range of medical effects,
vhich is the central orientation of the book. I believe that this is the first
nterdisciplinary examination of the consequences of nuclear war that gives
ignificant attention to the psychological and psychiatric aspects, which
urely are a major part of the problem—both pre- and postwar.

It is striking to see how many new results have been announced on
ubjects that everyone thought were well-understood. The immediate and
specially the long-term consequences of nuclear war seem to hold an
normous number of surprises, almost all of which are unpleasant. It is
s if we live in a field of stones that no one has ever looked under. When
inally we succumb to our curiosity and turn the stones over, we find a
est of vipers under many of them.

There is a kind of deadly embrace between the United States and the
oviet Union—their military establishments depend on each other—that
oes back at least to 1945 and that has led to the construction of a kind
f global doomsday machine, which has been almost entirely ignored until
ately. The population of the planet has, by and large, been sleepwalking
hrough the last 40 years. The consequences of nuclear war, even as they
vere known 20 or 30 years ago, did not permeate the public consciousness.
And that is still the case, although less so, as a kind of race transpires
etween how fast new and disquieting discoveries are made about the

nature of nuclear war and how fast these discoveries are absorbed, ofte with great reluctance, into the consciousness of the public and the go ernment.

In this summary I proceed in rough serial order through some of th topics presented in this volume and give a few impressions. On the nucle winter issue itself, there now seems to be a fairly broad consensus aft the original TTAPS[1] study that it is something worth worrying abou something probably very grave. Even the most conservative and careful phrased reports on this subject make that apparent. The National Researc Council's report[2] states that nuclear winter is a "clear possibility" an that the probability that the severity of nuclear winter would be wor than in the "baseline case" is roughly the same as the probability that would be better. Despite uncertainties, "the committee believes that lon term climatic effects with severe implications for the biosphere cou occur."

Much stronger statements were made in early 1985 in a report by th Royal Society of Canada[3] (it called nuclear winter a "formidable threat" in various Soviet publications,[4] and in September 1985 in the SCOPI ENUWAR (Scientific Committee on Problems of the Environment/E vironmental Effects of Nuclear War) report by the International Counc of Scientific Unions,[5] a real tour de force involving hundreds of scientis from some 20 or so nations over a period of 3 years. They conclude th "the risks of unprecedented [climatic] consequences are great for no combatant and combatant countries alike." I recommend that everyor take a close look at the first volume on the physical effects of nucle war. It is an excellent summary of what we currently know. And th second volume on the biological effects in many places plows importa new ground, which is especially useful because there is a curious reluc ance on the part of the U.S. government to fund work on the biologic consequences of nuclear winter. I will return to this question.

The issue of the reliability of nuclear winter must of course be raise The subject is not readily amenable to direct experimental verification– at least not more than once, and very few people wish to perform th experiment, as important as it is to know the answer. The issue of reliabilit has been described[6] as analogous to what in the United States, perhap unfortunately, is called Russian roulette. You have a revolver that has si chambers. It is filled with an unknown number of cartridges, but probabl more than zero. The chambers are spun; you put the revolver to you temple and are about to pull the trigger. How relevant is it that you hav some doubt about how many of the chambers are filled? Would you d something very different if only one chamber were filled or if five or si were filled?

Perhaps the greatest uncertainty at present has to do with the duration of the effects of nuclear winter, whether the atmosphere would cleanse itself in, say, weeks or months or whether it would take considerably onger. This is a real issue, especially considering the self-lofting of soot, which has been demonstrated in recent fully interactive general circulation models, such as those of Malone and colleagues[7] at Los Alamos National Laboratory. Also, the earth's atmosphere is restructured by the heating that occurs at high altitudes to produce a vast region of thermal inversion. Working in the other direction is the fact that some soot but not dust would be chemically attacked in the upper atmosphere, and so the chemical properties, the absorption coefficients of the fine particles, may to some extent decay with time.

There is a school of thought that says that as long as the effects of nuclear winter are uncertain, they should not be seriously considered—or at least they should not be taken into account in discussions of public policy.[8] It is a curious position because, among other reasons, the standard military posture in thinking about the Soviet Union is the worst case analysis. The argument is always that we must plan not on what the Soviet Union is likely to do but what is the worst that they can possibly do. But somehow that approach does not carry over, even a little bit, in the minds of these people into assessments of the consequences of nuclear war. Here it is argued just the other way around; that is, the best possible case should be adopted as the basis for strategic policy and doctrine until it is un-ambiguously demonstrated that a worse case is probable.

The issues of exactly how much the temperatures would fall and exactly how much sunlight would be attenuated are, of course, uncertain. "Un-certain" does not mean that we know nothing. Uncertain means simply that we are not certain.* But even for relatively small nuclear wars, involving roughly 1 percent of the 20,000 or so strategic warheads in the U.S. and Soviet nuclear arsenals, the effects appear to be devastating—especially if cities are targeted.[1] What is especially relevant is the vul-nerability of biological systems, including the webs of ecological inter-dependence of which humans are a part, to even small temperature declines—

---

*Most estimates of nuclear winter continental temperature declines from ambient for a midsummer central strategic exchange have remained around -10 to $-25°C$, beginning with the original TTAPS[1] paper. Anspaugh (this volume) takes us to task for presenting one-dimensional calculations for land and sea separately, although we explicitly indicated that allowance for the thermal inertia of the oceans was likely to make "temperature decreases in continental interiors . . . roughly 30% smaller than predicted here, and along coastlines 70% smaller."

declines smaller than many recent models, as well as the earlier TTAPS models, suggest may be the case.

Food arrives on the table, or at least in the kitchen, and I often eat it Sometimes I go so far as to visit the grocery store or supermarket. But rarely trace back the sequence of events that begins in a furrowed fiel or a water-covered paddy. Harwell presents in this volume a paper on the ecological consequences of nuclear war. It is good to remember that crop are tremendously vulnerable to temperature declines, because much of the food we eat has arisen by a process of artificial selection over thousand of years from plants that were originally tropical or semitropical varieties. Their sensitivity to temperature is marked. The Royal Society of Canada report[3] and the SCOPE/ENUWAR report[5] both describe how a temperature decline of two or three centigrade degrees in Canada does very little to harm the wheat and barley crops. But one additional degree—a temper ature decline in the growing season that is very modest compared with those that occur in many nuclear winter scenarios—causes the crops to fail altogether.

Global agriculture also requires many subsidies: pesticides, fertilizers seed stocks, fuel for tractors, and many other things. Those subsidies to nations that are not engaged in the nuclear war, that are not in the northern mid-latitude combat zone, would, of course, be cut off since they come mainly from the industrialized, nuclear-capable targeted nations.

Therefore, for such distant countries, the implications for food are serious even if no nuclear weapons fall on their territory. And this is not just true in places where subsistence is marginal. A nation like Japan imports more than 50 percent of its food supply. So in the unlikely case that in a major nuclear war no targets in Japan were hit, and no significant radioactive fallout arrived from China, and no nuclear winter effects oc curred in Japan itself, then the principal effects would be on food, fuel, and other imports. But that in itself would be sufficient to induce starvation on an unprecedented scale in Japan.

More generally, nations that have no part in the quarrel between the United States and the Soviet Union (if there are any) and nations that are far removed from the northern mid-latitude combat zone could nevertheless be utterly destroyed in a nuclear war.[9] This is part of the answer to the question that I am sometimes asked: "What is new about nuclear winter?" We all knew we were going to die anyway." Those of us in the United States and the Soviet Union perhaps imagined that we were going to die anyway in a major nuclear war. But people elsewhere in the world imag ined that their fate would be quite different. Now it appears that we are all at risk.

The SCOPE/ENUWAR report stresses that the carrying capacity of the planetary environment is limited. The report does not guarantee that this the consequence of nuclear war, but the following numbers they adduce eem well worth pondering: If every nation were reduced to subsistence n local agriculture, without the kinds of major subsidies from without nat I mentioned above, then the carrying capacity of the planet would be population only 10 percent that at present, some hundreds of millions f people. If humans were to be reduced to living off natural ecosystems, s our hunter-gatherer ancestors did, then another factor of 10 reduction n the human population would immediately follow, so that 50 million or o humans would be all that the planet could support. And this assumes hat there are no effects other than those from the destruction of agriculture, hat no one dies from blast, prompt ionizing radiation, fires, fallout, lisease, cold, dark, pyrotoxins, or an enhanced surface flux of solar iltraviolet radiation.

Clearly, the agricultural consequences of nuclear war through starvation ire much more serious than had been suggested only a few years ago.

I was struck by a number of new findings presented in this volume: for xample, the analysis by Rotblat that the acute mean lethal dose for humans LD_{50}) may be considerably less than was previously thought, provided he other wartime stresses (but no ecological factors) are considered. I was also struck by the findings of Greer and Rifkin on the vulnerability of human T cells, and therefore of the human immune system, to the various stresses, mainly radiation stresses, of nuclear war. This raises another set of issues. Let me mention two of them.

First, if the dose required for radiation sickness and death goes down, does the dose required to compromise the immune system also go down? The answer seems to be that it does. The amount of prompt radioactive fallout that is in the range, for example, in which the human immune system would be compromised corresponds to what fraction of the area of the northern mid-latitude combat zone? Some very quick and rough estimates suggest that as much as one-third to one-half of the northern mid-latitude land area might suffer radiation doses approaching 100 rads. In the vivid phrase of Greer and Rifkin, nuclear war carries with it a kind of global case of acquired immune deficiency syndrome (AIDS).

The second issue is that of synergism, where the overall consequences of several different environmental stresses can be more than the sum of their parts. Let me give an example. Birds are differentially vulnerable to temperature declines, low light levels, and high-radiation environments. Insects are relatively invulnerable to those same environmental stresses. Birds are one class of predators on insects. After a nuclear war, birds would die but the insects would just close up shop for the winter. When the fine particles producing nuclear winter fall out or are carried out of the atmosphere and the conditions return more or less to normal, the insects rub their eyes and go about their business, reproducing at an increased rate. But insects are disease vectors. At the same time, human immune systems would be compromised and sanitary systems and medical and hospital systems would be severely attenuated. It seems likely that, under these conditions, epidemics and pandemics would rage.

There are many other examples. Synergisms have not at all been examined in detail. This is generally difficult to do because ecosystems are complicated. In virtually every case, but not in all cases, the synergisms work to decrease, not increase, the likelihood of long-term survival of the populations exposed to them.

I was asked to say something about the issue of extinction. It is hard, of course, to be in any sense certain about it. The paper by Ehrlich[10] and 19 others—mainly biologists and ecologists—that was published in December 1983, following publication of the TTAPS paper, stressed that at least under some circumstances, the extinction of plants, animals, and microorganisms might be expected. They went on to make a statement that was properly cautious, that is, that the extinction of the human species could not be excluded under these circumstances; however, they did not say that it was guaranteed.

But extinction is the rule, not the exception, for life on Earth. By far most species that have ever existed are extinct today. There have been massive species extinctions, including the extinctions at the Cretaceous-Tertiary boundary 65 million years ago, in which most of the species of life on Earth died out. It is at least a good bet[12] that the K-T extinctions were produced by something like nuclear winter, caused by the impact on the Earth of a 10-kilometer-diameter object, an asteroid or cometary nucleus, that sprayed fine particles up into the atmosphere that took 1 or 2 years to fall out. There is one major difference: the dinosaurs were not responsible for their own demise.

Now, there is an announced American plan—the so-called national program—to study nuclear winter and its consequences. It was originally advertised to be funded at $50 million for 5 years. The first year of funding, however, turns out to be at a rate of $5.5 million, and much of that turns out to be for programs that are not very different from those already authorized before the discovery of nuclear winter. The research is very highly concentrated in the Department of Defense and the national weapons laboratories. Only $500,000 is allocated to the National Science Foundation. There is an uncomfortable tendency for this very small amount of money to go to institutions that may, more so than others, be captives of what passes for the prevailing wisdom.

In addition, it is a matter of policy that virtually none of this money goes for biological studies—on the grounds that you have to be "sure" of the post-war physical environment before you can trace the biological implications. Well, that is a prescription for never studying the biological consequences at all. In contrast, a wide range of biological studies can be done in which possible nuclear war effects are parameterized—for example, studies in which communities of organisms, biomes, are subjected to a wide range of environmental stresses that would simulate nuclear winter along with its collateral effects such as radioactivity, pyrotoxins, and, later, enhanced UV-B flux. Such experiments would also be of general ecological utility quite apart from the nuclear winter issue.

Another aspect of some of the papers presented in this volume that struck me was the explicit or implicit seriousness of nuclear wars that fall significantly short of engaging the full strategic arsenals. In the original TTAPS nuclear winter study,[1] a heuristic calculation was performed for a nuclear war scenario in which 100 downtowns were burned and nothing else was destroyed. It would have required some 0.8 percent of the strategic arsenals and was shown to be enough to produce a very major nuclear winter effect.

Here, Daugherty, Levi, and von Hippel also talked about the destruction of 100 cities and found a trail of death and destruction resulting from prompt effects alone to be much worse than had been discussed previously. Abrams showed—in many different ways—the enormous disparity between the medical facilities that would be available after a nuclear war and the urgent human needs that would actually exist. While there were different proportional disparities, some of them—intensive care units and especially burn beds—represented very large disparity factors: a factor of 100 or more for the Federal Emergency Management Agency (FEMA) 6,500-megaton attack scenario.

So, if there is, say, a factor of 100 disparity between what is available and what would be needed for the survivors of a 6,500-megaton attack, it is again possible to see that the consequences would be extremely serious for something far less than a full exchange. Thus, it has been shown in three different ways that the strategic arsenals are vastly—I would say obscenely—in excess of what is necessary to produce unparalleled death and destruction. This has a range of policy implications, including policy implications for Star Wars, the Strategic Defense Initiative (SDI).

Even under very optimistic assessments, SDI leaks. These are not impermeable systems, and not even the most fervent technically competent advocates of Star Wars foresee impermeable systems in the next two or three decades. A system that is, for example, 10 percent permeable in a contemporary full strategic nuclear exchange might let through as many as a thousand and certainly a few hundred Soviet strategic warheads. This is in the same ballpark as or in excess of the kinds of numbers mentioned above. The U.S. and Soviet arsenals could be reduced by a factor of 10 to 100 and still retain for each nation an invulnerable and devastating retaliatory capability, maintaining, if we think it desirable, the posture of strategic deterrence.

The possible failures of human and technological systems, especially under stress, also have been discussed in this volume. There is currently a field of technology that is subject to a great deal of public scrutiny, in which an enormous amount of national pride has been invested, in which the best minds work, and for which the major nuclear nations have powerful incentives not to have embarrassing failures: the civilian space program. Nevertheless, there have always been and there remain major unexpected failures at every level in the civilian space program. Just recently there was the spectacle of French President François Mitterand visiting French Guiana to witness a launch of an Ariane booster, which promptly blew up on the pad. An even more famous case is when Soviet Premier Nikita Khrushchev was at the United Nations in New York and a spectacular launch was planned from Tyuratum. Instead there was a spectacular explosion, which killed Field Marshal Nedelin and other members of the upper echelons of Soviet rocketry senior management. The explosion is easy to understand; that it killed a marshal is more difficult to understand.

And the space shuttle itself has had many failures: in the deployment of satellites, in its computers, and so on.* These examples are just reminders that technical failures are unavoidable, especially in a situation in which there is insufficient opportunity for testing because, as has been stated repeatedly, there can only be one nuclear war. There will not be much opportunity to learn from experience.

I would like to make a few remarks about the section of this volume on the psychosocial perspectives of images and risks of the nuclear arms race. I thought that this was extraordinarily useful and is perhaps the central topic of the nuclear war issue, namely, the human heart and mind. In the late winter and early spring of 1902, on the island of Martinique, there were a set of unmistakable premonitions of the forthcoming volcanic

---

*Note added in proof, May 9, 1986: Since I gave this presentation on September 22, 1985, my point has been tragically reinforced by the Challenger disaster and several subsequent NASA and DoD launch failures and, in the Soviet Union, by the Chernobyl disaster (for which the probability of meltdown was authoritatively stated by Soviet experts in 1985 as 0.0001/yr). With these sobering recent experiences before us, how sure are we of the improbability of accidental nuclear war or, if nuclear war happens, that the long-term consequences will fall short of the worst case? And if we are unsure, how should decisions on policy and doctrine be skewed? Also, what do these experiences tell us about the ultimate reliability of the proposed and vastly more complicated SDI systems?

explosion of Mt. Pelee. There were rumblings heard all over the island. There were ash deposits and a number of people on the island, including scientists, spoke out and urged prompt evacuation.

But civil authorities reassured everyone that there was nothing to worry about and vigorously opposed the idea of taking any precautions whatsoever. On May 8, 1902, the famous volcanic explosion occurred, which killed the entire population of the port of St. Pierre (some 26,000 people), except for a handful of prisoners in subterranean cells, and the like.

This is a dramatic illustration of denial: denial by public officials, denial in the face of the clear public interest. I give this as an existence theorem of what can happen, not hypothetically, but in the real world.

The psychiatric mechanisms that were discussed today—denial, displacement, and projection—are not part of the lexicon of political debate in this country or, indeed, as far as I know, anywhere else. And yet they are central issues of our time, especially, but by no means exclusively, for the nuclear war problem. Better education of national leaders and the world public on the existence and force of such unconscious motivations should have a high priority.

One of the principal difficulties of the nuclear war issue is a kind of failure of the imagination; that is, most of us have not experienced a nuclear war, and therefore it is hard to imagine. It has an abstract quality. It seems unreal. The principal, most effective means of transcending that failure of the imagination is to portray it in the news media, and especially on television.

We have heard about The Day After, but The Day After was, of course, a very bowdlerized version of nuclear war. The American Broadcasting Company (ABC) executives thought that even a bowdlerized version was too much for the American people and were unusually skittish and nervous about showing it. A television program much closer to the realities of a nuclear war—for example, the British Broadcasting Corporation (BBC) program Threads—was widely considered to be too difficult for Americans to see and was not shown by the commercial networks or even by the Public Broadcasting System. Only Ted Turner and WTBS had the courage to show it.

There is, here, an important tension between public education about these unpleasant possibilities and the understandable wish to avoid feeling rotten all the time. But it is essential that we understand what the stakes are if there is to be any likelihood that we can reduce the prospects of nuclear war.

It is noteworthy and surprising and distressing how infrequently television or films portray a hopeful future for the human species. Most television attempts to prognosticate what the future holds involve either a very unimaginative extrapolation from where we are today and/or som kind of global, usually nuclear, catastrophe. As a result, youngsters grow up expecting the worst, without any knowledge that major departures from the prevailing wisdom, in a benign direction, have occurred many time before in human history. They can happen again.

There was a time when the divine right of kings was powerfully ad vocated, in which national leaders and the clergy argued, to take an American example, that it was the specific intention of God Almighty that Americans should live under the yoke of King George III. Well, we now laugh at that. How could anyone have been so foolish as to believe that George III was divinely foisted upon us? But there was a time when the remark I have just made was treasonable.

The same is true of slavery, at least chattel slavery, in which people were bought and sold like cattle. That was also considered divinely or dained. Aristotle argued that chattel slavery is part of human nature, some humans (those in power) are "naturally" masters, others "naturally" slaves. And yet today, all over the world, with only a few exceptions, it is widely recognized that slavery is something monstrous; maybe our ancestors were comfortable with such an institution, but we in the enlightened present recognize it for what it is.

Similar remarks apply to cannibalism, smallpox, and many other social conventions and natural events that were once thought immutable. I suggest that our descendants—if we are wise enough to avoid the worst—will look upon our tolerance of nuclear weapons, or willingness to "live" with them, as we look on those tolerant of absolute monarchy or chattel slavery. I suggest that the nuclear war issue, which seems to be such a difficult nut to crack, also is a soluble problem, but only if, as Einstein urged upon us, we are willing to change our way of thinking.

NOTES

[1]Turco, R. P., O. B. Toon, T. P. Ackerman, J. B. Pollack, and C. Sagan. 1983. Nuclear winter: Global consequences of multiple nuclear explosions. Science 222:1283–1292. [TTAPS]

[2]National Research Council. Committee on the Atmospheric Effects of Nuclear Explosions. 1985. The Effects on the Atmosphere of a Major Nuclear Exchange. Washington, D.C.: National Academy Press.

[3]Royal Society of Canada. 1985. Nuclear Winter and Associated Effects: A Canadian Appraisal of the Environmental Impact of Nuclear War. Ottawa: Royal Society of Canada.

[4]Alexandrov, V., Update of climatic impacts of nuclear exchange, International Seminar on Nuclear War, Fourth Session, Erice, Italy, August 19–24, 1984; The Night After: Climatic and Biological Consequences of a Nuclear War, 1985, Moscow: Mir; see also Ehrlich, P. R., C. Sagan, D. Kennedy, and W. O. Roberts, 1984, The Cold and The Dark: The World After Nuclear War, New York: W. W. Norton.

[5]Pittock, A. B., T. P. Ackerman, P. J. Crutzen, M. C. MacCracken, C. S. Shapiro, and R. P. Turco, 1986, Environmental Consequences of Nuclear War, Vol. I: Physical and Atmospheric Effects, New York: John Wiley & Sons; Harwell, M. A., and T. C. Hutchinson, 1986, Environmental Consequences of Nuclear War, Vol. II: Ecological and Agricultural Effects, New York: John Wiley & Sons; see also Sagan, C., 1985, Nuclear winter: A report from the world scientific community, Environment 27(8):12–15,38–39.

[6]By S. Schneider in testimony, House Interior and Science and Technology Committees, March 14, 1985. (Proceedings in press, U.S. Government Printing Office, Washington, D.C.)

[7]Malone, R. L., L. H. Auer, G. A. Glatzmaier, M. C. Wood, and O. B. Toon. 1986. Nuclear winter: Three-dimensional simulations including interactive transport, scavenging, and solar heating of smoke. J. Geophys. Res., 91(D1):1059–1053; also see R. L. Malone, Atmospheric perturbations of large-scale nuclear war. This volume.

[8]See, e.g., Teller, E., 1984, Widespread after-effects of nuclear war, Nature 310:621–624; and the rebuttal, Sagan, C., 1985, On minimizing the consequences of nuclear war, Nature 317:485–488.

[9]Sagan, C. Nuclear war and climatic catastrophe: Some policy implications. 1983/1984. Foreign Affairs 62(2):257–292.

[10]Ehrlich, P. R., et al. 1983. Long-term biological consequences of nuclear war. Science 222:1293–1300.

[11]Sepkoski, J. John Jr. 1986. Phanerozoic overview of mass extinction, in Pattern and Process in the History of Life, D. M. Raup and D. Jablonski (eds.). Berlin: Springer-Verlag.

[12]Alvarez, L. W., W. Alvarez, F. Asaro, and H. V. Michel, 1980, Extraterrestrial cause for the cretaceous-tertiary extinction, Science 208:1095; Pollack, J. B., O. B. Toon, T. P. Ackerman, C. P. McKay, and R. P. Turco, 1983, Environmental effects of an impact-generated dust cloud: Implications for the cretaceous-tertiary extinctions, Science 219:287.

The Medical Implications of Nuclear War, Institute of
Medicine. © 1986 by the National Academy of Sciences
National Academy Press, Washington, D.C.

LONG-TERM CONSEQUENCES OF AND PROSPECTS FOR RECOVERY FROM NUCLEAR WAR: TWO VIEWS

View II

LYNN R. ANSPAUGH, PH.D.
Lawrence Livermore National Laboratory
Livermore, California

INTRODUCTION

I have been asked to comment on the information presented in this
volume and to speculate on the long-term consequences of nuclear war
and the prospects for recovery. In order to do that, it might be useful to
define long term. To me this means time frames of years to perhaps even
hundreds of years in terms of the ultimate response and recovery of large-
scale ecosystems. Such long time frames may seem excessive, but if some
of the speculated effects of nuclear war are actually realized, it may indeed
take centuries before native ecosystems restabilize.

Also, when referring to long-term effects of the magnitude required to
have a major impact on entire ecosystems, it is clear that the driving force
would not be the direct effects of nuclear war. Of potentially greater
significance would be the secondary effects mediated by the intermediate-
term impacts on global climate. Specifically, I refer to the speculative
impacts of major decreases in the heat and light fluxes reaching the Earth's
surface. Such changes are commonly referred to as "nuclear winter."

UNCERTAINTIES IN THE "NUCLEAR WINTER" SCENARIO

Because the long-term biological and ecological consequences depend
on the short- and intermediate-term perturbations on global climate, it is
necessary to translate these climatic effects into impacts on individual
organisms and ecological systems. This problem is enormously complex.

Any serious attempt to solve this biological and ecological problem must depend on accurate input data concerning the changes in global climate.

Thus it seems prudent to examine first the validity of the projected impacts on global climate and to view these projections with a healthy dose of skepticism. I hasten to add that I certainly do not know whether a "nuclear winter" would or would not occur, because we simply do not have a thorough technical understanding of this issue. A similar statement can be made about many of the other projections concerning what might occur as a consequence of nuclear war.

Figure 1 represents my reaction to much of what I have read in this volume. The projected impacts of global nuclear war involve extreme extrapolations beyond observational experience. There are a few things that are known with some certainty, such as the propagation of shock waves and thermal loadings. From this it is necessary to employ projections that involve a great deal of extrapolation, not only in terms of magnitude but of the processes themselves.

As an example, there is speculation that "superfires" might occur, but there are no firm data on which to base such speculations; and it is fair to say that there is simply no basic understanding of the physics of the process such that one can predict with any certainty the essential requirements for the production of a superfire. Furthermore, the whole concept of nuclear "winter" depends on fire phenomenology and how this translates into the injection of smoke into the atmosphere. One must rely on estimates of combustible material, of the fraction of combustible material that would actually burn, of the fraction of burned material that would become smoke, of where within the atmosphere the smoke would be injected, of the carbonaceous content of the smoke, and of the optical properties of the smoke particles.

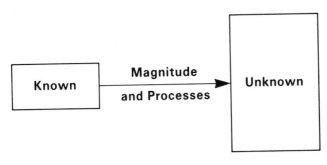

FIGURE 1 The projected impacts of nuclear war involve many extrapolations beyond observational experiences.

From these estimates of the smoke injected into the atmosphere, one must estimate the coagulation and scavenging of the injected smoke particles and their diffusion and spreading. Finally, the impact of the injected smoke must be estimated in terms of the physics of visible light absorption and scattering with due regard given to the changes in the optical properties of the atmosphere as they also affect the absorption of infrared radiation emanating from the Earth's surface. Even assuming that all of these effects have been calculated properly, it is then necessary to model correctly the changes in the structure of the atmosphere including the great differences that can be expected to occur over land as opposed to over the ocean.

Now, unfortunately, these projections are well beyond any existing data bases, and, more importantly, they are also well beyond current understanding of the processes that are involved. One of the central issues in the ''nuclear winter'' scenario is the very important question: Have we perceived and modeled correctly all of the relevant processes that might be important in this situation, which is far beyond our observational experiences? Of course, this concern is not one sided. It is not known whether the current imperfect understanding leads to over- or underestimation of the projected effects on the global climate.

The next desired step is to translate the projected effects on global climate into effects on biological and ecological systems. There is even a lesser ability to do this because there is not a long-range, broad-based program that attempts to model ecological systems on a sufficiently large scale. There has been a global climate modeling program for many years, and this has been applied to this problem with a great deal of success and with the achievement of substantial progress. Unfortunately, there is not an analog in biology and ecology that can be applied readily to this problem.

However, the biologists and ecologists do have one compelling advantage in that they can actually perform some of the relevant experiments. That is, they can put biological systems into conditions that simulate the predicted effects of ''nuclear winter'' and make actual experimental determinations. Up to this time, such studies have not been done, but they are to begin shortly.

I emphasize again that there is no global ecosystem model that can be applied to this problem. The best that there are at the moment are community-scale models that operate on a geographic scale about equal to the size of a stage in an auditorium. Even these models are based largely on empirical data and do not contain a thorough understanding of the relevant processes so that they may be applied reliably to predict situations that appear to be beyond observational experience. In terms of recovery, these models do not deal with some of the essential processes such as extinction and migration. Thus at present biologists and ecologists do not have an ecosystem-prediction model that can be coupled to the output from the global climate prediction models.

The global climate models are now being used to predict the effects known as "nuclear winter"; these effects generally consist of lower temperatures and lower light levels on the Earth's surface, and some predictions include lower amounts of rainfall. Typically, effects are predicted that are most severe for about 30 days, and then a return to normality is indicated. However, the further into time that these predictions are made, the more uncertain they become. It is fair to say that none of these predictions can be considered to be realistic and, if the predicted short-term effects should occur, it is an open question as to how long the effects might last. Some authors speculate that the modified atmosphere will restabilize with a situation that would reduce the scavenging processes; others postulate that the modified atmosphere, if modeled correctly, might be very unstable.

Examine some of the predictions of the effect of nuclear war on global climate and how these predictions have changed as a function of time. In Figure 2 are plotted some data on predicted changes in temperature on the Earth's surface that I have taken from Table 2 in a paper by Covey.[1] These data on predicted temperature changes are plotted as an approximate function of the study's completion date. The initial TTAPS study[2] was with a one-dimensional model, and later studies[3-7] have included three-dimensional interactive models that include the seasonal effects and other variables. What can be seen is that there has been a significant change in the predictions as the models have become more sophisticated. Moreover, the overall effect is toward less extreme changes (all changes shown here are roughly for midcontinent regions).*

---

*During the discussion period during the symposium, Dr. Sagan objected to my characterization of change as shown in Figure 2. He stated that the TTAPS paper[2] included a statement that, because of ocean buffering, "Actual temperature decreases in continental interiors *might* [emphasis added] be roughly 30 percent smaller than predicted here . . . ," and therefore the temperature change predicted by the TTAPS sutdy was −25°C, which is essentially the same as results of later calculations. However, I note that −35°C is used without caveat in their Figure 2, which is the key element of the paper. Furthermore, if the −35°C change is too large to represent changes in midcontinental temperatures, what does it represent? (Changes over the ocean and coastal areas would be smaller.) Finally, I note that the TTAPS paper had a companion paper (Ehrlich et al.[8]), of which Sagan was a coauthor, and it quotes a value from the TTAPS study of −40°C in the text and −43°C in its Table 1. If −25°C were the proper number, why the use of −40°C or −43°C in subsequent calculations?

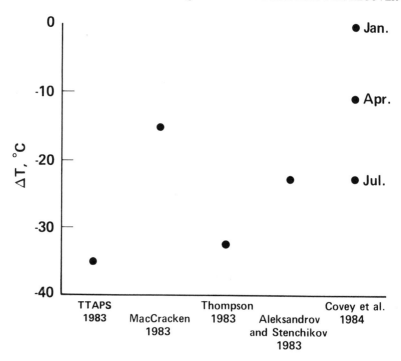

FIGURE 2   Predictions of changes in temperature as a function of time. Source: Data from Covey (1985, p. 565).[1]

As mentioned by Harwell in this volume,[9] these changes have an impact on the problem of predicting biological and ecological changes, too, in that they present a moving target of input data. The biological and ecological predictions would be much easier if the changes in global climate were so severe that the conclusion would be obvious. Now that the predicted temperature changes are more moderate, the problem of predicting biological and ecological effects has become more difficult.

The data plotted in Figure 2 are not the last word in predictions of changes in the global climate. Where the predictions might go from here is a question of great interest. I agree completely with the comment made by Turco[10] that astounding progress has been made in the ability to model and predict changes in global climate, and we can look to further advances in this ability. There also remains, however, the question of the validity of the input data that are used to drive these models. Covey[1] states, "The greatest uncertainty is the amount of smoke produced by fires." Carrier[11] considered the uncertainties in input data and made estimates of uncertainties for the following:

- fuel amount, factor of 2
- fuel that burns, factor of 2
- smoke-to-fuel ratio, factor of 3
- early scavenging of smoke, factor of 3

It is not obvious how these uncertainties should be propagated, but a simple root mean square of the above is a factor of 5.

A central question is what effect these uncertainties, which relate to the quantity of smoke particles injected into the atmosphere, might have on the predicted impacts on global climate. Plotted in Figure 3 are some data taken from MacCracken,[12] who has examined the sensitivity of his calculated changes in temperature to the amount of smoke injected. (The temperature changes plotted here are calculated for 10 days after smoke injection into the Northern Hemisphere between 20° and 70° n. lat.) Typical calculations for a base scenario have assumed that about 120 to 140 teragrams (Tg) of smoke are injected. As shown in Figure 3, the calculated change in temperature is quite sensitive to this assumption in a nonlinear way and the rate of change at 120 Tg is high. According to MacCracken's calculations,[12] essentially the entire predicted effect on temperature would disappear if the amount of smoke injected were less by a factor of 2 or 3.

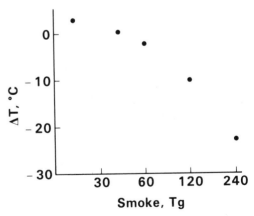

FIGURE 3   Sensitivity of calculated changes in temperature to amount of smoke injected into the atmosphere. Source: Data from MacCracken (1985, p. 26).[12]

In view of this sensitivity, it seems prudent to reexamine carefully all input data and processes that are involved in calculating the amount of smoke that would be injected into the atmosphere. A major step in these calculations is the seemingly simple tabulation of all the combustible material that might be available to burn during some postulated scenario of nuclear war. Unfortunately, even this step is not easy and is subject to major uncertainties. Bing[13] has recently attempted such a tabulation, and his results for this total combustible inventory are one-third or less than those of other studies. If correct, this might be sufficient to eliminate the entire postulated effect of "nuclear winter," and it is important that this issue receive more attention and analysis.

There are other issues as well. These involve the nature of the fuel and the resulting properties of the smoke that would be produced. As noted previously, important properties of smoke include its carbon content, its optical scattering and absorption properties, and whether the particles are wettable and able to serve as condensation nuclei. Thus, a major conclusion is that more data are needed to address these issues. Unfortunately, there seems to be very little work in progress to acquire such data. For example, two papers presented in this volume[10,14] refer to a managed forest fire in Canada. This fire appeared to have presented an opportunity to do some basic measurements on the smoke-to-fuel ratio and on the optical properties of the smoke particles, but neither of the presenters indicated that any such measurements had been made.

Finally, there is the main question at issue: What would be the biological and ecological effects from possible changes in the global climate as a result of a nuclear war? These predictions have been changing, too. Ehrlich et al.[8], with the assumption of a temperature change of about $-40°C$, predicted extremely dire consequences and questioned whether humans might survive as a species. Harwell[9] presented the results of the just completed Scientific Committee on Problems of the Environment (SCOPE) study. His presentation indicated that the SCOPE study had encountered difficulty in trying to predict biological and ecological consequences of "nuclear winter," when the predictions from the global climate models were undergoing substantial changes. They therefore attempted to present predictions that were normalized in terms of predicted biological changes per unit of change in global climate (particularly temperature). Harwell emphasized a possible severe impact on agricultural systems that, coupled with a breakdown of social and transportation systems, might result in mass starvation.

Generally, the ability to predict biological and ecological effects in response to climatic changes of any nature is poor. Even assuming that the predicted changes in global climate might be correct, there is not a good basis to predict changes in plant and animal populations. There are some good models of the physiological response of agricultural crops to lower temperatures, but, to my knowledge, there are no data on the response of crops to the simultaneous effects of lower temperature and lower levels of light flux. Furthermore, some predictions of changes in global climate[12] indicate that the diurnal cycle might be destroyed. These effects, coupled with the predicted subsequent occurrence of greatly increased ultraviolet radiation, leave us with essentially no observational experience on which to draw to make predictions.

Of greater interest over the long term are possible effects on native ecosystems. Native ecosystems are not like agricultural crops, which are annual and typically consist of tropical and subtropical plant species. There are no physiological models for native plants and there are even fewer relevant data that can be applied to this problem. The processes and interactions themselves are poorly understood. The simulation models that are available and that were used in the SCOPE study are limited and of questionable validity for the projected input conditions.

CURRENT CAPABILITY TO PREDICT BIOLOGICAL AND ECOLOGICAL CONSEQUENCES

The Lawrence Livermore National Laboratory (LLNL) and Stanford University recently cohosted a workshop[15] with the goal of examining the current state of knowledge that can be applied to predicting the biological and ecological effects of a postulated "nuclear winter." A major result of that workshop was that the ability to make quantitative predictions is very poor, but there is a large body of expert opinion that can be used to identify and classify ecosystems with regard to their sensitivity, resilience, etc. Figure 4 is one such example from the LLNL-Stanford Workshop, in which major ecosystems were classified with respect to their susceptibility to the stresses following a nuclear war. Harwell[9] showed similar attempts to classify ecosystems; a typical result is that the tropical rain forest is identified as the most sensitive ecosystem. This classification scheme, coupled with projected changes in global climate, allows derivation of some impression for the amount of damage to ecosystems that might result.

The next step is to examine the characteristics of the ecosystem types in terms of the features that might be important in the recovery of that system from damage. An attempt to do that is shown in Figure 5, which is also taken from the LLNL-Stanford Workshop.[15] Again, this is not a quantitative procedure, and it is only possible to classify and rank properties of resilience. This is because there is not a good understanding of

System	Cold	Low light	Fire	Toxic gas	Radiation
Tropical rain forest	High	High	Moderate	High	Moderate
Temperate forest	Moderate	Moderate	Moderate	Moderate	Moderate
Boreal forest	Low	Low	Low	Moderate	High
Grassland	Moderate	Moderate	Moderate	Moderate	Low
Savanna	High	High	Low	Low	Low
Desert	Low (?)	High	Low	Low	Moderate
Chaparral	Moderate	Moderate	Low	Low	Moderate
Tundra	Low	Low	Moderate	Low	Moderate

FIGURE 4 Susceptibility of the biomes to the stresses following a nuclear war

several processes that would be needed in order to do this in a quantitative way. These processes include succession, local extinctions, and migration of species. It is interesting to note that Figure 5 indicates that the tropical rain forest has the poorest prospect for recovery. Thus, this ecosystem has been identified as both highly sensitive to the effects of global climatic changes and as having a poor prospect for recovery from any induced damage.

Ecosystem	Environmental growth potential	Recovery Potential Seed bank	Resprouting ability	Breeding system	Symbiotic interactions
Tropical rain forest	High	Low	Low	Low	Low
Temperate forest	Moderate	Moderate	Moderate	Moderate	Moderate
Boreal forest	Low	Moderate	Moderate	High	High
Grassland	Moderate	High	Moderate	High	Moderate
Savanna	Moderate	Moderate	High	High	Low
Desert	Low	Moderate	High	Moderate	Moderate
Chaparral	Moderate	Moderate	High	Moderate	Moderate
Tundra	Low	Moderate	Low	Moderate	High

FIGURE 5 Components of resilience (recovery) of different biomes following death of the dominant species. High means that rapid recovery is likely.

WHAT IS NEEDED TO PREDICT BIOLOGICAL
AND ECOLOGICAL EFFECTS?

It would be desirable to have a suite of models, such as those shown in Figure 6, for the prediction of biological and ecological effects. One of the concepts illustrated in Figure 6 is the desirability of having models capable of dealing with a range of input data and having output specified as probability distributions. Reasonable models of global climate and individual organism response exist at present, but adequate ecosystem response and regional assessment models do not exist.

Also, there are not now adequate data for input to such models, even if the models did exist. Measurements of biological response have not been conducted under environmental conditions similar to those proposed for a "nuclear winter." These experiments to determine the response of individual organisms to the cold and dark are rather simple, and even more complex experiments are possible by building large exposure chambers over native communities.

One conclusion I offer is that we need additional research in order to understand the biological and ecological effects. The SCOPE study reported in this volume by Harwell[9] was a tremendous undertaking, but it was largely a volunteer, short-term effort that did not produce any new data. Rather, the objective was to synthesize existing data and to rely on

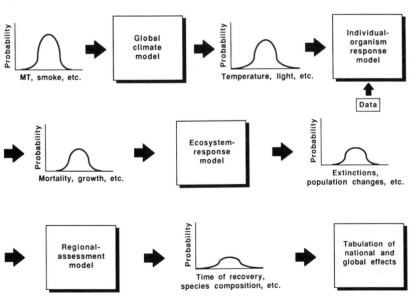

FIGURE 6   Nuclear winter assessment strategy.

- Studies to be done at the University of Wisconsin, Madison (J. Palta, B. McCown, T. Tibbitts)

- Initial studies with wheat, potato, soybean, loblolly pine

- Short-term

  — Minimum temperature of survival for different physiological periods in plant development

- Long-term

  — Simulate "nuclear winter" conditions predicted by MacCracken, et al. for continental N. America

  — Measure effects on plant productivity and mortality

FIGURE 7   Biological studies in controlled environments.

expert judgment and existing simulation models to make predictions. This effort represents an excellent beginning, but it still leaves important gaps in the needed data base and in the ability to simulate the required processes.

As mentioned by other speakers, there is currently not a major research program with the goal of predicting the biological and ecological effects of nuclear war. However, a modest program has been established at LLNL. One aspect of this program is experimental; its focus is outlined in Figure 7. This study will be conducted by the University of Wisconsin, Madison, under contract to LLNL. The goal is to acquire basic data on plant responses to conditions that mimic "nuclear winter."

At LLNL an attempt is also being made to develop new models that are capable of simulating large-scale ecosystems and which could deal with the "nuclear winter" conditions as input data. This is an activity that has a reasonable probability of success over several years and that could have a large payoff in application to other ecological problems of a global nature. Examples are the increasing level of carbon dioxide in the atmosphere and large-scale deposition of acid.

SPECULATIONS ON THE LONG-TERM CONSEQUENCES AND PROSPECTS FOR RECOVERY

Finally, I return to my assignment of speculating on the long-term consequences and the prospects for recovery. My opinion is that it simply is not known what the long-term biological and ecological effects would be, because there is not a firm grasp of what the effects of nuclear war would be on the global climate. Even if these effects were known, we would still fall far short of being able to translate accurately these climatic effects into biological and ecological effects.

However, it can be speculated that agricultural crops might be quite vulnerable and entire crops could be lost. Over the short term, this alone could produce a very serious problem for the surviving human population. Over the long term, agricultural crops could be reestablished, if the required energy and infrastructure are available.

I doubt that any major ecosystem would be completely destroyed. However, I have no way of knowing that, and any impact would be very sensitive to the actual changes in global heat and light fluxes. If substantial damage should occur to some ecosystems, they would undoubtedly restabilize over the long term to a structure that might or might not resemble the original.

OTHER REACTIONS TO THE MATERIAL PRESENTED

One interesting and surprising result presented in this volume by Rotblat[16] was his calculation of the dose that would produce 50 percent mortality (LD_{50}) for the Japanese exposed to radiation from the atomic bomb at Hiroshima. His calculated result was lower by about a factor of 2 than that which is commonly accepted. As Rotblat pointed out, his result is preliminary and awaits the conclusion of the major reassessment of the atomic bomb dosimetry that is now under way. If his result should stand, it may have a substantial impact on any assessment of casualties due to radiation exposure.

I was also surprised by the attention given to the paper presented by Greer and Rifkin,[17] wherein they pointed out that radiation and acquired immunodeficiency syndrome (AIDS) have somewhat similar effects on the immune system. While I follow the argument, this comparison fails on several significant fronts. The most important is that the effects of moderate doses of radiation on the immune system are neither critical nor life threatening and they are reversible, whereas the effects of AIDS on the immune system are the major effect of the disease and they are not reversible. Thus, I find the comparison to be superficial at best and a later characterization of nuclear war as a ''global case of AIDS''[18] to be substantially misleading. No one doubts that a large-scale nuclear war would be one of the worse, if not the worst, environmental disasters known to mankind; no exaggerations are needed to make that point.

Finally, I have had a strong impression of an unusual willingness of participants in the symposium to accept the offered predictive results and speculations at face value. It seems unusual for this to occur when these involve extrapolations that are so far beyond our observational experience. Perhaps a reason for this could be that the process has given way to emphasis on the desired and hoped for result: a final reason why global nuclear war *must* be avoided. While I have great sympathy for this view point, I believe that we as scientists will ultimately serve society best by examining every aspect of this issue more critically.

ACKNOWLEDGMENT

This work was performed under the auspices of the U.S. Department of Energy by the Lawrence Livermore National Laboratory under contract number W-7405-ENG-48.

NOTES

[1]Covey, C. 1985. Climatic effects of nuclear war. BioScience 35:563–569.

[2]Turco, R. P., O. B. Toon, T. P. Ackerman, J. B. Pollack, and C. Sagan. 1983. Nuclear winter: Global consequences of multiple nuclear explosions. Science 222:1283–1292.

[3]MacCracken, M. C. 1983. Nuclear War: Preliminary Estimates of the Climatic Effect of a Nuclear Exchange. Paper presented at the Third International Conference on Nuclear War, Erice, Italy, August 19–23, 1983. (Quoted in note 1.)

[4]Thompson, S. L. 1983. A Comparison of Baroclinic Eddy Heat Transport to a Simplified General Circulation Model. NCAR Cooperative Thesis No. 71, National Center for Atmospheric Research, Boulder, Colo. (Quoted in note 1.)

[5]Thompson, S. L., and C. Covey. 1983. Influence of Physical Processes in General Circulation Model Simulations of Massive Atmospheric Soot Injections. American Geophysical Union, Fall Meeting, San Francisco, December 1983. Washington, D.C.: American Geophysical Union. (Quoted in note 1.)

[6]Aleksandrov, V. V., and G. L. Gtenchikov. 1983. On the Modeling of the Climatic Consequences of Nuclear War. Moscow: The Computing Center of the USSR Academy of Sciences. (Quoted in note 1.)

[7]Covey, C., S. H. Schneider, and S. L. Thompson. 1984. Global atmospheric effects of massive smoke injections from a nuclear war: Results from general circulation model simulations. Nature 308:21–25. (Quoted in note 1.)

[8]Ehrlich, P. R., J. Harte, M. A. Harwell, P. H. Raven, C. Sagan, G. M. Woodwell, J Berry, E. S. Ayensu, A. H. Ehrlich, T. Eisner, S. J. Gould, H. D. Grover, R. Herrera R. M. May, E. Mayr, C. P. McKay, H. A. Mooney, N. Myers, D. Pimentel, and J. M Teal. 1983. Long-term biological consequences of nuclear war. Science 222:1293–1300

[9]Harwell, M. A., and C. C. Harwell. 1986. Nuclear famine: the indirect effects of nuclear war. This volume.

[10]Turco, R. P. 1986. Recent assessments of the environmental consequences of nuclear war. This volume.

[11]Carrier, G. F. 1986. Nuclear winter: the state of the science. This volume.

[12]MacCracken, M. C. 1985. Global atmospheric effects of nuclear war. Pp. 10–35 in Energy and Technology Review. UCRL-52000-85-5. Livermore, Calif.: Lawrence Livermore National Laboratory.

[13]Bing, G. 1985. Estimates of total combustible material in NATO and Warsaw Pact Countries. UCRL-93192. Livermore, Calif.: Lawrence Livermore National Laboratory.

[14]Brode, H. L., and R. D. Small. 1986. A review of the physics of large urban fires This volume.

[15]Kercher, J. R., and H. A. Mooney, eds. In press. Research agenda for ecological effects of nuclear winter. UCRL-53588. Livermore, Calif.: Lawrence Livermore National Laboratory.

[16]Rotblat, J. 1986. Acute radiation mortality in a nuclear war. This volume.

[17]Greer, D. S., and L. S. Rifkin. 1986. The immunological impact of nuclear warfare. This volume.

[18]Sagan, C. 1986. Long-term consequences of and prospects for recovery from nuclear war: view I. This volume.

Concluding Remarks

The Medical Implications of Nuclear War, Institute of Medicine. © 1986 by the National Academy of Sciences. National Academy Press, Washington, D.C.

Summary and Perspective: With Some Observations on Informed Consent

HERBERT L. ABRAMS, M.D.
Stanford University, Stanford, California

By accident, rather than by design, the symposium on the Medical Implications of Nuclear War took place almost exactly at the time that arms control negotiations between the Soviet Union and the United States resumed in Geneva. The papers in this volume constitute an argument of unparalleled persuasiveness for the superpowers to reach agreement before it is too late.

Physicians and scientists can take great pride in the role that they have played in raising the consciousness of America and the world to the threat of nuclear war and in educating themselves, the public, and policymakers. The papers presented in this volume are further examples of the educational process at work.

Let me present, in summary form, a series of propositions—some old, some new—that emerge from this meeting.

1. In the wake of a massive nuclear exchange, deaths from the acute effects will go far beyond those of any other period in human history.
2. While acute deaths will result from burn, blast, and radiation, the impact of fire will be far greater than anticipated, and thermal injury will be a dominating cause of the immediate casualties.
3. The effect of ionizing radiation may exceed that of prior projections; the LD_{50}—the dose at which 50 percent of all those exposed will die—may well be considerably less than previously accepted figures.
4. The estimated casualties both of countervalue and of counterforce attacks are formidable; the delicately crafted surgical strike that would

destroy the adversary's offensive weapons while doing little damage t•
the population is probably a fiction.

5. Climatic changes will occur with the injection of soot, smoke, an•
dust into the atmosphere; this may radically alter the conditions of life o1
the planet.

6. The degradation of agriculture by temperature change and the de
struction of the world's bread basket—the United States and Europe—
will cause tens of millions (possibly even billions) of deaths from star
vation.

7. Large amounts of oxides of nitrogen (nitric oxide) will alter th•
stratospheric ozone layer and expose the surviving population of the plane
to excessive, harmful ultraviolet B.

8. Other toxic chemicals and carcinogens, including dioxins, furans
and sulfates, will be emitted consequent to the fires and blast.

9. The synergistic effect of ionizing and ultraviolet radiation, trauma
burns, and malnutrition will create an acquired immunodeficiency con
dition in survivors that will augment the spread of exotic infections in th•
post-nuclear-war period and may underlie an increased incidence of can
cer.

10. The medical care system is highly vulnerable to disruption. In eithe
a massive exchange between the superpowers or a single one-megato1
attack on a large urban center, the system will be severely stressed, an•
there will be huge disparities between availability of and need for vita
medical resources.

11. Developing nations depend on the developed world for much o•
their drugs and medical supplies and equipment. Destruction of the source;
of supply will cripple their capacity to respond to injury and disease.

12. The threat of nuclear war engenders profound reactions of anxiet•
and concern among some children and adolescents.

13. It is said that Americans believe that nuclear war is unlikely, bu•
when asked, they estimate that there is a one-third or a 50/50 chance tha•
it will occur in their lifetime. If it occurs, they do not expect to survive
and they doubt that there is much they can do about it either way. Th•
issue of nuclear war is not central to their thinking and is far more remote
than bread and butter issues, but there is remarkably uniform support fo.
a nuclear freeze.

14. The managerial demands of modern weapons systems may excee•
the capacity to respond without error in times of crisis.

15. At any one time nuclear weapons personnel include numerous un
stable individuals—drug addicts, alcohol abusers, and psychotics.

16. Crisis-induced stress clearly affects the capacity of decision maker•
in times of international tension.

17. The two superpowers hold a mirror image of each other. The USSR and the United States each believes that the other is an expanding, aggressive, imperialist society intent on dominating large portions of the globe remote from its geographic borders. Methods to reduce mutual fear and mistrust are central to the maintenance of peace and avoidance of nuclear weapons use in the modern era.

18. In the short term, improvements in screening of nuclear weapons personnel, crisis prevention measures, and substantive changes in both structural design and day-to-day management of policymaking systems are essential to ensure our ability to cope with crisis and to avoid inadvertent nuclear war.

Most of the uncertainties have also been delineated:

1. How many deaths?
2. How much soot and smoke?
3. What degree of temperature change?
4. What time of the year?
5. How long will it last?
6. To what degree and in what time period can agriculture respond after a massive nuclear exchange?
7. How profoundly will the synergistic effects augment each other?
8. Will national leaders work together to handle the common threat?
9. How can that process be augmented by the social, political, and behavioral sciences?
10. How can the public be better educated and more involved?

The research agenda—the unanswered questions that remain—is a formidable compilation of work that lies ahead. Part of that work will resolve some of the uncertainties amenable to careful scientific scrutiny. But I am in full agreement that until that time, the truly conservative approach—and the conservation of life and health is the central concern of the physician—is to consider the uncertainties at the worst case level. This is how physicians best protect their patients: by a full consideration of the hazards of the illness that the patient confronts and of the possibilities of complications.

As we have wrestled with the weighty problems arising from the most intense and potentially catastrophic arms race in history, a number of oddities have become apparent. Does it strike you as extraordinary that this great National Academy of Sciences—with the best scientific minds in the country and many of the best in the world—could write a report on the ecological effects of nuclear war as recently as 1975 and totally neglect the impact of soot and smoke in producing climatologic changes?

Is there something peculiar about the new projections of fatalities based on the understanding that firestorms—studied in detail in Dresden and Hamburg—will be fiercely destructive and cause death in a range two to four times as great as those previously predicted? Is it unusual to hear in 1985 that the effects of fire will dominate those of blast and radiation as the central killer in the Third World War? Can we really be satisfied with the concept that nuclear winter emerged as a credible consequence only because *Ambio* asked Crutzen and Birks to write an article on nitrogen oxides, ozone, and dust?

I think not. The message presented in the papers in this volume is that just as we knew less about the effects of massive nuclear war on this planet in 1975 than we do in 1985, so by 1995 dimensions as yet totally unrealized and undescribed will then be apparent. Those effects will be worked out and scientifically validated within the limits of our methods.

My most profound hope is that none of these phenomena will have the kind of experimental verification that has established the credibility of modern science—that no one of us, in the near term or in a distant era, will have the opportunity to match the predictive brilliance of modern science with the empiric observations of the magnitude of these effects.

When Small, Brode, and Postol start with the fires; when Crutzen, Birks, and Carrier inject hundreds of tons of smoke and soot into the atmosphere; when Harwell and SCOPE define the effects on agriculture and the ensuing starvation in Asia, then it becomes manifest beyond question that the superpowers are engaged in an adventure that has potential ramifications extending far beyond their borders.

Physicians and scientists must emphasize that in the nuclear age, there are questions more profound and more serious than ever before as to the conduct and obligations of governments, not only toward their own citizens but toward all peoples who may be affected by their policies and actions.

Over a long period, the medical profession has worked out a set of criteria for appropriate behavior of physicians toward their patients. Their failure to use due care embodies negligence, or malpractice, for which the patient has legal recourse.

Is it possible that governments may be guilty of malpractice? Surely they have the same responsibility to populations as physicians have to individuals.

Due care, when referring to the affairs of nations, implies the use of ordinary skill and judgment in enhancing life, liberty, and the pursuit of happiness; conforming to international standards of reasonable conduct; acting in the light of current knowledge as to how conflicts can be resolved without the death of tens of hundreds of millions of people. When government departs from accepted practice, it must only be done if the people understand and if the people consent.

In medical malpractice cases, the standard of care most frequently applied has been the community standard. A change has now occurred in the locality rule, and a specialist is expected to perform at a level of care equivalent to that of other specialists in his field, regardless of geographic location. The community standard has been extended to embrace the national medical community.

In international discourse, it may equally be said that the national standard must be extended to embrace the international community. Activities or behavior which threaten third parties must be looked upon as an aberration from this rule.

In the general nuclear debate, the failure of the U.S. and Soviet policymakers to recognize the potential effect of their actions on the rest of the world goes hand in hand with the absence of any consideration of the doctrine of informed consent.

In recent years, the malpractice doctrine has been considerably broadened to include the physician's duty to obtain an informed refusal, to warn third parties, and to notify patients whenever past procedures or treatment are discovered to be potentially harmful. The physician has the duty to disclose information any and every time a risk is posed and must divulge information to related third parties when harm to others is reasonably foreseeable.

In the conduct of governmental affairs, far-reaching actions must also be explained: the risks, the potential benefits, the alternatives. The questions to be answered are not only those of the citizens of the involved nations but of all potentially affected countries. The uninvolved, the innocent bystanders, must understand that they are free to refuse or withdraw consent in the nuclear age.

It can hardly be said of the Soviet and American governments that they have systematically attempted to inform their own people fully, let alone those of other nations, of the potential consequences of their actions. Such actions have always been couched in terms of national security, rather than in terms of the extraordinary international insecurity they have produced.

Physicians have a responsibility to use appropriate diagnostic tests and to interpret them well. If a doctor makes a misdiagnosis on the basis of negligence, he is liable for malpractice. Unfortunately, if the diagnosis of the leaders of the superpowers is incorrect, and if the 50,000 nuclear weapons ultimately prove catastrophic to the Northern Hemisphere and much of the rest of the planet, there is no court of law in which they will be able to be tried.

The serious questions remain. How can governments be called on to account for their behavior? How can policymakers be placed in the courts not only of public opinion but of the developing world on whose lives their policies may impinge so radically? How can they be made to understand that the old Roman precept—if you desire peace, prepare for war—is, in the words of Lord Mountbatten, "absolute nuclear nonsense"

I cannot close without commenting on the notion expressed in some quarters that the grave matters dealt with in the papers in this volume are less than a proper subject to engage the energies of the Institute of Medicine. When we are asked to forego a scientific inquiry into the most important potential health and life issue of the century—to agree that we must leave it to the politicians or to the military—we know that to do so is to renounce our obligations in medicine and science. There is nothing political about knowledge. Educating the public is not a Republican or a Democratic or a Soviet Communist act. It is a traditional obligation that began in biblical times—indeed, at the dawn of civilization.

So when we are asked: Wasn't this a depressing symposium? Why spend your time in an auditorium confronting the apocalypse during the magnificent early autumn days of Washington? Isn't there something more bid about such a preoccupation? Then we can reply, with a sense of buoyancy and optimism, that we have asked the questions; we have obtained some, but not all, of the answers; we know more than we did yesterday; and our constituents—patients, the public, the policymakers—will all feel the ripple effect. They too will know in time, and it will affect their decisions and perhaps even the future of the world and of our grandchildren.

Glossary

Absorption optical depth: unit used to describe the attenuation at the earth's surface of sunlight passing through atmospheric smoke.

Albumin: most commonly used plasma protein for blood volume expansion.

Anoxia: failure of oxygen to gain access to, or be utilized by, the body tissues.

Barrier nursing: isolation of radiation victims whose immune systems are suppressed to prevent them from contracting infectious diseases.

BEIR: National Research Council Committee on the Biological Effects of Ionizing Radiations.

Beta particles: charged particles emitted from a nucleus during radioactive decay; a negatively charged beta particle is identical to an electron, and a positively charged particle is called a positron. Large amounts of beta radiation may cause skin burns, and beta emitters are harmful if they enter the body, but the particles are easily stopped by materials such as metal or plastic.

Bioaccumulation: the accumulation of a substance in a living organism.

Black rain: smoke from nuclear-initiated fires that is washed out of the atmosphere.

Blast lung: lesion caused when a shock wave compresses the chest wall against the spinal column and then suddenly releases it. Death can occur immediately from the sudden propagation of air emboli into cerebral and cardiac circulation, or later, from pulmonary hemorrhage and pulmonary edema.

Bone marrow: tissue occurring in the long bones and certain flat bones of vertebrates, the primary function of which is the generation of red and white blood cells.

Bone marrow transplants: bone marrow from matched donors may be use to restore immunologic competence in patients whose marrow function ha been destroyed by ionizing radiation.

Burn injuries: *first-degree* burns affect only epidermis and can cause de hydration and pain. *Second-degree* burns (partial thickness burns) result i blistering of the skin and will heal by slow regrowth of skin from the woun base. *Third-degree* burns substantially affect the dermis and will heal onl with skin grafts. *Flash* burns resemble first- and second-degree burns, al though with slightly less tissue swelling and fluid loss, and may occur o exposed surfaces as a result of direct thermal radiation.

C^3: the command, control, and communication functions of strategic weap ons systems, including early warning monitoring systems.

Carcinogen: an agent that causes development of a carcinoma or any othe sort of malignancy.

Casualty clearing station: a rudimentary hospital used within a few mile of the front line during World War I.

Cesium-137: long-lived radioactive isotope (half-life 33 years) which be haves like calcium and tends to accumulate in the cytoplasm of humans.

Circadian cycles: a rhythmic process within an organism occurring inde pendently of external synchronizing signals. In humans, this internal clock maintains a 24- to 25-hour cycle.

Crater: pit, depression, or cavity formed in the earth's surface by a surface or underground explosion.

Crisis relocation: planned evacuation of population centers in anticipation of nuclear war.

CRP-2B: a scenario of massive nuclear war, designed by the Federal Emergency Management Agency, based on a hypothetical attack of 6,559 Mt of nuclear explosives targeted primarily at military installations and population centers within the United States.

Cytostatic: an agent that suppresses cell growth and multiplication.

Decay, radioactive: disintegration of the nucleus of an unstable nuclide by spontaneous emission of charged particles, photons, or both.

Denial: a psychologic process by which what is consciously intolerable (facts, deeds, thoughts, feelings) is disowned by an unconscious mechanism of non-awareness; aspects of reality are regarded as non-existent or are transformed so that they are no longer unpleasant or painful.

Dioxins: any of several heterocyclic hydrocarbons that occur as persistent toxic impurities in herbicides or as the waste product of some industrial chemical reactions, suspected of causing birth defects, liver damage, or death.

Disaster syndrome: the tendency of victims to demonstrate apathetic, docile, indecisive, unemotional, or mechanical behavior.

Dose: general term denoting quantity of radiation or energy absorbed; *absorbed dose* is the energy imparted to matter by ionizing radiation per unit mass of irradiated material at the point of interest (expressed in rads or grays); *cumulative dose* is total radiation resulting from repeated exposures; *doubling dose* is the amount of radiation needed to double the natural incidence of a genetic or somatic anomaly; *genetically significant dose* is the gonad dose from all sources of exposure that, if received by every member of the population, would be expected to produce the same total genetic effect on the population as the sum of individual doses actually received; *threshold dose* is the minimum absorbed dose that will produce a detectable degree of any given effect.

Electromagnetic pulse: a sharp pulse of electromagnetic energy generated by a nuclear explosion, capable of damaging unprotected electric and electronic equipment at great distances.

Ethnocentrism: a habitual disposition to judge foreign peoples or groups by the standards and practices of one's own culture or ethnic group.

Fallout: particles of radioactively contaminated material which are dispersed in the atmosphere following a nuclear explosion and which subsequently settle to the earth's surface; *local fallout* refers to particles, generally larger than 1 micron, that reach the earth within 24 hours after a nuclear explosion; *global fallout* refers to fine particulate matter and gaseous compounds that ascend into the upper troposphere and stratosphere and may be widely distributed over a period of weeks or months (intermediate-fallout) to years (long-term fallout).

False consensus bias: the belief that others share our attitudes.

FEMA: Federal Emergency Management Agency.

Fireball: luminous sphere of hot gases that is formed by a nuclear explosion.

Firebreak: a cleared area of land intended to interrupt the spread of fire.

Firestorm: a large area fire in which heated air and gases rise rapidly, drawing in cooler air from surrounding areas, thus generating surface temperatures of 1000°C, winds up to 90 mph, and convection patterns with a relatively static boundary.

Fission: the splitting of heavy nucleus into two approximately equal parts, accompanied by the release of energy and neutrons.

Fuel loading: amount and types of combustible materials in a structure or geographical area.

Fusion: a nuclear reaction characterized by the joining together of light nuclei to form heavier nuclei.

Gamma radiation: high-energy, short wavelength electromagnetic emissions from the nucleus, frequently accompanying alpha and beta emissions and always accompanying fission. Gamma rays are similar to X-rays, but are usually more energetic. They are very penetrating and are best shielded agains by dense materials such as lead.

Global climate model: three-dimensional computer simulation describin, the actions of winds, temperature, moisture, and other factors throughout th global atmosphere.

GLODEP2: an empirical model used to estimate the fate of intermediate and long-term fallout particles in a normal atmosphere.

GRANTOUR: three-dimensional transport model driven by meteorologica data, used to estimate global fallout in a perturbed atmosphere.

Gray (Gy): 100 rads.

Ground zero: point on the earth's surface at which, above which, or belov which an atomic detonation has actually occurred.

Groupthink: a way of coping with stress that is characterized primarily b a shared illusion of invulnerability, an exaggerated belief in the competenci of the group, and a shared illusion of unanimity within the group.

Height of burst: height above the earth's surface at which a bomb is det onated in air. The optimum height can be selected for a weapon of specifiec energy yield to produce effect over the maximum possible area.

Hematopoietic syndrome: following exposure to 200–1000 rads, a victim may experience anorexia, apathy, nausea, and vomiting. Symptoms may subside after 36 hours, but lymph nodes, spleen, and bone marrow begin to atrophy, leading to abnormally low numbers of all formed elements in the blood.

Hotline: direct circuit between government installations in the United State and the U.S.S.R., available for immediate use without patching or switching

Hotspot: region in a radioactively contaminated area in which the level o radiation is noticeably greater than in neighboring regions in the area.

Hyperthermia: a disturbance of the body's heat-regulating mechanism, re sulting from exposure to excessive heat, characterized by prostration and circulatory collapse, and which can result in high fever and collapse, and sometimes in convulsions, coma, and death.

Hypervigilance: condition in which a decision maker, under crisis-inducec stress, searches frantically for a way out of the dilemma, rapidly shifting between alternatives, and then impulsively seizing on a hastily contrivec solution that seems to promise immediate relief.

Hypocenter: see *Ground zero.*

Hypovolemia: low blood volume arising from dehydration or hemorrhage.

Iatrogenic illness: abnormal state or condition inadvertently produced by medical intervention.

ICRP: International Commission on Radiological Protection.

Immune response: in humans, it is divided into humoral (antibody) and cellular or cell-mediated components. The humoral portion is mediated by *B-*

lymphocytes which are precursors of antibody-secreting cells; the cellular portion is mediated by *T-lymphocytes* which protect against certain bacterial infections and many viral and fungal infections, and which provide resistance to malignant tumors. Lymphocytes can be further differentiated as *effector T-lymphocytes*, which respond to target antigens, e.g., reject foreign tumors and eliminate virus-infected cells; *helper T-lymphocytes*, which stimulate the differentiation of B-lymphocytes into mature antibody-secreting plasma cells and activate effector T-lymphocytes; and *suppressor T-lymphocytes*, which suppress the initiation of specific immune responses.

Intercontinental ballistic missile (ICBM): weapon flying a ballistic trajectory after guided powered flight, usually over ranges in excess of 4000 miles (6500 km).

Ionizing radiation: any electromagnetic or particulate radiation capable of displacing electrons from atoms or molecules, thereby producing ions, e.g., alpha, beta, gamma, X-rays, neutrons, and ultraviolet light. High doses may produce severe skin or tissue damage.

Isotopes: forms of an element having identical chemical properties but differing in atomic masses (due to different numbers of neutrons in their respective nuclei) and in their radioactive properties.

Kazarma: Soviet military barracks.

Kerma: a measure of the intensity of a radiation field, in rads.

Kiloton (kt): an explosive power equal to 1000 tons of TNT.

Lapse rate: rate at which atmospheric temperature changes with altitude.

Latency period: the stage of a disease in which there are no clinical signs or symptoms.

LD$_{50}$: dose of a substance that will kill 50 percent of individuals in a population within a specified period (usually 60 days).

Leukemia: any of several acute or chronic malignancies of the blood-forming organs characterized by uncontrolled leukocyte proliferation.

Light-water reactors: reactors using ordinary water as coolant, including boiling water reactors and pressurized water reactors, the most common types used in the United States.

Lymphocytes: see *Immune response.*

Maximum permissible concentration: highest quantity per unit volume of radioactive material in air, water, and foodstuffs that is not considered an undue risk to human health.

Megaton (Mt): energy released by the explosion of 1 million metric tons of TNT.

Methaqualone: a sedative and hypnotic drug that is habit-forming and subject to abuse; also known as Quaalude.

(MIRV) Multiple, Independently Targetable, Reentry Vehicles: method of

delivering several warheads having individual yields of 100 to 500 kt on a single rocket.

Multiple myeloma: a primary bone malignancy characterized by diffuse osteoporosis, anemia, hyperglobulinemia, and other clinical features.

Mutagen: an agent that raises the frequency of mutation above the spontaneous rate.

Mutation: abrupt change in the genotype of an organism; genetic material may undergo qualitative or quantitative alteration, or rearrangement.

Mutual assured destruction (MAD): strategic policy to deter nuclear attack by assuring the destruction of any attacker in retaliation.

Neurosis: a category of emotional maladjustments characterized by some impairment of thinking and judgment, with anxiety as the chief symptom.

Neutron: an uncharged elementary particle with a mass slightly greater than that of the proton. The neutron is a constituent of the nuclei of every atom heavier than hydrogen.

NO_x: Oxides of nitrogen.

Nuclear fuel cycle facilities: nuclear power reactors, facilities for mining, milling, isotopic enrichment, fabrication of fuel elements, reprocessing of fissionable material remaining in spent fuel, re-enrichment of fuel material, refabrication into new fuel elements, and waste disposal.

Nuclear weapons: bomb, warhead, or projectile using active nuclear material to cause a chain reaction on detonation. *Strategic nuclear weapons* have long ranges and large yields; *tactical nuclear weapons* generally have a relatively short range (less than 100 km) and relatively small yields; *theater nuclear weapons* are medium range and medium yield.

Nuclear winter: global climatic perturbations triggered by the lofting of smoke and soot into the upper atmosphere from fires ignited by nuclear weapons.

Organ factor: proportion of a radioactive dose to the body surface that reaches the bone marrow.

Osteosarcoma: a malignant tumor derived from bone or containing bone tissue.

Overpressure: the transient pressure, in excess of normal atmospheric pressure, produced by the shock wave from an explosion.

Ozone depletion: reduction of the layer of ozone in the atmosphere that filters ultraviolet radiation, roughly between 10 and 50 km above the earth's surface.

Permissive action link (PAL): a coded lock to prevent the unauthorized release of nuclear weapons.

Personnel reliability programs: processes for screening individuals with access to and technical knowledge of nuclear weapons.

Photochemical smog: atmospheric pollutants resulting from chemical reactions involving hydrocarbons and nitrogen oxides in the presence of sunlight.

Polychlorinated biphenyls (PCBs): highly carcinogenic compounds produced by replacing hydrogen atoms in biphenyl with chlorine, used primarily as an insulating fluid in electrical equipment and to lend durability to hydraulic fluids and plastics. It has been found to accumulate in fish and to cause animal cancers.

Polyvinyl chlorides (PVCs): synthetic material in the family of vinyl resins, used for food packaging and in molded products such as pipes, fibers, upholstery, and bristles. Combustion products are very toxic, especially in combination with other agents.

Precipitation scavenging: removal of smoke from the atmosphere by rainfall.

Probit analysis: statistical measurement of probability based on deviations from the mean of a normal frequency distribution.

Prodromal syndrome: the early acute effects of exposure to radiation. See *Radiation sickness.*

Progeny testing: evaluation of the genotype of an animal in terms of its offspring, for the purpose of controlled breeding.

Psychosis: an impairment of mental functioning to the extent that it interferes grossly with an individual's ability to meet the ordinary demands of life; generally characterized by severe affective disturbance, withdrawal from reality, formation of delusions or hallucinations, and regression presenting the appearance of personality disintegration.

PUVA photochemotherapy: ultraviolet radiation therapy for patients with psoriasis.

Rad (Roentgen Absorbed Dose): absorbed dose of any nuclear radiation which is accompanied by the liberation of 100 ergs of energy per gram of absorbing material.

Radiation sickness: the complex of symptoms characterizing the disease known as radiation injury, resulting from excessive exposure of the whole body (or large part) to ionizing radiation. Earliest symptoms are nausea, fatigue, vomiting, and diarrhea, which may be followed by loss of hair, hemorrhage, inflammation of the mouth and throat, and loss of energy. In severe cases, where the radiation exposure has been relatively large, death may occur within 2 to 4 weeks. Those who survive 6 weeks after the receipt of a single large dose of radiation generally may be expected to recover.

Radionuclides: an unstable isotope of an element that decays or disintegrates spontaneously, emitting ionizing radiation.

Reactor core: central portion of a nuclear reactor containing the radioactive fuel elements.

Reactor vessel: a strong-walled container housing the core of most types of power reactors; it usually also contains the moderator, neutron reflector, thermal shield, and control rods.

Reinforced Mach front: a single vertical shock wave formed when the primary shock wave of a nuclear detonation reaches the earth's surface and coincides with a second wave generated by reflection. The overpressure is roughly twice that of either the primary or secondary shock.

Ringer's lactate: a balanced electrolyte solution used as a blood volume expander.

SCOPE/ENUWAR: Scientific Committee on Problems of the Environment of the International Council of Scientific Unions program on the Environmental Effects of Nuclear War; a project involving about 100 physical and atmospheric scientists and 200 agricultural and ecological scientists from more than 30 countries around the world in a unique undertaking to assess the global consequences of nuclear war.

Shock wave: the wave of air pressure produced by an explosion.

Sepsis: severe, toxic, febrile state resulting from infection with pyogenic microorganisms.

SLBM: submarine-launched ballistic missile.

SSBN: nuclear-powered ballistic missile-firing submarine.

SDI (Strategic Defense Initiative):   a program of advanced technological research initiated by Presidential directive in March 1983 for the purpose of "eliminating the threat of nuclear ballistic missiles"; also known by the sobriquet "Star Wars."

Stratosphere: atmospheric shell extending about 55 km above the tropopause, i.e., atmospheric layer between the troposphere and the mesosphere, in which temperature changes very little with altitude.

Strontium-90:   long-lived radioactive isotope (half-life 28 years) which tends to accumulate in the bones of humans.

Superfires: see *Firestorms.*

Surface bursts: nuclear explosions that contact land surfaces drawing up large amounts (about 100,000 tons per megaton of yield) of dust, soil, and debris with the fireball.

Synergism or synergy: the joint action of agents so that their combined effect is greater than the sum of their individual effects.

Teragrams: 1 teragram (Tg) = 10^{12} grams.

Teratogenic effects: formation of a fetal monstrosity or congenital anomaly, often leading to spontaneous abortion. Fetuses irradiated during the third and fourth months of development are particularly prone to brain damage.

Thermal fluence: amount of heat transferred across a surface of unit area in a unit of time.

Thermal pulse: brief but intense release of heat emanating from a nuclear fireball, roughly equivalent to one-third of the total yield of a 1-Mt weapon.

Thermal time: measure of the number of hours during the growing season that air temperatures exceed a specified base level by various amounts, calculated by multiplying the amount of time that the air temperature exceeds the base level times the increment of temperature above that level.

Threshold level value: average concentration of toxic gas to which a normal person can be exposed without injury for 8 hours per day, 5 days per week, for an unlimited period.

Total lymphoid irradiation (TLI):   therapy in which a patient's immune reactions are suppressed by delivering ionizing radiation in multiple doses to lymphoid tissue over a period of weeks.

Triage: the process of sorting casualties for the purpose of allocating resources and determining the priorities of medical response.

Tropopause: altitude at which the ambient air temperature begins increasing with altitude; it is viewed as the dividing line between the lower atmosphere and the stratosphere.

Troposphere: region of the atmosphere from the earth's surface to the tropopause, that is, the lowest 10 to 20 km, in which storms and rainfall occur, and in which temperature falls with increasing altitude.

Ultraviolet-B radiation (UV-B):   emissions in the wavelength range 280–320 nm, which is biologically damaging to plants and animals.

UNSCEAR: United Nations Scientific Committee on the Effects of Atomic Radiation.

Wind shears: local variations of wind vector or any of its components in a given direction.

World food reserves: measured by total cereal stores at any given time. In recent years they have amounted to about 2 months' supply.

X-rays: electromagnetic radiation, identical to gamma rays, but produced in processes outside the atomic nucleus.

Biographies of
Contributors

HERBERT L. ABRAMS, M.D., is Professor of Radiology at Stanford University School of Medicine and a Member-in-Residence of the Stanford Center for International Security and Arms Control (Stanford, CA 94305). From 1967 to 1985 he was the Philip H. Cook Professor of Radiology at Harvard Medical School and Chairman of Radiology at Brigham and Women's Hospital in Boston. Dr. Abrams was founding Vice-President of International Physicians for the Prevention of Nuclear War and has served as National Cochairman of Physicians for Social Responsibility.

LYNN ANSPAUGH, Ph.D., is the Division Leader for Environmental Sciences at the Lawrence Livermore National Laboratory (Livermore, CA 94450). Since 1963, he has been with the Biomedical and Environmental Research Program at LLNL and has performed research in the areas of aeolian resuspension of toxic materials, radiation-dose-model development, and risk assessment. Dr. Anspaugh is also Project Leader for LLNL's studies on the biological and ecological effects of global nuclear war.

WILLIAM R. BEARDSLEE, M.D., is Clinical Director of the Department of Psychiatry of Children's Hospital Medical Center and Assistant Professor at Harvard Medical School (Boston, MA 02115). He was a member of the 1982 American Psychiatric Association task force on nuclear issues and coauthor of its report *Psychosocial Aspects of Nuclear Developments*.

JOHN W. BIRKS, Ph.D., is Professor of Chemistry and Acting Director of the Cooperative Institute for Research in Environmental Sciences, University of Colorado, Boulder (80309). With Paul J. Crutzen, he co-authored the first paper on nuclear winter, which appeared in 1982 in a special issue of the Swedish international journal *Ambio*.

NIKOLAI P. BOCHKOV, M.D., is Director of the Institute of Medical Genetics of the Soviet Academy of Medical Sciences (UL. Solyanka 14, Moscow 109801, USSR). Academician Bochkov was a member of the steering committee for the World Health Organization's study of the effects of nuclear war and co-author of the 1984 WHO report *Effects of Nuclear War on Health and Health Services*.

SHLOMO BREZNITZ, Ph.D., is Director of the Jaffe Centre for the Study of Psychological Stress at Haifa University, Haifa, Israel. He has served as Provost of Haifa University and as Chairman of its Department of Psychology. From 1983 to 1985, he was Visiting Scientist at the National Institute of Mental Health, Rockville, Maryland. He edited the volume *The Denial of Stress*.

HAROLD L. BRODE, Ph.D., is Vice-President of Strategic Systems at Pacific-Sierra Research Corporation (Los Angeles, CA 90025). He is also Chairman of the Scientific Advisory Group for Effects (SAGE) for the Defense Nuclear Agency and co-founder of R&D Associates.

GEORGE F. CARRIER, Ph.D., is T. Jefferson Coolidge Professor of Applied Mathematics at Harvard University (Cambridge, MA 02138). He has received the Von Karman Medal of the American Society of Civil Engineers, the Timoshenko Medal of the American Society of Mechanical Engineers, and the Von Karman Prize of the Society of Industrial and Applied Mathematics. In 1983–1984, he chaired the National Research Council's Committee on the Atmospheric Effects of Nuclear Explosions.

HAROLD C. COCHRANE, Ph.D., is an Associate Professor of Economics and Co-Director of the Hazards Assessments Laboratory at Colorado State University (Fort Collins, CO 80523). He has written on the subjects of the economics of natural disasters and the economics of weather warnings.

WILLIAM DAUGHERTY earned a B.A. in politics from Princeton University in 1986 and is currently a graduate student in politics at Columbia University (New York, NY 10027).

OLE JOHAN FINNOY is a school psychologist in Trondheim, Norway. He is a research assistant on the project "Children and the Future" at the University of Bergen.

SUSAN T. FISKE, Ph.D., is Associate Professor of Social Psychology in the Department of Psychology, University of Massachusetts at Amherst (01003). She is co-author of *Social Cognition* and was co-editor of the 1983 *Journal of Social Issues* entitled "Images of Nuclear War."

JEROME D. FRANK, Ph.D., M.D., is Professor Emeritus of Psychiatry and Behavioral Sciences at the Johns Hopkins University School of Medicine (Baltimore, MD 21205). He is the author of *Sanity and Survival in the Nuclear Age* and numerous publications on intergroup relations and the psychology of the nuclear arms race.

ALEXANDER L. GEORGE, Ph.D., is the Graham H. Stewart Professor of International Relations at Stanford University and the Stanford Center for International Security and Arms Control (Stanford, CA 94305). He is a former research analyst with the Rand Corporation. Among his publications is *Presidential Decisionmaking in Foreign Policy: The Effective Use of Information and Advice.*

DAVID S. GREER, M.D., is Dean of Medicine and Professor of Community Health at Brown University (Providence, RI 02912). He was a member of the Institute of Medicine committee that produced the 1984 report, *Bereavement: Reactions, Consequences, and Care.* Dr. Greer has served on the Board of Directors of International Physicians for the Prevention of Nuclear War.

DAVID A. HAMBURG, M.D., is President of The Carnegie Corporation of New York. From 1975 to 1980, he was President of the Institute of Medicine. He is a member of the National Academy of Sciences Committee on International Security and Arms Control. Dr. Hamburg is a psychiatrist who has written extensively on aggression, stress, and coping in the context of ethology and human evolution.

TED F. HARVEY, Ph.D., is currently a member of the Atmospheric and Geophysical Sciences Division of Lawrence Livermore National Laboratory (Livermore, CA 94555). His current technical interests include numerical modeling of global and local fallout effects.

CHRISTINE C. HARWELL, J.D., is a consultant and lawyer specializing in environmental issues. She was technical editor and contributing author to the SCOPE 28 report, *The Environmental Consequences of Nucelar War Volume II: Ecological and Agricultural Effects.*

MARK A. HARWELL, Ph.D., is Associate Director of the Ecosystems Research Center at Cornell University (Ithaca, NY 14853). He is senior author of the recently published SCOPE 28 report, *The Environmental Consequences of Nuclear War. Volume II: Ecological and Agricultural Effects.*

ALEXANDER LEAF, M.D., is Ridley Watts Professor of Preventive Medicine at Harvard Medical School and Chairman of Preventive Medicine and Epidemiology at Massachusetts General Hospital (Boston, MA 02114). He was a member of the steering committee for the World Health Organization's study of the effects of nuclear war and co-author of the 1984 WHO report *Effects of Nuclear War on Health and Health Services.*

JENNIFER LEANING, M.D., is Chief of Emergency Services for the Harvard Community Health Plan (Boston, MA 02215). She is a member of the Executive Committee and Board of Directors of Physicians for Social Responsibility and co-chair of the Governor's Advisory Commission on the Impact of the Nuclear Arms Race on Massachusetts. Dr. Leaning co-edited *The Counterfeit Ark: Crisis Relocation for Nuclear War.*

BARBARA G. LEVI, Ph.D., is a member of the research staff at Princeton University's Center for Energy and Environmental Studies (Princeton, NJ 08540) and a contributing editor to *Physics Today.* Before joining the Princeton staff, Dr. Levi taught at the Georgia Institute of Technology.

ROBERT C. MALONE, Ph.D., pursues an interest in computer modeling of the earth's atmosphere and climate system at the Los Alamos National Laboratory (Los Alamos, NM 87545). Previously he conducted research on inertial confinement fusion, magnetic confinement fusion, and high-density plasma physics, also at Los Alamos.

ROBERT Q. MARSTON, M.D., is President Emeritus of the University of Florida and Professor of Medicine at the J. Hillis Miller Health Center, University of Florida (Gainesville 32610). He is a former director of the National Institutes of Health. He currently serves as Chairman of the Safety Advisory Committee of the General Public Utilities Nuclear Corporation. Dr. Marston chaired the steering committee for the 1985 Institute of Medicine Symposium, "Medical Implications of Nuclear War."

DENNIS MILETI, Ph.D., is Professor of Sociology and Co-Director of the Hazard Assessments Laboratory at Colorado State University (Fort Collins, CO 80523). He has published in the fields of human response to warnings and the organizational response to the threat of disaster.

PER OFTEDAL, Ph.D., holds a chair in General Genetics at the University of Oslo. He has worked and published extensively in the field of radiation genetics and contributed background papers on cancer and genetic aspects to the 1984 World Health Organization report *Effects of Nuclear War on Health and Health Services*.

KENDALL R. PETERSON, M.S., is an atmospheric physicist with Lawrence Livermore National Laboratory (Livermore, CA 94555). His research focuses on the transport and diffusion of radioactive pollutants over intermediate and global distances.

THEODORE A. POSTOL, Ph.D., is a physicist who has conducted research at Argonne National Laboratory, analyzed MX missile issues for the Congressional Office of Technology Assessment, and served in the Office of the Chief of Naval Operations. He is now at the Center for International Security and Arms Control at Stanford University (Stanford, CA 94305).

MAGNE RAUNDALEN, Ph.D., is Associate Professor of Clinical Child Psychology at the University of Bergen, Norway, where he directs the project "Children and the Future." He is co-editor of *War, Violence and Children in Uganda*.

LAWRENCE S. RIFKIN is a medical student in Brown University's Program in Medicine (Providence, RI 02912).

JOSEPH ROTBLAT, Ph.D., is Emeritus Professor of Physics at the University of London. An original signer of the Einstein-Russel Manifesto, Professor Rotblat was Secretary General of the Pugwash Conference on Science and World Affairs from 1957 to 1973. He is Past President of the British Institute of Radiology and was Editor-in-Chief of *Physics in Medicine and Biology*. His address is 8 Asmara Road, London NW2 3ST, England.

CARL SAGAN, Ph.D., is the David Duncan Professor of Astronomy and Space Sciences and Director of the Laboratory for Planetary Studies at Cornell University (Ithaca, NY 14853). He is a recent recipient of the Honda Prize in Ecotechnology, the Annual Award for Public Service of the Federation of American Scientists, and the Leo Szilard Award for Physics in the Public

Interest of the American Physical Society. He was co-editor of *The Cold and the Dark: The World After Nuclear War.*

CHARLES S. SHAPIRO, Ph.D., is Professor of Physics at San Francisco State University (San Francisco, CA 94132). Formerly, he studied radiation effects for 10 years at IBM. He currently is a consultant on fallout to the Lawrence Livermore National Laboratory. Professor Shapiro was co-editor and contributing author to the SCOPE 28 report, *Environmental Consequences of Nuclear War. Volume 1: Physical and Atmospheric Effects.*

RICHARD D. SMALL, Ph.D., is a Senior Scientist at Pacific-Sierra Research Corporation (Los Angeles, CA 90025), where he is responsible for fire research. Previously he was Visiting Assistant Professor at the University of California, Los Angeles, and Senior Lecturer at Tel Aviv University.

FREDRIC SOLOMON, M.D., is Director of the Division of Mental Health and Behavioral Medicine of the Institute of Medicine (Washington, DC 20418) where he co-edited the 1984 Institute of Medicine report, *Bereavement: Reactions, Consequences, and Care.* Since 1981, he also has served as staff officer to advisory committees to the Institute of Medicine's Council and President on medical consequences of nuclear war; he was Project Director for the 1985 symposium, "Medical Implications of Nuclear War."

JOHN D. STEINBRUNER, Ph.D., is Director of the Foreign Policy Studies Program at The Brookings Institution (Washington, DC 20036). He co-edited the 1983 Brookings publication *Alliance Security: NATO and the No-First-Use Question* and is co-editor of the forthcoming volume *Managing Nuclear Operations.*

SHERRY L. STEPHENS is a graduate student in the Department of Chemistry at the University of Colorado, Boulder (80309).

JAMES THOMPSON, Ph.D., is a Senior Lecturer in Psychology at University College London. He is a Fellow of the British Psychological Society and author of its official statement *Psychological Aspects of Nuclear War.* Dr. Thompson also serves as an adviser to the World Health Organization on the psychological aspects of nuclear issues and teaches in the psychiatry department of Middlesex Hospital (London, W1N 8AA).

RICHARD P. TURCO, Ph.D., is a Research Scientist and Program Manager at R&D Associates (Marina del Rey, CA 90295). He was co-editor and contributing author to the SCOPE 28 report, *The Environmental Consequences* *of Nuclear War. Volume I: Physical and Atmospheric Effects.* He is the recipient of the American Geophysical Union Editor's Citation, the H. Julian Allen Award, the American Institute of Aeronautics and Astronautics Service Award, and the Leo Szilard Award.

FRANK VON HIPPEL, Ph.D., is a Professor at Princeton's Woodrow Wilson School of Public and International Affairs and a senior research scientist at the University's Center for Energy and Environmental Studies (Princeton, NJ 08540). He earned a D.Phil. in theoretical physics as a Rhodes Scholar at the University of Oxford. Dr. von Hippel is a Past Chairman of the Federation of American Scientists (FAS) and is currently on the Board of Directors of *Bulletin of the Atomic Scientists.*

Index

A

Agricultural impacts
  air pollutants and fallout, 130
  farming methods, 376–377, 400
  grain crops, 123, 127–130, 132, 194,
    284, 286, 375–376, 558, 577; *see also*
    Food
  growing seasons, 118, 126, 130, 164, 286
  precipitation changes, 123, 286, 400
  reduced energy inputs, 127–128, 376, 558
  soil deterioration and losses, 286, 400
  sunlight reductions, 123, 127
  temperature declines, 118–119, 123–130,
    286, 558, 584
Air pollutants, 124–125, 130
Alcoholism
  British military, 504–505
  personnel screening for, 510, 512–516,
    518
  security risks because of, 506–508
  Soviet military, 503
  U.S. military, 496–498, 500
American Academy of Arts and Sciences,
  5–6
American Association for the Advancement
  of Science (AAAS), 4–5
American Physical Society, 6
Anti-Ballistic Missile (ABM) Treaty, 6

Antinuclear activism, 457–459, 462, 472,
  476
Arab-Israeli War, 361, 488–489
Arms control studies, 4
Arms race, psychology of power in,
  474–484; *see also* National leaders/
  decision makers
Atmospheric effects and responses
  chemically induced, 112–114, 156,
    163–164
  convective cloud formation from fire
    plumes, 108–109, 159
  environmental stresses associated with,
    156
  ozone layer reductions, 112–113, 156,
    160–163, 320, 584
  photochemical smog formation, 163–164
  radioactive cloud dispersal, 169
  smoke-related, 95, 110–112, 137,
    146–148, 184, 584
  stratospheric injection of fallout, 106, 179,
    184, 195
  structural modification, 143, 148, 154,
    184
  sulfuric acid removal, 164
  uncertainties in assessments of, 137
  see also Climatic impacts and responses;
    Nuclear winter; Tropopause;
    Troposphere

N